T0394949

The Palgrave Handbook of Workplace Innovation

Adela McMurray
Nuttawuth Muenjohn
Chamindika Weerakoon
Editors

The Palgrave Handbook of Workplace Innovation

palgrave
macmillan

Editors
Adela McMurray
College of Business, Government and Law
Flinders University
Adelaide, SA, Australia

Nuttawuth Muenjohn
School of Management
RMIT University
Melbourne, VIC, Australia

Chamindika Weerakoon
Faculty of Business and Law
Swinburne University of Technology
Hawthorn, VIC, Australia

ISBN 978-3-030-59915-7   ISBN 978-3-030-59916-4   (eBook)
https://doi.org/10.1007/978-3-030-59916-4

This Palgrave Macmillan imprint is published by the registered company Springer Nature Switzerland AG.
The registered company address is: Gewerbestrasse 11, 6330 Cham, Switzerland

To my parents and children, with love for all of time
Adela McMurray

To my family, Seangthong, Ladda, Napasorn, Peamawat, Bunnawat, Nakane,
and Teerawuth Muenjohn

Nuttawuth Muenjohn

To my husband, Sam Gamage, and my son Ryan Shenal for their uncondi-
tional love

Chamindika Weerakoon

Preface

With the extraordinary contributions from practitioners and scholars across the world, this handbook provides evidenced-based case studies identifying workplace innovation practices in developing and developed countries. Never before, under one cover, have the positive, negative, outlandish, and eccentric aspects of workplace innovation been presented as a collection of unique evidence-based case studies. As innovation is a large area of research, this handbook presents six different themes of workplace innovation. Each theme has its own setting and focus. The themes intend to link workplace innovation to various organizational aspects.

Under the first theme, workplace innovation in context, the handbook presents a novel macro model comprised of the six elements of climate, culture, structure, leadership, management, and environment. This model has utility for developing an assessment of an organization's innovation process and understanding the vital elements impacting on this process. Then, workplace innovation in the European Union context is explored to determine the challenge of technological innovation and the nature of workplace innovation as a journey of learning and experimentation. Finally, the theme examines the relationship between organizational culture and workplace innovation within the context of public sector. This helps public sector managers to invest in developing positive cultural environments to support the advancement of workplace innovation. Specific examples, and identified highlights, are found in the first five chapters under theme one.

Chapter 1: The Introduction: An Overview to Workplace Innovation Research (Weerakoon and McMurray)—The objective of this introductory chapter is to provide an evidence-based overview to workplace innovation research by identifying the growth trajectories and key knowledge domains of the workplace innovation literature and to rationalize the handbook's focus. By so doing this chapter provides the focus and the approach in this book.

Chapter 2: The Vital Elements of Organizational Innovation (Scott and McMurray)—This integrative study consolidates the literature to identify a novel macro model comprised of the six elements of climate, culture, structure, leadership, management, and environment. This model has utility for academics and practitioners when developing an assessment of an organization's innovation process and understanding its vital elements.

Chapter 3: Developing Workplace Innovation Policies in European Union (Pot, Totterdill, and Dhondt)—Developing organizational performance and job quality simultaneously has been an issue in some European countries for quite some time. From the 1990s, the European Union developed a series of policies on "participative organizational design," later called "workplace innovation." The newest challenge is to complement technological innovation with workplace innovation.

Chapter 4: Workplace Innovation in Practice: Experiences from the UK (Totterdill and Exton)—This chapter draws on UK experiences to demonstrate the nature of workplace innovation as a journey of learning and experimentation, one which can be stimulated and resourced by targeted support from policymakers. Lessons from these experiences are of wider relevance to enterprises, policymakers, and other stakeholders internationally.

Chapter 5: Workplace Innovation in Government Organizations and Its Relationship with Organizational Culture (Nuenham)—Governments enact innovation across the public sector through public sector organizations; however, little is known about how innovation works within them. This research identified a significant relationship between organizational culture and workplace innovation finding that public sector managers can invest in developing positive cultural environments to support the development of workplace innovation.

Part II: Theme 2—Determinants of Workplace Innovation

In the second theme, the handbook identifies the determinants of workplace innovation. Management support and reinforcement are found to be sources of guidance and motivation for innovativeness. By contrast, work discretion and time availability are sources of employee empowerment. The theme also elaborates that organizational culture is one of the important factors that contributes to workplace innovation. A study also finds that creativity willingness is a significant predictor of creative ideation and creative ideation is a more significant predictor of exploratory innovation. In addition, a chapter under this theme argues that the dialogical approach is an anti-positivist way of promoting workplace innovation. It does not prescribe ready-made models or tools, or researcher-led change processes, rather it establishes a set of principles for dialogical processes at the workplace and beyond, which support engagement, knowledge development, and communicative rationality. Finally, the theme reveals specific barriers that hinder a culture of innovation and organizational climate issues that stimulate a culture of innovation in the government sector. Specific examples, including highlights, are found within theme 2 which is comprised of Chaps. 6, 7, 8, 9, and 10.

Chapter 6: The Relationship Between Corporate Entrepreneurship Climate and Innovativeness: A National Study (McMurray, de Waal, Scott, and Donovan)—Management support and rewards/reinforcement are sources of guidance and motivation for innovativeness. By contrast, work discretion and time availability are sources of employee empowerment. The results indicate that employee guidance and motivation for corporate entrepreneurship are more important for innovativeness than are sources of employee empowerment.

Chapter 7: Diagnosing and Developing a Culture of Innovation: Exploring an INGO's Aspired Future in Changing Cambodia (Andrew Henck)—This case study takes place in the Cambodia country office of an international NGO (nongovernmental organization). During a three-month culture study in this Southeast Asian country, employees and senior leaders sought to better understand their current organizational culture in light of a forthcoming global strategic planning process. Through interviews, focus groups, participant observation, and the Organizational Culture Assessment Instrument (OCAI), the current and aspired culture is diagnosed, and priority gaps are identified.

Chapter 8: The Predictive Powers of Team Creativity, Creativity Willingness, Creative Ideation, and Leader Openness on Exploratory Innovation (Ogbeibu, Senadjki, Gaskin, and Awal)—They attempt to bolster the foundations of team creativity by examining and integrating the concept of "creativity willingness" into team creativity dimensions. They find that among other team creativity dimensions, creativity willingness is a more significant predictor of creative ideation and creative ideation is a more significant predictor of exploratory innovation.

Chapter 9: The Dialogical Approach to Workplace Innovation (Johnsen, Hildebrandt, Aslaksen, Ennals, and Knudsen)—This chapter presents a Nordic-based research approach, aimed at encouraging dialogical processes and broad participation at work, in order to support workplace innovation. The approach has been implemented in Norway and Sweden and has had an impact on Scandinavia and beyond. The dialogical approach is an anti-positivist way of promoting workplace innovation. It does not prescribe ready-made models or tools, or researcher-led change processes, rather it establishes a set of principles for dialogical processes at the workplace and beyond, which support engagement, knowledge development, and communicative rationality.

Chapter 10: The Factors that Impact on Innovation in Australian Public Sector Organisations (Mahmoud Moussa)—Public sector innovation in this chapter refers to major changes in processes in the Australian public sector. This chapter can serve as an indication of the extent to which the Australian government is providing the infrastructure to support or encourage innovation. In addition, this chapter might help public servants/decision-makers to identify the most favorable behaviors and characteristics that foster a culture of innovation. The findings revealed specific barriers that hinder a culture of innovation and leadership characteristics and organizational climate issues that stimulate a culture of innovation in the government sector.

Part III: Theme 3—Workplace Innovation as a Process

The third theme defines workplace innovation as a process. The theme argues that when organizations innovate, they sometime open to engage with external resources while remaining closed at other times. The pattern of being open and close across the innovation process leads to different innovation trajectories of development. Digitalization of workplace innovation processes is also examined through a framework for the future of industrial work. A case study of Unisinos is examined which created a hub, a locus for open innovation, enhancing companies' engagement in the technology transfer process. Furthermore, a chapter argues that innovation processes which constantly deliver innovation-powered projects can be prototyped. Then, prototyping is developed and explored as a stage in innovation process linking idea with refined solution. To find some insights, the authors examine a particular example of prototyping an innovation process step by step, materialize it in a software that enables to automatize and stabilize the process, and fine-tune it with employees in an inclusive approach in a medium-sized construction business. Specific examples, and identified highlights, are found in Chaps. 11, 12, 13, 14, 15, 16, 17, and 18 under theme three.

Chapter 11: Workplace Innovation as a Process: Examples from Europe (Peter R. A. Oeij, Paul T. Y. Preenen, and Steven Dhondt)—The three take-away messages are the following: insight in practices of European companies dealing with workplace innovation; since there is no one best way, companies can develop their own unique solutions; and insight in how management and employees cooperate in reaching shared goals, namely, competitive business performance and good-quality jobs.

Chapter 12: Innovation Trajectories: When to Open and Close the Innovation Process (Shukla and Shukla)—When organizations innovate, they sometime open to engage with external resources while remaining closed at other times. The pattern of being open and close across the innovation process leads to different innovation trajectories of development. This chapter explores the factors that influence the choice of innovation trajectory undertaken by any innovation development.

Chapter 13: Digitalization for Workplace Innovation: Service Engineering Research in Japan (Watanbe, Takenaka, and Okuma)—This chapter introduces a pioneering research project that bridges workplace innovation and digitalization at work: the service engineering research project, executed in Japan from 2009 to 2012. Based on two illustrative case studies including care and restaurant businesses, six principles for digitalization contributing to workplace innovation are introduced.

Chapter 14: The Paradox of Organized Innovation: Can Organizations Learn from Individual Innovators? (Shukla, Shukla, and Chawla)—Organizations tend to innovate in a structured and planned way. Since innovation inherently involves disruption and chaos, such innovation becomes suboptimal in spite of investment of huge resources. They study and contrast organizational innovation with individual innovation to seek ways to make organizational innovation more authentic and optimal.

Chapter 15: Digitalization of Work Processes: A Framework for the Future of Industrial Work (Hirsch-Kreinsen and Ittermann)—The chapter presents options and criteria of a human-oriented design of digitized industrial work. First, there are no clear prospects for the development of digital work; rather, very different development perspectives can be assumed. Second, the development of digitization has therefore to be regarded as a design project. A useful conceptual base for this is the approach of the socio-technical system. Third, based on this approach, a basic criteria for the design and implementation of human-oriented forms of digitized work can be systematically developed. Methodologically, the contribution draws on research findings that deal with the diffusion of digital technologies and the development of work in industrial sectors of Germany.

Chapter 16: The Locus for Open Innovation Arrangements: How Universities Can Engage Firms to Collaborate (Groehs, Faccin, da Silva, Bitencourt, and Puffal)—More and more entrepreneurial behavior is expected from the university. However, in some locations, such as Brazil, where universities have developed based on technology import models, collaboration with industry, and therefore technology transfer, is still challenging. They present the case of Unisinos, which created a hub, a locus for open innovation, enhancing companies' engagement in the technology transfer process. This hub has a specific physical structure to enhance companies' engagement with the university as it uses a set of expert-brokered interface processes capable of ensuring quality, improving project management, and making the best choice of partners for the company project.

Chapter 17: Innovation Strategies in Motion in Australian Public Sector Organisations (Moussa)—Public sector innovation in this chapter refers to major changes in processes in the Australian public sector. This chapter serves as an indication of the extent to which the Australian government is providing the infrastructure to support or encourage innovation. The findings revealed specific barriers that hinder a culture of innovation and leadership characteristics and organizational climate issues that stimulate a culture of innovation in the government sector.

Chapter 18: Prototyping Innovation as a Business Process (Sysko-Romańczuk and Bachnik)—The chapter proposes that only innovative companies can deliver sustainable performance over time. The authors claim that innovation processes which constantly deliver innovation-powered projects can be prototyped. So far prototyping was developed and explored as a stage in an innovation process linking idea with refined solution. They use prototyping as a method of getting innovation processes done. The chapter provides an example of prototyping an innovation process step by step, materializing it in a software that facilitates automatizing and stabilizing of the process and fine-tuning it with employees in an inclusive approach. The case study, set within a medium-sized construction business, discusses key factors in determining a sustainable innovation process based on a true understanding of the external environment and contextual business requirements.

Part IV: Theme 4—Workplace Innovation as an Outcome

Workplace innovation as an outcome is emphasized in the fourth theme. A new evidence is provided to indicate the importance of leader's creative role modelling for achieving higher levels of followers' task performance and organizational citizenship behavior. In addition, a study confirms that innovation endeavors have helped the university lecturers to unleash their self-potential in the world of innovation, encourage their quest for continuous professional improvement, and provide them the avenue to feel accomplished upon the recognition of their innovation. Then, a concept of frugal innovation is presented by using the concept of workplace innovation. The chapter also develops a framework for conceptualizing not only frugal workplace innovation but workplace innovation in general, and also for predicting workplace innovation-related outcomes. In this theme, the value of unsuccessful innovations is also recognized. The authors argue that recognizing the value of unsuccessful innovations is vital to continue innovating better. Sometimes it is necessary to refocus the whole innovation strategy and culture in a firm. The interactions between innovation and quality of the work life management are also examined. It contributes to workplace innovations both in terms of organizational behavior management models and the development of innovative skills. At the end of the theme, the impact of workplace innovation on organizational performance is investigated within the entrepreneurial venture context across developing and developed countries. It is interesting to find different outcomes between the countries. Specific examples, and identified highlights, are found under theme 4 which is comprised of Chaps. 19, 20, 21, 22, 23, and 24.

Chapter 19: Creative Leadership and Work Role Proficiency: The Mediating Role of Employee Innovativeness (Hernaus, Klindžić, and Marić)—Since the prevailing norm adopted by many successful businesses is that creativity is no longer an optional but a necessary feature of leadership, the present study develops and tests a model of the mechanisms linking various stages of the innovation process (delivered by different actors) and work role proficiency. Specifically, by examining a sample of 177 leader-member dyads from four public sector organizations based in a European Union member state, we showed that (1) leader creativity is positively related to employee organizational citizenship behavior (a direct effect) and (2) employee innovativeness mediates the positive relationship between leader creativity and employees' work role proficiency dimensions (an indirect effect). Thus, they provided new evidence on the importance of leader's creative role modeling for achieving higher levels of followers' task performance and organizational citizenship behavior.

Chapter 20: Academic Leadership Qualities Towards Innovation Endeavours in an Organisation: A Comparative Study of Malaysia and Singapore Perceptions (Quah, Sim, and Tan)—This study employed mixed method to explore the comparison between Malaysia and Singapore in terms of the contribution of leadership qualities attributes and impacts toward innovation endeavors. Findings revealed that operational focus and quality measurement attributes make the strongest unique contribution towards innovation endeavors. Findings also showed that innovation endeavors have promising impacts on Malaysia and Singapore university students towards enhancing, inspiring, and motivating their learning, besides providing them a sense of self-improvement, self-motivation, self-satisfaction, self-efficiency, and a sense of achievement. This chapter implies that innovation endeavors have helped the university lecturers to unleash their self-potential in the world of innovation, encourage their quest for continuous professional improvement, and provide them the avenue to feel accomplished upon the recognition of their innovation.

Chapter 21: Frugal Workplace Innovation Framework (Etse, McMurray, and Muenjohn)—The process by which frugal innovation is embedded in organizational DNA, and the mechanisms by which its related beneficial outcomes eventuate, however, remain unclear, as these have not been clarified in the literature. This chapter explores the process by which a frugal workplace innovation environment is created and develops a conceptual framework to depict relationships between various frugal workplace innovation predictors and related outcomes. The resultant conceptual framework identifies two independent variables, one mediating variable, and one outcome variable. This chapter extends the field of workplace innovation management and lays the groundwork for the development of a testable workplace innovation theory.

Chapter 22: Recognizing the Value of Unsuccessful Innovations: A Case Study from the Dairy Industry in Mexico (Ramirez-Portilla and Torres)—Traditional mature industries such as the dairy industry are focusing more on innovation. Operational excellence cannot be the only differentiator in competitive industries. Recognizing the value of unsuccessful innovations is vital to continue innovating better. Sometimes it is necessary to refocus the whole innovation strategy and culture in a firm.

Chapter 23: Innovation and Quality of the Work Life Management: Managers, Purpose of Life and Joy (Limongi-França, Barcauí, Mendes, da Silva, and Nogueira)—The interactions between innovation and quality of the work life management are multiple and continuous. The foundations of these relationships consider biological, psychological, social, and organizational approaches. This chapter studies happiness among executives, characteristics of the app 7Waves motivations for life objectives, and a description of Doctors of Joy. The contributions of these approaches refer to innovations both in terms of organizational behavior management models and the development of innovative skills in companies. The methodology teaching case used was the analysis of real cases from the perspective of added values to the management and practice of quality of life and changes in the organizational culture. The cases studied show new frontiers of perception by the directors, in relation to workshops that promote the expression of emotions.

Chapter 24: Impact of Workplace Innovation on Organisational Performance: A Cross Country Comparative Analysis of Entrepreneurial Ventures (Choudhary, McMurray, and Muenjohn)—Based on the resource-based view theory, this chapter identifies the relationship between workplace innovation and organizational performance in entrepreneurial ventures across Australia and Pakistan. Cross-sectional quantitative method was used to collect the data from top executives working in entrepreneurial ventures in both countries through an online and hardcopy survey. The results demonstrated that workplace innovation has a positive impact on organizational performance in a developed country, yet this relationship is nonsignificant in a developing country, showing a significant difference in both countries. The findings extend the literature of workplace innovation and empirically justify that there is a need to practically implement workplace innovation as a business growth strategy in ventures across developing countries.

Part V: Theme 5—Workplace Innovation and Transformations

In the fifth theme, the handbook observes workplace innovation as a tool to transform various aspects of organization. It argues that organizations that are not transforming to a more creative agile future are unlikely to survive without a mind-shift towards engagement, culture, and behavior. In addition, it is believed that design thinking or human-centered design and its focus on creating more desirable futures captures the imagination, energy, and human ingenuity to stimulate, nurture, and shape new ways of thinking and working, delivering collaborative new improved solutions across multiple organizational contexts, and enabling workplace innovation. Looking from another side, the dark side of using innovation for self-advantage is revealed. The chapter draws attention to the concept of unethical innovation process and highlight practices that characterize such a process. Using a case study, the authors explore the characteristics and facilitating factors of the unethical innovation process. The theme also reveals the role of innovation and creativity in the contemporary tourism industry that is transforming and sustaining competitive advantages. The evidence indicates that the innovation-enhancing leadership behaviors transform positively and significantly to employees' creativity and innovation. Specific examples, and identified highlights, are found in Chaps. 25, 26, 27, 28, 29, and 30 within theme 5.

Chapter 25: Innovation Unplugged: The Power of Mindsets, Behaviour and Collaboration in the Quest for Innovation (Boyes and Shelly)—An innovative workplace of the future will flourish by leading its people through iterative cycles of constant transformation and adapting to new challenges as they emerge. Organizations that are not transforming to a more creative agile future are unlikely to survive without a mind-shift towards engagement, culture, and behavior.

Chapter 26: The Role of Top Management Team Cognitive Diversity in a Global Sample of Innovative Firms: A Review (Simmers)—This chapter used secondary sources to examine the role of cognitive diversity among top management teams in a global sample of 38 innovative firms (19 headquartered in the USA and 19 headquartered in other countries). Top management team demographics, generation, firm tenure, gender, and race were collected, and firms were classified into four business life cycles. Firms in the maturity phase had less generational and geographic dispersion, but more gender and racial diversity, so that cognitive diversity might facilitate continuous innovation aimed at marketplace relevancy. Innovative start-ups were geographically dispersed but more cohort, gender, and racially concentrated. Perhaps this lack of cognitive diversity was necessary to maintain focus on the new business for survival in the early years.

Chapter 27: Design Thinking and Workplace Innovation Interface (Matthews)—Workplace innovation and its relevance to health, well-being, and prosperity continues to be a positive response to the challenging features of our time. Following a brief review of existing research on the application of design thinking, the chapter focuses on its contributions to workplace innovation. This chapter proposes that design thinking or human-centered design and its focus on creating more desirable futures captures the imagination, energy, and human ingenuity to stimulate, nurture, and shape new ways of thinking and working, delivering collaborative new improved solutions across multiple organizational contexts, and enabling workplace innovation.

Chapter 28: Unleashing Innovation Across Ethical and Moral Boundaries: The Dark Side of Using Innovation for Self-Advantage (Etse, McMurray, and

Muenjohn)—In this chapter they draw attention to the concept of unethical innovation process and highlight practices that characterize such a process. Using Theranos, a medical technology firm as our case study, and content analysis as our methodological approach, they explored the characteristics and facilitating factors of the unethical innovation process. The findings highlight eight major related characteristics and 11 major facilitating factors. This chapter makes three significant contributions to the field of innovation management by doing the following: it introduces the concept of unethical innovation process; highlights the major related characteristics; and identifies the major related facilitating factors.

Chapter 29: Innovation-Enhancing Leadership in the Australian Tourism Industry (Solmaz and Muenjohn)—Of all factors related to employees' behavior, leadership is found to be one of the most influential in supporting and encouraging subordinates' creativity and innovation. The chapter's purpose is to examine the influence of perceived innovation-enhancing leadership behaviors on employees' creativity and innovation. A survey of 292 hotels and resorts in Australia was conducted. The empirical findings indicate that the innovation-enhancing leadership behaviors relate positively and significantly to employees' creativity and innovation. The findings of this study will enable industry practitioners to develop innovative and sustainable organizational strategies in the competitive tourism industry, as well as useful directions for leadership coaching programs.

Chapter 30: Back to Basics in the Dairy Industry: Building Innovation Capabilities to Allow Future Innovation Success (Torres and Ramirez-Portilla)—Formulation and implementation of the innovation strategy is a contextual process. The building of innovation capabilities is a long-term endeavor that includes acquiring tangible and intangible assets. Innovation capabilities are dynamic capabilities, and they can be reconfigured to respond to the environmental conditions. Vision and top management decisions shape the renewal of core capabilities.

Part VI: Theme 6—Workplace Innovation Ecosystem

The final theme focuses on innovation ecosystem. It believes that the creation and consolidation of innovation ecosystems is one path. However, unlocking barriers to foster a culture of entrepreneurship and innovation remains a primary challenge. The theme also argues that an ecosystem perspective on workplace innovation may support better understanding of emerging health-care challenges and better workplace innovation strategies. Therefore, a practical method for collaboratively designing ecosystem workplace innovation is required. Using a socio-technical system theory, a prototype for designing workplace innovation is developed within a care ecosystem context. The findings show the potential of workplace innovation at the ecosystem level. Finally, the theme explores the implications of frugal innovation for socio-economic development. Two case studies are examined, and the findings suggest that frugal innovation's developmental effect is nuanced; while it may enhance living conditions at the micro level and serve as a useful stop gap measure for managing developmental challenges, it might not be adequate for addressing the underlying factors of socio-economic underdevelopment. Specific examples, and identified highlights, are found in theme 6 which is comprised of Chaps. 31, 32, 33, and 34.

Chapter 31: Brazil: Culture as a Key-Driver for Innovation (Spinosa, Reis, Schlemm)—Brazil is the ninth largest economy in the world and has been driving substantial efforts to develop new paths for socio-economic development. The creation and consolidation of innovation ecosystems is one path. Unlocking barriers to foster a culture of entrepreneurship and innovation remains a primary challenge. This chapter contributes to an understanding of the cultural factors that might inhibit these developments. Selected innovative ecosystems in Brazil are subjected to context-based analysis considering detailed constructs established in studies of America's Silicon Valley. Our main conclusion is that Brazil has the basic cultural conditions to foster workplace innovation, but the necessary cultural factors are not yet fully developed or structured in an integrated way.

Chapter 32: A Prototype for Designing Workplace Innovation Within a Care Ecosystem Context (Dessers and Mohr)—An ecosystem perspective on workplace innovation may support better understanding of emerging health-care challenges and better workplace innovation strategies. A practical method for collaboratively designing ecosystem workplace innovation is required. Using the Dutch/Belgian socio-technical system theory, they developed a prototype for designing workplace innovation within a care ecosystem context. Three cases of ecosystem workplace innovation in health and social care have been analyzed and supplemented by a series of iterative design dialogues. The findings of this exploratory work show the potential of workplace innovation at the ecosystem level. Future research is needed to further develop and validate the prototype.

Chapter 33: Innovation and Entrepreneurial Ecosystem in EdTech Start-Ups in India (Radhika and Banjarie)—The context of this study is set against the backdrop of Bengaluru, India, with a specific focus on understanding important factors affecting the growth of EdTech start-up firms. The study identified that the most important factors affecting the growth are "lack of conducive culture, infrastructure support, and finance."

Chapter 34: Frugal Innovation: A Developmental Implications Perspective (Etse, McMurray and Muenjohn)—This chapter explores the implications of frugal innovation for socio-economic development. Two case studies, eRanger motorcycle ambulance and Tata Swach water purifier, are examined using the qualitative content analysis methodology. The findings suggest that frugal innovation's developmental effect is nuanced; while it may enhance living conditions at the micro level and serve as a useful stop gap measure for managing developmental challenges, it might not be adequate for addressing the underlying factors of socio-economic underdevelopment.

The practical and provocative aspects of workplace innovation comprising this handbook are offered as case studies for use as learning tools for practitioners, academics, and students. The editors are confident that the handbook provides a sound source of research and practice for professional and academic communities in developing and developed countries. The editors would like to express their appreciation to all authors whose valuable contributions made this handbook possible.

Adelaide, SA, Australia   Adela McMurray
Melbourne, VIC, Australia   Nuttawuth Muenjohn
Hawthorn, VIC, Australia   Chamindika Weerakoon

Contents

Notes on Contributors

Hildegunn Aslaksen is a research fellow at the School of Business and Law, Department of Working Life and Innovation at the University of Agder, Norway.

Iddrisu Mohammed Awal is a research assistant in the Faculty of Business and Finance at Universiti Tunku Abdul Rahman, Perak, Malaysia. He holds a bachelor's degree in Business Administration (Hon) Banking and Finance and a Master of Philosophy degree in Social Science from the Universiti Tunku Abdul Rahman.

Katarzyna Bachnik is Professor of Marketing and Innovation and Research Fellow at Hult International Business School, Cambridge, MA, USA. She holds a PhD in Management from Warsaw School of Economics. Her teaching and research are in the fields of international marketing, cross-cultural management, innovation, and design thinking.

Jayanta Banerjee, PhD & MPhil (Management) has 20 years of teaching and industry experience. He is working as Associate Professor of Marketing at CHRIST Deemed to be University, Bangaluru, Karnataka, India. He regularly adjudicates doctoral thesis and supervises PhD scholars.

André Baptista Barcauí is a postdoctoral in Administration from FEA/USP and has a PhD in Administration from UNR and master's in Systems Administration from UFF. He holds both Information Technology and Psychology degrees. He is a consultant, professor, and speaker with six management published books.

Mark Boyes holds an EMBA degree, is an Innovation Capability Development Manager—Australian Pharmaceuticals Industries, and holds an Executive MBA (Distinction) and a PhD in Creative Thinking, with over 15 years of leadership experience in diverse project teams, information technology, and business transformation. During his research Boyes was also Lecturer in Technology and Innovation Strategy and Design Thinking at RMIT's Graduate School of Business and Law. His experience is broad having worked across numerous sectors including gaming, finance, retail, FMCG, security, pharmaceuticals, and human resources. He has co-developed the world's first technologies in the surveillance arena and more recently has been leading multi-million-dollar business intelligence projects. He is also a published illustrator, and he has facilitated innovation and visualization sessions in organizations such as NASA, RMIT University, Bangkok University, Hemisphere Design School in France, Creative Melbourne, and Creative Bangkok.

Sonam Chawla is an assistant professor at Jindal Global Business School and a fellow in Management from Management Development Institute, Gurgaon, Haryana (India), in the area of organizational behavior. She has done her MBA in HR from FORE School of Management, Delhi, and B.Com (Hons.) from Jesus & Mary College, Delhi University.

Ali Iftikhar Choudhary brings along a teaching and research experience of over seven years. Choudhary is doing a PhD in Management from School of Management at RMIT University, Melbourne, VIC, Australia. Choudhary has published more than 20 research articles in peer-reviewed research journals and presented his research work in four international conferences.

Silvio Bitencourt da Silva is Professor of Innovation Studies at Universidade do Vale do Rio dos Sinos—Unisinos, São Leopoldo, Brazil. He is also working as coordinator of technology transfer institutes. His research focuses on university-industry interactions, collaborative innovation, and innovation policies.

Rodolfo Ribeiro da Silva holds a Master of Administration degree from UNINOVE with specialization in Innovation and Entrepreneurship from Université Pierre-Mendès-France. He is founder and CEO of 7 Waves, a Brazilian start-up that works with analytics applied in people's life and corporate goals. Guest researcher in Quality of Work Life Research Group from FEA/USP.

Luciana Maines da Silva is Lecturer in Strategy and Innovation at the Universidade do Vale do Rio dos Sinos—Unisinos, São Leopoldo, Brazil. She is a PhD candidate in Business Administration at Universidade do Vale do Rio dos Sinos—Unisinos, Brazil. Her research focuses on responsible innovation, stakeholder inclusion, innovation management, and the healthcare sector.

Ezra Dessers, PhD is a research manager at HIVA—Research Institute for Work and Society and an assistant professor at the Centre for Sociological Research (KU Leuven, Leuven, Belgium). He holds graduate degrees in Sociology, Spatial Planning, and Information Technology. He has extensive experience in research, teaching, consultancy, and project management in the field of workplace innovation, in various societal sectors. He is the coordinator of Paradigms 4.0, a four-year, multidisciplinary research project on the digital transformation of industry. He has published on organizational challenges related to integrated care both in scientific and specialist journals and is an editorial board member of the International Journal of Care Coordination. In 2014, he spent six months as a visiting researcher at the Saw Swee Hock School of Public Health of the National University of Singapore.

Gerrit A. de Waal is Senior Lecturer in Entrepreneurship and Innovation at RMIT University in Melbourne, Australia. His research interests include corporate entrepreneurship and frugal innovation. He has published in a range of leading international journals, including *R&D Management*, *IEEE Transactions on Engineering Management*, and *Journal of Engineering and Technology Management*.

Steven Dhondt is a senior research scientist at TNO and professor at KU Leuven (chair: workplace innovation), Leuven, Belgium. He has been involved in large-scale EU projects (HiRes; Meadow; the European learning network on Workplace Innovation—EUWIN; SI DRIVE, SIMPACT, SHINE, BEYOND4.0) and projects for international organizations (ILO, EU-OSHA, Eurofound). He participated in the Eurofound study on *Workplace Innovation in European Companies*. He is the coordinator of the FWO/SBO Paradigms and the H2020 BEYOND4.0 projects which analyze the impact of digital transformation for manufacturing in Belgium and in Europe. He coordinates a major TNO research program on Smart Work.

Jerome D. Donovan is Senior Lecturer in Entrepreneurship and Innovation at Swinburne University of Technology, Melbourne, VIC, Australia. His research interests include corporate entrepreneurship, frugal innovation, and sustainability assessments. He has published in a range of leading international journals, including the *Journal of Business Ethics*, *Journal of Cleaner Production*, and *Environmental Impact Assessment Review*.

Richard Ennals is Professor Emeritus at Kingston University, UK, and Adjunct Professor at the Department of Working Life and Innovation, University of Agder, Grimstad, Norway, and the Norwegian University of Science and Technology, Norway. He is Editor in Chief of the *European Journal of Workplace Innovation*.

Daniel Etse is a PhD candidate and a research assistant at RMIT University, Melbourne, VIC, Australia. His research interests include sustainable procurement and sustainability; frugal innovation; corporate social responsibility; assessment and evaluation in education; and quality assurance.

Rosemary Exton is Founding Director of Workplace Innovation Europe CLG, Glasgow, UK. She has been a workplace innovation researcher and consultant since 2002, building on many years' experience as clinician, manager, and trade unionist in the UK's National Health Service where she instigated, drove, and delivered several complex change and improvement initiatives. She holds an MA in Leadership and Management degree and was an elected Director of the Royal College of Midwives from 2007 to 2013.

Kadígia Faccin is Professor in Innovation Management and Qualitative Research Methods at the Universidade do Vale do Rio dos Sinos—Unisinos, São Leopoldo, Brazil. After obtaining a PhD in Business Administration from Unisinos University, Brazil, and in Science of Information and Communication from the University of Poitiers, France, in 2016, she joined the Unisinos University as a postdoctoral fellow during 2016–2018 when she became a professor at this university. Her research focuses on interorganizational relations, collaborative innovation, interorganizational knowledge management, and innovation ecosystems.

James Gaskin is Associate Professor of Information Systems at Brigham Young University, Utah. He received his PhD in MIS from Case Western Reserve University. He has over 100 peer-reviewed articles published in top outlets, including MISQ, ISR, JMIS, JAIS, ISJ, CHB, JBR, IEEE, and JCP, among others.

Giulia Sandri Groehs is an expert on innovation and leadership management.

Andrew Henck is a doctoral student in Leadership Studies with an emphasis in Nonprofit Organizational Consulting in the Department of Leadership Studies at the University of San Diego, San Diego, CA, USA. He holds degrees in organizational communication and leadership and consults with leaders and teams as a Certified LEGO® Serious Play® Facilitator. He continues to speak and present across the globe on his research interests focusing on leadership, culture, and change across the third sector.

Tomislav Hernaus is an associate professor in the Faculty of Economics and Business at the University of Zagreb, Zagreb, Croatia, and a visiting professor at the University of Ljubljana, Slovenia. His multilevel research interests include organization design, process management, job design, knowledge hiding, and innovative work behavior. He received several awards and honors for his scientific contribution (e.g., Highly Commended Award Winner at the Literati Network Awards for Excellence, the Emerald/EMBRI Business Research Award for Emerging Researchers). His research has been published in journals such as *Human Resource Management Journal, Journal of Knowledge Management, Employee Relations*, and *Journal of Managerial Psychology*.

Clare Hildebrandt is a PhD research fellow at the School of Business and Law, Department of Working Life and Innovation, University of Agder, Grimstad, Norway.

Hartmut Hirsch-Kreinsen is Senior Professor of Economic and Industrial Sociology at the TU Dortmund University, Dortmund, Germany. Main areas of work are development of work, innovation processes, and technology development, in particular digitalization of industrial production.

Peter Ittermann is senior researcher in the field of Industrial and Work Research at the Social Research Center, TU Dortmund University, Dortmund, Germany. Main areas of work include Industry 4.0 and digitalization of work, low-skilled work in production and logistics, participation, and co-determination.

Hans Chr. Garmann Johnsen is a professor at the Department of Working Life and Innovation, University of Agder, Grimstad, Norway. In addition to his position at the University of Agder, Garmann Johnsen is a visiting professor at Deusto University in Spain. For several years, Garmann Johnsen has been involved in national research programs on collaborative innovation.

Maja Klindžić is an assistant professor in the Faculty of Economics and Business at the University of Zagreb, Zagreb, Croatia. Her research interests include work motivation and reward management, flexible work arrangements, and management skills. She has been awarded for both scientific work and teaching excellence. Her research has been published in journals such as *Employee Relations, Economic Research*, and *Journal of East European Management Studies*.

Jon P. Knudsen is a professor at the Department of Working Life and Innovation, University of Agder, Grimstad, Norway. Knudsen has a doctorate (PhD) in Social Geography from Lund University, Sweden. He has additional education in press management from Norway and the USA. Among other things, he has been employed by the Research Department at Statistics Norway, the University of Oslo, Agder Research, the University of Agder, and the Northern Region, Stockholm.

Ana Cristina Limongi-França is a senior full professor in the Business Department at FEA/USP—Universidade de São Paulo, São Paulo, Brazil. Deputy Provost for Culture (2016–2018) of the University of São Paulo. Psychologist. Participant of CPCL 2008 Harvard Business School. Eduardo Mondlane University and ISPU, MZ and Del Valle University, Cl. Ibero-American RIPOT Network and Flag Lusophone Forum. Research line: People management and quality of life.

Matija Marić is a PhD student in the Faculty of Economics and Business at the University of Zagreb, Croatia. His research interests include organization design, job design, organizational citizenship behavior, and innovative work behavior. His research has been published in journals such as *Journal of Managerial Psychology* and *Journal for General Social Issues*.

Judy Matthews B. Arts, B. Social Work, M. Social Work, PhD, is Senior Lecturer in Management in the School of Management, QUT Business School, Queensland University of Technology, Brisbane, QLD, Australia, where she teaches and researches innovation management and design approaches to problem framing, problem-solving, and entrepreneurship.

Adela McMurray is Professor of Management/HRM and Innovation at College of Business, Government and Law, Flinders University, Adelaide, SA, Australia, and has extensive experience researching in public and private sectors and implementing organizational change and development. She has published over 260 refereed publications. Her research is internationally recognized, and she is the recipient of four Australian Research Council grants, two industry Collaborative Research Centre grants, and various other grants totalling over AUD$5 million. She has won teaching and leadership awards and chaired numerous USA Academy of Management Committees and is a member of various journal Editorial Advisory Boards. Her research expertise addresses workplace innovation, organizational culture and climate, cultural diversity, and sustainability.

Paulo Bergsten Mendes holds a bachelor degree in Business Administration from FEA/USP. He is also a member of Research Group in New Work Morphologies from IEA/USP and Member of Research Group in Quality of Work Life from FEA/USP.

Solmaz (Sally) Moghimi completed her PhD in Management from School of Management, RMIT University, Melbourne, VIC, Australia. Her PhD thesis explored the influence of leadership behavior, organizational climate, and personal initiative on employee's creativity and innovation in Australian and Iranian hospitality industry. She has been working as a sessional academic member at RMIT University since 2012 in the field of business management, leadership and decision-making, occupational health and safety, as well as strategic human resources.

Bernard J. Mohr is Chair and President of the People Powered Innovation Collaborative Portland, Maine, USA, and a consulting social scientist and a co-founder, the past Dean of Complex Systems Change at the Institute for Applied Behavioral Science, an adjunct faculty in organizational innovation at Concordia University, and a guest lecturer at KU Leuven. He works throughout the USA, Central America, the Caribbean, Western Europe, Canada, and the Middle East on relational and strength-based workplace innovation of professional service practices in healthcare, education, and R&D. Representative clients include Baystate Health, British Petroleum, Canadian Broadcasting Corp., Elliot Health System, Faxton—St. Luke's Healthcare, GSK, Newark Beth Israel Medical Center, Novartis, Novo Nordisk, NYU Langone Medical Center, Tennessee Hospital Association, Tufts Medical Center, University of Maine System, and the World Health Organization. He has authored/co-authored five books and numerous articles dealing with workplace innovation and co-creating more humane and effective organizations.

Mahmoud Moussa is a PhD candidate in Management and a sessional lecturer at the College of Business and Law, School of Management at RMIT University, Melbourne, VIC, Australia. He is a member of the editorial board at *Emerald Emerging Markets Case Studies* (EEMCS) journal, Emerald Group Publishing. He has been teaching Business and Management courses for the undergraduate and postgraduate students in Thailand and Australia for the last 14 years. His current research interest involves innovation in Australian public sector organizations.

Nuttawuth Muenjohn is a researcher and educator at the School of Management, RMIT University, Melbourne, VIC, Australia. His research focuses on leadership studies. His continuing commitment to research has been achieved through various research collaborations with international networks in the Asia-Pacific region such as China, Japan, Singapore, Thailand, Vietnam, Malaysia, Hong Kong, India, and Australia. He has produced over

70 refereed publications including books, journal articles, book chapters, and best paper proceedings. His research works have been published with top international publishers and in high-quality journals. He has been invited to present his research works in Australian, Japanese, Chinese, and Thai universities.

Leonie Newnham is a sessional lecturer and research fellow in the School of Management at RMIT University, Melbourne, VIC, Australia. Previously a state government manager for over 30 years, she contributed to multiple industry forums, presenting over 25 papers as part of her over 30 publications. She completed a PhD at RMIT University in 2018. She is now researching public sector and workplace innovation, organizational change and culture, agility, and artificial intelligence.

Wellington Nogueira is the founder of Doctors of Joy in 1991 and an actor, clown at Artistic Department, Recursos Humorísticos, São Paulo, Brazil, and a social entrepreneur. He studied at the American Academy of Dramatic and Musical Theatres in New York, USA. That's when he met the Big Apple Circus Clown Care Unit, founded by actor and clown Michael Christensen in 1984. Guest researcher in Quality of Work Life Research Group from FEA/USP.

Peter R. A. Oeij is a senior research scientist at TNO, Innovation for Life, the Netherlands Organisation for Applied Scientific Research Leiden, The Netherlands. He has been involved in several EU projects and international projects for EU statutory organizations (such as OSHA, Eurofound). He was project leader of the Eurofound study on *Workplace Innovation in European Companies*. He holds a PhD in management science, and the focus of his work is on innovation management, workplace innovation, social innovation, and organizational and team dynamics.

Samuel Ogbeibu is a lecturer and program coordinator in the Faculty of Business, Department of Management, Curtin University, Miri, Sarawak, Malaysia. He holds a Doctor of Philosophy (PhD) degree from the Universiti Tunku Abdul Rahman (UTAR), Malaysia, and a Master of Business Administration degree from the University of Wales (Prifysgol Cymru), Cardiff, UK.

Takashi Okuma is a Senior Researcher at National Institute of Advanced Industrial Science and Technology, Chiba, Japan, and a team leader of the Smart Work IoH Research Team, Human Augmentation Research Center, AIST. He works on service process visualization and improvement using human behavior-sensing technologies. He is also working on virtual human-sensing, which uses virtual reality technologies to acquire human behavior data.

Frank Pot is Professor Emeritus of Social Innovation of Work and Employment, Radboud University, Nijmegen, The Netherlands, and former Director of TNO Work and Employment, the Netherlands.

Paul T. Y. Preenen is a senior researcher at TNO Innovation for Life, Leiden, The Netherlands. He has been involved with large-scale European research projects (EU FP7, H2020), such as the Eurofound study on *Workplace Innovation in European Companies*. He gained (inter)national policy advising and technology matchmaking experience working for The Netherlands Trade and Investment Office in Taiwan, the Ministry of Finance, and the Ministry of Infrastructure and Environment. He holds a PhD in Work and Organizational Psychology. His research focuses on consequences of digitalization for social and workplace innovation.

Daniel Pedro Puffal is Professor of Innovation Studies at Universidade do Vale do Rio dos Sinos—Unisinos, São Leopoldo, Brazil. He is also working as a manager of research, development, and innovation at Unisinos. His research focuses on university-industry interactions, innovation ecosystems, and collaborative innovation.

Cheng Sim Quah is a senior lecturer at Institut Aminuddin Baki, Ministry of Education, Nilai, Malaysia. She serves in the editorial board for *Horizon Research* journal and is a referee in the *Educational Management Administration & Leadership* journal under SAGE. She was the Vice President for ICAM/ICSI conference, USA, from year 2013 to 2018. She is the Vice President for the International Association of Applied Management conference, USA.

Andres Ramirez-Portilla is an associate professor and head of research at the Departamento de Estudios Empresariales of Universidad Iberoamericana, Mexico City, Mexico. He has a double degree PhD in Industrial Management and Industrial Engineering from KTH Royal Institute of Technology in Stockholm and Politecnico di Milano. He is a scientific panel member of ISPIM.

Rosana Silveira Reis is an associate professor in the Department of Economics, Market & Society at ISG—International Business School in Paris, France. She has 31 years of experience in human resources. Since 2000 she has been teaching international human resource management, organization behavior, and management of innovation in graduation, master's, and MBA programs. Following the International Partnership Program at ISG, she is also a visiting professor at Fundação Dom Cabral—FDC in Brazil and invited professor in MBA programs at IMPS Business School in Brno, Czech

Republic; at University of Bologna, Italy; and at Università Cattolica del Sacro Cuore in Rome, IT. In her research, she is working in the cross-border of organization behavior, innovation, and entrepreneurship. Her focus is on ecosystems of innovation, culture, creativity in global teams, and leadership. Her research has appeared in books and international journals published in English, Portuguese, and Chinese languages.

Marcos Muller Schlemm holds a bachelor degree in Business Administration—UFPR, M.Sc. in Management from Hult International School of Business, and a PhD in Public Policy from University of Southern California. He is also a visiting scholar at Haas School of Business, UC Berkeley. He is also a professor, executive in governmental planning, executive education, industrial food processing, telecommunications, software, and service organizations. His research interest includes entrepreneurship, management of innovation, cultures of innovation, and ecosystems. He has published on entrepreneurship, innovation, and design thinking.

Don Scott, BSc, MBA, PhD is Professor Emeritus at Southern Cross University, Lismore, NSW, Australia. His articles have been published in journals such as *Applied Economics*, *European Journal of Marketing*, *Human Resource Development Quarterly*, *International Migration Review*, *Journal of Business Research*, *Managerial and Decision Economics*, and *Women in Management Review*.

Abdelhak Senadjki is Assistant Professor of Economics at the Faculty of Business and Finance, Universiti Tunku Abdul Rahman (UTAR), Kampar, Perak, Malaysia. He obtained his PhD from Universiti Sains Malaysia (USM). He has been involved in various research grants and has published widely in several refereed journals.

Arthur Shelley is the founder of Intelligent Answers and producer of Creative Melbourne and a capability development and knowledge strategy consultant with over 30 years of professional experience and a PhD in PM soft skills. He held a variety of professional roles including managing international projects in Australia, Europe, Asia, and the USA. He has facilitated courses in master's programs on Executive Consulting, Leadership, Knowledge Management, Research Practice, and Entrepreneurship. He is the author of three books and a regular speaker at international professional development events. He has worked with a wide range of organizations including NASA, Cirque du Soleil, World Bank, Cadbury, Singapore government, education and research centers in several countries, and not-for-profits.

Shashwat Shukla has done his doctorate in entrepreneurship and is a research scholar in the University of Allahabad. He takes courses in economics, HRM, and labor law. He is an active member of the APA and has published leading research in area of leadership, decision-making, and psychology. He has previously worked in senior management positions in the Indian oil sector and Government of India. His research interests include entrepreneurship and organizational behavior.

Shantam Shukla is a strategy and innovation management professional. He is a fellow (PhD) of Indian Institute of Management, Ahmedabad, Gujarat, India, where he did his doctorate in Business Policy. His doctoral dissertation on innovation strategy titled "Exploring Openness in Innovation Process" spanned projects across America, Europe, and Asia. He is with Forbes Marshall as Lead Innovation Officer for the group, where he is responsible for making innovation as the bedrock for future growth plans of the firm. He has worked across diverse industries such as ITES, automotive, education, and manufacturing. He is a member of Innovation Task Force of CII—Western Region, India, and also delivers academic sessions in the field of management particularly on subjects of strategy, entrepreneurship, and innovation for students at IIM as an adjunct faculty. His research has been published and presented at leading academic platforms.

Sandra Phek Lin Sim is an associate professor at Academy of Language Studies, Universiti Teknologi MARA, Cawangan Sarawak, Kota Samarahan, Malaysia. Her areas of expertise are curriculum and pedagogy (TESL) and applied linguistics. She reviews books and journal articles. She was a board member of ICAM/ICSI conference, USA, from 2015 to 2018. She is the coordinator and Chief Editor for the documentation of quality management system in her institution.

Claire A. Simmers, PhD is Professor Emeritus at Management Department, Saint Joseph's University, Philadelphia, PA, USA. Her research interests are in the sociotechnical interfaces in the Internet-connected workplace, generational mixes, human capital contributions, and sustainability. She has over 95 scholarly works in her profile and over 900 citations. Her most recent book is: Simmers, C.A. & Anandarajan, M. (Eds.). *The Internet of People, Things and Services: Workplace Transformations*. 2018. She is a member of the Academy of Management and has served in various leadership positions in the International Theme Committee and the Organizations and Natural Environment division.

Luiz Marcio Spinosa is the Chief of Science, Technology and Innovation Office at Parana State Agency for Science, Technology and Innovation. He is also Academic and Scientific Director of the Humane and Smart Cities Lab. (LabCHIS) at Federal University of Santa Catarina (UFSC) in Florianópolis, Brazil. He is a visiting scholar at Haas School of Business, UC Berkeley, and Deputy Convener of the National Innovation Systems and Models of the Triple Helix Association issued from Stanford University. He holds a PhD degree in Production and Informatics and his Diplôme d'études approfondies in CIM Systems.

Sylwia Sysko-Romańczuk is Professor of Entrepreneurship and Innovation Management at Warsaw University of Technology, Warsaw, Poland. Her research as well as business application projects are focused on innovation-driven growth powered by lean start-up methodology and advanced technology solutions. She designs and leads in-company projects for managerial competences development.

Takeshi Takenaka works at the Human Augmentation Research Center, National Institute of Advanced Industrial Science and Technology, Chiba, Japan. He does research in service engineering, which promotes the improvement of service productivity, integration of service and manufacturing, and institutional design of service platform. He is particularly interested in re-design of service systems based on employee satisfaction, customer satisfaction, productivity, and social value.

Wee-Liang Tan is Associate Professor of Strategic Management at the Lee Kong Chian School of Business, Singapore Management University, Singapore, Singapore. He is Editor in Chief of the *Journal of Enterprising Culture* and Wilford White Fellow of the International Council for Small Business. He serves on the council of the Chartered Secretaries Institute of Singapore and consults as a lawyer.

Erick G. Torres is Associate Professor of Industrial Engineering in Departamento de Ingeniería Química Industrial y de Alimentos at Universidad Iberoamericana, Mexico City, Mexico. He has a PhD in Industrial Engineering from Anahuac University, a master's degree in Planning and Enterprise Systems, and a graduate degree in Chemistry at La Salle University. He is a member of the American Society for Quality.

Peter Totterdill is a researcher, consultant, and policy advocate for workplace innovation. He helped found Workplace Innovation Europe CLG, Glasgow, UK, a not-for-profit organization helping public and private sector organizations achieve enhanced performance and better working lives. He was Professor of Work Organization and Director of The Work Institute at Nottingham Trent University from 1995 to 2005 and is now holding visiting professorships at Kingston University London and Mykolas Romeris University, Vilnius.

Radhika Venkat is a PhD scholar at Jain University and ex-professor at CHRIST Deemed to be University, Bengaluru, Karnataka, India, and has an MBA degree from Strathclyde Business School, UK, with over 25 years of industry and teaching experience in India and UAE. The areas of expertise are strategic management, scenario planning, international business, leadership, and managing HR.

Kentaro Watanabe is a senior researcher at the Human Augmentation Research Center, National Institute of Advanced Industrial Science and Technology (AIST) in Chiba, Japan. His research domains are service engineering, design, and innovation. He is specifically interested in technology integration and digitalization in service systems.

Chamindika Weerakoon is an early career researcher and lecturer in the Faculty of Business and Law, Department of Business Technology and Entrepreneurship at Swinburne University of Technology, Australia. Her research focuses primarily on social enterprises, social innovation, and business model innovation. She has published in the *Journal of Small Business Management*, *Knowledge Management Research & Practice*, and the *Social Enterprise Journal*. Weerakoon's international teaching career spans across 11 years including Sri Lanka and Australia. She has won numerous awards including the Inspirational Teaching Award from the School of Management, RMIT University Melbourne.

List of Figures

List of Tables

List of Boxes

Theme I

Workplace Innovation in Contexts

1

The Introduction: An Overview to Workplace Innovation Research

Chamindika Weerakoon and Adela McMurray

Background

Workplace transformations have resulted from globalisation and the digitalisation of world economies which position workplace innovation as a pivotal requirement for organisations to be competitive in the marketplace (Durugbo, 2020). Workplace innovation is a contextual psychological construct identifying and measuring (McMurray, Islam, Sarros, & Pirola-Merlo, 2013) an individual's or team's behavioural aspects associated with innovation practices aimed at improving organisational management and technology (Totterdill, Cressey, & Exton, 2012). Workplace innovation provides strategic renewal in organising behaviour and is comprised of four resources: strategic orientation, product-market improvement, flexible work and smarter organising (Oeij & Vaas, 2016).

The objective of this introductory chapter is to provide an overview to workplace innovation research by identifying the growth trajectories and key knowledge domains of the workplace innovation literature and to rationalise

C. Weerakoon (✉)
Faculty of Business and Law, Swinburne University of Technology, Melbourne, VIC, Australia
e-mail: cweerakoon@swin.edu.au

A. McMurray
College of Business, Government and Law, Flinders University, Adelaide, SA, Australia
e-mail: adela.mcmurray@flinders.edu.au

© The Author(s), under exclusive license to Springer Nature Switzerland AG 2021
A. McMurray et al. (eds.), *The Palgrave Handbook of Workplace Innovation*,
https://doi.org/10.1007/978-3-030-59916-4_1

the focus of the book. Contrary to the traditional norm in presenting an introductory chapter, we follow a novel systematic approach to provide insights into the status of overall workplace innovation research and thereby to locate the rationale of the book. To this end, we employ bibliometric approaches including a citation network generated from VOSviewer bibliometric network software using the references gathered from a systematic literature search executed in Scopus database. By so doing we provide an evidence-based rationalisation to our focus and the approach in this book. Despite the growing research addressing workplace innovation, the field suffers from numerous issues. For example, there is no clear conceptualisation of workplace innovation (Prus, Nacamulli, & Lazazzara, 2017); narrow definitional focuses measuring workplace innovation at the individual task level often ignoring work environment (Tan, Resmini, Tarasov, & Adlemo, 2015); limited research from Asian, African and South and Central American contexts with higher concentration of workplace innovation scholarship conducted in the USA, Europe and Australia and higher focus on private and profit-oriented organisational contexts with limited exploration of public and not-for-profit contexts. Such loose applications of a concept with confinements limited to specific research contexts may be an impediment to the growth of workplace innovation research and thus, calling for systematic research capturing various dimensions and contexts of workplace innovation. Therefore, this timely book brings together a larger community of workplace innovation scholars across the world. We do this in order to identify the gaps in workplace innovation research, to establish connections in desperate literature, and to expand the boundaries of workplace innovation research in terms of conceptualisation, and to further the contextualisation and methodological design of workplace innovation research. To this end, we build on Crossan and Apaydin (2010) organisational innovation framework to define the book's focus, rationale and the chapter organisation. What follows is a brief account of the methods followed to achieve the chapter's objective and provide a detailed discussion on the growth and knowledge clusters in workplace innovation research thereby further clarifying the handbook's focus and structure.

Methodology

A systematic search was conducted utilising Boolean operations including the search tag of 'workplace innovation*' in keywords, abstracts and titles of the Scopus database which is one of the largest abstract and citation-based databases containing peer-reviewed literature including journals, books and conference proceedings (Kumar, Shivarama, & Choukimath, 2015). This initial search generated 157 references including 9 notes and an editorial. Analysis was limited to journal papers, conference papers, reviews, books and book chapters written in the English language making the emerging sample 144 publications in total. Figure 1.1 presents an overview of the distribution of these publications in terms of document type.

Nearly 75% of the publications are in the form of journal papers and Economic and Industrial Democracy (five), World Review of Entrepreneurship Management and Sustainable Development (five), International Journal of Action Research (four), International Journal of Human Resource Management (four) and Journal of Corporate Real Estate (four) were among the top five journals carrying these publications.

An ontological analysis (Cameron, Ramaprasad, & Syn, 2017; La Paz, Merigó, Powell, Ramaprasad, & Syn, 2020) was followed to map and represent the workplace innovation literature. Modern scientific advancements are triggered by the evaluation of scientific work (Rosas, Kagan, Schouten, Slack, & Trochim, 2011), and this evaluation can be performed by using bibliometrics which is the field of science that applies quantitative measures and indicators based on bibliographic information (Leeuwen, 2005). These analyses are founded on the claim that citations can be used as indicators of present and past activities of scientific work (Garfield, 2001). Bibliometric analysis has strong traditions in innovation and entrepreneurship research as shown by Schildt, Zahra and Sillanpää (2006) and Gregoire, Noel, Déry and Béchard (2006).

We employ a citation analysis to provide a holistic view of the workplace innovation knowledge sphere. Citation analysis is well-known in bibliometric

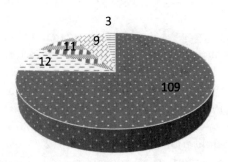

■ Article   ⌐ Review   ♪ Conference Paper   ∧ Book Chapter   ≡ Book

Fig. 1.1 Document type of workplace innovation research 1987–2020. Source: Authors. Note*: final count of the publications includes only up to July 2020

evaluations because citations provide a reliable indication of the specific interaction among researchers and research institutions (Kraus, Filser, O'Dwyer, & Shaw, 2014). Citation analysis is a '…quantitative oriented bibliographic approach…' (Gundolf & Filser, 2013, p. 178) which determines the most influential publications of a specific discipline area of concern and is considered to be reliable indicators of scientific interactions of scholarly ideas (Small, 1973). Moreover, the direct citations '…cluster documents more evenly across the time window, and tends to cluster a larger number of documents than either bibliographic coupling or co-citation processes…' (Boyack & Klavans, 2010, p. 2391). Further, direct citation relationships provide a higher accuracy of relatedness of publications than bibliographic coupling or co-citation indices (Van Eck & Waltman, 2017).

The 144 references identified above were exported into VOSviewer (Van Eck & Waltman, 2010) bibliometric software to generate a citation network (*see* Fig. 1.3). Following Schildt et al. (2006), this study's citation frequency threshold was adjusted to three minimum citations per publication so as to obtain a sufficient number of references for the analysis. Thus, within the 144 publications, there were only 17 highly connected publications meeting this criterion indicating the existence of 6 main knowledge clusters within the workplace innovation literature (*see* Fig. 1.2).

After generating the citation network, abstracts and introduction sections of each of these 17 publications were read to identify the main foci, methodological approaches and key study findings. Below is a detailed account of the findings from the systematic search and the citation network.

Growth of Workplace Innovation Research

The earliest publication we found in our search traced back into 1987. Figure 1.2 exhibits the growth of workplace innovation publications since 1987. Since then till July 2020, two clear periods of growth can be identified. The first period from 1987–2006 is a slow growth period with a few fluctuations, while the period from 2007–July 2020 indicates the growth of workplace innovation research. The period from 1987–2006 has produced nearly 27% of the total publications, while the rest 12.5 years period produced nearly 73% of the total workplace innovation publications in our sample. In addition, we found that the United States (34), the United Kingdom (25), Australia (17), the Netherlands (16) and Finland (9) were among the top five countries contributing to these 144 publications in our sample.

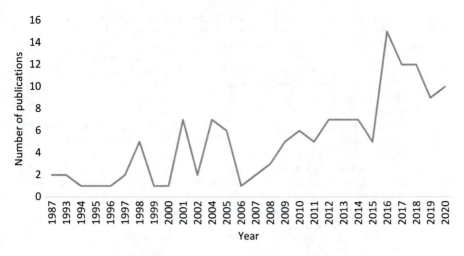

Fig. 1.2 Growth of workplace innovation publications. Source: Authors

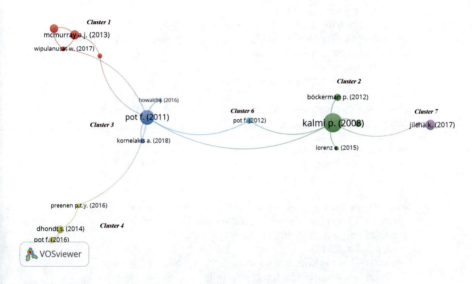

Fig. 1.3 Citation network for workplace innovation research 1987–2020

These five countries make up 101 publications (70%) of the total publications, and 50% of these publications are from European context. The citation network generated from 144 total references in our sample is presented in Fig. 1.3.

There are six main knowledge clusters within our sample of 144 publications and citation network with Fig. 1.3 showing only the highly connected 17 publications. The titles, authors and source of these 17 publications are summarised in Table 1.1.

Table 1.1 Titles, authors and sources of highly cited and connected publication

Cluster	Title and authors	Source title
1	Pathways to workplace innovation and career satisfaction in the public service: The role of leadership and culture (Wipulanusat, Panuwatwanich, & Stewart, 2018)	International Journal of Organizational Analysis
	Workplace Innovation: Exploratory and Confirmatory Factor Analysis for Construct Validation (Wipulanusat, Panuwatwanich, & Stewart, 2017)	Management and Production Engineering Review
	Design leadership, work values ethic and workplace innovation: an investigation of SMEs in Thailand and Vietnam (Muenjohn and McMurray 2017a)	Asia Pacific Business Review
	Workplace Innovation in a Non-profit Organization (McMurray et al., 2013)	Non-profit Management and Leadership
2	Work organisation, forms of employee learning and labour market structure: Accounting for international differences in workplace innovation (Lorenz, 2015)	Journal of the Knowledge Economy
	Innovative work practices and sickness absence: What does a nationally representative employee survey tell? (Böckerman, Johansson, & Kauhanen, 2012)	Industrial and Corporate Change
	Workplace innovations and employee outcomes: Evidence from Finland (Kalmi & Kauhanen, 2008)	Industrial Relations
	Re-evaluating the Finnish workplace development programme: Evidence from two projects in the municipal sector (Payne, 2004)	Economic and Industrial Democracy
3	Why are your reward strategies not working? The role of shareholder value, country context, and employee voice (Kornelakis, 2018)	Business Horizons
	Workplace innovation and social innovation: An introduction (Howaldt, Oeij, Dhondt, & Fruytier, 2016)	World Review of Entrepreneurship, Management and Sustainable Development
	Workplace innovation for better jobs and performance (Pot, 2011)	International Journal of Productivity and Performance Management

(*continued*)

Table 1.1 (continued)

Cluster	Title and authors	Source title
4	Workplace innovation: European policy and theoretical foundation (Pot, Totterdill, & Dhondt, 2016)	World Review of Entrepreneurship, Management and Sustainable Development
	Why job autonomy matters for young companies' performance: Company maturity as a moderator between job autonomy and company performance (Preenen, Oeij, Dhondt, Kraan, & Jansen, 2016)	
	The importance of organizational level decision latitude for well-being and organizational commitment (Dhondt, Pot, & Kraan, 2014)	Team Performance Management
5	Industrial occupational safety and health innovation for sustainable development (Jilcha & Kitaw, 2017)	Engineering Science and Technology, an International Journal
	Workplace innovation influence on occupational safety and health (Jilcha, Kitaw, & Beshah, 2016)	African Journal of Science, Technology, Innovation and Development
6	Social innovation of work and employment (Pot, Dhondt, & Oeij, 2012)	Challenge Social Innovation: Potentials for Business, Social Entrepreneurship, Welfare and Civil Society

Source: Authors

Cluster 1—Leadership, Organisational Culture and Workplace Innovation

There are four publications included in this cluster: McMurray et al. (2013), Muenjohn and McMurray (2017a) and Wipulanusat et al. (2017, 2018). The central focus of this cluster is the links between leadership, organisational culture and workplace innovation. McMurray et al. (2013) examine the links between leadership, organisational climate and workplace innovation in a non-profit organisational context, while another publication co-authored by the same lead author, Muenjohn and McMurray (2017a), proposes a three-dimensional model to clarify the links between design leadership, workplace value ethics and workplace innovation. Building on these studies, Wipulanusat et al. (2017) propose a new factor structure of workplace innovation construct arguing that organisational performance is improved by the new products, processes and services enabled by workplace innovation. In another recent work, Wipulanusat et al. (2018) propose leadership and organisational culture as two constructs of climate for innovation and study their impact on workplace innovation and career satisfaction. Looking at the methodologies and the research contexts of this cluster, this is a survey-research dominant group with a strong diversity in terms of context of the research: not-for-profit organisations (McMurray et al., 2013), public services departments (Wipulanusat et al., 2017, 2018) and small and medium enterprises (SMEs) (Muenjohn & McMurray, 2017a). However, all the publications are based in the Australian context except for Muenjohn and McMurray (2017a) which focuses on Thailand and Vietnam SMEs.

Workplace innovation is characterised by organisational innovation, organisational climate, individual innovation (McMurray et al., 2013; Muenjohn & McMurray, 2017a), team innovation and individual creativity (McMurray et al., 2013; Wipulanusat et al., 2017). While work value ethics and workplace innovation relationship is moderated by design leadership behaviour (Muenjohn & McMurray, 2017a), some aspects of transformational leadership and transactional leadership tend to have direct effects on workplace innovation fostering a healthy organisational climate (McMurray et al., 2013). While specifically an ambidextrous culture for innovation improves career satisfaction of employees (Wipulanusat et al., 2018), design leadership as a novel form of leadership which creates and sustains innovation design solutions in organisations is a crucial determinant not only of organisational climate but also of organisational, team and individual innovation dimensions of workplace innovation (Muenjohn & McMurray, 2017a). Thus, workplace environments need to be designed in such a way that encourages innovation and application of employee creativity which will subsequently create positive employee perceptions about their jobs (Wipulanusat et al., 2018).

Cluster 2—Forms of Work Organisation Quality of Work and Employment

Four publications including Lorenz (2015), Böckerman et al. (2012), Kalmi and Kauhanen (2008) and Payne (2004) form cluster 2 which brings a human resource management perspective in to the discussion. Especially, various aspects of 'forms of work organisation' and their concomitant relationships with quality of work and employment have been a major focus of this cluster. Lorenz (2015) examines the relationships between process innovation and the use of discretionary learning which is a form of work organisation. A policy discussion around institutional arrangements related to these topics was observed. For instance, while Lorenz (2015) discusses labour market policies for adopting discretionary learning, Payne (2004) examines the role of public policy in developing better forms of work organisation to further employee opportunities to exercise skill and discretion in their jobs. Moving the focus to outcomes of workplace innovation, Kalmi and Kauhanen (2008) address the competing views of workplace innovation outcomes: positive outcomes such as increased discretion, improved job security and enhanced job satisfaction versus negative outcomes including increased job intensity and mental strain and compromised job security. Along the same lines Böckerman et al. (2012) examine the effect of 'bundles' of innovative work practices including self-managed teams, information sharing, employer-provided training and incentive pay on the prevalence of sickness absence and accidents at work. This cluster is predominantly based in the European context and three out of four publications focus on aspects of workplace innovation in Finland. Usage of secondary data from data sets such as Finnish Quality of Work Life Survey (e.g. Böckerman et al., 2012; Kalmi & Kauhanen, 2008) and Labour Force Survey (e.g. Kalmi & Kauhanen, 2008) and qualitative approaches including interviews and case studies (e.g. Payne, 2004) inform the main methodological approaches in this cluster.

High levels of employee learning, problem-solving and discretion in work are key attributes of forms of work organisation (Lorenz, 2015). Thus, workplace innovations mainly create beneficial outcomes for employees (Kalmi & Kauhanen, 2008), but there's little impact on the overall health of employees by high-performance workplace systems (Böckerman et al., 2012). However, discretional learning is higher in nations with high levels of labour market mobility, unemployment protection and active labour market measures (Lorenz, 2015). This confirms that institutional labour markets may mediate workplace innovation outcomes (Kalmi & Kauhanen, 2008) and the absence of substantial, long-term investment on the part of policymakers may weaken the expected success of policy development (Payne, 2004).

Cluster 3—Employee Participation in Workplace Innovation

The third cluster is comprised of three publications written by Pot (2011), Howaldt et al. (2016) and Kornelakis (2018). The cluster examines the implications for research and practice regarding the social aspects of workplace innovation, especially employee participation and workplace practices. While Pot (2011) examines the need for workplace innovation policies and practice in Europe with a regional level focus in a programme evaluation, Howaldt et al. (2016) provides an introduction to a special issue focusing on the social innovation elements of workplace innovation. In a more recent work, Kornelakis (2018) deep dives into prescribing guidance on enhancing productivity and boosting employee satisfaction. From a methodological point of view, these publications are conceptual scholarly works based on secondary data.

Workplace innovation is '…the implementation of new and combined interventions…' such as '…performance-based pay, flexible job design, and employee involvement…' (Pot, 2011, pp. 404–405) in work organisation, human resource management and supportive technologies (Kornelakis, 2018). Thus, workplace innovation is necessary for organisational renewal given its complementary role to technological and business model innovation (Howaldt et al., 2016). Both employee quality of work and organisational success can be achieved through collaborative arrangements encouraging employee engagement (Howaldt et al., 2016) and employee participation in change projects (Pot, 2011). Further, building on Pot's (2011) definition, Kornelakis (2018) proposes to move away the focus of reward practices from shareholder-value reward to stakeholder reward as a workplace innovation mechanism to provide employees with a voice.

Cluster 4—Occupational Stress

Three publications form cluster 4 of the citation network illustrated in Fig. 1.3. These are Pot et al. (2016), Preenen et al. (2016) and Dhondt et al. (2014). These publications examine various aspects of occupational stress including job decision latitude, job demand, job control and provide insights into both implications for research and practice. Pot et al. (2016) note the fragmentation of workplace innovation policies in the EU. Advancing the organisational level analysis on the impact of job autonomy, Preenen et al. (2016) present a quantitative investigation into the links between employees' job autonomy and company performance growth (Preenen et al., 2016). In another work, Dhondt et al. (2014) look into the effects of job control dimensions on subjective well-being and organisational commitment. This cluster predominantly focuses on studies conducted in the European context. In terms of the research methodologies utilised in these studies, they tend to use a mix of methods including qualitative review techniques (Pot et al., 2016) and survey research (Dhondt et al., 2014; Preenen et al., 2016).

Locating the discussion at an organisational level, Preenen et al. (2016) and Dhondt et al. (2014) make very important conclusions related to occupational stress elements. While Dhondt et al. (2014) find that functional support and organisational level decision latitude tend to be strongly associated with subjective well-being and organisational commitment than job autonomy, Preenen et al. (2016) find the significant importance of adapting job autonomy-focused workplace innovation practices to achieve stronger performance targets especially in younger firms. In their national level focus, while calling for more research into obstacles and the mechanisms to promote workplace innovation implementation, Pot et al. (2016) stress the significant importance played by national programmes formed by various stakeholders such as employers' associations, trade unions, governments and research institutes thereby targeting policy levels.

Cluster 5—Occupational Safety and Health Innovation

Knowledge cluster 5 is comprised of two publications by the same co-authors Jilcha et al. (2016) and Jilcha and Kitaw (2017). These two publications focus on workplace safety and health interventions aligned with the concept of sustainable development. They introduce a new pillar of sustainable development including culture, political and technological dimensions and propose new research areas along the same lines (Jilcha & Kitaw, 2017) and effects of workplace innovation addressing occupational safety and health interventions (Jilcha et al., 2016). To this end, they followed various qualitative research methods and techniques including literature review, interviews and industry observations. Both Jilcha and Kitaw (2017) and Jilcha et al. (2016) note the limited focus of literature on the effects of workplace safety and health innovation approaches on sustainable development. While healthy people, safer workplace, reduced cost of accidents, controlled environment, managed workplace accidents and improved workplace safety knowledge contribute to sustainable development (Jilcha & Kitaw, 2017), the literature has no clear demarcation set between workplace innovation and new product development innovation (Jilcha et al., 2016).

Cluster 6—Innovation in Social Aspects of Organisation

Cluster 6 is the smallest cluster in the citation network with one book chapter by Pot et al. (2012) focusing on social innovation elements of workplace innovation. They particularly examine workplace innovation at the organisational level which is a prerequisite for achieving sustainable and inclusive growth in regions. They recommend including a focus of workplace innovation in EU policies given the social nature of workplace innovation '…both in ends (quality of working life, well-being and development of talents together with organisational performance) and in their means (employee participation and empowerment)…' (Pot et al., 2012, p. 261).

Based on the above discussion, we can make a few conclusions about the growing research field addressing workplace innovation. One of the main observations is that workplace innovation research tends to largely concentrate on organisational and individual levels of workplace innovation leaving group/team level less researched. Cluster 3 through to cluster 6 primarily focus on organisational level analysis, while clusters 1 and 2 focus on individual and managerial levels. Cluster 2 includes some presence of a national level focus in discussing the labour market policies and its relevance to workplace innovation. Therefore, much research is needed on addressing the group/team level aspects of workplace innovation. For instance, cluster 1 focuses on the effects of leadership and organisational culture on workplace innovation, yet upper echelon theory asserts that top management team characteristics (e.g. experience, diversity, industry ties) provide a stronger explanation on organisational outcomes rather than a leader's individual characteristics and behaviours (Talke, Salomo, & Kock, 2011). In addition, the managerial level of focus in this research stream seems largely to be limited to organisational culture. Further, another observation is that the literature tends to discuss the 'human resource management' elements of workplace innovation. Therefore, it is important to examine other organisational and multi-level variables supporting workplace innovation. For example, the effects of managerial levers such as missions/goals/strategies; structures and systems; knowledge management and learning and resource allocation are important areas to be considered (Crossan & Apaydin, 2010, p. 1171). For instance, there is a dearth of literature investigating the effects and formation on learning and knowledge creation processes within workplaces. Oeij, Dhondt, Rus and Van Hootegem (2019) propose the need for workplace innovation in building an inclusive economy through disruptive technology and social transformation. For instance, in the context of artificial intelligence, technological innovation is promoted by artificial innovation through the mechanisms of accelerating knowledge creation and technology spill over; improving learning and absorptive capacities of firms and increasing R&D and talent investment by firms. Therefore, it is imperative to investigate the way in which learning and knowledge creation processes support workplace innovation in organisations.

Another observation is that the literature largely discusses the policy context of workplace innovation. For instance, clusters 2 through to 6 primarily focus on outcomes, output and policy contexts. Yet, there is limited research addressing the process dimension of workplace innovation. The process dimension of innovation generally includes the aspects such as drivers, sources, locus and levels of innovation (Crossan & Apaydin, 2010). According to Fricke and Totterdill (2004, p. 3) 'workplace innovation should be seen as the product of a complex process of learning grounded in, for example, vertical and horizontal interaction within firms, networking between firms (industry associations, supply chain relationships, etc.), public policy, vocational training, industrial relations, the financial system and so on'. Thus, research into process elements may uncover the mechanisms of workplace innovation emergence. Moreover, workplace innovation provides strategic renewal in organising behaviour and is comprised of four resources: strategic orientation, product-market improvement, flexible work and smarter organising (Oeij & Vaas, 2016). Yet, rarely does the workplace innovation literature focus on workplace innovation and its link to strategic orientation dimensions other than organisational performance. Hence, another future research area to focus on would be the effects and mechanisms of workplace innovation driving various strategic orientations.

Workplace innovation is context driven (Muenjohn & McMurray, 2017b). Yet, the above analysis indicates that workplace innovation research has substantially emerged from the European context (e.g. clusters 2, 3, 4 and 6) and drawn from the for-profit organisational setting. Thus, it is essential to extend the focus of workplace innovation research into other country and regional contexts across the globe and organisational settings such as not-for-profit organisations, social enterprises and public organisations (e.g. government departments). An exception to this is the recent developments of workplace innovation research linking to social innovation (Oeij, Dhondt, Pot, & Totterdill, 2018; Totterdill et al., 2012). However, in the context of social innovation, Archibugi (2017) calls for new research focusing on social innovation given the growing value of digital technology in society and particularly in the era of Industry 4.0. This is evident through the introduction of concepts such as digital social innovation (Bonina, López-Berzosa, & Scarlata, 2020) and technology-enabled social innovation (Battisti, 2019) evidenced in recent scholarly work. Such new directions of research can be explored to contribute to the understanding of workplace innovation that generates social and business impact (Tracey & Stott, 2017).

A diverse set of methods have been used in this research including primary data-driven approaches—surveys, case studies, reviews and secondary data-based methods. However, the field suffers from issues such as the absence of a clear conceptualisation of the workplace innovation concept (Prus et al., 2017) and a narrow definitional focus in measuring workplace innovation at the individual task level often ignoring the work environment (Tan et al., 2015). Given this theoretical ambiguity associated with the concept of workplace innovation, theoretical and conceptual work clarifying the constructs of workplace innovation is a much-needed focus for future research to address (e.g. proposition development studies).

While the entirety of all this future research cannot possibly be addressed in one collection, below is a brief account as to how this book addresses some of these research areas and makes a contribution to the current workplace innovation literature.

Objectives and Approach of This Book

This handbook collection of chapters aims to contribute to the growing workplace innovation literature. We believe that innovation is a phenomenon which embraces complex causal relationships while also reflecting a basic sequential evolution process. Thus, the handbook chapters are based on the foundation of the '...organisational innovation framework...' by Crossan and Apaydin (2010). This framework focuses on two major areas which reflect the sequential view of innovation steeped in the determinants of innovation and innovation dimensions (process and outcome elements). The innovation determinants include group level, business process level and managerial level variables underpinned by upper echelon theory, process theory and resource-based view theory.

Innovation dimensions are formed by perspectives of innovation as a process and innovation as an outcome. Therefore, the book addresses workplace innovation at an organisational level which is couched within developed and developing countries and organised along six major themes: workplace innovation in contexts (Chaps. 1, 2, 3, 4), workplace innovation determinants (Chaps. 5, 6, 7, 8, 9), workplace innovation as a process (Chaps. 10, 11, 12, 13, 14, 15, 16, 17), workplace innovation as an outcome (Chaps. 18, 19, 20, 21, 22, 23), workplace innovation and transformations (Chaps. 24, 25, 26, 27, 28, 29) and finally, workplace innovation ecosystems (Chaps. 30, 31, 32, 33).

Another important contribution made by this book is to harbour workplace innovation research from a variety of contexts. The preceding analysis on workplace innovation research confirms that the workplace innovation literature is growing with strong traditions primarily set in the European context. This may be attributable to the long history of developing strong programmes to promote workplace innovation in Europe (Tan et al., 2015). A limited focus on central and south American, African and Asian workplace innovation contexts is visible. It is argued that one-size-fits-all strategies are not practical given the cultural and institutional differences across countries (Kornelakis, 2018). Thus, this book includes scholarly contributions from a diverse set of country contexts including Mexico (e.g. Chap. 29), India (e.g. Chaps. 11, 13 and 32), Brazil (e.g. Chaps. 15 and 30), Malaysia, Singapore (e.g. Chap. 19), Japan (Chap. 12), Cambodia (Chap. 6), Pakistan (Chap. 23) and Africa (Chap. 33) in addition to established research traditions in Australia (e.g. Chaps. 4 and 9), the USA (e.g. Chap. 25) and Europe (e.g. Chaps. 2, 3, 10). Furthermore, this book contains scholarly work drawn from both private and public sectors (e.g. Chaps. 4, 10, 15 and 32) and their unique approaches to workplace innovation.

By opening the contributions to a global representation, we build a global community of workplace innovation researchers and bring together a range of perspectives and examples from around the world. The authors included in this handbook are from a variety of backgrounds: academics, practitioners and policymakers with disciplinary backgrounds drawn from management, economics, entrepreneurship, not-for-profit, public sector, arts and sociology. The workplace innovation analysis identifies occupational stress, health and well-being, employee participation, forms of organisation, leadership and culture as concentrations of focus. While exploring these areas further, the collections in this book expand its intellectual inquiry in to many of the unexplored dimensions, fields and contexts related to workplace innovation. For instance, rather than limiting workplace innovation focus into an 'output' perspective, theme three of the handbook is comprised of eight chapters which investigate the 'process' aspect of workplace innovation.

Chapters 23, 24, 25, 26, 27, 28 and 29 provide a 'futuristic' perspective to workplace innovation. Chapters 30, 31, 32 and 33 centre on the 'innovation ecosystem' of workplace innovation. These are the main research areas that are overlooked in extant workplace innovation literature. Moreover, the scholarly community of researchers who have contributed to this book have focused on an emerging area of workplace innovation research. This includes the technological impact by discussing various aspects of digitalisation of workplace innovation processes (e.g. Chaps. 12 and 14).

Notably, Chaps. 26, 20, 27 and 21 provide insights into workplace innovation research by discussing novel and unexplored areas including design thinking, frugal innovation, dark side of innovation and unsuccessful innovations, respectively. While this is an interesting intellectual inquiry into workplace innovation, it splendidly showcases the multidisciplinary nature of workplace innovation research. Further, this book not only includes theoretical discussions but also policy debates so that it serves to codify and analyse practice in a way that can inform better organisational and research policy decision-making.

With this note we conclude the chapter and its over to you now! Do enjoy reading the cutting-edge knowledge shared by the community of workplace innovation scholars and industry leaders across the globe!

References

Archibugi, D. (2017). The Social Imagination Needed for an Innovation-Led Recovery. *Research Policy, 46*(3), 554–556.

Battisti, S. (2019). Digital Social Entrepreneurs as Bridges in Public–Private Partnerships. *Journal of Social Entrepreneurship, 10*(2), 135–158.

Böckerman, P., Johansson, E., & Kauhanen, A. (2012). Innovative Work Practices and Sickness Absence: What Does a Nationally Representative Employee Survey Tell? *Industrial and Corporate Change, 21*(3), 587–613.

Bonina, C., López-Berzosa, D., & Scarlata, M. (2020). Social, Commercial, or Both? An Exploratory Study of the Identity Orientation of Digital Social Innovations. *Information Systems Journal.*

Boyack, K. W., & Klavans, R. (2010). Co-Citation Analysis, Bibliographic Coupling, and Direct Citation: Which Citation Approach Represents the Research Front Most Accurately? *Journal of the American Society for information Science and Technology, 61*(12), 2389–2404.

Cameron, J. D., Ramaprasad, A., & Syn, T. (2017). An Ontology of and Roadmap for Mhealth Research. *International journal of medical informatics, 100*(1), 16–25.

Crossan, M. M., & Apaydin, M. (2010). A Multi-Dimensional Framework of Organizational Innovation: A Systematic Review of the Literature. *Journal of management studies, 47*(6), 1154–1191.

Dhondt, S., Pot, F. D., & Kraan, K. O. (2014). The Importance of Organizational Level Decision Latitude for Well-Being and Organizational Commitment. *Team Performance Management, 20*(1), 307–327.

Durugbo, C. M. (2020). Affordance-Based Problem Structuring for Workplace Innovation. *European Journal of Operational Research, 284*(2), 617–631.

Fricke, W., & Totterdill, P. (2004). *Action Research in Workplace Innovation and Regional Development* (Vol. Vol. 15). Amsterdam: John Benjamins Publishing.

Garfield, E. (2001). *From Bibliographic Coupling to Co-Citation Analysis Via Algorithmic Historio-Bibliography: A Citationist's Tribute to Belver C. Griffith, Lazerow.* Drexel University, Philadelphia, PA. Retrieved from http://garfield. library.upenn.edu/papers/drexelbelvergriffith92001.pdf

Gregoire, D. A., Noel, M. X., Déry, R., & Béchard, J. P. (2006). Is There Conceptual Convergence in Entrepreneurship Research? A Co-Citation Analysis of Frontiers of Entrepreneurship Research, 1981–2004. *Entrepreneurship Theory and Practice, 30*(3), 333–373.

Gundolf, K., & Filser, M. (2013). Management Research and Religion: A Citation Analysis. *Journal of Business Ethics, 112*(1), 177–185.

Howaldt, J., Oeij, P. R. A., Dhondt, S., & Fruytier, B. (2016). Workplace Innovation and Social Innovation: An Introduction. *World Review of Entrepreneurship, Management and Sustainable Development, 12*(1), 1–12.

Jilcha, K., & Kitaw, D. (2017). Industrial Occupational Safety and Health Innovation for Sustainable Development. *Engineering Science and Technology, an International Journal, 20*(1), 372–380.

Jilcha, K., Kitaw, D., & Beshah, B. (2016). Workplace Innovation Influence on Occupational Safety and Health. *African Journal of Science, Technology, Innovation and Development, 8*(1), 33–42.

Kalmi, P., & Kauhanen, A. (2008). Workplace Innovations and Employee Outcomes: Evidence from Finland. *Industrial Relations, 47*(3), 430–459.

Kornelakis, A. (2018). Why Are Your Reward Strategies Not Working? The Role of Shareholder Value, Country Context, and Employee Voice. *Business Horizons, 61*(1), 107–113.

Kraus, S., Filser, M., O'Dwyer, M., & Shaw, E. (2014). Social Entrepreneurship: An Exploratory Citation Analysis. *Review of Managerial Science, 8*(2), 275–292.

Kumar, A., Shivarama, J., & Choukimath, P. A. (2015). *Popular Scientometric Analysis, Mapping and Visualisation Softwares: An Overview.* Paper presented at the 10th International CALIBER-2015, HP University and IIAS, India.

La Paz, A., Merigó, J. M., Powell, P., Ramaprasad, A., & Syn, T. (2020). Twenty-Five Years of the Information Systems Journal: A Bibliometric and Ontological Overview. *Information Systems Journal, 30*(3), 431–457.

Leeuwen, T. V. (2005). Descriptive Versus Evaluative Bibliometrics. In H. F. Moed, W. Glänzel, & U. Schmoch (Eds.), *Handbook of Quantitative Science and Technology Research* (pp. 373–388). Dordretch: Springer.

Lorenz, E. (2015). Work Organisation, Forms of Employee Learning and Labour Market Structure: Accounting for International Differences in Workplace Innovation. *Journal of the Knowledge Economy, 6*(2), 437–466.

McMurray, A. J., Islam, M. M., Sarros, J. C., & Pirola-Merlo, A. (2013). Workplace Innovation in a Nonprofit Organization. *Nonprofit Management & Leadership, 23*(3), 367–388.

Muenjohn, N., & McMurray, A. (2017a). Design Leadership, Work Values Ethic and Workplace Innovation: An Investigation of Smes in Thailand and Vietnam. *Asia Pacific Business Review, 23*(2), 192–204.

Muenjohn, N., & McMurray, A. (2017b). Leadership and Workplace Innovation: An Investigation of Asian Smes The Palgrave Handbook of Leadership in Transforming Asia (pp. 201–212).

Oeij, P., Dhondt, S., Pot, F., & Totterdill, P. (2018). *Workplace Innovation as an Important Driver of Social Innovation*. Dortmund: Sozialforschungsstelle TU Dortmund.

Oeij, P. R., Dhondt, S., Rus, D., & Van Hootegem, G. (2019). The Digital Transformation Requires Workplace Innovation: An Introduction. *International Journal of Technology Transfer and Commercialisation, 16*(3), 199–207.

Oeij, P. R. A., & Vaas, F. (2016). Effect of Workplace Innovation on Organisational Performance and Sickness Absence. *World Review of Entrepreneurship, Management and Sustainable Development, 12*(1), 101–129.

Payne, J. (2004). Re-Evaluating the Finnish Workplace Development Programme: Evidence from Two Projects in the Municipal Sector. *Economic and Industrial Democracy, 25*(4), 485–524.

Pot, F. (2011). Workplace Innovation for Better Jobs and Performance. *International Journal of Productivity and Performance Management, 60*(4), 404–415.

Pot, F., Dhondt, S., & Oeij, P. (2012). Social Innovation of Work and Employment. In W. Franz, J. Hochgerner, & J. Howaldt (Eds.), *Challenge Social Innovation: Potentials for Business, Social Entrepreneurship, Welfare and Civil Society* (Vol. 9783642328794, pp. 261–274). Heidelberg: Springer.

Pot, F., Totterdill, P., & Dhondt, S. (2016). Workplace Innovation: European Policy and Theoretical Foundation. *World Review of Entrepreneurship, Management and Sustainable Development, 12*(1), 13–32.

Preenen, P. T. Y., Oeij, P. R. A., Dhondt, S., Kraan, K. O., & Jansen, E. (2016). Why Job Autonomy Matters for Young Companies' Performance: Company Maturity as a Moderator between Job Autonomy and Company Performance. *World Review of Entrepreneurship, Management and Sustainable Development, 12*(1), 74–100.

Prus, I., Nacamulli, R. C. D., & Lazazzara, A. (2017). Disentangling Workplace Innovation: A Systematic Literature Review. *Personnel Review, 46*(7), 1254–1279.

Rosas, S. R., Kagan, J. M., Schouten, J. T., Slack, P. A., & Trochim, W. M. K. (2011). Evaluating Research and Impact: A Bibliometric Analysis of Research by the Nih/Niaid Hiv/Aids Clinical Trials Networks. *PloS one, 6*(3), e17428.

Schildt, H. A., Zahra, S. A., & Sillanpää, A. (2006). Scholarly Communities in Entrepreneurship Research: A Co-Citation Analysis. *Entrepreneurship Theory and Practice, 30*(3), 399–415.

Small, H. (1973). Co-Citation in the Scientific Literature: A New Measure of the Relationship between Two Documents. *Journal of the Association for Information Science and Technology, 24*(4), 265–269.

Talke, K., Salomo, S., & Kock, A. (2011). Top Management Team Diversity and Strategic Innovation Orientation: The Relationship and Consequences for Innovativeness and Performance. *Journal of Product Innovation Management, 28*(6), 819–832.

Tan, H., Resmini, A., Tarasov, V., & Adlemo, A. (2015). Workplace Innovation in Swedish Local Organizations—Technology Aspect. In *Lecture Notes in Business Information Processing* (Vol. 228, pp. 139–147).

Totterdill, P., Cressey, P., & Exton, R. (2012). *Social Innovation at Work: Workplace Innovation as a Social Process Challenge Social Innovation: Potentials for Business, Social Entrepreneurship, Welfare and Civil Society* (Vol. 9783642328794, pp. 241–259).

Tracey, P., & Stott, N. (2017). Social Innovation: A Window on Alternative Ways of Organizing and Innovating. *Innovation, 19*(1), 51–60.

Van Eck, N., & Waltman, L. (2010). Software Survey: Vosviewer, a Computer Program for Bibliometric Mapping. *Scientometrics, 84*(2), 523–538.

Van Eck, N. J., & Waltman, L. (2017). Citation-Based Clustering of Publications Using Citnetexplorer and Vosviewer. *Scientometrics, 111*(2), 1053–1070.

Wipulanusat, W., Panuwatwanich, K., & Stewart, R. A. (2017). Workplace Innovation: Exploratory and Confirmatory Factor Analysis for Construct Validation. *Management and Production Engineering Review, 8*(2), 57–68.

Wipulanusat, W., Panuwatwanich, K., & Stewart, R. A. (2018). Pathways to Workplace Innovation and Career Satisfaction in the Public Service: The Role of Leadership and Culture. *International Journal of Organizational Analysis, 26*(5), 890–914.

2

The Vital Elements of Organizational Innovation

Don Scott and Adela McMurray

Introduction

It is argued that innovation is a key component in an organization's sustainability and success in today's marketplace (Cascio & Aguinis, 2019). Friedman (1970) argued that the main objective of a firm is to derive a profit and that such a focus will promote an orientation toward different types of innovations. This role of innovation in producing enhanced profits was similarly identified by the Profit Impact of Market Strategies (PIMS) study (Buzzell & Gale, 1987).

Porter (1985) in his writings on business strategy suggested that there are two types of strategic orientations that can be followed, a focus on producing new and innovative products or a focus on efficiency of manufacture process for product offerings that are more of a commodity in nature. However, the PIMS study has clearly shown that these types of approaches do not need to be exclusive of one another and that a mixture of innovation and cost orientations will lead to the highest returns for any business.

The modern economy provides an opportunity for businesses to develop new product offerings and to engage in innovative product development. This

D. Scott (✉)
Southern Cross University, Lismore, NSW, Australia

A. McMurray
College of Business, Government and Law, Flinders University,
Adelaide, SA, Australia
e-mail: adela.mcmurray@flinders.edu.au

© The Author(s), under exclusive license to Springer Nature Switzerland AG 2021
A. McMurray et al. (eds.), *The Palgrave Handbook of Workplace Innovation*,
https://doi.org/10.1007/978-3-030-59916-4_2

is spurred on by the internet, artificial intelligence, and by advances in manufacture such as 3D printing. The need for businesses to identify and to develop new innovative offerings has become even more important so that workplace innovation is now attracting great interest from policymakers. It has been argued that environmental uncertainty triggers innovation (Baldridge & Burnham, 1975) and the modern world is undergoing a major stage of uncertainty evidenced through climate change. Examples are economic and production changes causing a heightened state of uncertainty about the future, spurred on by the appearances of climate change promoters at public events and at the United Nations. This is leading to an enhancement of the need for the identification of the drivers of innovation, so that businesses and nations can utilize these to promote innovation. This has attracted much interest from policymakers and public policy researchers as it has been said to represent a major driver of economic growth potential for countries (Dhondt et al., 2014).

Innovation can take place under several guises. Thus, Beblavý et al. (2012, p. 2) defined workplace innovation as an integration of skills of employers and employee, technology innovation and human resources. In the same year, Fagerberg, Fosaas, and Sapprasert (2012) in their bibliometric analysis of innovation studies identified several phases in the evolution of the innovation literature. The early phase (up to 1970) saw the studies situated in the social sciences, economics and sociology fields. This was followed by the growth phase expanding into the economics and R&D and organizing innovation clusters. Then from the 1980s, the field entered the mature phase where professional associations focused on and promoted the field's growth. In a study of innovation in ten different types of workplaces Balkin, Tremblay, and Westerman (2001) identified a range of different types of innovation that they categorized into the following types specifically, Team Innovation, Organization Restructure, Work Schedule Innovation, Skill Mix Change, Bargaining Process Innovation, Empowerment Innovation, Individual Pay Innovation, Team Pay Innovation, Organization Pay Innovation, and Benefits Pay Innovation. Later, Totterdill and Exton (2014) suggested that there were four components of workplace innovation, namely, work organization, structure and systems, reflection and innovation, and workplace partnership.

Ritala, Schneider, and Michailova (2020) identified four methodological challenges within the innovation management literature. The first being the 'conceptual and empirical ambiguity' of the concept itself. This was followed by 'level multiplicity' which refers to the multiple layers of innovation. A third challenge is 'temporal interdependencies' which refers to the processual character of the concept, and finally there is 'contextual complexity' that refers to the way in which innovation is entrenched within organizations and is socially constructed.

Generally, innovation benefits organizations, and Camisón and Villar-López (2014) found that the development of technological innovation capabilities was brought about by organizational innovation. In concert with technological capabilities for products and processes, this could result in superior firm performance.

Exposito and Sanchis-Llopis (2018) suggested a multidimensional approach to investigating the relationship between innovation choices and business performance. Thus innovation possibilities and work systems that influence creativity (Do & Shipton, 2019) and permeate thorough any business or organizational activity are an aspect that requires taking into account as organizations are forced to compete in an environment of increasing levels of competition.

A range of elements of innovation have been identified by numerous researchers and fall into the categories of an organizational nature, organizational climate and culture, leadership and management, and processes required to promote innovation. These different aspects of the drivers of innovation will be individually discussed in the following sections and address the aim of this chapter which is to identify the seminal elements that impact an organization's innovation process and which is underpinned by the following research question:

RQ1 What are the seminal elements that impact an organization's innovation process?

Of note here is that the chapter adopts a general approach and is not specific to a particular type of organization or industry and therefore embraces multiple types of organizations and industry contexts.

Methodology

To address the research question, an in-depth systematic integrated literature review was conducted which included seminal and current studies investigating the organizational innovation processes. The key words utilized in the search were 'seminal elements innovation' and 'organizational innovation'. Both UK and US spelling were employed when searching for the key term 'organisation and organization'. The criteria for inclusion and exclusion of the selected articles followed consistency (Salkind, 2010) in that the articles had to be scholarly peer-reviewed articles and written in English. Therefore, the manual literature review was predominantly comprised of peer-reviewed journal articles, books, chapters, and conference papers. The search engines used in the review were EBSCO, Proquest, and Google Scholar. The first stage of the search generated 1793 potential references. These references ranged from seminal, highly cited literature to current prevalent literature and were subjected to detailed examination prior to 66 of the mainly more recent papers being identified as covering the material and being included in this chapter. The material was analyzed, and the findings were synthesized to develop a model that identifies the vital elements of an organization's innovation process.

Literature Review

Organizational Environment and Innovation

Kimberley and Evanisko (1981) found that environmental and organizational variables, especially industry, and organizational size affect organizational innovation, thus establishing the relationship between organization size and innovation. In this regard, Pienaar and Boshoff (1996) examined the relationship between creativity, innovation, and organizational climate in library settings, where they found that large organizations evidenced higher levels of innovation than smaller organizations. They concluded that the size of the organization has a direct influence on the level of innovation. In support of this finding, Divisekera and Nguyen (2018) identified organizational size as influencing innovation in the tourism industry. Naqshbandi (2018), in a study of Malaysian organizations, used six measures of inbound innovation and four measures of outbound innovation and established that there was a significant difference between organizations of different sizes in relation to levels of inbound and outbound open innovation. The cause of this effect was ascribed to the inflows and outflows of knowledge and information regarding the paths to market. Yet in contrast, other studies have found no significant relationship between the size of an organization and the implementation of innovation (Vakola & Rezgui, 2000).

Where it is found to exist, the effect of organizational size on innovativeness is viewed as being due to personnel and management practices (Stata, 1989; Stringer, 2000). To examine this aspect, Capaldo, Iandoli, Raffa, and Zollo (2003) introduced an innovation capability evaluating method with four resource sets—human, entrepreneurial, those arising from external linkages and economic sources. Each set contained several measures to assess both the degree of technological innovation and market innovation capability.

However, to be able to utilize such identified resource sets, it is necessary that an organization be structured in such a way as to allow for the utilization of these abilities. In this regard, Pavitt (1991) had identified five key aspects that should be possessed by innovative organizations. The first aspect was organization-specific abilities that could allow for the development of the direction and range of technological opportunities that the organization could exploit. This was followed by an organizational structure that was sufficiently decentralized to allow for effective implementation of new opportunities. The third aspect was associated with the type of organization needed to allow for the use of core technologies. The fourth aspect was anchored to the process of learning that would enable organizations to use their experience to improve their competencies, and the final aspect pertained to the methods of resource allocation that would support the development of innovative offerings.

Research by Thompson (1965) found that a rigid bureaucratic structure inhibits innovation but can be altered to increase innovativeness. This could be achieved by means of processes such as increased professionalization, a loose or a untidier organizational structure, decentralization, freer communication, greater reliance on group processes, modification of the incentive system, and changes in management practices. These types of less bureaucratic structures can be enhanced by the utilization of key innovation advocates such as internal champions, intrapreneurs, promoters, gatekeepers, and other staff roles which support, energize, and facilitate innovation (Rothwell, 1992). Other researchers have found that flat or matrix organizational structures and open communication pathways between departments and functions are likely to be more innovative than traditional hierarchical organizations, characterized predominantly by vertical communication and chain of command (e.g., West & Altink, 1996).

Martins and Terblanche (2003) suggested that the level of innovation was a context-specific evaluation which varied from one group, one organization, and one organizational culture to another. This suggested that the evaluation of innovation should be considered at the level of person, organization, industry context, staff role, profession, and wider. However, in contradiction to this, Bakx (2007) suggested that the degree of innovativeness is not dependent on the nature of the organization where the person works. In contrast, Galanakis (2006) asserted that knowledge creation and new product design including market success processes are shaped by an organization's internal elements as well as by external factors such as national policy.

The understanding of the role that is played by organizational knowledge had been stated earlier, in a broader manner by Ettlie and Reza (1992) who considered that new product development capability could be the result of a combination of external knowledge, the coordination capacity of internal relationships, and the collective organizational mind. Chang and Lee (2008) explored the effect of knowledge accumulation capability on organizational innovation. They found that the interaction between the external environment, the organizational culture, and the ability of the organization to accumulate knowledge would influence organizational innovation. Andreeva and Kianto (2011) suggested that knowledge creation is the most important aspect required to enhance the development of innovation in organizations, and Naqshbandi (2018) identified that knowledge acquisition in open innovation organizations was a driver of innovation. However, in order to utilize the level of knowledge that exists within an organization the knowledge needs to be shared among its members, and De Mayer (1985) had identified that the degree of innovation internally (upward, downward, and laterally) within an organization and outside can be influenced by organizational-wide communication.

Thus, having an organization that allows for its personnel to involve themselves in learning and knowledge creation can be a vital element in promoting innovation. Such learning can be enhanced by the length of tenure of organizational personnel, and as Sveiby and Simons (2002) have identified, employees with longer organizational tenure tend to foster a more collaborative culture and thus promote knowledge sharing and workplace innovation.

Organizational Climate, Culture, and Innovation

While it is evident that the type of organization and its system of management are elements that will influence innovation, there are other aspects that can have a major effect on an organization's innovative activity. Two of the foremost of these influences are the climate and culture of the organization. Empirical investigations have been found to support the concept that organizational climate effects innovation (Abbey & Dickson, 1983), while Rothwell (1992) suggested that a quality-oriented culture with an internal and external customer focus was an organizational aspect that would enhance innovation. Another research study reported by Delgado-Verde, Martín-de Castro, and Emilio Navas-López (2011) regarding an empirical analysis of 251 Spanish high and medium manufacturing firms has shown that higher product innovation capability can result from the organizational culture and the chief executive officer's commitment toward innovation. Similarly, Zain, Richardson, and Adam (2002) had determined that national culture could play an important function in the innovation process.

The organization's culture influences its organization's climate; however, the concept of climate is one that extends far beyond the simple concept of organizational cultural differences. It has been established that organizational climate is an antecedent to culture (McMurray & Scott, 2003) and that climate, the older concept, informs culture (Schneider, Ehrhart, & Macey, 2011) and impacts on organizational effectiveness. A number of researchers have therefore focused specifically on organizational climate and its relationship to the development of innovative offerings. Thus, following on from their findings, Baer and Frese (2003) proposed that cooperation within an organization would be an important factor in enhancing the development of innovative offerings. In addition, in expanding on what would represent cooperation, they suggested that there could be two climate dimensions of major importance. These were, firstly, support for an active approach toward work, where staff were comfortable to take interpersonal risks, and secondly, a climate where the organization placed a value on an individual's contributions to knowledge and skill that could be utilized in the work process, so that successful cooperation required the existence of a climate in which employees felt safe when displaying proactive behavior. Similarly, Siegal and Kaemmerer (1978) had identified support for creativity as being a major factor contributing to an innovative climate, and such a creative climate was defined by Tidd, Bessant, and Pavitt (2001, p. 314) as a '…positive approach to creative ideas supported by relevant reward systems'.

In their research, Baer and Frese (2003) focused on process innovation and examined the organizational climates of 47 medium-sized German companies to identify those climates that positively affected the relationship between process innovation and company performance. The aspects that they examined were the relationship between process innovations, climates for initiative, psychological safety, and firm performance, and they found a direct relationship between a climate for initiative, psychological safety, and firm performance. They concluded that climates for innovation and psychological safety were important means to use to increase company performance irrespective of the degree of change in process innovativeness and that such climate changes alone could result in higher levels of employee innovativeness.

Leadership and Management

Leadership and consideration of individuals was suggested by Parry and Proctor-Thompson (2003) to be linked to climate. Jaskyte (2004) also suggested that innovation would be dependent on leadership and that this would be affected by the organizational climate. However, when attempting to test this suggested relationship by means of correlational analysis, Jaskyte (2004) failed to demonstrate any such relationship between leadership and innovation although it was found that leadership did appear to affect organizational culture.

Meyer and Goes (1988) had shown that managerial or leadership variables were strong predictors of innovation processes, and Schoemaker, Heaton, and Teece (2018) identified the important role played by top management entrepreneurial leadership in influencing an organization's innovation processes. In terms of transformational leadership styles, Mokhber, Khairuzzaman, and Vakilbashi (2017) identified that there was a positive relationship between transformational leadership and innovation as did Xie et al. (2018). They conducted an empirical analysis and found that transformational leadership styles built trust and individual identity within teams. In turn, Hughes et al. (2018, p. 565) concluded that '…there is clear theoretical and empirical evidence demonstrating that leadership is an important variable that can enhance or hinder workplace creativity and innovation'.

Other leadership styles such as transactional leadership showed some influence, but this was not as strong in influencing organizational innovation as that arising from transformational leadership. In the educational sector, Elrehail, Emeagwali, Alsaad, and Alzghoul (2018) found that knowledge sharing interacted with transformational leadership and that this could be the differentiating factor influencing the development of innovation processes.

Guimaraes, Paranjape, Cornick, and Armstrong (2018) in studying the outcome of an innovative process as being the introduction of new products and the success of such introductions suggested that important determinants of such new product development success would fall into four main areas of strategic leadership specifically competitive intelligence, management of technology, specific characteristics of the company's innovation process, and the company's absorptive capacity to use available knowledge to produce and commercialize new products.

Many factors influence an individual's motivation and ability to innovate in the workplace. In addition to individuals feeling safe, these can relate to the nature and existence of any sanctions for making mistakes, the intrinsic value of tasks, and autonomy and control over work (West & Altink, 1996). Su and Baird (2017) have identified the need for service organizations to focus on new management practices, process structures, and techniques to promote organizational innovation. The effect of the use of innovative management techniques covering aspects such as knowledge management and entrepreneurial action has been investigated in Spain by Albors-Garrigos, Igartua, and

Signes (2018) who found that the utilization of such techniques had a direct effect on innovation activity but also that this effect could be moderated by the industry environment. This research into the influence on innovation of all these aspects of the management of an organization has highlighted the need for, and nature of, such management to be carefully considered.

However, for there to be successful implementation of an innovation process apart from an acceptance of mistakes and the allocation of extra 'thinking' time, it is necessary that there should be some perceptual rewards for the organizational members who are engaged in the process. This in turn requires that there should be some measurement of the achievements, and Williams and McMurray (2004) suggested that innovative practice could be supported by means of an appropriate performance appraisal system. The development of such a suitable appraisal system would be a function of the leadership of an organization.

In contrast to thoughts of imposing sanctions on employees for making mistakes, researchers such as Amabile (1998) have suggested that the generation and implementation of new ideas by employees would depend on creative behavior. This would need to be sustained and rewarded by the organization in order to ensure that it can develop to its fullest capacity. This aspect can be enhanced by means of documented management procedures and by the nature of an employment contract that is entered into by employees and organizational management. In reinforcement of this aspect, Dung, Thang, Janssen, and Hine (2017) examined 865 Vietnamese small and medium manufacturing enterprises. They found that the formality of the employment contract was a significant positive influence on product improvement and process innovation.

Required Innovation Processes

The potential influence of human resource management on innovation has been recently identified by Lee, Pak, Kim, and Li (2019) who determined that suitable human resource management practices such as rewards and performance appraisals could increase the proactivity of workforce members and thereby increase the levels of innovation in the workplace.

Luu and Inaba (2013), in an analysis of more than 2500 private manufacturing small and medium Vietnamese enterprises, expanded the range of aspects that would be important for innovation to occur within an organization when they found that international engagements, export, import of equipment and machinery, and support from foreign donors would be promoters of innovation.

Both product innovation known as outcome innovation and process innovation require firms to have capabilities related to technology and the market (Danneels, 2002) with many studies presenting innovation capability as a synthesis of such capabilities. From a process approach, Chiesa, Coughlan, and Voss (1996) proposed a formative measurement model for technological innovation capability which included product development capability, process innovation capability, concept generation capability, leadership capability, technology acquisition capability, capability in the effective use of systems and tools, and resource deployment capability.

It is evident that there are a range of organizational actions that need to be taken into account when examining the types of activities that are necessary to promote an organization to become innovative. Some of these relate to the basic climate and culture of the organization, as has been previously discussed, and others to the organization of the processes that will be necessary to bring about innovation. This was highlighted by Van der Panne, van Beers, and Kleinknecht (2003) in their identification of what they considered to be the seven factors that would be important if an organization were to create new and innovative product offerings. The first of these factors embrace a culture that is dedicated to innovation and explicitly recognizes the collective nature of innovation efforts. This is followed by previous experience with innovation projects. Thirdly, a multidisciplinary research and development team with a balance of technological and marketing skills, and the presence of a product champion. Fourthly, a clearly articulated innovation strategy and a suitable management style. The fifth factor addresses the compatibility of the product development project with the firm's core competencies. The sixth is the innovations product quality and price relative to those of established products, followed lastly by good market introduction timing.

Measurement of Innovation

A number of the elements that are necessary for innovation to take place have been reflected in instruments that have been developed in order to measure innovation. Thus, Becker and Whisler (1967) suggested that the innovation process could be measured based on the four stages of stimulus, conception, proposal, and adoption. Building on this work, McMurray and Dorai (2003) developed a 24-item Workplace Innovation Scale (WIS) that was designed to identify and to measure the behavioral aspects of innovation practices by individuals in their workplace. This measure was comprised of the four dimensions specifically addressing innovation climate, organizational innovation, team innovation, and individual innovation.

Another measurement scale that was aimed at the evaluation of innovation performance was suggested by Alegre, Lapied, and Chiva (2006). These authors considered that product innovation performance was a result of the existence of the two different dimensions of efficiency and efficacy. While innovation efficiency reflected the effort carried out to achieve a degree of success, innovation efficacy reflected the degree of success of an innovation.

Consolidation and Discussion

According to Dackert, Loov, and Martensson, 2004, there are four aspects of group innovation, in particular vision, participative safety, climate for excellence, and support for innovation. However, innovation requires an encouraging environment, suitable organizational structures, climate and culture, and the carrying out of a suitable process. The factors that influence innovation in organizations and that have been identified in the preceding discussion can therefore be summarized as follows:

Firstly, in terms of the nature of the organization in relation to its size, personnel and management practices, inflows of knowledge, and the types of technology and markets in which it is operating are important aspects. These will in turn be able to be utilized by the existence of a suitable decentralized, flat structure with good easy communication between employees possibly enhanced by personnel with longer tenures and the promotion of learning, proper resource allocation, and a suitable incentive scheme.

Secondly, the organizational environment will relate to the climate that exists within the organization and its culture both of which need to be quality and customer oriented. Personnel need to be encouraged to be creative and to accept risks with there being rewards for creativity and innovation, support for such innovation, and an absence of any sanctions that penalize failures of innovative efforts.

Thirdly, aspects of the organizational environment, climate, and culture will need to be promoted through entrepreneurial leadership that supports creativity and innovation and which may be transformational in its orientation. Innovation can therefore be promoted by support for the acquisition and utilization of competitive intelligence, the sharing of knowledge, the absence of any sanctions that inhibit risk-taking, a suitably accepting human resource management-based appraisal system, and employee contracts that recognize innovation.

Finally, it is necessary that any innovation be able to be transformed into competitive offerings that will appeal to customers, and this will require that there is a suitable level of technological capability and a sharing of knowledge together with the integration of employee skills, technology, and human resource management which may need to acquire any skilled personnel needed to support the developmental process that is required.

In order to determine whether an organization is suitably equipped to promote innovative activity, it will be necessary to measure the organization's capability, and this will require the utilization of an assessment instrument that is more wide ranging than the instruments that have hitherto been used.

These six required innovation elements are depicted in condensed form within the following foundational model (Fig. 2.1):

ELEMENTS OF INNOVATION

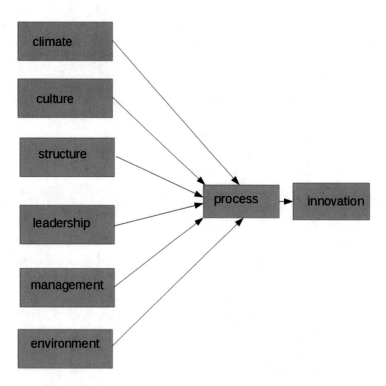

Fig. 2.1 Foundational Model: Elements of Innovation. Source: Authors

Conclusion

The purpose of this chapter was to identify the seminal elements that impact on an organization's innovation process. The six vital elements of culture, climate, structure, leadership, management, and environment were derived from the literature. These factors informed the development of the foundational innovation model that contributes to the literature through the identification of the foundation influences of the innovation process. Future research could expand this model to include the detailed components of each of the six elements as they relate to a specific organizational type or a specific industry.

A limitation of this chapter is that it is conceptual and only evaluated literature that was published in the English language.

References

Abbey, A., & Dickson, J. (1983). R & D Work Climate and Innovation in Semiconductors. *Academy of Management Journal, 26*, 362–368.

Albors-Garrigos, J., Igartua, J. I., & Signes, A. P. (2018). Innovation Management Techniques and Tools: Its Impact on Firm Innovation Performance. *International Journal of Innovation Management, 1850051*, 31. World Scientific Publishing Europe Ltd. https://doi.org/10.1142/S1363919618500512

Alegre, J., Lapied, R. A., & Chiva, R. (2006). A Measurement Scale for Product Innovation Performance. *European Journal of Innovation Management, 9*, 333–346.

Amabile, T. M. (1998). How to Kill Creativity, *Harvard Business Review*, September-October: 77–87.

Andreeva, T., & Kianto, A. (2011). Knowledge Processes, Knowledge-intensity and Innovation: A Moderated Mediation Analysis. *Journal of Knowledge Management, 15*, 1016–1034.

Baer, M., & Frese, M. (2003). Innovation is Not Enough: Climates for Initiative and Psychological Safety, Process for Innovations, and Firm Performance. *Journal of Organizational Behavior, 24*(1), 45–68.

Bakx, N. (2007). *Which Personality Traits do Innovative People Possess*, Masters Thesis, University of Amsterdam.

Baldridge, J., & Burnham, R. A. (1975). Organizational Innovation: Individual, Organizational and Environmental Impacts. *Administrative Science Quarterly, 20*, 165–176.

Balkin, D. B., Tremblay, M., & Westerman, J. (2001). Workplace Innovations in Large, Unionized Canadian Organizations. *Journal of Business and Psychology, 15*, 439–448.

Beblavý, M., Maselli, I., & Martellucci, E. (2012). *Workplace Innovation and Technological Change.* CEPS Special Report.

Becker, S. W., & Whisler, T. L. (1967). The Innovative Organization: A Selective View of Current Theory and Research. *Journal of Business., 40,* 462–469.

Buzzell, R. D., & Gale, B. T. (1987). *The PIMS Principles.* New York: The Free Press.

Camisón, C., & Villar-López, A. (2014). Organizational Innovation as an Enabler of Technological Innovation Capabilities and Firm Performance. *Journal of Business Research, 67,* 2891–2902.

Capaldo, G., Iandoli, L., Raffa, M., & Zollo, G. (2003). The Evaluation of Innovation Capabilities in Small Software Firms: A Methodological Approach. *Small Business Economics, 21,* 343–354.

Cascio, W. F., & Aguinis, H. (2019). *Applied Psychology in Talent Management* (8th ed.). Thousand Oaks, CA: Sage.

Chang, S.-C., & Lee, M. S. (2008). The Linkage Between Knowledge Accumulation Capability and Organizational Innovation. *Journal of Knowledge Management, 12,* 3–20.

Chiesa, V., Coughlan, P., & Voss, C. A. (1996). Development of a Technical Innovation Audit. *Journal of Product Innovation Management, 13,* 105–136.

Dackert, I., Loov, L. A., & Martensson, M. (2004). Leadership and Climate for Innovation in Teams. *Economic and Industrial Democracy, 25*(2), 301–318.

Danneels, E. (2002). The Dynamics of Product Innovation and Firm Competences. *Strategic Management Journal, 23,* 1095–1121.

De Mayer, A. (1985). The Flow of Technological Innovation in an R & D Department. *Research Policy, 4,* 315–328.

Delgado-Verde, M., Martín-de Castro, G., & Emilio Navas-López, J. (2011). Organizational Knowledge Assets and Innovation Capability: Evidence from Spanish Manufacturing Firms. *Journal of Intellectual Capital, 12,* 5–19.

Dhondt, S., Preenen, P., Oeij, P., Corral, A., Isusi, I., Totterdill, P., & Karanika-Murray, M. (2014). European Company Survey: Construction of the Workplace Innovation Index and Selection of Companies. (No. TNO 2014 R14131). TNO.

Divisekera, S., & Nguyen, V. K. (2018). Determinants of Innovation in Tourism Evidence from Australia. *Tourism Management, 67,* 157–167. https://doi.org/10.1016/j.tourman.2018.01.010

Do, H., & Shipton, H. (2019). High-performance Work Systems and Innovation in Vietnamese Small Firms. *International Small Business Journal, 37*(7), 732–753.

Dung, N. V., Thang, N. N., Janssen, F., & Hine, D. (2017). Employment Contract and SME's Innovation in Developing and Transition Economies: The case of Vietnam. *Journal of Developmental Entrepreneurship, 22,* 1750027.

Elrehail, H., Emeagwali, O. L., Alsaad, A., & Alzghoul, A. (2018). The Impact of Transformational and Authentic Leadership on Innovation in Higher Education: The Contingent Role of Knowledge Sharing. *Telematics and Informatics, 35*(1), 55–67. https://doi.org/10.1016/j.tele.2017.09.018

Ettlie, J. E., & Reza, E. M. (1992). Organizational Integration and Process Innovation. *Academy of Management Journal, 35*, 795–827.

Exposito, A., & Sanchis-Llopis, J. A. (2018). Innovation and Business Performance for Spanish SMEs: New Evidence from a Multi-dimensional Approach. *International Small Business Journal, 36*(8), 911–931.

Fagerberg, J., Fosaas, M., & Sapprasert, K. (2012). Innovation: Exploring the knowledge Base. *Research Policy, 41*(7), 1132–1153.

Friedman, M. (1970). *The Social Responsibility of Business Is to Increase Its Profits.* New York: The New York Times Magazine.

Galanakis, K. (2006). Innovation process. Make Sense Using Systems Thinking. *Technovation, 26*(11), 1222–1232.

Guimaraes, T., Paranjape, K., Cornick, M., & Armstrong, C. P. (2018). Empirically Testing Factors Increasing Manufacturing Product Innovation Success. *International Journal of Innovation and Technology Management, 15*(2), 1850019.

Hughes, D. J., Lee, A., Tian, A. W., Newman, A., & Legood, A. (2018). Leadership, Creativity, and Innovation: A Critical Review and Practical Recommendations. *The Leadership Quarterly, 29*(5), 549–569. https://doi.org/10.1016/j.leaqua.2018.03.001

Jaskyte, K. (2004). Transformational Leadership, Organizational Culture, and Innovativeness in Nonprofit Organizations. *Non Profit Management & Leadership, 15*(2), 153–168.

Kimberley, J. R., & Evanisko, M. J. (1981). Organizational Innovation: The Influence of Individual, Organizational and Contextual Factors on Hospital Adoption of Technological and Administrative Innovations. *Academy of Management Journal, 24*, 689–714.

Lee, H. W., Pak, J., Kim, S., & Li, L.-Z. (2019). Effects of Human Resource Management Systems on Employee Proactivity and Group Innovation. *Journal of Management, 45*(2), 819–846. 10.11/0149206316680029.

Luu, D. T., & Inaba, Y. (2013). External Engagements and Innovation of Firms: Evidence from Vietnamese Manufacturing SMEs. *The Journal of Social Science, 1*, 73–99.

Martins, E. C., & Terblanche, F. (2003). Building Organisational Culture that Stimulates Creativity and Innovation. *European Journal of Innovation Management, 6*(1), 64–74.

McMurray, A., & Scott, D. (2003). The Relationship between Organizational Climate and Organizational Culture. *Journal of American Academy of Business, 3*, 1): 1–1): 8.

McMurray, A. J., & Dorai, R. (2003). Workplace Innovation Scale: A New Method for Measuring Innovation in the Workplace. *Organizational Learning & Knowledge 5th International Conference.* Lancaster University, UK.

Meyer, A., & Goes, J. B. (1988). Organizational Assimilation of Innovations: A Multilevel Contextual Analysis. *Academy of Management Journal, 31*, 897–923.

Mokhber, M., Khairuzzaman, W., & Vakilbashi, A. (2017). The Moderator Role of Organization Support for Innovative Behaviors. *Journal of Management and Organization, 24*(1), 108–128.

Naqshbandi, M. M. (2018). Organizational Characteristics and Engagement in Open Innovation: Is there a Link? *Global Business Review, 19*(3), 1–20. https://doi.org/10.1177/0972150918757845

Parry, K. W., & Proctor-Thompson, S. B. (2003). Leadership, Culture and Performance: The Case of the New Zealand Public Sector. *Journal of Change Management, 3*(4), 376–399.

Pavitt, K. (1991). Key Characteristics of the Large Innovating Firm. *British Journal of Management, 2*, 41–50.

Pienaar, H., & Boshoff, A. B. (1996). Relationship Between Creativity and Innovation in University Libraries and the Organizational Climate. *South African Journal of Library and Information Science, 64*, 67–74.

Porter, M. E. (1985). *Competitive Advantage: Creating and Sustaining Superior Performance*. New York: Free Press.

Ritala, P., Schneider, S., & Michailova, S. (2020). Innovation Management Research Methods: Embracing Rigor and Diversity. *R&D Management, 50*(3), 297–308.

Rothwell, E. (1992). Successful Industrial Innovation: Critical Factors for the 1990s. *R & D Management, 22*(30), 221–239.

Salkind, N. J. e. (2010). *Encyclopedia of Research Design* (Vol. 1). Thousand Oaks: Sage.

Schneider, B., Ehrhart, M. G., & Macey, W. H. (2011). Perspectives on Organizational Climate and Culture. In S. Zedeck (Ed.), *APA handbooks in psychology®. APA handbook of industrial and organizational psychology, Vol. 1. Building and developing the organization* (pp. 373–414). Washington DC: American Psychological Association. https://doi.org/10.1037/12169-012

Schoemaker, P. J. H., Heaton, S., & Teece, D. (2018). Innovation Dynamic Capabilities and Leadership. *California Management Review, 61*(2), 15–42. https://doi.org/10.1177/0008125618790246

Siegal, S. M., & Kaemmerer, W. F. (1978). Measuring Perceived Support for Innovation in Organizations. *Journal of Applied Psychology, 63*, 553–562.

Stata, R. (1989). Organizational Learning: The Key to Management Innovation. *Sloan Management Review, Spring*, 63–74.

Stringer, R. (2000). How to Manage Radical Innovation. *California Management Review, 42*, 70–88.

Su, S., & Baird, K. (2017). The Role of Leaders in Generating Management Innovation. *The International Journal of Human Resource Management, 29*(19), 2758–2779. https://doi.org/10.1080/09585192.2017.1282533

Sveiby, K. E., & Simons, R. (2002). Collaborative Climate and Effectiveness of Knowledge Work: An Empirical Study. *Journal of Knowledge Management, 6*(5), 420–433.

Thompson, V. (1965). Bureaucracy and Innovation. *Administrative Science Quarterly, 1*, 20.

Tidd, J., Bessant, J., & Pavitt, K. (2001). *Managing Innovation Integrating Technological, Market and Organisational Change*. England: John Wiley & Sons Ltd.

Totterdill, P., & Exton, R. (2014). Defining Workplace Innovation: The Fifth Element. *Strategic Direction, 30*, 12–16.

Vakola, M., & Rezgui, Y. (2000). Organizational Learning and Innovation in the Construction Industry. *The Learning Organization, 7*, 174–183.

Van der Panne, G., van Beers, C., & Kleinknecht, A. (2003). Success and Failure of Innovation: A Literature Review. *International Journal of Innovation Management, 7*(3), 309–338. https://doi.org/10.1142/s1363919603000830

West, M. A., & Altink, W. M. M. (1996). Innovation at work: Individual, Group, Organizational, and Socio-historical Perspectives. *European Journal of Work and Organizational Psychology, 5*, 3–11.

Williams, L., & McMurray, A. J. (2004). Factors Effecting the Innovative Practice of Nurse Managers in Health Organisations. *Contemporary Nurse, 16*(1-2), 30–39.

Xie, Y., Xue, W., Li, L., Wang, A., Chen, Y., Zheng, Q., et al. (2018). Leadership Style and Innovation Atmosphere in Enterprises: An Empirical Study. *Technological Forecasting & Social Change, 135*, 257–265. https://doi.org/10.1016/j.techfore.2018.05.017

Zain, M., Richardson, S., & Adam, M. N. K. (2002). *The Implementation of Innovation by a Multinational Operating in Two Different Environments: A Comparative Study*. Oxford: Blackwell Publishers.

3

Developing Workplace Innovation Policies in the European Union

Frank Pot, Peter Totterdill, and Steven Dhondt

Introduction. The Urgency of Workplace Innovation

Workplace innovation, as it developed from the beginning of this century in Europe, is a member of the Sociotechnical Systems Design (STSD) family (Mohr & Van Amelsvoort, 2016), going back to the restructuring of Europe after the Second World War, starting more or less the same policies for productivity and industrial democracy in several Western European countries. Although consensus about the definition of workplace innovation is growing worldwide, and its policy profile is getting stronger, other different policy concepts are being used to describe and implement more or less the same approach (Kesselring, Blasy, & Scoppetta, 2014). Examples include 'innovative workplaces' (EESC, 2011; OECD, 2010), 'sustainable work

F. Pot (✉)
Radboud University, Nijmegen, The Netherlands
e-mail: frank.pot@ardan.demon.nl

P. Totterdill
Workplace Innovation Europe CLG, Glasgow, UK
e-mail: peter.totterdill@workplaceinnovationeurope.eu

S. Dhondt
TNO Innovation for Life, Leiden, The Netherlands

KU Leuven, Leuven, Belgium
e-mail: steven.dhondt@tno.nl

© The Author(s), under exclusive license to Springer Nature Switzerland AG 2021
A. McMurray et al. (eds.), *The Palgrave Handbook of Workplace Innovation*,
https://doi.org/10.1007/978-3-030-59916-4_3

systems' (e.g. Sweden, New Zealand), 'high involvement workplaces', 'high road', 'employee-driven innovation' (e.g. Norway, Denmark) and 'relational coordination' (USA, Hoffer Gittell, 2016). Although the terminology might differ, all these approaches place a premium on employee participation and a better utilisation of the already existing human talent within organisations, primarily by (re)designing the organisation of work and tasks to enable people to be more effective and creative. Moreover, the shared objective of these approaches is to simultaneously improve the quality of working life (competence development, stress reduction) and organisational performance (productivity, quality, innovative capacity).

Workplace Innovation: Process and Outcomes

The European Workplace Innovation Network (EUWIN), started in 2013, describes workplace innovation as follows: 'Workplace innovations describe new and combined interventions in work organisation, human resource management, labour relations and supportive technologies. It is important to recognise both process and outcomes. The term workplace innovation describes the participatory and inclusive nature of innovations that embed workplace practices grounded in continuing reflection, learning and improvements in the way in which organisations manage their employees, organise work and deploy technologies. It champions workplace cultures and processes in which productive reflection is a part of everyday working life. It builds bridges between the strategic knowledge of the leadership, the professional and tacit knowledge of frontline employees and the organisational design knowledge of experts. It seeks to engage all stakeholders in dialogue in which the force of the better argument prevails. It works towards "win-win" outcomes in which a creative convergence (rather than a trade-off) is forged between enhanced organisational performance and enhanced quality of working life' (Dhondt, 2012, p. 2).

There is a vast body of evidence to underpin the concept (Oeij, Rus, & Pot, 2017; Osterman, 2018). However, the evidence for generalisable outcomes such as higher profits, higher wages and lower absenteeism is much thinner than that for the intermediate impacts described above. In our opinion, this thinner evidence is not a surprise because many more determinants have to be taken into account in explaining these outcomes, including markets, economic conditions, institutions, laws and regulations to mention just a few.

This clearly poses difficult methodological issues. Questions of generalisability arise because so much of the evidence comes from case studies. A second question centres on the need for adequate control data. The third concern is that of selection (Osterman, 2018, p. 12). Quantitative research seems almost impossible because of the diversity, dynamics and different environments of organisations in any sample to be studied.

The emergence of interest in workplace innovation can be understood not by a simple linear relationship with performance but by looking at wider economic, technological and labour market developments. The broader context is that in the early 1990s, a significant shift in Europe's economy and businesses could be observed fuelled by information technology. This shift reversed the historical pattern where tangible capital was considered to be the main asset in companies. Around 1990, investments in intangible capital (in percentage of adjusted GNP) such as patents, R&D, marketing and organisational competences became higher than investments in tangible capital (Corrado & Hulten, 2010). As 'hard' technological innovations do not seem to explain persistent productivity differentials, Bloom and Van Reenen presented evidence on another possible explanation for persistent differences in productivity at the firm and the national level, namely, that such differences largely reflect variations in management practices (Bloom & Van Reenen, 2010). The OECD calls it 'knowledge-based capital' (KBC).

One conclusion of Bloom and Van Reenen is that 'There is certainly some element of contingency in management choices' (p. 221). That 'organisational choice' does exist was confirmed by Osterman's (2018) review. A further consideration regarding innovation is the growing conviction in Europe that 'social innovation' (work organisation, competence development, employee participation, etc.) is probably more important than 'technological innovation' in explaining company performance. Whereas some companies and public institutions still put their faith in technological innovation alone and focus their resources on 'digitalisation', others have come to realise the limitations of focusing blindly only on technological advancements. Organisations can only fully benefit from technological innovation if it is embedded in a proper work organisation (Brynjolfsson & McAfee, 2014, p. 138). This context explains the need to develop and utilise the skills and competences of the present and potential workforce to increase added value as part of a competitive and knowledge-based global economy (European Commission, 2014).

Next, there is a need to enhance labour productivity to maintain our level of welfare and social security in a near future with fewer people in the workforce due to the ageing population. Finally, societal values, sometimes translated into conventions or legislation, also play a role, for example, by promoting 'decent work' or 'good jobs', enabling people to develop during working life and earn at least a 'living wage'.

Summarising these contextual issues it is clear that workplace innovation does not only address organisational performance and job quality but wider policy issues as well. However, in spite of 'organisational choice' and the existing evidence of positive effects, workplace innovation was not widely adopted. This growing awareness of the need for new forms of work organisation stimulated successive waves of policy intervention at the European level, described in the following section.

Modernising the Organisation of Work (1995–2010)

During the mid-1990s representatives from national programmes and initiatives mobilised an influential coalition of researchers and policymakers, resulting in the publication in 1995 of 'Europe's next step: organisational innovation, competition and employment', a manifesto for the future of work organisation (Andreasen, Coriat, Den Hertog, & Kaplinsky, 1995). A seminal moment for those advocating the recognition of workplace innovation as a key dimension in EU strategy came in 1997 with the publication of the Commission's Green (consultation) Paper 'Partnership for a new organisation of work': 'The Green Paper invites the social partners and public authorities to seek to build a partnership for the development of a new framework for the modernisation of work. Such a partnership could make a significant contribution to achieving the objective of a productive, learning and participative organisation of work' (European Commission, 1997, pp. 5–6).

Interest in work organisation as a driver for European competitiveness and quality of working life had been growing, partly fuelled by national initiatives such as those in Norway, Sweden, Ireland, France, Germany and the Netherlands. Based on the responses to this consultation, a policy document 'Modernising the organisation of work—A positive approach to change' was published by the European Commission in 1998 (European Commission, 1998). A substantial volume of evidence for the positive effects of new forms of work organisation was provided by the European Work and Technology Consortium (1998). Meanwhile, Eurofound conducted a large-scale research project into 'employee participation in organisational change' which provided again evidence for the positive relation between employee participation and organisational performance (EPOC: Eurofound, 1997).

In this first period, work organisation became a clear topic with support from the European Commission, in particular its Directorate General for

Employment (DG EMPL), albeit this support was not translated into a clear policy vision directed towards companies and national governments. Networks bringing together researchers and policymakers played an important role, including the ACTEUR Group, the European Work & Technology Consortium and the European Work Organisation Network (EWON).

The type of influence that was chosen could be called 'soft regulation' (invitation, stimulation, research etc.), to be distinguished from 'hard regulation' (legislation, directives etc.). See Table 3.1.

In 2002, a European Social Fund (ESF) programme (DG EMPL) focused on the realisation of a more flexible labour market and work organisation. One of the main areas proposed for investment was the 'design and dissemination of innovative and productive methods of work organisation' (EWON, 2002). Research commissioned by DG Research and Innovation showed positive results of what was called 'the high road of work organisation' and represented the first substantial attempt to define the concept of 'workplace innovation' (Totterdill, Dhondt, & Milsome, 2002). There are instances in Finland, the Netherlands, Belgium, Germany and Sweden where these reports have been used as a foundation for national programmes or initiatives.

In 2004, facilitated by the 6th EU Framework Programme ERA-NET, the 'Work-In-Net' consortium (2004–2010) coordinated research in the field of 'Innovation of Work Organisation' (Alasoini, Ramstad, Hanhike, & Lahtonen, 2005; WIN, 2010). In the same period, the Employee-driven innovation (EDI) network was established, in particular by the Norwegian and Danish trade union confederations and researchers in the field of work organisation (Høyrup, Bonnafous-Boucher, Hasse, Lotz, & Møller, 2012).

Table 3.1 Policy options in the promotion of workplace innovation

Hard/indirect regulation	Hard/direct regulation	
Directives or binding rules which focus indirectly on workplace innovation through some other policy area (e.g. product market, labour market or occupational safety and health)	Directives or binding rules which focus directly on workplace innovation (e.g. work-related, organisational or management practices)	
Soft/indirect regulation	Soft/meso-level regulation	Soft/direct regulation
General policy frameworks and recommendations, conferences, 'good practice' guides, etc.	Educational and training programmes, coaching, research, learning networks, etc.	Subsidised consultancy, development and action-oriented research projects, tax credits, etc.

Source: Alasoini, Ramstad, & Totterdill, 2017, p. 29.

Since the EU's Lisbon Growth and Jobs Strategy in 2000, the European Employment Strategy's overarching objectives have encompassed not only full employment but also the promotion of quality and productivity at work. In the European Commission (2003), the 'design and dissemination of innovative and sustainable forms of work organisation' continued to be cited as a means of enhancing productivity, responsiveness and quality, as well as improving working life and the retention on the labour market of older employees.

Member States with a tradition of policies and programmes focused on workplace innovation such as those in the Nordic countries, the Netherlands, France and Germany continued to deliver such programmes; countries with no such tradition (e.g. Greece: Ioannou, 2006) continued by and large to ignore workplace innovation.

This lack of tradition was also the case in the 'new' EU Member States. For some of them, notably the former socialist countries in Central and Eastern Europe, implementing workplace innovation is even more difficult because they have another tradition in which concepts such as productivity, industrial democracy and social dialogue had different meanings than comparable concepts in Western Europe. In the 1980s, Central and Eastern European countries became familiar with the Japanese style of management and work organisation as most established productivity centres with Japanese aid funds and Japanese consultants (viz. Japanese ex-managers in their 'second career'). These centres were connected to Western European centres through their membership of the European Association of National Productivity Centres (EANPC). The EANPC (2005) promotes not only productivity but an integrated approach with quality of working life and sustainability. After these countries had entered the European Union, Japanese aid was discontinued.

Even in the Nordic countries, implementing workplace innovation was not a matter of course; in Sweden the programmes and research were partly discontinued by the new centre-right government in 2006 (Sandberg, 2013).

The outcome of this period is a European policy pattern that has remained largely fragmented: a series of separate EU policy fields such as competitiveness, innovation, employment, health and safety and social inclusion that add up to less than the sum of the parts.

Adoption of Workplace Innovation in EU Policy (2011–2016)

The formulation of the EU's Europe 2020 vision and strategy during 2009–2010 (European Commission, 2010) provided an important opportunity for European policymakers to learn from evidence of how innovation in working practices can address economic and social priorities and translate this into policies. Key influences on the European Commission included a 2011 Opinion of the European Economic and Social Committee (EESC—an advisory forum representing employers' associations, trade unions and NGOs) on 'Innovative workplaces as a source of productivity and quality jobs' (EESC, 2011) and the 'Dortmund-Brussels Position Paper' (Dortmund-Brussels Position Paper, 2012) signed by more than 30 experts and practitioners across the EU, both calling for more proactive interventions by the European Commission. DG Enterprise and Industry (ENTR) reacted to this Position Paper by organising a set of meetings to understand what they could do. After DG EMPL had been in the lead since the mid-1990s, the initiative was taken now by DG Enterprise and Industry (DG ENTR), related to industrial and innovation policy.

In 2012 DG ENTR adopted workplace innovation in its industrial and innovation policy and decided to support and fund a European Workplace Innovation Network (EUWIN) for four years, embracing all 27 EU Member States, EU candidate countries, Switzerland and Norway. EUWIN was designed to exchange good practices and establish 'workplace innovation alliances' of employers' associations, trade unions, governments and knowledge institutes.

According to DG Internal Market, Industry, Entrepreneurship and SMEs (DG GROW, the former DG ENTR) workplace innovation improves motivation and working conditions for employees, which leads to increased labour productivity, innovation capability, market resilience and overall business competitiveness. All enterprises, no matter their size, can benefit from workplace innovation, states DG GROW. It improves performance and working lives, encourages creativity of employees through positive organisational changes, combines leadership with hands-on, practical knowledge of frontline employees and engages all stakeholders in the process of change. This policy is also part of the 'Advanced Manufacturing Programme' (ADMA): 'Workplace innovation has to provide advanced solutions for manufacturing industry, based on the newest technologies' (European Commission, 2014, pp. 27–28).

In the words of DG EMPL: 'With the Europe 2020 Strategy it also became a priority to support workplace innovation aimed at improving staff motivation and working conditions with a view to enhancing the EU's innovation capability, labour productivity and organisational performance' (European Commission, 2015, pp. 169–70). One of the paragraph titles is 'Complementing technological innovation with workplace innovation' (p. 164).

European agencies supporting the policies of DG EMPL continued to supply new ideas and policy recommendations. Eurofound already organised the first seminar on workplace innovation in 2005 and developed the concept over the years in their European Working Conditions Survey (EWCS; Eurofound, 2012; Eurofound, 2016) and the European Company Survey (ECS; Eurofound, 2015). Core indicators are decision latitude and organisational participation. The European Agency for Safety and Health at Work connected workplace innovation to 'well-being at work' in both the research and policies priorities of occupational safety and health (EU-OSHA, 2013a, 2013b).

All these activities have helped the concept of workplace innovation to gain a higher policy profile with other EU institutions. The policy concept of workplace innovation was also used by the European Parliament (2013) and IndustriAll European Trade Union (IndustriAll European Trade Union, 2014) in their programmes for an industrial renaissance, as well as in national initiatives in Ireland and the UK, and in the translations of this concept into national programmes in other European countries (Alasoini et al., 2017). Outside Europe the concept is being used as well, for example, in the USA (e.g. Black & Lynch, 2003) and Australia (e.g. McMurray & Dorai, 2003).

Policies of work organisation and workplace innovation have never resulted in legislation or regulations at EU level. Mentioning the issue in the Employment Guidelines, which in effect have a purely advisory status for EU Member States, did not seem to help much nor did the evidence from the effective national legislation that exists in a small minority of Member States. Probably workplace innovation is not suitable for a regulatory approach, because its implementation depends very much on the social dialogue at European, national, sectoral and organisation levels. Furthermore, there is a strong feeling amongst policymakers that they should not interfere in company policies.

Nonetheless EU, national and regional authorities can stimulate dialogue and develop campaigns for knowledge dissemination and capacity building, described by Alasoini (2016, pp. 20-23) as 'soft regulation' compared to 'hard regulation' (legislation). Some of these authorities stimulated and resourced workplace innovation at enterprise level, but unfortunately only for a short period of time in Ireland, Norway, the Netherlands, Belgium (Flanders) and Portugal. France, Germany and Finland (Alasoini, 2016) are the exceptions, with programmes that have been renewed several times over the past decades. New ongoing programmes have been developed in Basque Country (Spain) and Scotland (UK) (Alasoini et al., 2017).

In the lobbying for and development of these policies, an important role has always been played by researchers and their networks. Policies were developed bottom-up by coalitions of European Commission officials and researchers who organised seminars, meetings and workshops to convince the Commission's Directors, Directors-General and finally EU Commissioners. Sometimes a few representatives of trade unions and/or employers' associations were also active in these networks. These coalitions have appeared to be successful in helping to put workplace innovation higher on the political agenda.

Complementing Technological Innovation with Workplace Innovation (2017 and Beyond)

In the present times all the reasons for workplace innovation mentioned in paragraph 1 are still relevant. However, policymakers also see the rise of digital technologies as setting a new policy scene for the workplace (Oeij, Rus, Dhondt, & Van Hootegem, 2019). The world has been muddling through several disruptive technological breakthroughs for some time now. Robotics, artificial intelligence and machine learning could fundamentally change the nature of work and impact the future viability of organisations as well as that of the general societal fabric. The debates on digital transformation and the future of work reveal new risks and opportunities. These risks and opportunities cannot be solved by technology alone.

Workplace innovation remains the main solution for organisations to stimulate the use of new technology (Putnik, Oeij, Dhondt, Van der Torre, & De Vroome, 2019) and to deal with the risks. Will part of the workforce be left behind or will everybody acquire new skills? Can we create more high-quality jobs or will the polarisation of jobs become even stronger? We suggest that workplace innovation is able to contribute to positive solutions. Being aware of 'organisational choice', managers can actively choose to take workplace innovation as a departure point for innovation. But in spite of the benefits, this strategy is not self-evident. Rodrik and Sabel (2019) argue that the shortfall in 'good jobs' can be viewed as a massive market failure—a kind of gross economic malfunction, and not just a source of inequality and economic exclusion. They make the case that this problem cannot be dealt with standard regulatory instruments. Binding agreements between companies, social partners and governments are necessary to start a 'good jobs' industrial policy, and they formulate the conditions for a different interplay of public policy, social partners and scientific communities. This new approach could send a message to the new European Commissioners—installed end of 2019—to keep workplace innovation in their industrial and innovation policy and stimulate social dialogue to prepare such agreements.

Recently the EESC published a new 'Own-Initiative Opinion' on 'Social Dialogue for Innovation in the Digital Economy'. One of the recommendations is to continue promoting workplace innovation: 'At national level initiatives by social partners to enhance the productivity and well-being of workers at workplace level are a promising method, that should be promoted in a wider European context. In this regard the EESC welcomes the initiatives and research of Eurofound and the European Workplace Innovation Network and proposes that the EU take action to develop the dialogue between social partners and other stakeholders in the context of participative approaches to promote workplace innovation' (EESC, 2019, p. 4).

The European Commission established the 'Industry 2030 High-Level Industrial Roundtable' with 8 independent experts and 12 representatives of employers' associations and trade unions. In their vision they agreed on social dialogue, innovative jobs, human-centred design of technology and investing in new skills. One of the recommendations for building an enabling environment for more sustainable business activities is: 'Promote the development of workplace innovation and other modern practices, which influence both well-being and economic performance of companies' (Industry 2030 High-Level Industrial Roundtable, 2019, p. 35).

In another publication, DG EMPL concluded this as well: 'Robust economic expansion in the EU cannot be sustained without higher total factor productivity growth, which relies more on the efficient use of productive factors, rather than just expanding their use. Total factor productivity thrives in Member States and regions with strong labour market institutions and in firms that invest in workers' training and innovative capital and processes. Policies that help to develop human capital and facilitate workplace innovation are most effective in increasing productivity in the long term, provided labour markets do not discriminate and firms can access the necessary capital' (European Commission, 2019a, p. 28).

The European Agency for Safety and Health at Work published a study, *Foresight on new and emerging occupational safety and health risks associated with digitalisation by 2025* (EU-OSHA, 2018) in which workplace innovation is used as an option to construct scenarios. In a recent Discussion Paper EU-OSHA uses the concept of 'social innovation in the workplace', meaning non-technical innovations that emphasise good quality jobs and employee participation. The argument is that the fourth industrial revolution should go together with social innovation in the workplace (EU-OSHA, 2019).

These high-level recommendations seem to reflect high levels of agreement about the positive impact of workplace innovation. However, the transposition of these recommendations to EU and national policies is not that self-evident. In particular the employers' representatives emphasise that work organisation and technology is their prerogative and responsibility. They decide when and how workers will be involved. No need for arrangements with trade unions and/or governments. Conducting research and training consultants is not seen as a priority issue. If joint programmes of social partners and governments are not feasible (at the moment), government initiatives seem obvious. Good examples include current programmes in France, Germany, Finland, the Basque Country and Scotland.

The lobbying continues, and workplace innovation's applied and action research community again has to draw its own plan. This is being achieved by revitalising EUWIN, this time without funding by the European Commission but with financial and in-kind contributions of—at the start—19 partners from 12 European countries. Current plans, co-ordinated by the HIVA Research Institute at the University of Leuven, include a programme of international events and the relaunch of a definitive Workplace Innovation Knowledge Bank, bulletin and social media campaign (led by Workplace Innovation Europe CLG).

Conclusions

For the European Commission, all these high-level recommendations are an extra reason to continue the policy of supporting workplace innovation. Workplace innovation could be easily integrated in EU policy agendas such as innovation, new skills, 'more and better jobs' and 'social dialogue'. On its innovation web page DG GROW refers to 'key enabling technologies, such as workplace innovation' (DG GROW, 2019). DG EMPL is in the lead of the 'New Start for Social Dialogue'. Obviously these policies should be extended to and embedded in broader policies of public interest such as social equality, social empathy, peace and the environment (André, 2019).

There is room for improvement. In the European Working Conditions Survey 2015, one question was: 'Are you involved in improving the work organisation or work processes of the department or organisation?' Of the responding employees in the EU-27 countries, 50% answered 'always' or 'most of the time'. More or less the same percentage responded positive to questions about 'involvement in target setting' and 'ability to influence decisions that are important for one's work' (Eurofound, 2016).

For a number of reasons many enterprises, hospitals and government departments, for example, do not implement workplace innovation as a matter of course, in spite of the obvious benefits for employees and employers (Dhondt, Vermeerbergen, & Van Hootegem, 2017, pp. 90–91). Recently several scientists from the USA emphasised the importance of the socio-economic system. The 'massive market failure', as Rodrik and Sabel call it, to create a 'good jobs economy' should be compensated by a better coordinated policy and more action by governments, social partners and research institutes. Osterman (2018, p. 25) argued 'that adoption of specific internal labor market practices is the result of a political contest within organizations in which groups advocate for policies that are in their self-interest. The impact of these groups is shaped by their power within the firm, by the needs of the firm and its competitive environment, and also by resources, regulatory and legal, that are provided by the external environment'. To support a 'good jobs economy', the development of 'countervailing power, or, to put it bluntly, coercion' (p. 27) is needed if creating a supportive environment that helps sustain stakeholder behaviour (soft regulation) is not enough. Trade unions, shareholders with broader goals for their investments, governments and the general public (values) could play their part in both strategies.

The emphasis on job quality is also supported by the MIT Task Force on the Future of Work: 'We must first understand that today's challenge, and likely tomorrow's, is *not* too few jobs. Instead, it is the quality and accessibility of the jobs that will exist and the career trajectories they will offer to workers, particularly to those with less education. Addressing this challenge means channeling technological progress and accompanying productivity growth into a strong labor market that delivers broadly distributed income growth and economic security, as occurred in the decades after World War II' (Autor, Mindell, & Reynolds, 2019, p. 46). The importance of job quality is also underlined in the conclusions of the evaluation of the Europe 2020 Strategy: the employment policy was rather successful but 'cannot encompass all the aspects of the changing workplace, in which the quality of jobs matters as much as their availability. In the future, greater attention should be given to the aspect of the quality of work' (European Commission, 2019b, p. 7).

Although the situation in Europe is slightly better than in the USA due to the social economy that dominates in Europe, the debate on proper policies continues. In Europe workplace innovation is considered not appropriate for hard/direct regulation. But the market failure is also visible in EU countries. Workplace innovation is still not widespread and the number of precarious and non-standard jobs has been increasing due to the economic crisis and new technologies. This is why the European Commission came forward in 2017 with the European Pillar of Social Rights, covering 20 rights in the fields of (a) equal opportunities and access to the labour market, (b) fair working conditions and (c) social protection and inclusion (European Commission, 2017). Governments and social partners are encouraged by the European Commission to apply these rights through social dialogue, but legislation is not excluded. Additionally it would not be surprising to see more workers and trade unions engage in industrial action and legal procedures.

EU and national authorities have shown that they can successfully stimulate social dialogue and develop campaigns for knowledge dissemination and capacity building. However persistent endeavours are needed, and it's a challenge to extend these programmes to European countries with less tradition and experience. An important trigger is that the highest benefits from new technologies can be obtained by complementing them with proper workplace innovation. Besides a better economic performance, this will create a good jobs economy as well.

References

Alasoini, T. (2016). *Workplace Development Programmes as Institutional Entrepreneurs. Why They Produce Change and Why They Do Not.* Aalto University (doctoral dissertations 12/2016).

Alasoini, T., Ramstad, E., Hanhike, T., & Lahtonen, M. (2005). *European Programmes on Work and Labour Innovation—A Benchmarking Approach.* Helsinki/Bonn: Work-In-Net.

Alasoini, T., Ramstad, E., & Totterdill, P. (2017). National and Regional Policies to Promote and Sustain Workplace Innovation. In P. R. A. Oeij, D. Rus, & F. Pot (Eds.), *Workplace Innovation. Theory, Research and Practice* (pp. 27–44). Cham, Switzerland: Springer.

André, J.-C. (2019). *Industry 4.0. Paradoxes and Conflicts.* London; Hoboken: ISTE Ltd./John Wiley & Sons Inc.

Andreasen, L. E., Coriat, B., Den Hertog, J. F., & Kaplinsky, R. (1995). *Europe's Next Step: Organisational Innovation, Competition and Employment*. Ilford: Frank Cass.

Autor, D., Mindell, D. A., & Reynolds, E. B. (2019). *The Work of the Future: Shaping Technology and Institutions*. Cambridge, USA: Massachusetts Institute of Technology.

Black, S. E., & Lynch, L. M. (2003). *What's Driving the New Economy?: The Benefits of Workplace Innovation* (FRBSF Working Paper 2003-23 final revision).

Bloom, N., & Van Reenen, J. (2010). Why Do Management Practices Differ across Firms and Countries? *Journal of Economic Perspectives, 24*(1), 203–224.

Brynjolfsson, E., & McAfee, A. (2014). *The Second Machine Age: Work, Progress, and Prosperity in a Time of Brilliant Technologies*. New York/London: W.W. Norton.

Corrado, C., & Hulten, C. (2010). How Do You Measure a Technological Revolution? *American Economic Review, 100*(5), 99–104.

DG GROW (European Commission). (2019). Retrieved August 30, 2019, from http://ec.europa.eu/growth/industry/innovation_en

Dhondt, S. (ed.) (2012). *European learning network for workplace innovation*, Section 4 technical proposal, call for tender no 212/pp/ent/cip/12/c/n02c04. Hoofddorp: TNO.

Dhondt, S., Vermeerbergen, L., & Van Hootegem, G. (2017). Evidence of Workplace Innovation from Organisational and Economic Studies. In P. R. A. Oeij, D. Rus, & F. Pot (Eds.), *Workplace Innovation. Theory, Research and Practice* (pp. 79–94). Cham, Switzerland: Springer.

Dortmund-Brussels Position Paper. (2012). *Workplace Innovation as Social Innovation*. Retrieved August 30, 2019, from http://www.kennisbanksocialeinnovatie.nl/nl/kennis/kennisbank/workplace-innovation-as-social-innovation/1009?q=dortmund

EANPC. (2005). *Productivity, the High Road to Wealth*. Brussels: European Association of National Productivity Centres.

EESC (European Economic and Social Committee). (2011). *Innovative Workplaces as a Source of Productivity and Quality Jobs*. [own-initiative opinion SC/043]. Retrieved August 26, 2019, from http://www.eesc.europa.eu/resources/docs/ces543-2011_ac_en.doc

EESC (European Economic and Social Committee). (2019). *Social Dialogue for Innovation in Digital Economy [own-initiative opinion SOC/577]*. Brussels: EESC.

Eurofound. (1997). *Employee Participation and Organisational Change: EPOC Survey of 6000 Workplaces in Europe*. Dublin: European Foundation.

Eurofound. (2012). *Fifth European Working Conditions Survey- Overview Report*. Luxembourg: Publications Office of the European Union.

Eurofound. (2015). *Third European Company Survey. Workplace Practices: Patterns, Performance and Well-being*. Luxembourg: Publications Office of the European Union.

Eurofound. (2016). *Sixth European Working Conditions Survey- Overview Report*. Luxembourg: Publications Office of the European Union.

European Agency for Safety and Health at Work (EU-OSHA). (2013a). *Priorities for Occupational Safety and Health Research in Europe: 2013–2020.* Bilbao: EU-OSHA.

European Agency for Safety and Health at Work (EU-OSHA). (2013b). *Well-being at Work—Creating a Positive Work Environment.* Bilbao: EU-OSHA.

European Agency for Safety and Health at Work (EU-OSHA). (2018). *Foresight on New and Emerging Occupational Safety and Health Risks Associated with Digitalisation by 2025.* Bilbao: EU-OSHA.

European Agency for Safety and Health at Work (EU-OSHA). (2019). *The Fourth Industrial Revolution and Social Innovation in the Workplace.* (Discussion Paper). Bilbao: EU-OSHA.

European Commission. (1997). *Partnership for a New Organisation of Work.* Brussels: Green Paper.

European Commission. (1998). *Modernising the Organisation of Work—A Positive Approach to Change'.* Policy Document. Brussels.

European Commission. (2003). *Council Decision of 22nd July 2003 on Guidelines for the Employment Policies of the Member States.* OJEC, 5.8.2003, L 197/13, para 14.

European Commission. (2010). *Europe 2020: A Strategy for Smart, Sustainable and Inclusive Growth.* COM(2010) 2020 final, 3 March 2010, Brussels.

European Commission. (2014). *Advancing Manufacturing—Advancing Europe— Report of the Task Force on Advanced Manufacturing for Clean Production.* SWD(2014) 120 final, Commission staff working document, Brussels.

European Commission. (2015). *Employment and Social Developments in Europe 2014.* Brussels: DG Employment.

European Commission. (2017). *European Pillar of Social Rights.* Brussels: European Commission.

European Commission. (2019a). *Employment and Social Developments in Europe 2019, Sustainable Growth for All: Choices for the Future of Social Europe.* Luxembourg: Publications Office of the European Union.

European Commission. (2019b). *Assessment of the Europe 2020 Strategy. Joint report of the employment committee (emco) and social protection committee (spc).* Luxembourg: Publications Office of the European Union.

European Parliament. (2013). *Report on Reindustrializing Europe to Promote Competitiveness and Sustainability.* 2013/2006(INI), Brussels.

European Work & Technology Consortium. (1998). *A Medium Term Plan for Collaborative Action.* Nottingham: Centre for Work & Technology.

EWON (European Work Organisation Network). (2002). *The Use of ESF Funds in Supporting the Modernisation of Work Organisation.* Unpublished report for the European Commission [online]. Retrieved August 30, 2019, from http://uk.ukwon.eu/File%20Storage/5032375_7_EC-Work-Organisation-ESF-Final-Report.pdf

Hoffer Gittell, J. (2016). *Transforming Relationships for High Performance. The Power of Relational Coordination.* Stanford: Stanford Business Books.

Høyrup, S., Bonnafous-Boucher, M., Hasse, C., Lotz, M., & Møller, K. (Eds.). (2012). *Employee-Driven Innovation: A New Approach*. London: Palgrave Macmillan.

IndustriAll European Trade Union. (2014). *Manifesto to Put Industry Back to Work*. Brussels: IndustriAll.

Industry 2030 high-level industrial roundtable. (2019). *A Vision for the European Industry Until 2030*. Brussels: European Commission.

Ioannou, C. A. (2006). Why Is Modern Work Organisation Lacking from Southern European Public Policies? The Case of Greece. *The International Journal of Comparative Labour Law and Industrial Relations, 22*(1), 19–37.

Kesselring, A., Blasy, C., & Scoppetta, A. (2014). *Workplace Innovation: Concepts and Indicators*. Brussels: European Commission.

McMurray, A. J., & Dorai, R. (2003). *Workplace Innovation Scale: A New Method For Measuring Innovation In The Workplace*, Organizational Learning & Knowledge 5th International Conference, 30th May–2nd June 2003—Lancaster University, UK.

Mohr, B., & Van Amelsvoort, P. (Eds.). (2016). *Co-creating Humane and Innovative Organizations: Evolutions in the Practice of Socio-technical System Design*. Portland: Global STS-D Network Press.

OECD. (2010). *Innovative Workplaces: Making Better Use of Skills Within Organizations*. Paris: OECD.

Oeij, P. R. A., Rus, D., Dhondt, S., & Van Hootegem, G. (Guest Eds.) (2019). Special issue of *Int. J. Technology Transfer and Commercialisation*, 16(3): Workplace Innovation in the Era of Disruptive Technologies.

Oeij, P. R. A., Rus, D., & Pot, F. (Eds.). (2017). *Workplace Innovation. Theory, Research and Practice*. Switzerland: Springer.

Osterman, P. (2018). In Search of the High Road: Meaning and Evidence. *ILR Review, 71*(1), 3–34.

Putnik, K., Oeij, P., Dhondt, S., Van der Torre, W., & De Vroome, E. (2019). Innovation Adoption of Employees in Logistics: Individual and Organizational Factors Related to the Actual Use of Innovation. *International Journal of Technology Transfer and Commercialisation, 16*(3), 251–267.

Rodrik, D., & Sabel, C. F. (2019). *Building a Good Jobs Economy*. Cambridge, MA/ New York: Harvard Kennedy School/Columbia Law School (Working Paper, April 2019).

Sandberg, A. (Ed.). (2013). *Nordic Lights: Work, Management and Welfare in Scandinavia*. Stockholm: SNS FÖRLAG.

Totterdill, P., Dhondt, S., & Milsome, S. (2002). *Partners at Work? A Report to Europe's Policy Makers and Social Partners*. Nottingham: The Work Institute.

Work-In-Net (WIN). (2010). *The Grand Societal Challenge: Sustainable European Work to Withstand Global Economic Change and Crisis*, Declaration 11–12 March, Berlin: WIN.

4

Workplace Innovation in Practice: Experiences from the UK

Peter Totterdill and Rosemary Exton

Why Workplace Innovation?

How do company decision-makers and change activists navigate a vast and growing body of research, dating back at least as far as the iconic Tavistock Institute studies[1] of the 1950s? And how should they learn from the experiences of European companies that had succeeded in achieving exemplary performance and enhanced capacity for product and service innovation at the same time as creating high-quality working lives for their employees?

Throughout the 1990s, several influential European policymakers and researchers began to focus on the increasingly apparent divide in strategies adopted by companies in response to the changing market environment, leading to quite different economic and employment consequences. According to the European Work and Technology Consortium (1998):

> On the one hand strategies for workplace flexibility which are motivated principally by cost-cutting will certainly decrease the demand for labour; as several studies of lean production methods suggest they are also likely to reduce quality of working life ('job enlargement without job enrichment'). However, strategies

---

[1] For example Trist and Bamforth (1951).

P. Totterdill (✉) • R. Exton
Workplace Innovation Europe CLG, Glasgow, UK
e-mail: peter.totterdill@workplaceinnovationeurope.eu; rosemary.exton@workplaceinnovationeurope.eu

© The Author(s), under exclusive license to Springer Nature Switzerland AG 2021
A. McMurray et al. (eds.), *The Palgrave Handbook of Workplace Innovation*,
https://doi.org/10.1007/978-3-030-59916-4_4

for flexibility which are geared towards the creation of new products or services, exploring new business activities and building new markets may have quite the opposite effect. We can therefore differentiate between a *high road* and a *low road* of innovation, built on quite distinctive approaches to the organisation of work. The defining characteristics of the high road are the creation of organisational spaces and the liberation of human creativity *in ways which achieve a dynamic balance between product and process innovations.*

One important issue remained. Beyond the high road and the low road of innovation, there was also an *old road* on which almost everything remains the same. This absence of any substantial change was seen to endanger employment even more than the low road approach, since many of those companies on the old road would fail to survive in the new climate of global competition. And there were still far more firms on the old road than on the new ones, not least in the UK (European Foundation, 1997; European Work & Technology Consortium, 1998).

In 2001, the European Commission requested a study from one of this chapter's authors designed to analyse evidence both from existing literature and from an international sample of more than 100 private and public sector organisations, each characterised by high performance and high quality of working life. The aim of the Hi-Res study (Totterdill, Dhondt, & Milsome, 2002), involving collaboration across eight EU countries, was to elaborate the 'high road' previously articulated by the European Work and Technology Consortium.

Many different terms were being used to describe these high road approaches including high-performance workplaces, high involvement workplaces and new forms of work organisation. Although terminologies might differ, all these approaches placed a premium on employee participation and a better utilisation of existing human talent within organisations, primarily by (re) designing the organisation of work and tasks to enable people to be more effective and creative. The shared objective, one underpinned by a substantial body of evidence, (see, e.g. Oeij, Rus, & Pot, 2017; Totterdill, 2015), was to improve the quality of working life and organisational performance simultaneously. Successive Swedish surveys, for example, found a very clear link between flexible, participative forms of work organisation and performance: flexible organisations were more productive (+20–60%), showed a much lower rate of personnel turnover (–21%) and a lower rate of absence due to illness (–24%) compared with traditionally organised operational units (NUTEK, 1996). Comparable findings can be found in studies from Finland (Antila & Ylöstalo, 1999) and Germany (Lay, Dreher, & Kinkel, 1996). Yet the proliferating vocabularies were doing much to obscure the real choices available to company decision-makers.

'Workplace innovation' was established by the Hi-Res study as a coherent, evidence-based and action-oriented framework and was aimed at company decision-makers as well as policymakers and researchers, building on diverse traditions beginning with the pioneering work of the Tavistock Institute, and including both Socio-Technical Systems Design (Mohr & Van Amelsvoort, 2015) and Scandinavian Democratic Dialogue (Gustavsen, 1992). Hi-Res summarised workplace innovation's defining characteristic as the creation of jobs and practices that "empower workers at every level of an organisation to use and develop their full range of knowledge, skills, experience and creativity in their day-to-day work", leading to high performance simultaneously with high quality of working life (Totterdill et al., 2002). It brought practices such as job design and self-managed teams together with employee involvement in innovation and representative participation in strategic decision-making. The concept highlights the ways in which these specific workplace practices connect skills development and skills utilisation, business performance, employee health, the retention of older workers and economic and social inclusion (Oeij et al., 2017; Totterdill, 2015).

In defining workplace innovation, it is important to recognise both process and outcomes. The term describes the participatory process of innovation which leads to empowering workplace practices which, in turn, sustain continuing learning, reflection and innovation. Most importantly workplace innovation is an inherently social process, building skills and competence through creative collaboration. It seeks to build bridges between the strategic knowledge of business leaders, the professional and tacit knowledge of frontline employees and the organisational design knowledge of experts, leading to self-sustaining processes of organisational development fuelled by learning and experimentation.

Thus workplace innovation does not offer a blueprint; rather it provides global concepts and practices as generative resources which organisational actors contextualise as 'local theories' to fit local circumstances, resulting in tangible changes in workplace practice. It is inherently *innovative* in that each instance is the outcome of contextualisation and customisation.

Workplace innovation is also a systemic approach, influenced in part by studies of failed organisational change which emphasise the role of 'partial change' in undermining the introduction of empowering working practices (see, e.g. Business Decisions Ltd, 2002). It is influenced by the European sociotechnical design tradition (Van Amelsvoort & Van Hootegem, 2017) in recognising the interdependency of organisational practices as well as by other bodies of research which emphasise the importance of internally consistent policies and practices. Combining different forms of representative and direct participation achieves superior outcomes for organisations and their employees which are greater than the sum of individual measures (Huselid, Jackson, & Schuler, 1997; Lado & Wilson, 1994; Teague, 2005).

The Spread of Workplace Innovation

Governments and business support organisations in several European countries came to recognise workplace innovation as a powerful resource in addressing diverse yet interconnected policy goals. If workplace innovation produces tangible economic and employee benefits at enterprise level (see, e.g. Dhondt, Vermeerbergen, & Van Hootegem, 2017), it is also likely to have wider impacts on the economy and labour market including employee health and the retention of older workers in employment.

Workplace innovation is now embedded in national and regional programmes from the Basque County to Finland (see Pot et al. in this volume; see also Alasoini, Ramstad, & Totterdill, 2017; Totterdill, Exton, Exton, & Gold, 2016). It is recognised within the OECD's Innovation Strategy (OECD & Centre for Educational Research Innovation, 2010; Organisation for Economic Co-operation Development International Labour Organisation, 2017) and now occupies an important place in EU innovation and competitiveness policy.[2] This subsequently led to the creation of the European Commission's Workplace Innovation Network (EUWIN)[3] in 2013, jointly led by Toegepast Natuurwetenschappelijk Onderzoek (TNO)[4] and Workplace Innovation Limited.[5] EUWIN has organised a succession of awareness-raising events in at least 15 European countries, attracting many hundreds of people in total, and in many cases creating networks of workplace innovation activists at national and regional levels. EUWIN's online Knowledge Bank[6] is a unique source of inspiration, knowledge and learning resources, attracting more than 8000 hits per month at peak.

---

[2] http://ec.europa.eu/growth/industry/innovation/policy/workplace/index_en.htm.

[3] http://uk.ukwon.eu/euwin-resources-new.

[4] https://www.tno.nl/en/focus-areas/healthy-living/roadmaps/work/healthy-safe-and-productive-working/euwin-the-european-workplace-innovation-network/.

[5] www.workplaceinnovation.eu.

[6] http://uk.ukwon.eu/euwin-knowledge-bank-menu-new.

The Challenge of Defining Workplace Innovation

The task set by EU policymakers following the inauguration of EUWIN in 2013 was to create a coherent and accessible roadmap for the adoption of workplace innovation by companies and public sector organisations. 'The *Essential* Fifth Element'[7] was developed by Workplace Innovation Limited as co-leader of EUWIN to guide practitioners through workplace innovation and provide guidance on its implementation (Totterdill, 2015).

Expanding the original Hi-Res framework, The *Essential* Fifth Element is grounded in an analysis of more than 200 articles and case studies (Totterdill, 2015). The analysis identified four bundles (or 'Elements') of working practices with a strong association between high performance and high quality of working life (see table below). Alignment between these Elements creates a synergy in the form of the 'Fifth Element', a system of mutually interdependent parts which leads to a sustainable culture of innovation and empowerment embedded throughout the organisation.

The *Essential* Fifth Element forms the basis for the Workplace Innovation Diagnostic®, an employee survey measuring direct experiences of workplace practices associated with high performance and high quality of working life.

Why Workplace Innovation Matters for the UK

The revival of concern about the UK's poor productivity record began in part as a response to the country's emergence from the international financial crisis, and has since been amplified by the prospect of Brexit. While much of the policy debate at national level has largely focused on the infrastructural drivers of productivity, the 'productivity paradox' gives rise to concerns about the structure of the UK's economy and labour market.

Sisson (2014) reviews evidence of multiple factors cited for the long-term 'productivity puzzle' including, amongst others, low pay and high levels of inequality, low levels of employee engagement, weaknesses in the supply and utilisation of 'intermediate skills', cost-based competitive strategies and the predominantly transactional nature of HR.

Other writers have described the interaction between these factors as creating a "low skill equilibrium" in the UK. In short, this describes an economy based on a vicious circle in which firms follow mass production strategies requiring low skills and Tayloristic forms of work organisation, where a

---

[7] http://uk.ukwon.eu/the-fifth-element-new.

predominantly low skilled workforce has low aspirations and little incentive to participate in education and training to raise qualification levels, and which is self-perpetuating through interaction with societal and state institutions that reinforce the status quo (Green, 2016; MIT, 2019; Wilson et al., 2003).

The low skill equilibrium may explain the slow pace at which UK employers have adopted high involvement working practices, creating an unfavourable comparison with several other Northern European countries (LLAKES, 2012; UKCES, 2009). The rate at which these evidence-based workplace practices are being adopted by UK enterprises is persistently low, not least in comparison with several other Northern European countries. Analysis of findings from the European Working Conditions Survey suggests that under 20% of UK workers are in 'Discretionary Learning Jobs', less than half that of countries such as Denmark and the Netherlands (Lundvall, 2014). Likewise, the Work Foundation (2018) argues that only 9% of businesses can be classified as high-performance workplaces.

Their limited spread can be understood in terms of several interwoven factors (Business Decisions Ltd, 2002; Organisation for Economic Co-operation Development International Labour Organisation, 2017; Totterdill et al., 2002) including an excessive tendency to see innovation purely in terms of technology; low levels of awareness of innovative practice and its benefits amongst managers, social partners and business support organisations; poor access to robust methods and resources capable of supporting organisational learning and innovation; barriers to the market for knowledge-based business services and the absence of publicly provided forms of support and the failure of vocational education and training to provide knowledge and skills relevant to new forms of work organisation. In the UK's case, a more adversarial tradition in industrial relations compared with other Northern European countries is also a factor, not least because of the absence of effective social partnership structures (Marginson & Sisson, 2006). The OECD study (2017) also points to the continuing ability of firms to make profits on the 'low road' of low skill, low cost, mass production in certain markets; moreover previous choices relating to human resources, capital investment and organisational culture can create path dependency, holding enterprises within a low skills, low-income (MIT, 2019) trap.

In seeking to break out of the low skills equilibrium, Wright and Sissons (2012) argued that the historic focus on supply-side skills interventions was insufficient to close the productivity gap with competitor nations. UKCES (UK Commission for Employment and Skills) (2009) sought to make the policy case for "a shift in focus to considering how we can ensure that skills are effectively *used* as well as developed in the workplace". Yet evidence of such a shift by the UK government is hard to find, and, as Keep (2014) suggested, for policymakers "… the underlying assumption was that competitive pressures and managerial wisdom would lead to organisations using workers productively".

Workplace Innovation in Scotland

The devolution of certain powers from the UK to an elected Scottish Parliament has opened a different trajectory for economic development and industrial policy in Scotland. The Scottish Government's Inclusive Growth strategy and its Fair Work Framework were both grounded in a commitment to win-win-win outcomes for companies and people: high levels of economic performance, high quality of working life and a high skill equilibrium in the labour market.

In little more than three years, Scottish Enterprise, the country's economic development agency, has developed an extensive programme designed to raise awareness of workplace innovation through workshops and masterclasses, provide direct support to companies implementing workplace innovation measures and help build a wider ecosystem of support for workplace innovation through its large team of specialist advisers.

Scottish Enterprise's new portfolio included the pilot Workplace Innovation Engagement Programme (WIEP). The programme's structure, suggested by Workplace Innovation Limited from its experience of designing and delivering comparable programmes elsewhere (Harris, Tuckman, Watling, & Downes, 2011; Sharpe & Totterdill, 1999; Totterdill, 2017), sought to combine specialist support with opportunities for peer-to-peer knowledge exchange, creating a community of practitioners on comparable journeys. The conceptual framework for the programme was provided by 'The *Essential Fifth Element*', providing the evidence base and shaping each of the activities described in following sections. Workplace Innovation Limited was subsequently selected by Scottish Enterprise to deliver the programme.

The first WIEP cohort of ten companies was recruited by Scottish Enterprise in Autumn 2016, and a second cohort of nine companies entered the programme in September 2017. Both cohorts represented considerable diversity in terms of size, sector and geographical location. 'Engagement' in one form or another was cited by the majority of companies as the principal motivation for joining the programme, whether to support anticipated growth, manage internal restructuring or to address a 'burning platform' created by changing market conditions. None of the 19 companies identified improvements in specific quantifiable indicators as a motive for participation.

In some cases, participation in WIEP was the sole support mechanism for change available to the company. For the majority, WIEP played a complementary role alongside other publicly supported programmes including leadership development courses, organisational development reviews and training in lean methods, or in support of corporate change programmes.

Two employees were nominated by each company to participate in the programme and act as catalysts in developing and implementing workplace innovation with support from Scottish Enterprise and the Workplace Innovation Limited team. It was intended that one participant should represent senior management, lending the weight of their authority to the change initiative; the other should be the leading 'change entrepreneur', stimulating and steering the process on the ground.

The structure of the programme is summarised below:

Inception Workshop

The programme commenced with an induction workshop designed to ensure a common understanding of its aims and structure, to provide an introduction to workplace innovation and to prepare participants for the Diagnostic stage (see below). There was also a focus on building cohesion amongst participants, helping them to realise that they faced common challenges and that they could learn from each other despite marked differences in size and sector.

Diagnostic Tool

Immediately following the workshop, each business initiated the Workplace Innovation Diagnostic®, an online employee survey tool using 49 evidence-based indicators drawn from The *Essential* Fifth Element. Employees and managers were asked to identify experiences of the four 'Elements' of workplace practice described in Table 4.1.

Results, presented as a spreadsheet in which cumulative answers to each question were given as a percentage of the maximum possible score, were coded red, amber or green to indicate the need for intervention. This was further broken down by department, team, professional group or other variables provided by individual companies. Discrepancies between senior manager and employee scores were given, indicating the extent to which the former understood workplace practices in their own organisations.

Table 4.1 The essential fifth element

Element	Indicative practices	Associated outcomes
Jobs, teams and technology	Individual discretion Job variety Constructive challenges Self-managed teams Collaboration within the team Reflective team practices People-centred technologies	Improved workflow Enhanced quality Better productivity Cost reduction Engagement and retention Improved workforce health
Employee-driven innovation and improvement	Productive reflection in teams Cross-team improvement groups Permission to experiment Company-wide innovation events	Enhanced capacity for innovation and improvement Enterprising behaviour Enhanced quality and performance Learning and development Engagement and retention Intrinsic job satisfaction
Organisational structures, management and procedures	Reduced hierarchies and silos Strengths-based career structure Coaching style line management Appraisals focused on learning and innovation Simplified procedures	Improved workflow Cost reduction Better productivity Engagement and retention Improved workforce health
Co-created leadership and employee voice	Openness and transparency Emotionally intelligent behaviours Visible leadership Delegated decision-making Representative participation	Strategic alignment Better decision-making Engagement and retention
The Fifth Element	A culture of empowerment and innovation	Win-win outcomes for the organisation and its employees

The Diagnostic was repeated towards the end of each cohort's programme, enabling companies to measure progress and to identify priorities for follow-up intervention to sustain the momentum of change.

Minor refinements were made to the questionnaire following a validation exercise on survey data from Cohort 1 using Principal Components Analysis.

Action Plans

Participants from each company were supported to develop an Action Plan based on their Diagnostic survey findings. Typical Plans included:

- Flattening existing hierarchies and devolving decision-making
- Defining and living organisational values and behaviours
- Implementing self-directed teamworking
- Creating empowered, cross-functional teams based on workflow rather than silos
- Establishing innovation forums and continuous improvement groups
- Rethinking traditional leadership and management roles and accountabilities
- Enhancing skills development and utilisation, training and coaching plans

Reflecting the systemic character of workplace innovation, the Action Plans helped companies to identify 'interdependencies' (other potential actions within the plan), shaping the impact of individual changes.

Structured Learning Sessions

A programme of seven interactive workshops focused on the principal practices associated with workplace innovation. During Session 3, participants were divided into two groups and presented their proposed actions in response to the Diagnostic results. Group members were invited to comment on each other's action plans as 'critical friends', recognising positives and identifying potential weaknesses and omissions. This provided a prelude to the subsequent action learning sets, described below.

Action Learning Sets

The implementation of action plans was facilitated through regular peer review in action learning sets, enabling participants to discuss challenges and how they were planning to meet them, while receiving constructive feedback. Participants were coached on the principles of action learning to ensure that the sets were conducted with mutual empathy and positive support. The peer-to-peer support within these sessions was particularly prized by participants, enabling them to share problems, discover new ideas and build personal resilience:

The action learning is fantastic; you take so much from that. Like a therapy session, you become emotional sometimes. You have the relationship with the other companies, you feel what the other people feel, and you can be more open. And then you want to know how the other companies are doing as well.

Fresh Thinking Labs

Participating companies also gained automatic membership of Fresh Thinking Labs,[8] an international platform for knowledge sharing between companies created by Workplace Innovation Limited. The platform offers online resources and opportunities for in person contact with good practice companies across the UK and in other European countries.

Content from the Structured Learning Sessions was provided on the Fresh Thinking Labs platform, enabling participants to access a wide range of learning material, case studies, films and practical tools to support change. Several participants took advantage of 'critical friend' in-company workshops involving other Fresh Thinking Lab members. Some also took part in international Fresh Thinking Labs events as speakers and active participants, hosted by partner organisations and companies in Denmark, Estonia, Sweden and Portugal.

Coaching and Facilitation

Throughout the programme, participants received continuous support from Workplace Innovation Limited's team and Scottish Enterprise Specialists. Each pair of participants received coaching visits and telephone calls from Workplace Innovation's experts at appropriate intervals, often involving their Scottish Enterprise Specialist. Typically, these sessions took the form of in-depth discussion of progress and obstacles and the provision of further suggestions, examples and practical tools. It also involved the facilitation of workshops for employees and/or senior teams.

Institute for Leadership and Management Awards

Several participants chose to take part in an optional course on Leadership for Workplace Innovation, gaining a Level 5 qualification (accredited by the Institute for Leadership and Management) as part of their WIEP coaching support. The course, delivered by members of Workplace Innovation Limited's team, was supported by Fresh Thinking Labs' interactive e-learning platform. Assessment was designed to avoid lengthy written assignments and was based on participants' action plans, learning logs and progress reports.

---

[8] www.freshthinkinglabs.com.

Impact of the Programme

Evaluation of the programme's impact on business performance presents several challenges, not least because of the paucity of reliable and relevant 'before and after' performance measures at company level (UKCES, 2016). Whilst productivity is an understandable priority for policymakers, none of the 19 companies measured it directly nor were there readily identifiable surrogate indicators. A second and equally challenging problem is that of attributing changes in specific indicators to the programme itself. For example, Company D (see below) achieved a £1.4m turnaround on profit without additional investment through increased volume and efficiency, entirely attributed by management to enhanced engagement and behaviour change. Yet this transformation had already started before WIEP, and there is no ready way of attributing a specific share of £1.4m to the programme.

We can draw two conclusions from the Company D example. Firstly, the attribution of a substantial profit turnaround exclusively to the introduction of practices related to workplace innovation is headline-grabbing in its own right, raising business awareness and strengthening the case for future public support. Outcomes from other companies may be less succinctly expressed but certainly add to this argument.

Secondly, it directs us to the key question underpinning evaluation: did WIEP play a role in these transformations that was critical to the outcomes? Again, the answer cannot be entirely straightforward: who can untangle the multiple sources of inspiration or evidence that inform the introduction of an innovative work practice? Yet those participating in WIEP from Company D, as well as its General Manager, claimed that the programme played an indispensable role in informing and sustaining the journey.

Although independent evaluation of WIEP was not available as in earlier projects (Harris et al., 2011), the following table is based on reports from an indicative sample of participants during the programme sessions, anonymous survey responses and post project interviews. The workplace changes and impacts reported in the following table were all identified by participants as having been a direct result of WIEP, rather than other internal or external change programmes running at the same time:

Each company participating in the programme made significant process improvements attributable wholly or in substantial part to WIEP. These improvements led to faster throughput time, greater efficiency, more effective problem-solving, enhanced competencies and/or greater capacity for innovation. In several cases, silo working was reduced by enhanced collaboration between functional departments, leading to less bureaucracy and fewer conflicts or delays. By empowering teams, time previously spent on micromanagement is freed up, leading to greater agility and speed of response.

Each of the companies also instigated mechanisms for stimulating and utilising employee ideas for product, service or process innovation, unleashing the potential for further generation well into the future.

While few of the companies have quantified the economic benefits of these improvements, examples such as:

- The reduction of throughput time at Company E by nearly a third
- The savings of £100k on a single improvement project at Company F
- The resolution of a business-critical problem at Company I
- The profit uplift in teams at Company R

  - All provide an indication of the overall benefits to the Scottish economy when aggregated across all 19 organisations

Each of the companies reports improved levels of engagement, validated by several participating organisations through their internal engagement survey results as well as by our interviews. This is likely to be reflected in better mental and physical health, the retention of older workers and enhanced skills development for younger employees.

I can see a difference in the two people that have been in this course and I can see how they are keen to see that change to be replicated within the business. For me it has exceeded all expectations, probably gone beyond the boundaries of where I thought it would go, it goes right under the skin of the business. I am happy that we are now at the other side of it, that it's made a big difference. Martin Welsh, MD, Booth Welsh

This programme affects the way people involved in change think and act, and gives a power to the change process. Sara Blanco Rodriguez, Manager, Kilco

This has been a really good journey for us for what we needed to do, bringing a coherence across the organisation. Rob Aitken, CEO, Institute of Occupational Medicine.

Multiplier effects can also be added to the assessment of impact. Elsewhere on the scale, enhanced innovation capacity at Company H, K, M and Q or improved competitive advantage at Company E is likely to stimulate further job growth.

WIEP was also designed to enhance the competence of individual participants in terms of management and leadership skills, change facilitation and knowledge of workplace innovation, as well as to support them and their companies in introducing new working practices. Each individual participant reported important benefits in terms of personal learning and development. These can be summarised as:

- Enhanced knowledge and experience of workplace innovation
- Exposure to wider experiences
- Increased confidence
- Ability to challenge established practice and influence others
- Changed management style
- Encouraging curiosity and 'learning to learn'
- Creative thinking
- Peer-to-peer learning

The importance of competence development is not limited to the individual alone; rather it reflects their continuing ability to drive positive changes forward. Over time, WIEP alumni will become an important asset for the future of the Scottish economy.

Sustainability and the avoidance of innovation decay lies at the heart of The *Essential* Fifth Element approach with its emphasis on the interdependent practices that can ensure the success or failure of changes. Each company considers that it has built a sustainable momentum of change through WIEP, though some recognise the need for further support especially those faced with adverse trading circumstances.

Finally, in evaluating the impact of WIEP, it is also important to consider the costs of participation for the companies concerned. For most participants, WIEP involved a commitment of 8.5 days away from the workplace plus an estimated 4–8 hours on the Fresh Thinking Labs platform. This would be a substantial commitment for a conventional leadership course in which there was only an indirect impact on the business. WIEP, however, offers a triple helix of benefits: personal development, practical support for workplace change and peer-to-peer network building. This combination of outcomes may explain the lack of any negative comment from participants about the overall time commitment. Overall, feedback suggested that the content of the sessions positively supported practical action in the workplace as well as personal learning, development and network building.

Implementation Challenges

Whilst all 19 companies reported tangible benefits by the end of the programme, some individual participants did not find the journey easy. Many had had very little briefing, either from Scottish Enterprise or their own companies, before arriving at the Induction Workshop. A few participants entered the programme with very limited business knowledge, experience and confidence and required extra coaching and support.

Since the programme avoids prescription and does not offer a 'one-best-way' blueprint, it places a particular onus on the sense-making abilities of participants. One summarised the overall approach with approval, explaining that his initial uncertainty about what to expect from WIEP was slowly replaced by a realisation that the programme's 'learning approach' was to expose participants to selected concepts and case studies, to help them analyse their meaning and relevance and to support them in contextualising the lessons within their own companies. Other participants, perhaps used to more prescriptive change models or none at all, needed more support to extract relevant learning from the sessions.

In certain cases, Diagnostic results presented the companies with an unexpectedly stark reality. Some participants found that their senior teams were in denial at first exposure to the results and had to be coaxed into accepting them. In a few cases this imposed considerable pressure and emotional strain on participants, though alleviated by support from other members of their action learning sets and by one-to-one coaching.

Senior leadership problems proved to be particularly intractable in some smaller enterprises characterised by a command and control culture where majority ownership or control lay with a single director or chief executive. WIEP participants, Scottish Enterprise Specialists and Workplace Innovation Limited's team all found these individuals to be almost completely inaccessible in certain cases, and even though tangible business benefits were achieved, the full potential value of the programme will not be realised without their buy-in. Once again, these challenges featured strongly in the action learning sessions and in-company facilitation.

These challenging experiences should come as no surprise, and in the majority of cases the individuals and companies concerned have emerged stronger and have gained greater confidence in pursuing their workplace innovation journeys.

One overarching lesson is that the funding cycle for the WIEP programme, based on cohorts of around ten months' duration, is too short a time period in which to assess the longer-term impact. However, the evidence does suggest that the programme has succeeded in establishing a sustainable momentum of change in each of the participating companies. Nonetheless future support for these companies will play an important role, not just in sustaining changes but in taking them to the next level.

Earlier in this chapter, we identified the European sociotechnical tradition (Van Amelsvoort & Van Hootegem, 2017) as a key part of the foundations on which the concept of workplace innovation was built, along with Scandinavian dialogical approaches. Whilst the former emphasises structural change in terms of organisational redesign, WIEP embraced companies with widely varying states of readiness for change. Only one (Company B, Table 4.2) entered the programme fully committed to organisational redesign; two more (H and K) embarked on some form of structural change during the programme. The other participating companies achieved tangible innovations in participatory working practices as well as a degree of culture change, but further work is required to assess WIEP's longer-term impact.

Conclusions

WIEP reinforces and elaborates findings from previous studies (notably UKCES, 2016; Work Foundation, 2018) on how to design and deliver public programmes to support workplace change. WIEP's experience not only provides guidance for those designing future programmes but also offers insights for in-company change leaders contemplating a potential roadmap for successful workplace innovation:

- **Target participants at the right level.** Programmes need to be sensitive to the unique configurations of influence and authority within each company. In some, middle managers will lead the change process and facilitate effective channels of communication to senior management. In others, effective change agents can include employee representatives, emerging leaders or simply people with a passion to see change happen. Elsewhere again, senior leaders themselves may be the right choice for participation in programmes, especially in smaller companies.
- **Blend competence development with workplace innovation.** Programmes can help individual participants to build the knowledge, skills and personal attributes required to stimulate, resource and sustain change. At the same time, the test of effectiveness lies in how these competencies are translated into effective and sustainable change within participants'

Table 4.2 Impact of WIEP on selected companies

Company	Workplace innovation	WIEP impact
D) Packaging *Previous and current GMs committed to culture change*	Enhanced teamworking Coaching style of management Morning meetings further developed FabLab sessions drive process improvement Cross-team collaboration Changed KPIs Revived Employee Forum	Reduced throughput time. Enhanced engagement Stronger focus on quality Transformed culture High involvement in innovation and creative thinking activities
E) Cycle Wear *Senior team commitment to culture change following collapse in financial performance*	Process mapping within and between departments Regular engagement events Middle managers huddle Senior commitment to engagement	Reduced throughput time from 6 to 4.1 weeks leading to financial savings and improved customer satisfaction Widespread workforce engagement in improvement and 'taking the initiative' Improved communication Reduced silos
F) Pharmaceuticals *Lean methodologies adopted to make the company attractive to a prospective buyer* *It was sold in April 2017 with resulting challenges of transition*	Regular opportunities for staff involvement in innovation and improvement activities Streamlined regulatory processes Office relocation to remove silos Workplace innovation to enhance 'lean' Adoption of coaching style by senior and middle management Workforce participation in strategy	Wider engagement in problem-solving and improvement: £100k saved in a single improvement project through workforce involvement Enhanced cross-functional working Improved communication and a more open culture

(continued)

Table 4.2 (continued)

Company	Workplace innovation	WIEP impact
H) Defence *Existing commitment to create a multidisciplinary team structure. Joined WIEP to support implementation*	Successful implementation of new team structure Appointment and development of new sub-team leaders New Innovation Hub Development of next generation	Improved Diagnostic scores Positive internal customer feedback Effective team culture and team leadership Reducing silos and strengthening cross-functional collaboration Innovation Hub enhances capacity for product and process innovation
K) Engineering services *Recently acquired by an Australian parent, the company sought to strengthen internal capacity for innovation and adoption of digital technologies*	Mission and values strategy day identified four work streams as the focus for employee participation Creation of an Innovation Lab and café space to enable employee-driven innovation Steering group to stimulate staff ideas through events Engagement initiatives aimed at staff on remote sites	Enhanced Diagnostic scores 60 employee-driven proposals generated MD argues that WIEP 'put the company 12 months ahead of the competition' and helped build a strong Industry 4.0 offer
M) Engineering R&D *Small company seeking to reverse emerging silos and of senior team distance before embarking on further growth*	Engaged staff in creating vision Volunteer 'guerrillas' to challenge poor workplace practices and stimulate fresh thinking Self-managed teamworking Employee groups facilitate problem-solving and improvement, creating a channel for employee voice Senior team study visit to an employee-owned company	Enhanced Diagnostic scores Improved project delivery and customer satisfaction Great capacity for innovation

(*continued*)

Table 4.2 (continued)

Company	Workplace innovation	WIEP impact
Q) Chemical manufacture *Poor working environment, lack of teamworking and team leadership, fragmented leadership*	Shop floor teams made responsible for the work environment Team leadership development and team practices strengthened Improved cross-functional communication Cross-sectional volunteer group of employees and managers created to drive improvement and innovation	Some improvements in Diagnostic scores, reflecting greater staff engagement in improvement and innovation Senior team issues still to be resolved
R) Specialist building restorers *Varying quality of team leadership and team practices across dispersed sites plus communication difficulties had negative impact on profits*	Introduction of weekly team meetings around structured whiteboard agendas focused on project targets and progress, plus lessons learned Greater transparency regarding sales and financial information Planned team leadership and team development programme	Improved Diagnostic results in all Elements Average 6% profit uplift in teams targeted by the programme

own organisations. In short, "there can be no learning without action and no action without learning" (Revans, 1998).

- **Combine multiple learning modes.** Text, film, personal stories, individual coaching and group dialogue can combine to create a mutually reinforcing learning milieu, recognising that many participants respond more effectively to some stimuli than others.
- **Embed peer-to-peer learning and support.** Participants consistently cited exchanges of experience and peer support as one of the most important resources offered by WIEP, whether through action learning sets or as a result of company-hosted 'critical friend' visits.
- **Establish a systemic view of change.** The concept of workplace innovation focuses on bundles of interdependent practices that must be aligned with proposed changes to ensure their success and sustainability. Non-alignment creates 'antibodies' that erode individual changes and lead to 'innovation decay'. The Workplace Innovation Diagnostic® is a key tool

designed to provide companies with a systemic direction towards the achievement of successful change from the outset of the process.

- **Create a relatively intensive momentum of change.** A structured programme of workshops and action learning helps to build and maintain a consistent level of activity. Monthly events that bring the whole cohort together builds pressure on participants to demonstrate progress to their peers, and the momentum of change is further supported by online activity and individual coaching between sessions.
- **Ensure a sustainable momentum of change.** Workplace innovation is never complete but leads to a continuing process of learning and development based on aspirations that grow with each success. Creating such a momentum is often the true test of a programme's effectiveness. This can be sustained beyond the life of a programme by continued peer-to-peer exchanges within learning networks that evolve over time.
- **Capture and disseminate generalisable knowledge and experience created by programmes.** As an international movement, workplace innovation is fuelled by shared learning and mutual support, especially through EUWIN. Programmes generate knowledge and experience that belong within the public sphere by means of publications and peer-to-peer networks, challenging established practitioners with fresh thinking and supporting new entrants.

Workplace innovation is a powerful but underutilised resource for achieving diverse economic and social policy goals in the UK, with its relatively slow uptake of organisational practices associated with high productivity and high quality of working life. Scotland has broken with the UK government's embedded indifference to internal workplace practices, and the Scottish Government is articulating a distinctive vision for the future of its economy. Workplace innovation is now firmly embedded within national policy frameworks, generating lessons of clear significance for many other countries.

References

Alasoini, T., Ramstad, E., & Totterdill, P. (2017). National and Regional Policies to Promote and Sustain Workplace Innovation. In *Workplace Innovation: Theory, Research and Practice*. Cham: Springer International Publishing.

Antila, J., & Ylöstalo, P. (1999). *Functional Flexibility and Workplace Success in Finland*. Helsinki: Ministry of Labour.

Business Decisions Ltd. (2002). *New Forms of Work Organisation: The Obstacles to Wider Diffusion*. Brussels: European Commission.

Dhondt, S., Vermeerbergen, L., & Van Hootegem, G. (2017). Evidence of Workplace Innovation from Organisational and Economic Studies. In P. Oeij, D. Rus, & F. D. Pot (Eds.), *Workplace Innovation: Theory, Research and Practice* (pp. 79–94). Cham: Springer International Publishing.

European Foundation. (1997). *Employee Participation and Organisational Change. EPOC Survey of 6000 Workplaces in Europe*. Dublin: European Foundation.

European Work & Technology Consortium. (1998). *A Medium Term Plan for Collaborative Action*. Nottingham: Centre for Work & Technology.

Green, A. (2016). *Low Skill Traps in Sectors and Geographies: Underlying Factors and Means of Escape*. Coventry: University of Warwick.

Gustavsen, B. (1992). *Dialogue and Development*. Assen/Maastricht: Van Gorcum.

Harris, L., Tuckman, A., Watling, D., & Downes, B. (2011). Unlocking Engagement: A Review of the 'Innovative Workplaces' Initiative. (ntu:23730). Retrieved from http://irep.ntu.ac.uk/id/eprint/23730/

Huselid, M. A., Jackson, S. E., & Schuler, R. S. (1997). Technical and Strategic Human Resource Management Effectiveness as Determinants of Firm Performance. *Academy of Management Journal, 40*(1), 171–188. https://doi.org/10.2307/257025

Keep, E. (2014). *Employment Relations Comment, October*. London: Acas.

Lado, A. A., & Wilson, M. C. (1994). Human Resource Systems and Sustained Competitive Advantage: A Competency-Based Perspective. *The Academy of Management Review, 19*(4), 699–727. https://doi.org/10.2307/258742

Lay, G., Dreher, C., & Kinkel, S. (1996). *Neue Produktionskonzepte leisten einen Beitrag zur Sicherung des Standorts Deutschland*. ISI Produktionsinnovationserhebung Nr. 1.

LLAKES. (2012). Skills and Employment Survey. Retrieved from www.llakes.org. www.llakes.org

Lundvall, B.-Å. (2014). Deteriorating Quality of Work Undermines Europe's Innovation Systems and the Welfare of Europe's Workers! *EUWIN Bulletin*. Retrieved from http://uk.ukwon.eu/File%20Storage/4670703_7_June%20Bulletin.pdf

Marginson, P., & Sisson, K. (2006). *European Integration and Industrial Relations: Multi-Level Governance in the Making*. London: Palgrave Macmillan.

MIT. (2019). *The Work of the Future*. Retrieved from https://workofthefuture.mit.edu/sites/default/files/2019-09/WorkoftheFuture_Report_Shaping_Technology_and_Institutions.pdf

Mohr, B., & Van Amelsvoort, P. E. (2015). *Co-creating Humane and Innovative Communities of Work: The Evolution of STS Design Practice and Perspective*. Leuven: Global STS-D Network.

NUTEK. (1996). *Towards Flexible Organisations*. Stockholm: NUTEK.

OECD, & Centre for Educational Research Innovation. (2010). *Innovative Workplaces: Making Better Use of Skills Within Organisations*. Paris: OECD.

Oeij, P., Rus, D., & Pot, F. (2017). *Workplace Innovation. Theory, Research and Practice*. Cham, Switzerland: Springer.

Organisation for Economic Co-operation Development International Labour Organisation. (2017). *Better Use of Skills in the Workplace: Why It Matters for Productivity and Local Jobs*. Paris: OECD Publishing.

Revans, R. (1998). *ABC of Action Learning*. London: Lemos & Crane.

Sharpe, A., & Totterdill, P. (1999). *An Evaluation of the New Work Organisation in Ireland Programme*. Dublin: Irish Productivity Centre.

Sisson, K. (2014). The UK Productivity Puzzle – Is Employment Relations the Missing Piece? *Acas Policy Discussion Papers*, September.

Teague, P. (2005). What Is Enterprise Partnership? *Organization*, (4), 567–589.

Totterdill, P. (2015). Closing the Gap: 'The Fifth Element' and Workplace Innovation. *European Journal of Workplace Innovation, 1*(1), 55–74.

Totterdill, P. (2017). Workplace Innovation as Regional Economic Development: Towards a Movement? *International Journal of Action Research*, (2), 129–153.

Totterdill, P., Dhondt, S., & Milsome, S. (2002). *Partners at Work? A Report to Europe's Policymakers and Social Partners*. Nottingham: The Work Institute.

Totterdill, P., Exton, R., Exton, O., & Gold, M. (2016). High-performance Work Practices in Europe: Challenges of Diffusion. *European Journal of Workplace Innovation, 2*(1), 63–81.

Trist, E. L., & Bamforth, K. W. (1951). Some social and Psychological Consequences of the Longwall Method of Coal-Getting: An Examination of the Psychological Situation and Defences of a Work Group in Relation to the Social Structure and Technological Content of the Work System. *Human Relations, 4*(1), 3–38.

UKCES. (2009). *High Performance Working: A Synthesis of Key Literature. Evidence Report 4*. Wath-upon-Dearne: UKCES.

UKCES. (2016). *Evaluation of the UK Futures Programme: Conclusions and Guidance*. Wath-upon-Dearne: UKCES.

Van Amelsvoort, P., & Van Hootegem, G. (2017). In O. P, R. D, & P. F (Eds.), *Towards a Total Workplace Innovation Concept Based on Sociotechnical Systems Design*. Cham: Springer.

Wilson, R., Hogarth, T., Bosworth, D., Dickerson, A., Green, A., Jacobs, C., et al. (2003). *Tackling the Low Skills Equilibrium: A Review of Issues and Some New Evidence. A Report for the DTI*. Coventry: University of Warwick.

Work Foundation. (2018). *Manufacturing Productivity in the UK*. Lancaster: The Work Foundation.

Wright, J., & Sissons, P. (2012). *The Skills Dilemma: Skills Utilisation and Low-Wage Work*. London: The Work Foundation.

5

Workplace Innovation in Government Organizations and Its Relationship with Organizational Culture

Leonie Newnham

Introduction

Understanding the process for innovative change within public sector organizations provides ideas and approaches on how to facilitate and foster workplace innovation. Improving public sector organization's innovation capacity will allow them to respond to a rapidly changing operational environment. The outcome from workplace innovation assists governments that work through public sector organizations, to implement policies and programmes, and to change the dynamics within an economy for the benefit of the state and the population (Newnham, 2018).

The relationship between organizational culture and workplace innovation was investigated in the context of a case study of a public sector department in Victoria. This research took place in Victoria, a state of Australia, in an organization within the state's public sector. Australia has the Westminster system of government, which is a common form of government for former members of the British Empire and applies across a number of countries (OECD, 2010). While the Westminster system is only one of many systems of government, it has characteristics that align with other systems so the findings may be applicable for other government organizations (Newnham, 2018).

L. Newnham (✉)
School of Management, RMIT University, Melbourne, VIC, Australia
e-mail: leonie.newnham@rmit.edu.au

© The Author(s), under exclusive license to Springer Nature Switzerland AG 2021
A. McMurray et al. (eds.), *The Palgrave Handbook of Workplace Innovation*,
https://doi.org/10.1007/978-3-030-59916-4_5

An explanatory sequential mixed methods approach was used which supports the complex nature of public sector organizations (Hendren, Luo, & Pandey, 2018; Mele & Belardinelli, 2018). It brings together organizational culture, workplace innovation and public sector management theory. In this study, culture was treated at three levels: public sector culture, organizational culture and group (department)-level culture.

The subject organization was a department of state, an entity rarely available for research. The research results empirically identified a significant relationship between public sector culture and workplace innovation. As an unusual and critical case the findings could be generalized to add to the public sector literature concerning culture, innovation and management. To date, there has been no similar research undertaken in a public sector organization in Victoria. Kelman (2005) posited that there is a paucity of information on public sector organizations due to a focus on the private sector, which is now changing as 'countries … (need to solve) … intractable public problems that have a strong management component' (Kelman, 2005, p. 967).

Literature Review

Innovation is increasingly recognized to be important to public sector success (OECD, 2015). Public sector innovation occurs in a different context from private sector innovation and this has been a neglected area of study as earlier studies focused on the private sector (Hartley, 2013). Public sector innovation research had focused on products and services with the emphasis on services as they are the main output of the public sector. The definition has been expanding to include other aspects of service delivery in terms of how the service is delivered, stakeholders it is delivered to and the special categories of governance, policy and the creation of public value (Considine & Lewis, 2007; Gruen, 2009; Moore & Hartley, 2008; Mulgan & Albury, 2003). Attention has been given to aspects of the individual within the organization, recognizing that innovation changes either begin or are put into effect at the workplace level (Koch & Hauknes, 2005; McMurray & Dorai, 2003; Pot, 2011).

Much of the existing innovation research and definitions have been developed by researchers based on work on product innovation in the private sector, resulting in the literature being 'context blind' (Hartley, 2013, p. 45), which has not allowed for understanding and explanation about innovation in the public sector. New research has argued for a framework to integrate the private and public sector innovation research while being aware of considering the differences in how innovation works in public and private sector organizations (Hodgkinson, Hannibal, Keating, Chester Buxton, & Bateman, 2017).

Innovation literature falls into two categories of process and outcome. Process innovation consists of processes and changes within organizations that create innovation (Arundel, Casali, & Hollanders, 2015; Moore & Hartley, 2008; Tidd, Bessant, & Pavitt, 2005). The workplace innovation scale used in this study measures process innovation (McMurray & Dorai, 2003). Outcome innovation leads to changes in what is delivered to individuals and entities outside the organization (Nählinder & Eriksson, 2019; Tidd et al., 2005). Earlier research by this author and others identified outcome innovation initiated by Department A, thus providing insight for this case study (Newnham & McMurray, 2007; Newnham & McMurray, 2020).

Workplace innovation is a term that encompasses the elements of innovation within an organization, which collectively enable the creation of products and services. It is a multidimensional, subjective and context-specific phenomenon (McMurray & Dorai, 2003) that includes the dimensions of organizational innovation, organizational climate for innovation, team and individual innovation (Muenjohn & McMurray, 2017).

There are differences between private and public sector organizational culture with the common perception being that the public sector is more bureaucratic, less innovative, more risk adverse and inwardly focused compared with the private sector. The public sector has more complex drivers than a purely profit motive, which affects how it delivers services (Alford, Douglas, Geuijen, & 't Hart, 2017; Hartley, Alford, Hughes, & Yates, 2015; Moore & Hartley, 2008). There is little directly published in the literature about public sector organizational culture. It is often referred to and its related aspects are studied (Bradley & Parker, 2006; Parker & Bradley, 2000; Su, Baird, & Blair, 2013); however, a detailed exploration or explanation has not been developed (IPA, 2011).

There a paucity of literature addressing workplace innovation, organizational culture and management in the public sector. Yet identifying how innovation works at the workplace level provides support and ideas on how to achieve benefits at the organization level that will flow through to the operations of the organization, other parts of the public sector and the larger government sector. Innovation in government organizations has been identified as a neglected and undeveloped research area (Brown & Osborne, 2013; Hartley, 2013; Olejarski, Potter, & Morrison, 2019; Stewart, 2014; Torugsa & Arundel, 2014). There is even less research on the Australian public sector, and less again on the state government of Victoria.

Research literature is silent on a number of aspects of organizational culture within public sector organizations, especially on how they work and how they innovate. Yet the public sector is important in supporting a country's productivity (OECD, 2010). Within Australia, there has been recognition of the need for additional research on public sector departments to support developing their innovation performance (Harrison & Baird, 2015).

Lastly, the constructs of organizational culture, workplace innovation and public sector management have all been studied using different methods: organizational culture primarily through qualitative analysis, workplace innovation through quantitative analysis and public sector management through a mixture of qualitative and quantitative research. Researchers have called for additional research, with Hartley (2013) calling for more innovation research from a public sector context and others (De Vries, Bekkers, & Tummers, 2016; Hendren et al., 2018; Mele & Belardinelli, 2018) specifically identifying a need to use mixed methods approaches to gain benefits from both qualitative and quantitative methods of research, and connecting to the existing research body that used either qualitative or quantitative approaches.

The literature review and analysis addressed the relationship between workplace innovation and organizational culture within a public sector organization government agency. The form of public sector organizations creates a particular organizational culture that impacts on workplace innovation. The relationship between organizational culture and workplace innovation in public sector organizations has not been the subject of academic research especially within an Australian context. This research was based on a variety of sources including government reports and publications, which are important source materials for public sector practitioners (Adams, Smart, & Huff, 2017). The public sector traditionally makes extensive use of reports to guide practice and develop policy with the potential contributions of such literature becoming apparent to researchers in this and other research fields (Benzies, Premji, Hayden, & Serrett, 2006; Rothstein, Sutton, & Borenstein, 2006). The conceptual framework model (Fig. 5.1) provides an overview of how all the elements of the research fit together.

The conceptual framework in Fig. 5.1 illustrates how the conceptual components of this research work together to address the omissions and research opportunities identified in the literature. The chapter investigates the relationship between the four dimensions of workplace innovation and the two aspects of public sector culture in the public sector within the frame of a Victorian public sector organization. The broader research identified how demographic factors and employment characteristics relate with public sector culture and workplace innovation, which is not covered in this work.

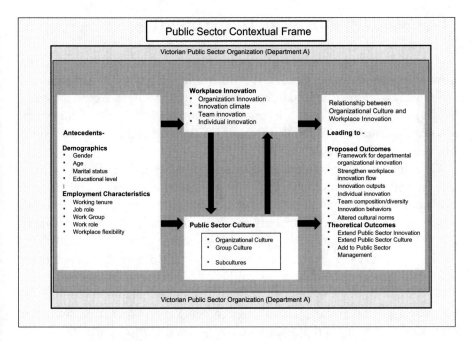

Fig. 5.1 Conceptual framework model

To investigate the omissions in the literature the following research question and supporting hypotheses were investigated—RQ. 1. What is the relationship between workplace innovation and public sector culture in the context of a Victorian public sector organization?

H1: Public sector culture has a significant effect on workplace innovation.

H1a: Public sector culture including organizational and group culture has a
    significant effect on workplace innovation climate.
H1b: Public sector culture including organizational and group culture has a
    significant effect on individual innovation.
H1c: Public sector culture including organizational and group culture has a
    significant effect on team innovation.
H1d: Public sector culture including organizational and group culture has a
    significant effect on organizational innovation.

The Case Organization: Department A

The research's focus was a department of state as this distinctive organizational form is very poorly understood. Departments deliver a range of functions and activities according to mandatory requirements that are set out in various legislation, regulations and conventions (Newnham, 2018). Departments are an organizational type difficult to access for research and so they present an unusual case (Yin, 2014).

Case details—Department A: The basis of this research included information gained by the researcher over 20 years working in and studying the Environment Department in Victoria. It had been documented through observation, documentary analysis and departmental meetings (Newnham, 2018; Newnham & McMurray, 2007; Newnham & McMurray, 2020).

Department A was created formally on 1 July 2013 with the merger of the former Environment Department with the former Agriculture Department (DEPI, 2014, p. 4). Department A had as its subject matter the public and private use of land and the natural environment. The organization comprised six main business areas that were commonly called groups, under the leadership of a deputy secretary. They were Regional Services; Land, Fire, Environment; Water and Catchments; Agriculture Group; Corporate Services; and Regulation and Compliance.

The department employed more than 3470 staff, working across Victoria. It had an annual income of around $1.69 billion (AUS) in 2013 to 2014 and its staff worked in 90 different locations across the state (DEPI, 2014). Its vision was as follows: 'Productive and competitive primary industries, a resilient and healthy environment and optimal use of public land to support Victoria's long-term prosperity' (DEPI, 2014, p. 10).

The existing cultural context was identified by internal research undertaken on Department A's culture and that of its preceding organizations using the organizational cultural index (OCI), a survey developed and used by Human Synergistics (HSI, 2015). The OCI provides the profile of an organization's operating culture in terms of the behaviours that members believe are required to 'fit in and meet expectations'. The results indicated that Department A's overall culture was dominated by behaviour norms and expectations from the passive/defensive group of behaviours, with the dominant being avoidance and dependence (Newnham, 2018). In addition, the department had a number of strong subcultures, with groups having very different professional backgrounds (Newnham, 2018); earlier studies had found subcultures can influence organizational culture (Hinings, 2012; Schein & Scheiner, 2016).

Methodology

The researcher used a pragmatic philosophical outlook where it was possible to review innovation objectively and its relationship to the more subjectively defined organization and culture (Cook & Reichardt, 1979; Creswell, 2010). The research is framed in a mixed methods approach to recognize the complementary strengths of the methods used (Teddlie & Johnson, 2009). The mixed methods approach allowed the development of an understanding of both the size of the relationship and the reasons behind the relationship.

An explanatory sequential mixed methods approach was used with a deductive Phase one quantitative analysis producing outcomes which informed the inductive Phase two qualitative stream of research. The two phases were linked as the final part of the mixed methods approach integrating understandings from the quantitative and qualitative research, identifying significant themes underlying the research and combining them into meta-inferences (Newnham, 2018).

For Phase one, data was collected in a web-based survey available to all members of Department A with 479 out of 3470 responding. The surveys represented a 14% response rate from the original population. This was a high response rate within this organization for organization-wide surveys (Newnham, 2018). Qualitative data was collected in the survey and through an analysis of documents externally and internally published by Department A, and externally published documents relating to the department. The researcher used NVivo 11 to provide an accurate and transparent picture of the data while providing an audit of the data analysis process as a whole (Bazeley, 2007; Merriam & Tisdell, 2015; Welsh, 2002). These research decisions were based in assessing methodology options from the research methods literature (Bazeley, 2007; Merriam & Tisdell, 2015).

The data was collected by a survey using the workplace innovation scale (WIS scale) chosen as a reliable, valid and proven measure of workplace innovation. The WIS scale has been used in a number of research studies in the private and not-for-profit sectors over the last 18 years with consistently high Cronbach Alpha scores from $a = 0.89$ to $a = 0.94$, establishing the instrument's reliability and validity (McMurray, Islam, Sarros, & Pirola-Merlo, 2013; Von Treuer & McMurray, 2012). Organizational culture was measured based on the Pace and Faules (1994) measure developed to capture information from organizational members on key values and shared concepts, to create their image of the organization. This measure was called 'public sector culture', collecting information on two aspects, organizational and group culture.

A Phase one quantitative analysis led to a Phase two qualitative study where the theoretical drive or priority in the core methods was quantitative and the supplementation qualitative method built on the findings from Phase one (Creswell, 2010; Morse, 2016). Additional confidence in the quantitative study was gained by using a two-stage data analysis approach using first-generation statistics in the form of linear regression for Stage 1 and the second-generation approach of structural equation modelling for Stage 2. The method was reinforced with the concepts from Phase one being used as the basis for theme creation for Phase two qualitative analysis, thus allowing a Stage 1 triangulation between these phases. A second stage of triangulation of the findings from both phases was undertaken as part of the integration of the data in a final mixed methods research question that confirmed the results of the two phases and integrated them together, allowing the development of six additional meta-inferences. This approach enabled the findings to be corroborated from both methods and provided additional depth and understanding of the results obtained, identifying congruence, complementarity and difference between the two results.

Findings

The results from the qualitative and quantitative methods are shown in Table 5.1, which triangulates and integrates the data. This is summarized in Table 5.2.

Table 5.1 provides the findings for the first part of the research relating to Hypothesis 1 and its component parts. The second part of the research considered the relationship between culture and workplace innovation related to a range of demographic and employment characteristics data, which is not included in this chapter. The first column identifies findings from the quantitative results that were used to triangulate the qualitative date. The second column gives the quantitative findings for Hypothesis 1 for both Stage 1 and 2 of the analysis. The results indicated that all hypotheses (1a, 1b, 1c and 1d) were supported. The qualitative findings are shown in the third column. The fourth column shows the results of the triangulation of the quantitative and qualitative results and identifies if they were in agreement.

For Findings 1 and 3 to 6 there was full agreement between the quantitative and qualitative results. Details about these findings follow: Finding 1—public sector culture has a significant effect on workplace innovation, Findings

Table 5.1   Conversion table showing the triangulation of quantitative and qualitative results against the findings identified

Findings	Quantitative findings	Qualitative findings	Results
Finding 1—Public sector culture has a significant effect on workplace innovation	Hypothesis 1 outcome: A significant effect was identified with **Stage 1:** Sigma $P<0.001$; predicted 24.6% variability (adjusted R^2) Supported by **Stage 2**: Positive—Sigma level of 1%	*Themes of public sector culture and workplace innovation* A strong interrelationship was shown between the two constructs	In full agreement. Both the quantitative and qualitative outcomes supported this finding
Finding 2—Group culture is more significant as a predictor of workplace innovation than organizational culture	A significant effect was identified for both aspects of public sector culture, group and organizational culture. Group culture had more impact, with a large effect on both organizational and team innovation, and a medium effect on workplace innovation climate and individual innovation. Organizational culture had a large effect on organizational innovation, a medium effect on team innovation and a low effect on workplace innovation climate and individual innovation	*Subthemes of organization and group culture and theme of workplace innovation* Group culture overall had a greater connection than organizational culture, which, however, was only connected with particular dimensions of workplace innovation	In partial agreement. Both the quantitative and qualitative outcomes supported this finding to a degree. The qualitative results indicated that group culture overall had a greater connection than organizational culture, which, however, was only connected with particular dimensions of workplace innovation

(*continued*)

Table 5.1 (continued)

Findings	Quantitative findings	Qualitative findings	Results
Finding 3—Public sector culture (PSC) including organizational and group culture has a significant effect on workplace innovation climate	Hypothesis 1a outcome: A significant effect was identified with **Stage 1:** Sigma $P<0.001$ for all; PSC predicted 10.9% variability (adjusted R^2) Organizational culture predicted 3.9% variability (adjusted R^2). Group culture predicted 11.3% variability (adjusted R^2) Supported by **Stage 2:** Positive—Sigma level of 1%	*Themes of public sector culture and subtheme of workplace innovation climate* The results showed that there was a strong relationship between workplace innovation climate and public sector culture	In full agreement. Both the quantitative and qualitative outcomes supported this finding
Finding 4—Public sector culture including organizational and group culture has a significant effect on individual innovation	Hypothesis 1b outcome: A significant effect was identified **Stage 1:** Sigma $P<0.001$ for all; PSC predicted 8.1% variability (adjusted R^2). Organizational culture predicted 3.3% variability (adjusted R^2). Group culture predicted 7.5% variability (adjusted R^2). Supported by **Stage 2:** Positive—Sigma level of 1%	*Themes of public sector culture and subtheme of individual innovation* The results showed that there was a strong relationship between individual innovation and public sector culture	In full agreement. Both the quantitative and qualitative outcomes supported this finding

(continued)

Table 5.1   (continued)

Findings	Quantitative findings	Qualitative findings	Results
Finding 5—Public sector culture including organizational and group culture has a significant effect on team innovation	Hypothesis 1c outcome: A significant effect was identified. **Stage 1:** Sigma $P<0.001$ for all; PSC predicted 15.6% variability (adjusted R^2). Organizational culture predicted 7.1% variability (adjusted R^2). Group culture predicted 14.3% variability (adjusted R^2). Supported by **Stage 2:** Positive—Sigma level of 1%	*Themes of public sector culture and subtheme of team innovation* The results showed there was a strong relationship between team innovation and public sector culture	In full agreement. Both the quantitative and qualitative outcomes supported this finding
Finding 6—Public sector culture including organizational and group culture has a significant effect on organizational innovation	Hypothesis 1d outcome: A significant effect was identified. **Stage 1:** Sigma $P<0.001$ for all; PSC predicted 24.0% variability (adjusted R^2). Organizational culture predicted 12.3% variability (adjusted R^2). Group culture predicted 20.3% variability (adjusted R^2). Supported by **Stage 2:** Positive—sigma level of 1%	*Themes of public sector culture and subtheme of organizational innovation* The results showed that there was a strong relationship between organizational innovation and public sector culture	In full agreement. Both the quantitative and qualitative outcomes supported this finding

3 to 6—public sector culture including organizational and group culture have a significant effect on workplace innovation climate, individual innovation, team innovation and organizational innovation, respectively; there was full agreement between the quantitative and qualitative results. The quantitative

Full agreement with both the quantitative and qualitative methods for:
Finding 1 - Public sector culture has a significant effect on Workplace Innovation.
Finding 3 - Public Sector Culture including Organizational and Group Culture has a significant effect on Workplace Innovation Climate.
Finding 4 - Public Sector Culture including Organizational and Group Culture has a significant effect on Individual Innovation.
Finding 5 - Public Sector Culture including Organizational and Group Culture has a significant effect on Team Innovation.
Finding 6 - Public Sector Culture including Organizational and Group Culture has a significant effect on Organizational Innovation.
Partial agreement with both the quantitative and qualitative methods for:
Finding 2 - Group Culture is more significant as a predictor of workplace innovation than Organizational Culture.

Fig. 5.2 Summary of findings for both the quantitative and qualitative methods

results found that public sector culture and its aspects are significantly related to those of the workplace innovation scale and its four dimensions with the qualitative results showing strong relationships between the themes of public sector culture and workplace innovation. Within the dimensions of workplace innovation, the analysis showed a strong relationship with public sector culture and all the named subthemes. Individual innovation was shown to be a less important dimension within Department A.

Finding 2 showed that the quantitative and qualitative results were in partial agreement. Finding 2 was that group culture is more significant as a predictor of workplace innovation than organizational culture. The qualitative data analysis confirmed overall that group culture had a greater overall connection to workplace innovation; however, this was only within three of the five themes and subthemes connected to workplace innovation, with these being climate, organizational innovation and team innovation. There were no references to workplace innovation and individual innovation where it connected to groups. Workplace innovation was not identified by the organization in its documentation, and the focus was on innovation as a broader concept; this translated to a silence by those in the organization who did not have a context within which to discuss workplace innovation. The quantitative analysis described workplace innovation through the survey questions and the results showed that workplace innovation was seen to be more strongly related to group culture.

There was confusion around the concept of individual innovation, which was identified in the theme of survey response. This was partly due to this concept not being identified by the organization in its documentation and due to the stronger focus on teams and team-oriented work projects. The connection to organizational innovation was through the way the organization referred to innovation in a number of its documents, where groups were mentioned in relation to organizational innovation initiatives. In the survey response, a large number of individuals mentioned that workplace innovation climate and team innovation connected to groups, which highlighted how important group culture was to supporting these aspects of innovation within Department A (Newnham, 2018).

The last step in the method included integrating the qualitative and quantitative research collection to link the understandings and findings from these components of the research. Significant themes underlying the research were identified and combined into meta-inferences, which confirmed the inferences or results obtained by the two phases of this research and highlighted an additional six significant inferences (Onwuegbuzie & Combs, 2010; Teddlie & Tashakkori, 2009). These are the following:

1. Group culture is more important than organizational culture in Department A in supporting workplace innovation.
2. Cultural change management in Department A was led by senior executives who were not engaging with staff at all organizational levels and this resulted in reduced cultural cohesion and workplace innovation.
3. There were divisions between different levels of the organization associated with support for workplace innovation. The managers were identified as an important group that had a significant impact on culture and workplace innovation in their groups.
4. Particular demographic groups were disadvantaged when Department A created new organizational structures, thus reducing their innovation capacity.
5. Organizational barriers were identified that impeded workplace innovation.
6. Department A's workplace structure impacted on workplace innovation.

These significant inferences assisted in providing an explanation as to why the quantative results were found.

Discussion and Implications

Public sector culture was identified as a significant antecedent of workplace innovation, predicting 24.6% of variation and identifying significant variation in individual innovation, organizational innovation, team innovation and workplace innovation climate, which impacted on employee's capacity to innovate. Group-level culture was particularly influential.

The case study of a public sector department of state for this research was both an unusual and a critical empirical case and it was possible to generalize the findings to extend the knowledge in public sector research literature (Eisenhardt & Graebner, 2007; Schein & Scheiner, 2016; Schwandt & Gates, 2017; Yin, 2014). The relationship between public sector culture and workplace innovation within a Victorian public sector organization could be confirmed for the first time.

The theory of public management (Hill & Lynn, 2004; Hughes, 2012, 2017) was extended, identifying that managers can develop conditions to support workplace innovation in public sector organizations. The importance of organizational culture to developing strong and productive organizations is an increasingly popular area of management focus. The high positive correlations between organizational culture and workplace innovation support public sector managers investing efforts in developing stronger organizational cultures to build workplace innovation.

The significant findings extend the existing public sector culture literature by empirically identifying the direct and strong relationship between public sector culture and workplace innovation. This extended Schein's Theory of Culture (Schein & Scheiner, 2016) that identified the importance of context in understanding the cultural manifestations in organizations where the espoused beliefs and values are set by political directions. The findings extended the theory by proving the relationship of culture as a significant antecedent to workplace innovation in the context of a public sector department of state. It builds on the work undertaken in the private sector by Büschgens, Bausch, and Balkin (2013)) on how aspects of organizational culture determined capacity for innovation with Von Treuer and McMurray (2012), focusing on the aspect of workplace climate. It supports recent work in the public sector that identified how some aspects of workplace climate impact innovation performance (Sherief, 2019).

The importance of group culture in influencing workplace innovations points to a need to build cultural cohesion across the organization by working with group subcultures to build a collaborative group rather than applying top-down change and development programmes. From the human resource management and managerial perspective, approaches, guides and performance systems that consider the team aspect of workplace innovation will allow more focus on this area of innovation and promote a variety of team composition that represents diversity. Teams with a range of people of different demographic and employment characteristics will optimize workplace innovation.

Understanding this relationship between culture and workplace innovation at the micro level in public sector organizations provides public sector managers with the ability to develop positive cultural environments that support the development of workplace innovation. Through understanding this they will understand that a negative culture at the macro or micro level of the organization will significantly impede workplace innovation. The decisions of senior policy makers in the public sector can be more congruent with what is known about how organizational and cultural change occurs; thus, changes can be most effectively achieved (Ferlie, Hartley, & Martin, 2003) within public sector workplaces.

The research finding extends the theory of public sector innovation by identifying that culture is a significant antecedent to workplace innovation by empirically proving the relationship and measuring the relationship of public sector culture to the workplace innovation scale as an operationalization of workplace innovation (McMurray & Dorai, 2003). The relationship between culture and innovation performance has been assumed in the research literature and this work empirically proves this within a public sector organization. These outcomes supported calls for more research in public sector innovation to build upon existing literature and emphasized theory development using more multi-method approaches (De Vries et al., 2016; Hendren et al., 2018; Mele & Belardinelli, 2018) and to highlight public sector innovation features to overcome the 'context-blindness' of innovation literature (Hartley, 2013). The research extended the literature describing workplace innovation as a multidimensional, subjective and context-specific phenomenon. This included the dimensions of organizational innovation, workplace innovation climate, team and individual innovation (McMurray & Dorai, 2003; Muenjohn & McMurray, 2017) by empirically proving the relationship between culture and workplace innovation and its four dimensions in the context of a public service organization.

Australia has a tradition of government being innovative ahead of other countries (Gruen, 2009, p.96). The initiative for innovation was originally at the political level and this is changing to focus on the role of public sector managers and organizations in delivering innovative performance (Newnham, 2018). Existing governmental innovation policies provide strategic direction but lack details on how to enact innovation (DPMC, 2015; Newnham, 2018). This is compounded by a lack of information on how innovation works within public sector organizations and an absence of approaches to foster innovation (Demircioglu & Audretsch, 2017; Moussa, McMurray, & Muenjohn, 2018). A rich body of literature covering innovation aspects around organizational issues in the private sector has found that organizations are the principal places where innovation is carried out (Balfour & Demircioglu, 2017; O'Connor, Roos, & Vickers-Willis, 2007). However, this is lacking for the public sector despite findings that a public sector organization's ability to innovate is regarded as a vital factor in its overall success (Arundel et al., 2015; Stewart-Weeks & Kastelle, 2015).

In Australia, cultures of bureaucracy and hierarchy persist in the public sector, with attendant emphasis on rules, conformity and attention to technical detail despite the introduction of innovative management techniques (Bradley & Parker, 2006; Parker & Bradley, 2000). In addition, governments 'like the private sector, are having to adjust to both the challenges and opportunities presented by globalisation and rapid technological change' (OECD, 2015, p. 3) and all organizations need to adapt to the new demands with new operating environments (Stewart-Weeks & Cooper, 2019). If public sector organizations want to create new ways of operating, a reshaping of the traditional bureaucratic organizational form may be required (Kreutzer, Neugebauer, & Pattloch, 2018; Stewart-Weeks & Cooper, 2019). Yet case studies of a number of digitally enabled service transformation projects in public sector institutions found some of the transformations can damage institutional stability and legitimacy and result in failure. This was evident if the complex institutional setting of the public sector were not adequately considered or acknowledged in the change effort (Weerakkody, Omar, El-Haddadeh, & Al-Busaidy, 2016). Understanding how culture and workplace innovation are connected can assist public sector organizations to navigate complex organizational dynamics to innovate successfully and create new organizational forms.

References

Adams, R. J., Smart, P., & Huff, A. S. (2017). Shades of Grey: Guidelines for Working with the Grey Literature in Systematic Reviews for Management and Organizational Studies. *International Journal of Management Reviews, 19*(4), 432–454.

Alford, J., Douglas, S., Geuijen, K., & 't Hart, P. (2017). Ventures in Public Value Management: Introduction to the Symposium. *Public Management Review, 19*(5), 589–604.

Arundel, A., Casali, L., & Hollanders, H. (2015). How European Public Sector Agencies Innovate: The Use of Bottom-Up, Policy-Dependent and Knowledge-Scanning Innovation Methods. *Research Policy, 44*(7), 1271–1282.

Balfour, D., & Demircioglu, M. (2017). Reinventing the Wheel? Public Sector Innovation in the Age of Governance. *Public Administration Review, 77*(5), 800–805.

Bazeley, P. (2007). *Qualitative Data Analysis with NVivo*. Wiltshire, UK: SAGE Publications Limited.

Benzies, K. M., Premji, S., Hayden, K. A., & Serrett, K. (2006). State-of-the-Evidence Reviews: Advantages and Challenges of Including Grey Literature. *Worldviews on Evidence-Based Nursing, 3*(2), 55–61.

Bradley, L., & Parker, R. (2006). Do Australian Public Sector Employees Have the Type of Culture They Want in the Era of New Public Management? *Australian Journal of Public Administration, 65*(1), 89–99.

Brown, L., & Osborne, S. (2013). *Handbook of Innovation in Public Services*. Cheltenham: Edward Elgar Publishing.

Büschgens, T., Bausch, A., & Balkin, D. B. (2013). Organizational Culture and Innovation: A Meta-Analytic Review. *Journal of Product Innovation Management, 30*(4), 763–781.

Considine, M., & Lewis, J. M. (2007). Innovation and Innovators Inside Government: From Institutions to Networks. *Governance, 20*(4), 581–607.

Cook, T. D., & Reichardt, C. S. (Eds.). (1979). *Qualitative and Quantitative Methods in Evaluation*. Beverly Hills, CA: Sage Publications.

Creswell, J. (Ed.). (2010). *Mapping the Developing Landscape of Mixed Methods Research* (2nd ed.). SAGE Handbook of Mixed Methods in Social & Behavioral Research. Sage: United States of America.

De Vries, H., Bekkers, V., & Tummers, L. (2016). Innovation in the Public Sector: A Systematic Review and Future Research Agenda. *Public Administration, 94*(1), 146–166.

Demircioglu, M. A., & Audretsch, D. B. (2017). Conditions for Innovation in Public Sector Organizations. *Research Policy, 46*(9), 1681–1691.

DEPI. (2014). *Annual Report 2014*. Melbourne, VIC: Department of Environment and Primary Industries, Government of Victoria.

DPMC. (2015). *National Innovation and Science Agenda*. Department of the Prime Minister and Cabinet, Australian Government, Canberra, Australian Capital Territory.

Eisenhardt, K. M., & Graebner, M. E. (2007). Theory Building from Cases: Opportunities and Challenges. *Academy of Management Journal, 50*(1), 25–32.

Ferlie, E., Hartley, J., & Martin, S. (2003). Changing Public Service Organizations: Current Perspectives and Future Prospects. *British Journal of Management, 14*, s1.

Gruen, N. (2009). Policy Forum: Enhancing the National Innovation System. Beyond Central Planning: Innovation in Government in the 21st Century. *The Australian Economic Review, 24*(1), 96–103.

Harrison, G. L., & Baird, K. M. (2015). The Organizational Culture of Public Sector Organizations in Australia. *Australian Journal of Management, 40*(4), 613–629.

Hartley, J. (2013). Public and Private Features of Innovation. In L. Brown & S. Osborne (Eds.), *Handbook of Innovation in Public Services*. Cheltenham: Edward Elgar Publishing.

Hartley, J., Alford, J., Hughes, O., & Yates, S. (2015). Public Value and Political Astuteness in the Work of Public Managers: The Art of the Possible. *Public Administration, 93*(1), 195–211.

Hendren, K., Luo, Q. E., & Pandey, S. K. (2018). The State of Mixed Methods Research in Public Administration and Public Policy. *Public Administration Review, 78*(6), 904–916.

Hill, C. J., & Lynn, L. E. (2004). Is Hierarchical Governance in Decline? Evidence from Empirical Research. *Journal of Public Administration Research and Theory, 15*(2), 173–195.

Hinings, B. (2012). Connections Between Institutional Logics and Organizational Culture. *Journal of Management Inquiry, 21*(1), 98–101.

Hodgkinson, I. R., Hannibal, C., Keating, B. W., Chester Buxton, R., & Bateman, N. (2017). Toward a Public Service Management: Past, Present, and Future Directions. *Journal of Service Management, 28*(5), 998–1023.

HSI. (2015). *Why Culture and Leadership Matter. Proving the People-Performance Connection.* Sydney, NSW: Human Synergistics Inc.

Hughes, O. (2012). *Public Management and Administration.* Great Britain: Palgrave Macmillan.

Hughes, O. (2017). Public Management: 30 Years On. *International Journal of Public Sector Management, 30*(6/7), 547–554.

IPA. (2011). Why Should Public Service Managers Concern Themselves with Organisational Culture? *Institute of Public Administration Newsletter, 1*(15), 1–4. Viewed 7 April 2018.

Kelman, S. (2005). *Unleashing Change: A Study of Organizational Renewal in Government.* Washington, DC: Brookings Institution Press.

Koch, P., & Hauknes, J. (2005). *On Innovation in the Public Sector – Today and Beyond.* Oslo, Norway: NIFU.

Kreutzer, R., Neugebauer, T., & Pattloch, A. (2018). *Digital Business Leadership: Digital Transformation, Business Model Innovation, Agile Organization, Change Management.* Berlin, Heidelberg: SpringerLink.

McMurray, A., & Dorai, R. (2003). Workplace Innovation Scale: A New Method for Measuring Innovation Support Practices in the Workplace. Paper Presented to Organizational Learning and Knowledge – 5th International Conference, Lancaster University Management School, England Friday, 30th May–Monday, 2nd June, 2003.

McMurray, A., Islam, M., Sarros, J., & Pirola-Merlo, A. (2013). Workplace Innovation in a Nonprofit Organization. *Nonprofit Management and Leadership, 23*(3), 367–388.

Mele, V., & Belardinelli, P. (2018). Mixed Methods in Public Administration Research: Selecting, Sequencing, and Connecting. *Journal of Public Administration Research and Theory, 29*(2), 334–347.

Merriam, S. B., & Tisdell, E. J. (2015). *Qualitative Research: A Guide to Design and Implementation.* San Francisco, CA: John Wiley & Sons.

Moore, M., & Hartley, J. (2008). Innovations in Governance. *Public Management Review, 10*(1), 3–20.

Morse, J. M. (2016). *Mixed Method Design: Principles and Procedures*. New York: Routledge.

Moussa, M., McMurray, A., & Muenjohn, N. (2018). A Conceptual Framework of the Factors Influencing Innovation in Public Sector Organizations. *The Journal of Developing Areas, 52*(3), 231–240.

Muenjohn, N., & McMurray, A. (2017). Design Leadership, Work Values Ethic and Workplace Innovation: An Investigation of SMEs in Thailand and Vietnam. *Asia Pacific Business Review, 23*(2), 192–204.

Mulgan, G., & Albury, D. (2003). *Innovation in the Public Sector* (pp. 1–40). London, UK: Strategy Unit, Cabinet Office.

Nählinder, J., & Eriksson, A. F. (2019). Outcome, Process and Support: Analysing Aspects of Innovation in Public Sector Organizations. *Public Money & Management, 39*(6), 443–449.

Newnham, L. (2018). The Relationship Between Workplace Innovation and Organizational Culture: A Case Study of a Victorian Public Sector Organization. Doctor of Philosophy Thesis, RMIT University, Melbourne. Retrieved from https://researchbank.rmit.edu.au/eserv/rmit:162438/Newnham.pdf

Newnham, L., & McMurray, A. (2007). Land Management Innovation and Sustainability: The Flow on Effects of Organizational Change. Paper Presented to ICSB World Conference June 2007, Turku, Finland,

Newnham, L., & McMurray, A. (2020). Land Management Innovation and Sustainability – A Longitudinal View. *Public Money & Management*, vol. Manuscript ID is RPMM-2019-0179.

O'Connor, A., Roos, G., & Vickers-Willis, T. (2007). Evaluating an Australian Public Policy Organization's Innovation Capacity. *European Journal of Innovation Management, 10*(4), 532–558.

OECD. (2010). *The OECD Innovation Strategy: Getting a Head Start on Tomorrow*. Paris, France: OECD Publishing.

OECD. (2015). *Achieving Public Sector Agility at Times of Fiscal Consolidation*. Paris, France. https://doi.org/10.1787/9789264206267-en

Olejarski, A. M., Potter, M., & Morrison, R. L. (2019). Organizational Learning in the Public Sector: Culture, Politics, and Performance. *Public Integrity, 21*(1), 69–85.

Onwuegbuzie, A. J., & Combs, J. P. (Eds.). (2010). Emergent Data Analysis Techniques in Mixed Methods Research: A Synthesis. In *Handbook of Mixed Methods in Social and Behavioral Research*. Thausand Oaks, CA: SAGE.

Pace, R. W., & Faules, D. F. (1994). *Organizational Communication*. Upper Saddle River, NJ: Prentice-Hall Inc.

Parker, R., & Bradley, L. (2000). Organisational Culture in the Public Sector: Evidence from Six Organisations. *International Journal of Public Sector Management, 13*(2), 125–141.

Pot, F. (2011). Workplace Innovation for Better Jobs and Performance. *International Journal of Productivity and Performance Management, 60*(4), 404–415.

Rothstein, H. R., Sutton, A. J., & Borenstein, M. (2006). *Publication Bias in Meta-Analysis: Prevention, Assessment and Adjustments*. John Wiley & Sons.

Schein, E., & Scheiner, P. (2016). *Organization Culture and Leadership*. New York, USA: John Wiley & Sons, Incorporated.

Schwandt, T. A., & Gates, E. F. (Eds.). (2017). Case Study Methodology (5th ed.). *SAGE Handbook of Qualitative Research*. London: SAGE Publications.

Sherief, M. (2019). Key Organizational Climate Elements Influencing Employees' Creativity in Government. *The Innovation Journal, 24*(1), 1–16.

Stewart, J. (2014). Implementing an Innovative Public Sector Program. *International Journal of Public Sector Management, 27*(3), 241–250.

Stewart-Weeks, M., & Cooper, S. (2019). *Are We There Yet? The Digital Transformation of Government and the Public Sector in Australia*. Haberfield, Australia: Longueville Media Pty Ltd.

Stewart-Weeks, M., & Kastelle, T. (2015). Innovation in the Public Sector. *Australian Journal of Public Administration, 74*(1), 63–72.

Su, S., Baird, K., & Blair, B. (2013). Employee Organizational Commitment in the Australian Public Sector. *The International Journal of Human Resource Management, 24*(2), 243–264.

Teddlie, C., & Johnson, R. (Eds.). (2009). Methodological Thought Since the 20th Century. In *Foundations of Mixed Methods Research: Integrating Quantitative and Qualitative Approaches in the Social and Behavioral Sciences*. Los Angeles, CA: SAGE.

Teddlie, C., & Tashakkori, A. (Eds.). (2009). *Foundations of Mixed Methods Research: Integrating Quantitative and Qualitative Approaches in the Social and Behavioral Sciences*. Los Angeles, CA: SAGE.

Tidd, J., Bessant, J., & Pavitt, K. (2005). *Managing Innovation Integrating Technological, Market and Organizational Change*. Great Britain: John Wiley and Sons Ltd.

Torugsa, N., & Arundel, A. (2014). Complexity of Innovation in the Public Sector: A Workgroup-Level Analysis of Related Factors and Outcomes. *Public Management Review, 18*, 1–25.

Von Treuer, K., & McMurray, A. J. (2012). The Role of Organisational Climate Factors in Facilitating Workplace Innovation. *International Journal of Entrepreneurship and Innovation Management, 15*(4), 292–309.

Weerakkody, V., Omar, A., El-Haddadeh, R., & Al-Busaidy, M. (2016). Digitally-Enabled Service Transformation in the Public Sector: The Lure of Institutional Pressure and Strategic Response Towards Change. *Government Information Quarterly, 33*(4), 658–668.

Welsh, E. (2002). Dealing with Data: Using NVivo in the Qualitative Data Analysis Process. Paper Presented to Forum Qualitative Sozialforschung/Forum: Qualitative Social Research.

Yin, R. K. (2014). *Case Study Research: Design and Methods* (5th ed.). Thousand Oaks, CA: Sage publications.

Theme II

Determinants of Workplace Innovation

6

The Relationship Between Corporate Entrepreneurship Climate and Innovativeness: A National Study

Adela McMurray, Gerrit A. de Waal, Don Scott, and Jerome D. Donovan

Introduction

The history of corporate entrepreneurship research may be traced back to the concept of entrepreneurial orientation (Covin & Slevin, 1989, 1991; Miller, 1983; Morris & Paul, 1987). This refers to the strategy or strategic orientation of an organization (Ireland, Covin, & Kuratko, 2009), which can be either entrepreneurial or conservative (Covin & Slevin, 1991; Rhee, Park, & Lee, 2010) and is context dependent on other organizational factors (Batra, Sharma, Dixit, & Vohra, 2018). The entrepreneurial end of the spectrum is more relevant to innovation (Hornsby, Naffziger, Kuratko, & Montagno,

A. McMurray (✉)
College of Business, Government and Law, Flinders University,
Adelaide, SA, Australia
e-mail: adela.mcmurray@flinders.edu.au

G. A. de Waal
RMIT University, Melbourne, VIC, Australia
e-mail: gerrit.dewaal@rmit.edu.au

D. Scott
Southern Cross University, Lismore, NSW, Australia

J. D. Donovan
Swinburne University of Technology, Melbourne, VIC, Australia
e-mail: jdonovan@swinburne.edu.au

© The Author(s), under exclusive license to Springer Nature Switzerland AG 2021
A. McMurray et al. (eds.), *The Palgrave Handbook of Workplace Innovation*,
https://doi.org/10.1007/978-3-030-59916-4_6

1993; Rhee et al., 2010) and, as such, it is considered an important domain of research inquiry.

Corporate entrepreneurship is the way we improve an organization's ability to harness and apply the entrepreneurial skills and abilities of their members (Rutherford & Holt, 2007) and assists in identifying how entrepreneurial an organization tends to be (Kuratko & Morris, 2018). This is generally indicated by the "development of new business ideas and opportunities within large and established organizations" (Hough & Scheepers, 2008, p. 17) and may be viewed as a process of organizational renewal in which organizational members pursue entrepreneurial opportunities (Ireland, Kuratko, & Morris, 2006a; Zahra, 1993).

Innovation has been extensively researched in the business and economics disciplines because of its positive relationship to performance (Gronum et al., Gronum, Steen, & Verreynne, 2016), regions and countries (Crossan & Apaydin, 2010; Schumpeter, 1942). For organizations, creativity (Kong, Chiu, & Leung, 2019) is critical to organizational performance, which leads to innovation and ultimately contributes to competitive advantage (Porter, 1990) and long-term success (Baden-Fuller, 1995; Baker & Sinkula, 2002). Improvements in organizations' competitive advantages lead to GDP growth at the regional and national levels and GDP growth is associated with improved standards of living (Ahlstrom, 2010). Innovation may be best defined as the implementation of new or significantly improved products (goods/services), processes, marketing methods and organizational methods (Manual, 2005). In short, it is what results when one transforms opportunities into ideas and applies them to practice (Tidd, 2001). Growing research into innovation, including ownership structures of patents (Hamada, 2017), has suggested that organizations may be able to increase innovation output through corporate entrepreneurship (Kuratko & Morris, 2018). Yet the literature is vague about this relationship, thus raising the need for further exploration of the possible association between corporate entrepreneurship and innovativeness.

Our study provides three contributions to the corporate entrepreneurship and innovation literature. Firstly, we evaluate the possible association between corporate entrepreneurship and innovation. Secondly, our study provides further clarification of the constructs that have been suggested to be components of corporate entrepreneurship as identified in the Corporate Entrepreneurship Assessment Instrument (CEAI) and in particular addresses the organizational boundaries construct that has been suggested by several researchers (e.g. Brizek, 2003; Rhoads, 2005; Wood, 2004) to not be a worthwhile contributor to the CEAI. Thirdly, the identification of a path model as the structural equations component of a structural equations model (SEM) evaluation of the relationships between the CEAI components and innovativeness has enabled path rules to be applied in order to determine the strengths of the associations between the CEAI-based constructs and innovativeness, through the assessment of an organization's corporate entrepreneurship climate (CEC).

Literature Review and Hypothesis Development

Determinants of Corporate Entrepreneurship Climate

Climate has been defined as "a collective set of individual perceptions regarding policies, practices, and procedures that an organization rewards and supports" (Spell & Arnold, 2007) and a CEC is suggested to comprise five constructs: (1) rewards/reinforcement, (2) resource/time availability, (3) managerial support, (4) organizational boundaries and (5) work discretion/autonomy as identified by the CEAI (Hornsby, Kuratko, Shepherd, & Bott, 2009; Hornsby, Kuratko, & Zahra, 2002; Ireland et al., 2006a; Ireland, Kuratko, & Morris, 2006b; Kuratko, Ireland, Covin, & Hornsby, 2005; Rutherford & Holt, 2007; Urban, 2017). The CEAI has been shown to have validity and has been used in a number of studies such as those by Hornsby, Kuratko, Holt, and Wales (2013), Mazouz, Naji, Jeljeli, and Shdaifat (2019) and Urban and Verachia (2019).

According to researchers such as Ireland et al. (Ireland et al., 2006a; Ireland et al., 2006b), Kuratko et al. (2005), and Kuratko and Morris (2018), a CEC has been assumed to contribute to organizational innovativeness but according to Hough and Scheepers (2008), Urban (2017) and Rutherford and Holt (2007), there is little empirical evidence to support these assumptions.

Innovativeness

Innovativeness is commonly recognized as having an important association with corporate entrepreneurship (Covin & Miles, 1999; Duygulu, 2009; Simon, 2009; Kmieciak, Michna, & Meczynska, 2012; Rubera & Kirca, 2012; Rust, Lemon, & Zeithaml, 2004). The concept of innovativeness is the most powerful way by which organizations can differentiate themselves from competitors and establish competitive advantage (Knight, 1997; Kreiser, Marino, & Weaver, 2002; Sharma & Lacey, 2004). It enables organizations to preserve market power over time through a constant output of innovations, turning momentary advantages from a single new product into persistent, competitive advantages comprising multiple new products (Sharma & Lacey,

2004; Srinivasan & Hanssens, 2009). An organization's innovativeness can be researched internally within an organization and externally through the regulatory environment (Jiao, Baird, & Harrison, 2019), although, to date, both research literatures are incomplete. Therefore, organizational innovativeness and its determinants within an organizational context across Australia are the focus of this research. The study investigates several assumptions within an Australian context by drawing on information obtained from a sample of 1415 respondents who were employed by a range of Australian organizations. We investigate (1) whether a CEC is an overarching (second-order) construct that comprises the five proposed CEAI constructs (Ireland et al., 2006a; Ireland et al., 2006b) and (2) whether the CEC is associated with innovativeness. This is the first study of its kind in Australia, incorporating a sample of respondents drawn from a wide cross section of industries, organizational departments, institutional types and sizes in major Australian cities.

To summarize, the study has proposed that the CEAI factors of management support, work discretion, organizational boundaries, time availability and rewards/reinforcement are significantly and positively associated with organizational innovativeness. Furthermore, we have proposed that the CEAI components will combine to form a second-order CEC construct.

The Organizational Climate and Innovativeness Relationship

The rationale for the relationships between CEC and innovativeness is described in the literature (Hornsby et al., 2002; Hornsby et al., 2009; Hough & Scheepers, 2008; Ireland et al., 2006a; Ireland et al., 2006b; Rutherford & Holt, 2007; Urban, 2017). Beginning with Hough and Scheepers (2008), we see conflicting evidence that provides support for some CEC aspects, but not all. Hough and Scheepers (2008) specifically looked at the relationship between five CEAI-based constructs and organizational innovativeness. Drawing on a sample of 315 South African organizations, they found that managerial support and rewards/reinforcement had a significant influence on innovativeness, while time availability, work discretion/autonomy and organizational boundaries did not. They, therefore, identified a lack of support for some of the five CEAI-based constructs. This was proposed to have possibly been due to bias in the data or to measurement problems and led them to call for further research.

Urban (2017) examined the same relationships, based on a sample of 784 employees of financial organizations in South Africa. He revealed positive and significant results for the determinants of rewards/reinforcement, resource/time availability and (flexible) organizational boundaries. Work discretion/autonomy and managerial support, however, were not significantly associated with innovativeness. Taken together with Hough and Scheepers (2008), this suggested that, in a South African context, work discretion/autonomy might not be important for innovativeness. Australian organizations, by contrast, may see greater benefit from work discretion as they are rated as having a high level of entrepreneurial employee activity (Global entrepreneurship monitor report, 2020, p. 80).

Rutherford and Holt (2007) surveyed 264 employees of a mid-sized American public organization, and revealed similar determinants of entrepreneurship, including communication climate, perceived organizational and leadership support, perceptions of co-workers and reward alignment. These were defined similarly to corresponding CEAI-based climate determinants of managerial support, rewards/reinforcement, time availability and organizational boundaries.

This chapter will use structural equations modelling (SEM) in order to evaluate whether a proposed model of a CEC and innovativeness relationship provided an acceptable fit to data that had been collected from respondents working in a wide range of companies.

Determinants of Innovativeness

There is growing empirical evidence to suggest the existence of innovativeness determinants, such as effective knowledge management (Chen, Huang, & Hsiao, 2010; Ferraresi, Quandt, dos Santos, & Frega, 2012; Sankowska, 2013); trust (Sankowska, 2013); strategic orientation (entrepreneurial, market and learning) (Ferraresi et al., 2012; Rhee et al., 2010); entrepreneurial, managerial and technical capabilities (Kyrgidou & Spyropoulou, 2013); IT capability (Kmieciak et al., 2012); adhocracy culture (Duygulu, 2009); proactivity (Ejdys, 2016) and realized absorptive capacity (Cepeda-Carrion, Cegarra-Navarro, & Jimenez-Jimenez, 2012).

The relationship of these factors to innovativeness is important because many of them closely resemble the five CEC constructs considered in our research. The conceptual overlap with the CEC constructs indicated the potential relevance of these to innovativeness. Trust, for example, as conceived in Sankowska's (2013) study, was viewed as helping mitigate the fear of risk and experimentation, which is necessary for innovativeness. This conception of trust closely resembles one proposed CEC construct—work discretion/

autonomy as, according to Ireland et al. (2006a), trust is a requirement of higher levels of work discretion/autonomy.

Similarly, entrepreneurial orientation, as conceived by Rhee et al. (2010), resembles one of the proposed five CEC constructs—managerial support. Managers are generally responsible for the strategic orientation of the organization, whether entrepreneurial or otherwise, and so this construct implies managerial support for corporate entrepreneurship. Furthermore, entrepreneurial and managerial capabilities, as conceived by Kyrgidou and Spyropoulou (2013), encapsulate three potential CEC constructs of resource/time availability, rewards/reinforcement and managerial support. Lastly, the adhocracy organizational culture as regarded by Duygulu (2009) is a dynamic and entrepreneurial place to work, where leaders are considered innovators or risk takers and individuals are provided the freedom to experiment and are encouraged to take initiative. This type of culture closely resembles the proposed CEC constructs of managerial support, work discretion/autonomy, rewards/reinforcement and organizational boundaries, suggesting their importance to entrepreneurship.

Ireland et al. (2006b) in their research into entrepreneurship and innovation created what they termed an entrepreneurial health audit instrument that they suggested could be used to determine the degree to which a company was oriented towards entrepreneurship and innovation. For this study four of the health audit instrument items which were considered to be good measures of innovativeness were selected to be used as an innovativeness measure.

Method

Based on a proposed structural model, we tested the fit of the proposed SEM model and its construct loadings to the data that was collected from surveyed respondents. This meant that the following relationships were tested:

1. Whether a model of the relationships between the aspects of corporate entrepreneurship created a second-order model of CEC.
2. Whether CEC is associated with innovativeness.
3. Whether the constructs of management support, work discretion, risk reward/reinforcement, organization boundaries and time availability were individually significantly associated with innovativeness.

Data Collection

The CEAI as developed by Hornsby et al. (2002), and based on the work of Kuratko, Montagno, and Hornsby (1990), was used to collect information from managerial level employees in a range of businesses operating in Australia and yielded 1415 usable responses.

The research was approved by the university's Human Research Ethics Committee and followed Jordan and Troth's (2020) suggested key strategies in the design and management of the study to control for any potential common method bias (CMB). For example, the study's purpose and clarity was provided to the respondents by means of an Ethics Participant Information Sheet and Consent form, which contained a 14-point extensive explanation of the purpose and the benefits of the research before a respondent accepted to proceed to complete an online Qualtrics survey. Common scale properties were addressed as the questionnaire items were anchored to a Likert-type scale where 1 represented 'Strongly Disagree' and 7 'Strongly Agree'. To improve item scale clarity all items were simple in order to avoid any double meanings with no items being double-barrelled questions. Another strategy to reduce CMB, as advised by Jordan and Troth (2020), was the inclusion of reversals within the survey in order to balance positive and negative items which we incorporated with the inclusion of nine strategically placed reversal items throughout the survey.

To further control for CMB, the survey was pretested on three industry participants to ensure the questionnaire item's clarity of content and instructions, thus also addressing content validity. This was followed by the launch of the pilot study where 140 responses were drawn from the target population and were analysed in order to determine questionnaire item validity and reliability. The Cronbach alpha scores for each proposed construct ranged between $\alpha = 0.8$ and $\alpha = 0.9$, with one slightly lower at $\alpha = 0.749$ and the highest at $\alpha = 0.978$. All of these scores were above 0.7, which indicated an acceptable level of reliability (Hair, Black, Babin, & Anderson, 2010).

In order to collect the data and to ensure a high response rate, we obtained the support of a professional research survey distributing company, CINT. CINT's opt-in panel sampling approach is widely accepted and used in entrepreneurship (Gupta, Wieland, & Turban, 2019; Lu, Akinola, & Mason, 2017) and management (Schaumberg & Flynn, 2017) research. Thus, the responses were collected from managerial level employees (single respondent) of Australian companies signed up to CINT's opt-in panel.

Sample Details

The sample represented a wide cross section of organizational departments, industries, institutional types and sizes. There were approximately 100 or more respondents from each type of department including general management (n = 417), marketing and sales (n = 143), accounting and finance (n = 170), research and development (n = 116), manufacturing (n = 112), operations (n = 250), human resources (n = 97) and other (n = 110). Of a total of 33 industries, the most prominent included information technology (applications, services, systems and hardware and internet services) (n = 211), banking and financial services (n = 156), retail (n = 100), healthcare (n = 98), education (n = 98), manufacturing (n = 96) and construction (n = 81). The majority of organizations were private (n = 898), with a good representation of public (n = 452) followed by not-for-profit organizations (n = 65).

Multinational enterprises comprised 441 of the organizations, while 460 were non-international. Other types included franchises (n = 195), joint ventures (n = 176), exporting (n = 100) and importing (n = 43) organizations. The majority were large organizations, employing 200 full-time staff or more (n = 880), with a good representation of medium-sized organizations, employing 20–199 full-time staff (n = 470). Only 33 were small organizations (Swanepoel & Harrison, 2015).

Most of the organizations could be considered entrepreneurial, with 68% of the respondents indicating that they had had an opportunity to innovate within the first 12 months of their employment. Geographically, the sample included organizations from all major Australian cities, including Sydney (n = 542), Melbourne (n = 409), Brisbane (n = 186), Perth (n = 103), Adelaide (n = 66) and Canberra (n = 48). Lastly, both male (n = 796) and female (n = 613) genders were well-represented, with six respondents identifying themselves as belonging to an 'other' category.

The SEM Model

There is significant empirical evidence to suggest that there should be a relationship between the CEAI constructs, a second-order CEC construct and a measure of innovativeness. This proposed relationship can be encapsulated in a SEM shown in Fig. 6.1 that illustrates an anticipated causal model that comprises five first-order CEAI-based reflective constructs leading to a reflective second-order CEC construct that influences an innovativeness construct.

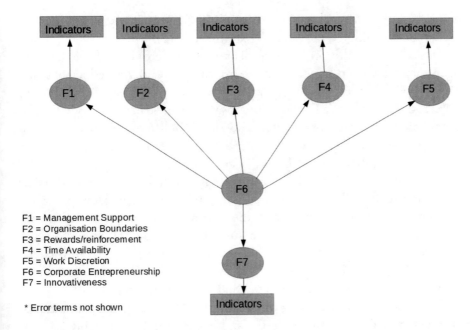

Fig. 6.1   SEM model

As was explained by Wright (1921), in relation to path models and as reported by Pearl (1998, p. 250), in terms of structural equations modelling, "[p]rior knowledge of the causal relationships is assumed as prerequisite". This model therefore outlines the authors' belief that corporate entrepreneurship climate would influence innovativeness and the structural equations model was created on the basis that the second-order CEC construct labelled as F6 would influence constructs F1 to F5, the CEAI-based constructs of management support, organizational boundaries, rewards/reinforcement, time availability and work discretion, as reflected by the measures provided by their indicator variables and that CEC would also influence an innovativeness construct labelled as F7.

As a preliminary stage to the evaluation of this model, the six first-order constructs were subjected to confirmatory factor analysis (CFA) in order to establish whether they provided an acceptable fit to the data. In conducting this analysis, the two-stage approach as recommended by Anderson and Gerbing (1988, p. 421), who have stated that "ideally, a researcher would want to split a sample, using one half to develop a model and the other half to validate the solution obtained from the first half", was adopted and the dataset was split into two halves yielding datasets of 707 and 708 respondents. The initial CFA evaluation was carried out with the first half of the dataset, using the EQS statistical software (Bentler, 1995) and employing a maximum likelihood technique (Hair et al., 2010; Kline, 2012).

This analysis resulted in the removal of seven indicator items from the management support construct and two items from the work discretion construct that all loaded at less than 0.5. Because the constructs were all reflective in nature, the removal of a few such items was acceptable because "indicators of a unidimensional concept are interchangeable" (Bollen & Lennox, 1991). An innovativeness construct was composed from four items chosen from the CECI health audit model of Ireland et al. (2006b).

An organizational boundaries construct is traditionally conceptualized as belonging to the CEC (see Ireland et al., 2006a) concept. However, when examined in the Australian context, the CFA revealed that the indicator variables that had been used to indicate this construct were not satisfactory and there was no fit. Consequently, the organizational boundaries construct was excluded from the final model to yield five first-order constructs in the final SEM model that was subjected to test and which is shown in Fig. 6.2.

This model was tested using the second half of the data and was found to fit the data well as shown in Fig. 6.3 and in the fit indices in Table 6.1. The construct indicator loadings that were determined in respect of this model are shown in Table 6.2.

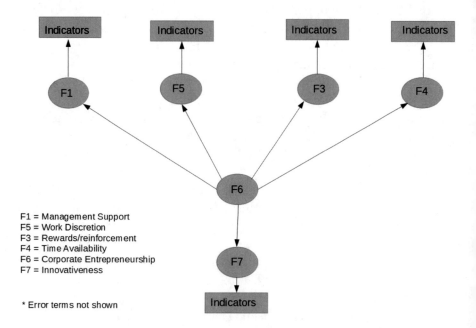

F1 = Management Support
F5 = Work Discretion
F3 = Rewards/reinforcement
F4 = Time Availability
F6 = Corporate Entrepreneurship
F7 = Innovativeness

* Error terms not shown

Fig. 6.2 Amended model

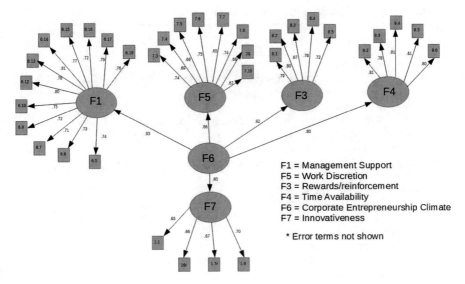

Fig. 6.3 Final model

Table 6.1 Model goodness of fit summary

Bentler-Bonett non-normed fit index	0.911
Comparative fit index	0.917
Bollen (IFI) fit index	0.918
Standardized RMR	0.046
Root mean square error of approximation (RMSEA)	0.058

The model fit to the data was evaluated by means of the NNFI, CFI, IFI, SRMR and RMSEA fit indices. The RMSEA was less than the maximum recommended value of 0.08, the CFI, NNFI and IFI values were more than the minimum recommended level of 0.90 and the SRMR was less than the maximum recommended value of 0.05 (see Cunningham, 2010; Hair et al., 2010; Kline, 2012). The standardized loadings for the measurement model indicators were all significantly greater than zero and exceeded the required minimum level of 0.5 (Hair, Black, Babin, Anderson, & Tatham, 2006, p. 795) and are shown in Table 6.2, while the model diagram with the construct loadings and path values is shown in Fig. 6.3.

The results showed that the second-order CEC construct was strongly and positively related to innovativeness (0.80), as well as to the CEC first-order constructs including management support for corporate entrepreneurship,

Table 6.2 Model indicators and standardized loadings

Code	Indicator	Standardized loading
F7	***Innovativeness***	
1.1	A high rate of new product/service introductions, compared to our competitors (including new features and improvements)	0.652
1.6r	A top management philosophy that emphasizes proven products and services, and the avoidance of heavy new product development costs (reversed scores)	0.662
1.7r	Cautious, pragmatic, step-at-a-time adjustment to problems (reverse scores)	0.667
1.8	Active search for big opportunities	0.703
F1	***Management support for corporate entrepreneurship***	
6.5	A promotion usually follows from the development of new and innovative ideas	0.744
6.6	Those employees who come up with innovative ideas on their own often receive management encouragement for their activities	0.726
6.7	The 'doers on projects' are allowed to make decisions without going through elaborate justification and approval procedures	0.709
6.9	Many top managers have been known for their experience with the innovation process	0.720
6.10	Money is often available to get new project ideas off the ground	0.751
6.12	There are several options within the company for individuals to get financial support for their innovative projects and ideas	0.800
6.13	People are often encouraged to take calculated risks with ideas around here	0.776
6.14	Individual risk takers are often recognized for their willingness to champion new projects, whether eventually successful or not	0.809
6.15	The term 'risk taker' is considered a positive attribute for people in my work area	0.772
6.16	My company supports many small and experimental projects, realizing that some will undoubtedly fail	0.722
6.17	An employee with a good idea is often given free time to develop that idea	0.785
6.18	There is considerable desire among people in the company for generating new ideas without regard for crossing departmental or functional boundaries	0.762
F5	***Work discretion***	
7.3	My company provides the chance to be creative and try my own methods of doing the job	0.741
7.4	My company provides the freedom to use my own judgement	0.692

(*continued*)

Table 6.2 (continued)

Code	Indicator	Standardized loading
7.5	My company provides the chance to do something that makes use of my abilities	0.691
7.6	I have the freedom to decide what I do on my job	0.754
7.7	It is basically my own responsibility to decide how my job gets done	0.654
7.8	I almost always get to decide what I do on my job	0.743
7.9	I have much autonomy on my job and am left on my own to do my own work	0.680
7.10	I seldom have to follow the same work methods or steps for doing my major tasks from day to day	0.668
F3	***Rewards/reinforcement***	
8.1	My manager helps me get my work done by removing obstacles and roadblocks	0.790
8.2	The rewards I receive are dependent upon my innovation on the job	0.797
8.3	My supervisor will increase my job responsibilities if I am performing well in my job	0.665
8.4	My supervisor will give me special recognition if my work performance is especially good	0.783
8.5	My manager would tell his/her boss if my work was outstanding	0.720
F4	***Time availability***	
9.2	I always seem to have plenty of time to get everything done	0.806
9.3	I have just the right amount of time and work load to do everything well	0.783
9.4	My job is structured so that I have sufficient time to think about wider organizational problems	0.808
9.5	I feel that I am only sometimes working with time constraints on my job	0.613
9.6	My co-workers and I always find time for long-term problem solving	0.803
F6	***Corporate entrepreneurship climate***	
F1	Management support	0.926
F3	Rewards/reinforcement	0.921
F4	Time availability	0.800
F5	Work discretion	0.857
F7	Innovativeness	0.798

rewards/reinforcement, work discretion and time availability. An evaluation of the path values in the structural model showed that there was a slight difference in the strength of the relationships between the four CEC constructs and innovativeness. The influence of time availability and work discretion on innovativeness was less (0.64 and 0.68) than that of management support and rewards/reinforcement (0.74 and 0.74). These path values are shown in Table 6.3.

Table 6.3 Path analysis model relationships and standardized loadings

Path analysis model relationships	Standardized loadings
Management support → Innovativeness	0.74
Rewards/reinforcement → Innovativeness	0.74
Work discretion → Innovativeness	0.68
Time availability → Innovativeness	0.64
Corporate entrepreneurship climate → Innovativeness	0.80

Discussion, Implications and Limitations

Implications for Theory

This study sought to investigate two assumptions, the first being that CEC is an overarching (second-order) construct comprising five constructs of management support, organizational boundaries, work discretion, rewards/reinforcement and time availability and a second assumption that CEC influences innovativeness.

By using empirical data from 1415 Australian respondents who were employed by a wide range of businesses and industries, our results have provided evidence that supports the existence of an overarching second-order entrepreneurial climate construct that we have termed CEC. The results have also supported the contention that CEC contributes to innovativeness. However, one of the five proposed CEAI-based constructs did not fit the data and the CEC was therefore found to be reflected by four constructs. This finding was in line with some researchers such as, for example, Brizek (2003), Wood (2004) and Rhoads (2005) who have queried the relevance of this construct, although its relevance has been supported by researchers such as Birkinshaw (2003) who has pointed out that organizational boundaries are one of four factors that contribute to corporate transformation and may be recorded or implicitly understood. He has asserted that boundaries are central to innovation management and are designed to improve organizational effectiveness and efficiency. Moreover, Birkinshaw (2003) has noted that organizational boundaries are dependent on specific organizational structures and may act as barriers to information sharing including innovation. To compensate for such developments, managers engage in boundary spanning and perhaps this could be one explanation as to why the measurement of organizational boundaries did not fit the data in this study. Boundary spanning might rather be what is required to be evaluated as a potential CEC measure.

The study results make a contribution to the corporate entrepreneurship literature by determining that there is a strong positive relationship between CEC and innovativeness (0.80). Unlike in the South African context (see Hough & Scheepers, 2008; Urban, 2017), in Australian organizations, work discretion as a component of CEC has been found to have a positive effect on innovativeness. Importantly, we have observed that the CEAI-based components of management support and rewards/reinforcement show a stronger influence on innovativeness (0.74 and 0.74) than work discretion and time availability (0.68 and 0.64). The constructs of management support and rewards/reinforcement may be viewed as sources of guidance and motivation for innovativeness. By contrast, work discretion and time availability may be seen as sources of employee empowerment. These results indicate that employee guidance and motivation for corporate entrepreneurship are more important for innovativeness than are sources of employee empowerment. Taken together, sources of employee guidance, motivation (for CEC) and empowerment comprise a CEC that is strongly related to innovativeness.

Implications for Practice

As the first study of its kind in Australia, the results provide important implications for all levels of management in many types of Australian industries, organizations, departments and institutional types. The findings are particularly applicable to larger private or public Australian organizations operating in the information technology industry or in retail, healthcare, education, manufacturing, construction, banking and financial services.

In this context, the four-construct CEAI (see Table 6.2) may be used by Australian managers to self-assess the extent to which their organizational climate reflects a CEC. By extension, managers may also assess the extent to which their organizational climate is aligned with innovativeness. Importantly, a CEC value could be used by Australian managers to identify potential levels of improvement in innovation orientation.

Managers can take proactive actions to improve their organizational climate. To this end, the first construct that is most influential in promoting an entrepreneurial climate is management support. The encouragement and willingness of managers to support innovative activities serves a pivotal role in shaping employees' beliefs and expectations about innovation (Hornsby et al., 2002). Managers can exhibit support for entrepreneurial actions through a variety of ways, including the promotion, recognition or encouragement of individuals who champion innovative ideas, the provision of resources or expertise as necessary, the promotion of risk-taking and the support of small and experimental projects. Management support for entrepreneurial behaviour will inspire employees to seek out innovative solutions to problems, to act proactively and to be prepared to pursue novel projects.

Further to management support, rewards and reinforcement must be used appropriately. This requires managers to seek out and remove obstacles and roadblocks that affect innovative work and ensure that exceptional work performance is rewarded through special recognition and increased responsibility. In addition, managers should ensure there is sufficient challenge or room for entrepreneurial activities in an employee's work and ensure that there are suitable rewards for such initiatives. The implementation of an effective reward and reinforcements system, as such, motivates entrepreneurial activity and develops managers' inclination to become involved.

An entrepreneurial climate requires that organizational members be provided with sufficient work discretion and time availability. Managers can ensure that employees have sufficient work discretion by providing opportunities for employees to use their own judgement, to be creative and to try their own methods of doing their job and to have the freedom to decide what to do in their job. Providing employees with opportunities to rarely have to follow the same work methods or steps for doing major day-to-day tasks and to be left on their own to do their own work will assist in developing a climate of entrepreneurship. Managers also need to ensure that employees are provided with sufficient time to engage in entrepreneurial thinking and actions by alleviating time constraints and structuring work roles and tasks in a way that provides employees with sufficient time to think about solutions for wider organizational problems.

Limitations and Suggestions for Future Research

The evidence and rationale provided in this study should be considered in view of its limitations. Firstly, this study is based only on Australian organizations. Furthermore, in our analysis we did not control for any potential influencing effects of organizational size or research and development intensity.

The study opens up several areas for future research to address. For example, it would be beneficial to replicate this Australian study in different country contexts or to merge the research design to incorporate external regulatory variables such as those investigated by Jiao et al. (2019) in order to become the first study to identify internal and external influences of firm innovativeness. Furthermore, it could be interesting to test the second-order corporate entrepreneurship climate model in relation to alternative measures of types of organizational boundary effects. Finally, our population sample comprising managers and future research may find it beneficial to include and examine other staff in the population sample.

Acknowledgement   The authors would like to thank Dr V. Vranic for his research assistant work.

References

Ahlstrom, D. (2010). Innovation and Growth: How Business Contributes to Society. *Academy of Management Perspectives, 24*(3), 11–24.

Anderson, J. C., & Gerbing, D. W. (1988). Structural Equations Modelling in Practice: A Review and Recommended Two-Step Approach. *Psychological Bulletin, 103*(3), 411–423.

Baden-Fuller, C. (1995). Strategic Innovation, Corporate Entrepreneurship and Matching Outside-in to Inside-Out Approaches to Strategy Research 1. *British Journal of Management, 6*, S3–S16.

Baker, W. E., & Sinkula, J. M. (2002). Market Orientation, Learning Orientation and Product Innovation: Delving into the Organization's Black Box. *Journal of Market-Focused Management, 5*(1), 5–23.

Batra, S., Sharma, S., Dixit, M. R., & Vohra, N. (2018). Does Strategic Planning Determine Innovation in Organizations? A Study of Indian SME Sector. *Australian Journal of Management, 43*(3), 493–513.

Bentler, P. M. (1995). *EQS Structural Equations Program Manual*. Encino, CA: Multivariate Software, Inc.

Birkinshaw, J. (2003). The Paradox of Corporate Entrepreneurship. *Strategy and Business*, 46–57.

Bollen, K., & Lennox, R. (1991). Conventional Wisdom on Measurement: A Structural Equation Perspective. *Psychological Bulletin, 110*(2), 305–314.

Brizek, M. G. (2003). *An Empirical Investigation of Corporate Entrepreneurship Intensity Within the Casual Dining Restaurant Segment*. Falls Church, VI: Virginia Polytechnic Institute and State University.

Cepeda-Carrion, G., Cegarra-Navarro, J. G., & Jimenez-Jimenez, D. (2012). The Effect of Absorptive Capacity on Innovativeness: Context and Information Systems Capability as Catalysts. *British Journal of Management, 23*(1), 110–129.

Chen, C. J., Huang, J. W., & Hsiao, Y. C. (2010). Knowledge Management and Innovativeness: The Role of Organizational Climate and Structure. *International Journal of Manpower, 31*(8), 848–870.

Covin, J. G., & Miles, M. P. (1999). Corporate Entrepreneurship and the Pursuit of Competitive Advantage. *Entrepreneurship Theory and Practice, 23*(3), 47–63.

Covin, J. G., & Slevin, D. P. (1989). Strategic Management of Small Firms in Hostile and Benign Environments. *Strategic Management Journal, 10*(1), 75–87.

Covin, J. G., & Slevin, D. P. (1991). A Conceptual Model of Entrepreneurship as Firm Behavior. *Entrepreneurship Theory and Practice, 16*(1), 7–26.

Crossan, M. M., & Apaydin, M. (2010). A Multi-dimensional Framework of Organizational Innovation: A Systematic Review of the Literature. *Journal of Management Studies, 47*(6), 1154–1191.

Cunningham, E. G. (2010). *A Practical Guide to Structural Equation Modelling Using Amos.* Melbourne, VIC: Statsline.

Duygulu, E. (2009). The Effects of Leadership Styles and Organizational Culture on Firms Innovativeness. *African Journal of Business Management, 3*(9), 475–485.

Ejdys, J. (2016). Entrepreneurial orientation vs. Innovativeness of Small and Medium Size Enterprises. *Journal of Engineering, Project, and Production Management, 6*(1), 13–24.

Ferraresi, A. A., Quandt, C. O., dos Santos, S. A., & Frega, J. R. (2012). Knowledge Management and Strategic Orientation: Leveraging Innovativeness and Performance. *Journal of Knowledge Management, 16*(5), 688–701.

Global Entrepreneurship Monitor Report. (2020). *The Global Entrepreneurship Research Association.* London, UK: London Business School. ISBN: 978-1-9160178-2-5.

Gronum, S., Steen, J., & Verreynne, M. L. (2016). Business Model Design and Innovation: Unlocking the Performance Benefits of Innovation. *Australian Journal of Management, 41*(3), 585–605.

Gupta, V. K., Wieland, A. M., & Turban, D. B. (2019). Gender Characterizations in Entrepreneurship: A Multi-level Investigation of Sex-Role Stereotypes About High-Growth, Commercial, and Social Entrepreneurs. *Journal of Small Business Management, 57*(1), 131–153.

Hair, J. F., Black, W. C., Babin, B. J., & Anderson, R. E. (2010). *Multivariate Data Analysis* (7th ed.). Upper Saddle River, NJ: Prentice Hall.

Hair, J. F., Black, W. C., Babin, B. J., Anderson, R. E., & Tatham, R. L. (2006). *Multivariate Data Analysis* (6th ed.). Upper Saddle River, NJ: Pearson Education Inc.

Hamada, K. (2017). Incentive for Innovation and the Optimal Allocation of Patents. *Australian Journal of Management, 42*(4), 692–707.

Hornsby, J. S., Kuratko, D. F., Holt, D. T., & Wales, W. J. (2013). Assessing a Measurement of Organizational Preparedness for Corporate Entrepreneurship. *Journal of Product Innovation Management, 30*(5), 937–995.

Hornsby, J. S., Kuratko, D. F., Shepherd, D. A., & Bott, J. P. (2009). Managers' Corporate Entrepreneurial Actions: Examining Perception and Position. *Journal of Business Venturing, 24*(3), 236–247.

Hornsby, J. S., Kuratko, D. F., & Zahra, S. A. (2002). Middle Managers' Perception of the Internal Environment for Corporate Entrepreneurship: Assessing a Measurement Scale. *Journal of Business Venturing, 17*(3), 253–273.

Hornsby, J. S., Naffziger, D. W., Kuratko, D. F., & Montagno, R. V. (1993). An Interactive Model of the Corporate Entrepreneurship Process. *Entrepreneurship Theory and Practice, 17*(2), 29–37.

Hough, J., & Scheepers, R. (2008). Creating Corporate Entrepreneurship Through Strategic Leadership. *Journal of Global Strategic Management, 2*(1), 17–25.

Ireland, R. D., Covin, J. G., & Kuratko, D. F. (2009). Conceptualizing Corporate Entrepreneurship Strategy. *Entrepreneurship Theory and Practice, 33*(1), 19–46.

Ireland, R. D., Kuratko, D. F., & Morris, M. H. (2006a). A Health Audit for Corporate Entrepreneurship: Innovation at All Levels: Part I. *Journal of Business Strategy, 27*(1), 10–17.

Ireland, R. D., Kuratko, D. F., & Morris, M. H. (2006b). A Health Audit for Corporate Entrepreneurship: Innovation at All Levels: Part II. *Journal of Business Strategy, 27*(2), 21–30.

Jiao, L., Baird, K., & Harrison, G. (2019). Searching in the Regulatory Environment: The Impact of Regulatory Search on Firm Innovativeness. *Australian Journal of Management, 45*(1), 153–171.

Jordan, P. J., & Troth, A. C. (2020). Common Method Bias in Applied Settings: The Dilemma of Researching in Organizations. *Australian Journal of Management, 45*(1), 3–14.

Kline, R. B. (2012). *Principles and Practice of Structural Equation Modelling* (3rd ed.). New York: Guilford.

Kmieciak, R., Michna, A., & Meczynska, A. (2012). Innovativeness, Empowerment and IT Capability: Evidence from SMEs. *Industrial Management and Data Systems, 112*(5), 707–728.

Knight, G. A. (1997). Cross-Cultural Reliability and Validity of a Scale to Measure Firm Entrepreneurial Orientation. *Journal of Business Venturing, 12*(3), 213–225.

Kong, H., Chiu, W. C., & Leung, H. K. (2019). Building Creative Self-Efficacy Via Learning Goal Orientation, Creativity Job Requirement, and Team Learning Behavior: The Key to Employee Creativity. *Australian Journal of Management, 44*(3), 443–461.

Kreiser, P. M., Marino, L. D., & Weaver, K. M. (2002). Assessing the Psychometric Properties of the Entrepreneurial Orientation Scale: A Multi-country Analysis. *Entrepreneurship Theory and Practice, 26*(4), 71–93.

Kuratko, D. F., Ireland, R. D., Covin, J. G., & Hornsby, J. S. (2005). A Model of Middle–Level Managers' Entrepreneurial Behavior. *Entrepreneurship Theory and Practice, 29*(6), 699–716.

Kuratko, D. F., Montagno, R. M., & Hornsby, J. S. (1990). Developing an Entrepreneurial Assessment Instrument for an Effective Corporate Entrepreneurial Environment. *Strategic Management Journal, 11*, 49–58.

Kuratko, D. F., & Morris, M. H. (2018). Corporate Entrepreneurship: A Critical Challenge for Educators and Researchers. *Entrepreneurship Education and Pedagogy, 1*(1), 42–60.

Kyrgidou, L. P., & Spyropoulou, S. (2013). Drivers and Performance Outcomes of Innovativeness: An Empirical Study. *British Journal of Management, 24*(3), 281–298.

Lu, J. G., Akinola, M., & Mason, M. F. (2017). "Switch On" Creativity: Task Switching Can Increase Creativity by Reducing Cognitive Fixation. *Organizational Behavior and Human Decision Processes, 139*, 63–75.

Manual, O. (2005). Oslo Manual: Guidelines for Collecting and Interpreting Innovation Data. *Committee for Scientific and Technological Policy, OECD-OCDE, Paris, 57*, 70–80.

Mazouz, A., Naji, L., Jeljeli, R., & Shdaifat, F. (2019). Innovation and Entrepreneurship Framework Within the Middle East and North Africa Region. *African Journal of Science, Technology, Innovation and Development.* https://doi.org/10.108 0/20421338.2019.1573959

Miller, D. (1983). The Correlates of Entrepreneurship in Three Types of Firms. *Management Science, 29*(7), 770–791.

Morris, M. H., & Paul, G. W. (1987). The Relationship Between Entrepreneurship and Marketing in Established Firms. *Journal of Business Venturing, 2*(3), 247–259.

Pearl, J. (1998). Graphs, Causality and Structural Equations Models. *Sociological Methods and Research, 27*(2), 226–284.

Porter, M. E. (1990). *The Competitive Advantage of Nations.* New York: The Free Press.

Rhee, J., Park, T., & Lee, D. H. (2010). Drivers of Innovativeness and Performance for Innovative SMEs in South Korea: Mediation of Learning Orientation. *Technovation, 30*(1), 65–75.

Rhoads, G. R. (2005). *Initiating an Entrepreneurial Mindset in the Department of Defense (DoD): Testing a Comprehensive Model.* Ohio: Air Force Institute of Technology, Wright-Patterson Air Force Base.

Rubera, G., & Kirca, A. H. (2012). Firm Innovativeness and Its Performance Outcomes: A Meta-analytic Review and Theoretical Integration. *Journal of Marketing, 76*(3), 130–147.

Rust, R. T., Lemon, K. N., & Zeithaml, V. A. (2004). Return on Marketing: Using Customer Equity to Focus Marketing Strategy. *Journal of Marketing, 68*(1), 109–112.

Rutherford, M. W., & Holt, D. T. (2007). Corporate Entrepreneurship: An Empirical Look at the Innovativeness Dimension and Its Antecedents. *Journal of Organizational Change Management, 20*(3), 429–446.

Sankowska, A. (2013). Relationships Between Organizational Trust, Knowledge Transfer, Knowledge Creation, and Firm's Innovativeness. *The Learning Organization, 20*(1), 85–100.

Schaumberg, R. L., & Flynn, F. J. (2017). Clarifying the Link Between Job Satisfaction and Absenteeism: The Role of Guilt Proneness. *Journal of Applied Psychology, 102*(6), 982–992.

Schumpeter, J. (1942). Creative Destruction. *Capitalism, Socialism and Democracy, 825*, 82–85.

Sharma, A., & Lacey, N. (2004). Linking Product Development Outcomes to Market Valuation of the Firm: The Case of the US Pharmaceutical Industry. *Journal of Product Innovation Management, 21*(5), 297–308.

Simon, H. (2009). *Hidden Champions of the Twenty-First Century: The Success Strategies of Unknown World Market Leaders.* Springer Science and Business Media.

Spell, C. S., & Arnold, T. J. (2007). A Multi-level Analysis of Organizational Justice Climate, Structure, and Employee Mental Health. *Journal of Management, 33*(5), 724–751. https://doi.org/10.1177/0149206307305560

Srinivasan, S., & Hanssens, D. M. (2009). Marketing and Firm Value: Metrics, Methods, Findings, and Future Directions. *Journal of Marketing Research, 46*(3), 293–312.

Swanepoel, J. A., & Harrison, A. W. (2015). The business size distribution in Australia - research paper 5/2015. In Department of Industry, Innovation and Science (Ed.). Canberra: Australian Government: Office of the Chief Economist.

Tidd, J. (2001). Innovation Management in Context: Environment, Organization and Performance. *International Journal of Management Reviews, 3*(3), 169–183.

Urban, B. (2017). Corporate Entrepreneurship in South Africa: The Role of Organizational Factors and Entrepreneurial Alertness in Advancing Innovativeness. *Journal of Developmental Entrepreneurship, 22*(3), 1750015.

Urban, B., & Verachia, A. (2019). Organisational Antecedents of Innovative Firms: A Focus on Entrepreneurial Orientation in South Africa. *International Journal of Business Innovation and Research, 18*(1), 128–144.

Wood, C. C. (2004). *Entrepreneurial Mindset in Department of Defense (DoD) Organizations: Antecedents and Outcomes.* Ohio: Air Force Institute of Technology, Wright-Patterson Air Force Base.

Wright, S. (1921). Correlation and Causation. *Journal of Agricultural Research, 20*, 557–585.

Zahra, S. A. (1993). A Conceptual Model of Entrepreneurship as Firm Behavior: A Critique and Extension. *Entrepreneurship Theory and Practice, 17*(4), 5–21.

7

Innovating for the Future: Understanding Organizational Culture in Changing Cambodia

Andrew Henck

Introduction

This case study took place in the Cambodia country office within an international NGO focused on humanitarian aid and development. The sector, as recognized today, is widely considered to have been born in Article 71 of the UN Charter in 1945 where the term nongovernmental organization appears (UN Charter, n.d.). The NGO analyzed in this case study functions across the globe in nearly 100 countries and has operated in Cambodia for more than 40 years. With more than 800 staff employed in the capital city of Phnom Penh and nine provinces across the country, the NGO provides vital nutrition support, education programming, and other services to more than 2.7 million children and their families each year across Cambodia. Senior leaders in Phnom Penh sought to better understand their current organizational culture and its impact on the forthcoming global strategic planning process. With several new members to the senior leadership team, the aim was to seek clarity and consensus around the cultural dynamics and factors critical for future success. Subsequently, a three-month culture study in Summer 2017 was conducted to engage the organization from frontline staff in rural field offices to managers and senior leaders with country-wide responsibilities across Cambodia. The researcher spent the entirety of the culture study inside the

A. Henck (✉)
Department of Leadership Studies, University of San Diego, San Diego, CA, USA
e-mail: ahenck@sandiego.edu

© The Author(s), under exclusive license to Springer Nature Switzerland AG 2021
A. McMurray et al. (eds.), *The Palgrave Handbook of Workplace Innovation*,
https://doi.org/10.1007/978-3-030-59916-4_7

NGO, based in the country office headquarters, to explore, measure, and observe these organizational realities at play.

While the dynamic nature of this organizational culture effort was taking place, it's important to note the broader changes happening across the Cambodia context. This Southeast Asian nation has continued to experience tremendous growth in development, reaching lower middle-income status in 2015 and is on its way to middle-income status by within the next decade, according to the World Bank (2020). Notably, the total number of NGOs working in the country has also grown exponentially over the last 30 years (Cooperation Committee for Cambodia, n.d.). Nonetheless, this case study provides a unique framework for exploring organizational culture within a developing country context and the pursuit of workplace innovation in an international NGO environment.

Theoretical Background

Organizational Culture

Schein (2010) defines this phenomenon as "the basic tacit assumptions about how the world is and ought to be that a group of people share and that determines their perceptions, thoughts, feelings, and overt behavior" (p. 17). Over the course of the chapter, this definition will frame the discussion on organizational life within this developing world context. The three major levels of Schein's cultural analysis also offer a relevant frame for considering this case study: (1) artifacts, (2) espoused beliefs and values, and (3) basic underlying assumptions. Other dynamics important here include, but are not limited to, observed behaviors, group norms, and climate. Perhaps most at the heart of the literature here involves these espoused values lived within an organizational culture. According to Schein (1985), espoused values first begin as a shared value then become shared assumptions within the workplace. Naturally, the challenge within organizations here involves the transition from these espoused values actually being lived for members to tangibly see and experience.

Hofstede (1983) offers another critical and multifaceted lens on organizational culture as (1) holistic, (2) historically determined, (3) related to anthropological concepts, (4) socially constructed, (5) software, and (6) difficult to change. Ultimately, he offers a definition of organizational culture as "the collective programming of the mind which distinguishes the members of one organization from another" (1983). One of the main distinctions and connections to the broader literature on culture comes through his distinction between the "software" for national cultures primarily expressed in values and the "software" for organizational cultures, which is typically revealed through practices. In additional research, this subfield of the culture literature would provide a valuable foundation within international organizations composed of diverse workforces. Concurrently, it is important to note the focus on historical determinants within Hofstede's organizational culture definition. With a growing number of new industries and sectors impacting the world of work today, additional scholarship is needed to validate the relevance of this claim amidst continued change.

While the literature in organizational culture is expansive, there is little existing within the relevant bodies of NGO scholarship. Walkup (1997) argues the dysfunctional dynamics within humanitarian organizations, often identified as a part of the organizational culture, as integral factors shaping not only internal beliefs and behaviors but external relationships with stakeholders from beneficiaries to donors to governments. Ultimately, the culture impedes the ability of the organization to learn and innovate into its future. Given the unique organizational contexts like humanitarian settings, Stephenson (2005) presents the case for NGOs to reconsider their cultures entirely to focus on cooperation and trust with other actors. Nonetheless, in these environments, the value placed on humanitarian principles is critical to ensure quality performance. After research at MSF Holland, Hilhorst and Schmiemann (2002) posit that these principles contribute to the organizational culture through providing a "glue" to interpersonal relationships throughout the system.

Similarly, Adler (2002) defines culture, in part, as something that "shapes behavior and structures one's perception of the world." It is here where the literature offers a relevant analysis at a deeper level to the underlying dynamics of culture that Adler acknowledges. With the basic tacit assumptions that Schein acknowledges, there is room for further exploration of those that are unsaid, unconscious, and perhaps even contradictory to the espoused values of an organization. Nonetheless, the expansive literature recognizes organizational culture as a dynamic phenomenon, complete with elements and factors that contribute to our ongoing experiences at work. However, the tension, as Morgan (1986) describes, emerges when we attempt to reduce culture to discrete variables rather than recognizing it as an ongoing construction of reality, both individually and as organizations. Rather than one uniform organizational culture, there might be a series of competing value systems that create a broader mosaic of organizational realities (1986).

Competing Values Framework

This metatheory was developed to explain the differences in values underlying models of organizational effectiveness (Quinn & Rohrbaugh, 1981). The framework focuses on a series of tensions within an organization with a primary emphasis on (1) conflict between stability and change and (2) conflict between the internal organization and external environment. Through subsequent decades of organizational effectiveness research, the Competing Values Framework has been utilized to study a variety of phenomena, including organizational culture. Specifically, Cameron and Quinn (2011) developed the Organizational Culture Assessment Instrument (OCAI) that is utilized widely across the globe as a diagnostic frame for organizational culture and change management initiatives. The instrument assesses the organization based on Wilkins and Ouchi's (1983) typology of cultures: clan, market, adhocracy, and hierarchy.

Another utilization of the Competing Values Framework is outlined in Quinn and Cameron's (1983) research on organizational life cycles. Their research hypothesized certain effectiveness criteria present within each stage of organizational development: (1) entrepreneurial stage, (2) collectivity stage, (3) formalization and control stage, and (4) elaboration of structure and mirror the culture types offered in the OCAI. Additionally, Quinn and Rohrbaugh (1981) utilize the framework to provide models of organizational effectiveness, each embedded in a set of competing values: (1) human relations model, (2) open system model, (3) rational goal model, and (4) internal process model. Ultimately, the framework recognizes that the importance of these criteria will differ across conditions and time in organizations.

Workplace Innovation

Organizational innovation in developing world contexts is an underexplored topic within the literature, even as it shares significant overlap in characteristics with creativity (Angle, 1989). Through the meta-analytic review work of Büschgens, Bausch, and Balkin (2013), the literature has yet to extensively explain any theoretical relationship between organizational culture and innovation, especially in developing countries. Nonetheless, there are ample frameworks to consider at this critical nexus for some of our world's largest and complex actors seeking to solve some of our most pressing global challenges.

Burns and Stalker (1961) provide an organizational design approach to utilize in navigating the related complexities in business environments. Their environmental deterministic view of organizations shows how entities can deal with unpredictability and volatility in the broader environment. Similarly, Kanter (1988) examines the environments in which innovation is best practiced and posits that the following six elements have to be present: (1) integrative structures, (2) an emphasis on diversity, (3) structural linkages in and out of the organization, (4) intersecting territories, (5), collective pride and faith in people's talents, and (6) and emphasis on collaboration and teamwork (p. 383).

The innovation literature offers few frameworks to consider in light of the intersection for practice with organizational culture. Axtell et al. (2000) consider innovation as the "generation, adoption, implementation and incorporation of new ideas, practices, or artifacts within organizations." However, it is critical to identify the inverse reality for organizations unable to innovate. Dougherty and Heller (1994) posit that innovation has the possibility of failing in the case where stability is valued within an organizational culture. Specifically, the negative correlational impact of hierarchical cultures on innovation is notable (Jaskyte, 2004). Additionally, it is important to note the tangible impact that an organization's values can have on the capacity and conditions for innovating. As mentioned previously, while the literature offers frameworks for organizational innovation, it is important to note that rarely are these found within the NGO or nonprofit sectors. As a result, while the literature exists within the intersection of organizational culture and innovation, the gap remains for practitioners outside of the corporate world.

Within the broader international NGO sector, Green (2015) acknowledges that innovation is inherently challenging to consistently achieve within larger organizations like the one in this case study with a myriad of accountability and reporting requirements. Furthermore, some argue the broader sector of international NGOs working in humanitarian aid and development, like the organization in this case study, has a culture that fosters staying closed and averse to innovation (Bennett, Foley, & Pantuliano, 2016). Regardless, the pursuit of workplace innovation within the context of this case study is ripe with challenges both locally and systemically for an entity like this international NGO in Cambodia.

Methodology

Over the duration of the three-month culture study, a variety of methods were used to analyze and examine the organization's culture. Semi-structured interviews were conducted with a diverse roster of 30 participants employed by the organization across Cambodia. Purposive sampling techniques were utilized to ensure interview participants were able and willing to speak candidly about their experiences in different divisions and offices within the organization. Three employee focus groups, composed of ten participants each, were facilitated in different provinces across the country to ensure a diversity of perspective outside of Phnom Penh. Convenience sampling was utilized as the participating provinces were selected based on pre-scheduled travel with employees from the country office. Additionally, through the researcher's regular presence in the country office, participating in shared meals, organizational events, and travel to provinces with employees, participant observation offered a critical method for studying cultural dynamics. This broad set of methods was designed for the goal of collecting thoroughly rich data, especially given the abbreviated three-month span of the study.

The Organizational Culture Assessment Instrument (OCAI) was distributed to a total of 16 employees, with an equal number of senior leaders and employees from across divisions and office locations in the country. A purposive sampling strategy was utilized to ensure a balance of positions as well as divisional representation in the organization. This instrument assessed six key characteristics of the organizational culture: (1) dominant characteristics, (2) organizational leadership, (3) management of employees, (4) organization glue, (5) strategic emphases, and (6) criteria of success. Ultimately, these characteristics measured the current and aspired levels of Wilkins and Ouchi's (1983) typology of cultures: clan, market, adhocracy, and hierarchy. Cameron and Quinn (2011) rightly acknowledge that their framework helps organize culture types and offers a way to consider key elements but is not comprehensive of all cultural phenomena in organizations. The OCAI was selected for its credibility across the globe as the "dominant model in quantitative research on organizational culture today" (Kwan & Walker, 2004).

Data Analysis and Discussion

Each of the questions in the OCAI corresponds with one of the four culture types as briefly described below (Cameron & Quinn, 2011). Based on the responses collected from the 16 participants, the results below show the current culture and preferred culture of the future for the organization in this case study.

Clan

A very friendly place to work where people share a lot of themselves. Success is defined in terms of sensitivity to customers and concern for people. The organization places a premium on teamwork, participation, and consensus.

Adhocracy

A dynamic, entrepreneurial, and creative place to work. People stick their necks out and take risks. The leaders are considered to be innovators and risk takers. The glue that holds the organization together is commitment to experimentation and innovation. The emphasis is on being on the leading edge.

Market

A result-oriented organization. People are competitive and goal oriented. The leaders are hard drivers, producers, and competitors. They are tough and demanding. The glue that holds the organization together is an emphasis on winning. Reputation and success are common concerns. The organizational style is hard-driving competitiveness.

Hierarchy

A very formalized and structured place to work. Procedures govern what people do. The leaders pride themselves on being good coordinators and organizers, who are efficiency-minded. Maintaining a smoothly running organization is most critical. Formal rules and policies hold the organization together.

In the table of results (Table 7.1), a number of gaps are shown between the current and preferred cultures. Notably, both groups desired the most

Table 7.1 OCAI results by group

	Senior leaders ($n = 8$)		Staff ($n = 8$)	
	Current	Preferred	Current	Preferred
Clan	32.8	34.5	26	32
Adhocracy	18.8	26.8	23.2	25.6
Market	20.3	23.2	24.5	22.4
Hierarchy	28.1	15.5	26.3	20

significant change in *decreasing the hierarchy* culture type. Additionally, a desire to *increase the adhocracy* culture type was mutually shared. This is a key finding as it relates to the organization's collective desire to promote and reward innovation at work in Cambodia.

Through the OCAI results and conversations with employees across the organization, the desire for a *stronger agile culture was clear.* On the most practical level, this applies to the common processes and policies that employees engage with in their daily work. Consistent feedback was gathered, and the OCAI results support a desire to improve this area to maximize time in the future. Through feedback sessions with senior leaders and employee focus groups, a general consensus was observed to reduce the number of overall policies and implement Kaizen-like mindsets in more daily work processes. When this process improvement takes place and the emphasis on a policy-driven work environment is reduced, an agile *culture of adhocracy can begin to strengthen itself and innovation can be more clearly embodied across the organization.*

A consistent finding through the series of interviews and focus group discussions involved the overwhelmingly strong OCAI scores for Clan culture type. Various senior leaders and employees alike mentioned the family-like atmosphere of the organizational culture and referred to colleagues as "sisters" and "brothers." It is important to acknowledge that both groups rated the Clan culture type as the strongest and desired for that to continue, even at a greater presence in the preferred future for the organization.

Ultimately, the findings in this case study chapter will give evidence to this organization's broader pursuit of innovative behaviors to strengthen as a foundation for creating their shared future together in a changing Cambodia.

Discussion and Implications

At the conclusion of the three-month study, the researcher presented the initial findings and facilitated two extended meetings for senior leaders to discuss the previous key themes and determine implications for the forthcoming global strategic planning process.

Inherently, the operations of any organization in today's globalized world involves engaging a myriad of stakeholders with often conflicting priorities and competing values, especially within the context of this case study. This reality not only exists external to organizational boundaries but within our increasingly expansive and interdependent cultures that transcend borders of nations and sectors. As a result, there are complex challenges for organizations to regularly consider as they navigate their respective contexts, most likely continuing to go through rapid change.

Through the course of this culture study, it is clear where the organization is seeing itself now and where it desires to go collectively into the future. After receiving the final report of the study findings, senior leaders participated in a guided futuring activity to discuss practical behaviors to (1) start, (2) stop, and (3) do more of as an organization. Notably, there was unanimity that the organization should start *rewarding failures* and *encouraging risks* as well as stop leading with a central guiding focus on policy and procedure and focus on innovating for the unknown future. The question remains how these systemic tensions and competing values will be acknowledged by other organizations in and outside of the international NGO sector. When organizational circumstances require high levels of control and stability to ensure safety and well-being of vulnerable children and families, it would be understandably rare for risk taking and innovating to be encouraged. Additionally, as Green (2015) notes, the broader international NGO system in which this entity belongs has its own innate proclivities toward certain efforts of change and innovation, given its growing call for accountability and reporting from within the sector.

One of the key challenges of diagnosing or changing organizational culture is best articulated in Morgan's (1986) recognition of the tension between reducing culture to discrete variables versus recognizing culture as an ongoing construction of reality. While identifying workplace behaviors was a key prompting exercise for senior leaders to encourage innovation in the organization, it was simply one facet of the continuing work in understanding and changing cultural dynamics. Nonetheless, the researcher challenged them to consider promoting and rewarding creative and innovative behaviors across the organization. This included developing a cross-functional think tank of employees to incubate ideas for ongoing growth and improvement as well as developing a platform for employee innovation each year through an annual prize for creative thinking.

Moving forward, the implications from this case study are numerous for local organizations to consider within large international NGO environments. Through the heightened calls for systemic change within the work of humanitarian aid and development (Green, 2015; Konyndyk & Worden, 2019), the role of these actors continues to be up for discussion and debate in an increasingly volatile, global climate.

Conclusion

Within the previous discussion on limitations in the literature, a foundation exists for future research into organizational cultures of NGOs and their capacity and conditions for innovating. The case study discussed in this chapter highlights the practical value for this research but presents limitations as well. How does a country office of an international NGO seek behaviors they would deem as "innovative" while aligning to the broader norms and expectations of the global federation? Where we look for best practices across an international sector like this, do organizations truly provide the parameters and resources for innovation or simply espouse this as a value to stakeholders? In this case, the extent for thorough ethnographic research was limited as the duration was just three months. Additionally, while the culture study was designed to balance the input and perspective of senior leaders and rank-and-file members of the organization, challenges were evident with the surrounding English language, technology, and travel realities across this developing context. There is also much to be explored around Khmer cultural norms across Cambodia and their seeming influence on employee participation in a study on organizational culture like this. In the future, case study research in developing country contexts could provide a comparative analysis in the future for consideration across Association of Southeast Asian Nations (ASEAN) member states (i.e., Myanmar, Vietnam, etc.). Nonetheless, continued research is warranted to explore the dynamics of organizational culture within developing contexts like this, where local entities are interdependent with the broader cultures and systems of larger networks like an international NGO sector.

References

Adler, N. J. (2002). *International Dimensions of Organizational Behavior*. Mason, OH: Thomson/South-Western.

Angle, H. L. (1989). Psychology and Organizational Innovation. In A. H. Van de Ven, H. L. Angle, & M. S. Poole (Eds.), *Research on the Management of Innovation: The Minnesota Studies* (pp. 135–170). New York: Harper & Row.

Axtell, C. M., Holman, D. J., Unsworth, K. L., Wall, T. D., Waterson, P. E., & Harrington, E. (2000). Shopfloor Innovation: Facilitating the Suggestion and Implementation of Ideas. *Journal of Occupational and Organizational Psychology, 73*(3), 265–285.

Bennett, C., Foley, M., & Pantuliano, S. (2016). *Time to Let Go: Remaking Humanitarian Action for the Modern Era*. London: HPG/ODI.

Burns, T., & Stalker, G. M. (1961). *The Management of Innovation*. London: Tavistock.

Büschgens, T., Bausch, A., & Balkin, D. B. (2013). Organizational Culture and Innovation: A Meta-Analytic Review. *Journal of Product Innovation Management, 30*(4), 763–781.

Cameron, K. S., & Quinn, R. E. (2011). *Diagnosing and Changing Organizational Culture Based on the Competing Values Framework*. Reading, MA: Addison-Wesley.

Cooperation Committee for Cambodia FAQ. (n.d.). Retrieved from https://www.ccc-cambodia.org/en/about-us/faq

Dougherty, D., & Heller, T. (1994). The illegitimacy of successful product innovation in established firms. *Organization Science, 5*(2), 200–218.

Green, D. (2015). *Fit for the Future? Development Trends and the Role of International NGOs*. Oxfam GB.

Hilhorst, D., & Schmiemann, N. (2002). Humanitarian Principles and Organisational Culture: Everyday Practice in Médecins sans Frontiè res-Holland. *Development in Practice, 12*(3–4), 490–500.

Hofstede, G. (1983). The Cultural Relativity of Organizational Practices and Theories. *Journal of International Business Studies, 14*(2), 75–89.

Jaskyte, K. (2004). Transformational Leadership, Organizational Culture, and Innovativeness in Nonprofit Organizations. *Nonprofit Management and Leadership, 15*(2), 153–168.

Kanter, R. M. (1988). When a Thousand Flowers Bloom: Structural, Collective and Social Conditions for Innovation in Organizations. In B. M. Straw & L. L. Cummings (Eds.), *Research in Organizational Behavior* (Vol. 10, pp. 123–167).

Konyndyk, J., & Worden, R. (2019). *People-Driven Response: Power and Participation in Humanitarian Action*. CGD Policy Paper, 155.

Kwan, P., & Walker, A. (2004). Validating the Competing Values Model as a Representation of Organizational Culture through Inter-Institutional Comparisons. *International Journal of Organizational Analysis, 12*(1), 21.

Morgan, G. (1986). *Images of Organization*. Newbury Park, CA: Sage Publications.

Quinn, R. E., & Cameron, K. (1983). Organizational Life Cycles and Shifting Criteria of Effectiveness: Some Preliminary Evidence. *Management Science, 29*(1), 33–51.

Quinn, R. E., & Rohrbaugh, J. (1981). A Competing Values Approach to Organizational Effectiveness. *Public Productivity Review*, 122–140.

Schein, E. H. (1985). Defining organizational culture. *Classics of organization theory, 3*(1), 490–502.

Schein, E. H. (2010). *Organizational Culture and Leadership* (Vol. 2). John Wiley & Sons.

Stephenson Jr., M. (2005). Making Humanitarian Relief Networks More Effective: Operational Coordination, Trust and Sense Making. *Disasters, 29*(4), 337–350.

UN Charter. (n.d.). Full Text. Retrieved from https://www.un.org/en/sections/un-charter/un-charter-full-text/

Walkup, M. (1997). Policy Dysfunction in Humanitarian Organizations: The Role of Coping Strategies, Institutions, and Organizational Culture. *Journal of Refugee Studies, 10*(1), 37–60.

Wilkins, A. L., & Ouchi, W. G. (1983). Efficient Cultures: Exploring the Relationship between Culture and Organizational Performance. *Administrative Science Quarterly*, 468–481.

World Bank in Cambodia. (2020). Retrieved from https://www.worldbank.org/en/country/cambodia/overview

8

The Predictive Influences of Team Creativity, Creativity Willingness, Creative Ideation, and Leader Openness on Exploratory Innovation

Samuel Ogbeibu, Abdelhak Senadjki, James Gaskin, and Iddrisu Mohammed Awal

Introduction

In an ever-changing world and uncertain financial future, organisations are increasingly leveraging team creativity, leader openness, and exploratory innovation initiatives (Bai, Lin, & Li, 2016; Hunter, Cushenbery, & Jayne, 2017; Troster & Van Knippenberg, 2012) to drive and implement objectives that promotes organisational innovation (Ogbeibu, Emelifeonwu, Abdelhak, Gaskin, & Kaivo-oja, 2020). Team creativity and exploratory innovation are positive drivers of organisational innovation and long-term survival (Caniels

S. Ogbeibu (✉)
Faculty of Business, Department of Management, Curtin Univeristy,
Miri, Sarawak, Malaysia
e-mail: samuel.ogbeibu@curtin.edu.my

A. Senadjki • I. M. Awal
Faculty of Business and Finance, Universiti Tunku Abdul Rahman,
Kampar, Perak, Malaysia
e-mail: abdelhak@utar.edu.my; Awaaal41@1utar.my

J. Gaskin
Information Systems, Brigham Young University, Provo, Utah, USA
e-mail: james.gaskin@byu.edu

© The Author(s), under exclusive license to Springer Nature Switzerland AG 2021
A. McMurray et al. (eds.), *The Palgrave Handbook of Workplace Innovation*,
https://doi.org/10.1007/978-3-030-59916-4_8

135

& Rietzschel, 2015; Gilson & Litchfield, 2017). In emerging economies, team creativity and exploratory innovation are gaining increasing attention due to their relevance for creating and sustaining organisational competitive advantages (Ogbeibu et al., 2020). However, particularly in Nigeria (and in other nations with similar civil, societal, and business conditions), few are willing to pursue creative solutions, leader openness is rare, and innovation initiatives are scarce (Dimnwobi, Ekesiobi, & Mgbemena, 2016; Ogbeibu, Senadjki, & Gaskin, 2018). It is therefore challenging for leaders to drive organisations towards achieving exploratory innovation outcomes (Caniels & Rietzschel, 2015).

To date, team creativity and exploratory innovation have received a plethora of attention (Anderson, Potocnik, & Zhou, 2014). Team creativity refers to team member attributes that cause the origination and development of creative ideas that lead to innovation (Baer, 2012; Dane, Baer, Pratt, & Oldam, 2011). Consistent with the componential theory of individual creativity (CTIC) by Amabile (1997), team creativity can be multifaceted as the CTIC embodies constructs such as expertise, creativity skills, and task motivation. *Expertise* characterises all factual knowledge, potential, and technical proficiencies across distinct task domains (Amabile, 1997; Birdi, Leach, & Magadley, 2016). Likewise, *creativity skills* are generalisable competencies that aid to process thoughts divergently to formulate original ideas (Runco, 2013). *Task motivation* relates to the perception of enjoyment, strong interests, or goal accomplishment desires experienced when engaging in a defined task (Burr & Cordery, 2001).

Yet, despite several attempts to provoke deeper creativity and innovation insights via a team level of analysis, a persistent limitation is prevalent (Hennessey & Amabile, 2010). While team creativity qualifies as a multidimensional phenomenon (Amabile, 1997), it is usually operationalised as a unidimensional construct (Bai et al., 2016). This simplified measurement prevents a holistic empirical analysis of the team creativity undergirding as extant research continues to overlook the theorisations of the CTIC (Amabile, 1997). Therefore, these works and others (Gilson & Litchfield, 2017) may suffer from endogeneity because of a failure to empirically examine probable dimensions of team creativity (Antonakis, Bendahan, Jacquart, & Lalive, 2010). Equally, extant research further advanced insights associated with the team creativity phenomenon by accentuating the concept of *creative ideation* as a consequence of team creativity (Pannells & Claxton, 2008).

Runco (2013) further supports that creative ideation refers to the useful and authentic product of divergent and creative thinking which highlights true originality. Despite recent efforts (Ogbeibu et al., 2020), several scholarly works yet champion the assumption that creative ideation is a facet of team creativity (Baer, 2012; Gilson & Litchfield, 2017). Conversely, creative ideation is often speculated to be a feature of exploratory innovation occurrence (Anderson et al., 2014). Consequently, it is unclear from the literature what exact role creative ideation plays, and its inconclusive association with team creativity or exploratory innovation provokes further attention. Additionally, an investigation into the plausible roles of creative ideation via the CTIC lens is yet to be given adequate empirical attention (Birdi et al., 2016). These clear gaps partially motivate our study and guide our theoretical contributions.

According to Birdi et al. (2016), exploratory innovation exists as a result of the acceptance and implementation of creative ideation. Huang, Ding, and Chen (2014) highlight that *exploratory innovation* deals with the departure from prevailing information, to offerings of new designs, development of new distribution channels, and the creation of new markets. Congruently, we argue that, to successfully engender exploratory innovation, organisational leaders ought to engage in fundamentally different innovative approach which reflects adequate openness to their subordinates (González-López & Fernández-Montoto, 2018). Similarly, driving an organisation via the capabilities of a leader who advocates openness could likely increase an organisation's chance for exploratory innovations (Vahter, Love, & Roper, 2014). The degree to which leaders engage with creative ideas and suggestions from subordinates in a transparent and unbiased manner is known as *leader openness* (Troster & Van Knippenberg, 2012).

In an effort to achieve organisational innovative outcomes, leaders may employ several measures to help subordinates pursue initiatives that might provoke creative ideation and diffusion of creative ideas (Bai et al., 2016). Nevertheless, leaders are bound to face severe challenges when subordinates become unwilling to participate in such initiatives (Chandy & Tellis, 1998). Auernhammer and Hall (2014) indicate that creative ideation requires the *willingness* of subordinates. Subordinates' unwillingness to be creative might spring up from avoidance of extra responsibilities, or when the creative process is perceived to be a threat to their health, work-life balance, or job security (Amabile & Pillemer, 2012). Therefore, *creativity willingness* deals with the prime and most compelling unit of thought processes that influences conscious and deliberate choice to voluntarily exhibit specific creative behaviours (Auernhammer & Hall, 2014; Chandy & Tellis, 1998).

Few studies have examined creativity willingness (Auernhammer & Hall, 2014; Chandy & Tellis, 1998). Moreover, the CTIC largely neglects creativity willingness and how it influences creative ideation. Although Amabile (1997) and Ogbeibu et al. (2018) argued for the importance of engendering creative ideation by giving adequate consideration to the CTIC dimensions, they did not empirically examine the predictive powers of the CTIC dimensions on creative ideation. Likewise, the CTIC does not consider the mediating role of creative ideation.

By investigating these gaps, we seek to deepen prior knowledge on how creativity willingness may further engender exploratory innovation via creative ideation. Manufacturing organisations in emerging economies, such as Nigeria (Ogbeibu et al., 2018), strive to benefit from the advantages of committing adequate resources towards team creativity, creativity willingness, leader openness, and exploratory innovation initiatives (Bai et al., 2016; González-López & Fernández-Montoto, 2018). The Nigerian manufacturing industry is a significant contributor to Nigeria's economic growth (Dimnwobi et al., 2016). However, studies (Dimnwobi et al., 2016; Emeka, Ifeoma, & Emmanuel, 2015) lament that the Nigerian manufacturing industry yet suffers an accelerating decline in innovation capabilities and prospects.

Extant research shows that, before the late 1980s, the Nigerian manufacturing industry was at a 78% score in its creativity and innovation prowess. However, it has struggled recently to rise beyond 29.3% (Emeka et al., 2015). Nigeria is no longer even classified as one of over 139 nations in the Global Creativity Index (GCI) (Ogbeibu et al., 2018). Furthermore, evidence from the 2015 Global Innovation Index (GII) relate that Nigeria ranks 128 among over 141 highlighted nations across the globe (Dimnwobi et al., 2016). This, therefore, calls for closer attention to be given to creativity in the Nigerian manufacturing industry (Ogbeibu et al., 2018).

Unfortunately, several Nigerian manufacturing organisations are managed by hierarchical and often autocratic leadership that promotes secretiveness rather than openness (Gabriel & Kpakol, 2014). Naranjo-Valencia, Jiménez-Jiménez, and Sanz-Valle (2016) lament that this has a negative influence on exploratory innovation. A stringent form of leadership tends to produce fear in subordinates and consequently weakens the bonds they may have with their leaders (Ogbeibu et al., 2018). This is evidenced in the attitudes of distinct subordinates across Nigerian manufacturing organisations, as they tend to become unresponsive and unwilling to pursue exploratory innovation initiatives (Gabriel & Kpakol, 2014). Lebel (2016) emphasises that leaders who advocate openness within the workplace are likely to help provoke creative ideation within the organisation because creative ideation is a product of team creativity leading towards exploratory innovations (Baer, 2012).

We attempt to challenge and advance contemporary theoretical underpinnings by attempting to integrate creativity willingness into team creativity dimensions and investigating their predictive powers on creative ideation. To deepen previous understanding on how team creativity might engender exploratory innovation, we attempt to investigate the predictive powers of creative ideation and leader openness on exploratory innovation. Our findings should help bridge the gap between how team creativity, creativity willingness, and leader openness truly act to advance exploratory innovation while accounting for the distinct mediating role of creative ideation in the Nigerian context. We also anticipate that our findings could mirror a substantive resource for other developing economies.

Hypothesis Development

One of the most crucial drivers of team creativity is the level of team members' expertise (Amabile & Pillemer, 2012), which is positively associated with creativity (Tang, Shang, Naumann, & Von Zedtwitz, 2014). The CTIC argues that experts are equipped mentally or technically to process novel information more than novices (Amabile & Pillemer, 2012). Tang et al. (2014) emphasise that expertise causes faster formulation and execution of creative ideation due to experts' greater comprehension of underlying strategies and philosophies that could aid to define and uncover problems' origins and areas for innovation (Birdi et al., 2016). Mumford, Medeiros, and Partlow (2012) theorised that expertise provides knowledge of constraints and errors and cognitive models that could aid in several phases of the creativity process.

Likewise, Birdi et al. (2016) have stressed that the creativity skills dimension is an essential aspect of the CTIC that has been relatively neglected. Creativity skills reflect a style of thinking of diverse aspects of methods to solving problems (Runco, 2013). Runco (2013) argued that creativity skills have a positive association with creative ideation when it is exhibited via strong divergent thinking capabilities. Amabile (1997) advocated that task motivation, most especially intrinsic motivation, is the key for creativity. Thus, studies (Birdi et al., 2016; Dewett, 2006) argue that task motivation is favourable to creativity, and this is such that task-motivated team members tend to exhibit behaviours that mirror flexibility, risk taking, and spontaneity towards creative ideation initiatives.

Though the CTIC expounded on the grave importance of task motivation in creativity initiatives, it overlooked the significance of team members' willingness to engage in the creative ideation process (Auernhammer & Hall, 2014). Numerous studies (Bordia & Bordia, 2015; Melkonian, Monin, & Noorderhaven, 2011; Van Vianen, Dalhoeven, & De Pater, 2011) investigated the willingness concept as a behavioural outcome. While this approach may have yielded substantial results over the years, it might have likewise inadvertently orchestrated a disregard for the probable role(s) of creativity willingness as a plausible antecedent of creative ideation (Auernhammer & Hall, 2014). Similarly, Dewett (2006) and Bordia and Bordia (2015) highlighted that creativity willingness often involves risk-taking, and this reflects a positive influence on the creative ideation process. It is thus argued that leaders could achieve more innovative outcomes when they have a team of willing members at their disposal (Van Vianen, Dalhoeven, & De Pater, 2011).

H1a : *Expertise increases creative ideation.*

H1b : *Creativity skills increase creative ideation.*

H1c : *Task motivation increases creative ideation.*

H1d : *Creativity willingness increases creative ideation.*

Creative ideation reflects meaningful authentic novelty, and its positive relevance is highly advocated by organisational leaders who constantly strive to harness the creative suggestions and knowledge of their subordinates (Anderson et al., 2014). Baer (2012) argued that creative ideation is a fundamental action of the early phases of exploratory innovation. Likewise, the results that leaders are able to obtain and exploit during the creative ideation phase may have a high impact on a later idea exploration phase that manifests as exploratory innovation (Huang et al., 2014). The work of Gilson and Litchfield (2017) reflects that cultivating a sufficient stream of creative ideas from team members is thus argued to be a prerequisite for efficient exploratory innovations. This strategy helps to foster creative ideation capture that is expedient for increased realisation of exploratory innovative outcomes (Baer, 2012).

H2 : *Creative ideation increases innovation.*

The works of Troster and Van Knippenberg (2012) and Lebel (2016) suggest that engendering exploratory innovation would require a certain degree of openness which creates room for the exchange of creative ideas. By listening to, pondering upon, and occasionally executing actions based on subordinates' propositions and feedback, leaders can promote exploratory innovation (Vahter et al., 2014). When leaders exhibit behaviours that reflect openness, subordinates could find them more approachable to exchange creative ideas

(Ogbeibu et al., 2018). Vahter et al. (2014) further espoused that leader openness fosters stress reduction and high levels of professional independence that contributes to innovation performance. Equally, viewing leaders as liberal, kind, and flexible could inspire subordinates to comfortably take informed risks that might eventually provoke exploratory innovations (Cui, Wu, & Tong, 2018). Hence, the works of Lebel (2016) and Troster and Van Knippenberg (2012) and Birdi et al. (2016) indicate that leader openness may be positively associated with exploratory innovation.

H3 : *Leader openness increases exploratory innovation.*

In retrospect of the vexing debate encompassing the nexus and conceptual definitions undergirding the creativity and innovation literature, a logical inference thus arguably rests on the creative ideation underpinning (Baer, 2012; Gilson & Litchfield, 2017). This could be further empirically examined from the lens of team creativity and exploratory innovation conceptualisations, which our study investigates to more closely capture the definitive role(s) of creative ideation as an independent, yet often overlooked factor (Anderson et al., 2014). As studies simultaneously or respectively integrate creative ideation into the team creativity and exploratory innovation underpinnings, it further becomes unclear what and where the distinction of the creative ideation role lies (Baer, 2012; Gilson & Litchfield, 2017). Additionally, considering their distinct philosophical conceptions, studies (Amabile, 1997; Ogbeibu et al., 2018) explicate that creative ideation stems from the overarching ideology associated with the CTIC dimensions. However, Cui et al. (2018) notes that creative ideation is a precursor of, and core requirement for, any innovative outcome. So far, relative extrapolations of extant research (Caniels & Rietzschel, 2015; Cui et al., 2018) yet raise serious concerns of conjectural inconclusiveness and statistical incongruity regarding the theoretical position and probable conceptual roles(s) of creative ideation. The following theorisations are consequently highlighted (Fig. 8.1).

H4a : *Creative ideation mediates the positive effect of expertise on exploratory innovation.*

H4b : *Creative ideation mediates the positive effect of creativity skills on exploratory innovation.*

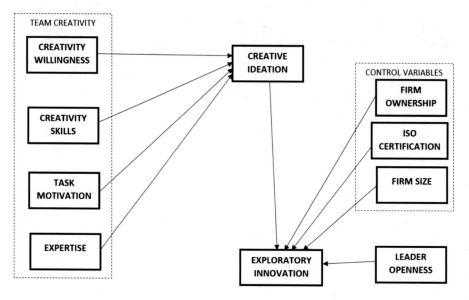

Fig. 8.1 Conceptual framework

H4c : *Creative ideation mediates the positive effect of task motivation on exploratory innovation.*

H4d : *Creative ideation mediates the positive effect of creativity willingness on exploratory innovation.*

Methodology

The target population of this study includes research and development (R&D) and information technology (IT) team members (leaders and their subordinates) in the headquarters (HQ) of 15 different manufacturing organisations in Nigeria. We employed the Krejcie and Morgan (1970) sample size determinant to guide in obtaining a stratified proportionate sampling of participants. Out of 400 distributed questionnaires, 350 were sufficiently complete, indicating an approximately 88% usable response rate. Respondents were between 20 and 60 years old. Regarding gender, 46.2% of the respondents reported as female, thus suggesting that male respondents have not been overrepresented in this study. 54.2% of respondents were from IT departments, compared to 45.8% of respondents who were employees from R&D departments. Moreover, 44% of respondents had undergraduate degrees, 33% of respondents had a master's degree, 7.2% had a PhD, and only 15.8% had a diploma or equivalent.

Three senior researchers and experts assisted in evaluating this study's questionnaire items prior to distribution. Likewise, research assistants (RAs) were engaged and trained for the purpose of data collection. Fifty participants from three distinct manufacturing organisations were involved in the pilot study. SPSS (v22) was used to evaluate the pilot study data. During an EFA, poorly loaded items were dropped (Sarstedt, Ringle, & Hair, 2017).

Measures

The questionnaire utilised for data collection was comprised of 5-point Likert scales of agreement and demographic questions, prepared in English. Consistent with studies of Podsakoff, MacKenzie, and Podsakoff (2012) and Roese and Vohs (2012), in order to pre-empt common method bias (CMB), participants were assured of their anonymity, and team leaders assessed subordinates regarding measures of all team creativity dimensions (excluding task motivation). While subordinates assessed their task motivation and leader openness measures, all team members assessed innovation measures. Furthermore, with Kock's (2015) recommendations on identifying if a model is free from CMB, Table 8.1 of this study shows that the highest variance inflation factor (VIF) (2.002) does not exceed the threshold of 3.3. Hence, CMB did not influence participants' responses.

For task motivation, four items were adapted from Burr and Cordery (2001) and one item from Birdi et al. (2016) (0.79 reliability), for example, "I am strongly motivated by the recognition I can get from my company". For creativity skills, seven items were adapted from Birdi et al. (2016) (0.90 reliability), for example, "This subordinate is skilled at generating more than one solution to a problem". For expertise, two items were adapted from Kaufman (2012) and four items from Birdi et al. (2016) (reliability scale—0.76), for example, "This subordinate is able to address almost any problem in his/her job". For creativity willingness, six items were self-developed based on the work of Dewett (2006), for example, "This subordinate is willing to think of a creative idea despite the possibility of potential rejection". For creative ideation, six items were adapted from Runco, Plucker, and Lim (2001) (reliability scale—0.90), for example, "This team member often produce ideas no one else has". For exploratory innovation, six items were adapted from Jansen, Vera, and Crossan (2009) (reliability scale—0.91), for example, "My organisation creates new products and services". For leader openness, three

Table 8.1 Measurement model factor analysis, reliability, validity, and prediction-oriented assessments

Construct	Composite reliability (CR)	VIF Values	rho_A	AVE	PLS Predict RMSE	LM RMSE
Creative ideation (CI)	0.962	1.722	0.948	0.865		
CI items						
• CI5					**0.644**	0.676
• CI2					**0.691**	0.696
• C13					**0.622**	0.646
• C14					**0.669**	0.685
Creativity skills	0.970	1.400	0.965	0.866		
Creativity willingness	0.964	2.002	0.950	0.870		
Expertise	0.925	1.704	0.905	0.713		
Exploratory innovation (EI) items	0.936		0.919	0.746		
EI items						
• EXP4					**0.832**	0.862
• EXP6					**0.729**	0.741
• EXP1					**0.632**	0.646
• EXP3					**0.830**	**0.810**
• EXP2					0.673	**0.670**
Firm ownership	1.000	1.688	1.000	1.000		
Firm size	1.000	1.386	1.000	1.000		
ISO certification	1.000	1.200	1.000	1.000		
Leader openness	0.984	1.439	0.975	0.952		
Task motivation	0.880	1.793	0.820	0.646		

Note: AVE (average variance extracted); VIF (variance inflation factor)

items were adapted from Troster and Van Knippenberg (2012) (reliability scale—0.90), for example, "Good ideas receive serious deliberations from my leader". Congruent with Ogbeibu et al. (2020), we control for ISO certification, firm ownership, and firm size.

Data Analysis and Empirical Results

Our study employed the SmartPLS 3 software for prediction analysis. The use of SmartPLS for statistical predictions analysis is strongly recommended by extant literature (Ogbeibu et al., 2020; Shmueli et al., 2019). We used variance-based SEM (VB-SEM) due to its assumptions of easy distributions of model specification and complexity, interpretation ease, and ability to simultaneously deal with several dependency associations and provide greater statistical efficiency (Ringle, Sarstedt, Mitchell, & Gudergan, 2018). In contrast to theory testing found in covariance-based SEM, our study's primary objective is grounded on an exploratory and prediction-oriented nature (Shmueli et al., 2019).

Given the relatively close construct scores evidenced in the standard deviation (0.91–1.1) and mean (4.2 to 4.7) outputs, it thus suggests no substantial disparity among investigated variables. Likewise, skewness (-0.157 to 0.82) and kurtosis (-0.069 to 0.758) values for all variables indicate normal distribution (Hair, Ringle, & Sarstedt, 2011). Figure 8.2 shows that substantial value is contributed by all the measurement items towards their respective constructs (Sarstedt et al., 2017). In Table 8.1, composite reliability and rhoA confirm internal consistency and reliability of all constructs, and the AVE values suggest convergent validity (Ogbeibu et al., 2018). Moreover, the values of heterotrait-monotrait ratio (HTMT) (Table 8.2) confirm the discriminant validity of respective constructs (Ringle et al., 2018). Congruent with the convincing recommendations of Sarstedt et al. (2017) and Ringle et al. (2018) and, as demonstrated by Ogbeibu et al. (2020), in place of model fit assessment criteria, prediction-oriented studies using VB-SEM should uphold

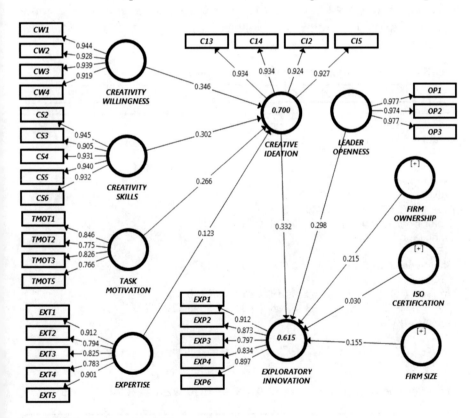

Fig. 8.2 Measurement model

a causal-predictive method and consequently rely on model's predictive power, relevance, and accuracy (VB-SEM RMSE values compared to LM RMSE values, Q^2, β, R^2). Consequently, the structural model is estimated (Fig. 8.3).

In Fig. 8.2, R^2 values of 0.700 ($t = 23.435$, $p \leq 0.000$) and 0.615 ($t = 13.191$, $p \leq 0.000$) indicate a relatively large and moderate degree of variance explained in creative ideation and exploratory innovation respectively (Ringle et al., 2018). Similarly, results of Figs. 8.2 and 8.3 suggest that creativity willingness is the strongest positive predictor of creative ideation, and this is followed by creativity skills, task motivation, and expertise. These findings support H1a, b, c, and d. Effect sizes (f^2) for creativity willingness (0.200), creativity skills (0.217), task motivation (0.132), and expertise (0.030) suggest a medium, medium, moderate, and small effects respectively (Ogbeibu et al., 2018). Likewise, creative ideation is the strongest positive predictor of exploratory innovation compared to leader openness. Nevertheless, f^2 values for creative ideation (0.167) and leader openness (0.160) indicate they exhibit moderate effect sizes. This evidence supports H2 and H3. Among the control variables, firm ownership shows the strongest predictive and positive influence on exploratory innovation, followed by firm size. f^2 values for firm

Table 8.2 Heterotrait-monotrait ratio (HTMT) test

	CI	CS	CW	EXT	EI	FO	FS	IC	LOP	TMOT
Creative ideation (CI)										
Creativity skills (CS)	0.669									
Creativity willingness (CW)	0.766	0.499								
Expertise (EXT)	0.647	0.449	0.646							
Exploratory innovation (EI)	0.721	0.504	0.730	0.757						
Firm ownership (FO)	0.554	0.371	0.529	0.561	0.618					
Firm size (FS)	0.412	0.263	0.479	0.452	0.507	0.502				
ISO certification (IC)	0.325	0.243	0.296	0.401	0.356	0.320	0.232			
Leader openness (LOP)	0.533	0.421	0.559	0.556	0.637	0.384	0.277	0.342		
Task motivation (TMOT)	0.769	0.512	0.691	0.623	0.670	0.472	0.429	0.380	0.459	

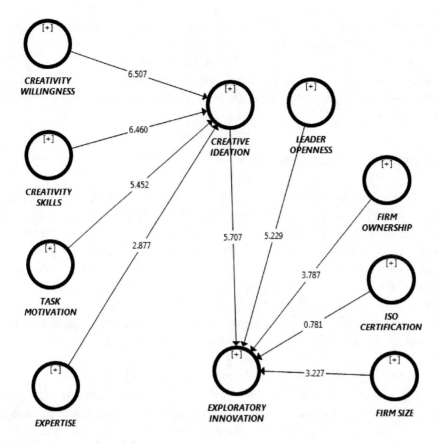

Fig. 8.3   Structural model

ownership (0.071) and firm size (0.045) indicate small effects. Moreover, ISO certification has no influence on exploratory innovation.

We examine specific indirect effects (Nitzl, Roldan, & Cepeda, 2016) to test mediation. The results indicate that creative ideation plays a mediating (β = 0.115, t = 4.009, $p \le 0.000$) and a complementary role (β = 0.157, t = 2.537, $p \le 0.011$) between creativity willingness and exploratory innovation. Creative ideation also plays a mediating (β = 0.041, t = 2.424, $p \le 0.015$) and a complementary role (β = 0.243, t = 4.477, $p \le 0.000$) between expertise and exploratory innovation. Similarly, creative ideation mediates the relationship between task motivation (β = 0.100, t = 4.940, $p \le 0.000$) and exploratory innovation. Creative ideation also mediates the relationship between creativity skills and exploratory innovation (β = 0.243, t = 4.477, $p \le 0.000$). The results support H4a, b, c, and d. Moreover, Q^2 values for creative ideation (0.581) and exploratory innovation (0.437) provide support for its predictive accuracy and relevance (Shmueli et al., 2019). Finally, values of PLSpredict RMSE and LM RMSE relate insights into our model's out-of-sample predictive power (Table 8.1). Consequently, the results indicate that our model has a large predictive power for predicting creative ideation and has a moderate power for predicting exploratory innovation (Ogbeibu et al., 2020; Shmueli et al., 2019).

Discussion and Conclusion

Our findings indicate that while all included dimensions of team creativity are positive predictors of creative ideation, creativity willingness demonstrates the strongest predictive power on creative ideation. These findings are consistent with extant studies that advocate the positive roles of expertise, creativity skills, and task motivation (Birdi et al., 2016; Van Vianen, Dalhoeven, & De Pater, 2011)). Bearing in mind that not all creative ideas can result in exploratory innovation (Baer, 2012), our results show that creative ideation is a substantial predictor of exploratory innovation, consistent with extant literature (Gilson & Litchfield, 2017). Similar to extant literature (Cui et al., 2018; Troster and Van Knippenberg 2012), our findings show that leader openness is a positive predictor of exploratory innovation. Nevertheless, this finding stands in relative dissonance with that of previous literature that suggest a negative influence of leader openness (Kratzer, Meissner, & Roud, 2017; Vahter et al., 2014). Despite the assertions of prior research on the positive effect of creative ideation on exploratory innovation (Birdi et al., 2016; Gilson & Litchfield, 2017), we demonstrate that creative ideation and leader openness each have moderate effect sizes on exploratory innovation. This finding challenges contemporary insights that have championed the perception that creative ideation reflects the strongest influence on exploratory innovation.

Our findings show that creative ideation plays multiple roles. Creative ideation is a mediator between team creativity dimensions and exploratory innovation. We also find that creative ideation is a complimentary mediator between creativity willingness, expertise, and exploratory innovation. Thus a portion of the effects of creativity willingness and expertise on exploratory innovation are mediated through creative ideation. Thus, team members with relevant expertise who are willing to exhibit creativity may not need to rely on creative ideation for exploratory innovation to occur. These findings challenge extant literature (Baer, 2012).

Theoretical and Managerial Implications

The method of examining team creativity in several extant researches, and its influence on exploratory innovation in several other scholarly works, has raised endogeneity concerns due to a lack of investigation on all core dimensions undergirding team creativity. By investigating all team creativity dimensions, this study has helped to reveal new insights on how creative ideation is predicted by the powers of expertise, creativity skills, task motivation, and more especially creativity willingness. As a key theoretical contribution, this study also advanced prior theoretical insights by investigating and attempting to integrate creativity willingness into the CTIC underpinning. This attempt has further helped to provoke new insights into the much overlooked significance and role of creativity willingness. Creativity willingness is consequently demonstrated to exhibit the strongest positive prediction of creative ideation, and proves to be the most important when compared to other creativity dimensions in our study. Therefore, to engender exploratory innovation, leaders and policymakers should endeavour to give ample considerations towards team creativity dimensions, and especially fostering of *willingness* to demonstrate creativity in the workplace. To ensure informed decisions that could drive creative ideation towards exploratory innovations, policymakers and practitioners may want to consider determining and instituting initiatives that allow for and provoke willingness to share creative ideas without being criticised.

Likewise, given the conflicting perspectives surrounding the phenomenon of creative ideation in the innovation and creativity literature, our study suggests creative ideation is independent of itself and serves as a mediating entity. This finding further harmonises prior contemporary insights that have argued concerning the nexus between team creativity and exploratory innovation. However, our study challenges recently advanced theoretical conceptualisations and those relative to the CTIC, by exemplifying that creative ideation does not always function as an intermediary but also as a complementary mediating phenomenon. We advance prior theoretical assumptions by showing that by mainly housing a portion through which experienced and willing team members may establish exploratory innovations, creative ideation is demonstrated to not be the only cognitive access point to exploratory innovation. Therefore, as not all team members might have the luxury or potential to easily produce creative ideas, policymakers and leaders may develop initiatives and facilities that can help team members to tap into their prior experiences, and inspire their willingness to further foster exploratory innovation. Such initiative also consequently provokes novel and deeper understanding into prior creativity and innovation discrepancies evidenced in extant research. Furthermore, we show that creative ideation and leader openness are both direct and moderate level predictors of exploratory innovation, given their similar sizes of effect. This finding challenges prior theoretical assumptions and empirical extrapolations of extant literature championing the notion that creative ideation may possess the strongest positive prediction of exploratory innovation. Consequently, policymakers may endeavour to further develop and institute workplace ethics that guide and inspire creative ideation and control for consistent behaviours which mirror leader openness.

Limitations and Future Directions

Considering that this study's research has been initiated on a team level analysis, individual and organisation level insights and implications should not be inferred. Therefore, the authors call on future researchers to execute similar research from individual- and organisational-level points of analysis (see Kelley & Kelley, 2015). This recommendation could help to advance the insights of this study towards a much broader perspective. Application of cross-sectional design might have constrained the possibility of advancing this study's insights beyond its current form. However, executing a longitudinal study would intensely escalate the cost relative to a cross-sectional design. Moreover, since findings of this study further demonstrate results that are consistent with and reinforce extant research, the authors therefore recommend that future replications of this study should be attempted via a longitudinal approach to foster results comparability across disparate periods and contexts. Finally, generalisation of this study's results ought to be attempted with caution, given that data collection information originated from mainly 15 manufacturing organisations' HQ in Nigeria. Nevertheless, its reliability remains valid as investigations were executed from nationally recognised and reputable manufacturing organisations whose HQ wholly mirrored the central objectives and aims of this study.

References

Amabile, T. M. (1997). Motivating Creativity in Organisations: On Doing What You Love and Loving What You Do. *California Management Review, 40*(1), 39–58.

Amabile, T. M., & Pillemer, J. (2012). Perspectives on the Social Psychology of Creativity. *The Journal of Creative Behavior, 46*(1), 3–15.

Anderson, N., Potocnik, K., & Zhou, J. (2014). Innovation and Creativity in Organizations: A State-of-the-Science Review, Prospective Commentary, and Guiding Framework. *Journal of Management, 40*(5), 1297–1333.

Antonakis, J., Bendahan, S., Jacquart, P., & Lalive, R. (2010). On Making Causal Claims: A Review and Recommendations. *The Leadership Quarterly, 21*, 1086–1120.

Auernhammer, J., & Hall, H. (2014). Organisational Culture in Knowledge Creation, Creativity and Innovation: Towards the Freiraum Model. *Journal of Information Science, 40*(2), 154–166. https://doi.org/10.1177/0165551513508356

Baer, M. (2012). Putting Creativity to Work: The Implementation of Creative Ideas in Organizations. *Academy of Management Journal, 55*(5), 1102–1119.

Bai, Y., Lin, L., & Li, P. P. (2016). How to Enable Employee Creativity in a Team Context: A Cross-Level Mediating Process of Transformational Leadership. *Journal of Business Research, 69*(9), 3240–3250.

Birdi, K., Leach, D., & Magadley, W. (2016). The Relationship of Individual Capabilities and Environmental Support with Different Facets of Designers' Innovative Behavior. *Journal of Product Innovation Management, 33*(1), 19–35.

Bordia, S., & Bordia, P. (2015). Employees' Willingness to Adopt a Foreign Functional Language in Multilingual Organizations: The Role of Linguistic Identity. *Journal of International Business Studies, 46*, 415–428.

Burr, R., & Cordery, J. L. (2001). Self-Management Efficacy as a Mediator of the Relation between Job Design and Employee Motivation. *Human Performance, 14*(1), 27–44.

Caniels, M. C., & Rietzschel, E. F. (2015). Organizing Creativity: Creativity and Innovation under Constraints. *Creativity and Innovation Management, 24*(2), 184–196.

Chandy, R. K., & Tellis, G. J. (1998). Organizing for Radical Product Innovation: The Overlooked Role of Willingness to Cannibalize. *Journal of Marketing Research, 35*(4), 474–487.

Cui, T., Wu, Y., & Tong, Y. (2018). Exploring Ideation and Implementation Openness in Open Innovation Projects: IT-Enabled Absorptive Capacity Perspective. *Information & Management, 55*(5), 576–587.

Dane, E., Baer, M., Pratt, M. G., & Oldam, G. R. (2011). Rational versus Intuitive Problem Solving: How Thinking 'Off the Beaten Path' Can Stimulate Creativity. *Psychology of Aesthetics, Creativity, and the Arts, 5*(1), 3–12.

Dewett, T. (2006). Exploring the Role of Risk in Employee Creativity. *Journal of Creative Behavior, 40*(1), 27–45.

Dimnwobi, S. K., Ekesiobi, C. S., & Mgbemena, E. M. (2016). Creativity, Innovation and Competitiveness in Nigeria: An Economic Exploration. *International Journal of Academic Research in Economics and Management Sciences, 5*(3), 29–52.

Emeka, N. H., Ifeoma, A. J., & Emmanuel, O. I. (2015). An Evaluation of the Effect of Technological Innovations on Corporate Performance: A Study of Selected Manufacturing Firms in Nigeria. *The International Journal of Business & Management, 3*(1), 248–262.

Gabriel, J. M., & Kpakol, A. G. (2014). Mediating Role of Power Distance on the Association of Perceived Managerial Competency and Employee Trust in the Nigerian Manufacturing Industry. *International Journal of Managerial Studies and Research, 2*(10), 1–12.

Gilson, L. L., & Litchfield, R. C. (2017). Idea Collections: A Link between Creativity and Innovation. *Innovations, 19*(1), 80–85.

González-López, M., & Fernández-Montoto, J. (2018). The Role of Intercultural, Scientific and Technological Openness on Innovation in European Regions. *Innovation: The European Journal of Social Science Research, 31*(3), 278–292. https://doi.org/10.1080/13511610.2017.1348934

Hair, J. F., Ringle, C. M., & Sarstedt, M. (2011). PLS-SEM: Indeed a Silver Bullet. *Journal of Marketing Theory and Practice, 19*(2), 139–151.

Hennessey, B. A., & Amabile, T. M. (2010). Creativity. *The Annual Review of Psychology, 61*, 569–598.

Huang, S., Ding, D., & Chen, S. (2014). Entrepreneurial Leadership and Performance in Chinese New Ventures: A Moderated Mediation Model of Exploratory Innovation, Exploitative Innovation and Environmental Dynamism. *Creativity and Innovation Management, 23*(4), 453–471.

Hunter, S. T., Cushenbery, L. D., & Jayne, B. (2017). Why dual leaders will drive innovation: Resolving the exploration and exploitation dilemma with a conservation of resources solution. *Journal of Organizational Behavior, 38*(8), 1183–1195. https://doi.org/10.1002/job.2195

Jansen, J. J., Vera, D., & Crossan, M. (2009). Strategic Leadership for Exploration and Exploitation: The Moderating Role of Environmental Dynamism. *The Leadership Quarterly, 20*, 5–18.

Kaufman, J. C. (2012). Counting the Muses: Development of the Kaufman Domains of Creativity Scale (K-DOCS). *Psychology of Aesthetics, Creativity, and the Arts, 6*(4), 298–308.

Kelley, D., & Kelley, T. (2015). *Creative Confidence: Unleashing the Creative Potential within Us All*. HarperCollins Publishers. London, United Kingdom, 1–244.

Kock, N. (2015). Common Method Bias in PLS-SEM: A Full Collinearity Assessment Approach. *International Journal of e-Collaboration, 11*(4), 1–10.

Kratzer, J., Meissner, D., & Roud, V. (2017). Open Innovation and Company Culture: Internal Openness Makes the Difference. *Technological Forecasting and Social Change, 119*, 128–138.

Krejcie, R. V., & Morgan, D. W. (1970). Determining Sample Size for Research Activities. *Educational and Psychological Measurement*, 1–4.

Lebel, D. R. (2016). Overcoming the Fear Factor: How Perceptions of Supervisor Openness Lead Employees to Speak Up When Fearing External Threat. *Organizational Behavior and Human Decision Processes, 135*, 10–21.

Melkonian, T., Monin, P., & Noorderhaven, N. G. (2011). Distributive Justice, Procedural Justice, Exemplarity, and Employees' Willingness to Cooperate in M&A Integration Processes: An Analysis of the Air France-KLM Merger. *Human Resource Management, 50*(6), 809–837.

Mumford, M. D., Medeiros, K. E., & Partlow, P. (2012). Creative Thinking: Processes, Strategies, and Knowledge. *The Journal of Creative Behavior, 46*, 30–47.

Naranjo-Valencia, J. C., Jiménez-Jiménez, D., & Sanz-Valle, R. (2016). Studying the Links between Organizational Culture, Innovation, and Performance In Spanish Companies. *Revista Latinoamericana de Psicología, 48*(1), 30–41.

Nitzl, C., Roldan, J. L., & Cepeda, G. (2016). Mediation Analysis in Partial Least Squares Path Modeling: Helping Researchers Discuss More Sophisticated Models. *Industrial Management & Data Systems, 116*(9), 1849–1864.

Ogbeibu, S., Senadjki, A., & Gaskin, J. (2018). The Moderating Effect of Benevolence on the Impact of Organisational Culture on Employee Creativity. *Journal of Business Research, 90C*, 334–346.

Ogbeibu, S., Emelifeonwu, J., Abdelhak, S., Gaskin, J., & Kaivo-oja, J. (2020). Technological Turbulence and Greening of Team Creativity, Product Innovation, Human Resource Management: Implications for Sustainability. *Journal of Cleaner Production, 244*, 118703.

Pannells, T. C., & Claxton, A. F. (2008). Happiness, Creative Ideation, and Locus of Control. *Creativity Research Journal, 20*(1), 67–71.

Podsakoff, P. M., MacKenzie, S. B., & Podsakoff, N. P. (2012). Sources of Method Bias in Social Science Research and Recommendations on How to Control It. *Annual Review of Psychology, 63*, 539–569.

Ringle, C. M., Sarstedt, M., Mitchell, R., & Gudergan, S. P. (2018). Partial Least Squares Structural Equation Modeling in HRM Research. *The International Journal of Human Resource Management, 31*(12), 1–27.

Roese, N. J., & Vohs, K. D. (2012). Hindsight Bias. *Perspectives on Psychological Science, 7*(5), 411–426.

Runco, M. A. (2013). Assumptions of Divergent Thinking and New Research Directions. In M. A. Runco (Ed.), *Divergent Thinking and Creative Potential* (pp. 395–400). Cresskill, NJ: Hampton Press.

Runco, M. A., Plucker, J. A., & Lim, W. (2001). Development and Psychometric Integrity of a Measure of Ideational Behavior. *Creativity Research Journal, 13*(3–4), 393–400.

Sarstedt, M., Ringle, C. M., & Hair, J. F. (2017). Partial Least Squares Structural Equation Modelling AG. In C. Homburg et al. (Eds.), *Handbook of Market Research* (pp. 1–40). Springer International Publishing AG.

Shmueli, G., Sarstedt, M., Hair, J. F ., Cheah, J.-H., Ting, H., Vaithilingam, S., & Ringle, C. M. (2019), "Predictive model assessment in PLS-SEM: guidelines for using PLSpredict". *European Journal of Marketing, 53*(11), 2322–2347. https://doi.org/10.1108/EJM-02-2019-0189

Tang, C. Y., Shang, J., Naumann, S. E., & Von Zedtwitz, M. (2014). How Team Identification and Expertise Identification Affect R&D Employees' Creativity. *Creativity and Innovation Management, 1*(1), 1–14.

Troster, C., & Van Knippenberg, D. (2012). Leader openness, nationality dissimilarity, and voice in multinational management teams. *Journal of International Business Studies, 43*, 591–613.

Vahter, P., Love, J. H., & Roper, S. (2014). Openness and Innovation Performance: Are Small Firms Different? *Industry and Innovation, 21*(7–8), 553–573. https://doi.org/10.1080/13662716.2015.1012825

Van Vianen, A. E., Dalhoeven, B. A., & De Pater, I. E. (2011). Aging and training and development willingness: Employee and supervisor mindsets. *Journal of Organizational Behavior, 32*, 226–247. https://doi.org/10.1002/job.685

9

The Dialogical Approach to Workplace Innovation

Hans Chr. Garmann Johnsen, Clare Hildebrandt, Hildegunn Aslaksen, Richard Ennals, and Jon P. Knudsen

Introduction

Recent debate on workplace innovation (e.g. Oeij, Rus, & Pot, 2017) has emphasised individual workplaces and practices, often within the context of socio-technical systems thinking. Similarly, there is a Scandinavian contribution to this debate, emphasising employee participation in innovation processes (Høyrup, Bonnafous-Boucher, Hasse, Møller, & Lotz, 2012). In contrast to this, there is a longstanding Norwegian model for workplace innovation, based on broad participation, that has received attention as a *democratic and dialogical approach* to enhancing business development. The approach has been developed through national programs, as we will demonstrate in this chapter. Furthermore, the focus was not the individual

H. C. G. Johnsen (✉) • C. Hildebrandt • H. Aslaksen • J. P. Knudsen
Department of Working Life and Innovation, University of Agder,
Grimstad, Norway
e-mail: hans.c.g.johnsen@uia.no; clare.hildebrandt@uia.no; hildegunn.m.aslaksen@uia.no; jon.p.knudsen@uia.no

R. Ennals
Department of Working Life and Innovation, University of Agder,
Grimstad, Norway

Kingston University, London, UK

Norwegian University of Science and Technology, Trondheim, Norway

© The Author(s), under exclusive license to Springer Nature Switzerland AG 2021
A. McMurray et al. (eds.), *The Palgrave Handbook of Workplace Innovation*,
https://doi.org/10.1007/978-3-030-59916-4_9

workplace, rather attention was on how to develop *systemic preconditions for dialogical development.*

The underlying governance model for this dialogical approach, known as the tripartite model, was gradually constructed in a co-operation between the Norwegian government and the social partners in the post-war period. From the 1980s, the processes of broad participation in business development through democratic dialogue were conceptualised by the late Prof. Bjørn Gustavsen. His philosophy was put into practice, first through the Swedish Leadership, Organisation and Co-determination programme (the LOM-programme) from 1985 to 1990, and then through three large Norwegian work life research programmes between 1995 and 2017. This chapter refers to some of the findings from the three Norwegian programmes.

The intention of the chapter is to (a) present the theoretical underpinning related to the dialogical approach to workplace innovation; (b) present findings from the three large successive workplace innovation programmes based on this foundation in Norway; (c) connect (a) and (b) by presenting the programme designs, evaluations and research output and finally (d) reflect upon learning points from this programme history. The overall thesis is that the dialogical approach to workplace innovation has taken a large step forward through the Norwegian programmes. There is potential to further develop both the theoretical foundation for this approach and the methodology of dialogical change.

Theoretical Background

Context

A basic agreement between the Employees Confederation and Confederations of Trade Unions in Norway was signed in 1935 after a period of heavy work life conflicts in the 1920s and early 1930s. This agreement became a cornerstone in the reconstruction after World War II, not least because of peaceful relations in the workplace, and the parties' dedication to co-operation. Parallel to this, a historical agreement was made between the Agrarian Party and the Labour Party, settling a compromise for the economic policy for the country and bringing the political climate to tempered parliamentarian standards.

The work life research programmes initiated by the Norwegian government in the post-war period were formalised by a collaboration between Norwegian researchers and researchers from the Tavistock Institute in London in the

1960s. Tavistock had adopted an Action Research methodology that built on Kurt Lewin's thinking on experiments in practice (Lewin, 1947; Trist, 1981), combined with a systems approach to organisational development (Emery & Trist, 1965). The collaboration also took as a theoretical point of departure, both Human Relations theories developed in the USA and socio-technical theory (STS) developed at Tavistock. Thus, both the psycho-social work environments, together with the interaction and organisational structure in production, were central issues of what became the work life research program in Norway.

Together, Norwegian and Tavistock researchers conducted a series of real-life *collaborative experiments*, aimed at supporting participatory processes in industry (Pasmore & Khalsa, 1993). Concepts such as autonomous work groups, job rotation and self-steering groups were inspired by the outcome of these experiments. These new work organisation forms were largely based on indirect participation, on the representative system (Emery & Thorsrud, 1976; Gustavsen, 2011a). Development was taken forward through negotiations and agreements between the parties in the tripartite collaboration.

A new programme history that started in the early 1980s, constituted a renewal of the thinking that went into the collaborative studies. The dialogical approach was developed by a group of researchers under the leadership of Bjørn Gustavsen, Professor and Research Director at the Work Research Institute (AFI) in Oslo and Professor at the Arbetslivcentrum in Stockholm. His ideas represented a theoretical break with earlier programmes.

The LOM programme in Sweden in the 1980s was the historical starting point for the operationalisation of the *dialogical approach*. The programme was motivated by calls for more collaboration within enterprises. During the programme period, 800 dialogue conferences were conducted (Gustavsen & Naschold, 1993). A similar initiative went in parallel in Norway, where some 450 conferences were held in the same period. In these conferences, representatives from all layers of an organisation worked together to define common tasks related to challenges. These could vary, from small quality of work improvements to more strategic initiatives. However, when summarising experiences and considering evaluations of these initiatives, Gustavsen (1992) argued that there was a need for a more comprehensive programme that would follow up on these conferences and facilitate further development. This initiative took work life research in a totally new direction, emphasising the lifeworld experience of the employee. Also, the dialogical approach represented a more radical, constructivist approach to social science (Toulmin & Gustavsen, 1996).

Thus, with the LOM programme experience and a renewed theoretical foundation, Gustavsen managed to mobilise the Norwegian Research Council (NFR), together with the Confederations of Trade Unions (LO) and the Employees Confederation (NHO) to support new national initiatives for workplace development in Norway.

The Theory of the Dialogical Approach

The dialogical approach to workplace innovation was based on a distinct theoretical foundation. Despite common reference to Action Research, a main distinction can be drawn between the dialogical approach and socio-technical system theory. As a background for understanding the dialogical approach, we recall the work of Kurt Lewin. He had participated in the Vienna Circle before the war and was strongly influenced by logical positivism, which promoted a strict, logical and fact-based foundation for science. In contrast to this, Gustavsen rejected the positivist point of departure. Hence, strong anti-positivism and anti-instrumentalism became key features of the dialogical approach, with its focus on continuous improvement, participation, delegation and bottom-up processes, emphasising individual reflexivity and organisational dialogue.

More specifically, the *epistemological position* was that we as social scientists cannot generalise from the lifeworld of others. Gustavsen (2002) used the term *constructivism*, to describe his own approach, which implies that one can influence the social structure and the direction of social and economic development at a certain level without believing that it is possible to intervene in the particular and local social practices. Thus, he was reluctant to prescribe specific organisational models or management practices.

The dialogical approach was built on the linguistic turn (Rorty, 1992) in social science, emphasising how we conceptualise our understanding of the world through language. Thus, language plays and important role in how we perceive the world and therefore linguistic practice becomes a main point of interest. Gustavsen writes:

> Everyday language, however, is not so much a series of pictures of reality as a set of instruments enabling people to deal with reality. Each word is an arbitrary collection of signs or sounds: its meaning is found in its use. It can consequently be argued that, in order to create 'new theory,' research must restructure the language out of which theory can grow. In order to do this, it is necessary to restructure those forms of practice to which the relevant ele-

ment of everyday language can be bound. In this way, a theory of science argument for Action Research can be identified, following up the lines of reasoning and evolutionary patterns that emerges from the attack on positivism. (Gustavsen, 1996, p. 7)

The inspiration comes from Jürgen Habermas' theory of communication. For Habermas, democracy is an arena for self-reflection. It is a system of common rules in combination with autonomy that allows one to conceptualise life experience, rather than joint culture, conformity or unity.

In the Norwegian work life programmes, this anti-positivistic emphasis on the importance of everyday language and Habermas' thoughts on democratic self-reflection were downscaled to the organisational level (Habermas, 1981; Toulmin & Gustavsen, 1996). The theoretical argument was that interpretation of words and sentences relates to experiences that are local and situational. Words transmit experiences from one context to another. In the same way, the formulation of interests and positions uses the medium of language. By searching for the experiences that create the foundation for our use of words, and for the underlying meaning to that which is said, one has the possibility to develop common understanding beyond interests (Gustavsen, 2010a). This is summarised in Table 9.1.

In Table 9.1, the dialogical concept for organisational change is based on a set of basic principles, where reaching individual participation and reflexivity is central. As an expansion of this, critical dialogue is preferred to unity or agreement. This means creating an environment for dialogue, with a prerequisite level of institutional design and communicative competence.

Table 9.1   A comparison between experiment-oriented and dialogue-oriented projects

	Experiment-oriented	Dialogue-oriented
Project logic	Linear	Interactive
Theoretical foundation	Socio-technical theory, socio-physiological theory, organisational theory	Theory of participatory and deliberative democracy
Leading actors	Few	Many
Defining point of departure	Zero-point analysis	Existing processes
Situation assessment	Highly structured	Low structure level
Improvement	Leaps forward	Continuous

Source: Gustavsen, 1990, p. 40, authors translation

The Concept of Dialogical Development

According to Habermas, a democratic regime allows individuals to interpret the context, intentions and actions in a social situation. The communicative process is not a decision process, but a process of reaching a higher level of rationality. This rationality is achieved through critical discussion, reflexivity and the willingness to be convinced by a better argument. The dialogical approach presupposes that individuals involved in communicative action do not use strategic means in the communicative process: they are involved in illocutionary conventions.

The specified role for change agents or researchers in a communicative process is that of mediation and facilitation of discourse (Gustavsen, 2000). The methodology prescribed is Action Research: the researcher takes an active part in the process and contributes to the generation of new practice, while at the same time providing theoretical foundations for this new practice. This must be understood as an alternative to orthodox instrumentality, explaining how a researcher can have a strategy without taking a dominant or authoritarian position.

This dialogue requires some design of arenas. Dialogue from a Habermasian perspective has three principles which underpin the development of the communicative concept for organisational change: the individual desire to participate in a non-strategic way, the frames for the arena where the dialogue takes place and the individual's competence for participating. Habermas himself has been reluctant to prescribe institutional design. However, there is also the underlying idea that it should somehow be possible to neglect other structures (like power or position), while taking part in the dialogue.

In the Nordic research programmes, these principles were translated into practical measures at two levels: on the company level and on the research group level. On the company level, the researchers were supposed to facilitate dialogical processes, hopefully resulting in new and better practices. At the same time, by utilising established networks, the new practices would ideally be diffused and further developed or applied by others, creating an optimal premise for workplace innovation and company transformation. At a research group level, the idea was that researchers report academically about their experience, thus adding insight into how linguistic practices transform social reality (Gustavsen, 2002).

Although the programme thinking had translated the communicative principles into workable guidelines, some would argue that the output of these processes was not sufficiently predictable. This may partly explain why the dialogical approach eventually ran into difficulties.

Design Principles of Dialogical Participation

Gustavsen and Engelstad (1995) identify four groups of arenas, depending on how comprehensive the task is and who the participants are. Category 1 is a small meeting with limited participation and a specific task (project group). Category 2 is a large group with a specific task (working group). Category 3 is a small group with a wide span of themes (strategy forum). Finally, category 4 is a large group with a comprehensive theme (dialogue conference).

Furthermore, Gustavsen defined a set of criteria for democratic dialogue (Gustavsen, 1992, p. 3). These criteria were meant to guide the dialogical process ensuring that everyone was able to speak, to express their thoughts and to listen to others. The idea was that consensus should come as a voluntary process based on the best arguments. Communicative action is, as mentioned, different from strategic action or negotiation. It is an open-ended dialogue, where active participants are willing to reconsider their arguments against better arguments (Gustavsen, 1992; Habermas, 1981, 2018).

In designing the work life programmes, Gustavsen (2011a) acknowledged that Human Relations theory, as well as Nordic quality of work theories, had been important for the development of quality at work in the Nordic countries (and elsewhere). However, he argued that this does not happen as a result of the theory; rather it is a result of somebody using and implementing the theory. Furthermore, as a theory only says something general, it must be interpreted and implemented in a local situation.

Subsequently there are four categories for possible results from dialogical processes and these are presumably interrelated (as indicated in Fig. 9.1). A dialogical process based on the principles above, will change the pattern of communication. Through this change, new issues and aspects of interpretation will evolve in the dialogue probably initiating change in the work organisation. As language and practice change, new aspects of how to work and how to organise work will develop. Thus, the dialogical approach was operationalised in a way that would create a link between dialogical practice and organisational change.

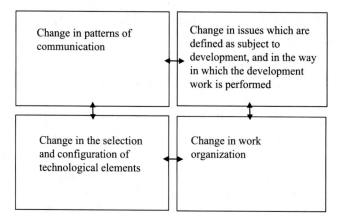

Fig. 9.1 The four categories of dialogical process results. (Source: Gustavsen, 1992, p. 70)

Methodology

The Three Programme Designs

Based on the discussion above, we now turn to analysing how the dialogical approach was applied in three successive national innovation programs in Norway from the mid-1990s onwards. As mentioned, the LOM program in the 1980s in Sweden had paved the way for the three Norwegian programs but also demonstrated that the program design had to be improved in order to support change in work life. Thus, as we will demonstrate below, there was an evolution of the three following programs.

In the following we analyse through a meta-study the outcomes of the three dialogue-based programmes that were conducted in Norway between 1995 and 2017. We present findings from a meta-study, summarising several projects within the national programmes.

The meta-study includes three evaluation reports from the respective programmes. In addition, the programmes arranged several researchers' conferences, with papers and discussions on the progress of the programme. We have also considered some of the theoretical contributions that came alongside the programme, expanding on its theoretical foundation. Bjørn Gustavsen, the key architect behind the programmes, produced several articles reflecting on the outcome of and learning from these programmes.

In analysing this literature, our focus is on the impact of democratic dialogue on workplace innovation. Of particular interest are foundational changes in communicative structure and in understanding. Such development of understanding can provide insight into how relations between these processes and conditions are leading to enterprise development and workplace innovation. Before analysing the outcome of the programs, we shortly present the three programmes below.

Enterprise Development 2000: From Dialogue Conference to Development Coalition

The key concept of the Enterprise Development 2000 (ED2000) programme that was launched in the mid-1990s was the development coalition, initiated both at a network level and inside participating enterprises. The development coalition entailed attention to the follow-up activity succeeding the dialogue conferences and was based on the following four criteria: (1) legitimacy in enterprise development should be created through broad participation. (2) The enterprise development process should be based on problems as they are defined by the enterprise. (3) The process should be integrated into the ongoing development processes in the enterprise. (4) The process should be based on the vision that future challenges are met by internal development coalitions.

Goals at the programme level were to contribute to the establishment and development of models for structuring and developing Norwegian industry, by increasing competitiveness for the participating enterprises, given the new challenges in their environment. One would apply both existing research approaches and those developed through the programme as it unfolded, by experimenting with a number of new models for combining research and other resources (such as external allies) with enterprise development, so as to yield better results for both research and business. The creation of a collaborative constellation between relevant research (and educational) institutions was both intended at serving the R&D needs of industry and strengthening organisational research.

The programme required some output targets, even though the programme was based on non-instrumental theoretical foundations. This target list was made mostly processual, indicating a sort of compromise between the constructivist, dialogical approach and the management needs of the Norwegian Research Council. This contradiction would increasingly become an issue of tension throughout the programme history.

Value Creation 2010: From Development Coalition to Regional Development Coalition

When Value Creation 2010 (VC 2010) was launched in 2001, regionalisation was a hot topic in Norway as the government planned for regional reform. Enterprise development was seen alongside this reform, especially as much of the explicitly defined regional policies were targeting the business sector. The programme was still researcher driven, but the partnerships related to the programme were extended. The intention was to move the "ownership" of the programme from a national to a regional level. Thus, the regional development coalition was initiated. Several regional institutions were engaged, and a core aim of the programme was to establish a communicative infrastructure in the regions affected.

The goal was to have development coalitions in all regions of Norway, putting county council authorities in charge of the coalitions, increasing the regional commitment through their co-financing of the programme. However, the constructivist dimension of the programme was retained, supported by a conference in Stockholm in 2002, with the title *Action Research, Constructivism and Democracy* in collaboration with the American Academy of Management. International scholars like John Shotter, Peter Reason and Kenneth Gergen met with Scandinavian scholars and Norwegian researchers engaged in the VC 2010 programme.

The key outcome of this further development of the constructivist perspective was not so much a change of direction in the programme as an increase in scope. The objectives of the programme now stretched beyond enterprises, incorporating regional development and democracy at large. Specifically, the goal of VC 2010 was to:

- Contribute to increased value creation by involving the social partners in participative processes at the company and the network levels
- Support regional development strategies
- Strengthen the knowledge base in the field (of organisational innovation, networking and regional development) through scientific production and publication

The point about scientific production was an acknowledgement of the need to strengthen not only practical development but also academic reflection related to the programme. This was institutionalised through a PhD programme called Enterprise Development and Working Life (EDWOR), managed by Norwegian University of Science and Technology (NTNU) (Arnold,

Muscio, Næhlinder, & Reid, 2005). Furthermore, the VC2010 programme had a stronger focus on innovation than the previous programme. It thereby initiated activities aimed at strengthening innovation through:

- Intra-firm organisational processes
- Inter-firm organisation and networking
- Intra-regional social and political processes

The last point also implied that the programme aimed at addressing regional organisation and regional innovation policy through active participation of the main organisations of the social partners (NHO and LO) and widespread participation by employees in development processes, utilising working life researchers as development actors, in co-operation with private companies. The companies set the agenda and could draw on research capabilities in the areas of organisation, management, productivity and working environment. The tight coupling of the programme's activities to regional business development strategies, and to regional actors of importance, was meant to produce value creation and innovation, increasing the effectiveness of the total public effort. The development of the scientific knowledge would contribute to increasing the relevance of the research and education institutions.

VRI:[1] From Regional Development Coalition to Regional Innovation Policy

In VRI, the programme was split into two: one part dealing with development and one part focused on research. Development was now run by a secretariat and was co-ordinated with other innovation instruments, most notably the business cluster programmes in Innovation Norway (the national innovation agency). The programme lasted for ten years and was terminated in 2017.

The main goals of VRI were to develop knowledge of, and ability for, interaction and innovation processes in the regions and promote research-based innovation in working life by:

- Strengthen interaction and knowledge flow between companies, research environments and public actors
- Mobilise and increase the quality of research-based development projects in companies, public enterprises, networks and regions
- Conduct innovation research with regional significance

---

[1] VRI = Virkemidler for regional innovasjon, translated to Instruments for regional innovation.

A new key term in the programme was co-generation of knowledge. This co-generation of knowledge was to be achieved through competence broker-age, business projects, personal mobility, dialogue, wide participation and dialogue methods. From the mere listing of goals and tools, a more instru-mentalist turn is easily detected.

When VRI was terminated in 2017, the three programmes ED 2000, VS 2010 and VRI had, over more than 20 years, consumed more than one billion Norwegian kroner (NOK), thousands of enterprises had been involved, and hundreds of researchers engaged, resulting in tens of PhD theses and numer-ous books and articles. However, probably two thirds of these outcomes took place in the last VRI period. Thus, VRI could be seen as an upscaling of the initiative started in the mid-1990s.

Table 9.2 summarises the three Norwegian programmes and their Swedish predecessor (LOM) to give a rough overview of the progress and development of this programme history.

Table 9.2 The "construction" of organisational and social development

Program	LOM programme 1985–1990	Enterprise development 2000 1995–2000	Value creation 2010 2001–2007	VRI 2007–2017
Main activity	Dialogue conferences	From dialogue conference to development coalition	From development coalition to regional development coalition	Democratisation of innovation, co-generation of knowledge
Participants	Organisation	Network	Triple helix	Decentralising innovation policy
Structural targets	Broad participation in organisation	Horizontal networks	Vertical networks	Combining horizontal-vertical networks
Unit of analysis	Organisation-specific conferences	Seven modules	19 counties involved in 9 regional development coalitions	15 co-generation projects, 36 innovation research projects
Role of research	Researcher initiated together with social partners	Researcher driven, facilitating development coalitions	Researcher driven but strategies developed by a regional partnership	Separation of research activity and development activities

Data Analysis and Discussion

Programme Evaluations

None of the evaluations of the three programmes (Oscarsson (1999), Arnold et al. (2005), and NFR (2017)) have a specific focus on dialogical processes or change in communicative patterns. The word dialogue is hardly mentioned, and where it is mentioned it refers to the use of dialogue conferences. This is not surprising, as evaluations often focus on programme goals rather than their underlying theoretical foundation, and subsequently, all the reports have also a focus on the output of the programme. As such, we note a paradigmatic mismatch between the rationales of the programmes under evaluation and the tools used to evaluate them.

The midterm evaluation of VC 2010 was the final evaluation. This is significant, since the report initiated a comprehensive change that resulted in the new programme, referred to as VRI. The report was based on more extensive interviews with people involved in the programme and a larger company survey, compared with the ED 2000 report. The report tells about a substantial intensification in activity in the programme. As a natural consequence of the project expansion to include all 19 regions in Norway, the budget for the project was greatly increased. However, although the regional project in VC 2010 organised regional development coalitions, the report argues that these had not been institutionalised regionally, and therefore did not result in regional partnerships. A second main conclusion from the report is that, since researchers had to both organise the activities and carry out research activity, both processes suffered. Research outcome was weaker than expected, as was the specific impact for businesses. Thus, VC 2010 to some extent fell between the two stools of development and research. Also, it is striking that the evaluation does not look into the research outcome, or even consider the vast number of academic texts that had been produced.

The final evaluation of the VRI programme in 2018 argued that more than 50 new companies had been founded, and more that 250 new or improved products were due to the programme. The programme had contributed to more R&D activity in businesses, the university sector had become more relevant for businesses, the county councils had adopted their new task as development agents in their region, and the triple-helix co-operation had been strengthened. In addition to this, the report argued that innovation research in Norway had been strengthened. However, from a methodological perspective, given both the length of the programme and how integrated it was with other regional institutions and policy instruments, it is difficult to know to what these should be ascribed.

Research Reports

The ED 2000 programme intended to relate internal processes of participation to innovation and strategic issues in the enterprise. The main tool was broad participation with emphasis on the dialogical aspects of participation. The underlying idea of the ED 2000 programme was that each workplace exists in a context that contains different groups within the organisation, as well as different partners, including external actors and organisations, customers and enterprises surrounding the organisation. This context also includes research institutions. These actors and groups can play a constructive role in developing the organisation and in making it more innovative through their dialogical processes. Gustavsen, Finne and Oscarsson (2001) refer to this as a supportive context. The main research focus of the programme was to investigate how such a supportive context could be created. The programme aimed to connect actors, in order to strengthen the innovative capacity of the organisation.

The official report finds that the ED2000 programme had not met all its targets. In particular, the report specifies that it is hard to ascribe particular business innovations to the programme initiative. At an organisational level, there is positive feedback from companies on the usefulness of the activity in the programme. The report finds that the seven research groups (modules) in the programme had different approaches and used Action Research to different degrees. Significant resources had been used to establish these research groups and build relations to companies. In order to get more effect out of the efforts, the report suggests a continuation of the programme with a stronger relation to regional institutions. As a result, the regional development coalition was suggested. The NFR (2002) report argues that the activity of constructing new social meeting places that occurred in ED2000 had the effect of bringing actors into new arenas for sharing experiences and discussing mutual challenges. The main argument is that people bring their ideas and interest into these arenas and through interaction, new perspectives and understandings emerge. Summarising the activity in the seven modules of ED2000, NFR (2002) found strong support for this effect on the programme.

NFR (2003) report from the seven modules stipulates which type of actors, businesses and activities were related to each module, describing a variety of initiatives throughout the country. A key concept at this stage in the programme development was partnership. VC 2010 emphasises the need to create regional partnerships and a culture of commitment in these partnerships. The 2003 report suggests that the foundation for this process had started in all regions as a result of ED 2000.

The NFR (2004) report focused on how to make the transfer, from the institutional setup of networks and partnership to the more specific, practical working harmony of these structures. At this stage in the programme development, the idea was that having established a communicative infrastructure, new practices would materialise. The report found that the variety of activities between the regions supported the idea that the programme communicates with regional and local realities. The report argues that the most striking and promising aspect of the programme is the plurality of communicative arenas. Close to 30 different communicative forms (arenas) were identified among the regional projects—in the social constructive interpretation, this is an indication of new social realities in the making.

Anthologies

The three programmes also produced several books. Some of these address the research outcome of the programmes. Concepts like mentoring, networks, learning cycles and development organisations are discussed and operationalised (Gustavsen, Colbjørnsen, & Pålshaugen, 1998).

In Levin (2002) there are several research papers on experiences from the ED 2000 programme and partly from the then new VC 2010 programme. The book summarises these in some thematic chapters, addressing programme development, new research practice, networking and action research, enhancing innovation as well as democracy, participation and communicative change. The core argument in the book is that the programmes have taken on ambitions to organise activities and achieve several objectives that need more thorough discussion. In example the discussion of work organisation versus development organisation was judged not conclusive.

In Ekman, Gustavsen, Asheim and Pålshaugen (2011), the focus is on the regional innovation system and the issue of learning. Several chapters argue for a bottom-up approach to regional innovation and argue that the Norwegian road into regional innovation systems has gone from the business level to the regional level. Accordingly, the VRI programme undertook to investigate further avenues for innovation policies in a more strongly regionalised policy regime (Fitjar, Isaksen, & Knudsen, 2016), but in this perspective the dialogue legacy was tacitly omitted. It had become overtaken by the new paradigm of partnerships.

Organisational Analysis

The evaluation reports more or less ignored the scientific discourse related to the programme initiative of Gustavsen. A series of articles and books tried to further develop an organisational theory based on a dialogical philosophy. Øyvind Pålshaugen, Olav Eikeland and others contributed to this theoretical development (Eikeland, 2008; Johnsen, 2002; Pålshaugen, 2002; Pålshaugen, Gustavsen, Østerberg, & Shotter, 1998). A key argument in this literature is that different dialogical practices exist alongside each other in an organisation, not least in the relation between a development organisation and work organisation. Eikeland (2008) promoted the idea that a development organisation alongside a work organisation allows for a kind of backstage arena, a "room" for rehearsal and exercise, independent of being exposed to the market and outside world.

The Wider View

One of Gustavsen's ambitions was the diffusion of the ideas of *dialogical change*. He took an active part in establishing the journal *Concepts and Transformations* (later *International Journal of Action Research*) and a book series related to this journal. In specific discussions, he engaged in transferring the Nordic experience to an international context, specifically through strong relations to Britain and Holland. Ennals and Gustavsen (1999) focus on the theme of work organisation and regard Europe as a development coalition in which much can be learned from different cases. Ennals, Totterdill and Ford (2001) present the UK Work Organisation Network and show how lessons were learned from the Scandinavian experience and applied in the different context of the UK, where tripartite relationships were much weaker. Fricke and Totterdill (2004) brought together papers describing practical experience with Action Research in both workplace innovation and regional development.

Johnsen and Ennals (2012) consider the idea of creating a regional knowledge economy, referring to the idea that regional-specific learning processes can result in knowledge creation that support innovation in the region. The assumption behind this is that innovation comes from knowledge creation and that knowledge creation is a result of collaboration. At the same time, collaboration requires shared perspective and common understanding that might be easier to achieve in regional and local settings, compared to larger entities like nations.

Gustavsen's Reflections

Bjørn Gustavsen, the architect of the programmes, wanted to construct the *systemic conditions* for peaceful and creative collaboration and business development, through participation and democratic dialogue. The underlying idea was that change is local, that people in the workplace themselves are the best to know what is most important and that the local reality is mirrored in and shaped by the linguistic practices. Creating dialogue, communication and participation therefore is an important aspect of this enterprise development. In 2001 he wrote:

> There is a need for connectedness between the people with whom we work, and it is a major part of an Action Research effort to help create this connectedness. (Gustavsen et al., 2001)

Even though the programmes were changed over more than 20 years, there was a turning point in 2007 following the midterm report by Arnold et al. (2005). The programmes after 2007 went into a more instrumental stage. Although Gustavsen continued to be a key figure in expanding the programme into what became VRI, there was a tension between the original constructivist idea of the programme and the kind of outside evaluation conducted by Arnold et al. (2005). The evaluation report simply ignored the whole linguistic argument.

Gustavsen comments on this in his 2008 article "Learning form Workplace Development Initiatives: External Evaluations versus Internal Understandings". The tension is related to the local learning and insights that require participation versus positivistic ideas that external observers can form relevant knowledge about reality from a distance. This rather more pessimistic attitude is reinforced in a 2010 article. He writes:

> However, while action research has already won most of the debates on epistemology and ethics in research, it has also lost most of the debates on research policy. Much of the research performed under the heading of action research has failed to convince other actors in society that this is a form of research worth investing in. (Gustavsen, 2010b, p. 145)

Conclusion

We emphasise four main aspects of the experience from the programmes we have presented: firstly, the methodological challenge in the form of expectations for the role of social science; secondly, the challenge of conversion of the philosophical foundation to programme design; thirdly, the tension between non-instrumentality and instrumentality and finally what we see as the dilution of the theoretical foundation for the programmes.

The Methodological Challenge

The dialogical approach that was implemented in four national programmes, one in Sweden and three in Norway, met several methodological challenges. Foremost among these was the role of social science in workplace innovation and enterprise development be emphasised. The core idea of the dialogical approach was to achieve hard results in form of organisational development and innovation, based on soft means, in the form of dialogue (Gustavsen et al., 2001). The anti-positivistic approach to social science was used in an instrumental setting of enterprise development. The methodological challenge, as we see it, was that many of the participants in the program apparently did not comprehend this tension.

Gustavsen's reluctance to more instrumental thinking, for instance, in the form of providing "best practice", was based both on his *epistemological position* and as a response to the positivist criticisms of action research, articulated by among others Bødtker Sørensen (1991). The argument was that although researchers cannot generalise from single cases, it is possible to observe structural dimensions, for instance, linguistic practices, that provide insight into mechanisms of social interaction (Gustavsen, 2011b). The data presented suggests that the expectations for the contribution from social science research in the mentioned programmes towards specific innovation or organisational development results far exceed the observation of structural dimensions.

From Philosophical Foundation to Programme Design

The Habermasian theory of dialogical development and communicative action is a philosophically informed sociological theory that challenges fundamental institutions in society. In a normative sense, it prescribes an ideal of reaching mutual understanding under conditions of universal, communicative structure. When these principles are downscaled to the organisational level, the question is: can they thrive in an institutional environment that has not bought into deliberative thinking?

Although the Nordic history of workplace collaboration indicates a potential for deliberative processes in work life, one might ask whether there was sufficiently widespread support and understanding of this communicative foundation at an institutional level (both in regions and at the national level). Learning from the previously described research programmes suggest that these structural and institutional preconditions are imperative for the successful implementation of the dialogical approach and should have been more deliberatively specified in the programme design.

From Non-Instrumentality to Instrumentality

We have presented the philosophical and theory of science foundation of the three programmes and indicated that the programme history took a new turn in 2007. This new turn was based on evaluations that argued for stronger institutionalisation of the programme, including specification of tools that could induce innovation and organisational development initiatives in businesses. The result of this institutionalisation was a stronger instrumental approach to research and evaluation (Gustavsen, 2008).

It is natural that stakeholders expect certain outcomes for their investment in the programme; however the non-instrumental foundation of the initiative was stated and expressed through conferences and research reports. It is therefore surprising that this founding philosophy is so absent in the evaluations and that the modules deviated from this foundation, without approaching the fundamental debate regarding the new direction of the programmes. Seen from a Habermasian point of view, the tension between knowledge and interests is apparent; however the transcending of this tension by communicative structure seems not to be widely understood. This supports the first point, suggesting that the intellectual maturity and shared understanding of key actors in the programmes was not sufficiently secured.

Dilution of the Theoretical Foundation

Gustavsen's constructivist ambition was to make a social impact. He deliberately wanted the programmes to be large, to connect with a wide range of companies, researchers and institutions. His vision was to create a communicative infrastructure that would be a foundation for democratic dialogue. The conditions for peaceful, democratic development in society are not something we can take for granted, but something we need to create. This implies that democratic, dialogical development is not something that just happens, rather it is founded in a deliberate intention that people share. From this point of view, it is astonishing and surprising, as well as disappointing, that this aspect of innovative thinking more or less vanished during the programme history.

One might argue that Gustavsen's grand vision of *constructivism* presupposed a broad social support for the direction this would take in terms of structural change. As the programmes merged into processes leading to regional reforms in Norway, it is not clear whether the structural role of the county authority corresponded with the original ideas of the work life programmes. With hindsight, one might argue that these preconditions should have been agreed upon at an earlier stage. The VRI project ended up being less about enterprise development and innovation, and more about developing regional innovation systems.

This insight opens a potential for both action and further research. One might choose to see the case of the work life programmes in Norway as an experience in the positioning of dialogical development processes in business and society. It could have been assumed that the Nordic work life model of participation and collaboration provided an optimal foundation for a dialogical approach to the research of workplace innovation. However, the analysis of this chapter paves the way for further development of the dialogical approach and highlights a need to address some of the challenges experienced in these extensive research programmes.

References

Arnold, E., Muscio, A., Næhlinder, J., & Reid, A. (2005). *Mid-Term Evaluation of the VS2010 Programme. A Report to the Research Council of Norway.* Oslo: Norwegian Research Council.

Eikeland, O. (2008). *The Ways of Aristotle: Aristotelian Phronesis, Aristotelian Philosophy of Dialogue, and Action Research* (Vol. 5). Peter Lang.

Ekman, M., Gustavsen, B., Asheim, B. T., & Pålshaugen, O. (Eds.). (2011). *Learning Regional Innovation: Scandinavian Models.* Basingstoke: Palgrave Macmillan.

Emery, F. E., & Trist, E. L. (1965). The Causal Texture of Organizational Environments. *Human Relations, 18*(1), 21–32.

Emery, F. E., & Thorsrud, E. (1976). *Democracy at Work.* Leiden: Nijhoff.

Ennals, R., & Gustavsen, B. (1999). *Work Organization and Europe as a Development Coalition*. Amsterdam: John Benjamins Publishing Company.

Ennals, R., Totterdill, P., & Ford, C. (2001). The UK Work Organisation Network: A National Coalition for Working Life and Organisational Competence. *Concepts and Transformation, 6*(3), 259–273.

Fitjar, R. D., Isaksen, A., & Knudsen, J. P. (2016). *Politikk for Innovative Regioner*. Oslo: Cappelen Damm Akademisk.

Fricke, W., & Totterdill, P. (Eds.). (2004). *Action Research in Workplace Innovation and Regional Development*. Amsterdam: John Benjamins Publishing Company.

Gustavsen, B. (1990). *Strategier for utvikling i arbeidslivet*. Oslo: Tano.

Gustavsen, B. (1992). *Dialogue and Development: Theory of Communication, Action Research and Restructuring of Working Life*. Assen: Van Gorcum.

Gustavsen, B. (1996). Development and Social Sciences: An uneasy relationship. In: Toulmin, Stephen and Gustavsen, Bjørn (eds.) *Beyond Theory: Changing Organizations through Participation*. Amsterdam: John Benjamins Publishing Company.

Gustavsen, B. (2000). Theory and Practice: The Mediating Discourse. In H. Bradbury & P. Reason (Eds.), *Handbook of Action Research*. Thousand Oaks: Sage Publishing, Inc.

Gustavsen, B. (2002). Constructing New Organisational Realities; The Role of Research. *Concepts and Transformations, 7*(3), 237–260.

Gustavsen, B. (2008). Learning from Workplace Development Initiatives: External Evaluations Versus Internal Understandings. *International Journal of Action Research, 4*, 15–38.

Gustavsen, B. (2010a). In Memory of Stephen Toulmin. *International Journal of Action Research, 6*(1), 5.

Gustavsen, B. (2010b). Relational Being. Beyond Self and Community. *International Journal of Action Research, 6*(1), 139.

Gustavsen, B. (2011a). The Nordic Model of Work Organisation. *Journal of the Knowledge Economy, 2*(4), 463–480.

Gustavsen, B. (2011b). Innovation, Participation and 'Constructivist Society'. In M. Ekman, B. Gustavsen, B. T. Asheim, & Ø. Pålshaugen (Eds.), *Learning Regional Innovation*. London: Palgrave Macmillan.

Gustavsen, B., Finne, H., & Oscarsson, B. (Eds.). (2001). *Creating Connectedness. The Role of Social Research in Innovation Policy*. Amsterdam: John Benjamins Publishing Company.

Gustavsen, B., & Naschold, F. (1993). *Constructing the New Industrial Society*. Maastricht: Van Gorcum.

Gustavsen, B., Colbjørnsen, T., & Pålshaugen, Ø. (Eds.). (1998). *Development Coalitions in Working Life*. Amsterdam: John Benjamins Publishing Company.

Gustavsen, B., & Engelstad, P. H. (1995). The Design of Conferences and the Evolving Role of Democratic Dialogue in Changing Working Life. In O. Eikeland

& H. D. Finsrud (Eds.), *Forskning og handling: Søkelys på aksjonsforskning*. Oslo: Arbeidsforskningsinstituttets skriftserie no. 1.

Habermas, J. (1981). *Theori des Kommunikativen*. English Translation: Thomas McCarthy. (1997). *The Theory of Communicative Action: Vol. 1: Reason and the Realization of Society, Vol. 2: Lifeworld and System: A Critique of Functionalist Reason*. London: Polity Press.

Habermas, J. (2018). *Philosophical Introductions: Five Approaches to Communicative Reason*. Cambridge: Polity.

Høyrup, S., Bonnafous-Boucher, M., Hasse, C., Møller, K., & Lotz, M. (Eds.). (2012). *Employee-Driven Innovation: A New Approach*. Palgrave Macmillan.

Johnsen, H. C. G. (2002). Discourse and Change in Organisations. *Concepts and Transformation, 7*(3), 301–321.

Johnsen, H. C. G., & Ennals, R. (Eds.). (2012). *Creating Collaborative Advantage: Innovation and Knowledge Creation in Regional Economies*. London: Routledge.

Levin, M. (Ed.). (2002). *Researching Enterprise Development. Action Research on the Co-operation Between Management and Labour in Norway*. Amsterdam: John Benjamins Publishing Company.

Lewin, K. (1947). Frontiers in Group Dynamics: Concept, Method and Reality in Social Science; Social Equilibria and Social Change. *Human Relations, 1*(1), 5–41.

NFR. (2002). *Mellom tekst og virkelighet: Samarbeid om utvikling mellom bedrifter og forskning (Between Text and Reality: Collaboration on Development Between Business and Research)*. Oslo: Norges forskningsråd.

NFR. (2003). *Bedriftsutvikling og regionalt partnerskap (Business Development and Regional Partnership)*. Oslo: Norges forskningsråd.

NFR. (2004). *Nettverk: abstrakte kategorier eller konkret arbeidsfelleskap (Network: Abstract Categories or Specific Work Partnerships)*. Oslo: Norges forskningsråd.

NFR. (2017). *Sluttrapport fra VRI programmet 2007–2017*. Oslo: Norwegian Research Council.

Oeij, P. R. A., Rus, D., & Pot, R. (Eds.). (2017). *Workplace Innovation: Theory, Research and Practice*. Switzerland: Springer.

Oscarsson, B. (1999). *Benchmarking of Enterprise Development 2000: An Impact Evaluation and a Comparative Analysis of Programme Design*. Oslo: Norwegian Research Council.

Pålshaugen, Ø. (2002). Discourse Democracy at Work: On Public Spheres in Private Enterprises. *Concepts and Transformation, 7*(2), 141–192.

Pålshaugen, Ø., Gustavsen, B., Østerberg, D., & Shotter, J. (1998). *The End of Organization Theory?* John Benjamins Pub.

Pasmore, W. A., & Khalsa, G. S. (1993). The Contributions of Eric Trist to the Social Engagement of Social Science. *Academy of Management Review, 18*(3), 546–569.

Rorty, R. (Ed.). (1992). *The Linguistic Turn: Essays in Philosophical Method*. University of Chicago Press.

Sørensen, A. B. (1991). *Evaluering av den anvendte arbeidslivsforskning i Norge*. Oslo: Nordisk råd for anvendt samfunnsvitenskaplig forskning (NORAS).

Toulmin, S., & Gustavsen, B. (Eds.). (1996). *Beyond Theory: Changing Organizations Through Participation*. Amsterdam: John Benjamins Publishing Company.

Trist, E. (1981). The Evolution of Socio-Technical Systems. *Occasional Paper, 2*(1981).

10

Barriers on Innovation in Australian Public Sector Organisations

Mahmoud Moussa

Background and Significance

The public sector is a complex environment; thus, it is fundamental to keep up with the changes in the services they are providing in Australia in order to be competitive in a changing global economy. There is consensus over the necessity to create an ideal environment to allow innovation to flourish. Arguably, public administrations are based on bureaucratic processes with traditional administrative models that hinder innovation processes (Criado et al., 2020). According to Divisekera and Nguyen (2018), the need to be innovative has become a prerequisite for the survival and future growth of modern organisations operating in a highly competitive global economy. Despite the extensive research on innovation in the public sector in the literature, seminal research still recommends the need to investigate how public sector organisations can support processes of innovation (Lopes & Farias, 2020). This chapter presents the factors that impact on innovation in Australian public sector organisations, serves as a contribution to the current literature on innovation and develops an understanding of the crucial factors that impact on innovation in State government departments in Australia. Specifically, data were collected and analysed from secondary data in the Department of Education, the Department of Environment, the Department

M. Moussa (✉)
School of Management, RMIT University, Melbourne, VIC, Australia
e-mail: mahmoud.moussa@rmit.edu.au

of Health and Human Services and the Department of the Premier and Cabinet across all states of Australia.

Literature Review

Several scholars investigated potential barriers to the generation and exploitation of innovation in the public sector. A flexible structure can contribute to better informality, effective communication and participation among the organisation's members, which in turn develops a more innovation-friendly culture (Sousa, Ferreira, & Vaz, 2020). Further, the literature concludes that leaders provide a key factor in the promotion of innovation (Mumford, Scott, Gaddis, & Strange, 2002). Moussa, McMurray, and Muenjohn (2018a) stated that leadership competencies influence the ability to innovate in public sector organisations. Concisely, the theory of leadership has emerged considerably over time in response to growing and changing understandings of organisations, communities and societies (Grint, 2011). Subsequently, many definitions and theories of leadership have been developed; however, there is little consensus on how leadership should be defined (Yukl, 2012). One reason driving this dilemma is that the key concept definitions differ according to the focus of the studied phenomenon. Furthermore, changes in the organisational climate make knowledge obsolete rapidly, and it is critical to develop dynamic capabilities that allow organisations to update its ordinary capabilities to be able to innovate (Jimenez-Jimenez, Martinez-Costa, & Rabeh, 2018). Moreover, organisations' concerns for employees' well-being and health can affect employees' perceptions of reforms and innovations (Moussa, McMurray, & Muenjohn, 2018b). Notably, while 'innovativeness' refers to the organisation's culture and thinking, 'innovation' is perceived as an outcome (Detre, Johnson, & Gray, 2011).

Methodology

This chapter employs a qualitative research design. Glesne and Peshkin (1992) concluded that qualitative researchers hope to identify terms not fully appreciated through their descriptions and analysis of the complex data. David (2006: 4, p. 16) noted that "…qualitative research strives to understand how all the parts work together to form a whole". Interpretation is not reading but a process that creates appropriate ideas from the text (Creswell, 2009). Further, Eriksson and Kovalainen (2008) noted that the

analysis of textual documents offers meaningful ideas in a qualitative investigation, through the use of secondary sources of information (Cavana,
Delahaye, & Sekaran, 2001). This involves using published or unpublished
documents (e.g. articles, newspapers and reports) (Silverman, 2004).
Relevant documents are regarded as significant tools that scholars may use
to develop inferences and offer relevant interpretation of the subject matter
(Yin, 2009). In the data collection process in this chapter, the application
of this method was based on several justifications. First, the analysis of
secondary data, such as government websites, newsletters and reports,
enhanced the author's level of understanding in undertaking this study
(Myers, 2009), in which these documents offered some insights into the
topic understudied (Merriam, 1998). Another justification for applying
this method was that these records were viewed as non-reactive, unobtru-
sive sources of information. This was due to the documents used in this
chapter have been developed during or before the research, and, hence, it
cannot be impacted by the researcher's investigation. Nonetheless, the
researcher followed specific criteria for specifying the validity of the data
for the research because of the significant amount of information available
from this method.

These criteria could assist researchers in avoiding the downsides of applying
this method, such as gathering irrelevant data or obsolete data and therefore
not being able to satisfy the research objectives (Cavana et al., 2001).
Subsequently, to enhance the quality assurance for this chapter, the researcher
applied Forster's (2006) five practical phases of analysing and accessing documents, which involved (a) accessing appropriate documents; (b) examining
authenticity; (c) understanding the documents; (d) analysing the data and (e)
using the data. 'Thematic analysis' and 'content analysis' were the two main
techniques of data analysis that were employed. In qualitative research, thematic analysis is known as the major concepts that have been revealed in
NVivo Pro 11 and 12 from the research data (Bernard & Ryan, 2010) and
which arise as being vital to explore the topic under scrutiny (Fereday &
Muir-Cochrane, 2006). The rationale behind the thematic analysis method is
to offer a structured way of comprehending how to create thematic codes.
After generating the crucial themes that aided the researcher to identify factors that enhance innovation in the public sector, the researcher employed the
content analysis. Content analysis is an endeavour to quantify qualitative data
by identifying frequencies of words and important events associated with the
research data (Crowther & Lancaster, 2009). Hence, the qualitative analysis
answered the research questions: (a) What are specific barriers to overcome to
innovate in public sector organisations in Australia? (b) What are the

leadership characteristics that promote a culture of innovation in public sector organisations in Australia? (c) In what way the organisation's climate impact the ability to innovate in public sector organisations in Australia?

Findings

The in-depth analysis involved open coding, and the researcher attempted to comprehend all themes that emerged from the data through conceptualising line-by-line. This process ultimately resulted in the production of specific codes. Themes were eventually categorised into three main themes and its constituents. These were organisational barriers (e.g. rules and regulations and funds and budget); leadership characteristics (e.g. strategic leadership, national leadership and inclusive leadership); and organisational climate issues (e.g. workplace planning, measurement tools, initiatives, embracing diversity and collaboration and networking).

Organisational Barriers

Rules and Regulations

It was found that public servants in the Australian Capital Territory (ACT) are aware that rules and regulations in the Department of Education can hinder a culture of innovation (ACT Department of Education & Training, 2015). For example, one barrier in the existing funding system involves insufficient incentives that may encourage universities to enrol students in undergraduate degrees at the expense of other qualifications in the higher education or vocational education (ACT Department of Education & Training, 2016). As one public servant noted:

> To drive innovation, fairness and excellence in Australian higher education, Australian higher education providers need to be held accountable and meet national standards, particularly to be eligible for government subsidies and to be able to offer student loans. Our tertiary education system must be affordable. Individuals and the country as a whole benefit from the higher education system. A sustainable system needs to strike the right balance between public and private contributions, while ensuring that up-front barriers to participation are minimised. (ACT Department of Education & Training, 2016, p. 46)

Notably, in Tasmania (TAS), "we all face barriers to education and employment. Whether we lack the capacity, support or resources, or experience a system that is blocking us, there is always something that hinders our transition through education and employment" (TAS Department of Education, 2014, p. 18). In the Department of Environment in New South Wales (NSW), the allocated time to process proposals and renewals of accreditation, or a refusal to provide a certificate of accreditation, is considered a barrier to innovate (NSW Department of Planning & Environment, 2014). Other barriers found in the Department of Environment in SA were partnerships projects that increased the acceptance of no-till sowing techniques, improved grazing management and other practices (SA Department of Environment, Water, & Natural Resources, 2014). In the Department of Health, the ACT's emergency departments are re-assessing their policies and collaborating with their colleagues throughout the hospitals to minimise barriers that delay access to particular services (ACT Health Directorate, 2016).

Funds and Budget

It was found that other barriers that hinder a culture of innovation in the selected departments involved funds and budget. For example, it was proposed by the Department of Education in the ACT to contribute towards the cost of study for students supported by Commonwealth through the 'Commonwealth Grant Scheme' (CGS) and eliminate upfront cost barriers via the provision of 'income-contingent loans' under the 'Higher Education Loan Programme' (HELP) (ACT Department of Education & Training, 2015). In TAS's Department of Education, "there are barriers and potential dangers for many citizens, in terms of costs of Internet, literacy and the ability to comprehend complex information, commercialisation of information, privacy, cyber safety and security" (TAS Department of Education, 2015, p. 56). In VIC, the Department of Education will continue to restructure the Technical and Further Education (TAFE) and training sector to enhance the Victorians' competencies for current and future jobs (VIC Department of Education & Training, 2018a). This involves eliminating the financial barriers for students, who are eager to develop their competencies that prepare them for jobs; providing vulnerable Victorians sufficient training to develop crucial literacy and numeracy skills and leading reforms to identify quality apprenticeships and traineeships.

In the ACT's Department of Environment, due to the limited resources, some national collaborative initiatives were delayed (ACT Department of the

Environment & Energy, 2016), whereas, in South Australia (SA's) Department of Environment, "Building Upgrade Finance is a voluntary mechanism designed to overcome barriers to investment in improving the energy, water or environmental performance of existing commercial buildings" (SA Department of Environment, Water, & Natural Resources, 2017, p. 44). Similarly, in the Department of Health in NT, the economic burden accompanied with the increasing demand for health services, while not sufficient to the NT, embodies a substantial financial challenge to the department. Therefore, "changing demographics, adoption of new technologies, service expansion and innovation all contribute to the demand on fiscal resources" (NT Department of Health, 2015, p. 82).

Leadership Characteristics

Strategic Leadership

Several government reports emphasised that strategic leadership plays a crucial role in promoting innovation in Australian public sector organisations. For example, in TAS's Department of Education, strategic leadership provides opportunities to identify a plethora of frameworks, research and standards, leading to the improvement of quality of teaching and learning (TAS Department of Education, 2017). Likewise, the Northern Territory (NT's) Department of Environment enhances its strategic leadership across the agency, providing expert advice and guidance to enhance the development and delivery of government priorities and initiatives (NT Department of Environment & Natural Resources, 2017).

The ACT's Department of Health provides strategic leadership and advice on the quality approach to promote individual-centred, safe and effective care and strategic frameworks in governance and quality across ACT health (ACT Health Directorate, 2017). The NSW's Health Department is investing in its workforce through the establishment of 'the District Clinical Council', who provides strategic leadership and oversights of clinical engagement in service planning and delivery (NSW Health, 2016). In NT's Department of Health, the 'Corporate Services Bureau' promotes strategic leadership and service delivery of centralised corporate support functions with an emphasis on innovation and efficiency (NT Department of Health, 2017).

National Leadership

Another desirable leadership characteristic found was 'national leadership'. It is noted that the progress and the performance of the ACT's Department of Education is demonstrated through maximising the prosperity for their workforce and their community through their national leadership role in training and education (ACT Department of Education & Training, 2018). In the ACT's Department of Environment, "the Australian Heritage Strategy supports the long-term protection of Australia's heritage places by establishing a 10-year framework to deliver actions against three high-level outcomes: national leadership, strong partnerships and engaged communities" (ACT Department of the Environment & Energy, 2016, p. 5). By undertaking a strategic approach, the NT's Health Department provides national leadership for a model linking health outcome targets and health service reform (NT Department of Health, 2014). In the ACT's Department of the Premier and Cabinet (PM&C), the first 'Special Adviser on Cyber Security' was selected within PM&C as a crucial point for national leadership and support on cyber security policy and to drive the application of the Cyber Security Strategy (ACT Department of the Premier & Cabinet, 2016). Additionally, in TAS's PM&C, national leadership leads and coordinates tasks across the State service to assist the Premier's participation at the 'Council of Australian Governments' (COAG) on issues associated with 'Reform of the Federation', 'the National Disability Insurance Scheme' and 'Family Violence' (TAS Department of Premier & Cabinet, 2017).

Inclusive Leadership

Another crucial leadership characteristic found was 'inclusive leadership'. For example, the TAS's Department of Education established a dataset to identify strategies that examine specific barriers and issues impacting on gender diversity to increase the proportion of females in leadership roles (TAS Department of Education, 2017). The executive board participated in 'a four-phase unconscious bias training program'. The four phases were 'inclusive leadership health check survey', 'one-on-one debriefing session', 'inclusive leadership and unconscious bias awareness training session' and 'post workshop coaching session' (TAS Department of Education, 2017). In VIC's Department of Education, flexible work, gender equality, generational diversity and LGBTI are outlined in the annual plan with initiatives to promote inclusive leadership and to combat processes and systems that can sometimes be barriers (VIC Department of Education & Training, 2018b).

The VIC Department of Environment is committed to developing an inclusive work environment that uses the full potential of employees and embraces diversity of thought to spur innovation and improve service delivery for the community (VIC Department of Environment, Land, Water, & Planning, 2017). This is enhanced through the development of the inclusive leadership program for their senior leaders. In TAS's Department of PM&C, heads of agencies and deputy secretaries across all State service departments have recently completed training and coaching in diversity and inclusive leadership (TAS Department of Premier & Cabinet, 2017). They are now implementing more inclusive strategies in their respective organisations.

Organisational Climate Issues

Workplace Planning

In VIC Department of Education, they support a high-performing workforce with effective leadership and a culture of integrity and respect. It is articulated that:

> The 'Investing in our People' strategy contains five key areas that represent a clear focus for action: leadership capability, workforce capability, culture of integrity and respect, safe and inclusive workplaces, and accountability for outcomes. These elements work together to provide a holistic and balanced approach to ensuring our people are capable; able to perform at their best; and feel empowered, valued and supported. (VIC Department of Education & Training, 2016, p. 9)

In SA's Department of Environment, it is noted that several approaches have been applied to organisational change. For example, organisational programs (e.g. think one team and values workshops) and targeted leadership and management programs (e.g. manager and leader forums and leadership information packages) and individual and team behavioural change programs (e.g. the culture network and internal 90-day change projects) (SA Department of Environment, Water, & Natural Resources, 2015). In TAS, the Department of the PM&C emphasises the development of an inclusive workplace that includes reviews of their performance management and development process, end-to-end recruitment practices and capability development initiatives for managers and staff to support and promote inclusive work practices (TAS Department of Premier & Cabinet, 2017). The Department of the PM&C in WA is supporting their workforce through development opportunities to produce the best leaders and services; providing support through monitoring, coaching and coordinating; providing effective and timely policy recommendations to support the Premier and Cabinet and delivering quality services to support the government (WA Department of the Premier & Cabinet, 2014).

Measurement Tools

In the ACT's Department of Education, "the implementation of strategies are underpinned by a range of people-related evidence, metrics and data including the aggregated results of the department's people capability framework self-assessments and results from the Australian Public Service Commission (APSC)" (ACT Department of Education & Training, 2015, p. 82). In addition, the department monitors progress against workplace diversity through self-assessment using a variety of assessments of workforce demographic data and 'Australian Public Service (APS) census results' (ACT Department of Education & Training, 2018). Likewise, in QLD's Department of Environment, measures for success involve effective decision-making and strategic approaches to capture and record data, open access to information and a framework for evaluation of pilot programs and environmental performance (QLD Department of Environment & Heritage Protection, 2014). The outcome-based risk management measures encourage ongoing innovation in environmental protection and allow industry to contain cost-related risk management as low as possible (QLD Department of Environment & Heritage Protection, 2017). In NT's Department of Health, initiate or participate in evaluation programs enhance clinical and health system outcomes and drive system-wide innovation, development, and improvement (NT Department of Health, 2018). Lastly, in QLD's PM&C, components for success involve survey results of innovation, job empowerment and engagement and organisational leadership (QLD Department of the Premier & Cabinet, 2018).

Initiatives

In QLD's Department of Education, fostering industry innovation and growth is undertaken by promoting the 'Queensland Government's Advance Queensland' initiatives to innovative training providers and employers (QLD

Department of Education & Training, 2017). In SA's Department of Environment, five innovations in agriculture fora were carried out across the State that led to substantial interest in new technologies (e.g. the use of drones) (SA Department of Environment, Water, & Natural Resources, 2015). SA's Department of Health developed the 'Carers-Partnering with you' web page, encouraging carers to provide feedback and information on how carers can engage with healthcare sites in service planning, designing care, measuring and evaluating health services and further information to local and national carer support services (SA Department of Health and Ageing, 2018). In VIC Department of Health, 'Safer Care Victoria' through 'Better Care Victoria' continued to lead on the testing and implementation of innovation to identify several targeted objectives for future work (VIC Department of Health & Human Services, 2017).

A number of transformational initiatives and projects were developed in QLD to drive innovation and partnership and create choice to meet the future challenges of the public sector. For example, the department hosted the 'Advance Queensland Innovation and Investment Summit' and attracted the best visionaries in the world in the fields of innovation, entrepreneurship and technology to inspire and empower Queenslanders (QLD Department of the Premier & Cabinet, 2016). The SA's Department of the PM&C established an 'Ageing Well Living Laboratory', a dedicated facility located at the 'Tonsley Innovation Precinct' called 'LifeLab' to enhance innovation and growth in the development of new products and services designed for seniors (SA Department of the Premier & Cabinet, 2018). Lastly, the Department of the PM&C in VIC actively strengthened innovation practices, with the launch of the 'Public Sector Innovation Fund' to support projects that experiment new approaches to tackle intricate policy challenges and the creation of the 'Behavioural Insights' unit to enable the integration of behavioural insights into public policy, service design and delivery (VIC Department of Premier & Cabinet, 2016).

Embracing Diversity

In TAS's Department of Education, "workforce diversity is well established within the department's culture and management systems. Initiatives align with key drivers of the department's 'Learners First Strategy', 'an Innovative Workforce', and 'Inspired Leadership" (TAS Department of Education, 2015, p. 82). VIC Department of Education's 'Workforce Diversity and

Inclusion Strategy' reflects the department's commitment to a corporate workplace culture that demonstrates respect, promotes diversity and supports their people's qualities and skills (VIC Department of Education and Training, 2017).

The QLD's Department of Environment implements strategies to promote an environment that values the contributions from Aboriginal and Torres Strait Islander peoples, women, individuals from diverse cultural backgrounds and people with a disability (QLD Department of Environment & Heritage Protection, 2015). Lastly, in VIC Department of the PM&C, diversity and inclusion priorities involve promoting diversity and inclusion as a source of strength to drive innovation and achievement (VIC Department of Premier & Cabinet, 2017).

Collaboration and Networking

QLD's Department of Education uses strategic partnerships to promote innovative and practical solutions to major problems and drives innovation in schools through collaboration and innovation strategies (QLD Department of Education & Training, 2017). In WA's Department of Education, "27 teacher development STEM Innovation Partnership schools engaged with 34 other schools on innovative STEM practices. Feedback from partner schools suggested the program improved confidence to implement STEM education and led to teachers changing their teaching and learning practices" (WA Department of Education, 2018, p. 29). In QLD's Department of Health, the 'Clinical Excellence Division' (CED) collaborates with consumers and clinicians to promote an ongoing effort in patient care, spur innovation and develop a culture of service excellence across the Queensland's health system (QLD Department of Health, 2018).

QLD's Department of the PM&C collaborates with agencies across government to deliver on the government's objectives for the community to create safe and connected communities, encourage innovation and investment, accommodate more jobs and strengthen Queensland's diverse economy (QLD Department of the Premier & Cabinet, 2018). Whereas the WA's Department of the PM&C continued to collaborate with 'the Department of Finance' in implementing 'the whole-of-government plan' to revive regulatory reform to enhance innovation and eliminate barriers to investment, employment and productivity (WA Department of the Premier & Cabinet, 2016).

Discussion and Implications

Despite the advances in the literature on innovation, recent studies call for the need to investigate how different management strategies influence innovation processes in the public sector (Agger & Sorensen, 2018; Torfing, 2019). State government departments across all states of Australia have developed numerous actions and strategies to put innovation in motion. These actions and strategies emerged based on what is practical and already occurring in government departments. However, some strategies or actions flourish more than others; therefore, constant change is required to deliver better outcomes for the community. Moreover, it is vital to acknowledge that innovation is not solely in the hands of the government; it also depends on non-government organisations (NGOs), businesses, education institutions, individuals and ultimately the entire society. Most importantly, innovation is a tricky term that requires context to ensure its understanding and relevance. This chapter described and displayed three crucial factors that could stimulate or hinder a culture of innovation in specific State government departments across all states of Australia.

Although barriers are considered antecedents of innovation and predictors of outcomes (De Vries, Bekkers, & Tummers, 2016), to date there is limited understanding of the existing barriers within the public sector innovation process (Cinar, Trott, & Simms, 2019). Bureaucracies rely on old organisational models with one-way communication style, compliance, order and control rather than on new and creative organisational models that foster commitment and enhance communication among all members of an organisation. As a caveat, Raipa and Giedraityte (2014) stated that barriers to innovation are context specific; hence, may differ from one organisation to another and from one nation to another. Nevertheless, in this study, the researcher found that the most noticeable barriers that hinder a culture of innovation in Australian public sector organisations involved rules and regulations and funds and budget. For example, it is found that the Australian government's capacity to enhance innovation through direct funds for encouraging innovation projects is inadequate. Notably, the Australian public sector has an intricate decision-making and structures that tailor the conditions for and impact on innovation. Hence, this chapter supports calls for further research about strategies/structures that overcome barriers such as rules and regulations and funds and budget to spur innovation in government departments across all states of Australia. Another significant barrier found was insufficient resources and support that can be barriers to innovation. While individuals may be given the opportunity to implement their ideas, they are offered inadequate support, and they may not have the resources to pursue their ideas. Moreover, innovative public servants may point to frustration with approval processes to pursue their projects. Additionally, government departments often support uniformity and metrics rather than brainstorming. In other words, there is a propensity to return to previous structures and models, which hinder a culture of innovation. Although the ontology of innovation and initiatives require us to change how we operate, innovation can sometimes be a challenge for government departments when novel ways of operating are proposed. Therefore, it is critical to investigate in future research whether State government departments are equipped with the required competencies to promote innovation.

According to Shafique, Ahmad and Kalyar (2019), despite the existence of numerous studies on the relationship between leadership characteristics and organisational innovation, this stream of research remains underdeveloped. One of the primary objectives of this chapter was to systematically trace the impact of leadership characteristics on innovation in several departments across all states of Australia. Hence, the investigation of leadership characteristics in this chapter extends the theory of leadership, particularly in the context of Australian public sector organisations and supports calls for more research about strategic, national and inclusive leadership across State government departments in Australia. However, as a caveat, leadership theories/models conceptualised to influence organisational performance and effectiveness are not generalisable to creativity and innovation (Mumford & Licuanan, 2004). Furthermore, in this chapter, the researcher aimed at understanding in what way the organisation's climate impacts the ability to innovate in public sector organisations in Australia. Organisational-level research clearly suggests that organisational climate that is conducive to innovation acts as a facilitator of change in specific industries and organisations (Khazanchi, Lewis, & Boyer, 2007), but what is still vague is how these organisational climates are manifest as facet-specific climates for innovation. Lopes and Farias (2020) conducted a systematic literature review to contribute to our understanding of the dynamics of innovation processes in the public sector and recommended that future studies should address the role of organisational climate that fosters innovation strategies. Thus, the comprehension on the impact of organisational climate on workplace innovation is considered as one contribution to the existing literature. Nonetheless, more research is needed about the impact of organisational climate on innovation at the individual, organisational and team levels in Australian public sector organisations.

Conclusion

This chapter revealed the dynamics of innovation in specific State government departments across the eight states of Australia. This involved three major themes and its constituents: (a) barriers, which consist of rules and regulations, and funds and budget; (b) leadership characteristics, which consist of strategic leadership, national leadership and inclusive leadership and (c) organisational climate issues, which consist of workplace planning, measurement tools, initiatives, embracing diversity and collaboration and networking. The analysis allowed for certain observations regarding the relationship between the levels of government and their innovation efforts. In other words, the findings indicated the extent to which innovation policy and practice is consistent, and acts in concert, across each of these levels of government.

References

ACT Department of Education and Training. (2015). *Annual Report 2014–2015: Opportunity Through Learning*. Department of Education and Training: Australian Government.

ACT Department of Education and Training. (2016). *Annual Report 2015–2016: Opportunity Through Learning*. Department of Education and Training: Australian Government.

ACT Department of Education and Training. (2018). *Annual Report 2017–2018: Opportunity Through Learning*. Department of Education and Training: Australian Government.

ACT Department of the Environment & Energy. (2016). *Annual Report 2015–2016*. Department of the Environment & Energy: Australian Government.

ACT Department of the Premier and Cabinet. (2016). *Annual Report 2015–2016*. Department of the Premier and Cabinet: Australian Government.

ACT Health Directorate. (2016). *Annual Report 2015–2016*. ACT Government Health Directorate.

ACT Health Directorate. (2017). *Annual Report 2016–2017*. ACT Government Health Directorate.

Agger, A., & Sorensen, E. (2018). Managing Collaborative Innovation in Public Bureaucracies. *Planning Theory, 17*(1), 53–73.

Bernard, H. R., & Ryan, G. W. (2010). *Analyzing Qualitative Data: Systematic Approaches*. Los Angeles: Sage.

Cavana, R. Y., Delahaye, B. L., & Sekaran, U. (2001). *Applied Business Research: Qualitative and Quantitative Methods*. Milton, QLD: John Wiley & Sons, Australia.

Cinar, E., Trott, P., & Simms, C. (2019). A Systematic Review of Barriers to Public Sector Innovation Process. *Public Management Review, 21*(2), 264–290.

Creswell, J. W. (2009). *Research Design: Qualitative, Quantitative, and Mixed Methods Approaches* (3rd ed.). Thousand Oaks, CA: Sage Publications.

Criado, J. I., Dias, T. F., Sano, H., Rojas-Martín, F., Silvan, A., & Filho, A. I. (2020). Public Innovation and Living Labs in Action: A Comparative Analysis in Post-New Public Management Contexts. *International Journal of Public Administration.* https://doi.org/10.1080/01900692.2020.1729181

Crowther, D., & Lancaster, G. (2009). *Research Methods: A Concise Introduction to Research in Management and Business Consultancy* (2nd ed.). Amsterdam, Boston; London: Butterworth-Heinemann.

David, S. (2006). *Interpreting Qualitative Data: Methods for Analysing Talk, Text and Interaction* (3rd ed.). London: Sage.

De Vries, H., Bekkers, V., & Tummers, L. (2016). Innovation in the Public Sector: A Systematic Review and Future Research Agenda. *Public Administration, 94*(1), 146–166.

Detre, J. D., Johnson, A. J., & Gray, A. W. (2011). Innovativeness and Innovation: Implications of the Renewable Materials Supply Chain. *International Food and Agribusiness Management Review, 14*(2), 17–34.

Divisekera, S., & Nguyen, V. K. (2018). Determinants of Innovation in Tourism Evidence from Australia. *Tourism Management, 67*, 157–167.

Eriksson, P., & Kovalainen, A. (2008). *Qualitative Methods in Business Research.* Thousand Oaks, CA: Sage Publication.

Fereday, J., & Muir-Cochrane, E. (2006). Demonstrating Rigor Using Thematic Analysis: A Hybrid Approach of Inductive and Deductive Coding and Theme Development. *International Journal of Qualitative Methods, 5*(1), 80–92.

Forster, N. (2006). The Analysis of Company Documentation. In J. Scott (Ed.), *Documentary Research* (Vol. IV). London: Sage Publications.

Glesne, C., & Peshkin, A. (1992). *Becoming Qualitative Researchers: An Introduction.* New York: Longman.

Grint, K. (2011). A History of Leadership. In A. Bryman, D. Collinson, K. Grint, B. Jackson, & M. Uhl-Bien (Eds.), *The Sage Handbook of Leadership.* London: Sage Publications.

Jimenez-Jimenez, D., Martinez-Costa, M., & Rabeh, H. A. D. (2018). Fostering New Product Success Through Learning Competencies. *Technology Analysis & Strategic Management, 30*(1), 58–70.

Khazanchi, S., Lewis, M. W., & Boyer, K. K. (2007). Innovation-Supportive Culture: The Impact of Organizational Values on Process Innovation. *Journal of Operations Management, 25*(4), 871–884.

Lopes, A. V., & Farias, J. S. (2020). How Can Governance Support Collaborative Innovation in the Public Sector? A Systematic Review of the Literature. *International Review of Administrative Sciences, 0*(0), 1–17.

Merriam, S. B. (1998). *Qualitative Research and Case Study Applications in Education.* San Francisco, CA: Jossey-Bass.

Moussa, M., McMurray, A., & Muenjohn, N. (2018a). A Conceptual Framework of the Factors Influencing Innovation in Public Sector Organisations. *the Journal of Developing Areas, 52*(3), 231–240.

Moussa, M., McMurray, A., & Muenjohn, N. (2018b). Innovation and Leadership in Public Sector Organisations. *Journal of Management Research, 10*(3), 14–30.

Mumford, M. D., & Licuanan, B. (2004). Leading for Innovation: Conclusions, Issues, and Directions. *The Leadership Quarterly, 15*(1), 163–171.

Mumford, M. D., Scott, G. M., Gaddis, B., & Strange, J. M. (2002). Leading Creative People: Orchestrating Expertise and Relationships. *The Leadership Quarterly, 13*(6), 705–750.

Myers, M. D. (2009). *Qualitative Research in Business and Management.* London: Sage.

NSW Department of Planning & Environment. (2014). *2013–2014 Annual Report.* State of NSW Department of Planning and Environment.

NSW Health. (2016). *Annual Report 2015–2016.* State of NSW Department of Health.

NT Department of Environment and Natural Resources. (2017). *Annual Report 2016–2017.* Northern Territory Department of Environment and Natural Resources: Northern Territory Government.

NT Department of Health. (2014). Annual Report 2013–2014. Northern Territory Department of Health: Northern Territory Government.

NT Department of Health. (2015). *Annual Report 2014–2015.* Northern Territory Department of Health: Northern Territory Government.

NT Department of Health. (2017). *Annual Report 2016–2017.* Northern Territory Department of Health: Northern Territory Government.

NT Department of Health. (2018). *Annual Report 2017–2018.* Northern Territory Department of Health: Northern Territory Government.

QLD Department of Education & Training. (2017). *Strategic Plan 2017–2021.* QLD Department of Education & Training: Queensland Government.

QLD Department of Environment and Heritage Protection. (2014). *Annual Report 2013–2014.* Department of Environment and Heritage Protection: Queensland Government.

QLD Department of Environment and Heritage Protection. (2015). *Annual Report 2014–2015.* Department of Environment and Heritage Protection: Queensland Government.

QLD Department of Environment and Heritage Protection. (2017). *Annual Report 2016–2017.* Department of Environment and Heritage Protection: Queensland Government.

QLD Department of Health. (2018). *Annual Report 2017–2018.* Department of Health: Queensland Government.

QLD Department of the Premier and Cabinet. (2016). *Annual Report 2015–2016.* Department of the Premier and Cabinet: Queensland Government.

QLD Department of the Premier and Cabinet. (2018). *Annual Report 2017–2018*. Department of the Premier and Cabinet: Queensland Government.

Raipa, A., & Giedraityte, V. (2014). Innovation barriers in public sector: A comparative analysis in Lithuania and the European Union. *International Journal of Business Management, 9*(10), 10–20.

SA Department of Environment, Water and Natural Resources. (2014). *Annual Report 2013–2014*. The Department of Environment, Water and Natural Resources: Government of South Australia.

SA Department of Environment, Water and Natural Resources. (2015). *Annual Report 2014–2015*. The Department of Environment, Water and Natural Resources: Government of South Australia.

SA Department of Environment, Water and Natural Resources. (2017). *Annual Report 2016–2017*. Department of Environment, Water and Natural Resources: Government of South Australia. Adelaide SA.

SA Department of Health and Ageing. (2018). *Annual Report 2017–2018*. Department of Health and Ageing. Government of South Australia.

SA Department of the Premier and Cabinet. (2018). *Annual Report 2017–2018*. Department of the Premier and Cabinet: Government of South Australia.

Shafique, I., Ahmad, B., & Kalyar, M. N. (2019). How Ethical Leadership Influences Creativity and Organizational Innovation: Examining the Underlying Mechanisms. *European Journal of Innovation Management, 23*(1), 114–133.

Silverman, D. (2004). *Qualitative Research Theory, Method and Practice*. London: Sage Publications.

Sousa, M. J., Ferreira, C., & Vaz, D. (2020). Innovation Public Policy: The Case of Portugal. *Management and Economics Research Journal, 6*, 1–14.

TAS Department of Education. (2014). *Annual Report 2013–2014*. Department of Education: Tasmanian Government.

TAS Department of Education. (2015). *Annual Report 2014–2015*. Department of Education: Tasmanian Government.

TAS Department of Education. (2017). *Annual Report 2016–2017*. Department of Education: Tasmanian Government.

TAS Department of Premier and Cabinet. (2017). *DPAC Annual Report 2016–2017*. Department of Premier and Cabinet: Tasmanian Government.

Torfing, J. (2019). Collaborative Innovation in the Public Sector: The Argument. *Public Management Review, 21*(1), 1–11.

VIC Department of Education and Training. (2016). *Annual Report 2015–2016*. The Education State. Victoria State Government.

VIC Department of Education and Training. (2017). *Annual Report 2016–2017*. The Education State. Victoria State Government.

VIC Department of Education and Training. (2018a). *Annual Report 2017–2018*. The Education State. Victoria State Government.

VIC Department of Education and Training. (2018b). *2018–2022 Strategic Plan*. The Education State. Victoria State Government.

VIC Department of Environment, Land, Water and Planning. (2017). *Annual Report 2017*. Victoria State Government: Environment, Land, Water and Planning.

VIC Department of Health and Human Services. (2017). *Annual Report 2016–2017*. Victorian Department of Health and Human Services: Victoria State Government.

VIC Department of Premier and Cabinet. (2016). *Annual Report 2015–2016*. Department of Premier and Cabinet: Victoria State Government.

VIC Department of Premier and Cabinet. (2017). *Annual Report 2016–2017*. Department of Premier and Cabinet: Victoria State Government.

WA Department of Education. (2018). *Annual Report 2017–2018*. Department of Education: Government of Western Australian.

WA Department of the Premier & Cabinet. (2014). *Annual Report 2013–2014*. Department of the Premier & Cabinet: Government of Western Australian.

WA Department of the Premier & Cabinet. (2016). *Annual Report 2015–2016*. Department of the Premier & Cabinet: Government of Western Australian.

Yin, R. K. (2009). *Case Study Research: Design and Methods* (4th ed.). Thousand Oaks, CA: Sage.

Yukl, G. A. (2012). *Leadership in Organizations* (8th ed.). Pearson Education, Limited.

Theme III

Workplace Innovation as a Process

11

Workplace Innovation as a Process: Examples from Europe

Peter R. A. Oeij, Paul T. Y. Preenen, and Steven Dhondt

Introduction

Redesigning organisations and work processes can lead to better organisational performance and jobs in general (e.g., Bloom & van Reenen, 2010; Boxall, 2012; Boxall & Macky, 2009). Workplace innovation (WPI), a specific approach focusing on participative organisational redesign, is beneficial for both business performance and the quality of jobs. The benefits of WPI have been documented for both employees and organisations across a range of organisational and national contexts. For example, WPI has been linked to both improved individual-level outcomes, such as indices of the quality of working life and improved organisational performance (Dhondt & van Hootegem, 2015; Dhondt, Vermeerbergen, & van Hootegem, 2017; Oeij, Rus, & Pot, 2017). Hence, companies that care about their performance and employees could consider the adoption and implementation of WPI.

In fact, WPI might be more relevant than ever in the current times of ongoing change and competition in which many companies focus strongly on

P. R. A. Oeij (✉) • P. T. Y. Preenen
TNO Innovation for Life, Leiden, The Netherlands
e-mail: peter.oeij@tno.nl; paul.preenen@tno.nl

S. Dhondt
TNO Innovation for Life, Leiden, The Netherlands

KU Leuven, Leuven, Belgium
e-mail: steven.dhondt@tno.nl

© The Author(s), under exclusive license to Springer Nature Switzerland AG 2021
A. McMurray et al. (eds.), *The Palgrave Handbook of Workplace Innovation*,
https://doi.org/10.1007/978-3-030-59916-4_11

technological and business (model) innovation and efficiency to face today's demands. However, competitiveness is not realised merely through stimulation of new technological developments and adoption of cost-cutting efficiency policies but needs to go hand in hand with organisational innovation, such as WPI (Pot, 2011), in order for (technological) renewal to be adopted by employees (Putnik, Oeij, van der Torre, de Vroome, & Dhondt, 2019). In our view, WPI is an essential link between technological innovation (and other types of renewal and change in organisations) and desired improvement in organisational performance.

Despite such positive results, many policymakers and companies lack the knowledge to implement WPI practices. It is relevant to look at the current practice of WPI to develop an understanding of the core workings of WPI. This information can help other companies to adopt a more realistic approach to implementing WPI. This chapter discusses the Eurofound study of European companies that apply WPI, shows why they apply WPI and describes the main characteristics of the process of implementation (Oeij et al., 2015). We investigated the implementation of WPI in 51 companies across Europe. We will first describe the concept of WPI. Subsequently, results will be presented, including three company case examples of the implementation of WPI practices. We end with practical implications and a discussion. This can help policymakers, (applied) researchers and companies to better understand and implement WPI strategies.

Theory: The Concept of WPI

The Concept of WPI

WPI is a successfully applied, participative renewal of the structure and/or culture of the workplace; the workplace ranges from the immediate working environment—one's work station or desk—to the organisation as a whole, that is, the organisation of which employees are members through their employment relationship. More specifically, we define WPI as an integral set of participative mechanisms for interventions that relate structural (e.g., organisational design, division of labour) and cultural (e.g., leadership, coordination and organisational behaviour) aspects of the organisation and its people with the objective to simultaneously improve the conditions for performance (i.e., productivity, innovation, quality) and the quality of working life (i.e., well-being at work, competence development, employee engagement). In this definition, 'participative mechanisms for interventions' are synonymous with employee engagement in decision-making processes and represent a precondition for WPI (Oeij & Dhondt, 2017, p. 66; see also Oeij et al., 2015, pp. 8, 14). Employee engagement is related to employee-driven innovation (EDI). EDI means that employees, who are not per se responsible for renewal and inventions, nonetheless develop innovations; that is, employees generally contribute actively and systematically to the innovation process (Høyrup, 2012). To the extent employees have decisional power, one can speak of employee involvement, which goes a step further than engagement. For our purpose, it suffices to assess employee participation in the innovation process and whether the consequences are beneficial to the employees and the quality of their jobs. WPI differs from EDI in the sense that WPI deals not with innovation per se, like technological innovation, but with organisational renewal that enables technological innovation to become embedded; that is, it supports innovation adoption and technological acceptance (Putnik et al., 2019). WPI thus stimulates employee engagement more broadly and not only with regard to innovation.

Strategy and WPI

For WPI to succeed, it is important that it is part of the organisational strategy. Strategies can be rational or not, and there are at least ten different schools of thought in this regard (Mintzberg, Ahlstrand, & Lampel, 1998). From a rational planning perspective, strategy can be defined as the determination of the long-term goals and objectives of an enterprise, the adoption of courses of action and the allocation of resources necessary to carry out these goals (Chandler, 1962, p. 13). Strategies are rooted in management philosophies, which in turn reflect the political, economic and social preferences of those decision-makers that are in power within organisations. It is an assumed condition for WPI to be applied that these decision-makers have a positive image of mankind with respect to employees at every level of the organisation. Such positive, humanistic views could be observed in management trends such as the *human relations movement* (Trist & Murray, 1993), *quality of working life*, *Humanisierung der Arbeit* (humanising of work) in Germany, modern socio-technical thinking in Nordic countries and the Lowlands (Cummings & Srivastva, 1977; De Sitter, Den Hertog, & Dankbaar, 1997) and even in lean management (Womack & Jones, 2003). A humanised or humanistic approach to work and labour (Smith, 2017) means that work is designed such that people can develop their talents and have safe and healthy working conditions in addition to being productive. Humanised quality of work is the opposite of alienation, degradation, unfreedom and indecency, as it nurtures security, equity, individuation and democracy (Herrick & Maccoby, 1975). In organisations that strive not only for economic goals and efficiency but also for social goals, top management may have a serious eye for humanised quality of work. Not because such managers are merely human and empathic, but because they understand that successful competition is dependent on deploying human talents in the right way. Such managers are keen to create workplaces that allow employees to develop their talents and have a say in how the company progresses. WPI may help them achieve these goals.

WPI's Structure and Culture Orientation Practices

Structure follows strategy, according to Chandler (1962). The WPI's 'structure orientation' contains practices that allow for restructuring work organisation and job design (De Sitter et al., 1997; Oeij et al., 2015). These practices concern, for example, the division of labour between managers and employees and between people and machines, as well as the division between controlling ('managing') and executing tasks. In the case of strategies with attention to humanised jobs, it is possible to give employees structural influence over their own work, certain management tasks and parts of the production system through, for example, co-creation in work design, employee budget or planning control or establishing self-organising and self-steering teams. An example of this is management engaging employees in the acquisition of new IT tools, machines or other capital goods.

It is important to observe that such an approach goes beyond HR-dominated streams (such as high-performance work practices and high-involvement work practices—Appelbaum, Bailey, Berg, & Kalleberg, 2000; Boxall, 2012; Boxall & Macky, 2009; Huselid, 1995; discussed in Oeij et al., 2015; also Osterman, 2018), as it is rooted in the choices made about how to design the production system and an organisational structure for the work. One can say that structural approaches in engaging employees allow employees to participate in the root causes of their job design, whereas most HR measures do not affect the root causes of how design influences jobs but only give employees the influence to deal with symptoms. An example may clarify what we mean. Suppose sick leave and employee complaints are high due to heavy workload issues. A company could introduce stress management programmes and gym facilities, but such HR measures would merely combat symptoms of fatigue and work overload. A root cause type of measure would be to redesign the production process and job content in a way that allows employees to regulate the workload such that production targets are still met but stress risks are reduced. In the first situation, the employees lack the autonomy to change the organisational conditions, but they are able to do so in the second situation. Structure-oriented practices, therefore, can stimulate employee control or autonomy and provide the ground for employee (and employee representative) voices. These are crucial for individual-level motivation and innovative behaviour (Preenen, Oeij, Dhondt, Kraan, & Jansen, 2016).

The 'culture orientation' of WPI contains practices that provide opportunities for employees to participate in various ways, for example, in organisational decision-making through dialogue (Oeij et al., 2015), and are focused on enhancing employee engagement and participation to create a participative culture. An example of such a practice would be visits by higher management to the shop floor in order to engage in dialogue with the employees. These culture-oriented practices do not only concern employees, but they could also include employee representatives, as in the case of social dialogue and collective bargaining. Culture-oriented practices can stimulate commitment and provide employees (and employee representatives) with a voice (Totterdill & Exton, 2014).

This conceptualisation of WPI implies that one needs to look at the organisation as a whole and consider the reciprocal effects of strategy, structure and culture if one is to reap the benefits associated with WPI (Howaldt, Oeij, Dhondt, & Fruytier, 2016). For instance, hierarchical organisational structures may lead to more directive leadership styles and human resource management (HRM) practices that focus on a clear division of labour and control, whereas less hierarchical structures may lead to leadership styles and HRM practices that are geared at promoting employee involvement, engagement and commitment (MacDuffie, 1997; Pot, 2011). Therefore, to fully understand WPI, it is essential to not only focus on certain types of HRM practices and their consequences but to also take into consideration the organisational structure and the management philosophy underlying strategic choices (Howaldt et al., 2016; Karanika-Murray & Oeij, 2017).

The Methodology of the Eurofound Study

The Eurofound Study

The Eurofound study *Workplace Innovation in European Companies* (Oeij et al., 2015) is a multiple case study among 51 companies from 10 EU Member States. The companies were selected as leading cases of WPI among a database of 30,000 companies from Eurofound's European Company Survey 2013. One of its purposes was to explore why and how companies apply WPI in order to provide recommendations to policymakers in Europe for how to pursue and stimulate WPI across Europe. We focused on three central questions: (1) Why do companies apply WPI and are there differences in the strategies that they use? (2) How do these companies implement WPI interventions and provide employees with a role in that process? (3) What types of WPI interventions are being implemented and what are the (expected) effects of such interventions? More technical information about the methods and fieldwork are described in the original study (and in Oeij, Dhondt, Žiauberytė-Jakštienė, Corral, & Preenen, 2017). In summary, the methodology followed these steps:

- Selecting the best cases from the European Company Survey
- Conducting a case study of each company using face-to-face interviews with managers, (a group of) employees and employee representatives
- Writing 51 mini-case study reports based on a qualitative and quantitative analysis of WPI practices
- Recoding the main variables that explain the presence of WPI practices and performing a qualitative comparative analysis (QCA) to assess patterns of strategies that companies are using

In this chapter, we will present the main findings of the Eurofound study in a different order than that of the original report. No new analyses were performed. We will discuss:

- The company strategies behind WPI practices based on the QCA analysis
- Examples of WPI practices provided by the case study data
- The motives of companies to apply WPI practices
- The implementation process of WPI in the companies
- Three examples of the implementation process of WPI

The chapter closes with conclusions, points of discussion and practical pointers.

Data Analysis and Results

Strategies of Companies Using WPI: QCA Analysis

The Eurofound study showed that organisations that applied WPI could be characterised by patterns of related variables, which can be regarded as implicit strategies employed by these companies. The research showed the emergence of three sets of factors, namely, the structure of the company, cultural elements of workplace practices and the process to motivate employees during the implementation. Before we explain this, we must introduce the research model (Fig. 11.1). Figure 11.1 shows the elements under research, the so-called conditions, that could contribute to the outcome, substantial WPI. The term 'substantial' stands for performing relatively well in terms of WPI. 'Performing well' mimics the fact that these companies score highly on

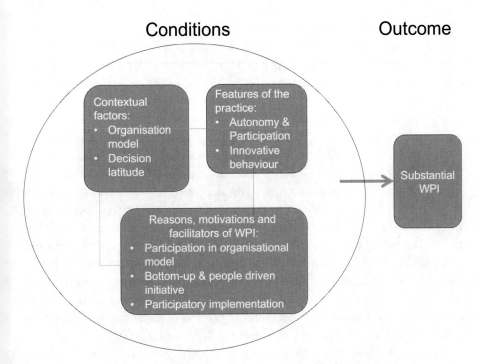

Fig. 11.1   Conditions that enable WPI (Oeij et al., 2015, p. 29)

a set of variables that together constitute a WPI index (see Oeij et al., 2015). About half of the cases were marked as substantial WPI. In each of the companies, we assessed the 'WPI practices'. These WPI practices could be related to structural (re)design of the organisation and jobs or resemble HR-related measures that improve the deployment of employees. The structural measures are regarded as a causal influence on the performance of both the organisation and the employees, whether or not the HR-related measures are directed at productive and healthy behaviours of employees without changing the structural conditions. Therefore, the first type of practices is 'structural' and the second type 'cultural'; in other words, root causes of better performance and symptomatic stimulators of desired behaviour. Reducing workloads by reorganising the production process is an example of a structural measure and a stress management programme of a cultural measure.

The study investigated (1) 'features of (WPI) practices', that is, the degree to which practices that were implemented stimulated autonomy and participation of employees and innovative behaviour of employees; (2) 'contextual factors', such as the degree of hierarchy of the organisational model and the decision latitude of the company to freely choose its own WPI practices; and (3) 'reasons, motivations and facilitators of WPI', namely, the degree to which employees participate in moulding the organisational model, whether WPI practices were developed bottom-up and people-driven and if employees played a role in the participatory implementation of WPI practices.

The structure elements in Fig. 11.1 are linked to decision latitude, the organisational model, participation to co-decide in the organisational model and autonomy and participation. The cultural elements are connected to innovative behaviour, bottom-up and people-driven initiative and participatory implementation. Box 11.1 describes the seven 'conditional' variables.

In the study, we analysed whether the companies used combinations of these seven variables that associate with 'substantial WPI' and that could be understood as an implicit strategy. For this purpose, we used a technique called fuzzy set qualitative comparative analysis (fsQCA) that supports finding patterns, and we distilled five 'strategic' patterns or paths that are used by those companies that could be assessed as successful workplace innovators. The fsQCA in Table 11.1 shows these five paths that altogether explain half of the cases with a high level of consistency (81.1%). Consistency indicates to what degree cases are in line with the assumed theoretical conditions reflected in the factors of Fig. 11.1. The remaining cases have paths that are not consistent enough and score lower as 'substantial WPI' companies.

Table 11.1 shows five paths in the first column. For each of the five paths, a black dot, '●', indicates the relevance of a variable for that specific path or

Box 11.1 Conditional Variables

- Structure

  - Decision latitude of the organisation: the company has a certain degree of freedom to introduce self-chosen WPI practices. (DECLAT)
  - Organisation model: this mirrors a preference for limited or significant division of labour. (ORGMOD)

- Culture

  - Innovative behaviour of employees: employees perform in such a way that initiatives are taken, knowledge is shared, processes are improved, and new information is sought, or they are supported to do so. (INNOBEH)
  - Autonomy and participation: employees can decide in their jobs and share tasks (in teams); at the same time, there is open communication and much participation. (AUTPAR)

- (Process of) adoption and implementation

  - Participation in organisational model: participation in decisions about the organisational model. It reflects the participatory role in organisational design of middle management and first-line workers. (PARTMOD)
  - Bottom-up and people-driven initiative: whether the initiative for WPI is bottom-up and people driven. The initiative can be either bottom-up or top-down, and it can either be people driven by intrinsic arguments to improve the situation of employees or organisation driven by extrinsic arguments, namely, to account for business and market circumstances. (BOTUPIN)
  - Participatory implementation: the presence of a control orientation during the implementation process. It informs whether WPI is implemented participatorily and supported by employees. Implementation can be participative/participatory or top-down, and the change process for the WPI practices can be characterised by more or less support from employees. (CONOR)

pattern; the sign 'O' indicates that the variable must not be present in the pattern, while a blank space (empty position) points to the irrelevance of a variable.

The results show varying patterns that all lead to 'substantial WPI'. These paths, however, are not mutually exclusive for the outcome. In other words, different combinations can lead to the same results; therefore, different roads 'lead to Rome'. The paths or patterns are interpreted as follows:

Table 11.1 Configurations explaining substantial workplace innovation (WPI) (parsimonious solution)

Path (or configurations)	Causal conditions							Consistency, %
	ORGMOD	DECLAT	INNOBEH	AUTPAR	PARTMOD	BOTUPIN	CONOR	
1—Top-guided WPI						○	●	84.1
2—Autonomy-driven WPI	○	●						83.5
3—Integral WPI	●	●	●	●	●	●		83.7
4—Employee-driven WPI		●	●		●	●	●	82.7
5—Innovative behavioural-driven WPI	●		●		○			68.6
	Contextual factors		Feature of WPI		Adoption and implementation aspects			

Source: Oeij et al., 2015

"●"—causal condition is present, "○"—causal condition is absent

Model consistency is 0.811 (81.1%)

- 'Top-guided WPI' states that 84% of the companies with the characteristics, in conjunction, of innovative behaviour, the absence of bottom-up initiatives (i.e., the presence of top-down initiatives), and a participatory implementation process are high-scoring WPI companies.
- 'Autonomy-driven WPI' states that 83% of the companies with four characteristics in conjunction are high-scoring WPI companies, namely, those in which employees participated in developing the organisation's model, employees have job autonomy in combination with employee participation; the organisation itself has decision latitude to make its own choices; and the organisation is not featured by a preference for limiting the division of labour.
- 'Integral WPI' states that 84% of the companies with four characteristics in conjunction are high-scoring WPI companies, namely, those in which employees show innovative behaviour, the implementation process is a bottom-up initiative, the organisation itself has decision latitude to make its own choices; and the organisation is featured by a preference for limiting the division of labour.
- 'Employee-driven WPI' states that 83% of the companies with the characteristics, in conjunction, of employee participation in developing the organisation's model, an implementation process that is a bottom-up initiative, a participatory implementation process, and an organisation that itself has decision latitude to make its own choices are high-scoring WPI companies.
- 'Innovative behavioural-driven WPI' states that 68% of the companies with three characteristics in conjunction are high-scoring WPI companies, namely, those where employees have not participated in developing the organisation's model, where employees show innovative behaviour and where the organisation is featured by a preference for limiting the division of labour.

These results indicate that the implemented practices are varied and that every company gives its own twist to specific 'structural' or 'cultural' measures. There is not 'one best way of organising'.

Examples of WPI Practices

WPI practices are measures that companies have implemented to improve their performance, deploy personnel, or a combination of both. Companies can undertake all kinds of measures to support their goals. In the studied 51 cases, we found that companies have implemented a variety of measures, often more than one. Overall, we counted 168 different measures, of which 14% were targeted at improving the quality of the organisational performance, 18% at improving the quality of work and 69% at both goals simultaneously. In a next step, we looked at those measures from the viewpoint of whether they had a focus on the structure of the organisation and jobs, on the culture and behaviour of organisation members, or on something else. We analysed and distributed the measures into five categories: measures focusing on (1) WPI structure (14%), (2) WPI culture (20%), (3) a mix of WPI structure and culture (19%), (4) traditional HR (39%) and (5) a miscellaneous category of 'other' (8%) (Oeij et al., 2015, p. 21). Half of these practices (53%) are thus focused on WPI. A rather high proportion of identified practices were assessed as being exclusively HR practices, which are 'typical' or 'traditional' HR practices in the fields of, among others, personnel recruitment, training, competence development, performance appraisal, working conditions, remuneration, flexibility and health and risk and safety measures. The category 'other' consists of practices such as cost-effectiveness, efficiency improvement and ICT practices that also do not qualify as WPI. Some examples (Oeij et al., 2015) are given in Table 11.2 to provide an idea of what counts for WPI measures.

Motives for the Implementation of WPI Practices

Although companies did choose varying paths to WPI and selected different (combinations of) WPI practices, their reasons for initiating WPI reflect much commonality. Moreover, in each company, we interviewed managers, employees and employee representatives, and they all gave similar answers (Oeij et al., 2015, p. 27). For example, when asked what the main reason was to introduce WPI practices for the 'organisation as a whole', all three groups prioritised to 'improve efficiency', 'gain competitive advantage' and 'enhance innovative capability'. In a similar vein, when asked to give the main reason to introduce WPI practices from 'the managers' and employees' perspective', all three groups prioritised 'economic and business goals', 'learning and development opportunities' and 'performance'. Apart from these motives, we asked the three groups what they see as the most important leverage factors that drive the successful implementation of WPI practices. They answered 'employee involvement', 'top management commitment' and 'leadership or the involvement of a powerful person'. Again, this was reported by all three groups in similar order.

Table 11.2   Types of WPI practices

WPI: Structure orientation

- In an educational organisation, self-managing teams were introduced as a system for organising day-to-day duties and activities. This approach ensures that the team members have sufficient flexibility to decide how to implement their tasks taking into account their own capacities and time schedules.
- In a research organisation, the minimising of organisational levels and, thus, the enhancing of autonomous teams is done by ensuring that there are no more than two hierarchical levels between the lowest and the highest levels. This facilitates self-managed working teams to gain the freedom to organise themselves.
- A news and journalism organisation created job enlargement by expanding the sales jobs with account management tasks, thereby giving employees more autonomy; cross-functional teams were installed to realise innovation projects across departments, thus allowing employees a voice in organisational renewal.

WPI: Culture orientation

- A museum developed a partnership with unions. New projects and organisational changes are debated in a joint committee with union representatives, OSHA representatives and management representatives. This committee is initiating new practices such as training and support for new employees.
- An energy company introduced a 'knowledge management system' which is a voluntarily developed IT-based information sharing system. All employees can share and gain new knowledge via this system.
- A postal organisation installed 'Loyalty Day', which aims to enhance communication and knowledge sharing between managers and first-line workers. Managers voluntarily visit workers at their work site and gather information about specific processes and possible issues. Loyalty Day increases sustainability, efficiency and good organisational communication.

WPI: Mixed

- A research organisation introduced flexitime practices that allow workers to have a say regarding their working times: they can adjust their starting and exiting hours, and ad-hoc exits (with manager's permission) are also allowed.
- A financial service company implemented a special initiative for personal development: every year teams of 1–2 people take part in a challenge defined by the top management. New ideas can thus be passed from young talents to the top. Young talents are supported by coaching sessions and assessment tools. They gain a very useful experience.
- A pet food processor puts a focus on the development of 'overall competences' to improve employability of employees. An overall qualification/training was given to the production staff, enabling these employees to take over every job in the production line. After the mechanisation of certain parts of the production, most of the employees had the chance to upskill themselves and be able to take over a skilled workers' task.

The dominant view from these interviews is that reasons and motives to start WPI often point to business-related arguments but that employee involvement seems a sine qua non when it comes to adoption and implementation. During the interviews, it seemed clear that many companies understand that achieving economic goals largely depends on the good involvement of employees. This is perhaps not really a surprise because when we asked the three groups what the impacts of WPI practices were, they said that it would improve employee engagement and longer-term sustainability for the organisation (Oeij et al., 2015, pp. 28–29).

Sometimes there are problems underneath these motives, such as a situation of crisis or company performance difficulties that require significant changes to survive, or a take-over from (or merger with) another (multinational) company that brings in new forms of work organisation and new work practices, systems, etc. that involve WPI. In several of the Eastern European case studies, the privatisation of public enterprises and the associated reorganisation processes served as a background to the implementation of WPI that resulted in greater efficiency and employee involvement that were previously lacking.

In sum, the three different respondent groups tended to largely agree with each other. They found that economic goals are triggering the initiation of WPI and that employee involvement is a key factor in the introduction of WPI. Hence, in many instances, the *process* of introducing WPI practices tends to improve not only economic performance but also employee engagement and the quality of working life.

How Do Companies Implement WPI?

The process of initiation, adoption and implementation of WPI practices reveals a common pattern across companies. Our research suggests that it is often management that initiates WPI and that the main motive is economic. Once this decision has been taken, employees are involved to help design and implement the intervention. Moreover, consulting with employee representatives is common among those companies who advocate communication and employee interests. There are mature employment relationships that allow for open dialogue. The way that WPI practices get implemented reveals a generally applied pattern (Fig. 11.2):

1. The initiative of a WPI often has an economic purpose and very often this is dominant (see 1 in Fig. 11.2). However, in many cases, WPI practices are not solely targeted at economic goals. Often they are combined with or embedded in organisational, job and HR-related measures.

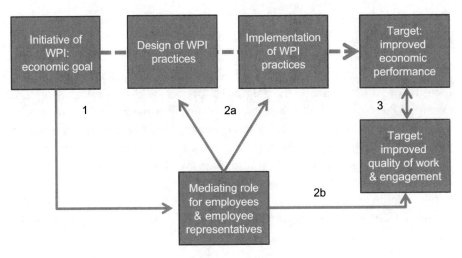

Fig. 11.2   Pattern of implementing WPI practices (Oeij et al., 2015, p. 59)

2. Once the WPI initiative has been refined into a measure or set of measures, employees (and often employee representatives) play an important role in co-designing and developing the WPI practice and its implementation (see 2a in Fig. 11.2). This happens because management tends to realise that it is impossible to implement WPI without the engagement of employees. Given that employee participation in the design and implementation phase is inextricably linked to employee engagement and possibly improved quality of working life, this can result in the achievement of employee-favourable targets (see 2b in Fig. 11.2).
3. The target of improved economic performance is often not only a direct effect of the implemented WPI practice but is, in most cases, also indirectly influenced by employees and employee representatives. When economic targets are achieved, they may well coincide with the targets of improved quality of working life and employee engagement. Vice versa, an improved quality of working life and employee engagement can contribute to improved economic targets (see 3 in Fig. 11.2).

It appears that (initial) reasons and motives to initiate WPI are mainly economic. In the next phase, concrete WPI practices are designed and implemented. Here, it becomes apparent that employees get to play a major role, especially because the most important leverage factor for adoption and implementation is employee involvement. Importantly, managers, employees and employee representatives seem to agree that employee engagement in the whole process is a necessary condition for WPI.

Three Company Examples of the WPI Implementation Process

We present three examples of WPI implementation from the United Kingdom, Denmark and Lithuania (Oeij et al., 2015, pp. 53–54). The United Kingdom example shows how leadership enables employee participation, while the Danish example mirrors a stepwise approach of management engaging in partnerships with unions. The Lithuanian case exemplifies the establishment of dialogue between management and employees, which is relatively new to the region. Although these examples are different in terms of the interplay between management, employees and their representatives, they are all similar in the sense that cooperation between actors is fundamental to improve the business.

Box 11.2   Examples of the WPI Implementation Process

United Kingdom example: Leadership in an energy company

'We want this to be a business where views are listened to and where communications are open and honest. We also want this to be a workplace where positive ideas are encouraged and where achievements are celebrated' says the Head of HR. The introduction of Open Forums replaced the previous company-wide meetings and suggestion schemes which had struggled to stimulate open and constructive dialogue and feedback. The CEO's open leadership creates trust and employees feel confident about the future. According to one employee: 'It is interesting isn't it, you go to the Open Forums and people will say what they think and absolutely nobody will turn round and go, I can't believe he said that … They might not agree with you but nobody will actually knock anyone for having a view because we are encouraged to have a view. That's really empowering I think.'

Danish example: Partnership with unions

Organisational changes are discussed by the manager and the union representatives. They have a partnership and value each other's opinions. The manager explains: 'It is nice to have representatives who are not afraid to step up against me in a constructive dialogue'. The implementation approach consisted of (1) management took initiative, (2) external consultants supported the process, (3) experiments were conducted (a work team tested new meeting practices or the like), (4) 'invitation' to the same knowledge for all training and (5) implementation of the practices, but not necessarily in the same way everywhere. Both management and employees believe that it is important to design the process in a manner that creates 'enthusiasts' amongst the employees. The union representative explains: 'It gives a huge boost to the company that we work together to create a great workplace. … That's what made us "the best workplace" (a Danish award)'. The employees believe that, even though the management determines the direction, they have to have the trust to be able to discuss it: 'It should be perfectly legal to say our outspoken opinion to our manager—and it is. There may well be disagreement, but you have to be able to discuss things' (employee).

Lithuanian example: Dialogue with personnel

The WPI practice 'Think Guest Feedback' consists of regular middle management meetings where middle managers from all departments (Front Office, Reservations, Conference Hall, Lobby, Restaurant, Sky Restaurant, Room Service, Marketing and others) regularly meet and review hotel ratings on dedicated social media platforms. They discuss particular guest feedback cases and joint actions that could improve guest stay experiences (and feedback as a result), brainstorm on how guest feedback could be stimulated and collectively addressed, take important information back to the teams of their departments for further action, produce minutes of their observations and recommendations to top management on improvement of various hotel operational aspects and share experiences with each other. Think Guest Feedback involves, for example, prompt reaction to guest feedback (especially when negative) before they leave the hotel and constant organisational learning from any mistakes made. It implies staff empowerment not only in the sense that they could solve emerging problems straight away but also that each of them could feel like owners of the business and be pro-active in preventing negative guest experiences.

Conclusion and Discussion

Conclusions

At the outset, we formulated three questions. Why do companies apply WPI and do they use different strategies? How do these companies implement WPI interventions and provide employees a role in that process? What types of WPI interventions are being implemented, and what are the (expected) effects of such interventions?

The initiative to start WPI practices usually comes from management, and their reasons to start applying WPI are mostly economic. However, these managers understand that the involvement and participation of employees and employee representatives is crucial for WPI to be successful and to help them reach benefits in terms of company performance and sustainability. Typically, the reasons driving management's decision to implement WPI practices are related to efficiency, competitiveness and innovation enhancement. The objective of WPI introduction is not to merely improve the working conditions or the working environment as such, but that, in order to enhance employee involvement and their contribution to the company's performance and innovation processes, to recognise that a good set of working conditions is required. Thus, WPI is a means, not a goal.

The companies in our sample used five different paths or strategies to become WPI mature organisations, meaning they applied different combinations of WPI practices and stressed different organisational choices. Although companies differ in their implementation strategies, constructive cooperation between management and employees seems to be a key factor for successful WPI, as our three case descriptions imply. We conclude that these five paths are an empirical reduction of the theoretical 128 possibilities within our dataset of 51 cases (remember there are 7 variables that could explain the outcome 'substantial WPI', thus $7^2 = 128$ possible combinations of variables). Additionally, the way that WPI practices are implemented seems to reveal a general pattern of management-employee (representatives) cooperation across companies (Fig. 11.2). A relevant remark is that the companies themselves do not speak in terms of WPI, as they do not use such abstract words. They speak of these practices as measures that are both 'good for the company and the employees'.

Pointers for Practice

We started the chapter with the assertion that WPI shows promise for companies, but that few companies follow this path. To change this situation, it is insufficient to merely develop more methodologies for companies. Learning from the practice of WPI practitioners is needed. If practitioners intend to develop and implement WPI practices to improve organisational performance and quality of work, particular attention should be given to the following considerations:

- WPI is not a goal in itself; it is a means to achieve better performance and jobs as desired outcomes.
- WPI is not 'just an HR thing'. Balancing the implementation of organisational, technological or business model renewal with desired outcomes requires a 'systems approach' to understand how outcomes can be traced back to root causes (MacDuffie, 1997). In our view (Oeij, Rus, & Pot, 2017), designing WPI interventions connects strategic, structural and cultural choices (as in sociotechnical systems theory and its newer branch modern sociotechnics, De Sitter et al., 1997).
- Today's world of work is a knowledge-based economy in which the successful mobilisation and deployment of good staff depends on employers successfully meeting employee wishes for challenging jobs. The jobs that attract most employees are those in which they can develop their skills and

apply their talents. Such jobs allow for job autonomy, learning opportunities, balancing the workload with work risks and the work-life relationship (De Sitter et al., 1997; Karasek Jr., 1979).

- The process of developing and implementing WPI practices clearly benefits from 'democratic dialogue' (Ennals, 2018) and a humanised view on employment relations, as this study has shown. Mature employment relations are like social relations in which members of the working community care for one another's health and well-being (Herriot, 2001).

Discussion and Themes for Further Research

This contribution is part of the book's theme of 'Innovation as a Process'. WPI is a throughput variable in the input-throughput-output model because we see WPI as a means that affects the output. Throughput is equivalent to the transformation process (i.e., the production process), and WPI measures are actions taken to intervene in the transformation process for the purpose of influencing the outputs (Achterbergh & Vriens, 2010, pp. 62–63). As such, WPI interventions are located at the organisational level and differ in this respect from WPI constructs that measure individual behaviour and its effects, as in Theme 4 'Workplace Innovation: Innovation as an Outcome'. In the 'workplace innovation scale', for example, WPI is viewed as a psychological construct that is context specific. The scale intends to identify and measure the behavioural aspects of innovation practices by individuals in their workplace and is comprised of the four dimensions of organisational innovation, innovation climate, individual innovation and team innovation (see, e.g., the 'workplace innovation scale' of McMurray, Islam, Sarros & Pirola-Merlo, 2013, and elsewhere in this book). Here innovative behaviours of persons are affected by, for example, leadership and organisational climate. Perhaps future research undertakings could develop a multilevel approach to WPI that combines organisational-level variables with individual-level variables.

Another relevant question for further research could be: Which WPI practices improve both company performance and quality of working life; how can such practices be co-developed between management and employees; what organisational conditions favour employee engagement; and which individual characteristics enable employee behaviour to contribute to innovations and make them easier to adopt? Since WPI is a means and not a goal, research could focus on its mediating and moderating role between strategic choices and the desired effects of interventions in study designs. We assume such studies may lay bare that structural aspects prove to be more substantial and significant than cultural aspects.

With these insights, we assume that policymakers, (applied) researchers and companies will better understand and implement WPI strategies for the benefit of both companies and their workers.

Acknowledgement This chapter is based on the study 'Workplace innovation in European companies' (Oeij et al., 2015). Parts of this chapter were published elsewhere. The authors and publisher gratefully acknowledge the following permission to use the material in this book:

Oeij, P., Dhondt, S., Žiauberytė-Jakštienė, R., Corral, A., & Preenen, P. (2017). Implementing Workplace Innovation: Why, How and What. In P. R. A. Oeij, D. Rus, & F. D. Pot (Eds.), *Workplace Innovation: Theory, Research and Practice* (Aligning Perspectives on Health, Safety and Well-Being) (pp. 149–170). Cham (Switzerland): Springer; Oeij, P., Dhondt, S., Žiauberytė-Jakštienė, R., Corral, A., & Preenen, P. (2017). Implementing Workplace Innovation Across Europe: Why, How and What? *EWOP in Practice, Special Issue on Workplace Innovation (1)*, 46–60; Oeij, P., Dhondt, S., Žiauberytė-Jakštienė, R., Corral, A., & Totterdill, P. (2016). Implementing Workplace Innovation Across Europe: Why, How and What? *Economic and Social Changes: Facts, Trends, Forecast, 5*(47), 195–218; Howaldt, J., Oeij, P. R. A., Dhondt, S., & Fruytier, B. (2016). Workplace Innovation and Social Innovation: An Introduction. *World Review of Entrepreneurship, Management and Sustainable Development, 12*(1), 1–12.

We thank our research partners of the Eurofound study: IKEI Research & Consultancy (Spain), Workplace Innovation Limited (United Kingdom), ARC Consulting EOOD (Bulgaria), Centre for Working Life Research, Roskilde University (Denmark), Gesellschaft für Empirische Arbeitsforschung und Beratung, GEA (Germany), Institute for Modelling and Analysis of Public Policies, IMAPP (Poland), Mykolas Romeris University (Lithuania), University of Piraeus Research Centre (UPRC) (Greece).

References

Achterbergh, J., & Vriens, D. (2010). *Organizations. Social systems conducting experiments.* (2nd ed.; 1st ed. 2009). Berlin: Springer.

Appelbaum, E., Bailey, T., Berg, P., & Kalleberg, A. L. (2000). *Manufacturing Advantage. Why High-Performance Work Systems Pay Off.* Ithaca, NY: Cornell University Press.

Bloom, N., & van Reenen, J. (2010). Why Do Management Practices Differ Across Firms and Countries? *Journal of Economic Perspectives, 24*(1), 203–224.

Boxall, P. (2012). High-Performance Work Systems: What, Why, How and for Whom? *Asia Pacific Journal of Human Resources, 50,* 169–186.

Boxall, P., & Macky, K. (2009). Research and Theory on High-Performance Work Systems: Progressing the High-Involvement Stream. *Human Resource Management Journal, 19,* 3–23.

Chandler, A. D. (1962). *Strategy and Structure: Chapters in the History of American Industrial Enterprises.* Boston, MA: MIT Press.

Cummings, T. G., & Srivastva, S. (1977). *Management of Work: A Sociotechnical Systems Approach.* Kent, OH: Kent State University Press.

De Sitter, L. U., Den Hertog, J. F., & Dankbaar, B. (1997). From Complex Organisations with Simple Jobs to Simple Organisations with Complex Jobs. *Human Relations, 50*(5), 497–534.

Dhondt, S., & van Hootegem, G. (2015). Reshaping Workplaces: Workplace Innovation as Designed by Scientists and Practitioners. *European Journal of Workplace Innovation, 1*(1), 17–25.

Dhondt, S., Vermeerbergen, L., & van Hootegem, G. (2017). Evidence of Workplace Innovation from Organisational and Economic Studies. In P. R. A. Oeij, D. Rus, & F. D. Pot (Eds.), *Workplace Innovation: Theory, Research and Practice* (Aligning Perspectives on Health, Safety and Well-Being) (pp. 63–78). Cham (Switzerland): Springer.

Ennals, R. (2018). Democratic Dialogue and Development: An Intellectual Obituary of Björn Gustavsen. *European Journal of Workplace Innovation, 4*(1), 11–26.

Herrick, N. Q., & Maccoby, M. (1975). Humanizing Work: A Priority Goal of the 1970's. In L. E. Davis & A. B. Cherns (Eds.), *The Quality of Working Wife. I* (pp. 64–66). New York, NY: Free Press.

Herriot, P. (2001). *The Employment Relationship: A Psychological Perspective.* Routledge: Hove.

Howaldt, J., Oeij, P. R. A., Dhondt, S., & Fruytier, B. (2016). Workplace Innovation and Social Innovation: An Introduction. *World Review of Entrepreneurship, Management and Sustainable Development, 12*(1), 1–12.

Høyrup, S. (2012). Employee-Driven Innovation: A New Phenomenon, Concept and Mode of Innovation. In S. Høyrup, C. Hasse, M. Bonnafous-Boucher,

K. Møller, & M. Lotz (Eds.), *Employee Driven Innovation: A New Approach* (pp. 3–33). New York, NY: Palgrave Macmillan.

Huselid, M. A. (1995). The Impact of Human Resource Management Practices on Turnover, Productivity, and Corporate Financial Performance. *Academy of Management Journal, 38*(3), 635–672.

Karanika-Murray, M., & Oeij, P. R. A. (2017). The Role of Work and Organisational Psychology for Workplace Innovation Practice: From Short-Sightedness to Eagle View? In *European Work and Organisational Psychology in Practice* (Special Issue on Workplace Innovation) (Vol. 1, pp. 19–30).

Karasek Jr., R. A. (1979). Job Demands, Job Decision Latitude, and Mental Strain: Implications for Job Redesign. *Administrative Science Quarterly, 24*(2), 285–308. https://www.jstor.org/stable/2392498

MacDuffie, J. P. (1997). The Road to "Root Cause": Shop-Floor Problem-Solving at Three Auto Assembly Plants. *Management Science, 43*(4), 479–502.

McMurray, A., Islam, M. M., Sarros, J. C., & Pirola-Merlo, A. (2013). Workplace Innovation in a Nonprofit Organization. *Nonprofit Management & Leadership, 23*(3), 367–388.

Mintzberg, H., Ahlstrand, B., & Lampel, J. (1998). *Strategy Safari. The Complete Guide Through the Wilds of Strategic Management.* London: Prentice-Hall.

Oeij, P., Dhondt, S., Žiauberytė-Jakštienė, R., Corral, A., & Preenen, P. (2017). Implementing Workplace Innovation: Why, How and What. In P. R. A. Oeij, D. Rus, & F. D. Pot (Eds.), *Workplace Innovation: Theory, Research and Practice* (Aligning Perspectives on Health, Safety and Well-Being) (pp. 149–170). Cham (Switzerland): Springer.

Oeij, P. R. A., & Dhondt, S. (2017). Theoretical Approaches Supporting Workplace Innovation. In P. R. A. Oeij, D. Rus, & F. D. Pot (Eds.), *Workplace Innovation: Theory, Research and Practice* (Aligning Perspectives on Health, Safety and Well-Being) (pp. 63–78). Cham (Switzerland): Springer.

Oeij, P. R. A., Rus, D., & Pot, F. D. (Eds.). (2017). *Workplace Innovation: Theory, Research and Practice* (Aligning Perspectives on Health, Safety and Well-Being). Cham (Switzerland): Springer.

Oeij, P. R. A., Žiauberytė-Jakštienė, R., Dhondt, S., Corral, A., Totterdill, P., & Preenen, P. T. Y. (2015). *Workplace Innovation in European Companies.* Study Commissioned by Eurofound. Luxemburg: Office for Official Publications of the European Communities.

Osterman, P. (2018). In Search of the High Road: Meaning and Evidence. *ILR Review, 71*(1), 3–34.

Pot, F. D. (2011). Workplace Innovation for Better Jobs and Performance. *International Journal of Productivity and Performance Management, 60*(4), 404–415.

Preenen, P. T. Y., Oeij, P. R. A., Dhondt, S., Kraan, K. O., & Jansen, E. (2016). Job Autonomy Matters for Young Companies' Performance Growth. *World Review of Entrepreneurship Management and Sustainable Development, 12*(1), 74–100.

Putnik, K., Oeij, P., van der Torre, W., de Vroome, E., & Dhondt, S. (2019). Innovation Adoption of Employees in Logistics: Individual and Organisational Factors Related to the Actual Use of Innovation. *International Journal of Technology Transfer and Commercialisation, 16*(3), 251–267.

Smith, N. H. (2017). Arendt's Anti-Humanism of Labour. *European Journal of Social Theory, 22*(2), 175–190. https://doi.org/10.1177/1368431017746326

Totterdill, P., & Exton, R. (2014). Defining Workplace Innovation: The Fifth Element. *Strategic Direction, 30*(9), 12–16.

Trist, E., & Murray, H. (1993). *The Social Engagement of Social Science: A Tavistock Anthology*. Philadelphia, PA: University of Pennsylvania Press.

Womack, J. P., & Jones, D. T. (2003). *Lean Thinking: Banish Waste and Create Wealth in Your Corporation* (2nd ed.). New York, NY: The Free Press.

12

Innovation Trajectories: When to Open and Close the Innovation Process

Shantam Shukla and Shashwat Shukla

Introduction

> With the Rise Prize, the Mahindra Group wants to provoke big disruptive ideas that can dramatically change lives. We are offering a big incentive for fresh thinking among the new generation of innovators in our country. ~ Anand Mahindra on "Rise Prize"[1]

On 27 February, 2014, Mahindra Group announced India's biggest innovation prize—the "Rise Prize" which offered USD 1 million to solve the Mobility Challenge, which invites solutions for driverless cars in India, and the second Solar Challenge which aims to make solar energy products more accessible to the population at large. This was one of the first large open innovation efforts by Mahindra and Mahindra (M&M), a leading automobile manufacturer in the Indian automobile industry. In the past, innovations at M&M were developed either internally or through selective practice of openness, where M&M would build an alliance with the leading solution

---

[1] Mahindra challenges India to drive disruptive innovation. (2014). *Mahindra and Mahindra*. Retrieved from http://www.mahindra.com/News/Press-Releases/1393504217

S. Shukla (✉)
Indian Institute of Management, Ahmedabad, Gujarat, India
e-mail: shantams@iima.ac.in

S. Shukla
University of Allahabad, Allahabad, Gujarat, India

providers from the developed world. However, with the announcement of the Rise Award, M&M has attempted a new approach to innovation development, which is open to all. This, however, does not mean that M&M is open for all innovation projects in its organization. There are still innovation projects for which it is close or opens selectively to few individuals. For instance, it was reported that Mahindra and Mahindra, along with Samsung SDI, ZF, and Continental, was developing the world's first hybrid technology that can be deployed in vehicles with manual transmission and can enhance fuel efficiency by almost 20%. Also, there are developments where the internal teams at Mahindra and Mahindra have launched new innovative products through their own internal ingenuity. This variance in approach suggests that openness across innovation process is a strategic choice of the organization where engagement with external members of an organization varies across different innovation projects. This study explores the factors that influence the strategic choice of organizations to open or keep closed their innovation project for participation from agents external to the organization. The development path through the innovation process which results from the organization's choices are referred to as "innovation trajectory" in this study.

Theoretical Background

Research in the last couple of decades has shown that organization innovation performance can improve if they engage with economic and social actors outside the organization boundary. Though this has been the focus of popular management literature related to "open innovation" in last decade (Chesbrough, 2003), the practice of engaging with outside actors has also been documented in academic literature on user-led innovations (Hippel, 1988), innovations at the margins of society (Gupta, 1987, 1999), and open communities of practice (Foray & Perez, 2006).

Lakhani, Jeppesen, Lohse, and Panetta (2007) have shown that openness in innovation leads to better results than closed development of innovations. In a study on scientific problem-solving, the research showed that openness led to over 1/3rd more success in finding solutions to problems than a closed approach. Co-development and sharing of information during execution and development have been found to improve value proposition of the development (Allen, 1983) while also limiting organization exposure to risk and uncertainty (Eisenhardt & Schoonhoven, 1996; Podolny, 1994). Open approach to development has also been found to rationalize costs of development (Hagedorn, Linl, & Vorontas, 2000). In fact, research suggests that openness can assist organization innovation efforts across the innovation cycle, starting with securing better ideas for new developments (Dahlander & Frederiksen, 2011; Salter, ter Wal, Criscuolo, & Alexy, 2012) or improving speed in development during product development phase (Rothaermel & Deeds, 2004) or even improving product adoption in later stages (West, 2003).

Additionally, openness in organization's innovation process can also lead to positive spillover in society. The impact of openness in innovation process can result in a positive sum game benefitting several members of the ecosystem and not just the business organization. Arguing from an economic stand point, Foray, Thoron, and Zimmermann (2007) suggest that openness supports the objective of welfare with no monopoly distortions and spillovers, which do not reduce but increase innovator's incentives. An important social initiative in India, the Honey Bee Network, has documented over 200,000 ideas, innovations, and traditional knowledge practices in a database. The platform encourage free and open sharing among users highlighting that not only a large number of innovations emerge outside the formal economy and boundaries of traditional organizations, but the practice of free revealing of innovations is also a widely practiced.

Research Perspective on Factors Influencing Decision to Open

For all the benefits of "open" approach to innovation, there exists the practice of "close" innovation as well. The focus on internal process and the need for internalization typifies the "closed" approach of innovation development. The fundamental arguments by scholars for having a "closed" innovation process are related to theories of competitive advantage, resulting from proprietary knowledge (Porter, 1980); high transaction costs in coordinating innovation activity (Kogut & Zander, 1992); and concerns regarding appropriating rent from innovative developments. Several researchers have explored closed innovation practices like secrecy, patent protection, being first to market, and availability of strategic resources as a mean to increase appropriability (Ceccagnoli, 2009; Cohen, Nelson, & Walsh, 2000).

Though we have alternate opinions on the practice of open and close approach to innovation development, there is limited research of the antecedents that influence the decision to open or close the innovation development in an organization (West & Bogers, 2014). The few limited studies have looked at organization level factors such as culture (Herzog, 2011; Van der

Meer, 2007) and absorptive capacity (Cohen & Levinthal, 1990; King & Lakhani, 2011; Rothaermel & Alexandre, 2009). Though we have evidences of open practices of innovation from diverse industries like high-tech industries (Chesbrough, 2003; Kirschbaum, 2005), mature industries (Chiaroni, Chiesa, & Frattini, 2010), or SMEs (Van De Vrande, De Jong, & Vanhaverbeke, 2009), we still do not have an integrated framework to understand factors influencing openness. Afuah and Tucci (2012) and Drechsler and Natter (2012) are some notable exceptions who have attempted to broaden the scope of antecedent for open innovation practice.

A critical challenge with most of these studies is that they have explored openness at the organization level, whereas in practice the choice to open or close is made at the project level, as organizations open for some projects and close for others. Further most of these studies do not make a distinction between different levels of openness; as a result factors that influence limited openness like in the case of alliances and completely open practices are not well received. To enhance our understanding of these variances in open and close innovation practices which lead to different innovation trajectories, we explored five eclectic cases with differing patterns of openness. This chapter highlights our learning from one of the first studies which looks at the openness in innovation development not at organization level but at the innovation process level and also identifies different levels of openness.

Emergence of Innovation Trajectories for Development

As discussed "innovation trajectory" reflects the diversity in choices to open across the innovation process. The five cases of innovation development in this study highlight the variance in "innovation trajectory" resulting from the organization response to two critical questions: (1) "Where to open?" (What activities/innovation stage to collaborate upon?) and (2) "How much to open?" (i.e. level of openness).

Where to Open: Innovation Process

Innovation is an evolutionary process where an idea evolves through several stages to realize into a physical product or service. The innovation management literature has discussed innovation development in organizations as a linear model where the development proceeds from one stage to another

(Cooper, 2008; Hansen & Birkinshaw, 2007). According to these research studies, "innovation process can be visualized as a series of stages" (Cooper, 2008). Rothwell and Zegweld (1985) consider innovation model as "…a logically sequential, though not necessarily continuous process, that can be divided into a series of functionally distinct but interacting and interdependent stages". There exists an alternate view in practice as well as research, which argues that innovation process is not linear but consists of multiple feedback loops and recursive processes between the stages and also a great role of serendipity which makes it difficult to categorize innovation as a simple linear process (Kline, 1985; Rosenberg & Nelson, 1994).

It is important to highlight that both approaches consider innovation as a set of activities with differing opinions on the timing and sequence of these steps. For this study we take the simplistic three stages of process categorization discussed by Tushman (1977) and Hansen and Birkinshaw (2007) to suggest that innovation process largely comprises of three stages, namely, ideation, execution, and value capture. The three categories are like classes, which contain different activities as part of the innovation process. Idea stage identified as the first stage of any innovation development task is related to the search for new directions, solutions, suggestions, etc. Execution stage relates to experiments, research and development, development of prototypes, testing, and manufacturing which focuses on the conversion of intangible inputs received in idea stage into tangible final products, ready for delivering to the market. The critical difference between activities in idea and execution stage is the level of investment in the development process. Whereas in idea stage the organization makes limited investment in the form of money, manpower, and physical resources, execution stage requires investment to realize ideas into the final product. Unlike the earlier studies which have considered the final stage as diffusion of innovation, we expand the activity set and call it as "value capture stage". The value capture stage contains activities related to diffusion of innovation such as marketing, licensing, and promotion as well as open sharing of development as observed in recent years.

How Much to Open: Levels of Openness

Working with external members is a necessary but not sufficient condition to identify a task as open. A critical challenge with earlier studies on openness has been that they have classified any attempt to work with external members as open innovation. Thus, they have considered openness as a binary where no outside association is a close approach to innovation and even one outside interaction is an open innovation approach. Such an analysis fails to distinguish between practices such as alliances or networks in which an organization has discretion to select its partners and open source developments. Where alliances are like quasi arrangements which provide organization's flexibility to choose their partners, open practices such as those observed in Procter and Gamble's (P&G's) Connect and Develop program or open source development of Linux are examples where anyone can participate in the process. The decision to be selective open or all open is an important choice which has not received adequate attention.

In our classification, the highest level of openness, i.e. "open innovation", is when the organization is not selective about the external members who could participate in the process. We argue that the different levels of openness depend on the opportunity for external members to participate in the organization's innovation process and can be ascertained through simply answering "whether the opportunity for outside actors to engage in organization's internal process is restricted or not". Using the suggested approach to classify levels of openness, we can say that organizations which do not open out are closed; when organizations open selectively to particular members outside the organization, it is a semi-open approach; and when any and every one can participate, i.e. open to all then, it is completely open.

Figure 12.1 shows the innovation trajectories undertaken in the five cases that form part of this research study and highlights the choice of different levels of openness across the innovation stages.

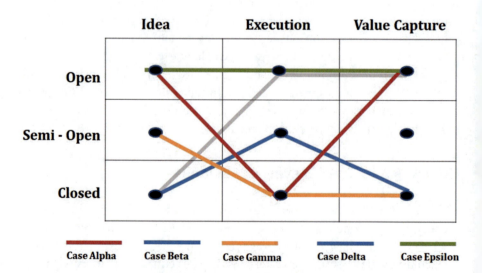

Fig. 12.1 Exploring openness across the innovation process

Methodology

The choices to open across the different stages of innovation process as discussed in the previous section lead to varied innovation trajectories which are highlighted in Fig. 12.1. To explore the factors that influence variation in innovation trajectories, we adopted a case-based methodology. Few prior studies have used survey-based research design to explore the nature of aspects like environment (Drechsler & Natter, 2012; Sofka & Grimpe, 2008), organization culture (Herzog, 2011), and absorptive capacity (De Faria, Lima, & Santos, 2010) on openness in innovation. Such an approach is limited by two major challenges which are measuring openness as just diversity of external sources and second, and more important, the inability of research to link openness to a specific project as data collection is largely at the organization level. Though there are a few qualitative studies such as Hughes and Wareham (2010) and Bogers (2011) where factors for openness have been explored at the organization level, we are not aware of any study on openness at the innovation process level which has been used in this study. Also, the levels of openness have not been explored in detail in existing literature. Though Keupp and Gassman (2009) argue for the level of openness in their research, they do not explore the relation of levels of openness across the innovation stages as attempted in this study.

Darke, Shanks, and Brodbent (1998) suggest that there are three main goals that lead to adopting case study as a method: to provide descriptions of phenomena, develop theory, and test theory. In our study we look to describe the diversity in developmental approaches for innovative products and develop theory as to the nature of openness practiced in each case study. We undertake purposive sampling to select projects in different organizations to fit categories of the open innovation, namely, close, semi-open, and open categories. By selecting specific cases for the study, one can ensure that significant aspects related to the context are covered (Huberman & Miles). Also, purpose sampling assisted in the selection of contrasting cases of openness in innovation process, which facilitated analysis by making certain processes "transparently observable" (Pettigrew, McKee, & Ferlie, 1988).

The primary objective during case selection was to ensure that cases reflect "open" and "close" activities along the innovation process. The study selected cases related to the development of new and innovative products only. The research is agnostic about the innovation content and the concerns regarding innovativeness of the new development. The study follows prior research definition for innovation according to which innovation is defined with respect to the team engaged in the activity, i.e. the individual or unit of adoption (Rogers, 1995; Zaltman, Duncan, & Holbeck, 1973). The objective of the study is to explore the internal and external factors that influence organization decision to "open" or "close" during their innovation process. The study assumes that as long as the organization considers their product as innovative, the research into their actions to "open" or "close" shall hopefully remain consistent.

The study documents five cases of innovative developments and provides description of their innovation processes for the study. Following purposive sampling approach, we engaged with cases where we had diversity across levels of openness in each stage of the innovation process. For instance, Case Alpha and Case Beta provide extreme choices at idea stage; similarly, Case Delta and Case Beta as well Case Epsilon provide diverse choices at execution stage and Case Epsilon and Case Beta as extreme choices in value capture stages. Such choice of cases provides us with discrete event analysis and an opportunity to understand the influence of factors for openness at each stage. Additionally, to control for industry variables and understand how industry variables may influence the results, we took three cases, namely, Case Alpha, Case Beta, and Case Epsilon, from the automotive sector. Case Gamma represents a slow-evolving industrial good firm, while Case Delta represents a fast-moving technology sector. Thus, through selective selection of cases for study, we ensure that the decision factors are adequately covered and discussed in this research. A brief detail of the innovation trajectories is highlighted in Fig. 12.1.

Data Analysis and Discussion

The organization environment and its ability to respond to the challenge of developing a new innovative product for the market shapes the trajectories that organizations follow across the innovation process. The requirements and needs of development vary across the innovation stages and so does the factors, which influence openness. This study argues that organizations which intend to pursue open innovation strategy for innovative product development need to evaluate decision to open at the level of innovation stages. Primarily, organizations need to decide how much to open for the three critical stages of idea, execution, and value capture stage.

The three levels of openness, namely, "close", "semi-open", and "open" across the three stages, which are "idea", "execution", and "value capture", present 27 unique trajectories for the organization. The study finds that organizations do behave differently for openness across innovation stages depending on their strategic choice. Our study finds that that there is little correlation between the action undertaken in one stage and the action undertaken in another stage. This is an important finding as it suggests that innovation management for openness needs to be evaluated at each stage and not once at the beginning of the product development.

Opening at Idea Stage

The first stage of idea, as defined here, focuses on broad search activities where the primary goal is to attract diverse ideas and suggestions for particular challenges confronting the development. This is essentially a collection exercise in a project and is influenced by availability of valuable resources in the external world and the organization's ability to collect and evaluate the diverse submissions. Our analyses highlight that openness at idea stage is an interplay between the external environment and internal context of the organization.

The results from the case study unambiguously suggest firms open out more in an uncertain environment. Environment uncertainty is studied through the factors of dynamism, heterogeneity, and hostility in this study. Environment dynamism is captured with regard to the frequency of new product introduction in the market. Markets which evolve rapidly demand higher rate of innovation, as observed in Case Delta and not Case Alpha, Case Beta, and Case Gamma. The cases highlight that rapidly evolving markets encourage organizations to open out for ideas. Also, markets which are heterogeneous where there is high degree of variation in consumer demand and expectations, openness has been observed. In Case Alpha and Case Delta, openness was practiced to include diverse groups and their views for conceptualizing new developments. In contrast in Case Beta where the market was fairly homogenous and where ideas for new development were already established, openness was limited. Thus, our study finds that in highly dynamic and heterogeneous markets, organizations show propensity to open out as a scanning mechanism for new ideas for development. This supports existing earlier research by Kessler and Bierly (2002) as well as the study by Eisenhardt (1989) according to which increasing uncertainty encourages organizations to seek more information, as a key argument for openness at the idea stage.

The study makes a strong observation with regard to hostile environment where pressure to remain closed was moderated by the dynamism of the environment. It emerged through Case Beta and Case Delta that though organizations are skeptical to open in a hostile environment, the decision gets strengthened or diminished depending on whether the environment dynamism is low or high.

Deeper exploration of cases found that irrespective of external environment orientation, openness is also influenced by the organization's ability to absorb external resources at the idea stage. Case Alpha relates to a firm with very high absorptive capacity than to a firm in Case Beta or Case Gamma, which influences the decision to open at the idea stage. The study clears the conundrum observed in the impact of absorptive capacity on openness where contradictory findings were reported by Barge-Gil (2010) and de Faria, Lima, and Santos (2010). Our study finds unequivocal evidence for positive influence of absorptive capacity on openness at the idea stage, with the same becoming a hindrance at a later stage of execution. This is perhaps because of the not-invented-here syndrome that has been found to be a dominant factor for openness at execution stage and not idea stage in this study. Case Alpha and Case Gamma highlight that when slack is available openness, is pursued as a choice, unlike in Case Epsilon where lack of resources demanded opening out. Availability of slack provides organization with a buffer against failure which encourages organizations to experiment and undertake risky projects (Cyert & March, 1963; Singh, 1986). Extending the argument this research finds that the availability of slack encourages exploration tasks for new and diverse ideas.

Interestingly, project characteristics did not exhibit influence on openness in idea stage. The influence of project characteristics like nature of project, time, or cost on openness at idea stage was not observed in this study. It is perhaps a reflection fact that in the idea stage, an organization is exploring opportunities without making any committing of resources. However, the role of innovation champion which has been discussed as a critical factor for innovation performance in literature was identified as a factor for openness only at the idea stage as identified in Case Alpha, Case Gamma, and Case Epsilon (Fig. 12.2).

Opening at Execution Stage

A dominant theme emerging from the cases relating to openness at execution stage highlights the theme of "certainty" and "caution" in approach to openness in execution stage. Unlike the idea stage where the key success factor may be identifying new opportunities, the execution stage demands realization of the idea into a product through investment of time, money, effort, and other scarce resources which leads to preference for internalization and control of

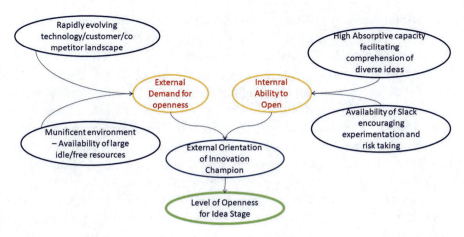

Fig. 12.2 Opening out at idea stage

development (Pisano, 1990). The study finds that product and project managers work toward ensuring that the organization investments secure fair results for their investment by increasing certainty and reducing risks over time during the execution stage.

In Case Beta and Case Gamma, we find that uncertainty of outcome was high for the organizations in the project. Additionally, in Case Beta the project was a priority for competitive market positioning, and so propensity to open was higher for organization to reduce uncertainty, while in Case Gamma it deferred its openness decision as the project though uncertain was not a priority. This approach to address organization challenges of uncertainty and risk has been documented in research on antecedents for alliances such as Gulati (1998) and Chaharbaghi, Adcroft, Willis, Todeva and Knoke (2005).

The research finds that while uncertainty and risk mitigation encourages organizations to open, the level of openness is moderated by the duration of engagement and requirement of specialized assets. In Case Epsilon, it was observed that low duration for collaborating tasks was an important aspect to manage task uncertainty by limiting negative downside for participating members. In developments which required long continuous and sustained development efforts, firms opted for internal development or close partnerships with selected external members as observed in Case Beta and Case Gamma. Similarly, when engagement requires specialized or capital intensive equipment for task collaboration, openness opportunity is limited as observed in Case Alpha, Case Beta, Case Gamma, and Case Delta. Established organizations which have the opportunity to engage in semi-open arrangements such as joint venture or alliance tend to prefer them over open-ended relations to address their requirements of reducing uncertainty and hedge risk.

The other reason for limited openness in execution stage results from team resistance also documented as a not-invented-here syndrome by Katz and Allen (1982). Our study finds strong validity for reluctance to open in execution stage, especially in established teams as in Case Alpha and Case Beta. The teams identify opening in idea stage as reflection of organization in their ability to realize wishes of external members, while openness in execution stage is perceived as the lack of confidence in internal team capabilities. Thus, when organizations open selectively for complementary resources for development, teams function well; however, opening to all is perceived as desperation or being lost for solution. The study also found that when organizations have high level of slack resources, openness at execution may be further muted. This provides some answer into earlier research, which has found contradictory results for availability on slack on innovation performance (Cyert & March, 1963; Nohria & Gulati, 1995). The study suggests that unlike in the idea stage, the availability of slack inhibits openness at the execution stage (Fig. 12.3).

Opening at Value Capture Stage

The final stage of development, termed as value capture stage, considers openness as free sharing of intellectual property, process, and outcome with external members in the society. According to our study, the fundamental argument in support of open sharing is to aid diffusion of new innovative product and service or to manage dependence of product ecosystem as observed in Case

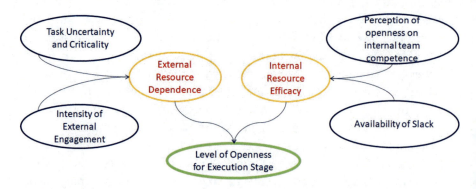

Fig. 12.3 Opening out at execution idea stage

Delta and Case Epsilon. Literature has identified appropriability regime and specialized complementary assets as two important factors determining the ability of organizations to profit from innovation (Ceccagnoli & Rothaermel, 2008; Teece, 1986). When organizations have access to specialized or co-specialized complementary resources, they may be more than willing to share their innovation development as in Case Delta. Other than access to complementary assets, interdependency on external members was found to be a significant factor for openness at value capture stage because of which Case Epsilon demonstrates openness; however, in Case Beta where all resources were available internally, we find limited discussion for openness at this stage. This supports the work of Iansiti and Levien (2004) and Adner (2006) who have argued that organizations may need to work in close proximity with external members for developing a viable ecosystem.

Another aspect of openness in value capture stage results from the strategic orientation of the developing team. There are studies which discuss about free revealing behavior of economic agents (Antikainen, Mäkipää, & Ahonen, 2010; Henkel, 2006). However, we did not find strong arguments for sharing of knowledge or innovation by organizations, without expectations of any monetary return. In a couple of cases where openness was observed as in Case Alpha and Case Epsilon, the product was not complete and could not have been commercialized, suggesting the intent of openness to maximize nonpecuniary gains. This aspect of free revealing of knowledge with limited value has also been observed by Henkel (2006). Thus, we conclude that organizations may open strategically to either build long-term viability of offering or secure social and moral capitals for the organization (Fig. 12.4).

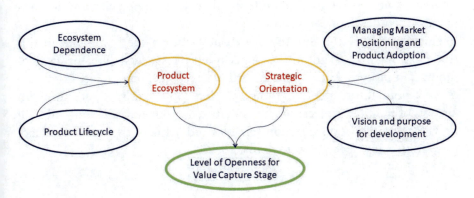

Fig. 12.4 Opening at value capture stage

Conclusion

Open and close are not binary choices; rather there are over 27 pathways, i.e. innovation trajectories, for any new developments to undertake across the innovation process. Our study makes two important contributions to research of open innovation. The categorization of open innovation practices across "close", "semi-open", and "open" addresses a prime challenge in open innovation literature where any research with external definition on open practices is loosely defined. As a result even organization practices of alliances and networks get introduced along with crowdsourcing practices as open innovation. As we move forward, this study should help make a distinction in open approaches for analyzing organization practices. The second important contribution that the study makes is highlighting the importance of understanding openness at project level and not organizational level. An organization may have say ten different innovation projects, where not all may have the same pattern of openness. Thus, exploring factors of openness at organization level can be misleading. Also, by exploding the innovation process, we are better able to address the confounding results observed for certain antecedents of openness in research. The study provides an insight into factors that influence organizations to adopt one of the 27 innovation trajectories.

The approach to study openness at the level of innovation stages also helps us answer some of the contradictory findings with regard to open practices reported in earlier study. For instance, the role of absorptive capacity or availability of slack, or disposition of innovation champion as discussed in previous section, suggests that the same antecedent may have an opposite influence on openness across the stages of innovation. Linking the extant literature on innovation process is critical to understand behavior of organizations to open or close their development process.

Finally, we hope that future research builds upon the framework in this study to bring new insights into practice of openness across different stages of innovation process. Also, where this study largely had one project from each organization, future research should explore opportunity where in-depth analysis of multiple projects can be undertaken at one organization. This will provide control over organization variables and help in better analysis of factors, influencing openness at the project level.

Appendix: Brief Details on Cases Analyzed in Study

Case name	Case Alpha	Case Beta	Case Gamma	Case Delta	Case Epsilon
Organization context	This case pertains to crowdsourcing initiative attempted by one of the leading automotive firms in the world with over a 100-year history of automotive development	This case pertains to an innovative development in a leading automotive firm in emerging market which also happens to be a global leader in tractor manufacturer	The case pertains to the development of three innovative offerings in a firm operating industrial good space and having over 70 years of legacy of leading in its market space	The case discusses about development of a technological handheld device much before the advent of smartphones. It was led by a group of academicians and technology entrepreneur with a vision to democratize technology adoption	The case discusses an open development of an automobile in line with open software development experience of Linux. The purpose of the project was to build the most fuel-efficient car
Geography	Initiative led by Latin America	India	India	India	Worldwide—with base in the USA
Project description	Development of a concept car to address the future demands of consumer. The firm opened out for ideas for development of concept car and also released the designs under creative common license	A new market offering for underpenetrated segment in agriculture tractor was launched. The conceptualization was done internally, while execution and development was outsourced. The final product was marketed by the focal company alone	Three developments of innovative product have been discussed here. The case highlights a preference of the firm to pursue selective openness across the innovation process, typically at execution stage. These products were marketed solely by the focal firm	MIT Technology Review hailed the development as one of the 7 Hottest Startups globally, in 2001. The handheld device was conceptualized to serve as a technology solution for the underprivileged section of society who did not have access to computers	The project was pursued with an objective to build 100 mpeg efficient automobile. Given the constraints and limitation of established firms, this development was undertaken as open source software development with individuals contributing to platform development from around the world

References

Adner, R. (2006). Match Your Innovation Strategy to Your Innovation Ecosystem. *Harvard Business Review, 84*(4), 98–107.

Afuah, A., & Tucci, C. L. (2012). Crowdsourcing as a Solution to Distant Search. *Academy of Management Review, 37*(3), 355–375.

Allen, R. C. (1983). Collective Invention. *Journal of Economic Behavior and Organization, 4*, 1–24.

Antikainen, M., Mäkipää, M., & Ahonen, M. (2010). Motivating and Supporting Collaboration in Open Innovation. *European Journal of Innovation Management, 13*(1), 100–119. https://doi.org/10.1108/14601061011013258

Barge-Gil, A. (2010). Open, Semi-Open and Closed Innovators: Towards an Explanation of Degree of Openness. *Industry & Innovation, 17*(6), 577–607. https://doi.org/10.1080/13662716.2010.530839

Bogers, M. (2011). The Open Innovation Paradox: Knowledge Sharing and Protection in R&D Collaborations. *European Journal of Innovation Management, 14*(1), 93–117. https://doi.org/10.1108/14601061111104715

Ceccagnoli, M. (2009). Appropriability, preemption, and firm performance. *Strategic Management Journal, 30*, 81–98.

Ceccagnoli, M., & Rothaermel, F. T. (2008). Appropriating the Returns from Innovation. In *Technological Innovation: Generating Economic Results Advances in the Study of Entrepreneurship, Innovation and Economic Growth* (Vol. 18, pp. 11–34) https://doi.org/10.1016/S1048-4736(07)00001-X

Chaharbaghi, K., Adcroft, A., Willis, R., Todeva, E., & Knoke, D. (2005). Strategic alliances and models of collaboration. Management decision.

Chesbrough, H. W. (2003). *Open Innovation: The New Imperative for Creating and Profiting from Technology*. Boston: Harvard Business Press.

Chiaroni, D., Chiesa, V., & Frattini, F. (2010). The Open Innovation Journey: How Firms Dynamically Implement the Emerging Innovation Management Paradigm. *Technovation, 31*(1), 34–43.

Cohen, W. M., & Levinthal, D. A. (1990). Absorptive Capacity: A New Perspective on Learning and Innovation. *Administrative Science Quarterly, 35*, 128–152.

Cohen, W. M., Nelson, R. R., & Walsh, J. P. (2000). Protecting their intellectual assets: Appropriability conditions and why US manufacturing firms patent (or not) (No. w7552). National Bureau of Economic Research.

Cooper, R. G. (2008). Perspective: The stage-gate® idea-to-launch process—update, what's new, and nexgen systems. *Journal of Product Innovation Management, 25*(3), 213–232.

Cyert, R. M., & March, I. G. (1963). *A Behavioral Theory of the Firm*. New Jersey: Prentice-Hall.

Dahlander, L., & Frederiksen, L. (2011). The Core and Cosmopolitans: A Relational View of Innovation in User Communities. *Organization Science, 23*(4), 988–1007.

Darke, P., Shanks, G., & Broadbent, M. (1998). Successfully completing case study research: combining rigour, relevance and pragmatism. *Information Systems Journal, 8*(4), 273–289.

De Faria, P., Lima, F., & Santos, R. (2010). Cooperation in innovation activities: The importance of partners. *Research Policy, 39*(8), 1082–1092.

Drechsler, W., & Natter, M. (2012). Understanding a Firm's Openness Decisions in Innovation. *Journal of Business Research, 65*, 438–445.

Eisenhardt, K. M. (1989). Making Fast Strategic Decisions in High-Velocity Environments. *Academy of Management Journal, 32*, 543–576. https://doi.org/10.2307/256434

Eisenhardt, K. M., & Schoonhoven, C. B. (1996). Resource-Based View of Strategic Alliance Formation: Strategic and Social Effects in Entrepreneurial Firms. *Organization Science, 7*(2), 136–150.

Foray, D., & Perez, L. H. (2006). The economics of open technology: collective organization and individual claims in the 'Fabrique Lyonnaise'during the old regime. New Frontiers in the Economics of Innovation and New Technology: Essays in Honour of Paul A. David, 239–54.

Foray, D., Thoron, S., & Zimmermann, J.-B. (2007). Open software: knowledge openess and cooperation in cyberspace. In E. Brousseau & N. Curien (Eds.), *Internet and digital economics: Principles, methods and applications* (pp. 368–390). New York: Cambridge University Press.

Gulati, R. (1998). Alliances and networks. *Strategic Management Journal, 19*, 293–317.

Gupta, A. K. (1987). *Scientific Perception of Farmers Innovations in Dry Regions: Barriers to the Scientific Curiosity* (No. 699).

Gupta, A. K. (1999). *Securing Traditional Knowledge and Contemporary Innovations: Can Global Trade Links Help Grassroots Innovations? Honey Bee perspective.* World Trade Forum.

Hagedorn, J., Linl, N. A., & Vorontas, S. N. (2000). Research Partnerships. *Research Policy, 29*, 567–586.

Hansen, M. T., & Birkinshaw, J. (2007). *The Innovation Value Chain.* June: Harvard Business Review.

Henkel, J. (2006). Selective Revealing in Open Innovation Processes: The Case of Embedded Linux. *Research Policy, 35*(7), 953–969.

Herzog, P. (2011). *Open and Closed Innovation Different Cultures for Different Strategies.* Springer.

Hippel, E. v. (1988). *The Sources of Innovation.* New York: Oxford University Press.

Hughes, B., & Wareham, J. (2010). Knowledge Arbitrage in Global Pharma: A Synthetic View of Absorptive Capacity and Open Innovation. *R&D Management, 40*(3), 324–343.

Iansiti, M., & Levien, R. (2004). Strategy as Ecology. *Harvard Business Review, 82*(3), 68–78.

Katz, R., & Allen, T. J. (1982). Investigating the Not Invented Here (NIH) syndrome: A look at the performance, tenure, and communication patterns of 50 R & D Project Groups. *R&d Management, 12*(1), 7–20.

Kessler, E. H., & Bierly, P. E. (2002). Is Faster Really Better? An Empirical Test of the Implications of Innovation Speed. *IEEE Transactions on Engineering Management, 49*(1), 2–12.

Keupp, M. M., & Gassmann, O. (2009). Determinants and archetype users of open innovation. *R&d Management, 39*(4), 331–341.

King, A. A., & Lakhani, K. R. (2011). *The Contingent Effect of Absorptive Capacity: An Open Innovation Analysis* (No. 11–102).

Kirschbaum, R. (2005). Open Innovation in Practice. *Research-Technology Management, 48*(4), 24–28.

Kline, S. J. (1985). Innovation is not a Linear Process. *Research Management, 28*(4), 36–45.

Kogut, B., & Zander, U. (1992). Knowledge of the Firm, Combinative Capabilities, and the Replication of Technology. *Organization Science, 3*(3), 383–397. https://doi.org/10.1287/orsc.3.3.383

Lakhani, K. R., Jeppesen, L. B., Lohse, P. A., & Panetta, J. A. (2007). The Value of Openness in Scientific Problem Solving (pp. 7–50). Boston, MA: Division of Research, Harvard Business School.

Nohria, N., & Gulati, R. (1995). Is Slack Good or Bad for Innovation? *The Academy of Management Journal, 39*(5), 1245–1264.

Pettigrew, A., McKee, L., & Ferlie, E. (1988). Understanding Change in the NHS. *Public Administration, 66*(3), 297–317.

Pisano, G. (1990). The R&D Boundaries of the Firm: An Empirical Analysis. *Administrative Science Quarterly, 35*(1), 153–176.

Podolny, J. M. (1994). Market Uncertainty and the Social Character of Economic Exchange. *Administrative Science Quarterly, 39*(3), 458–483.

Porter, M. E. (1980). *Competitive Strategy: Techniques for Analyzing Industries and Competitors*. New York: Free Press.

Rogers, E. M. (1995). *Diffusion of Innovations*. New York: Free Press.

Rosenberg, N., & Nelson, R. R. (1994). American Univesities and Technical Advance in Industry. *Research Policy, 23*, 323–348.

Rothaermel, F. T., & Alexandre, M. T. (2009). Ambidexterity in Technology Sourcing: The Moderating Role of Absorptive Capacity. *Organization Science, 20*(4), 759–780.

Rothaermel, F. T., & Deeds, D. L. (2004). Exploration and Exploitation Alliances in Biotechnology: A System of New Product Development. *Strategic Management Journal, 25*(3), 201–221. https://doi.org/10.1002/smj.376

Rothwell R., & Zegveld. (1985). Reindustrialization and Technology. Harlow, U.K.: Longman.

Salter, A., ter Wal, A., Criscuolo, P., & Alexy, O. (2012). *Open for Ideation: Individual-level Openness and Idea Generation in R & D*. DRUID 2012 on June 19 to June 21 at CBS, Copenhagen, Denmark.

Singh, J. V. (1986). Performance, Slack and Risk-Taking in Organizational Decision Making. *Academy of Management Journal, 29*, 562–585.

Sofka, W., & Grimpe, C. (2008). *Managing Search Strategies for Open Innovation – The Role of Environmental Munificence as Well as Internal and External R & D* (No. 08–075). Retrieved from ftp://ftp.zew.de/pub/zew-docs/dp/dp08075.pdf

Teece, D. J. (1986). Profiting from Technological Innovation. *Research Policy, 15*(6), 285–305.

Tushman, M. L. (1977). Special Boundary Roles in the Innovation Process Special Boundary Roles in the Innovation Process. *Administrative Science Quarterly, 22*(4), 587–605.

Van De Vrande, V., De Jong, J. P. J., & Vanhaverbeke, W. (2009). Open Innovation in SMEs: Trends, Motives and Management Challenges. *Technovation, 29*, 423–437. https://doi.org/10.1016/j.technovation.2008.10.001

Van der Meer, H. (2007). Open innovation–the Dutch treat: challenges in thinking in business models. *Creativity and Innovation Management, 16*(2), 192–202.

West, J. (2003). How Open is Open Enough? Melding Proprietary and Open Source Platform Strategies. *Research Policy, 32*, 1259–1285.

West, J., & Bogers, M. (2014). Leveraging External Sources of Innovation: A Review of Research on Open Innovation. *Journal of Product Innovation Management, 31*(4).

Zaltman, G., Duncan, R., & Holbeck, J. (1973). *Innovation and Organisations*. New York: Wiley.

13

Digitalization Toward Innovative Workplaces: Service Engineering Research in Japan

Kentaro Watanabe, Takeshi Takenaka, and Takashi Okuma

Introduction

The recent evolution of digital technologies promotes dynamic changes in organization, industry, and society. The impact of these technologies stimulates the expectation toward technological innovation in a variety of workplaces. In fact, technologies such as sensors, mobile devices, machine learning techniques, and robotics are being implemented in industrial and service workplaces. Digitalization or digital transformation using such technologies is a global trend in a variety of industries (D'Emidio, Dorton, & Duncan, 2015; Howaldt, Kopp, & Schultze, 2017; Vial, 2019).

Although digitalization is a recent term, the utilization of information and communication technologies (ICT) at workplaces has been an effective approach for improving and innovating work practices (OECD, 2004; Sundbo, 1999). Meanwhile, as emphasized by existing studies on workplace innovation (Oeij, Preenen, van der Torre, van der Meer, & van den Eerenbeemt, 2019; Pot, Rus, & Oeij, 2017) and some related concepts such as employee-driven innovation (Høyrup, 2012), innovation at workplaces is not created only by such technologies but also requires non-technological, organizational

K. Watanabe (✉) • T. Takenaka • T. Okuma
National Institute of Advanced Industrial Science and Technology, Chiba, Japan
e-mail: kentaro.watanabe@aist.go.jp; takenaka-t@aist.go.jp; takashi-okuma@aist.go.jp

© The Author(s), under exclusive license to Springer Nature Switzerland AG 2021
A. McMurray et al. (eds.), *The Palgrave Handbook of Workplace Innovation*,
https://doi.org/10.1007/978-3-030-59916-4_13

change. Simply forcing workers to use new technologies may lower their productivity and motivation.

In this chapter, we specifically focus on digitalization in service fields. It is expected that the aforementioned new types of technologies will increase the productivity and quality of working life in service industries (D'Emidio et al., 2015). To make the most use of digital technologies in service workplaces, a variety of studies emphasize the active role of employees in technology integration and utilization. Oeij et al. (2019) highlight the importance of employee engagement in technology adoption, though initiatives of technological innovation tend to be top-down. The scholars of service innovation also consider a human-centered, participatory approach as effective for the digitalization in service (Toivonen & Saari, 2019). Participatory design and co-design with users are commonly adopted in the design and development process of ICT to support work practices at workplaces (Greenbaum & Kyng, 1991; Sanders & Stappers, 2008). Meanwhile, the research on employee-driven innovation highlights that ICT can support innovative behavior and organizational learning for productive workplaces (Høyrup, 2012). These studies indicate that technology integration in work practices and innovative behavior through active engagement by workers would lead to more productive workplaces. However, the methodological aspect of digitalization toward innovative workplaces is still insufficiently studied. Therefore, in our research, we examined how digital technologies could be successfully integrated with work practices and innovative behavior at workplaces in the service industry.

This chapter introduces the research on service engineering in Japan. Although service engineering has several origins and research focuses (Bullinger, Fähnrich, & Meiren, 2003; Tomiyama, 2001; Watanabe, Mochimaru, & Shimomura, 2016), this chapter introduces research aiming to develop and integrate digital technologies to workplaces in service sectors, mostly driven by the lower productivity of service sectors in Japan in the 2000s. The Ministry of Economy, Trade and Industry (METI) in Japan promoted the policy-level initiative to encourage new research and development activities for service sectors. The ministry-funded project for service engineering kicked off in 2008, focusing on labor-intensive services such as restaurants, hotels, care work, and tourism (Mochimaru, 2011). Investments in research and development in these service sectors were traditionally very limited. The most significant feature of this project was to take both the data-driven and participatory approaches in technology development, integration, and use. Service engineering research does not push technology-led solutions to service fields, but co-develops and co-integrates technologies, data-assisted service operations, and innovation activities with service workers and managers. This project has remained very advanced, and the service engineering research has been conducted even after the project ended in 2012 (Watanabe et al., 2016). This service engineering approach could provide meaningful insights for the current digitalization trend in workplaces, especially in service industries.

In the following sections, we first illustrate the situation of service sectors and the government policy in Japan as the context of this chapter. Then, we introduce the overview and features of the service engineering research project funded by METI, Japan. From this project, we demonstrate two illustrative cases that exemplify the integration of technological and non-technological innovations at service workplaces. Based on the case studies, we summarize six principles for realizing digitalization for innovating work practices and promoting innovative behavior by the service engineering approach. Finally, we provide recommendations for future service engineering research.

Japanese Service Sectors and Government Policy

As the local context of this study, in this section, we first introduce industrial and policy situations of the case study.

Japan has become one of the world economic powers since the 1980s, and its main driver was the advantage in manufacturing technologies. However, after the collapse of the bubble economy in the early 1990s, the nominal growth rate decreased sharply and experienced negative growth in 1998. Consequently, the Japanese economy entered into deflation, and it became difficult for industries to invest significantly in capital and human resources. Accordingly, the unemployment ratio increased dramatically from the late 1990s to the early 2000s (Statistics Bureau of Japan, 2019). Another significant change related to employment was that the number of employees in manufacturing industries started to decrease in the mid-1990s and that of service industries increased (Statistics Bureau of Japan, 2015). Although this trend was also common in other developed countries in the 2000s, the impact of this shift was substantial in Japan as the Japanese economy heavily depended on manufacturing in terms of GDP, compared with other countries. Furthermore, the importance of service sectors in the Japanese economy was underestimated, as they were regarded simply as the source of employment in rural areas in Japan.

Against this backdrop, the Japanese government placed productivity improvement of service sectors as a top priority in their economic growth strategy of 2006 (Council on Economic and Fiscal Policy, 2006). First, they highlighted lower labor productivity and total factor productivity of service sectors compared with other countries such as the United States (Morikawa, 2007). Additionally, some challenges peculiar to Japanese service sectors, such as lower investment in information technology (IT) (Fukao, 2015), have been indicated as a cause of low productivity.

At the same time, many service businesses in Japan suffered from the worldwide economic downturn and personal consumption declined in the early 2000s. The progressing deflation compelled companies to pursue the efficiency of services and accelerated severe price competition in almost all service sectors. In the restaurant industry, for example, many major restaurant chains performed cost reductions, for example, in cooking processes, by introducing a central kitchen system. Thereafter, the economic downturn precipitated by the Lehman Brothers bankruptcy in 2008 compelled companies to reduce prices further to cope with the severe decline of personal consumption. This caused worse work conditions and led to a bad reputation, such as long working hours and low salaries of some restaurant chains, which was covered in the news from the late 2000s to the early 2010s. Accordingly, the restaurant industry started struggling with severe labor shortages, lasting even until today, and the improvement of productivity has remained a serious issue. The other types of service sectors, such as accommodation, welfare services, and local tourism, also suffer from similar challenges.

Service Engineering Research Project

Because of recognized lower productivity of Japanese service industries compared with other countries, the Japanese government started to emphasize the importance of science and technology for improving the productivity of service industries. Until the mid-2000s, there were only a few research fields that contribute to service industries in Japanese universities, such as marketing, management science, and industrial engineering, including operations research. A new scientific approach was anticipated, especially for developing technologies applicable to service industries.

At almost the same time in the United States, the government and industries stressed the need for education program in universities, which could teach both ICT and management science for the further growth of ICT industries. Based on this background, service science research started in the mid-2000s in the US service science aimed to understand and innovate service systems based on service marketing theory and an ICT-driven approach (Spohrer & Kwan, 2009).

In contrast, the Japanese government placed a greater emphasis on the importance of engineering and improvement activities, because they had promoted the growth of manufacturing industries in the past. For example, "Kaizen" as continuous improvement is known as a strong industrial culture in which all employees are actively engaged in improving daily operations. In fact, some service industries had already started adopting such improvement activities.

For improving processes, data collection and analysis in the production processes are essential. However, data collection at workplaces was considered insufficient in Japanese service industries. Collecting data in service fields is not easy, compared with automated manufacturing processes. In addition, the mindset of managers of service industries was also a barrier, as they tended to rely only on their own experiences. Against these backdrops, the Japanese government started preparing a research project on "service engineering" through a discussion with academia and service industries from 2006. Many researchers claimed the importance of a scientific methodology based on (big) data collected in actual service processes.

Through the discussion of the concept of service engineering, the service optimum design loop was proposed as a fundamental methodology. The service optimum design loop is an iterative design process using a data-driven approach (Mochimaru, 2011). As shown in Fig. 13.1, the design loop consists of four phases: "observation," "analysis," "design," and "application." In the observation phase, the data of stakeholders, service processes, and environment are collected by technological (e.g., sensors) and methodological (e.g., observation method) approaches. The collected data are analyzed to develop a

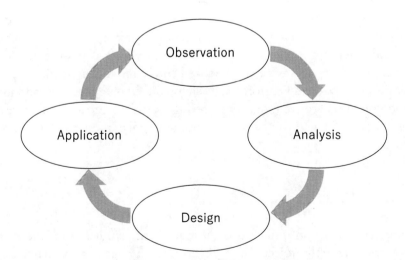

Fig. 13.1 Service optimum design loop (based on Mochimaru, 2011)

model to represent a target service in the analysis phase. Based on the model, service elements such as service processes and technological systems are designed as a solution in the design phase. The designed solution is applied in the field in the application phase. Finally, the solution is reassessed from the same or different perspectives in the observation phase.

Additionally, the importance of human-centricity was emphasized because services include many human factors related to satisfaction and decision-making of customers, employees, and managers. The participatory approach at service fields is the core for investigating the needs and challenges, as well as integrating the knowledge and experiences of employees and managers into the research process. The aforementioned service design optimum loop is conducted in collaboration with service workers. In addition, social sciences such as psychology, sociology, and management science were important research fields for service engineering to take care of the human aspect of services. Meanwhile, computer science and engineering research on sensing technologies, data analysis, simulation, optimization, and robotics were regarded as necessary research elements for service engineering. Therefore, service engineering was established as an inter-/transdisciplinary research field from its start.

Based on the discussion above, a national project on service engineering started in 2008 in Japan. Simultaneously, the Center for Service Research was established as a core organization for service engineering research at the National Institute of Advanced Industrial Science and Technology (AIST), a research institute under METI. Additionally, some universities were chosen as participants of the research project.

The target industries of service engineering that researchers focused on were mainly labor-intensive industries including retail, restaurant, nursing care, and entertainment services, as shown in Fig. 13.2. The aforementioned labor-intensive services were characterized with complex interactions among multiple employees and customers. Therefore, technology research and intervention under the conventional engineering research approach used to be difficult for them. Hence, this became the research goal of the service engineering research project.

Case Studies

In this section, we introduce two illustrative case studies from the service engineering research project. The following cases are specifically characterized by the in-depth participation of employees in the research activity and their

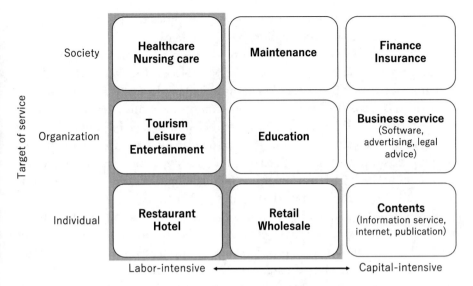

Fig. 13.2 Target industries of the service engineering research project

autonomous innovative behavior using developed technologies. The role of the researchers in both cases was to facilitate the technology-enabled innovative behavior by applying the service optimum design loop. Based on the existing project reports and documents, we examined the technology development and integration process and innovative behavior in each case to clarify the important factors for digitalization toward innovative workplaces.

Case 1: Mobile Communication as a Source of Innovation at a Care Facility

The first case concerns the support for employee-driven innovation through a mobile communication system at a care facility. This facility consisted of 3 floors with 150 beds. Approximately ten employees were working on each floor. The research orientation was to empower service employees using the support of ICT developed in collaboration with them.

For the understanding of the service process at the care facility, a time-and-motion study (Pigage & Tucker, 1954) was conducted. The measurements revealed that sharing and recording of care information took up a large amount of the caregivers' working time. As the first action by the care facility, the outsourcing of the information recording process was conducted and caregivers were able to use more time for direct care work (Miwa, Fukuhara, & Nishimura, 2012). This result led to stronger commitment of the management and employees involved in the project. The next target for improvement was the information handover between working shifts. The communication between working shifts had been done through verbal communication and shared notebooks at the workplace. However, it was difficult to share information by notebooks among many employees on time. According to this analysis, the co-design of a mobile communication system among caregivers started in 2011 (Fukuda, Nakajima, Nishimura, & Nishimura, 2017). The system was called DANCE. Several caregivers participated in the co-design process, providing ideas, testing the prototype, and encouraging other employees to use it. After the period of field testing, the developed system was successfully integrated into work practices in 2014.

This system functioned not only as a daily communication tool but also as an innovation source among employees. After the implementation of DANCE, data on daily care practices were accumulated in the system database. Based on the collected data, a workshop was conducted to create ideas for improvements in care work (Watanabe, Fukuda, & Nishimura, 2015). The workshop process was based on the aforementioned optimum design loop as shown in Fig. 13.3. The data collected from DANCE for the workshop correspond to the observation results. For the analysis, a co-occurrence network analysis was conducted, which is a text analysis technique for showing how frequently words are used as well as for identifying their correlation in graph format. The participating caregivers looked at the visualized graph

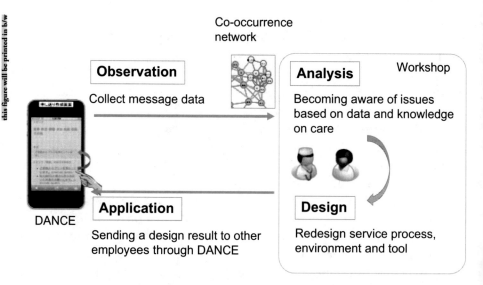

Fig. 13.3 Workshop process using DANCE (based on Watanabe et al., 2015)

and discussed the potential risk issues based on their knowledge at work. Then, they ideated the solution to the risk issue as a design result of employees. This design result may include service processes, environment, and tools for care. Finally, the design result is applied by sharing the idea with other colleagues using DANCE. This workshop demonstrated how service activities could be innovated in an employee-driven and technology-assisted manner.

Case 2: Computer-Supported Quality Control Circle at a Restaurant Business

The second case is related to improvement activities with the computational support at a restaurant business. The project was conducted at a Japanese-style restaurant. Traditionally, the quality control circle (QCC) activity—a form of Kaizen activity within a small group of employees—has been used to improve work practices in manufacturing and, more recently, service sectors in Japan (Watanabe, 1991). The studied restaurant had originally adopted QCC. An indoor positioning technology made the flow analysis of a number of people technically possible. With the cooperation of Ganko Food Service Co., Ltd., the flow analysis using indoor positioning technology was applied for quantitative analysis in QCC (Ueoka, Shinmura, Tenmoku, Okuma, & Kurata, 2012). Based on the strong commitment of management, a dedicated employee group was assigned to this project. The collected data from the sensors were visualized and utilized for the analysis in this improvement activity, which was called the computer-supported quality control circle (CSQCC) (Ueoka et al., 2012).

The first trial of CSQCC was held in 2011 (Ueoka et al., 2012). Collected data from wearable sensors was visualized for CSQCC by combining point-of-sales data of the restaurant. The employees were able to make plans for improving their processes using the visualizations of their activities. Figure 13.4 demonstrates the CSQCC.

At first, this activity was just an extension of conventional QCC. Measured and visualized human activities only helped the members of QCC find problems. Using human intelligence for daily work practices, the participants were able to derive effective solutions for work challenges. In other words, they utilized the human ability to find problems from visualized behavior at the first stage.

Through iterative applications, the improvement activities and the applied support systems were updated and sophisticated (Fukuhara, Tenmoku, Ueoka, Okuma, & Kurata, 2014). As the efforts progressed, intermediate indicators for service processes that can quantify the results of efforts were developed.

Fig. 13.4 CSQCC activity

For example, it was confirmed that the effects of this improvement could be measured with an increased stay ratio of employees in dining areas, which was defined as a KPI by circle members. Another impact of the improvement was shown as the increased number of additional orders. It is also meaningful to measure distance traveled at a workplace which accommodates the physical burden of employees. Moreover, the assessment method was further sophisticated by focusing on the relationship between "role" and "location" of employees (Fukuhara et al., 2014). By utilizing such metrices, the relationship between improvement activities and results can be analyzed more clearly.

In addition, the indoor positioning technology which was originally developed for navigation was customized in various ways as a service process analysis technology, improving operability on-site. The applied technologies are still being improved. By combining simulations based on measurement data, research into verifying the effectiveness of improvement measures in advance will become possible.

Findings

Based on the case studies, we have summarized the following six principles for successful digitalization for work practices and innovative behavior, as shown in Table 13.1. They are categorized into three topics: workplace-centered development, project management, and human-technology relation.

Table 13.1 Principles for service engineering approach

Workplace-centered development	Co-development with stakeholders
	Design for autonomy in workplace
Project management	Management commitment
	Trust-building process
Human-technology relation	Duality in technology
	Human-in-the-loop approach

Workplace-Centered Development

Co-Development with Stakeholders

The integration of technology tends to be cumbersome when simply pushing it onto the workplace. The approach applied in the above-presented cases was characterized by the deep understanding of work practices and co-development of technology and its use in collaboration with stakeholders such as service employees. For example, in Case 1, the researchers first conducted the service process analysis and then specified the cost for information sharing, specifically information handover between work shifts through discussion with the caregivers. In addition, the DANCE system was co-developed with the caregivers, which contributed to its successful implementation at the workplace. In Case 2, the support systems were also continuously redesigned in response to user feedback. This approach is meaningful also from the aspect of worker motivation regarding the use of developed technologies.

Design for Autonomy in the Workplace

The development target in the case studies includes the employees' activities and community for continuous technology use and data analysis. This is crucial for the autonomous use of data in workplaces toward workplace innovation (Watanabe et al., 2015). In Case 1, the workshop method was introduced to have caregivers figure out the issues to be improved and ideate solutions based on their practical knowledge at work. In Case 2, the sensing and visualization system was integrated into the QCC activity as CSQCC at the restaurant, which helped employees improve their service practices. As implied by the case study results, small group activities and workshops are effective.

Project Management

Management Commitment

Although the autonomy in the workplace is a key for the service engineering approach, management commitment is necessary for the projects, as the existing studies on innovative behavior have already pointed out (Hasu et al., 2015). In both cases mentioned above, there was strong support from the management. Therefore, the employees were able to fully contribute to the projects.

Trust-Building Process

Large-scale changes in the workplace are less acceptable without the trust for the research members. We emphasize the importance of the trust-building process, starting with a small, practical solution to provide the workplace with a sense of success and then extending the approach into more complicated, challenging issues. For example, the service process analysis in Case 1 was mainly conducted by the researchers. The collected data illustrated how much the caregivers spent their time on indirect tasks, such as information sharing and recording, and it provided meaningful insights for both employees and managers. Therefore, they were able to take another step to change the situation through the co-design process which requires their own participation.

Human-Technology Relation

Duality in Technology

Technologies for simple data collection in workplaces tend to be less acceptable, because their application causes the anxiety of employees and lower work efficiency, at least in the short term. Desirably, technologies need to have two features: instant functioning for service work and data collection as a result of its use.

DANCE in Case 1 is a typical example of such a technology. As an instant impact, the caregivers at the care facility were able to communicate with each other smoothly and immediately, by using DANCE. Meanwhile, collected data were available for data analysis to clarify issues to be solved in care work. Though the sensing device in Case 2 itself was mainly for collecting data, the visualization system made the collected data meaningful for workers. Therefore, it is important to at least provide feedback from whom the data was collected.

Human-in-the-Loop Approach

Data from a sensor or a device only show one aspect of service practices. For the interpretation and utilization of data, human intelligence is necessary (Watanabe et al., 2015). The "human-in-the-loop" approach is important when implementing digital technologies in workplaces. This means that the occasion for employees' interpretation of data should be intentionally included in the work practices.

The workshop in Case 1 represents a good example of data analysis based on the knowledge of caregivers. In addition, DANCE enabled the workshop participants to share the developed knowledge among other caregivers. This indicates that human knowledge based on data from digital technologies can be utilized also with the support of the same digital technologies. CSQCC in Case 2 was a further autonomous approach for improving service practices based on data collected in workplaces.

Discussion and Implications

The principles obtained from the case study provide meaningful insights for bridging the two studied topics: workplace innovation and digitalization at workplaces. The research on workplace innovation emphasizes non-technological innovation, whereas technology development and integration tend to be relatively minor issues. On the one hand, some principles such as co-development, duality in technology, and the human-in-the-loop approach provide practical clues when digital technologies are utilized for workplace innovation. On the other hand, digitalization at the workplace should be aligned to work practices. These principles will have important practical implications for technology developers and integrators who would like to develop and utilize digital technologies in service sectors. In addition, the trust-building process with both management and employees is also important to encourage technology integration and autonomous innovative behavior at work. These principles will contribute to innovative workplaces utilizing technological features and foster the current digitalization trend in a more human-centered way (Toivonen & Saari, 2019).

Although the case studies presented herein are limited to care and restaurant services, the technologies and approaches in the cases were also applied to different types of workplaces. For example, the technology set in Case 2 was applied to the warehouse business as well (Ichikari et al., 2019). The cases are still limited to a Japanese setting, but there is potential for applying them in other cultural settings.

The following items are the ongoing and future topics for research.

Multi-Actor Consideration

The service engineering research has included multi-actor perspectives in its development and application process. The assessment method of service systems from the perspectives of various actors including customers, managers, and other actors such as citizens should also be studied.

Long-Term Impact of Digital Technology

Digital technology attracts attention from both positive and negative aspects. The anxiety toward digitalization is an important issue that needs to be tackled. The long-term impact of digital technology at workplaces is another topic to be discussed for the technology development and integration process (Watanabe, Kishita, Tsunetomo, & Takenaka, 2020).

Acknowledgments The cases in this article were supported by the Ministry of Economy, Trade and Industry, Japan, in a service engineering research project (2009–2012).

References

Bullinger, H. J., Fähnrich, K. P., & Meiren, T. (2003). Service Engineering: Methodical Development of New Service Products. *International Journal of Production Economics, 85*(3), 275–287.

Council on Economic and Fiscal Policy. (2006). *Economic Growth Strategy* (in Japanese). Retrieved February 6, 2020, from https://www5.cao.go.jp/keizai-shimon/minutes/2006/0626/item2.pdf

D'Emidio, T., Dorton, D., & Duncan, E. (2015). Service Innovation in a Digital World. *McKinsey Quarterly*, February.

Fukao, K. (2015). Seisansei, Sangyokozo to Nihon no Seicho (Productivity, Industrial Structure, and the Growth of Japan). *RIETI Policy Discussion Paper Series*, 15-P-023. (In Japanese).

Fukuda, K., Nakajima, M., Nishimura, S., & Nishimura, T. (2017). Non-Routine Knowledge Sharing in Elderly Care-Facility for Better Services. In *Proceedings of the 18th European Conference on Knowledge Management* (pp. 326–333). ACPI.

Fukuhara, T., Tenmoku, R., Ueoka, R., Okuma, T., & Kurata, T. (2014). Estimating Skills of Waiting Staff of a Restaurant Based on Behavior Sensing and POS Data Analysis: A Case Study in a Japanese Cuisine Restaurant. In *Proceedings of the 5th International Conference on Applied Human Factors and Ergonomics (AHFE2014)* (pp. 4287–4299). AHFE Conference.

Greenbaum, J., & Kyng, M. (1991). *Design at Work: Cooperative Design of Computer Systems*. Erlbaum.

Hasu, M., Saari, E., Honkaniemi, L., Tuominen, T., Lehtonen, M. H., & Kallio, K. (2015). Trajectories of Learning in Practice-based Innovation–Organizational Roles at Play in Sustainable Innovation Management. In M. Elg, P. E. Ellström, M. Klofsten, & M. Tillmar (Eds.), *Sustainable Development in Organizations* (pp. 127–152). Edward Elgar Publishing.

Howaldt, J., Kopp, R., & Schultze, J. (2017). Why Industrie 4.0 Needs Workplace Innovation—A Critical Essay about the German Debate on Advanced Manufacturing. In P. Oeij, D. Rus, & F. D. Pot (Eds.), *Workplace Innovation* (pp. 45–60). Springer.

Høyrup, S. (2012). Employee-driven Innovation: A New Phenomenon, Concept, and Mode of Innovation. In S. Høyrup, C. Hasse, M. Bonnafous-Boucher, K. Møller, & M. Lotz (Eds.), *Employee-driven Innovation: A New Approach* (pp. 3–33). Palgrave Macmillan.

Ichikari, R., Kaji, K., Shimomura, R., Kourogi, M., Okuma, T., & Kurata, T. (2019). Off-site Indoor Localization Competitions based on Measured Data in a Warehouse. *Sensors, 19*(4), 763.

Miwa, H., Fukuhara, T., & Nishimura, T. (2012). Service Process Visualization in Nursing-Care Service Using State Transition Model. In J. C. Spohrer & L. E. Freund (Eds.), *Advances in the Human Side of Service Engineering* (pp. 3–12). CRC Press.

Mochimaru, M. (2011). A Research Project for Human Centered Service Engineering. *IEICE Technical Report Software Interprise Modeling, 111*(189), 1–6. (In Japanese).

Morikawa, M. (2007). Is Productivity in the Service Industries Low? An Analysis Using Firm-Level Data on the Dispersion and the Dynamics of Productivity. *RIETI Discussion Paper*, 07-J-048. (In Japanese).

OECD. (2004). *OECD Information Technology Outlook 2004*. OECD.

Oeij, P. R. A., Preenen, P. T. Y., van der Torre, W., van der Meer, L., & van den Eerenbeemt, J. (2019). Technological Choice and Workplace Innovation: Towards Efficient and Humanised Work. *European Public & Social Innovation Review, 4*(1), 15–26.

Pigage, L. C., & Tucker, J. L. (1954). Motion and Time Study. *The University of Illinois Bulletin, 51*(73), 3–48.

Pot, F. D., Rus, D., & Oeij, P. R. (2017). Introduction: The Need to Uncover the Field of Workplace Innovation. In P. Oeij, D. Rus, & F. D. Pot (Eds.), *Workplace Innovation* (pp. 1–8). Springer.

Sanders, E. B. N., & Stappers, P. J. (2008). Co-creation and the New Landscapes of Design. *CoDesign: International Journal of Cocreation in Design and the Arts, 4*(1), 5–18.

Spohrer, J., & Kwan, S. K. (2009). Service Science, Management, Engineering, and Design (SSMED): An Emerging Discipline-Outline & References. *International Journal of Information Systems in the Service Sector, 1*(3), 1–31.

Statistics Bureau of Japan. (2015). *Labor and Wage, Statistics in Japan.* Retrieved November 21, 2019, from https://www.stat.go.jp/data/nihon/back15/16.html. (In Japanese).

Statistics Bureau of Japan. n.d. *Unemployment Rate [by Age Group].* Retrieved November 14, 2019, from https://www.stat.go.jp/english/data/roudou/lngindex.html

Sundbo, J. (1999). Empowerment of Employees in Small and Medium-Sized Service Firms. *Employee Relations, 21*(2), 105–127.

Toivonen, M., & Saari, E. (Eds.). (2019). *Human-Centered Digitalization and Services.* Springer.

Tomiyama, T. (2001). Service Engineering to Intensify Service Contents in Product Life Cycles. In *Proceedings of Second International Symposium on Environmentally Conscious Design and Inverse Manufacturing* (pp. 613–618). IEEE.

Ueoka, R., Shinmura, T., Tenmoku, R., Okuma, T., & Kurata, T. (2012). Introduction of Computer Supported Quality Control Circle in a Japanese Cuisine Restaurant. In *Advances in the Human Side of Service Engineering* (pp. 379–388). CRC Press.

Vial, G. (2019). Understanding Digital Transformation: A Review and a Research Agenda. *Journal of Strategic Information Systems, 28*(2), 118–144.

Watanabe, K., Fukuda, K., & Nishimura, T. (2015). A Technology-Assisted Design Methodology for Employee-Driven Innovation in Services. *Technology Innovation Management Review, 5*(2), 6–14.

Watanabe, K., Kishita, Y., Tsunetomo, K., & Takenaka, T. (2020). Socially-Conscious Service System Design in the Digital Era: Research Agenda. In T. Takenaka, S. Han, & C. Minami (Eds.), *Serviceology for Services. ICServ 2020. Communications in Computer and Information Science, 1189* (pp. 266–274). Springer.

Watanabe, K., Mochimaru, M., & Shimomura, Y. (2016). Service Engineering Research in Japan: Towards a Sustainable Society. In A. Jones, P. Ström, B. Hermelin, & G. Rusten (Eds.), *Services and the Green Economy* (pp. 221–244). Palgrave Macmillan.

Watanabe, S. (1991). Japanese Quality Control Circle: Why it Works. *International Labour Review, 130*(1), 57–80.

14

Organizational and Individual Reality of Innovation: Similarities and Differences

Shashwat Shukla, Shantam Shukla, and Sonam Chawla

Introduction

Innovation has come to occupy a central place in the literature of strategy (Cusumano, Gawer, & Yoffie, 2019). The various fundamental views of organizational strategy focus on the ability of an organization to handle competition. In an increasingly isomorphic world, an organization has to manage competition and create competitive advantages for itself (Udriyah, Tham, & Azam, 2019). Therefore, the role of innovation, to use the resources creatively and in creating unique edges for an organization, becomes critical. Thus, various attempts are made by the organization to do innovation. However, the processes which the organization uses to do innovation hinder innovation in the first place.

This is so because innovation inherently involves chaos and disruption, and a planned approach to chaos or disruption hinders the quality of innovation. Yet, the organization as an entity in itself is a construct of "organizing" and

The original version of this chapter was revised. The correction to this chapter can be found at
https://doi.org/10.1057/978-3-030-59916-4_35

S. Shukla (✉)
University of Allahabad, Allahabad, Uttar Pradesh, India

S. Shukla
Indian Institute of Management, Ahmedabad, Gujarat, India
e-mail: shantams@iima.ac.in

S. Chawla
Jindal Global Business School, Sonipat, Haryana, India
e-mail: sonam@jgu.edu.in

therefore is inherently systematic even in its most basic transactions. As a consequence of this, a lot of the activity which happens under the rubric of innovation in organizations does not give the desired results (Stefflre, 1985). At the same time, it is common to find that under similar circumstances and with far less resources, individual innovators have been able to come up with disruptive innovations (Bhaduri & Kumar, 2011).

One way to look at this situation is to look at organizational innovation and individual innovation as separate entities. However, in this article, we take a different view and elaborate on the fact that most innovations have a group of people working behind them. Thus even individual innovators when looked closely are a group of collaborating individuals. In this sense a comparison between individual innovators and organizational innovation can be made.

In such a comparison, the key feature is to analyze the manner in which the group collaborates under conditions of individual innovation, as compared to the group processes which take place under organizational settings. This contrast may throw up some issues, which can be used to make organizational innovation more efficient and effective. This is the objective of this article, and in order to do so, we first illustrate the methodology followed by an individual innovator through a case study. Following which we juxtapose it with the generic process which is adopted in an organization to undertake innovation. In the concluding section of the chapter, we highlight the insights which have been made evident by the comparison of an individual innovation and organizational innovation.

Theoretical Background

At a fundamental level innovation can be identified as a psychological process (Schweizer, 2006). Innovation as a psychological phenomenon involves both intrapsychic and interpsychic elements. Therefore, in order to understand such a complex psychological phenomenon, we take the theoretical framework of transaction analysis (TA). Though a detailed description of TA is beyond the scope of this chapter, a brief theoretical background is being given which is of relevance to the present case. TA describes the human personality of an individual as being composed of three ego states. The ego states represent the three parts of our personality.

In a technical language, ego state may be described phenomenologically as coherent system of feelings, and operationally as a set of coherent behavior patterns...This repertoire is sorted out into the following categories:

1. Ego states which resemble those of parental figures

2. Ego states which are autonomously directed towards objective appraisal of reality
3. Those which represent archaic relics, still active ego states which were fixated in early childhood. (Berne, 2011)

These ego states can be called as the parent, adult and child ego states, receptively. At any given point, an individual is said to be acting from one of the ego states. To a healthy individual, all the ego states are available, and he can act from the appropriate ego state as per the requirements of the situation. The parent ego states pertain to the ego state which we use when we are issuing instructions or commands to other people primarily based from norms, values and conventions. The adult ego state is related to reasoning and analyzing of information. The child ego state is related with intuition, creativity, spontaneous drive and enjoyment. Furthermore, the child ego state is split into two parts which are the adapted child and the natural child ego states. The natural child is an ego state wherein intuition, creativity, spontaneous drive and enjoyment reside, while the adapted child ego state exhibits either compliant behavior or withdrawal as a consequence of parental training. In most of the individuals, the natural child ego state is not readily available. This is especially true in the case of organizational settings wherein the individual has to follow a lot of norms and rules, which can effectively be done in the adapted child ego state.

Innovative behavior is built on acts of creativity and intuition and therefore requires the natural child ego state to be active. However, the organizational settings predispose us to functioning more from an adapted child which is related with compliance and rule orientation. Thus the TA perspective would say that innovation would involve the high usage of the natural child ego state, followed by medium use of the adult ego state and little use of the parent ego state. While usual management activities which are productivity oriented would involve high usage of the adult ego state, medium use of the adapted child ego state and little use of the parent ego state. In the light of this paradigm, we shall examine our scripts of innovations which we create from the analysis of our case study.

Methodology

We use two complimentary research frameworks to develop our research methodology to test the propositions which we have set forth in the previous section. These frameworks are the case study methodology and transaction analysis (Hancock & Algozzine, 2017). Using the (TA) perspective and case study methodology, we create scripts for organizational innovation and the individual innovator. These scripts comprise the various stages through which an organization or an individual innovator has to go through in an innovation process. These stages are an interplay of psychological factors, management action and microeconomics. Through the contrast of the script's organizational innovation and individual innovator, we identify the key psychological and philosophical differences between the two forms of innovation practices. In the concluding section, we use these psychological and philosophical stances to blend the individual innovator in an organizational setting. In our view this allows the organization to handle the paradox of managing efficiency and innovation at the same time.

Data Analysis and Discussion

Nisha Madhulika is one of the most active YouTubers in India. Her channel on YouTube has 8.1 million subscribers, and her videos are watched not only in India but across the globe. Her channel description as posted on YouTube is "Nishamadhulika makes vegetarian Indian recipes that are easy to cook and good to eat. Watch our videos to discover interesting and delicious recipes and go to our website www.nishamadhulika.com to connect with more food lovers." The number of views her channel gets per month is more than 18 million, and the number of average views per day is between 575,000 and 625,000. She is one of the top ten YouTubers in terms of popularity and subscriber base in India.

Her recipes are about various kinds of Indian dishes and are explained in a very simple and uncomplicated language to the viewers. The cooking videos she posts are accompanied by written instructions for future reference. She uses simple ingredients available at home and her cooking process is easy to follow. This no-nonsense approach in explaining the recipes without any pretense has made her channel the favorite place for people who want to learn about Indian cuisines.

Nisha Madhulika is 56 years old and started her channel in the year 2011. At the time of starting the channel, she had not visualized that what was starting as her hobby and passion would go on to become a phenomenon and a very profitable financial venture. Nisha Madhulika was an accountant who used to work in New Delhi in an information technology company which was formed by her husband. In the year 2006, the couple shifted their residence to Noida, a satellite town on the outskirts of New Delhi.

The time to commute from their new residence to their office in New Delhi was very cumbersome and time-consuming. This made Nisha Madhulika decide to quit her job and stay at home. However, as an active person, she was searching for some meaningful activity in which she could participate. After trying many things, she stumbled upon a food blog while surfing the net one day. She had been a good cook and foodie herself, and the food blog sparked an idea of creating her own.

In 2007, she created her own blog and started posting recipes on it. Gradually the blog started to become very popular due to its no frills approach. The users of the blog gave her very positive feedback which inspired her further to incorporate pictures to illustrate the cooking process of the recipes. Soon she started reviving feedback from the viewers that if she posted videos of her recipes then it would be even more helpful.

The number of recipes on the blog was increasing at a rapid pace, and it was becoming difficult for Nisha Madhulika to organize and manage the blog for easy accessibility. This prompted her to create a website with the help of her son who is a software executive. Thus, the website was launched in 2008. The website further enhanced the quality of recipes which Nisha Madhulika was posting. The website became a vibrant community for food lovers and learners. One of the reoccurring feedbacks from this community to Nisha Madhulika was to post videos of her recipes. By this time YouTube was becoming popular in India, and a number of videos of Indian food recipes were being published online on the platform of Youtube. However, many of the videos which were being posted came from Indians living abroad and targeted the offshore audiences. Even the few numbers of the videos which were posted from India came from chefs and were either complicated to follow or were about exotic dishes rather than regular India cuisine.

In such a scenario, Nisha Madhulika launched her YouTube channel in 2011. The channel became an instant hit. It was supported by an already existing vibrant community of her followers. At the same time, Nisha Madhulika was able to translate her easy and simple approach to cooking in her videos as well. Her channel started to post authentic, easy to cook India dishes, something, which the viewers were interested in knowing rather than the complex and exotic dishes which were being posted by celebrity chefs. In the initial period, making videos was a difficult process for Nisha Madhulika. She was being assisted by her husband, who would shoot the videos for her. However, after the runaway success of the channel, Nisha created a studio setup in her home for shooting the videos. She formed a team of few assistants to help her in the process of making videos and writing recipes on the website while she focused on the cooking aspects. As of today, she and her small team shoot recipes for two days and the rest of the week is spent on attending the feedback, researching and planning for future recipes. Till date she has posted 1507 videos on her YouTube channel.

She earns a healthy sum of money through the YouTube revenue sharing model and has received many offers by corporates for endorsements of their product in her recipes. Interestingly she has refused all these offers and she does not endorse any specific brand. With the popularity of Indian cuisine growing worldwide, Nisha Madhulika has big plans for the future.

Scripts of Innovation

Nisha Madhulika's case provides some interesting insights of disruption, deviation and novel solutions. The case is interesting on many fronts. To start off with, Nisha Madhulika has redefined and rewritten the rules as to how young generations of Indians learn and collaborate about a very important cultural heritage, i.e., cuisine. Traditionally the Indian food culture and its knowledge were passed on from parents to their children, especially from mothers to daughters. Of course, there existed recipe books and magazines on the subject, but those were too sterile to capture the liveliness and social aspects of learning of such an important cultural heritage. The present generation of India has seen greater mobility of young people moving out of their home cities in search for jobs. At the same time, they also face great social pressures for making a professional career. Therefore, the learning process of this intangible culinary wisdom was being disrupted.

It is here that there existed an opportunity to come up with innovative solutions which could cater to the needs of this influential group of people. It was an apt opening for several organizations in the business of fast-moving consumer goods category to build such online platforms. These platforms would have greatly enhanced the brand equity and consumer outreach of the organizations. However, we find that no credible attempts were made in this direction and even those which were made lacked the connect with the end users. It is in this context that Nisha Madhulika was able to fill in this space. It is important to note that she was able to build this using open source tools and very meager resources. Many organizations who were putting in a lot of resources in planning and creating new innovations were not able to come up with such solutions. These organizations had professional chefs, exorbitant advertisement spend, established brands and event outreach programs to create online platforms, online communities in their product categories, yet most such initiatives have failed to find any traction with the consumers.

Thus, the important question is that how an individual innovator was able to create something which an organization with more resources was unable to do? It is this vital question which we seek to address through our case analysis. It is our assertion that organizations approach innovation in the same way as they approach efficiency. According to us such an approach severely jeopardizes the quality of innovation. In the following sections, we try to test this assertion in the light of the case.

The script of Nisha Madhulika case starts off with a phase of fertile void. The concept of fertile void is taken from gestalt psychotherapy. The concept essentially says that individuals as cognitive beings absorb a lot of stimuli from the environment in the form of observation and sensing. They then go through a phase of inactive processing, whereby this data/observation is given some meaning. In studies of creativity, such phases have been called the incubation-illumination phases. The characteristic of this phase is unhindered observation and period of quiet reflection. In Nisha Madhulika case, we find that Nisha was going through a lot of online and offline resources on recipes without any specific objective. This was a period of fertile void for her wherein she was absorbing stimuli relating to this subject in an unhindered way. At the same time, since she had no set objective of achieving any particular end result from this process, she was able to do unconscious reflection on the subject.

The result of such a process was that she was able to get some vital insights regarding the recipe resources as they had existed at that time. Her own comments are quite indicative of the feeling an individual has when he develops an insight on an issue. Such times are associated with a sudden excitement and a new understanding which the person didn't have. She says, "I always loved cooking even as a young girl. And when I read the blog that showed pictures of all stages of cooking, it blew my mind." The excitement which is built in the first phase is a very important outcome along with the insights which were garnered in this phase of fertile void.

The second phase of the case can be termed as the experiment phase. On the basis of the insights garnered in the earlier phase, simple experiments can be done. These experiments are the application of the insights which are the outcome of the first phase. The experiments generally represent a new way or a deviation in combining the subsystems of an existing process. In the present case, the insight was built around the fact that the recipes can be written in a much simpler and easy language. Secondly, the dishes should be useful to the viewers rather than complicated and exotic dishes which few people require. Lastly, the cooking process of the dishes should be simple and easy to follow.

As the experiment phase proceeds ahead, it results into the formation of a working model or a prototype. The working model is shared with end users at this stage itself, who start using the working model and generate reliable and pertinent feedback for the design team in a quick turnaround time. On the basis of the feedback important refinements are made. This loop of refinement and feedback leads to quick and continuous improvements in the design of the working model. In the present case, the author started to write the recipes in a regional language in a blog. She received a feedback that the recipes would be more illustrative if she included actual picture of the various steps in the cooking process. This was incorporated which increased the popularity of the blog further. The readers subsequently proposed that videos of recipes could be made and that they would be really helpful. This feedback sparked the idea of creating videos of recipes which went onto become one of the core ideas of the phenomenal success of this venture.

Let us contrast this, with how an organization would have proceeded, if they had to come up with some innovation relating to YouTube and recipes. To start off, an organization would begin with an objective to innovate because organizations understand the importance of innovation and its significance to their competitive edge. However, this starting point itself cuts off a significant part upon which innovations are based. Innovations involve a lot of absorption of the already occurring processes. When the objective of a working group is to innovate, the unhindered absorption of experiential data does not take place, because the objective is in the background and it fixes the frame of reference to some extent.

Frequently, once the organization has set its goal to innovate, they proceed to conduct group and creativity exercises that aid in the innovation process. After warming up, with these exercises, the members of the working group are encouraged to think in a similar manner upon the issues for which an innovative solution is required. This phase is often christened as the ideation phase. The ideation phase is used to generate several ideas. From these set of ideas, some important ideas are shortlisted, around whom the organization decides to build an innovative solution.

The shortlisted ideas are placed before an interdepartmental or cross-functional team. Herein, the working group/design team has to justify the viability of the idea, so that the organization may allocate the necessary funds for the innovation project. In order to get the ideas approved, the working group adds a lot of inorganic elements into the proposal of the innovative solution. The cross-functional team discusses the proposal from a critical perspective, and various additions/alterations are made to it due to the quasi political process to evolve a consensus. Thus, the final idea after the various additions and alterations is now more of an incremental solution rather than a disruptive innovative solution. In the following table we highlight the differences in the scripts of innovation as they occur in individual innovation and organizational innovation.

A comparison of both the scripts is presented in Table 14.1.

In the script of the individual innovator we find that the initial phase of the innovation building process is characterized by exploratory behavior. During such times, the person is acting from the natural child ego state and thus is fully able to utilize his creative or intuitive potential. These are ripe conditions for the germination of deviant solution or disruptive ideas. After this phase the person enters into the experimentation stage wherein the novel idea is translated into a working model by the creative use of the resources. Again, the natural child ego state is dominant. As the working model progresses the innovator needs assistance from other people and therefore the role of the adult ego state becomes important. The adult ego state allows the individual to build a flexible network of resources and in collaboration with other individuals. Once an innovation has reached the stage of maturity, it is shared with the end users. It is at this stage some usage of the parent ego state is required to deal with some issues raised by the end users.

In contrast the organizational script starts with an objective which is usually mandated by an organizational policy. The employees need to comply with the stated organizational objective and exhibit innovative behavior. As a consequence, the individuals start the innovation process from the adapted child ego state and therefore are likely to exhibit more of compliance behavior of the adapted child rather than the intuitive, creative behavior which resides in the natural child. To overcome this organizational handicap, some organizations hold brainstorming sessions to allow individuals to enter into the natural child ego state. Interventions like these do allow individual to access their natural child ego state, but it happens only to a limited extent. It is hindered by many handicaps such as the interventions do not happen in real time, i.e., when the innovation process is happening, rather the participants have to rely on their memory or recorded data which effects the quality of the ideas.

Once the ideas are generated, they are debated, discussed and critically analyzed to select the most feasible ideas. This process again pushes the participants in the adult ego state as they reason the feasibility of the ideas. The selected idea is then processed for approval, which primarily involves the usage of adult and parent ego states. After this stage the idea is executed. In this phase some part of natural child ego state is used; however, the idea is executed not with a spirit of experimentation but rather to meet deadlines and standard requirements which again makes use of the adult ego state as the main ego state.

Table 14.1 Comparison of individual and organizational innovation scripts

Script 1: Individual innovation	Script 2: Organizational innovation
Innovation starts with a phase of unhindered, nonobjective absorption of stimuli and data	Innovation starts with the intent to innovate to address a specific issue or problem which requires a new solution or to achieve competitive advantage. In order to achieve this, there is a formal meeting, wherein this objective is officially stated and recorded by means of a bureaucratic process
Individual innovator focuses more on sensing the data in an unhindered way	Typically, organizations engage in initiatives such as brainstorming sessions wherein the participants are encouraged to think in an unhindered way rather than sensing of data in an unhindered way
The sensing of data is done as the phenomena are taking place	The data which is used for the innovative solution has already been recorded or is being recollected from memory of the participants
The idea of innovation is worked upon to construct a working model before it is shared with other people. Some people may help in making the working model; however, their role is largely that of assistants in execution rather than critical working partners who influence the building of the working model. The model is shared with the end users who perform the dual role of consumers and collaborators. They are able to give feedback regarding the functioning of the innovation from the point of view of end users. The innovation develops organically with several cycles of exchange between the innovators and end users, till it attains a level of maturity	The focus is on generation of several ideas from each individual of the innovation team. All the individual ideas are then pooled together, and a few ideas are selected out of the pool ideas after intense debate and scrutiny. The ideas generated are deliberate act of thinking wherein the objective is to change and alter the process of preexisting thing. All the selected ideas are evaluated for their viability and ranked, and the most feasible idea is selected from this list of ideas
No such process is followed by the individual innovator	The selected idea is converted into a proposal of an inorganic way by addition of various elements such as existing organizational presumptions and presuppositions. This proposal of the innovation is then put before an interdepartmental committee or cross-functional team for approvals. After this stage the innovation projects is executed, and the outcome is offered to the end users

(continued)

Table 14.1 (continued)

Script 1: Individual innovation	Script 2: Organizational innovation
The innovator and end users are very close and show and overlap of roles of collaborators and end users	If the end users might give some feedback, it is passed on to the execution team, which in turn passes it onto the design team. The design team might make some changes as per the feedback, but they have to go through a process of obtaining the necessary approvals. In this process of approvals and critical analysis, changes might not be approved or alternatively some changes are approved and again presented to the end users. Thus, there is much time lag in this process of feedback
In terms of resources individual innovator works more likely with frugal, open source means to generate the working model. This approach cuts down the cost of production of the innovation.	The organizational resources are mobilized to produce the innovation. Often the cost of production by open resources is less than organizational resources, which are viable only under conditions of economies of scale.

Innovation being a creative, intuitive process requires high usage of the natural child ego state, followed by medium use of the adult ego state and little use of the parent ego state. We find that the first script of the individual innovator is closer to this condition as compared to the organizational script. Thus, TA perspective would prescribe that the experiential stances of the individual innovator script are built in into the organizational innovation process so that it meets the psychological requirements of the innovation process more aptly. We elaborate on these aspects in the concluding section.

Conclusion

The concept of organization presupposes the act of organizing. In other words, at a deep philosophical level, even in their smallest unit of transactions, organization are performing an organizing act. The net effect of such an effort is seen in the form of efficiency and consistency. Therefore, when the organization tries to perform the transaction of innovation, it invariably tries to do organized innovation. Organized innovation is an oxymoron because innovation essentially involves disruption which is the antithesis of organizing. Thus, the ability of organizations to innovate is significantly depleted.

However, with the rapid pace of technology and information dissemination, the competitive advantage of organization is constantly being eroded. One of the ways to rejuvenate the competitive advantage is by coming up with disruptive innovations. Thus, it creates a peculiar situation wherein innovation is required by the organization but the very nature of organizations makes it difficult for organizations to innovate. However, if we apply some of the philosophical stances which are taken by individual innovators then the potential of organizations to innovate may be increased. In this section we focus on some of these stances and elaborate on ways in which they can be incorporated in organizations so that organized innovation is avoided.

The first important stance of individual innovators valuable to organizations is that of nonobjectiveness. In other words, instead of making innovation as a goal, the organization should focus on the conditions which allow innovation to take place. In the case of individual innovators, the urge to innovate is an organic process and not a key responsibility area fixed and pre-decided in advance. Similarly, organizations should allow individuals to innovate when they have the urge to innovate rather than making it mandatory or as deliberate effort.

This brings us to the second stance which is a common pool of resources. Once an individual has the urge to innovate, then he must have access to areas within the organization wherein he can go and use open, common resources to innovate. These common centers can consist of some basic infrastructure both in terms of hardware and software which allows individuals to start working on their innovation. Herein the innovator can bring in other people from within and outside the organization to assist him in the creation of his working model.

The third stance is regarding the funding pattern. As we have pointed out earlier, organizations have an elaborate mechanism of approvals for funding an innovation. However, this is a generic process which is useful when a large sum of expenditure is required. Innovation can also be seen as microfinance issue wherein small sums of money are required till the stage of creating a working model. Therefore, the process of funding should be based on concepts of microfinance which are simple and quick. At later stages when the working model has matured and large sums are required, then elaborate approval mechanism can be followed.

These stances bring back a lot of the fluidity to the organizational innovation process. This may lead to a quasi-individual-driven innovation process happening under organizational settings, which results in a more authentic and genuine innovation. There are many spin-offs of this process which can act as important adjunct to the innovation process. One of them is the deepening of an innovation culture which is organically constructed rather than driven by the top management. For example, the creation of common resource centers bereft of organization rules of interaction can serve as the places wherein an innovation culture which gets formed among employees. Extant research on innovation places great value to the requirement of such a culture which is robust, dynamic and participative.

The other spin-off could be that when innovation is attempted in this way then it becomes an ongoing activity wherein many small innovations continue to take place in the organization all the time. In other words, the organization is not focused toward the big disruptive innovation only. The small innovations collectively give the organization significant competitive advantage and beat organizational isomorphism. And once in a while, such fertile conditions lead to a big disruptive game-changing innovation.

Bill gates has once quipped that "Software innovation, like almost every other kind of innovation, requires the ability to collaborate and share ideas with other people, and to sit down and talk with customers and get their feedback and understand their needs." All this happens in an environment which celebrates experimentation and is open to slack. Therefore, the organizational space must provide room for such numerous small oasis of innovation. These oases are constructed within the organizational setting using the psychological and philosophical stances of individual innovation. In this way the organization would be able to blend together efficiency and disruption in a meaningful way, leading to authentic and genuine innovation.

References

Berne, E. (2011). *Games People Play: The Basic Handbook of Transactional Analysis.* Tantor eBooks.

Bhaduri, S., & Kumar, H. (2011). Extrinsic and Intrinsic Motivations to Innovate: Tracing the Motivation of 'Grassroot' Innovators in India. *Mind & Society, 10*(1), 27–55.

Cusumano, M. A., Gawer, A., & Yoffie, D. B. (2019). *The Business of Platforms: Strategy in the Age of Digital Competition, Innovation, and Power.* New York, NY: HarperCollins.

Hancock, D. R., & Algozzine, B. (2017). *Doing Case Study Research: A Practical Guide for Beginning Researchers.* Teachers College Press.

Schweizer, T. S. (2006). The Psychology of Novelty-Seeking, Creativity and Innovation: Neurocognitive Aspects within a Work-Psychological Perspective. *Creativity and Innovation Management, 15*(2), 164–172.

Stefflre, V. (1985). Organizational Obstacles to Innovation: A Formulation of the Problem. *Journal of Product Innovation Management: An International Publication of the Product Development & Management Association, 2*(1), 3–11.

Udriyah, U., Tham, J., & Azam, S. (2019). The Effects of Market Orientation and Innovation on Competitive Advantage and Business Performance of Textile SMEs. *Management Science Letters, 9*(9), 1419–1428.

15

Digitalization of Work Processes: A Framework for Human-Oriented Work Design

Hartmut Hirsch-Kreinsen and Peter Ittermann

Introduction

The diffusion of digital technologies in the industrial sector will have far-reaching consequences for jobs and skills. This is especially true for highly industrialized countries like Germany, where this sector accounts for roughly 26 percent of the country's gross domestic product (GDP) (Germany Trade & Invest, 2019). It is expected that the diffusion of digital technologies will alter work processes in the industrial sector with potentially disruptive social and economic consequences (Avant, 2014). In the international debates, this perspective is referred to as the "second machine age" (Brynjolfsson & McAfee, 2014) and the "third industrial revolution" (Rifkin, 2011), or, in Germany, the topic is discussed intensively under the heading "fourth industrial revolution" resp. "Industry 4.0" (Forschungsunion & acatech, 2013). Of course, the diffusion of Industry 4.0 and increased digitalization is changing the world of work. These changes will become commonplace in the future, but predicting the consequences of digitalization for jobs and skills is a much harder task.

This chapter refers to this discussion and the respective open questions. It draws on the research on the development of industrial work in the context of the diffusion of digital technologies in the industrial sector of Germany.

H. Hirsch-Kreinsen (✉) • P. Ittermann
TU Dortmund University, Dortmund, Germany
e-mail: hartmut.hirsch-kreinsen@tu-dortmund.de;
peter.ittermann@tu-dortmund.de

A. McMurray et al. (eds.), *The Palgrave Handbook of Workplace Innovation*,
https://doi.org/10.1007/978-3-030-59916-4_15

Especially, the authors focus on the prerequisites and chances of a human-centered design of digitized industrial work; in other words, it asks for the possibilities of *workplace innovation* in a digitized world of labor. Hence, in the chapter, the following theses will be outlined:

- First, there are no clear prospects for the development of digital work; rather, very different development perspectives can be assumed (see "Divergent Perspectives on the Future of Industrial Work" section).
- Second, the development of digitization and Industry 4.0 are therefore to be regarded as a design project. A useful conceptual base for this is the approach of the *socio-technical system* (see "Socio-Technical Approach" section).
- Third, based on this approach, basic criteria for the design and implementation human-oriented forms of digitized work can be systematically developed (see "Options for Human-Oriented Work Design" section).

Methodologically, the contribution draws on the results of the qualitative empirical analysis that deal with the diffusion of digital technologies and the development of work in industrial sectors in the highly industrialized country of Germany, and which was carried out by the authors and their research group between 2015 and 2018. In detail, two methodological approaches have been pursued: on the one hand, the reasoning is based on the results of ongoing analysis of the relevant literature and the public and scientific discourse on digitization and the change of work. Additionally, the results of existing statistical-quantitative analyses are summarized. On the other hand, the analysis uses the results of a series of case studies of industrial companies and of additional expert interviews with scientists, policymakers, representatives of industrial associations, and union members in Germany.

All in all, the research sample includes 23 case studies with companies from mechanical engineering, electrical engineering, the furniture industry, and logistics. Most of the companies are small- to medium-sized companies with up to 500 employees (14 companies), some are larger companies (9 companies), and some have more than 1000 employees at the production sites examined. The introduction and operational consequences of various components and systems of digital technologies were examined in the factories. For example, the subject was the introduction of assembling robots, planning and control systems, digital assistance systems as well as networked transport and logistics systems, and their consequences for work and employment.

Divergent Perspectives on the Future of Industrial Work

Many studies suggest that digital technologies will change the nature of work in almost all sectors, including manufacturing—from the activities on the shop floor to related areas such as planning, control systems, and product development. Consequently, the demands on leadership and management will also change significantly: There will be new requirements on the design of workplace innovations and the participation of employees (Oeij & Dhondt, 2017; Howaldt, Kopp, & Schultze, 2018). Although studies predict thorough reorganization of work within companies and in the relationships between companies and their value chains, they do not agree about how industrial work will change and what those changes will mean in terms of job opportunities and skill requirements. Therefore, the thesis is that there are no clear prospects for the development of digital work; rather, very different development perspectives can be assumed (see "Introduction" section). Based on our considerations and empirical findings, the following development perspectives of digitized industrial work can be highlighted (Hirsch-Kreinsen, 2016; Hirsch-Kreinsen, Ittermann, & Niehaus, 2018):

A Pessimistic Perspective

One line of arguments can be characterized as pessimistic about how the future development of industrial work will affect workers. According to this perspective, the rapid development and dissemination of digital technologies and an increasingly growing gap between the new demands of technology and the difficulties in skilling or re-skilling workers will mean fewer opportunities for employees.

This argument contends that the demand for many tasks and qualifications will decline, reducing the number of available jobs. Many jobs will be replaced by digitalization. The well-known authors Frey and Osborne support this view in a study of the US labor market. They show that very significant potentials for job losses go hand in hand with the use of digital technologies. They conclude that approximately 47 percent of all activities in the American labor market over the next one or two decades could be threatened by automation (Frey & Osborne, 2017). Other authors present similar findings for the European and German labor markets (Bowles, 2014; Dengler & Matthes, 2015, 2018).

Studies with a pessimistic view of technology argue also that increasing adoption of technology will erode jobs requiring medium-level skills, while those in jobs demanding higher qualifications or jobs that cannot be routinized easily will benefit. This "skill-biased technical change", as it is frequently referred to, will exacerbate labor market inequalities. Following these authors, labor-intensive manufacturing work such as automotive installation and system monitoring and many routine administrative and service activities that require medium skill levels are also more routinized and can therefore be replaced by automation more easily (Autor, 2013). Complex activities in high-wage areas, such as management, consulting, or financial services, and low-wage jobs such as simple manual but due to particular material characteristics not routinizable tasks on the shop floor like specific assembly activities and social work in healthcare, however, will continue to enjoy high demand as they are not as easy to automate. Goos and Manning characterize this trend as the emergence of "lousy and lovely jobs" (Goos & Manning, 2007).

Similar trends toward a differentiated structure of activities have been elucidated in research on industrial work in the context of intelligent network logistics systems—automated systems for managing supply and distribution that rely on digital technologies, such as the self-controlling storage systems used by manufacturing companies. A clear job polarization is already taking place (e.g. Warnhoff & Krzywdzinski, 2018): On the one hand, sophisticated, more high-skilled occupations such as managers and supervisors have been created to run the new technological systems. On the other hand, low-value-added tasks and simple activities like packaging and assembling were retained, since the cost of automating these tasks is still higher than the cost of paying a low-skilled workforce to execute them. Companies often avoid fully automated systems due to high technological complexity and high cost, but the tasks they automate are those that would have been performed by middle-skilled workers (Hirsch-Kreinsen, Ittermann, & Falkenberg, 2019).

An Optimistic Perspective

Another strand of research predicts more positive effects of digitalization: job creation, increased skill requirements, and a general revaluation of jobs and skills, together constituting a "new, more humane turn" (Zuboff, 2010). These optimistic studies suggest that the efficiency gains, new products, new markets, and new employment opportunities in the longer term will compensate the negative employment effects of technological change in the short-term. Evangelista et al. see, on the basis of a detailed review of the international literature in anticipation of the adoption of digital technologies little clear impact on employment. In particular, they emphasize that it is particularly difficult to attribute causal effects on employment to this technology (Evangelista, Guerrieri, & Meliciani, 2014).

In Germany's Industry 4.0 debate, experts predict high productivity gains and higher economic growth rates (Bauer, Schlund, & Ganschar, 2015) as well as consistently better jobs of greater technology adoption. Thus, the vast majority of manufacturers expect the share of the workforce employed in industrial production to remain relatively stable and significant over the next few years and do not expect large negative employment effects. The same result is found in a study by the Boston Consulting Group, which predicts a 6 percent increase in employment in German manufacturing over the next 10 years, or about 390,000 jobs between 2015 and 2025 (BCG, 2015).

With respect to skills, many authors predict that digitalization of work will bring a growing appreciation or an "upgrading" of worker qualifications. First, this is considered to be the result of increasing automation of simple jobs such as machine monitoring or simple and highly routinized assembly work that are extensively substituted. Second, upgrading will affect all employee groups. In this perspective, digitalization of work is a process of computerization, which makes a wide variety of information about ongoing processes increasingly available. The complexity and possible applications of technology result in fundamentally new and as yet unknown requirements for all job-related activities. For example, under these conditions skilled machine operators are able to make decisions about work flow sequences on the basis of an optimized control and information system.

Generally spoken, the new technology provides data and evaluation capabilities that allow for a much higher degree of transparency in the production processes. The optimistic perspective emphasizes that a general upgrading of qualifications in the future will not only be possible but will inevitably be materialized. Following this perspective, the model of work in manufacturing industries may evolve into a pattern which can be characterized by a very limited division of labor, high flexibility, and an increasing skill level.

Yet adopting the technology and establishing the corresponding work environments is not easy. Complex production systems are very susceptible to interference and may have nontransparent and unpredictable effects (Grote, 2005). Therefore, workers will require a high degree of flexibility and problem-solving skills going forward. Finally, the life cycle of complex systems can always involve new system states that are difficult to control: unexpected start-up problems as well as unexpected disturbances in normal operation.

Socio-Technical Approach

Without doubt, there are opposing perspectives on how the digitalization of work will affect workers of different skill levels and the nature of jobs. Of course, the pessimistic perspective does present a possible scenario. In other words, there is no linear relation between new technologies and work; rather alternative development perspectives of work exist. Therefore, as highlighted with the second thesis (see "Introduction" section), the development of digitization and Industry 4.0 have to be regarded as a design project. As shown below, a useful conceptual base for this is the approach of the *socio-technical system*.

This thesis can be justified with reference to the common wisdom of labor research; there is no technological determinism. Rather, it is a matter of a complex and reciprocal relationship shaped by the influence of multiple economic, social, and labor-political factors that ultimately determines in what way the given new technological application potentials will actually be put to work and what outcomes for labor will emerge (Evangelista et al., 2014). Moreover, as research in the sociology of work of recent decades has shown, it is often the form of the labor-organization's embeddedness and the ultimate form of the new technologies that are the determining factors for their use. It has become clear particularly that technical and organizational design alternatives always exist that remain the domain of company and labor policy decision-making processes. Finally, the way that industrial work evolves in response to technological advancements will depend strongly on how policies and stakeholders shape work design. Work design refers to the way labor is deployed in a particular company or institution—the way jobs are executed and the kinds of tasks and interactions they involve. Work design affects the skill variety and autonomy of given job. Multiple economic and social factors and labor market policies have also a bearing on work design and the complex interaction between technology and jobs. These factors will ultimately determine how new technology will be adopted and how it will shape the future of work.

Therefore, digitization and Industry 4.0 are understood as a *design project*. Following our analytical and conceptual considerations, this perspective should be based on the approach of the *socio-technical system*. The main goal of this approach should be to realize both efficient and human-oriented forms of digital work. To realize this, the socio-technical approach emphasizes the interactions and interdependences between technology, humans, and the organization as a whole. Although research has not always been consistent in its definitions, a socio-technical system can be understood as a production unit consisting of interdependent technology, personnel, and organization subsystems (Trist & Bamforth, 1951; Rice, 1963). Though the technological subsystem can limit the design possibilities of the two other subsystems, these display the independent social and psychological characteristics that in turn affect the functioning of the technological subsystem.

If digitization and Industry 4.0 are understood as socio-technical system, the subsystem technology includes, e.g. new technologies as innovative transport technologies and "smart objects" that autonomously steer themselves through the manufacturing processes. The subsystem personnel includes skill requirements, employment structures, and participation modalities of the employees. And, the subsystem organization refers to changed workplace structures, new management functions, and innovative business models. Naturally in the design of the total system, the structures and economic requirements of each field of application and the various knowledge domains of Industry 4.0 must be taken into account. The company interests are here explicit in the sense that they want efficient technologies and competitive conditions of production. Furthermore, the socio-technical system is embedded in strategic and institutional framework and socioeconomic context factors (Fig. 15.1).

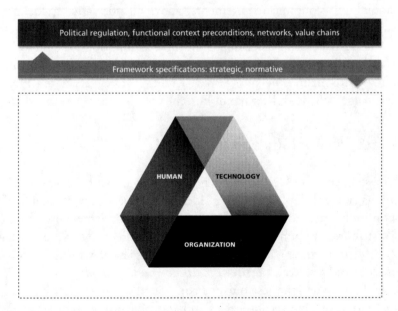

Fig. 15.1 Concept of socio-technical system (own source)

In this approach it is not a question of *either technology or the individual,* but rather a *complementary* design should be striven for with the single system elements adjusted to one another in a total socio-technical system (Trist & Bamforth, 1951). Complementarity means here that, depending on the situation, the specific strengths and weaknesses of the technology and humans are equally considered. In the complementary design of the total system, the leading criterion should of course always be to exploit as well as the potential advantages of a human-oriented work design. In other words, the concept of the socio-technical system highlights the principle of *joint optimization* of work, organization, and technology.

Options for Human-Oriented Work Design

The third thesis can thus be taken up and discussed that based on the approach of the socio-technical system, basic criteria for the design and implementation of human-oriented forms of digitized work can be systematically developed (see "Introduction" section). To this end, the design criteria should be linked not to the functional modes of the single subsystems, but rather to the *interdependencies* between the technology, personnel, and organization: *In other words, it is a matter of designing the interfaces between the technical, the personnel, and the organizational subsystems.* For the concrete configuration, besides functional and economic requirements, above all normative guidelines for human-oriented work, as well as divergent social and labor policy interests, play an important role. Proceeding from these assumptions, the present state of research and our own analyses, the options for work design can be outlined as follows (Ittermann, Niehaus, Hirsch-Kreinsen, Dregger, & ten Hompel, 2016; Dregger, Niehaus, Ittermann, Hirsch-Kreinsen, & ten Hompel, 2016):

Interface: Technology and Personnel

The design of the interface between the technological and the personnel subsystems is not only an issue of considering the well-known criteria of the ergonomically oriented dialogue design, but rather fundamentally a matter of the "distributed responsibility for action" (Rammert & Schulz-Schäffer, 2002). This is because, with the digital technologies, new forms of *function-distribution and interaction between machine and the human worker* are made possible. How to design these must be considered one of the key questions in the realization of digitized processes and Industry 4.0. This aspect refers to *alternative solutions to the design* of the human-machine interface: On the one hand, it is a matter of the fundamental question of the substitution of tasks and activities as a consequence of automated systems. On the other hand, divergent perspectives collide that regard the distribution between workers and machines of tasks and control. Assistance systems can make possible a greater variety of work and support on-the-job learning processes but also, through strict process guidelines, limit the space for action of workers.

In regard to the stated principle of complementary system interpretation, an interface design must make possible above all a satisfactory functional capability of the total system. This requires a holistic and collaborative view of the human-machine interaction that identifies the specific strengths and weaknesses of human work and technological automation. A central tenant here is that human work should attain and conserve transparence and control possibilities over production processes; gain and develop the often indispensible practical knowledge; and be supported in this by intelligent assistance systems.

This form of interface design leads to a broadening of the employees' task spectrum, fulfilling the need for challenging, learning-friendly work and opening new possibilities for workers' involvement in design and decision-making. The work situation is thus characterized by a digitally widened field and the need for new skills. For example, assistance systems should be able to be contextually or locally adjusted by the single workers to their individual needs and performance capabilities.

Interface: Personnel and Organization

The interface between the subsystems personnel and organization refers to the change in scope of actions, work-time models, and new demands on standards of training and skills. A key question in this respect is how resources in the form of available competences and experiential knowledge of employees can be used for the design of Industry 4.0 systems. Furthermore, the organizational design of digitized work is decisive for the completeness of operational tasks, as well as for the development of the scopes of action, and learning and qualification opportunities.

In a skill-oriented perspective, the given design spaces can be used to achieve a sustainable revaluation of activities and qualifications. This could make possible efficient forms of work organization as well as work situations with particular qualification demands and in certain circumstances a high degree of behavioral scope, the polyvalent deployment of workers, and a multitude of opportunities for "learning on the job". Relevant competences are self-acquired in the process, or in the form of job-related and job-integrated approaches: This means individual learning, e.g. through job rotation, as well as forms of "learning islands" or "learning factories". Learning-promotive work organization and qualification strategies should orient themselves here on the heterogeneous levels of experience and different competence bundles of the various employee groups. A central characteristic is that the tasks will rarely be addressed to single workers; rather, a "work collective" acts in a self-organizing way, highly flexible, and situationally determined according to the problems to be solved in the technological system.

This organizational pattern can be referred to a "holistic work organization" or, metaphorically, "swarm organization": a loose network of qualified and differently specialized employees (Hirsch-Kreinsen, 2016). The central feature of this organizational model is the absence of defined tasks for individual employees. Rather, the "work collective" functions in a highly flexible, self-organized, and situationally determined way, adapting its behavior to the problems that need to be solved around the technological system. In order for this new work model to be successful, workers need to be appropriately trained and continually upgrade their knowledge on-the-job. Furthermore, the argument is that cooperative work processes especially characterized by high work autonomy can help skilled workers effectively harness digitalized systems to their advantage (Lee & Seppelt, 2009).

The design of revaluated and broadened scopes of action is also a crucial precondition to the deployment of personnel of different abilities and performance capacities in one and the same process area, because a broad spectrum of tasks will be available. This possibility can on the one hand be used to deploy employees for specific activities, but on the other hand also rotations and exchange of tasks are possible, encouraged by broad qualification processes. The different design possibilities are not least also of great importance with regard to the possibility of age-mixed teams, in order to at least mitigate the consequences of the demographic turn of the workforce.

Interface: Organization and Technology

At the interface between the organizational and technological subsystems new design options are emerging referring to redesigning the overarching process and organization of the whole company. This addresses the change of the direct value chain processes in terms of function and hierarchy, as well as the structuring and the link between the core processes of the production and the associated management and support processes. New design options result in these dimensions from the fact that with the new digital systems and their local and simultaneously networked intelligence, a far-reaching departure from the earlier centralized IT systems can take place. These developments allow a shift to decentralization and dehierarchization—often within already relatively "flatly" structured company organizations. Furthermore, the company organization can not only be decentralized but also permanently flexibilized. Generally, the flexibility of the new technological systems suggests a highly individualized production, in some cases a "minimum batch size 1". Therefore, an organizational structure based on autonomous, self-controlling systems with a *decentralized control and intelligence* should be taken account.

This concerns not only the manufacturing area but also the hierarchical dimension of the entire company organization, as well as the logistics. Social media functionalities and with them the changed forms of communication affect also indirect areas such as planning, control, and engineering as well as direction and management functions. Connected with this is the reorganization of management functions, for example, in production and business managements, in consequence of the change in their decision-making competences and shifts in responsibilities to subordinate levels.

Finally, based on networked planning and control systems and the application of data mining methods, new forms of value chain structures and *new business models* become possible. In the "smart networked factory", industrial value creation is no longer limited to what takes place within the traditional organizational boundaries. Rather, a decentralized control and intelligence is required that still remains controllable. In consequence of this digitization process, new business models come into use to meet the technology- and organization-related challenges and their interrelations. Changes to the entire value chains are conceivable that may significantly transcend previous forms of inter-company division of labor and outsourcing. With that the organizational requirements are given for overcoming company barriers to an intensified service and customer orientation as well as to change in business models.

Basic Guidelines for Work Design

The outlined options in the design of the interfaces between personnel, technology, and organization are summarized in the following. It has already been stressed that in this, the key aim is to elaborate the socio-technical design criteria for human-oriented industrial work under the conditions of the application of digital technologies. It must be however underscored here that the design criteria reach back to the established knowledge stores of labor research and work design. To be mentioned here are, for example, the "classical" criteria of human-oriented work design, such as self-organization, encouragement of learning, or decentralization (Ulich, 2005). However, the technological functions of the new technologies open up not only new options for realizing the design objectives but there also emerge new challenges for work design. The following basic guidelines for work design can be highlighted:

Hybrid interaction between machines and humans: The criteria for the design of new forms of the interaction between machine and human being can be summarized as follows:

- *Context sensitivity and adaptivity*—these criteria comprise aspects of the ergonomically oriented adjustment of digital systems to specific working conditions and loads, eventually a systematic load monitoring, or the automation of especially difficult processes. Moreover, this is an issue of situation-specific, optimal provision of data and information to ensure a disturbance-free work flow and avoid stress-causing, costly interruptions and slowdowns. Necessary is an intelligent capability to adjust the information and assistance systems to individual, partly differing worker skill levels, in order to thereby ensure on the personnel side the possibilities for continual learning and qualification processes. Finally, the deployment of assistance systems should support the often essential tacit, resp. practical knowledge of employees.
- *Complementarity*—this criterion focuses on two central aspects of the human-machine interaction: One deals with a flexible, situation-specific division of functions between human and machine, and the other aspect is the preconditions for a sufficiently transparent and controllable system the employees are given. Relevant design aspects are here: assure human-machine interaction through intuitively serviceable and rapidly learnable hardware as well as targeted and situation-specific access to digital information in real time, in order to make thereby the employees' digitally supported decision-making and behavioral options secure and modifiable.

The interaction between smart systems and worker behavior can generally be characterized as *hybrid*. In contrast to a traditional perspective on technology as a passive object, the role of a behaving actor is ascribed in digital technology, with the consequence that not only the division of labor but also the decision-making competences in a specific way must be continually re-established between the new technology and personnel. With that, an until now fully unresolved question is posed: in how far, in human-machine interactions, we can speak of "machine responsibility" as the equal to "human responsibility"? This fundamental, legally, and ethically highly controversial question has been up to now only discussed in relation to the use of autonomous automobiles; in the future however, this discussion will be intensified in the case of autonomous Industry 4.0 systems.

Flexibly integrated work: The key criteria for the design of work activities at the interface of human being and organization can be summed up in the following catchwords:

- *Holism*—this criterion means the completeness of activities in a double sense: for one, an activity should comprise not only executive but also dispositive (organizing, planning and controlling) tasks. For another, this criterion aims for an appropriate, load-reducing mix of more and less demanding tasks. For example, this design objective can be realized in the context of new forms of robot-human collaboration. Moreover, holism of activities is the central requirement for a greater freedom of action as well as the self-organization of work.
- *Dynamics*—with this criterion the following issues are addressed: Firstly, the design of the work-organizationa should make on-the-job learning processes possible and encourage them. Secondly, the new social media functions promote interdisciplinary communication and cooperation between differently specialized employees and thus increase the innovation capacity of the work. Here it is particularly important to be able to "try it out on the shop floor" in order to cope with rapid technological change. At the same time, in the contexts of loosely structured forms of work, also the deployment of employees of differing abilities and output capacities becomes possible, e.g. in age-mixed work groups. Thirdly, low-structured, dynamic work processes are often the precondition for decisions and interventions to effectively solve unexpected emerging disturbances.

With this it becomes clear that the realization of these criteria suggests an organization of work that was termed above (see "Interface: Personnel and Organization" section) as a "holistic work organization" or "swarm organization" which comprises a loose network of qualified and differently specialized employees. This model is remarkable for its high structural openness, a very limited division of labor, self-organized activities, and great flexibility.

Decentralized systems: The central design guideline for the interface between organization and technology is considered to be the introduction of decentralized organization segments. On the one hand, the design potential of the new and particularly decentralized digital technologies will be organizationally exploited. On the other hand, through self-organized (i.e. autonomous), production and logistic systems new possibilities for creating the technical-organizational preconditions for new forms of flexibly integrated and innovative industry work are developed. Catchwords here are the overcoming of company-internal departmental barriers, employee participation, the self-organization of company segments and functions, and interdisciplinary project groups.

On the organizationally horizontal dimension, it is a matter of the flexible integration of differently specialized function areas. On the vertical dimension, the previous division of labor between executing factory-floor functions and the indirect areas will tend to be abandoned and replaced by new forms of flexible and interdisciplinary cooperation including many company functions. Finally, a reorganization of management functions such as production and business managements will be indispensable to the change in their decision-making competences and the shift in responsibilities to lower levels. As addressed above (see "Interface: Organization and Technology" section), decentralization and decentralized systems are also important organizational requirements for companies' intensified opening to the outside and for an intensified service and customer orientation, as well as for the shift in business models.

Altogether, these design criteria fulfill adequately the prerequisites for exploiting the technological and economic potential of the automated, and possibly the individualized, production system. Here one does not—as in an exclusively technology-centered perspective where controlling structures dominate—relegate to the work-behavioral capacity of personnel only fragmentary, residual functions, but rather, new design possibilities for skill-oriented work are explicitly emphasized. Incontrovertible is also that this design perspective on work makes industrial work, firstly, age- and aging-friendly and secondly, it can make industrial jobs attractive again to young generations as qualified, self-responsible, "high-tech" work. The basic criteria for a human-oriented system design in Industry 4.0 are summarized in Fig. 15.2.

Indispensible Additional Conditions

To sum up, it must be stressed that a successful diffusion and implementation of the described design criteria of human-oriented work depend on a number of *additional conditions*. These concern, firstly, the company level and

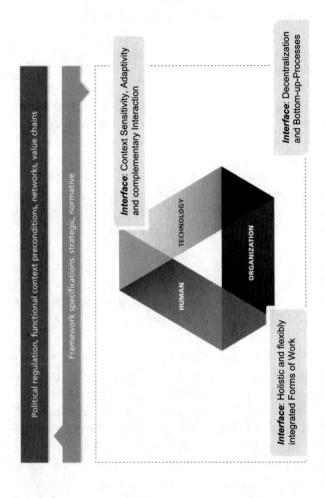

Fig. 15.2 Basic criteria of a human-oriented socio-technical system design (Own source)

secondly, the societal level. In regard to the company level, here two aspects should be emphasized:

First, the *acceptance* of Industry 4.0 systems and with that the resulting work design possibilities, both on the side of the work force, and on the management side, should not be overlooked. That this factor plays an important role is shown not least in the current Industry 4.0 debate. In order to mitigate reservations held by some of the labor force precisely with regard to the new features of work design—e.g. fears over possible job losses—new sources of stress with increased demands for flexibility, problems resulting from data protection, and an intensified surveillance capacity of work performance must be addressed. The reorganization processes to be expected may conceal multiple, new, and in part also contradictory demands on workers for flexibility and self-organization. If there is a disproportion between current needs and resources, stressful behavioral dilemmas could appear for personnel out of the need to manage immediate demands. Effective approaches to solutions to these problems could lie in methods of participative processes for employees and their interest representatives during the introductory and design and implementation process of Industry 4.0 systems. On the management side, above all frequent objections may arise to the far-reaching measures transforming established workplace and company organizational practices. In order to overcome such reservations, the targeted *transfer of knowledge and experience* should be introduced resp. further developed, in which successful and exemplary good-practice cases are presented and the success potential of humanly oriented work forms is communicated.

Second, there are challenges resulting from change in management functions and leadership styles. It has to be assumed that, in the face of the general challenges of the new technologies and in particular the implementation of skill-oriented forms of work, previous hierarchically established management practices and structures will become dysfunctional and obsolete. The direction of necessary change points to the growing importance of "soft skills" as well as high communication and teamwork capabilities: instead of control, it's now leadership and "motivation at a distance"; instead of hierarchic direction, it's now "orchestration" of co-workers and "peer-to-peer" communication and encouragement of worker participation that are becoming the key features of management success. Generally company management must, through a changed status consciousness, take account of the tendency that, through digitization and transformed forms of work, the functional and social boundaries between management and co-workers will erode, and under some circumstances even be reversed. In any case the dominant status differences of the past between "blue collar" and "white collar" will be increasingly blurred.

The objective envisioned is that new forms of self-organization and control will establish themselves, oriented of course to company objectives but characterized by fluid, problem-oriented forms of management. Admittedly, out of this breakup of past management models and the emphasis on bottom-up processes results a certain contradiction: that a sustainable and successful digital transformation in companies is emerging at the same time through functioning top-down processes. However, because of many open questions, this issue must be the object of intensive future research activity.

On the societal level, factors play a role that have as object the transformation and further development of labor policy and social policy regulation forms and at least indirectly affect the introduction of skill-oriented digital forms of work. The issues here are, for example, the regulation of flexibilization, work-time, and co-decision-making as well as continued education and training. Necessary in these areas is often a new labor-political compromise of interests, for only then can obstacles to and reservations over the transformation of work be avoided which emerge from unresolved conflicts and objections. Here cannot be valued too highly the significance of numerous measures in continued training and education as well as in competence development for the spread of humanly oriented forms of work in the context of the digital transformation. A central aim of such measures must be above all to resolve the multiple "digital divides": First, the competence differentials between technology-intensive companies and less technology-intensive ones must be evened out and second, the competence and performance divergences between different employee groups referring to different skills, gender, age, etc. Here, low-qualified work must be taken particularly into account in order not to separate these employees from general developments in qualifications. Overall however, "competence development" means those key educational and social policies required to realize on a broad societal front the skill-oriented and human-oriented forms of work.

Conclusion

To sum up the central arguments of the contribution, it can generally be stated that there is no "one best way" of digital work. It becomes clear that there are no clear, deterministically derivable social effects of digital technologies. The following could be shown in detail:

- First, future industrial work can go in different development paths. On the one hand, negative perspectives, in particular significant job losses and a progressive polarization of work, cannot be ruled out. On the other hand, positive development perspectives can also take hold. This concerns above all the tendencies of a long-term compensation of job losses through new jobs and a trend of a general, many activities of comprehensive upgrading of qualifications paired with an increasing flexibility of work. It must be emphasized, of course, that the different development trends of work are only analytically distinguishable tendencies. Rather, it is more realistic to assume that, depending on the specific company application conditions, intermediate work patterns can be expected. This means that the development trends outlined are in no way mutually exclusive; rather they overlap and can coexist on the sectoral and operational level, complement each other, and develop dynamically.

- Second, digitization and Industry 4.0 have to be understood as a design project. The relation between technology and work is shaped by the influence of multiple economic, social, and labor-political factors that ultimately determines in what way the given new technological application potentials will actually be put to work and what outcomes for work will emerge. The analytical concept for understanding this complex context is the approach of the socio-technical system. In this approach it is not a question of either technology or the individual, but rather a complementary design should be striven for with the single system elements adjusted to one another in a total socio-technical system. In other words, the concept of the socio-technical system highlights the principle of joint optimization of work, organization, and technology.

- Third, on the basis of the socio-technical approach, digitized work can be systematically designed in a human- and skill-oriented way. The new digital technologies offer extensive options for this. It has been shown that the key design spaces are the interdependencies between the technological, personnel, and organizational subsystems: concretely, it is a matter of designing the functional relations or interfaces between the technical, human, and organizational dimension of the socio-technical system. For the concrete configuration, besides functional and economic requirements, above all normative guidelines for human-oriented work play an important role.

However, it must be stressed that a successful diffusion and implementation of human-oriented digital work depend on additional social and political conditions both on the company and societal levels. As shown, on the company level, the acceptance of Industry 4.0 systems and with that the resulting work design possibilities, both on the side of the work force, and on the management side, should not be overlooked. Furthermore, there are challenges resulting from the change in management functions and leadership styles. It has to be assumed that, in the face of the general challenges of the new technologies and in particular the implementation of skill-oriented forms of work, previous hierarchically established management practices and structures will become dysfunctional and obsolete. On the societal level, the transformation and further development of labor policy and social policy regulation forms are an indispensable precondition to realize and implement successfully human-oriented patterns of digital work.

References

Autor, D. (2013). The "Task Approach" to Labor Markets: An Overview. *Journal for Labour Market Research, 46*(3), 185–199.

Avant, R. (2014). The Third Great Wave. *The Economist*, Special Report.

Bauer, W., Schlund, S., & Ganschar, O. (2015). *Industrie 4.0—Volkswirtschaftliches Potential für Deutschland*. Stuttgart: FhG IAO.

BCG (The Boston Consulting Group). (2015). *Industry 4.0—The Future and Growth in Manufacturing Industries*. Retrieved November 5, 2019, from https://www.bcg.com/de/publications/2015/engineered_products_project_business_industry_4_future_productivity_growth_manufacturing_industries.aspx

Bowles, J. (2014). *The Computerisation of European Jobs—Who Will Win and Who Will Lose from the Impact of New Technology Onto Old Areas of Employment?* Retrieved November 5, 2019, from http://bruegel.org/2014/07/the-computerisation-of-european-jobs

Brynjolfsson, E., & McAfee, A. (2014). *The Second Machine Age: Work, Progress, and Prosperity in a Time of Brilliant Technologies*. New York and London: Norton.

Dengler, K., & Matthes, B. (2015). Folgen der Digitalisierung für die Arbeitswelt. Substituierbarkeitspotenziale von Berufen in Deutschland. *IAB-Forschungsbericht* 11/15. Nürnberg.

Dengler, K., & Matthes, B. (2018). Wenige Berufsbilder halten mit der Digitalisierung Schritt. IAB-Kurzbericht 4/2018. Nürnberg.

Dregger, J., Niehaus, J., Ittermann, P. Hirsch-Kreinsen, H., & ten Hompel, M. (2016). *The Digitization of Manufacturing and its Societal Challenges. A Framework for the Future of Industrial Labor*. 2016 IEEE International Symposium on Ethics in Engineering, Science and Technology (ETHICS), Vancouver, BC, Canada, pp. 1–3.

Evangelista, R., Guerrieri, P., & Meliciani, T. (2014). The Economic Impact of Digital Technologies in Europe. *Economics of Innovation and New Technology, 23*(8), 802–824.

Forschungsunion & acatech. (2013). *Recommendations for Implementing the Strategic Initiative INDUSTRIE 4.0. Final Report of the Industry 4.0 Working Group.* Frankfurt/Main.

Frey, C. B., & Osborne, M. A. (2017). The Future of Employment: How Susceptible are Jobs to Computerisation? *Technological Forecasting & Social Change, 114*(1), 254–280.

Germany Trade & Invest. (2019). *Economic Overview Germany: Market, Productivity, Innovation.* Berlin: Germany Trade and Invest.

Goos, M., & Manning, A. (2007). Lousy and Lovely Jobs: The Rising Polarization of Work in Britain. *The Review of Economics and Statistics, 89*(1), 118–133.

Grote, G. (2005). Menschliche Kontrolle über technische Systeme—Ein irreführendes Postulat. In K. Karrer, B. Gauss, & C. Steffens (Eds.), *Beiträge der Forschung zur Mensch-Maschine-Systemtechnik aus Forschung und Praxis* (pp. 65–78). Düsseldorf: Symposion.

Hirsch-Kreinsen, H. (2016). Digitization of Industrial Work: Development Paths and Prospects. *Journal for Labour Market Research, 49*(1), 1–14.

Hirsch-Kreinsen, H., Ittermann, P., & Falkenberg, J. (Eds.). (2019). *Szenarien digitalisierter Einfacharbeit. Konzeptionelle Überlegungen und empirische Befunde aus Produktion und Logistik.* Baden-Baden: Nomos.

Hirsch-Kreinsen, H., Ittermann, P., & Niehaus, J. (Eds.). (2018). *Digitalisierung industrieller Arbeit. Die Vision Industrie 4.0 und ihre sozialen Herausforderungen* (2nd ed.). Baden-Baden: Nomos.

Howaldt, J., Kopp, R., & Schultze, J. (2018). Zurück in die Zukunft? Ein kritischer Blick auf die Diskussion zur Industrie 4.0. In H. Hirsch-Kreinsen, P. Ittermann, & J. Niehaus (Eds.), *Digitalisierung industrieller Arbeit* (2nd ed., pp. 347–363). Baden-Baden: Nomos.

Ittermann, P., Niehaus, J., Hirsch-Kreinsen, H., Dregger, J., & ten Hompel, M. (2016). *Social Manufacturing and Logistics. Gestaltung von Arbeit in der digitalen Produktion und Logistik* (Soziologisches Arbeitspapier 47). Dortmund: TU Dortmund.

Lee, J. D., & Seppelt, B. (2009). Human Factors in Automation Design. In S. Nof (Ed.), *Handbook of Automation* (pp. 417–436). Berlin: Springer.

Oeij, P. R. A., & Dhondt, S. (2017). Theoretical Approaches Supporting Workplace Innovation. In P. R. A. Oeij, D. Rus, & F. D. Pot (Eds.), *Workplace Innovation: Theory, Research and Practice* (pp. 63–78). Cham: Springer Verlag.

Rammert, W., & Schulz-Schäffer, I. (2002). Technik und Handeln. Wenn soziales Handeln sich auf menschliches Verhalten und technische Abläufe verteilt. In W. Rammert & I. Schulz-Schäffer (Eds.), *Können Maschinen handeln. Soziologische Beiträge zum Verhältnis von Mensch und Technik* (pp. 11–64). Frankfurt and New York: Campus.

Rice, A. (1963). *The Enterprise and Its Environment.* London: Tavistock.

Rifkin, J. (2011). *The Third Industrial Revolution. How Lateral Power is Transforming Energy, the Economy, and the World.* Basingstoke: Palgrave Macmillan.

Trist, E., & Bamforth, K. (1951). Some Social and Psychological Consequences of the Long Wall Method of Coal-Getting. *Human Relations, 4*(1), 3–38.

Ulich, E. (2005). *Arbeitspsychologie*. Stuttgart: Schäffer-Poeschel.

Warnhoff, K., & Krzywdzinski, M. (2018). Digitalisierung spaltet. Gering qualifizierte Beschäftigte haben weniger Zugang zu Weiterbildung. *WZB-Mitteilungen, 162*, 58–60.

Zuboff, S. (2010). Creating Value in the Age of Distributed Capitalism. *McKinsey Quarterly*. Retrieved November 5, 2019, from http://glennas.files.wordpress.com/2010/12/creating-value-in-the-age-of-distributed-capitalism-shoshana-zuboff-september-2010.pdf

16

The Locus for Open Innovation Arrangements: How Universities Can Engage Firms to Collaborate

Kadígia Faccin, Luciana Maines da Silva,
Giulia Sandri Groehs, Silvio Bitencourt da Silva,
and Daniel Pedro Puffal

Introduction

In recent decades, there has been a considerable increase in the entrepreneurial role of universities around the world, especially in developed countries. The volume of scholarly publications devoted to understanding the interaction between university and business as a source of innovation has grown exponentially, especially after the term "open innovation" was defined by Chesbrough (2003). Most studies focus it on at American universities such as Massachusetts Institute of Technology (MIT) and Stanford or in European countries such as the United Kingdom and Sweden; very little is found about the phenomenon in Asia or Latin America.

The rise in entrepreneurship in universities can be attributed in part to the industry's increasing demand for technological innovation in recent decades, as universities are recognized as a significant source of innovation (Rothaermel, Agung, & Jiang, 2007; Etzkowitz, 2013).

K. Faccin (✉) • L. M. da Silva • S. B. da Silva • D. P. Puffal
Universidade do Vale do Rio dos Sinos—Unisinos, São Leopoldo, Brazil
e-mail: kadigiaf@unisinos.br; lucianamaines@unisinos.br;
sibitencourt@unisinos.br; dpuffal@unisinos.br

G. S. Groehs
Porto Alegre, Brazil

Theorists have been proposing conceptual models to explain the entrepreneurial university phenomenon for almost two decades (Clark, 1998; Etzkowitz & Leydesdorff, 2000; Etzkowitz, 2004; Sporn, 2001; Rothaermel et al., 2007; Guerrero & Urbano, 2012). At the same time, empirical studies analyzed this phenomenon in universities around the world and indicated relevant conclusions related to the identification of some universities considered examples of entrepreneurial universities: their main factors, their adaptation processes, their organizational changes, their internal and external strategies, and their different types of business activities and academic characteristics, environmental pressures, practical recommendations, and academic uses, among others.

The interaction between scientific production and technological production plays an essential role in national innovation systems (Mazzoleni & Nelson, 2007; Sierra, Vargas, & Torres, 2017). In developed countries, it is possible to identify the existence of positive feedback circuits between these two dimensions, where there are two-way flows of information and knowledge (Cohen, Nelson, & Walsh, 2002). Universities and research institutes produce knowledge that is transmitted to companies in the productive sector, while the accumulation of technological knowledge produces essential questions for the scientific elaboration and the orientation of the qualification of human resources. In less developed countries, such as Brazil and others, the national innovation system is still not very dynamic in terms of interactions established between universities and companies (Suzigan & Albuquerque, 2011). In this sense, recent studies, such as Sierra et al. (2017), Johnston and Huggins (2017), and Fu and Li (2016), have been dedicated to identifying factors that increase university-industry (UI) interaction and the transfer of technology.

Given this problem, this chapter aims to understand how universities can engage companies for technology transfer. To answer the research problem, we sought a unique case study, capable of demonstrating the actions taken by a university to broaden engagement with local companies. Among the leading private universities in Brazil is the University of Vale do Sinos, Unisinos, which has had for over 20 years a Technology Park with renowned global companies and dozens of incubated startups and has developed in South Brazil a business model with unique and pioneering technology transfer.

In this chapter, we will present the case of this Brazilian university, which, from the creation of a locus for open innovation, managed to increase the interaction between the university and the companies of the regional ecosystem. Throughout the text, we present some in vivo transcripts from a set of interviews with companies and others involved in the case study. The study allowed us to relate some actions taken by the university that enhanced the companies' engagement in collaborative projects such as the construction of a specific physical structure to enhance the companies' connection with the university and the offer and development of specific interface processes, which will be presented throughout the chapter.

The Entrepreneurial University

The late nineteenth century witnessed a revolution in academia in which the production of knowledge, through scientific research, was introduced as the mission of these organizations, in addition to the fundamental role of teaching. Such a movement became known as the first academic revolution. The transition from a closed university to a more open and market-related model emerges at an early stage in the United States, where, due to the lack of research funding, individual and collective initiatives in search of resources are emerging (Etzkowitz, 2003). Many universities around the world are still experiencing this paradigm. However, the growing importance of knowledge and economic development research has opened the door for a second revolution, which has brought about an academic "third mission": the role of the university as an agent of socioeconomic development (Etzkowitz & Leydesdorff, 2000; Yusof & Jain, 2010). Since the early 1980s, US universities have considerably increased their business activities in several dimensions: patenting and licensing; setting up incubators, science parks, and technology centers; and investing in startups, among other activities related to applied research (Siegel, 2006). This transition to a more socioeconomically engaged model initially took place at MIT due to its close relationship with industry. However, the fundamental model of the entrepreneurial university shifted to Stanford, where a culture of applied research was introduced in the mid-twentieth century (Etzkowitz, 2003).

As pointed out by Yusof and Jain (2010), an entrepreneurial university can be considered a university that strategically adapts to the entrepreneurial mindset throughout the organization, practicing academic entrepreneurship at various levels. This entrepreneurial thinking influences the climate and organizational work environment of the university, enabling and facilitating technology transfer activities (Kirby, 2006; Yusof & Jain, 2010). These activities and business development not only tend to contribute to organizational growth, profitability, and wealth creation at the university but also impact the external environment and the economy as a whole, increasing productivity, improving best practices, creating new industries, and reinforcing the competitiveness of its surroundings (Yusof & Jain, 2010).

Studies such as Razak and Saad (2007) in Malaysia and Leitch and Harrison (2005) at Queen's University, Belfast Incubator (QUBIS); Rasmussen, Borch, and Sørheim (2008) in Canada; Luengo and Obeso (2013) in Spain; Freitas and Verspagen (2017) in Holanda; Silva, Furtado, and Vonortas (2017) in Brazil have shown that partnerships between universities, industry, and government have become increasingly common and that some recent innovations result from this kind of interorganizational arrangement. These studies show that the production of specialized technical knowledge (such as availability of scientists) and knowledge transfer are the two main activities of entrepreneurial universities (Smith & Bagchi-Sen, 2010).

Table 16.1 summarizes the main conceptual models of the entrepreneurial university, providing an overview of critical elements that provide a basis for identifying factors and antecedents that can determine or influence entrepreneurial activities

The entrepreneurial university extends the prism of ideas to practical activities, capitalizing on knowledge, organizing new entities, and managing risks. It promotes institutional change in various spheres. From this perspective, academia becomes an elastic institution, capable of periodically reinventing itself and incorporating multiple missions, such as teaching and research, with each benefiting from the other even when they persist in creative tension (Etzkowitz, 2013). In essence, the entrepreneurial university can be seen as an effort to integrate the best of both ideals of an educational and research

Table 16.1 Proposed elements of an entrepreneurial university

Clark (1998)	Etzkowitz and Leydesdorff (2000)	Etzkowitz (2004)	Rothaermel et al. (2007)
Compromised central nucleus	Internal transformation	Capitalization of knowledge	Entrepreneurial behavior of research
Strong insertion in the surroundings	Inter-institutional impacts	Interdependence with industry and government	Productivity of technology transfer
Diversification of revenue sources	Interface processes	Independent institutions	Creation of new ventures
Academic nucleus stimulated	Recursive effects	Hybrid organization	Joint innovation actions with other actors
Integrated entrepreneurial culture		Reflexivity and reciprocity	

Source: by the author, based on Bitencourt. A Influência das práticas empreendedoras de uma universidade na formação de ecossistemas de inovação: Um Estudo da Teoria do Trabalho Institucional. TESE/PPGA UNISINOS. Porto Alegre, 2019 institution: high-quality and robust research orientation with a relevant social and economic approach; in which education, innovation, and social responsibility are integrated with research through new inter- and transdisciplinary initiatives (Stensaker & Benner, 2013).

University-Industry Interaction

A large number of studies pay attention to the existence of links between universities and industry, including Bonaccorsi and Piccaluga (1994), Fritsch and Schwirten (1999), Mowery and Sampat (2007), Cohen et al. (2002), and Bruno and Orsenido (2003). However, the location of the studies has been predominantly in developed countries.

Klevorick, Levin, Nelson, and Winter (1995) present empirical evidence on the role of universities and science as an essential source of technological opportunities for industrial innovation. The study by Klevorick et al. (1995) shows how distinct industrial sectors assess the relative importance of universities and science for their innovative capabilities.

The research by Fritsch and Slavtchev (2007) conducted in Germany, for example, indicates that the intensity and quality of research conducted by the university, as well as a policy of distributing these institutions in the country, have a significant effect on regional innovation. Another important result of the research was the finding that the size of the university and its research budget do not correlate significantly with regional innovation. However, obtaining external resources by the university has a positive relationship, which may be an indicator of the importance of university-business-government interaction.

The university-business interaction consolidates and develops the national innovation system and must be understood as its constituent part. However, the intensity of the relationships depends on the structural absorption capacity of those involved, according to Meyer-Krahmer and Schmoch (1998). The characteristic of university-business interaction is country-specific, dependent on the national science and technology infrastructure. For Rapini and Righi (2007), in Brazil, a significant part of the relationships in university-business interaction has a unidirectional flow. For companies, it comes from universities and institutions.

For Andrade (2007),

Innovation depends less on capital intensive investment and technical inventiveness, and more on the creation of networks of information and knowledge circulation. The problem of innovation becomes less technological and more pedagogical, acquiring an economic (distributive) and social (cohesion) meaning that transcends the operational and functional dictates of technical objects. (pp. 320)

Traditionally, there are two ways for companies to develop their technological innovations: through the development of autonomous research activities and/or through alliances with university scientific laboratories or public research institutes (Nelson & Rosenberg, 1993). The universities are responsible for assisting, through research and development, in the process of innovation in companies, contributing to the generation of new knowledge and gaining greater relevance for the productive sector (Berni, Gomes, Perlin, Kneipp, & Frizzo, 2015). In this sense, an incentive for universities to establish cooperative relationships with industry is the possibility of acquiring practical inspirations in the formulation of research projects (Ipiranga & Almeida, 2012).

To bridge the gap between science and industry, many universities design specific programs or units. An example of this is the Technology Transfer Offices (ETT), which would be a bridge between academics and companies, and their main objective is to facilitate the process of knowledge and technology transfer between the university and the company, while transmitting an entrepreneurial research culture (Olvera, Berbegal-Mirabent, & Merigó, 2018).

For Perkmann and Walsh (2007), although research on university-industry relations has traditionally been involved in intellectual property transfer (IP) (patenting, licensing, commercialization), several other channels or mechanisms that function as informational pathways to technology transfer are identified, and which are exchanged or co-produced by universities and industry. Besides, a wide variety of channels can be used, such as consultancy and contract research, joint research, training, meetings and conferences, and the creation of new physical resources. The choice of which channels to use depends on the individual characteristics of the researchers involved and their area of knowledge and also on the institutional characteristics, i.e., how is the environment in which knowledge is produced and used (Bekkers & Freitas, 2008; Dias & Porto, 2014).

Perkmann and Walsh (2007) and Agustinho and Garcia (2018) argue that university-industry cooperation has different models that may include collaborative research, projects, research contracts, or scientific consulting. Consulting refers to research or consulting services provided by individual academic researchers to their industry clients. In this sense, Pagani (2016) and

Zammar (2017) realize that service-based activities in university-industry interaction processes happen every day in developing countries.

Widespread criticism of the relationship between universities and industries includes the lack of knowledge of university dynamics and adds the time factor as another difficulty. Universities aim to create new knowledge and educate, while companies are focused on attracting only that knowledge that can be leveraged for competitive advantage. Also, university communication channels are often poor, and low interest in academic research is another reason that impedes cooperation between universities and companies (Bruneel, D'este, & Salter, 2010). In the same way, Mota (1999) and Rodrigues (2004) state that one should be aware of the cultural differences of individuals from universities and companies due to the different forms of communication.

According to Siegel (2007), there is one significant barrier in the university-industry relationship: the inflexibility and rigidity of universities in the process of negotiating a licensing agreement with companies. For the most part, individuals who trade for universities have poor technical, marketing, and even negotiating skills, having a "public domain" mentality about innovation. Therefore, the author proposes that universities adopt a more flexible stance in negotiating technology transfer agreements. Ideally, universities should be hired by licensing managers and experienced technology transfer office managers to have a more commercial and substantial stance. Malik (2002) also points to the lack of trust, collaboration, and confidentiality issues as a barrier, as well as the lack of information, as it happens that many companies do not know how to take the first step toward interaction with the university.

Thus, the relationship between university and company has mutual benefits, but may have several barriers in this cooperation as well.

Methodology

This study is a unique case study. The case chosen is original, as Unisinos inaugurates a new model for engaging firms for technology transfer in Brazil. The traditional models and characteristics associated with entrepreneurial universities found in the literature fail to capture the complexity of the Brazilian economic scenario. Data collection was done through interviews using a script containing semi-structured questions that served as a guide to assist the interviews with the analysts responsible for the university's relationship with companies, researchers who transfer technology/knowledge, and companies that relate to the university. The script has been pre-validated with expert input linked to the university-industry interface. Data collection also includes reports from participant observation, since two of the authors of this chapter work directly in the engagement of technology transfer firms.

In total, there are 12 respondents, in more than eight hours of interviews, including the coordinator of Portal de Inovação, two Technological Institutes (ITT) market relations analysts, two innovation research and development management analysts, three coordinators of Technological Institutes (ITT), two researchers, and two company managers.

In addition to the interviews, this study has secondary data accessed directly from the university's website. In the next section, the survey results will be discussed. For data analysis, we chose to use the narrative to present the details of the structure adopted by Unisinos to increase the university's collaboration with industry.

The Context of the Brazilian University

The Brazilian university has unique characteristics in its formation that end up interfering with actions aimed at the development of innovation in the country. The largest Brazilian universities are public and largely depend on public policies to develop insertion actions in the industry.

The Brazilian university based its development on technology imports. In the period before the 1980s, it created the so-called extension rectories, with the function of having a human character and training human resources capable of absorbing imported technology. Since 1980, some critical changes in the political landscape, such as the end of import substitution policy, the creation of science and technology (S&T) policies, and the opening of markets in 1990, mean the Brazilian nation has begun to understand the importance of innovation for maintaining business competitiveness. It is in this scenario that entrepreneurs begin to consider the possibility of approaching universities and research institutes.

However, only from the 2000s onward did Brazilian universities begin to prepare to become "entrepreneurial universities," as suggested by the international literature. Within the scope of government regulation and incentive, Innovation Law No. 10,973/2004, as well as subsequent legislation, seeks to develop technological innovation in the country, making universities the locus of this applied knowledge creation process. Studies such as those by Moura, Mendes-da-Silva, and Fischmann (2008), which sought to investigate the insertion of universities in the R&D policy of Brazilian industries, highlight the fact that strategic alliances between companies and universities are in a stage of growth and consolidation. Other articles, such as Gomes, Gonçalo,

Pereira, and Vargas (2014) note that the university-company relationship has intensified, and, within this context, educational and research institutions can contribute efficiently to the generation of new technologies and knowledge, manifesting itself as an alternative of innovation along with private initiative. Soria and Ferreira (2009), when studying the generation of patents in federal universities, point out that patents generated in research groups are still new. The authors point out that groups still need to undergo adaptations. Although there is interaction with companies, the process does not seem to be carried out in an integrated manner between agents. This separation, as well as the difference in vision between university and company, seems to be the main limiting element in the evolution of the development of these relationships and, consequently, in the generation of patents in universities. Studies such as those by Faccin and Balestrin (2015) indicate that the university is an exciting partner for different industries as it can provide business infrastructure, but it is not the leading partner for research and development cooperation. Findings like this are similar in studies such as Oliveira and Balestrin (2015), where they explore the case of a Brazilian university in the south of the country that had to use strategies for the development of absorptive capacity, given the challenge of working in a collaborative project with the semiconductor industry.

Moreover, it seems possible to state clearly that all Brazilian universities have invested in the development and expansion of their capacities to support the demands of the market and the environment in which they operate; however, it is not yet known what the actions, practices, and processes are that employees in the process of interaction with universities are capable of when promoting important results for the environment in which they operate. Thus, the possibility of developing comparative studies between Brazilian universities and European universities will allow for further study and possibly will result in proposed actions for the university and the Brazilian government regarding public policies to direct resources to activities for university-university interaction with a view to economic and social development.

How Unisinos Engage Firms to Collaborate? Creating a Physical Structure

Unisinos is a private, nonprofit, community-based university in southern Brazil, in the state of Rio Grande do Sul. It has a qualified research structure, with 26 postgraduate programs, more than 120 specialized laboratories with around 130 research groups (Unisinos, 2019). In its Institutional Plan, Unisinos demonstrates the importance of contributing to regional development, being one of the university's three strategic drivers, described as "Integration in society and participation in the scientific, technological, cultural, welfare and environmental efforts to build human development, social and economic development of the region" (Unisinos, 2014, p. 20).

The university has one of the best technology parks in Brazil, with 35 incubated startups and 60 consolidated companies, generating approximately 6000 direct jobs, and it also has five Technology Institutes. Three hundred research and development projects are carried out annually through 250 researchers, and more than a third of them in partnership with companies from the region, from other parts of the country, and eventually companies from other countries (Unisinos, 2019).

At the university, there are five technology institutes (ITT) focused on different market sectors. ITT Chip is the Semiconductor Technology Institute, ITT Fossil develops basic and applied research in micropaleontology, ITT Fuse conducts project analysis and qualification testing for functional safety products and processes, ITT Nutrifor conducts research and provides services to food and beverage companies, and ITT Performance is the Technological Institute in Performance and Civil Construction. The institutes are mainly engaged in applied research and experimental development, contributing with consultancies and technical advisory services (tests, analysis, evaluations, certifications, inspections, product development, and prototyping), with the training of people and other specialized technical services. Some of these services are accredited by institutions such as Inmetro and Associação Brasileira de Normas Técnicas (ABNT), among others.

The university also has a project office, which is a nucleus that facilitates the relationship between the university, companies, and public agencies, helping the management of research projects developed by the university. The office assists in the modeling of business projects, making it more attractive for fundraising, as well as providing infrastructure for project management and development (Unisinos, 2019).

Despite standing out in the Latin American scenario for its significant numbers, Unisinos has created a structure capable of facilitating the university's engagement with the regional entrepreneurship ecosystem. This structure has become the locus for open innovation arrangements, called the Innovation Hub.

Portal da Inovação was created to facilitate the university's relationship with companies in the region. One respondent points out that "[...] dealing with universities is horrible. It's weird to hear from university, but it's too bad.

There are academic studies that prove this. Because it is bad? First, it is difficult to establish university dialogue. What is speech? Who do I talk to when I
look for a university? Am I going straight to the dean? One of the rectories?
To one of the academic directors? Or do I look for a course coordinator? What
if my problem is not a simple solution? No one will look for a university to
solve a problem that is solved simply. It often requires a multidisciplinary
approach, a laboratory, another department, with researchers from another
field. How do I deal with it inside the university?" (E1).

In addition to the problem of dialogue, already presented in studies by
Bruneel et al. (2010), the difference in "language" also stands out: "teachers
often tend to speak difficult and in a complex and exaggerated way in their
status." (E1). In addition, there are also barriers linked to the university's
response time to industry demands: "Many times those looking for a university to solve a problem will hear the following "Cool! There will be a selection
process next year for the master's and doctoral program, and I will try to raise
a scholarship for a student to do research on their topic (E1). Interlocution,
language, and time are some of the primary examples of corporate pain, which
we recognize as true and seek here at Unisinos, to get out of that more ordinary model and advance to a state of excellence in this relationship" from the
implementation of the Portal da Inovação (E1).

The model was developed based on the best technology transfer centers in
the world. "This Unisinos model was well researched, long research, we visited
centers of excellence around the world and were inspired to create the idea of
the Portal da Inovação for Unisinos." (E12). In 2017, Unisinos inaugurated
the Portal da Inovação, a structure within the university where companies that
want the institution can reach and be directed in the best way. It is a physical
as well as a virtual structure that connects companies to university resources
(UNISINOS, 2019).

Portal da Inovação was established to reinforce the university's interaction
with companies and the government, thus stimulating technological innovation. To properly support these relationships, Portal da Inovação integrates a
set of agents and different collaborative practices. Figure 16.1, taken from
Portal da Inovação website, shows the set of actors and elements that constitute the university's science, technology, and innovation system. It can be seen
that Portal da Inovação is the central figure of this network of actors, which
already existed in the university environment.

It is noteworthy that after the creation of the physical structure of the university's Portal da Inovação, the Innovation Academy was also created, and the
existing project office became part of the physical structure of the Portal da
Inovação. The academy aims to disseminate different approaches to

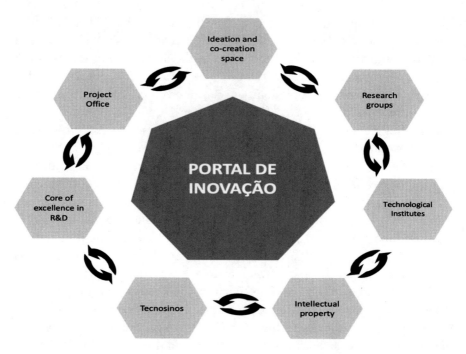

Fig. 16.1 Actors and elements of Portal da Inovação. (Source: by the author, based on Unisinos. Portal da Inovação. Available at: http://www.unisinos.br/portal-de-inovacao/sobre. Accessed on Oct 30, 2020)

innovation, contemplating the combination of methods and tools that originated from strategic design, strategic management, innovation management, and engineering. Thus, different approaches are disseminated through the promotion of workshops, workshops, lectures, and technological capabilities that will foster the adoption of the necessary approaches to accelerate the process of innovation in companies and ensure greater assertiveness. The academy is responsible for the ideation and co-creation spaces in the Portal da Inovação.

The Portal da Inovação is "[…] much more than a hub that connects all areas of the university, it is where all those entities and companies that do not have a communication channel with the university come here to understand what we can do to help them out. From here we qualify the demands and we will distribute those demands to those who can develop." (E1).

It can be said that technology transfer at Unisinos occurs through the Portal da Inovação, being organized in two ways basically: through the Technological Institutes when there is a demand for technological services or applied research and through the Graduate Programs (PPGs) and Centers of Excellence, when the demand is more robust, applied research, or basic research. In this article, we will focus on analytical efforts on how the Portal da Inovação engages businesses around it for technology transfer and innovation promotion.

Portal da Inovação is a university unit focused on meeting business needs and consists of a team of four Research Project Analysts, four Technology Institute Services Analysts, a Technology Institute Administrative Coordinator, a Research and Development Manager. It should be noted that the Portal da Inovação has a Technology Transfer and Innovation Center (TTIC), which is responsible for discussing intellectual property, royalties, and patent registrations, i.e., it is also the Technology Transfer Office (TTO) of the university. Therefore, one of the most significant differentials of the Unisinos technology transfer model is that it offers a physical space to facilitate the dialogue with the business demands. Having a team prepared to deal with the market, which integrates all information from the university experts in one place, facilitates communication between all those involved with knowledge transfer at the university.

How Unisinos Engage Firms to Collaborate? Creating Interface Processes

One of the major problems with university-industry relations is the cultural differences that exist between them. "The company has a language, a very different mental model from the university, the company is running after its month of reckoning, and the university wants to write an article, publish, have relevant projects and put those two in the same tune is a challenge." (E4). In this sense, the Portal da Inovação has become an interaction agent where this cultural barrier is softened through the creation of interface processes. Analysts play a very significant role in business, prospecting as they attend trade shows, events, and workshops: "We go there from booth to booth, demonstrating how technology transfer institutes work, how we can help by demonstrating that there are real situations we can solve. Just a little bit of a problem you have been facing within the company or a solution that you never thought could improve the product, we showed that we could help" (E5). In addition to analysts, institute coordinators are also involved in prospecting for open innovation arrangements.

Still, "there are cases that the process comes from the researcher who has something of interest, for example, if there is a public notice that directs resources to a particular area, and we have this area very well established in the university, and the notice foresees participation of companies, we can see a company from our relationship circle."(E4).

It can be seen that the engagement of companies can be motivated by different sources: researchers, companies, or even by the emergence of a public notice offering financial resources. In the case of the front researchers, it occurs when the university develops a research theme and naturally came to an application of that scientific knowledge and are looking for a company that fits the theme: "The researcher can come up with something he is researching and developing, and we can look for companies that align themselves in this research to contribute and also from there discuss and follow this project." (E9). However, "This is not linear. When the company arrives, we find the researcher or the opposite. That is, the company may come here with a problem, we hear her problem and indicate meetings with researchers that we believe can help" (E9).

These interaction channels allow us to ensure the quality of the university's approaches. Centralizing business demands on Portal da Inovação guarantees the best partner choices for the project. This assumption also makes sure that the university can prioritize researchers who have the skills to relate to the market because, often, "just as it is complicated to put companies in the language of the university, it is difficult to place researchers in the language of the project [...]" (E5).

Regarding the demand environment, it is emphasized that companies often want help from the university to innovate, but do not know exactly how the university can help. Often "[...] clients can simply come very openly: How can the university help me? And then it's up to us to explain everything we have here and identify what we can do to help" (E7). Realizing this, Portal da Inovação created an additional service, which is a Service of Creation and Selection of Ideas, the most initial and creative phase of the innovation process, where everything is defined with the company. The company directs its own employees for a 1–2-day immersion, along with university experts, and selects ideas for innovation. All of this is done for free, so it is still a way to attract companies. Collaborative initiatives to attract companies are favorable for the university-industry relationship because the relationship with the company begins even before a formal interaction and from this, the University can observe if the company is aligned with the research that the university conducts, and thus, offer the execution of a research project ideal for the needs of the company.

Considering this set of actions that allow us to improve project management, "[...] we are working with collaborative projects, in which the company gets involved from the first day to the last to reach the final result. It has been increasingly common. Today these collaborative projects have grown a lot, as well as consulting, but to a lesser extent" (E8). Accomplishing collaborative projects is a knowledge transfer that implies joint development. It is not the knowledge developed in isolation by one of the parties, leading to the elaboration of an even more complete solution/creation. Collaborative projects result in high relational involvement, and, according to Perkmann and Walsh (2007), relationship-based mechanisms contribute to the innovation processes in a broader sense than just providing university-generated innovations and innovative technologies.

Another important activity that ensures the increased interface between the university and business is prospecting funding for research. "We know the university's postgraduate expertise, and we use it as a general reference in choosing edicts. We research everything there is for research funding, looking for opportunities from 50 sources or so." Lists of funding opportunities are made available monthly to researchers as well as to university network companies. Thus, the university mitigates the problem of a lack of resources of many companies and provides the opportunity to conduct research applied by the university.

In addition to the pro-activity in attracting services and research to the University, we highlight the flexibility with which Unisinos negotiates with companies. Siegel, Waldman, Atwater, and Link (2004) identified that the inflexibility and rigidity of universities in the process of negotiating a licensing agreement with companies becomes a barrier in the university-industry relationship. At Unisinos, "we have a model contract, agreement, all pre-approved by the university. Rarely do companies accept first, so we have to adjust and negotiate for the best of both parties" (E7). Companies that have already collaborated with Unisinos point out that: "The contracts we have signed are not very restricted, we can talk a lot, it is flexible. We explain, and we have slightly different needs, but we always come to an agreement" (E12). It is soon apparent in the interviewees' speech that this is not a barrier to the university, as the contract is adapted according to the company's needs, considering that they have already had the effort to find researchers interested in conducting the research.

Final Remarks: What Does Unisinos Teach About the Engagement of Firms and Universities

Evidence suggests that the university from a specific environment orchestrates its different fronts to activate and support the demands of companies in research, development, and innovation, composing a local Science, Technology, and Innovation System (SCTI) that seeks to generate proposals to transform and leverage ideas into business-applied solutions. For this purpose, it acts in the formation of people and stimulating joint research between the university and company and provides technological services (technology consulting and advisory services and specialized technical services) and support for innovation by assisting entrepreneurs and incubating or setting up businesses. The environment acts as a type of hardware-based hub (meeting room infrastructure, ideation, collaborative, and support spaces, as well as space to accommodate projects under development with companies), software (methodologies, methods, and tools provided for generation and selection of innovative ideas and their development in connection with the university such as a living laboratory, as well as points of interaction with project and service flows such as project office, market relations, etc.), and humanware (intermediation of university specialists).

It is a transformative environment that contributes to the development of technological innovations in companies by integrating into the innovation networks the university itself and its different fronts of action and specialists, companies, government, and a wide range of social actors in a fourfold model. The Unisinos hub allows us to verify the importance of integrating all the expertise and infrastructure information that the university has, whether in a physical structure or a platform, so that companies can find all the information they need to partner.

Moreover, to soften the cultural differences of individuals in the U-I relationship, analysts guarantee the interface of processes. Analysts and coordinators are prepared to master the language, behavior, and expectations of companies, facilitating this interaction. These agents are knowledgeable about everything the university can offer and are responsible for prospecting new companies to become partners (whether in the form of publications, conference presentations, prospecting for public tenders and public notices), negotiating agreements, and maintaining a lasting relationship. In this way, the university will have a proactive position in the U-I relationship. Moreover, to break the barrier defined by Siegel et al. (2004), it is essential to have a flexible posture in negotiating the agreements.

Table 16.2 Proposed elements of an entrepreneurial university

Clark (1998)	Etzkowitz and Leydesdorff (2000)	Etzkowitz (2004)	Rothaermel et al. (2007)	What do we learn at Unisinos?
Compromised central nucleus	Internal transformation	Capitalization of knowledge	Entrepreneurial behavior of research	Interaction-oriented infrastructure
Strong insertion in the surroundings	Inter-institutional impacts	Interdependence with industry and government	Productivity of technology transfer	Centralizing framework for offering solutions
Diversification of revenue sources	Interface processes	Independent institution	Creation of new ventures	Flexibility and individuality in negotiations
Academic nucleus stimulated	Recursive effects	Hybrid organization	Joint innovation actions with other actors	Interface processes focused on qualifying business demand: ideation, strategic design tools
Integrated entrepreneurial culture		Reflexivity and reciprocity		Expert intermediation: ensuring quality, project management, and choice of partners

Source: by the author, based on Bitencourt. A Influência das práticas empreendedoras de uma universidade na formação de ecossistemas de inovação: Um Estudo da Teoria do Trabalho Institucional. TESE/PPGA UNISINOS. Porto Alegre, 2019

After the company becomes interested in partnering with the university, it is necessary to define which technology transfer channel to use, such as patenting and licensing, consulting, contract research, collaborative research, training, meetings, and conferences, among others (Bekkers & Freitas, 2008). The setting for choosing the transfer channel is defined in conjunction with the company. The same author believes that the choice of which channels to use depends on the individual characteristics of the researchers involved and their area of knowledge as well as the institutional characteristics (Bekkers & Freitas, 2008).

Interaction agents are responsible for maintaining the relationship with the company (project management) and investing in long-term relationships. In this way, cooperation will be strengthened, creating social bonds of trust and commitment. Furthermore, as with business to business (B2B) marketing, U-I collaboration is based on retention and mutual benefits where evolution is shared. It should also be borne in mind that industrial partners evaluate the project's professionalism, timing, market, and feasibility (Boehm & Hogan, 2013).

Considering the actions implemented by Unisinos in its Portal da Inovação, the university has created a real locus for open innovation. Thus, based on this case study, it seems possible to offer a set of characteristics of the entrepreneurial university to emerging countries. The actions taken by the Unisinos technology transfer model differ substantially from those presented in studies by entrepreneurial universities in developed countries. Based on the case of Unisinos, we made an update of the proposed elements reference frame (Table 16.2).

This hub has a specific physical structure to enhance companies' engagement with the university, enhancing interaction channels and qualifying the demand environment. In addition, it has created a set of university-brokered interface processes that ensure quality, improve the project management, and make the best choice for partners for the company project. This approach has offered an enterprising behavior for research and broadens the insertion of the university in its surroundings. It is worth mentioning that these are considered actions taken in this first stage of the technology transfer model development and are more specifically linked to the hub created.

References

Agustinho, E., & Garcia, E. N. (2018). Inovação, transferência de tecnologia e cooperação. *Direito e Desenvolvimento, 9*(1), 223–239.

Andrade, T. N. (2007). O Problema da Experimentação na Inovação Tecnológica. *Revista Brasileira de Inovação, 6*(2), 311–329.

Bekkers, R., & Freitas, I. M. B. (2008). Analysing Knowledge Transfer Channels between Universities and Industry: To What Degree Do Sectors also Matter? *Research Policy, 37*(10), 1837–1853.

Berni, J. C. A., Gomes, C. M., Perlin, A. P., Kneipp, J. M., & Frizzo, K. (2015). Interação universidade-empresa para a inovação e a transferência de tecnologia. *Revista Gestão Universitária na América Latina-GUAL, 8*(2), 258–277.

Bitencourt, A. C. (2019). *A Influência Das Práticas Empreendedoras De Uma Universidade Na Formação De Ecossistemas De Inovação: Um Estudo A Luz Da Teoria Do Trabalho Institucional.* Tese. Programa de Pós-Graduação em Administração. Unisinos. Porto Alegre, Brazil.

Boehm, D. N., & Hogan, T. (2013). Science-to-Business Collaborations: A Science-to-Business Marketing Perspective on Scientific Knowledge Commercialization. *Industrial Marketing Management, 42*(4), 564–579.

Bonaccorsi, A., & Piccaluga, A. (1994). A Theoretical Framework for the Evaluation of University-Industry Relationships. *R&D Management, 24*(3), 229–247.

Bruneel, J., D'este, P., & Salter, A. (2010). Investigating the Factors That Diminish the Barriers to University–Industry Collaboration. *Research Policy, 399*(7), 858–868.

Bruno, G. S. F., & Orsenido, L. (2003). Variables Influencing Industrial Funding of Academic Research in Italy: An Empirical Analysis. *International Journal of Technology Management, 26*(2–4), 277–302.

Chesbrough, H. W. (2003). The Era of Open Innovation. *MIT Sloan Management, 44*(3), 35–41.

Clark, B. R. (1998). *Creating Entrepreneurial Universities: Organizational Pathways of Transformation.* New York: Pergamon.

Cohen, W., Nelson, R., & Walsh, J. (2002). Links and Impacts: The Influence of Public R&D on Industrial Research. *Management Science, 48*(1), 1–23.

Dias, A. A., & Porto, G. S. (2014). Como a USP transfere tecnologia? *Organizações & Sociedade, 21*(70), 489–507.

Etzkowitz, H. (2003). Innovation in Innovation: The Triple Helix of University-Industry-Government Relations. *Social Science Information, 42*(3), 293–337.

Etzkowitz, H. (2004). The Evolution of the Entrepreneurial University. *International Journal of Technology and Globalization, 1*(1), 64–77.

Etzkowitz, H. (2013). Anatomy of the Entrepreneurial University. *Social Science Information, 52*(3), 486–511.

Etzkowitz, H., & Leydesdorff, L. (2000). The Dynamics of Innovation: From National Systems and "Mode 2" to a Triple Helix of University–Industry–Government Relations. *Research Policy, 29*(2), 109–123.

Faccin, K., & Balestrin, A. (2015). Práticas colaborativas em P&D: um estudo na indústria brasileira de semicondutores. *RAM. Revista de Administração Mackenzie (Online), 16*, 190–219.

Freitas, I. M. B., & Verspagen, B. (2017). The Motivations, Institutions and Organization of University-Industry Collaborations in the Netherlands. *Journal of Evolutionary Economics, 27*(3), 379–412.

Fritsch, M., & Schwirten, C. (1999). Enterprise-University Cooperation and the Role of Public Research Institutions in Regional Innovation Systems. *Industry Innovation, 6*(1), 69–83.

Fritsch, M., & Slavtchev, V. (2007). Universities and Innovation in Space. *Industry and Innovation, 14*(2), 201–218.

Fu, X., & Li, J. (2016). Collaboration with Foreign Universities for Innovation: Evidence from Chinese Manufacturing Firms. *Journal Technology Management, 70*(2/3), 193–217.

Gomes, M. S., Gonçalo, C. R., Pereira, C. D., & Vargas, S. L. (2014). A inovação como conexão para o desenvolvimento de parcerias entre universidade-empresa. *Navus-Revista de Gestão e Tecnologia, 4*(2), 78–91.

Guerrero, M., & Urbano, D. (2012). The Development of an Entrepreneurial University. *The Journal of Technology Transfer, 37*(1), 43–74.

Ipiranga, A. S. R., & Almeida, P. C. D. H. (2012). O tipo de pesquisa e a cooperação universidade, empresa e governo: uma análise na rede nordeste de biotecnologia. *Organizações & Sociedade, 19*(60), 17–34.

Johnston, A., & Huggins, R. (2017). University-Industry Links and the Determinants of Their Spatial Scope: A Study of the Knowledge Intensive Business Services Sector. *Papers in Regional Science, 96*(2), 247–260.

Kirby, D. A. (2006). Creating Entrepreneurial Universities in the UK: Applying Entrepreneurship Theory to Practice. *Journal of Technology Transfer, 31*(5), 599–603.

Klevorick, A. K., Levin, R. C., Nelson, R. R., & Winter, S. G. (1995). On the Sources and Significance of Inter-industry Differences in Technological Opportunity. *Research Policy, 24*, 185–205.

Leitch, C. M., & Harrison, R. T. (2005). Maximising the Potential of University Spin-Outs: the Development of Second-Order Commercialisation Activities. *R&D Management, 35*(3), 257–272.

Luengo, M. J., & Obeso, M. (2013). El efecto de la triple hélice en los resultados de innovación. *RAE-Revista de Administração de Empresas, 53*(4), 388–399.

Malik, K. (2002). Aiding the Technology Manager: A Conceptual Model for Intra-firm Technology Transfer. *Technovation, 22*(7), 427–436.

Mazzoleni, R., & Nelson, R. (2007). The Roles of Research at Universities and Public Labs in Economic Catch-up. *Research Policy, 36*(10), 1512–1528.

Meyer-Krahmer, F., & Schmoch, U. (1998). Science-based Technologies: University–Industry Interactions in Four Fields. *Research Policy, 27*, 835–851.

Mota, T. L. N. D. G. (1999). Interação universidade-empresa na sociedade do conhecimento: reflexões e realidade. *Ciência da Informação, 28*(1), 79–86.

Moura, G. L. D., Mendes-da-Silva, W., & Fischmann, A. A. (2008). Vantagem competitiva por meio de alianças estratégicas: examinando a inserção das universidades brasileiras. Anais.

Mowery, D. C., & Sampat, B. N. (2007). Universities in National Innovations Systems. In J. Fagerberg, D. Mowery, & R. Nelson (Eds.), *The Oxford Handbook of Innovation*. New York: Oxford University Press.

Nelson, R., & Rosenberg, N. (1993). *National Innovation Systems: A Comparative Analysis*. New York: Oxford University Press.

Oliveira, S. R. D., & Balestrin, A. (2015). Cooperação universidade-empresa: um estudo do projeto UNISINOS-HT Micron para o desenvolvimento de capacidade absortiva na área de semicondutores. *Gestão & Produção, 25*(3), 595–609.

Olvera, C., Berbegal-Mirabent, J., & Merigó, J. (2018). A Bibliometric Overview of University-Business Collaboration between 1980 and 2016. *Computación Y Sistemas, 22*(4), 1171–1190. https://doi.org/10.13053/cys-22-4-3101

Pagani, R. N. (2016). *Modelo de transferência de conhecimento e tecnologia entre universidades parceiras na mobilidade acadêmica internacional*. 2016. Tese. Programa de Pós-Graduação em Engenharia de Produção, Universidade Tecnológica Federal do Paraná—Campus Ponta Grossa., Ponta Grossa, PR, Brazil.

Perkmann, M., & Walsh, K. (2007). University–Industry Relationships and Open Innovation: Towards a Research Agenda. *International Journal of Management Reviews, Wiley Online Library, 9*(4), 259–280.

Rapini, M. S., & Righi, H. M. (2007). Interação universidade-empresa no Brasil em 2002 e 2004: Uma aproximação a partir dos grupos de pesquisa do CNPq. *Revista Economia, 8*(2), 248–268.

Rasmussen, E., Borch, O. J., & Sørheim, R. (2008). University Entrepreneurship and Government Support Schemes. In *The Dynamic between Entrepreneurship, Environment and Education* (pp. 105–130). Edward Elgar Publishing.

Razak, A. A., & Saad, M. (2007). The Role of Universities in the Evolution of the Triple Helix Culture of Innovation Network: The Case of Malaysia. *International Journal of Technology Management & Sustainable Development, 6*(3), 211–225.

Rodrigues, R. S. (2004). *Modelo de planejamento para cursos de pós-graduação à distância em cooperação universidade-empresa*. Tese (doutorado). Universidade Federal de Santa Catarina. Centro Tecnológico. Programa de Pós-graduação em Engenharia de Produção.

Rothaermel, F., Agung, S., & Jiang, L. (2007). University Entrepreneurship: A Taxonomy of the Literature. *Industrial and Corporate Change, 16*(4), 691–791.

Siegel, D. S. (2006). *Technology Entrepreneurship: Institutions and Agents Involved in University Technology Transfer* (Vol. 1). London: Edgar Elgar.

Siegel, D. S. (2007). Quantitative and Qualitative Studies of University Technology Transfer: Synthesis and Policy Recommendations. In *Handbook of Research in Entrepreneurship Policy* (pp. 186–199). Edward Elgar.

Siegel, D. S., Waldman, D. A., Atwater, L. E., & Link, A. N. (2004). Toward a Model of the Effective Transfer of Scientific Knowledge from Academicians to Practitioners: Qualitative Evidence from the Commercialization of University Technologies. *Journal of Engineering and Technology Management, 21*(1–2), 115–142.

Sierra, L. M. P., Vargas, M. E. M., & Torres, V. G. L. (2017). An Institutional Framework to Explain the University-Industry Technology Transfer in a Public University of Mexico. *Journal Technological Management Innovation, 12*(1), 4–12.

Silva, D. M., Furtado, D. R., & Vonortas, N. S. (2017). University-Industry R&D Cooperation in Brazil: A Sectoral Approach. *The Journal of Technology Transfer, 3*(2), 285–315.

Smith, H. L., & Bagchi-Sen, S. (2010). Triple Helix and Regional Development: A Perspective from Oxfordshire in the UK. *Technology Analysis & Strategic Management, 22*(7), 805–818.

Soria, A. F., & Ferreira, G. C. (2009). *Geração de Patentes em Universidades: um estudo exploratório sobre o processo e seus condicionantes.* Encontro Associação Nacional Pós-Graduação em Administração (Unisinos, 2017). *Anais do* XXXIII ENANPAD (pp. 1–16). ENANPAD, São Paulo, Brazil.

Sporn, B. (2001). Building Adaptive Universities: Emerging Organizational Forms based on Experiences of European and US Universities. *Tertiary Education and Management, 7*(2), 121–134.

Stensaker, B., & Benner, M. (2013). Doomed to be Entrepreneurial: Institutional Transformation or Institutional Lock-Ins of "New" Universities? *Minerva, 51*(4), 399–416.

Suzigan, W., & Albuquerque, E. M. (2011). The Underestimated Role of Universities for Development. *Brazilian Journal of Political Economy, 31*(1), 3–30.

Unisinos. (2014). *Oportunidades de Pesquisa, Desenvolvimento e Inovação.* Retrieved out. 30 October 2019, from http://www.unisinos.br/pesquisa-e-inovacao/nitt/oportunidades-de-pesquisa-desenvolvimento-e-inovacao.

Unisinos. (2017). *Plano de Desenvolvimento Institucional. PDI.* Fonte: Missão e Perspectiva. Retrieved May 3, 2019, from http://www.unisinos.br/minha-unisinos/images/conteudo/pdi-2014-2017.pdf.

Unisinos. (2019). *Portal da Inovacao.* Retrieved out. 30 October 2019, from http://www.unisinos.br/portal-de-inovacao/sobre.

Yusof, M., & Jain, K. (2010). Categories of University-Level Entrepreneurship: A Literature Survey. *International Entrepreneurship and Management Journal, 6*(1), 81–96.

Zammar, G. (2017). *Interação universidade-indústria: um modelo para transferência de tecnologia.* Tese (Doutorado em Engenharia de Produção). Universidade Tecnológica Federal do Paraná, Ponta Grossa, p. 140 f.

17

Examining and Reviewing Innovation Strategies in Australian Public Sector Organisations

Mahmoud Moussa

Introduction

Research in organisational innovation in both the public and the private sectors is primarily focused on factors/conditions that enhance innovation processes and subsequently improve productivity in the workplace. The investigation of how to develop a productive innovation climate has been critical in research on public sector organisations (Osterberg & Qvist, 2020). Public sector organisations are confronting significant structural, financial, and environmental pressures; thus, it is important to develop innovation processes that capture and capitalise on specialised knowledge from different contributors (Coulon et al., 2020). This chapter involved the analysis of the innovation strategy in each Australian state, which revealed the dynamics of innovation that influence innovation processes in Australian public sector organisations. Examining and reviewing innovation strategies in the Australian public sector would provide theoretical evidence and help individuals and organisations identify the dynamics of innovation in the government sector. In other words, a better understanding of how to enhance and encourage innovation can assist the Australian government in reinvigorating its structures in the government sector for the benefits of the entire nation.

M. Moussa (✉)
School of Management, RMIT University, Melbourne, VIC, Australia
e-mail: mahmoud.moussa@rmit.edu.au

© The Author(s), under exclusive license to Springer Nature Switzerland AG 2021
A. McMurray et al. (eds.), *The Palgrave Handbook of Workplace Innovation*,
https://doi.org/10.1007/978-3-030-59916-4_17

Theoretical Background

A considerable number of studies on the organisational barriers in the current literature can be associated with the internal environment in which innovation takes place. According to Cinar, Trott, and Simms (2019), the most identifiable type of organisational barriers in the literature involves the management of the innovation process activities. This is due to the 'New Public Management' approach to examine innovation, which highlights organisations and managers as the unit of analysis. The unique characteristics of public organisations (e.g. goal ambiguity, organisational structures, decision-making processes, and incentive structures) and environmental components for public organisations (e.g. the political economy of public institutions, performance criteria for government organisations, and different actors with power and authority over public organisations) may lead to barriers to innovation in public sector organisations (Demircioglu & Audretsch, 2017). This may suggest that public sector employees who identify barriers to innovation could use their knowledge and experience to minimise those barriers (Torugsa and Arundel, 2016). In other words, innovative employees are more able to recognise barriers to innovation in their organisations.

Further, leaders are a key factor in the promotion of innovation and creativity (Mumford et al., 2002). Vroom and Jago (2007) defined the characteristics of innovative leaders as those who stimulate others to work cohesively to achieve significant outcomes. Leaders determine priorities, affect decision-making, and have both the power and commitment to enhance organisational performance. Moreover, Trevino, Hartman, and Brown (2000) noted that leadership characteristics for innovative work behaviour include direct, meaningful, and transparent communication style.

Furthermore, the current literature depicts that organisational climate has been interpreted in different ways. Climate has been construed based on its effect on organisational processes, such as problem-solving and communication, and psychological processes, such as committing and motivating (Ekvall and Ryhammar 1999). As a caveat, how innovation is perceived and how it is interpreted can be subjective, which in turn may have resulted in some measurement errors (Rivera & Landahl, 2019). Therefore, future research should seek how public employees perceive the concept of innovation, whether it is perceived as occurring within the existing organisational policies or if it is organisationally transformative in the endeavour to be more effective. Organisational climate researchers have examined different aspects of organisational climate for various reasons, such as a climate for initiative (Baer & Frese, 2003) or for innovation (Hunter, Bedell, & Mumford 2007).

Methodology

The qualitative data analysis applied in this chapter is a non-mathematical analytical approach, where the researcher examined the words' meaning(s) and the government departments' philosophies (Maykut & Morehouse, 1994). In this chapter, the researcher collected a tremendous amount of data and meticulously analysed and interpreted the most relevant data to find out answers to the research questions. Therefore, the researcher applied the six steps of qualitative data analysis developed by Creswell (2009) to assist in the analysis and the interpretation of the qualitative data. These were (a) organising and preparing the data, which involved drafting and redrafting to gain in-depth understanding of the contents; (b) reading all data and developing general idea(s) that might be appropriate for answering the research questions; (c) coding the data for later stage of analysis; (d) developing a description of categories or themes from the coded data, which examined the codes to identify significant themes; (e) representing the themes in the qualitative comprehension to determine that they are appropriate for answering the research questions—in this step, themes were refined, combined, or discarded; and (f) interpreting the data. The researcher used NVivo Pro 11 and 12 statistical software packages to gain in-depth understanding of the qualitative data collected from several sources.

Thus, the analysis segment permitted the researcher to review the information published on the government departments' websites as well as the review of recent publications in innovation in the public sector. It further allowed the researcher to organise data according to the issues raised in a coherent order and to develop some codes from the published materials. In addition, comprehensive descriptions and illustrations were made, and categories and themes were developed. The differing data were compared and contrasted with the purpose of synthesising the documents into an inclusive portrayal of the completed process by drafting and redrafting. Moreover, thematic analysis and content analysis were applied in this chapter. Thematic analysis helped the researcher identify crucial factors that stimulate or hinder innovation in the public sector. Likewise, the employment of content analysis or 'constant comparative method' in this chapter aimed to enhance the themes that were developed by conceptualising the subject matter under study and patterning of the data (Boeije, 2012).

Data Analysis

The coding process involved the selective coding to identify the main themes that best illustrate the dynamics of innovation in Australian public sector organisations. This process reflected the thematic analysis, which helped the researcher to define the themes and generate appropriate outcome through NVivo. Themes were eventually categorised into three main themes and its constituents. These were organisational barriers (old organisational models; lack of support and autonomy; lack of professional development plans; and budget and funding); leadership characteristics (supportive; risk-taker; practical; lead by example; decision-making); and organisational climate (a culture of sharing; policy development; networking; measurement tools; incentives; embracing diversity; and commitment).

Organisational Barriers

The organisational barriers' thematic analysis explores the barriers that hinder innovation in public sector organisations in Australia and discusses several perspectives revealed from state government departments' reports.

Old Organisational Models

The content analysis revealed that the first barrier to innovation is old organisational models. For example, in South Australia (SA), it is found that common barriers to success relate to the broader conditions for innovation within the government (Vanstone, Ryan, & McPhee 2017). Whereas in Victoria (Vic), public servants are advised to change the traditional mindset and have an agile mindset (Victoria State Government, 2017). According to the Victorian government, in order to put innovation in motion, the existing vertical structures across departments may limit the ability to share ideas, experiences, and knowledge across the government (Victoria State Government, 2017). Therefore, horizontal structures are needed to enhance coordination among individuals and across departments. Other significant barriers to innovation involve systems that do not stimulate collaboration with diverse organisations. Hence, the Victorian government indicated that the dilemma is that government largely operates in silos-departments or agencies.

Lack of Support and Autonomy

The second barrier to innovation is lack of support and autonomy. The content analysis revealed that in South Australia (SA), factors cited as stopping people 'thinking outside the square' involved insufficient time and permission (Vanstone, Ryan, & McPhee 2017). In a report published by the 'Australian Innovation Research Centre' in Tasmania, it is indicated that one of the problems for innovators in Tasmania is the responsibility of several agencies whose responsibilities do not include sponsoring innovation (West, 2009). Thus, any change to the way things are implemented presents several challenges. In other words, if what the innovator suggests is not consistent with the organisational culture/system presents a threat to the organisation. Similarly, one public servant in Victoria (Vic) articulated, 'unfortunately some of us have tried to change things and been held back, either because we were not given the autonomy or we were denied the practical support to pursue a great idea' (Victoria State Government, 2017, p. 25). Another perspective in Victoria (Vic), 'pockets of good practice exist across the public sector but, as a rule, we do not encourage our people to constantly search for better ways of doing things, to learn and adapt as we go, and to ponder to "what if"?' (Victoria State Government, 2017, p. 26). In Western Australia, public servants acknowledged that work in innovation in Western Australia (WA) remains ad hoc and many skilled individuals leave WA to find opportunities in other states (Office of the Government Chief Information Officer, 2016). Hence, it is recommended, in the same report, that greater coordination, transparency, and access to information would improve this.

Lack of Professional Development Plans

The third barrier to innovation is lack of professional development plans. However, the researcher found this barrier to innovation in Victoria (Vic) State only. In the report of 'Putting Innovation in Motion', public servants acknowledged their need for more opportunities to develop their competencies and perspectives to enhance their work (Victoria State Government, 2017). Others noted the need to build their internal capability and to develop their skills to rise to the challenge of solving the community's problems (Victoria State Government, 2017). Hence, this report recommended Victorians, the need to value learning more than they value, as they do not need to be always at the cutting edge.

Budget and Funding

The fourth barrier to innovation is budget and funding. According to the Australian Innovation Research Centre in Tasmania, the content analysis revealed that this barrier only exists in Tasmania (TAS), where few Tasmanian and Australian investment capital is available for innovation (West, 2009).

Leadership Characteristics

The leadership characteristics thematic analysis explored the leadership characteristics that promote innovation in Australian public sector organisations. The content analysis revealed the following views and perspectives from the selected reports

Supportive, Risk-Taker, Practical, Lead by Example, and Decision-Making

The content analysis suggested that one of the favourable leadership characteristics to innovate in South Australia (SA) and Victoria (Vic) is to be a supportive leader. For example, in South Australia's innovation strategy report, it is noted that:

> coaching helps find best fit-methods, assists in identifying and assessing the conditions for innovation surrounding a project or within a department, implications of this for the project and advising on remedies where required or re-scoping the project where remedies are not available. (Vanstone, Ryan, & McPhee, 2017, p. 36)

In Victoria's 'Putting Innovation in Motion' report, there is a need for leaders who value and understand innovation and individuals who innovate. There is a need for leaders who will get behind their people, who clear a path through the 'blocks' in the system (Victoria State Government, 2017). Among the desired leadership characteristics found in all the government's reports and newsletters is risk-takers. Particularly the Victorian government emphasised the need for leaders who have the propensity to innovate (Victoria State Government, 2017). Besides the need for leaders who are risk-takers, the Victorian government calls for leaders who understand that innovation is not a threat to the system and may reduce risks. Since the Victorian government appreciates and values innovation, they attempt to develop opportunities for leaders to model the desired behaviours in their workplace (Victoria State Government, 2017). In South Australia (SA), a continued frustration expressed by several government officials was the difficulty in reaching a decision in the allocated time when multiple stakeholders or a large number of people are involved (Vanstone, Ryan, & McPhee 2017). In Victoria (Vic), there are several calls for leaders who understand their power can have a wide impact (Victoria State Government, 2017). As described by a public servant, you want leaders to be involved in the process so if you create a practical idea, you get the support (Tobias, 2014). A central issue with innovation in large organisations including the 'Australian Public Service' (APS) is the joint problems of groupthink and consensus decision-making (Management Advisory Committee, 2010). Decision-makers should invest in areas that offer the most potential and make the most of the organisation's investments and ideas, which may require dismantling the hierarchical mindset so that all individuals feel empowered to innovate (Tobias, 2013).

Organisational Climate

The organisational climate thematic analysis explored organisational climate issues that promote innovation in Australian public sector organisations. The content analysis revealed the following views and perspectives from several government reports, newsletters, and websites, as follows.

Culture of Sharing

In New South Wales (NSW), the government collaborates across different levels to minimise obstacles for businesses. However, it is noted in the 'government innovation strategy report' that the NSW government should play a significant role in promoting collaboration and developing an environment in which industries and government can collaborate to resolve problems (NSW Innovation Strategy, 2015). In Queensland (QLD), it is indicated that the government engages with industry and collaborate with QLD government agencies to eliminate regulatory hurdles to business innovation (Department of Science, Information Technology, Innovation and the Arts, 2013). A culture of sharing with partner organisations and other governments facilitates the delivery of practical innovation and information necessary for the market. In Victoria (Vic), a culture of sharing is developed through collecting and sharing innovation across the Victorian public service to inspire and stimulate innovation (Victoria State Government, 2017). In Western Australia (WA), the government is committed to bring successful expatriates home to share their experiences (Office of the Government Chief Information Officer, 2016).

Policy Development

In the Australian Capital Territory (ACT), policy development is perceived fundamental to enhance a culture of innovation. In New South Wales (NSW), the government should allow product development and new processes to flourish (e.g. (a) removing hurdles to the use of technologies, which weaken businesses and markets; (b) making purchasing rules that stimulate change and addressing market problems that hinder innovation; (c) highlighting research and novel ideas that are developed in NSW and promoting NSW as the innovation centre of Australia; (d) enhancing NSW research and development to enhance social and economic factors; (e) ensuring the right competencies are developed and retained in NSW and preparing existing and future workforce to develop opportunities and technologies for the future; (f) adopting a greater 'user-centric' approach and developing appropriate means for engagement that deliver better outcomes; and, importantly, (g) making it easier to collaborate with the government) (NSW Innovation Strategy, 2015). In addition, start the NSW Innovation Concierge (NIC) service which involves the digital interface 'Ask NIC', to access information and people in the government (NSW Innovation Strategy, 2015). It will be crucial for innovative ideas, which corresponds with state priorities. Moreover, develop 'regulatory sandboxes' where products and services can be experimented while preserving current protections (NSW Innovation Strategy, 2015). The initiative of regulatory sandboxes will promote more experimentation and permit industries to enhance innovation in NSW.

In the Northern Territory (NT) strategic directions 2017–2021 report, it is required to enhance and expand new products and services, innovation, and creativity (Northern Territory Government, 2017). In addition, shape an agile and diverse workforce. In Queensland (QLD), the government should propose suitable recommendations on evolving trends that have an impact on QLD's science and innovation system and promote mechanisms for enhancing research and development (R&D) and innovation across various sectors including government agencies, industries and universities, and international partnerships (Department of Science, Information Technology, Innovation and the Arts, 2013). Interestingly, to enhance government rules about what funds are necessary in future endeavours, the QLD government has created the 'Science and Innovation Investment Framework' and developed the 'Accelerate Queensland Science and Innovation Program' (Department of Science, Information Technology, Innovation and the Arts, 2013). In South Australia's (SA) 'Innovation Strategy Report', there are endeavours to introduce new methods for public sector problem-solving and support to explore how they could be applied to projects (Vanstone, Ryan, & McPhee 2017). Innovation systems in Tasmania (TAS) can be thought of individuals' competencies. For human resource development activities to promote innovation, they must optimise sectors that Tasmanian industries are willing to devote the competencies required for innovation activities. The infrastructure and the allocated capital that are necessary to enhance innovation may be different from that designed to achieve different purposes (West, 2009). 'No successful innovating country today relies on free markets alone to finance innovation' (West, 2009, p. 21). Alternatively, it is recommended that the Tasmanian government partner with private capital providers to minimise risks while accepting a less market rate of return on investment. Other options involve the development of a 'circuit breaker' that permits innovators to experiment the practicality of their projects before a regulatory approval is granted (West, 2009).

In Victoria (Vic), the government works in a unique way to improve its community. This involves developing internal systems, applying different techniques for policy development or restructuring current services to fulfil people's needs, and developing prototypes that could be critiqued and experimented efficiently (Victoria State Government, 2017). In Western Australia (WA), policies should be designed to inspire and unify WA towards a shared vision, stimulate collaboration, enhance WA's innovation system, and support structural change, as noted in the 'WA Innovation Strategy Report' (Office of the Government Chief Information Officer, 2016). In addition, opportunities for innovation in WA could be optimised by exposing innovators to international markets and allowing them to expand their networks.

Networking

In the Australian Capital Territory (ACT), industry collaboration is supported through various programs such as 'CollabIT' and the 'CBR Innovation Network (CBRIN)' through networking with research and education institutions and small and medium enterprises (Cumming, 2016). They pursue procurement activity such as the 'Small Business Innovation Program' and engage with local industries to stimulate participation. In addition, they develop networks among individuals and the existing commercial groups to promote opportunities for sales and development on the global platform (Cumming, 2016). In New South Wales (NSW), the government aspires to strengthen the linkages between research and the economy. Frequently, researchers are sceptical about who in the industry could benefit from their work, and businesses are frequently uninformed of the existing opportunities that might enhance collaboration with researchers (NSW Innovation Strategy, 2015). However, there are strategic relationships between educational institutions and the NSW government. This relationship management function will actively inspire dialogue to assist with problem-solving and collaboration and connect institutions with the government. In Queensland's (QLD) 'Innovation Action Plan', it is noted that collaboration between industry, research, government, and education is crucial to innovation. However, more endeavours are necessary to demonstrate the significance of science and innovation to the community. Collaboration and knowledge sharing will support Queensland's goals to have active networks between universities and businesses and have the community involved in science and innovation (Department of Science, Information Technology, Innovation and the Arts, 2013). In Victoria's 'Innovation Strategy Report', significant innovations often happen from networking with outstanding academics and effective organisations (Victoria State Government, 2017). It is perceived that by working with new partners, they can bridge silos and learn from one another. This not only delivers novel ideas and insights, it can also develop new competencies and relationships that support their day-to-day roles. In other words, engaging with different perspectives and skills that defy their own is fundamental to a more responsive public sector. The Western Australia's (WA) 'Innovation Strategy Report' outlines their collaboration with small firms and researchers to endorse particular notions in the market (Office of the Government Chief Information Officer, 2016). Bringing investors and innovators together can inspire action and promote innovative ideas.

Measurement Tools

In Queensland (QLD) program managers in their departments are monitoring and evaluating their programs (Department of Science, Information Technology, Innovation and the Arts, 2013). If required, changes are made to enhance efficiency and effectiveness. In Tasmania (TAS), innovation risk can be assessed by three dimensions. These are scale, duration, and intensity. *Scale* implies the minimum required investment to deliver innovation to market. *Duration* implies the minimum period required before revealing an outcome. *Intensity* implies the possibility that the product will be introduced in a particular market (West, 2009). The greater the scale and the duration, and less the intensity, the greater the project's risk. In addition, it is recommended to pursue an effective audit of Tasmanian regulation to measure its influence on innovation risk and incentive (West, 2009). In Victoria (Vic), the trend is to innovate on specific outcomes they are being measured on (Victoria State Government, 2017), whereas in Western Australia (WA), metrics are developed to evaluate WA's innovation performance and effectiveness at the state level and more specifically in effectiveness of the funds allocated (Office of the Government Chief Information Officer, 2016).

Incentives

In New South Wales (NSW), the government provides incentives to industry and universities to collaborate, for example, providing 'technology vouchers' that organisations can exchange through partnerships with research institutions to solve particular problems in their organisations (NSW Innovation Strategy, 2015). In Victoria (Vic), it is recommended not only to value innovation but also to make their stories more visible and develop strategies to reward commitment to achieve things that matter (Victoria State Government, 2017). In the meantime, establish significant events that identify and incentivise practical innovation across government.

Embracing Diversity

The nexus of diversity, innovation, and collaboration in the Australian Capital Territory (ACT) brings a unique power. As noted in the 'Innovation Strategy Report', 'it is the engine of accelerated evolution' (Cumming, 2016, p. 6). In other words, they are a community that promotes diversity in culture and thinking. In New South Wales (NSW), the NSW government can be a leader in innovation by embracing more external ideas and new perspectives to enhance their service delivery to the community. In Victoria (Vic), the trend is to diversify beyond traditional providers to include smaller innovative organisations to recognise new ways of thinking and working (Victoria State Government, 2017). Hence, engaging and networking with diverse people across government helps to reaffirm their commonalities. In Western Australia

(WA), innovation is promoted by encouraging diversity to pursue excellence (e.g. gender diversity, different generations, and people from diverse cultural backgrounds and experiences) (Office of the Government Chief Information Officer, 2016).

Commitment

There is a commitment to collaboration to reveal innovative solutions to enhance economic and social forces in New South Wales (NSW) (NSW Innovation Strategy, 2015). Similarly, in Queensland (QLD), the 'Science and Innovation Action Plan' is assessed after a year of operation to reaffirm that the goals and actions remain current and practical (Department of Science, Information Technology, Innovation and the Arts, 2013). This assessment enables outcomes of the QLD's plan to be considered and incorporated whenever required. In South Australia (SA), the government is building innovation capability within the state through a plethora of initiatives: programs to encourage entrepreneurial activity (e.g. SA Early Commercialisation Fund and SA Venture Capital Fund); infrastructure that supports innovation and the hi-tech industry (e.g. Gig City, SAHMRI, and Tech in SA); a strengthened focus on the use of government data and digital solutions (e.g. Digital Transformation Strategy, Digital by Default Declaration, and GovHack open data competition); experimentation with open-source and participatory approaches to public problem-solving through 'Better Together' (e.g. Adelaide to Zero Low Carbon Entrepreneur's Prize and Fund My Community); and appointment of a chief advisor on innovation (Vanstone, Ryan & McPhee, 2017). In Victoria (Vic), as public servants noted:

> While innovation requires a fundamental commitment from us as public servants, we also recognise that innovation can come from anywhere. We should engage all levels of the public sector to value practical innovation and those who deliver it, to recognise and share the work that is already happening; introduce actions to help connect people, ideas and work underway, and to build shared tools and resources for the future; grow our capabilities and understanding of practical innovation across all areas of government; and review impact and learn from strategy implementation to drive the next iteration and continue to build visibility. (Victoria State Government, 2017, pp. 10–12)

In Western Australia (WA), the 'Western Australian Innovator of the Year Program' acknowledges the success of the Western Australian innovators; promotes engagement with industry for promotional purposes; strengthens industry-government research collaborations and networking; and involves communities throughout WA districts (Office of the Government Chief Information Officer, 2016). In addition, there is a commitment to continue their endeavours to cut red tape to make it more efficient for industries to flourish and transform their operations to become a model of innovation.

Discussion and Implication

Innovation is a concept that is still underdeveloped, and delimitation and new concepts are developing as 'collaborative innovation', 'open innovation', 'green innovation' and others that create even more complexity but also create new possibility of developing a culture of innovation for organisations (Sousa, Ferreira & Vaz, 2020). It is apparent that the literature on innovation indicates a plethora of tactics that promote a culture of innovation in complex environments. For example, leadership characteristics, organisational climate, and competencies are constantly found to have positive impact on innovation (Moussa, McMurray, & Muenjohn, 2018a, 2018b). However, there is no consensus among scholars on which strategies/policies are most influential in the government sector in a changing global economy. Further, several scholars have suggested that budget constraints negatively impact innovation. Although Bernier and Hafsi (2007) concluded that organisations perform better when resources can be easily accessible and higher and long-term budgets (Denford, Dawson & Desouza, 2015) are fundamental for innovation, this chapter suggested that budgets at the state level are not considered a barrier to innovate in Australia except Tasmania. However, Demircioglu and Audretsch (2017) argued that limited budgets do not have any statistical impact on public sector employees' ability to innovate. Moreover, Albury (2005) and Bommert (2010) recommended a framework that outlines barriers to innovate in the public sector such as short-term budgets and planning prospects, insufficient competencies in taking risks, and administrative burdens. Nonetheless, this chapter suggested that generalising barriers to innovate in the public sector may not be feasible, as each organisation in each country/state has its unique climate.

According to Arrona, Franco, and Wilson (2020), public innovation drivers are diverse in nature and come from a variety of sources: from institutions which are distant to concrete daily practices, from experiences of different administrations, from within the organisation itself, and from the external environment such as external stakeholders and citizens. According to Lopes and Farias (2020), to date, most studies address the investigation of the innovation process; however, few empirical researches address leadership characteristics in the innovation process in the public sector. Although the researcher attempted to display the most favourable leadership characteristics that promote a culture of innovation, it remains an open question for future studies to identify leadership characteristics that contribute to the implementation of innovation that leads to improvement or transformation in public services (Moussa, McMurray, and Muenjohn 2018a, 2018b). The originality of this chapter lays in the tremendous amount of data garnered through relevant documents published in several government reports, newsletters, and websites which provided formative explanations of the dynamics of innovation in public sector organisations in Australia. Future research should seek how public employees perceive the concept of innovation, whether it is perceived as occurring within the existing organisational policies or if it is organisationally transformative in the endeavour to be more effective (Rivera & Landahl, 2019). There is a paucity of research exploring the processes inherent in innovation in public sector organisations in Australia compared with the plethora of studies evaluating the antecedent factors to innovation. Thus, this chapter provided an original contribution to the existing literature on innovation. In addition, the inclination for public sector organisations to innovate has implications for policy development. In other words, examining and reviewing innovation in this chapter would enhance our understanding of the dynamics of innovation in the public sector. This chapter can enhance public servants' level of awareness of the complexities of the dynamics of innovation in the government sector. Ultimately, this chapter can assist decision-makers tailor their employees' tasks/work in ways that promote innovation.

Conclusion

In this chapter, the author argues that from an innovation systems perspective, organisational barriers to innovation, leadership characteristics, and organisational climate are activities that influence innovation processes in the Australian public sector. The vital role that leadership plays in developing a culture of innovation in the government sector has become increasingly significant in the last decade. Thus, the objective in undertaking this review is to present a constructive critical review of the growing literatures on innovation in the public sector. This chapter aimed at enhancing our understanding of the factors that impact on innovation in Australian public sector organisations. It suggested crucial relationships such as organisational barriers, leadership characteristics, and organisational climate that impact the ability to innovate in the public sector.

References

Albury, D. (2005). Fostering Innovation in Public Services. *Public Money and Management, 25*(1), 51–56.

Arrona, A., Franco, S., & Wilson, J. R. (2020). Public Innovation through Governance in Place-Based Competitiveness Policymaking: The Case of Bizkaia Orekan. *Competitiveness Review: An International Business Journal*, 1–18. https://doi.org/10.1108/CR-03-2018-0023

Baer, M., & Frese, M. (2003). Innovation is Not Enough: Climates for Initiative and Psychological Safety, Process Innovations, and Firm Performance. *Journal of Organisational Behavior, 24*(1), 45–68.

Bernier, L., & Hafsi, T. (2007). The Changing Nature of Public Entrepreneurship. *Public Administration Review, 67*(3), 488–503.

Boeije, H. R. (2012). *Analysis in Qualitative Research*. Thousand Oaks, CA: Sage Publications.

Bommert, B. (2010). Collaborative Innovation in the Public Sector. *International Public Management Review, 11*(1), 15–33.

Cinar, E., Trott, P., & Simms, C. (2019). A Systematic Review of Barriers to Public Sector Innovation Process. *Public Management Review, 21*(2), 264–290.

Coulon, T., Templier, M., Bourdeau, S., Amandine, P., & Vieru, D. (2020). Open Innovation in the Public Sector: A Dynamic Capabilities Perspective and the Role of Information Technology. In *Proceedings of the 53rd Hawaii International Conference on System Sciences*, pp. 5942–5951.

Creswell, J. W. (2009). *Research Design: Qualitative, Quantitative, and Mixed Methods Approaches* (3rd ed.). Thousands Oaks, CA: Sage Publications.

Cumming, J. (2016). *ACT Government Digital Strategy 2016–2019*. ACT Government, Australia.

Demircioglu, M. A., & Audretsch, D. B. (2017). Conditions for Innovation in Public Sector Organizations. *Research Policy, 46*(9), 1681–1691.

Denford, J. S., Dawson, G. S., & Desouza, K. C. (2015). An Argument for Centralization of IT Governance in the Public Sector. In *Paper Presented at the 48th Hawaii International Conference on System Sciences (HICSS)*, Kauai, Hawaii.

Department of Science, Information Technology, Innovation and the Arts. (2013). *Science and Innovation Action Plan: Turning Great Ideas into Great Opportunities*. State of Queensland: Queensland Government.

Ekvall, G., & Ryhammar, L. (1999). The Creative Climate: Its Determinants and Effects at a Swedish University. *Creativity Research Journal, 12*(4), 303–310.

Hunter, S. T., Bedell, K. E., & Mumford, M. D. (2007). Climate for Creativity: A Quantitative Review. *Creativity Research Journal, 19*(1), 69–90.

Lopes, A. V., & Farias, J. S. (2020). How Can Governance Support Collaborative Innovation in the Public Sector? A Systematic Review of the Literature. *International Review of Administrative Sciences, 0*(0), 1–17.

Management Advisory Committee. (2010). *Empowering Change: Fostering Innovation in the Australian Public Service*. Commonwealth of Australian, ACT.

Maykut, P. S., & Morehouse, R. (1994). *Beginning Qualitative Research: A Philosophic and Practical Guide*. London and Washington, DC: Falmer Press.

Moussa, M., McMurray, A., & Muenjohn, N. (2018a). A Conceptual Framework of the Factors Influencing Innovation in Public Sector Organisations. *The Journal of Developing Areas, 52*(3), 231–240.

Moussa, M., McMurray, A., & Muenjohn, N. (2018b). Innovation and Leadership in Public Sector Organisations. *Journal of Management Research, 10*(3), 14–30.

Mumford, M. D., Scott, G. M., Gaddis, B., & Strange, J. M. (2002). Leading Creative People: Orchestrating Expertise and Relationships. *The Leadership Quarterly, 13*(6), 705–750.

Northern Territory Government. (2017). *DTBI Strategic Directions 2017–2021. Vision: A Vibrant and Resilient Economy for all Territorians*. Northern Territory Government.

NSW Innovation Strategy. (2015). *Bringing Big Ideas to Life*. State of New South Wales, Department of Finance, Services, and Innovation.

Office of the Government Chief Information Officer. (2016). *Western Australian Innovation Strategy*. The Office of the Government Chief Information Officer, Western Australia.

Osterberg, E. E., & Qvist, M. (2020). Public Sector Innovation as Governance Reform: A Comparative Analysis of Competitive and Collaborative Strategies in the Swedish Transport Sector. *Administration Society, 52*(2), 292–318.

Rivera, J. D., & Landahl, M. R. (2019). An Environment Conducive to Bureaucratic Innovation? Exploring the Potential for Public Entrepreneurship within FEMA. *Journal of Urban Management, 8*(2), 272–281.

Sousa, M. J., Ferreira, C., & Vaz, D. (2020). Innovation Public Policy: The Case of Portugal. *Management and Economics Research Journal, 6*, 1–14.

Tobias, J. (2013). *How to Be An Innovative Leader: Lessons from the Experts*. The Strategy Group Pty Ltd, NSW, Australia.

Tobias, J. (2014). *Who Should Be on Your Innovation Team?* NSW, Australia, The Strategy Group Pty Ltd.

Torugsa, N. A., & Arundel, A. (2016). Complexity of Innovation in the Public Sector: A Workgroup-Level Analysis of Related Factors and Outcomes. *Public Management Review, 18*(3), 392–416.

Trevino, L. K., Hartman, L. P., & Brown, M. (2000). Moral Person and Moral Manager: How Executives Develop a Reputation for Ethical Leadership. *California Management Review, 42*(4), 128–142.

Vanstone, C., Ryan, M., & McPhee, L. (2017). *Solving Tough Problems. Seizing New Opportunities: A Model for an Innovation Lab for the South Australian Public Sector.* Tacsi (The Australian Centre for Social Innovation).

Victoria State Government. (2017). *Public Sector Innovation Strategy: Putting Innovation in Motion.* Retrieved from publicsectorinnovation.vic.gov.au.

Vroom, V. H., & Jago, A. G. (2007). The Role of the Situation in Leadership. *American Psychologist, 62*(1), 17–24.

West, J. (2009). *An Innovation Strategy for Tasmania: A New Vision for Economic Development. Conceptual Overview and Options Outline.* Australian Innovation Research Centre, University of Tasmania.

18

Prototyping Innovation as a Business Process

Sylwia Sysko-Romańczuk and Katarzyna Bachnik

Introduction: Country and Context

Considered a moderate innovator (European Innovation Scoreboard, 2018), Poland is similar to other developed countries in Central Europe. Since the 1990s, the country highlights numerous examples of forerunners on an organizational level through organizations that were able to grow successfully in international markets with innovation-driven offerings. Selena Solaris and KGHM represent solid examples of innovation success.

Innovation is no longer a buzzword, it is the main driver of sustainable business performance and therefore the entire economy (Osterwalder, 2016). It has been treated as a remedy to embrace uncertainty associated with the exhaustion of post-transformation order, deep crisis of global capitalism, and rapid cultural and technological changes. Globalization, cost and tax optimization, as well as incremental innovations have been the driving force behind organizational growth in the last three decades. This engine has burned out, with consequences resulting in bankruptcies, acquisitions, or a radical renewal of business models (McKinsey, 2015). Informed CEOs understand that our

S. Sysko-Romańczuk
Warsaw University of Technology, Warsaw, Poland
e-mail: sylwia.sysko.romanczuk@pw.edu.pl

K. Bachnik (✉)
Hult International Business School, Cambridge, MA, USA
e-mail: katarzynabachnik@gmail.com

© The Author(s), under exclusive license to Springer Nature Switzerland AG 2021
A. McMurray et al. (eds.), *The Palgrave Handbook of Workplace Innovation*,
https://doi.org/10.1007/978-3-030-59916-4_18

next phase of business growth calls for a better understanding of innovation-driven processes. Rita McGrath (2018) was blunt and direct when stating "You can't really talk about strategy without taking about innovation. As we are moving to the world, where competitive advantage lasts shorter and shorter period of time, innovation becomes a process by which, you renew your transient competitive advantage," during the Global Peter Drucker Forum 2018. As creating this process remains the biggest challenge in theory and practice, it may be most beneficial to learn from those who experiment constantly and tirelessly learning on the way. The chapter focuses on one such organization in the construction industry.

For years, the construction industry was convinced that three things matter in the property market: location, location, and location. However, the last economic cycle undermined this assumption. The construction industry is not only about location anymore. It is timing, marketability, and location that constitute a new postcrisis real estate paradigm (Vergara-Alert & Gutes, 2019). Industry experts agree that most real estate investments pursued at the peak of the real estate bubble were an economic disaster, while investments made at the bottom of the business cycle were very successful regarding the location of real estate assets (Vergara-Alert & Gutes, 2019). The process of recovery from the last real estate crash has demonstrated that giving the optimal market use to each building plus its characteristics (potential different uses of the assets, different quality standards, design, technology, sustainability standards) is an essential factor when investing in real estate. Marketability of assets is both a transformative business purpose and source of innovation in the construction market. It is a new competitive paradigm and a chance to transform incumbent business models. It puts investors and construction companies outside their current comfort zone of maintaining market position and achieving satisfactory business results.

Introduction: Background and Significance

It is easy to talk about innovation, but it is difficult to implement it. There are a lot of studies offering a rich source of good practices and failed attempts in the context of innovative products and services. More often than not, these studies employ a result-oriented approach. The results are much more visible and tangible than the process that leads to creative outcomes. Business practice shows that the quality of the result is inherently related to the quality of the process from which the result arises. Gedeon Werner, CEO of Aquarius Management, stated that only innovative companies can sustainably deliver innovative solutions. In the light of these observations, prototyping innovation process, ensuring a robust pipeline of innovative projects to build an innovative company, becomes very relevant. The overall aim of innovation design and implementation is to deliver sustainable performance for the company over time. This chapter challenges and examines this research question.

Napollo, a middle-sized Polish developer in the construction industry, offers experiment-driven insight in the field. The case illustrates how to use a prototyping method to design an innovation process step by step, to materialize it in a software that enables automatization and stabilization, and then to fine-tune it with the inclusion of employees. The anticipated outcome is to present a business process, which generates sustainable business value and enables transient competitive advantage exploitation. The case discusses key factors determining what constitutes a sustainable innovation process, based on a true understanding of the external environment. Although rooted in construction specifics, the presented approach can gain broader application.

The case of Napollo suggests that a single organization equipped with leadership with strong determination, trust from employees, and structuralized innovation process can achieve two important goals. Firstly, it can cope with challenging external conditions, such as rapid urbanization, climate change, resource scarcity, and demographic and social changes with technological breakthroughs. Secondly, it can explore marketability of assets, a new competitive paradigm in the construction industry, as a solid source of innovation to cope with a transient competitive advantage.

Lean methodology is heavily grounded in the business research and practice. A key component of it, prototyping, was developed and explored as a stage in the innovation process linking ideas with refined solutions. It relies upon experimentation, refinement, and business assumption testing. It is also about visualization: "To build a prototype you need to transform your ideas into a physical form so that you can experience and interact with them and, in the process, learn and develop more empathy" (D.school, 2017; Liedtka, Ogilvie, & Brozenske, 2014). The creation of a physical representation of an idea allows engagement with end users to gather their feedback and introduce improvements (Curedale, 2013). As such it also closes a gap between ideation (exploration) and implementation. Numerous iterations allow for constant learning. As the proverb says: Progress and you will find perfection. Prototyping also enforces the notion of failing often and fast (Kelley, Littman, & Peters, 2001). Although failure is not widely accepted in the business world, it is an inevitable part of generating innovations. As Edmondson (2011) puts it: "The wisdom of learning from failure is incontrovertible. Yet organizations that do it well are extremely rare." Thirty-one percent of respondents of a Boston

Consulting Group survey identified a risk-averse culture as a key obstacle to innovation. In contrast to Western European respondents, lack of entrepreneurial heritage and negative country of origin effect are two key obstacles to innovation in post-Soviet countries (Prats, Sosna, & Sysko-Romańczuk, 2015). Birkenshaw and Haas (2016) advocate strongly that companies should increase their acceptance of failure by improving the return on it. In order to do this, they should rigorously extract and document the takeaways of failed projects.

Theoretical Background

Executives agree on the importance of innovation but are often dissatisfied with the results and lack of clarity on what the problem is and how to improve (McKinsey, 2019). In the last 15 years, 52% of S&P 500 companies have disappeared (Anthony, Viguerie, Schwartz, & Van Landeghem, 2018), which shows how transitory unsustainable businesses are. Such level of risk and uncertainty calls for more flexible and agile adaptation to internal and external factors (Sull, 2009). The CEOs of global giants like Google admit that organizations fail mostly because they could not foresee where the customers and industry were heading. Such statements bring innovation to the forefront as a necessity to survive and thrive. While easy to talk about innovation, it is much harder to design sufficient processes, get them to work in organizational ecosystem, and consequently build innovation capital (Dyer, Furr, & Lefrandt, 2019).

Some of the academic literature refers to innovation as an output/offering (Kahn, 2018), mindset, or collaborative culture, including co-creation (Kahn, 2018; Kolko, 2015; Ramaswamy, 2009). Others focus on innovation as a process leading to customer-driven offerings, championing approaches such as design thinking (Kelley et al., 2001; Liedtka & Ogilvie, 2011; Martin, 2009). New products and services are perceived as the usual, typical output of innovation. In the mindset-oriented approach innovation addresses the "internationalization of innovation by individual members of the organization where innovation is instilled and ingrained along with the creation of a supportive organizational culture that allows innovation to flourish" (Kahn, 2018). Dyer, Gregersen, and Christensen (2011) identify five skills that "push new ways of thinking, spur and support innovation, and represent distinguishing features of organizations known for innovation": associating, questioning, observing, experimenting, and networking. The cultural approach to innovation highlights the need to focus on users' experiences, to examine complex problems, to use prototypes, to explore potential solutions, and to tolerate failure. Design thinking serves as an example of a process leading to customer-driven offerings (Kelley et al., 2001; Liedtka & Ogilvie, 2011; Martin, 2009). It describes a way of thinking about business with the use of rigor and order assigned to designers. Design thinking can be briefly introduced as a five-stage process of problem recognition and solution finding. It is based on observation and experimentation, which involves testing and prototyping. The efficiency of the process is guaranteed through teamwork, leveraging on the expertise of individuals and a belief that there is no single best solution. Design thinking is about having many ideas and working on them through divergent and convergent iterative cycles (Liedtka & Ogilvie, 2011; Martin, 2009). Companies such as GE, Target, Procter & Gamble, IDEO, and Intuit have successfully applied this approach to design.

Some authors turn toward business model innovations (Amit & Zott, 2012; Christensen, Bartman, & van Bever, 2016; Johnson, Christensen, & Kagerman, 2008; Mitchell & Bruckner Coles, 2004). According to an Economist Intelligence Unit survey, 54% of respondents (senior managers) favored new business models over new products and services as a source of future competitive advantage. Findings from IBM make the case more extreme, suggesting companies whose operating margins had grown faster than their competitors over the previous five years were twice as likely to emphasize business model innovation, as opposed to product or process innovation (Amit & Zott, 2012). Following this line of thought, great business models can reshape industries and drive spectacular growth. However, successful business models must identify, in the simpler form, customer value proposition, profit formula, as well as key resources and processes (Johnson et al., 2008) and, in the more extensive, customer segments, value propositions, channels, customer relationships, revenue streams, key resources, key activities, key partnerships, and cost structure (Osterwalder & Pigneur, 2010).

Other authors recognize innovation as a learning process. Govindarajan and Trimble (2010) advocate for the disciplined approach to innovation. They make a convincing argument that sustainable innovation requires strong leadership and relentless motivation but also a lot of structure. They underline how difficult it is to build a team with a custom organizational model that will be aligned with the expectations of a "performance engine." They also explain that when planning innovative initiatives, creating and revising of the plans shall be guided by a rigorous learning process. In Kahn's view (2018), innovation as a process "attends to the way in which innovation should be organized so that outcomes can come to fruition—as such this includes an overall innovation process and a new product development process." The innovation process of PDMA (2015) illustrates this idea. However, innovation perceived as a business process embracing internal creativity that is managed horizontally (not vertically, via R&D department or business development) calls for deeper study.

Methodology

Although embedded in the specific context of a construction company, the presented research methodological approach is a part of current academic discussion fueled by the question: What if research had to make practical contribution with theoretical implications, rather than theoretical contribution with practical implications?

The chapter is based on outcomes developed during the science-driven project ordered by Aquarius Management, private equity company, for its portfolio company—Napollo, Polish construction developer.[1] The aim of the project was to build a comprehensive innovation management system for the company and generate practical, business contribution with theoretical implications. The project had a defined business need, which the owner wanted to solve using the existing theoretical knowledge in innovation theory. The project was conceived as a creative process of prototyping innovation as a business process—a solution that is currently not available on the market. For this reason, the adopted formula of the project was not consulting like, but a science-driven business one.

Through the completion of a three-phase project over the course of three years, a five-step process to generate sustainable innovation in small to medium businesses was developed and executed. The research team consisted of one academic faculty, tech consulting company, Napollo Management Board, Napollo Marketing Director, and the owner's representative. During the third phase all employees from Napollo were incorporated into the project.

The project explored prototyping as a methodological approach for business process design. It was developed in three phases: diagnose, educate, and prototype and experiment (Sysko-Romańczuk & Afifi, 2017). Those three

---

[1] The project was designed and led by S. Sysko-Romańczuk and U. Afifi from DEConsulting in years 2017–2019. The adopted formula of science-driven business project as well as related outputs are subject to copyright. This publication presents unpublished frameworks subject to their authors' IP rights: (1) methodological approach based on three pillars: diagnose, educate, and prototype and experiment—authors: S. Sysko-Romańczuk and U. Afifi DEConsulting; (2) the concept of Business Innovation composed of three components: creativity (time-to-idea), delivery process (time-to-market), and results (time-to-profit)—author: S. Sysko-Romańczuk; and (3) Five Steps of Innovation Cycle—author: S. Sysko-Romańczuk.

phases had different research team composition, timing, methodological designs, and outputs. These were as follows:

(1) May to July 2017 (Diagnose): Innovation Readiness Audit aiming at assessing the innovation competency gap—it involved structured interviews (owner and board of directors) and questionnaires (employees). Outcome: report highlighting innovation competency gap.

(2) October 2017 to March 2018 (Educate): Innovation Academy to backfill identified innovation competence gap. Based on the report findings, a tailor-made managerial competency development program was created, named Innovation Academy. It resulted in an increase in innovation competency for members of the board of directors and key company employees. Outcome: proof of concept for the innovation business process.

(3) February to June 2019 (Prototype and Experiment): Prototyping innovation process to bring acquired innovation competence into action. Focusing on pivoting and testing with the aim to design and materialize the actual innovation process using experiment-driven methodology. Two outcomes: (1) five-step innovation life cycle tailored to Napollo's organization structure and (2) dedicated software of the innovation life cycle in the form of intranet website.

The chapter uncovers insights from the third phase and zeroes on prototyping of Napollo's innovation life cycle. During February and March 2019, the research team was meeting every Monday to prototype the next versions of Napollo's innovation life cycle. Finally, the research team developed five versions, and the last one, numbered 5.0, was decided to be transferred to a software solution. Having that Napollo employees were involved in feedback and co-creation in prototyping in May. In June innovation life cycle MVP (minimum viable product) was successfully tested and then incorporated into Napollo's organizational structure (Sysko-Romańczuk & Afifi, 2019).

Data Analysis

Napollo is a mid-sized company (100 employees) operating since 2007. The scope of the operations includes acquisition of new land, coordination of construction works, financing, commercialization, sale of apartments, property management, and marketing communication. Although the company is focused on obtaining the highest margin from core operations, namely, residence building, commercial building, and property management, it is also involved in experiments with new business lines, including beekeeping on the roof of their apartment buildings. So far, such initiatives have emerged from spontaneous ideas from the owner of Napollo, and not the active seeking of new sources of revenue from employees and the company managers. The growing pressure from the owner to improve the company's results and the influx of uncontrolled, creative ideas forced the Napollo Management Board to deal with innovation professionally and shape it in the business process regular bases.

The projects methodological design was built on two business assumptions: (1) Innovation is a business process, and (2) innovation as a business process can be prototyped. The first assumption was verified thanks to developing a definition of business innovation understood by all employees of the company, its structural components as well as their different types and their business impact. Innovation in a business, proposed for discussion to Napollo, as a creativity applied to some purpose to create value via three key components (Sysko-Romańczuk, 2017): (1) creativity (time-to-idea), (2) delivery (time-to-market), and (3) results (time-to-profit). These three components, when working together, bring innovation in a business to life, because creativity is achieved when ideas are backed by appropriate processes to deliver business value. Following discussion with the research team, a definition of business innovation at Napollo was developed:

It's best to define it with a change. A change for the better and easier for the customer/recipient. It can solve a problem, break down an obstacle, meet an existing or unconscious need. The most everyday is an incremental innovation. It changes/automates repetitive activities, makes work lighter, gives it momentum, frees time and strength for important matters. The idea does not have to be groundbreaking. Just start acting differently. Change something in relationships, structure, processes, thinking. A breakthrough innovation may seem to be a course for advanced users. But it is only through this radical epithet. It is groundbreaking because it breaks the existing order. And even the simplest idea or thing can be groundbreaking. However, on a large scale, they influence the change in the environment, industry or life of the customers—our customers. Anyone in the company and anyone else can be customers. Don't be afraid to be radicalized when it comes to innovation! Innovation starts with ourselves. Our ideas, ideas, released imagination. To create a new quality out of it, it's worth to collide these ideas with the outside world—friends, clients, colleagues. Then we can find new meaning and meaning for existing solutions, products or services. It is not necessary to invent something that does not yet exist. You can find a new reason for someone to use an existing solution or product, just giving them a new way. (Napollo, 2019).

Developing a common definition of business innovation for Napollo enabled the transition to the verification of the second business assumption and the start of prototyping innovation as a business process. At the beginning the research team was introduced to the theoretical concept: "Steps of innovation life cycle—version 1.0" (Sysko-Romańczuk, 2019a). Finally, a five-step innovation process called Napollo's innovation life cycle was prototyped (Sysko-Romańczuk, 2019a). Each step was equipped with templates helping to measure progress on the way.

Step 1: Crystallization of the idea: the aim here is to give the idea a specific form and determine the most important parameters. It involves deciding whether the concept can be later transformed into incremental (efficiency or sustaining) or breakthrough innovation. An incremental innovation is defined as an innovation that optimizes work, tasks, changes and/or streamlines existing activities. Breakthrough innovation is defined as an idea, action, thing, even very simple, which can ultimately change the operation of the industry, market, or lifestyle of recipients. The ideator[2] is asked to answer the most important questions for this phase of creative thinking: Who is the customer—the recipient of my idea? What is their problem or challenge? How does my solution help them? Is it different from what is already known and practiced? What makes it attractive or useful? The idea does not have to meet market assumptions yet nor resemble an actual full-scale project. If the idea is fully formed, then a proper idea summary is prepared. There are separate Idea Templates designed to support the ideator with idea fine-tuning.

Step 2: Structurization of the idea: this is the level of defining the idea according to market systematics: how to sell it, how to make money from it, how to distance it from competition, and how will the project team and plan be supported with the Business Concept Template.

The ideator is helped to organize their thinking about the proposed solution or product not only in terms of what it is, who it serves, and what problems it solves. The Business Concept Template helps to translate an idea into a business case. Thanks to deep mental and analytical iteration, they develop the conceptual knowledge examining (1) problem/challenges/obstacles and needs of the recipient/customer of the idea/solution; (2) proposed solution/idea; (3) revenue model/monetization strategy; (4) direct, indirect, and substitution competition and the secret to the innovation/uniqueness

---

[2] Every employee that has an idea and wants to peruse it, through the new five-step process, is named an "ideator."

of the idea/solution; (5) promotion and sales plan; (6) composition of the team; (7) schedule and action plan; and (8) target location of the project in the structure/business of Napollo. The ideator is asked to answer the template questions as accurately as possible. The more it is distilled to the essence, the easier it will be for the ideator to work on the marketization of the idea.

Step 3: Presentation of the idea: reaching this stage means that the originator has completed conceptual work and business planning, both highly rated by the investment decisive body. This is the moment when the chances of materializing an idea are very high. The ideator prepares the Business Concept Presentation Template here that presents the business case in full detail. A direct meeting with the company investment body decides next whether to invest in the idea or not. At the presentation stage, even if the presentation does not end with an investment, everyone who reaches this step will receive a reward for this achievement.

Step 4: Implementation of the project: the winning funding idea becomes a project with a business plan, schedule, budget, and place in the company structure. The ideator becomes the leader responsible for completing the project team and the reliable testing of business assumptions and the delivery of achievable results. From now on, the project leader and team are required to implement the project standards in accordance with the methodology used in the organization. Such an approach helps reduce organizational uncertainty when implementing innovative projects.

Step 5: Settlement of the project: the completed project is equal to an implemented innovation. It can be a process, procedure, product, or service. Project impact is assessed via multi dimensions and analyzed by all the stakeholders in the company, from the project team, to the investment decisive body, and to the Management Board. This new product or service may remain in the company, be sold, or shut down. The work is rewarded, included in the company's targets and in the best practice annals that all employees can access. Again step 1 can be entered.

The whole process works in cycle (see Fig. 18.1) and is implemented horizontally in contrary to traditional business processes (finance, production, R&D, and etc.). Napollo's Innovation Life Cycle is managed collectively by employees with the support of the dedicated innovation process animator rather than the innovation director. Collegiality cannot be improvised. Those involved must learn how to listen, exchange views, share opinions, and bring out the best in each person in organization.

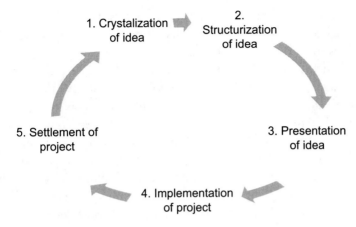

Fig. 18.1 Steps of innovation life cycle. (Source: Sysko-Romańczuk, 2019a)

The authors believe that the innovation process prototyped and implemented in Napollo is extraordinary, because it is simple, effective, and engaging. It operates in the horizontal dimension of the organizational structure, crushing walls between hierarchical business silos (departments; business lines). Napollo started a five-step innovation process in June 2019, which was preceded by three rounds of workshops with all employees in May 2019. After the workshops, the Board received many constructive comments and proposals to modify elements and relations in the proposed innovation life cycle, which were immediately discussed and some of them implemented before June. This had a significant effect on employee involvement in the new business process and on their sense of ownership of the process (perceived as "their own" and not "external and imposed").

Discussion and Conclusions

The chapter assumes that only innovative companies can deliver sustainable performance over time. Innovative companies can ensure a robust pipeline of innovative projects to build a sustainable portfolio. The authors claim that innovation processes which constantly deliver innovation-powered projects can be prototyped. So far prototyping was developed and explored in research as a stage in the innovation process linking concepts with refined solutions. The case of Napollo shows that prototyping can be used as a method to enable and implement innovation processes.

The authors realize that the innovation process described in the chapter addresses one company only. To prove its more universal application, further empirical research is needed. Yet, they see this example as a good starting point and benchmark. In light of the realization that experimentation is vital to business success (Davenport, 2009), this case presents practical insight into this phenomenon. The cycle-based approach of the company falls in line with the notion that innovation should not be a sole event but a continuous endeavor in every company's DNA (Holtzman, 2014). The company-wide effort to empower employees to be part of the process and contribute to organizational creativity aligns with assumptions that building an innovative ecosystem/infrastructure increases the chances of success (Davenport, 1998; Iyer & Davenport, 2008). Napollo also builds the process of knowledge transfer. The takeaways from the first steps in the innovation process constitute a basis for the design and execution of the next steps. By doing so, Napollo advocates for taking strategic and structural approach to innovation (Reeves, Fink, Palma, & Harnoss, 2017). Oeij, van der Torre, Vaas, and Dhondt (2019) tried to verify if social innovation could be treated as an innovation process, by applying the innovation journey model. The authors believe that the five-step innovation process presented here is worth experimenting with in other organizations to enhance performance. For companies in the region, Napollo is a great inspiration to dare to look beyond industry standards, have faith in internal capabilities, observe and analyze external environment carefully, and ideate and innovate sustainably in an ongoing manner.

The implementation of the two-year project was an opportunity to answer the research question raised at the beginning of the chapter: How to ensure a robust pipeline of innovative projects to build a sustainably innovative company? The approach to building innovative companies benefits from a three-phase project methodology, a five-step innovation life cycle, and a conscious commitment from owners and Management Boards to answer following questions:

1. How do we bring new ideas into the process?
2. What do we do with new ideas?
3. How do we turn new ideas into sustainable business value?

Iterative cycles provide more options, help establish a comprehensive innovation management system, and build a heritage of innovation capital in every company. This case demonstrates that great leadership practice accelerates this cycle. Jeff Bezos (Amazon), Elon Musk (Tesla), Marc Benioff (Salesforce), Indra Nooyi (PepsiCo), and Shantanu Narayen (Adobe) know that creativity and processes of commercialization are not enough. They succeed not only because of their ideas but because they also had the vision, reputation, and networks to win the necessary support and contribution of various stakeholder groups. Innovation perceived as a business process embracing internal creativity and managed horizontally is the example of an effective solution for solving innovators' dilemma on how to deal with innovation in organizations. The chapter presents a simple innovation life cycle that, no matter the company size, can assist to implement innovation with greater success.

References

Amit, R., & Zott, C. (2012). Creating Value Through Business Model Innovation. *MIT Sloan Management Review, 53*(3, Spring), 41–49.

Anthony, S. D., Viguerie, S. P., Schwartz, E. I., & Van Landeghem, J. (2018). Corporate Longevity Forecast: Creative Destruction is Accelerating. *Innosight*. Retrieved November 15, 2019 from https://www.innosight.com/wp-content/uploads/2017/11/Innosight-Corporate-Longevity-2018.pdf.

Birkenshaw, J., & Haas, M. (2016, May). Increase Your Return on Failure. *Harvard Business Review, 94*, 88–93.

Christensen, C. M., Bartman, T., & van Bever, D. (2016). The Hard Truth about Business Model Innovation. *MIT Sloan Management Review, 58*(1, Fall), 31–40.

Curedale, R. (2013). *Design Thinking: Process and Methods Manual*. Topanga, CA: Design Community College Inc.

D.school. (2017). The Design Thinking Process. Retrieved February 17, 2017, from http://dschool.stanford.edu/redesigningtheater/the-design-thinking-process/.

Davenport, T. H. (1998, July–August). Putting The Enterprise into the Enterprise System. *Harvard Business Review, 76*, 121–131.

Davenport, T. H. (2009, February). How to Design Smart Business Experiments. *Harvard Business Review, 87*, 2–8.

Dyer, J., Furr, N., & Lefrandt, C. (2019). *Innovation Capital*. Boston, MA: Harvard Business Review Press.

Dyer, J., Gregersen, H., & Christensen, C. M. (2011). *The Innovator's DNA*. Boston, MA: Harvard Business Review Press.

Edmondson, A. C. (2011, April). Strategies for Learning from Failure. *Harvard Business Review, 89*, 100–106.

European Commission (2018). European Innovation Scoreboard 2018: Europe must deepen its innovation edge. Retrieved November 8, 2002, from https://ec.europa.eu/growth/content/european-innovation-scoreboard-2018-europe-must-deepen-its-innovation-edge_en.

Govindarajan, V., & Trimble, C. (2010). *The Other Side of Innovation: Solving the Execution Challenge*. Boston, MA: Harvard Business School Publishing.

Holtzman, Y. (2014). A Strategy of Innovation through the Development of a Portfolio of Innovation Capabilities. *Journal of Management Development, 33*(1), 24–31.

Iyer, B., & Davenport, T. H. (2008). Reverse Engineering Google's Innovation Machine. *Harvard Business Review, 86*, 1–12.

Johnson, M. W., Christensen, C. M., & Kagerman, H. (2008, December). Reinventing Your Business Model. *Harvard Business Review, 86*, 50–59.

Kahn, K. B. (2018). Understanding Innovation. *Business Horizons, 61*, 453–460.

Kelley, T., Littman, J., & Peters, T. (2001). *The Art of Innovation: Lessons in Creativity from IDEO, America's Leading Design Firm*. New York, NY: Random House.

Kolko, J. (2015, September). Design Thinking Comes of Age. *Harvard Business Review, 93*, 2–7.

Liedtka, J., & Ogilvie, T. (2011). *Designing for Growth: A Design Thinking Tool Kit for Managers*. New York, NY: Columbia Business School Publishing.

Liedtka, J., Ogilvie, T., & Brozenske, R. (2014). *The Designing for Growth Field Book: A Step-by-Step Project Guide*. New York, NY: Columbia Business School Publishing.

Martin, R. (2009). *The Design of Business: Why Design Thinking is the Next Competitive Advantage*. USA: Harvard Business Press.

McGrath, R. (2018). Presentation. Vienna Leadership Summit. Panel 1: A New Innovation Landscape. Global Peter Drucker Forum 2018. Retrieved February 6, 2019, from https://www.youtube.com/watch?v=vgAF6OtqoFs.

McKinsey. (2015). Playing to Win: The New Global Competition For Corporate Profits. Retrieved November 15, 2019, from https://www.mckinsey.com/~/media/McKinsey/Business%20Functions/Strategy%20and%20Corporate%20Finance/Our%20Insights/The%20new%20global%20competition%20for%20corporate%20profits/MGI%20Global%20Competition_Full%20Report_Sep%202015.ashx.

McKinsey. (2019). McKinsey Global Innovation Survey. Retrieved September 10, 2019, from https://www.mckinsey.com/business-functions/strategy-and-corporate-finance/how-we-help-clients/growth-and-innovation.

Mitchell, D., & Bruckner Coles, C. (2004). Establishing a Continuing Business Model Innovation Process. *The Journal of Business Strategy, 25*(3), 39–49.

Napollo. (2019). Company Internal Website. Retrieved November 15, 2019, from www.innowacje.napollo.pl.

Oeij, P. R. A., van der Torre, W., Vaas, F., & Dhondt, S. (2019). Understanding Social Innovation as an Innovation Process: Applying the Innovation Journey Model. *Journal of Business Research, 101*, 243–254.

Osterwalder, A. (2016). "Innovation" is Dead. Long live "innovation". Retrieved February 6, 2019, from https://www.strategyzer.com/blog/posts/2016/12/19/innovation-is-dead-long-live-innovation.

Osterwalder, A., & Pigneur, Y. (2010). *Business Model Generation: A Handbook for Visionaries, Game Changers and Challengers*. NY, NY: John Wiley and Sons.

PDMA. (2015). *The Innovation Cycle*. Chicago, IL: Product Development and Management Association.

Prats, J., Sosna, M., Sysko-Romańczuk, S. (2015). *Entrepreneurial Icebreakers. Insights and Case Studies from Internationally Successful Central and Eastern European Entrepreneurs*. UK, London: Palgrave Macmillan.

Ramaswamy, V. (2009). Are you Ready for the Co-Creation Movement? *IESE-Insight Magazine, 2*, 29–35.

Reeves, M., Fink, T., Palma, R., & Harnoss, J. (2017). Harnessing the secret Structure of Innovation. *MIT Sloan Management Review, 59*(1, Fall), 36–41.

Sull, D. (2009, February). How to Thrive in Turbulent Markets. *Harvard Business Review, 87*, 78–88.

Sysko-Romańczuk, S. (2017). *Science-driven Innovation*. Project Documentation Prepared for Aquarius Management, May–July.

Sysko-Romańczuk, S. (2019a). *Steps of Innovation Life Cycle—Version 1.0. Prototyping Versions of Innovation Life Cycle*. Project Documentation Prepared for Aquarius Management, February–June.

Sysko-Romańczuk, S. (2019b). *Prototyping Versions of Napollo's Innovation Life Cycle—Versions 2.0-5.0*. Project Documentation Prepared for Aquarius Management, February–June.

Sysko-Romańczuk, S., & Afifi, U. (2017). *Comprehensive Innovation Management System: Innovation Readiness Audit—phase I*. Project Documentation Prepared for Aquarius Management, May–July.

Sysko-Romańczuk, S., & Afifi, U. (2019). *Comprehensive Innovation Management System: Prototyping Innovation Process—Phase III*. Project Documentation Prepared for Aquarius Management, February–June.

Vergara-Alert, C., & Gutes, J. (2019, September). *Timing, Marketability and Location. The New Real Estate Paradigm*. Middletown: Vergara-Alert, Gutes Publishing.

Theme IV

Workplace Innovation as an Outcome

19

Creative Leadership and Work Role Proficiency: The Mediating Role of Employee Innovativeness

Tomislav Hernaus, Maja Klindžić, and Matija Marić

Introduction

The preferred competitive position and established market share of high-performing organizations has been increasingly achieved by underlying the micro-foundations of innovation. A large number of scholars highlight the essential role of employees in introducing new products/services, building new technologies, improving or redesigning business processes, or applying new working methods (e.g., De Spiegelaere, Van Gyes, & Van Hootegem, 2012; Hernaus, Černe, & Pološki Vokić, 2016). Both theory and practice confirm that innovative work behaviors (IWBs)—the intentional creation, introduction, and application of new ideas within a work role, group, or organization (West & Farr, 1990)—drive the delivery of market-differentiating improvements.

Following ongoing calls about "the rise of the creative class" (Florida, 2002, 2005, 2012), as well as bearing in mind some of the most inspiring leadership success stories (e.g., Steve Jobs, Jack Welch, Bill Gates, Alan G. Lafley), we explore creative and innovative behavior in organizations that has nowadays become relevant for the entire workforce (above and beyond the cohort of the research and development professionals; see Yuan & Woodman, 2010). Hereby, it should be acknowledged that IWB is a complex, multi-dimensional

T. Hernaus (✉) • M. Klindžić • M. Marić
Faculty of Economics and Business, University of Zagreb, Zagreb, Croatia
e-mail: thernaus@efzg.hr; mklindzic@efzg.hr; mmaric@efzg.hr

© The Author(s), under exclusive license to Springer Nature Switzerland AG 2021
A. McMurray et al. (eds.), *The Palgrave Handbook of Workplace Innovation*,
https://doi.org/10.1007/978-3-030-59916-4_19

(e.g., different levels and different types of innovation), and multi-stage construct (e.g., idea exploration, idea generation, idea promotion, and idea implementation) that captures various multi-player roles.

Creativity and innovativeness are similar, closely related, time-dependent constructs (e.g., Anderson, Potočnik, & Zhou, 2014; Beckett & O'Loughlin, 2016). According to King and Anderson (2002), the innovation process starts with the creativity-driven stage (i.e., idea exploration and generation) which encompasses the production and adoption of an idea that represents a novel or adopted solution for a recognized problem (e.g., performance gaps, low-quality service, or internal competitive wars). As such, this creative effort ends when a manager makes the idea implementation decision. The second, innovation-driven stage (i.e., idea promotion and idea implementation) is a social-political process (Van de Ven, 1986) which often depends on employee team effort and their application behavior to successfully implement the generated (previously approved) idea. In other words, "idea implementation means putting the creative ideas into practice" (cf. Ren & Zhang, 2015), that is, "converting creative ideas into actual innovations such as new and improved products, services, or ways of doing things" (Baer, 2012). Obviously, the production of ideas and idea application are positively related concepts (Axtell et al., 2000), although they may be only loosely coupled (Baer, 2012). After all, we should be aware that in many organizations fewer than 5 percent of all ideas have been implemented (Desouza, 2011).

Acknowledging both differences and relatedness between idea exploration/generation and promotion/implementation, this chapter is focused on explicating distinct roles that managers/leaders and employees/followers play in these two main phases of the job-level innovation process. Our initial assumption is that different sources of individual creativity and innovativeness concurrently influence the innovation's odds of success. Specifically, by targeting the job-level phenomena, we expect that leaders' efforts supplemented with employees' efforts eventually contribute to the innovation process.

The Successful Innovation Process: From Creative Leadership to Employee Innovativeness and Work Role Proficiency

The vast majority of existing research confirms that leadership (i.e., transformational leadership, empowering leadership, leader-member exchange) is a major contextual predictor of employee IWB (e.g., Hammond et al., 2011;

Shalley & Lemoine, 2018). It has been demonstrated that leaders can have more or less direct influence on the innovative behavior of their followers. For instance, employees might follow a formal path to innovativeness by positively reacting to job innovation requirements, that is, managerial expectation to generate or implement new solutions (Shin, Yuan, & Zhou, 2016). As such, idea implementation can be significantly enhanced by setting solution-driven goals and making job innovation requirements more explicit (Hernaus, Marić, & Černe, 2019). According to David Skok, Boston Globe digital advisor, "the leader must change the structure or the tasks that people do to allow that innovation to happen" (Wilpers, 2015).

Alternatively, a less formal path to employee innovativeness is also possible through observational learning. Leaders indeed can be creative themselves (Wen, Zhou, & Lu, 2017) and thus might serve as role models (Škerlavaj, 2018). Surprisingly, the role of leader creativity has not yet received adequate attention in pursuing innovativeness of their subordinates. The accumulated evidence about creative co-workers (Zhou, 2003) signals how role modelling in general shapes employee attitudes and behaviors (Agarwal et al., 2012), including IWB (e.g., De Jong & Den Hartog, 2003).

Although studies that consider creative leaders as role models are limited (e.g., Koseoglu, Liu, & Shalley, 2017; Wen, Zhou, & Lu, 2017), it is similarly expected (e.g., social cognitive theory; see Bandura, 1986) that followers often imitate their leaders or are at least being inspired by how leaders think and act (Shalley & Perry-Smith, 2001; Mathisen, Einarsen, & Mykletun, 2012). Moreover, not only that innovating is recognized as a major dimension of leadership behavior (De Jong & Den Hartog, 2007; Langford, Dougall, & Parkes, 2017), but a large-scale CEO-based survey displays that creativity is a leadership competency most crucial for future success (IBM, 2010).

Thus, leaders with creative abilities practice entrepreneurial behavior, are more effective at identifying novel and useful ideas, successful in promoting positive change, and skillful in encouraging subordinates to implement new ideas (Mueller, Goncalo, & Kamdar, 2011). A good example of a creative leader is Elon Musk, the CEO and CTO of SpaceX, CEO of Tesla Motors, and Chairman of SolarCity. Not only that he is a visionary whose creative personality has led to several incredible entrepreneurial successes, but he also enables and encourages his employees to step out of the "traditional" way of thinking and to put all new ideas forth (see Musk & Watson, 2016).

Irrespective of the path taken, understanding the cause-and-effect relationship between employees' innovation-oriented behavior and their subsequent work role proficiency (i.e., task performance and organizational citizenship behaviors [OCB] as "two distinct dimensions of work behavior that can contribute independently to effectiveness outcomes for organizations"; cf. Griffin, Neale, & Neale 2001) is particularly important for decision-makers. Although the meta-analytic findings (Harari, Reaves, & Viswesvaran, 2016) verified the existence of the positive relationship between IWB and task performance, as well as between IWB and OCB (Deng & Guan, 2017), we need to apply rigorous longitudinal research designs to further investigate their causality across different organizational and work settings.

Research Context and Methodology

A quantitative time-lagged research has been conducted to answer the call for more evidence and to explore how leader creativity is related to workplace behaviors leading to innovation and performance. We used two rounds of the field survey to collect 177 dyadic responses from leaders and their direct reports employed by four Croatian public sector organizations different in size (small- to mid-sized public agencies and two large-sized state-owned enterprises). The chosen research context represents one of the post-transition countries and the youngest EU member country that moved to the free-market economy (Pološki Vokić, Klindžić, & Hernaus, 2018) and had undergone an extensive privatization process in the 1990s (see Franičević, 1999). The sampled organizations operate in four sectors—ICT, education, postal services, and professional, scientific, and technical activities. We narrowed our focus on knowledge-based jobs including positions such as HR specialists, quality experts, project counselors, and others.

Surveyed employees (N = 177; M = 42.69; SD = 9.17) and their corresponding leaders (N = 39; M = 41.06; SD = 7.40) were on average of similar age. Employees' sample was gender-biased (79.1% of female respondents), while we had similar percentage of men and women within the supervisors' sample (53.4% were male respondents). Furthermore, exploratory data analysis showed that employee respondents have spent distinctively more time in their current job position (M = 7.70; SD = 8.21) in comparison with their supervisors (M = 4.32; SD = 3.47). The modal number of employee respondents per supervisor was 3, and the average number was 4.54 (SD = 5.12). Only 3 out of 39 leaders who took part in our research had a span of control larger than 10.

Separate survey questionnaires (supervisor-based and employee-based) were developed by using previously validated measures, and the translation/ back translation procedure was applied. We used Likert-type frequency and agreement scales where respondents had to report the level of frequency

(1—not at all to 5—always; used for the assessment of leader creativity and employee innovativeness) or the level of their (dis)agreement with the statement at hand (1—strongly disagree to 5—strongly agree).

Leaders (i.e., supervisors) self-reported in Time 1 on their demographics and creativity (5-item scale on idea exploration and idea generation adopted from Janssen, 2000), as well as evaluated job innovation requirements (4-item scale taken from Yuan and Woodman, 2010) and innovation-driven behavior of their employees (5-item scale on idea promotion and implementation likewise adopted from Janssen, 2000). We used leaders' self-ratings of their creativity for the convenience, as previous work found that self-ratings of innovative behavior were correlated with supervisors' ratings (see Purc & Laguna, 2019). In Time 2 (nine months later), the same (leader) respondents valued their employees' task performance (4-item scale taken from Liden, Wayne, & Stilwell, 1993) and OCB (11-item scale adopted from Ilies, Scott, & Judge, 2006). The former addresses the proficiency with which employees carry out the core requirements of their jobs, such as those tasks that are specified in a job description (Motowidlo, Borman, & Schmit, 1997). The latter represents discretionary behaviors that, while not formally recognized as constituting performance in a given job, nonetheless contribute to the functioning of organizations (Borman & Motowidlo, 1993).

On the other hand, employees were asked in Time 1 to indicate the extent to which they agreed or disagreed with statements related to the nature of their jobs (work autonomy and job complexity scales were adapted from the Work Design Questionnaire developed by Morgeson and Humphrey, 2006; person-environment fit was measured following the 9-item scale proposed by Cable & DeRue, 2002). In addition, they provided information on demographic (age and gender, job tenure) and other personal characteristics (self-efficacy was measured using the 8-item scale developed by Frese et al., 1997; and personal initiative was self-reported using the 7-item scale taken from Chen, Gully, & Eden, 2001).

We followed best-practice recommendations (Bernerth & Aguinis, 2016) to include control variables relevant for our research. Specifically, we controlled for respondents' gender, age, and job tenure (except for leaders' age due to missing values that would significantly decrease the size of our sample) because they have been shown to influence innovative behavior and task performance (Scott & Bruce, 1994; Aryee et al., 2012). Beyond demographics, we also controlled for main job design predictors of IWB recognized by meta-analysis research (work autonomy, job complexity, and job innovation requirements; see Hammond et al., 2011) as well as for person-environment fit and highly relevant personal resources such as self-efficacy and personal initiative.

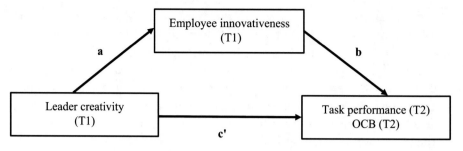

Fig. 19.1   Research model

Our theoretical assumptions and research model (see Fig. 19.1) were initially tested using descriptive statistics and Pearson's correlations. In addition, cross-tabulations were run to further analyze the performance data along two dimensions of the innovation process: leader creativity and employee innovativeness. Finally, multi-variate statistics were applied, that is, mediation regression analyses using PROCESS template 4 in SPSS (Hayes, 2018) were performed for each of the dependent variables (i.e., task performance and OCB, respectively).

Data Analysis

Means, standard deviations, and Pearson's correlations between four main study variables are reported in Table 19.1. In addition, we collected data on employees' individual characteristics (self-efficacy: $M = 4.12$, $SD = .47$; personal initiative: $M = 3.90$, $SD = .53$), as well as about self-perceived (work autonomy: $M = 3.45$, $SD = .79$; job complexity: $M = 3.76$, $SD = .73$) and other-rated job characteristics (job innovation requirements: $M = 3.49$, $SD = .78$).

Compared to true score correlations derived from recent meta-analytic findings examining similar bivariate relationships across samples (see Harari, Reaves, & Viswesvaran, 2016), our data on individual work role proficiency dimensions follow a general trend (values shown above the diagonal) although obtaining somewhat lower scores. Employee innovativeness is positively related to task performance and OCB, providing an initial evidence that causal relationships between these performance dimensions are possible.

According to supervisors' ratings, leaders are on average more creative ($M = 3.60$, $SD = .46$) than their employees are innovative ($M = 2.99$, $SD = .79$).

Table 19.1 Descriptives and correlations between main study variables

		Mean	SD	1	2	3	4
1	Leader creativity	3.60	.46	(.684)	–	–	–
2	Employee innovativeness	2.99	.79	.193[a]	(.897)	.55	.56
3	Task performance	3.57	.84	.126	.425[b]	(.886)	.74
4	OCB	3.61	.84	.185[a]	.371[b]	.823[b]	(.957)

Note: Cronbach's alphas are shown in parentheses on the diagonal.
[a]Correlation is significant at the .05 level
[b]Correlation is significant at the .01 level

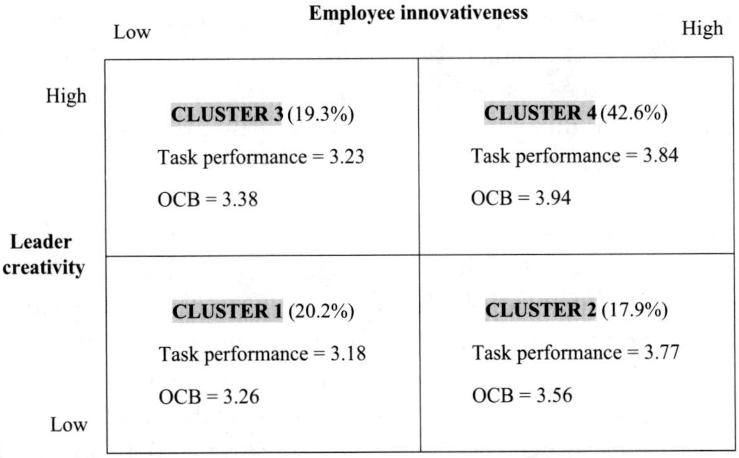

Employee innovativeness
Low   High

Leader creativity

High

CLUSTER 3 (19.3%)

Task performance = 3.23

OCB = 3.38

CLUSTER 4 (42.6%)

Task performance = 3.84

OCB = 3.94

CLUSTER 1 (20.2%)

Task performance = 3.18

OCB = 3.26

CLUSTER 2 (17.9%)

Task performance = 3.77

OCB = 3.56

Low

Fig. 19.2 Leader creativity-employee innovation clusters

Nevertheless, an average subordinate provides satisfactory levels of task performance ($M = 3.57$, $SD = .84$) and OCB ($M = 3.61$, $SD = .84$).

Next, we grouped and assigned our employee respondents to four clusters according to the respective modality of the leader creativity–employee innovativeness relationship. A mean split was used for making cluster grouping decisions, and a 2x2 matrix has been created (see Fig. 19.2). As expected, the highest task performance ($M = 3.84$) and OCB scores ($M = 3.94$) were obtained when both high leader creativity and high employee innovativeness were present (Cluster 4; 42.6% of the sample). On the other hand, the lowest level of task performance ($M = 3.18$) and OCB ($M = 3.26$) existed in a low-low situation (Cluster 1; 20.2% of the sample). Interestingly, significantly higher performance levels were reported when we had less creative leaders but more innovative employees (Cluster 2; 17.9% of the sample) in comparison with a situation where creative leaders co-existed with less-innovative employees (Cluster 3; 19.3% of the sample).

Additionally, we wanted to test and further extend the underlying assumption of the leadership–creativity/innovation research that leaders can, either directly or indirectly, influence the frequency of the subordinates' innovative behavior (e.g., Hughes et al., 2018) which might in turn shape job incumbents' work role proficiency habits. In such manner, we accept the view that leadership is a relational and goal-oriented process (Fischer, Dietz, & Antonakis, 2017) by which (creative) leaders influence followers' distal outcomes (i.e., work role proficiency) through more proximate mediating variables (e.g., employee innovativeness). Examining these leadership–performance mediational processes might be integral to the further development of theory and could offer beneficial practical recommendations, especially because previous research on the topic is scarce. An exception is a study conducted by Aryee et al. (2012); they provided empirical evidence that creative leadership fosters innovative behavior and consequently task performance of employees.

Our more refined research model was similarly examined by performing mediation analyses. All direct and indirect effects were estimated based on bootstrapped samples. Initially, we examined direct effects (see Table 19.2). The regression analyses showed that leader creativity as an independent variable was significantly and positively related to employee innovativeness (B = .369, SE = .132, p = .006). Furthermore, employee innovativeness was positively related to work role proficiency outcomes in each of the examined models, that is, task performance (B = .403, SE = .073, p = .000) and OCB (B = .336, SE = .077, p = .000) as dependent variables. In addition, leader creativity was not significantly associated with task performance as an outcome variable (B = .191, SE = .127, p = .134), although the significantly positive direct relationship exists in the case of OCB (B = .327, SE = .133, p = .015).

Finally, a bootstrapping technique with 10,000 repetitions was applied to estimate indirect (mediating) effects, that is, to explore whether leader creativity exert influence on employees' work role proficiency dimensions through employee innovativeness as a mediator variable. The mediation analyses showed that the indirect effect on task performance was significant (B = .149, SE = .069, 95% CI [.030, .303]), as well as on OCB outcome (B = .124, SE = .061, 95% CI [.030, .279]). The significance of the mediated (indirect) effects was additionally confirmed by the Sobel tests (z' = 2.463, $p < 0.05$ for the task performance model; z' = 2.315, $p < 0.05$ for the OCB model). Therefore, we may conclude that leader creativity is indeed a relevant predictor of individual work outcomes. In the case of task performance, creative leaders may indirectly influence how employees carry out the core requirements of their jobs by boosting implementation-oriented behavior (i.e., full mediation). When aiming for discretionary employee behaviors such as OCB, they could use both direct and indirect paths of influence (i.e., partial mediation).

Table 19.2 Regression model results

	Dependent variable					
	Model 1 Employee innovativeness		Model 2 Task performance		Model 3 OCB	
Predictor variable	B	SE	B	SE	B	SE
Intercept	.814	.803	3.427[b]	.757	3.094[b]	.790
Employee age (E)	−.009	.008	−.013	.007	−.011	.008
Employee gender (E)	−.204	.151	−.402[a]	.156	−.204	.151
Employee job tenure (E)	−.005	.008	−.014	.008	−.005	.008
Self-efficacy (E)	−.087	.193	.219	.199	−.087	.193
Personal initiative (E)	.186	.177	−.246	.182	−.199	.174
Work autonomy (E)	−.052	.088	−.002	.091	−.016	.086
Job complexity (E)	.021	.084	−.002	.087	−.040	.083
Job innovation requirements (S)	−.009	.092	−.113	.095	−.098	.091
Person-environment fit (E)	.159	.102	.189	.105	.217[a]	.101
Leader gender (S)	.294[a]	.133	−.117	.137	−.058	.132
Leader job tenure (S)	−.007	.018	−.013	.018	−.044[a]	.017
Leader creativity (S)	.456[b]	.138	.320[a]	.142	.456[b]	.138
Employee innovativeness (S)	–	–	.426[b]	.074	.341[b]	.077
R^2	.123		.316		.267	
F	1.914[a]		5.804[b]		4.560[b]	

Note: E, employee self-reported; S, supervisor self-reported
[a]Correlation is significant at the .05 level
[b]Correlation is significant at the .01 level

Control variables of sociodemographics (employee age, employee job tenure, leader gender), employees' personal characteristics (self-efficacy and personal initiative), and perceived job characteristics (work autonomy, job complexity, job innovation requirement) did not contribute systematically to the observed effects in our research model and as such should be neglected. A single exception has been noted in Model 2 (task performance as a dependent variable) for employee gender, as well as regarding person-environment fit and leader job tenure in Model 3 (OCB as a dependent variable). Nevertheless, we may conclude that the given results support the consistency of our findings across different jobs and individuals.

Discussion with Implications

The popular press is overwhelmed with charismatic leadership success stories. For instance, each year the *Fortune* magazine produces the list of the World's 50 Greatest Leaders (Fortune, 2019). Similarly, *Fast Company* (2017) recognizes the Most Creative People in Business list, while *Forbes* (2018) introduces the 5 Top Innovative Leaders. These premium business sources describe how creative leaders have engaged their workforce to achieve a competitive outreach. Despite numerous positive examples, we still lack more academically rigorous evidence. Therefore, in the present study, we were motivated to explore a piece of the leadership–innovation puzzle, that is, whether (and to what extent) an "average" leader (and not only "superstars") might increase employees' work role proficiency through their idea innovation-related behavior.

The dyadic empirical evidence from the public sector setting confirmed that creative leaders indirectly increase task performance of their immediate subordinates by fostering employees' idea promotion and implementation efforts. Such mediational process might be characterized as an example of creative role modelling. In terms of OCB as a desired outcome, we found that it could be shaped by creative leaders both directly and indirectly. In other words, creative leadership *per se* will motivate employees to go above and beyond their call of duty and practice citizenship behavior directed both toward the organization and individuals (co-workers).

From the results obtained, it appears that creative leadership is relevant for individual work role proficiency (high levels of creative leadership reach higher levels of employees' task performance than low levels of creative leadership). However, employee innovation-oriented behavior seems to be a much stronger determinant of work role proficiency outcomes. On one hand, effect size statistics clearly show that the difference in task performance between low- and high-creative leadership when having either low- (Cohen's d = .06) or high-employee innovativeness (d = .08) is rather small. Similar is also valid for OCB as an outcome variable when employee innovativeness is low (d = .14). However, in the situation of high-employee innovativeness, the effect size difference significantly increases (d = .45). On the other hand, the comparison between low- and high-employee innovativeness manifests meaningfully larger differences between group means. The large effect relative size exists in the case of task performance (d = .70 for the low- and d = .73 for high-creative leadership context), and medium-to-large effect relative size is present for OCB performance measure (d = .36 for low- and d = .66 for high-creative leadership context).

To get additional insights on this intriguing topic, we further analyzed our clustered data. As such, we observe and conclude that the highest work role proficiency results emerged from the fit situation at the high level of creativity and innovation (Cluster 4). This would mean that organizations can benefit the most by having both creative leaders and innovative employees. Synchronous efforts across different hierarchical levels would mean that all parties face a new problem collaboratively and thus strive to add value by recognizing and implementing the innovative solution. Some firms, like IDEO and Apple, have introduced design thinking and related tools to nurture creativity and foster innovation in such manner through a loosely structured organizational process (Brown, 2009).

Contrary, the lowest scores were reported when neither leader nor employees are behaving creatively and/or innovatively (Cluster 1). This lack of such behaviors means no progress, that is, an organization would be repeating the same patterns which eventually lead to stagnation, and leaves an organization unable to perform or meet change (Serrat, 2009). Two examples of such occurrence are video-rental company Blockbuster (stubbornly relied solely on its established brand name) and mobile phone producer Blackberry (had been actively rejecting the touch screen-based technology). Unfortunately, both companies failed to address shifts in consumer demands (see Ricketts, 2016).

Particularly interesting is to notice that the presence of creative leaders does not make a significant difference in work role proficiency if employees are not innovative (Cluster 3). Such results are in line with the anecdote "being lonely at the top" (Wright, 2012) and further support historical evidence on co-worker role models that the presence of observational learning had no positive effects on observers' creativity and may even lead the observers to exhibit relatively low levels of creativity (e.g., Halpin, Halpin, Miller, & Landreneau, 1979). Potentially, if the leader is too creative, he or she might seem unattainable to employees and make them to feel inferior (Hoyt & Simon, 2011; Morgenroth, Ryan, & Peters, 2015). Moreover, a multi-study research conducted by Mueller et al. (2011) showed that creativity might not necessarily signal leadership capability. Specifically, they found an evidence that individuals who expressed more creative ideas were viewed as having less, not more, leadership potential (with an exception of charismatic leaders). The same is valid for idea novelty; the radically novel ideas are less likely to be deployed than moderately novel ideas and thereby represent lower innovation potential (Škerlavaj, Černe, & Dysvik, 2014).

Ultimately, the Cluster 2 situation displays that employee innovativeness is really recognized by leaders (no matter of the level of their creativity) to be beneficial for both task performance and OCB. Managers are just one potential source of the idea, and they are increasingly not the source of the idea (Amabile & Khaire, 2008). Actually, having innovative and perhaps even creative employees might compensate for the lack of such creative abilities from the side of a leader. As employees are often the first to see issues on the front lines, their input can really help managerial decision-making (Sherf, Tangirala, & Venkataramani, 2019). For instance, Google's founders Sergey Brin and Larry Page tracked the progress of ideas that came from them versus ideas that bubbled up from the ranks—and discovered a higher success rate in the latter category. In addition, Philip Rosedale, the chairman of the fast-growing company Linden Lab, says that "the greatest successes come from workers' own initiatives" (Amabile & Khaire, 2008). No matter of these underlying reasons, our data clearly signal that there is no a one-size-fits-all approach; instead, creative role models seem to have positive impact on creative (see Zhou, 2003) and innovative efforts under specific conditions.

Study findings offer sound practical implications. Firstly, we advise human resource managers to search for and develop creative individuals both for managerial and nonmanagerial positions. The selection process should include an assessment of creative personality; job design needs to enable and encourage new (nonroutine) individual efforts, which should be followed by a performance measurement system that acknowledges creativity and innovation as desired behavior. Secondly, general managers need to practice creative leadership and should become creative role models for their workforce. Larger organizational benefits might be achieved if they are first among the equals (being surrounded with creative and entrepreneurial followers). Thirdly, creative employees themselves indeed make a performance difference and thus should not restrain their own creative ideas and innovative actions. Each individual should strive to increase his or her job-level innovativeness, as such change-oriented behavior has been recognized and appreciated both from creative and noncreative leaders.

Our study is not without limitations. The reader should be aware of the single source (i.e., leaders) used for collecting data on our independent and dependent variables. Although we had two time points, it is still not possible to exclude potential sources of bias and explicate the cause-and-effect relationship between constructs. We should also be aware of a potential halo error which occurs when raters hold a particular impression of a ratee that influences their performance ratings similarly across dimensions (Thorndike, 1920). The specific context of current research should be likewise acknowledged, preventing us to make generalizations beyond the public sector of a specific post-transition country.

While some questions have been answered, many others wait to be asked. For instance, future research should focus on potential "positive" and "negative" moderators (e.g., Hughes et al., 2018) approached from different levels of analysis (i.e., individual, dyadic, group, organizational, and occupational) to provide additional insights into complexity of the creative leadership–employee innovation relationship. For instance, identification with the leader, risk-taking climate, creative personality, and leader-member exchange differentiation represent just few of possible boundary conditions. Moreover, different research contexts should be observed to see whether the same patterns or important idiosyncrasies exist in creative and innovative behavior across different markets, organizations, teams, or jobs. An interesting line of inquiry might also be to get more familiar with different aspects of leader creativity (i.e., worker-role creativity and manager-role creativity; see Wen, Zhou, & Lu, 2017) and how these different roles influence employees' innovation differently.

Conclusion

Theory and practice confirm that innovative work behaviors drive the delivery of market-differentiating improvements and are now actively promoted as desirable actions for leaders and employees likewise. By acknowledging the fact that innovative work behaviors represent a complex, multi-dimensional, and multi-stage construct that captures various multi-player roles, we conducted a study in the public sector setting and examined the interplay between leader creativity and follower innovativeness and their relationship to employee work role proficiency (i.e., task performance and OCB). The empirical evidence confirmed that creative leaders indirectly increase task performance of their immediate subordinates by fostering employees' innovation-oriented behavior. The highest work role proficiency results emerged from the leader–follower fit situation at the high level of innovative work behaviors. This would mean that organizations would benefit the most by having both creative leaders and innovative employees.

References

Agarwal, U. A., Datta, S., Blake-Beard, S., & Bhargava, S. (2012). Linking LMX, Innovative Work Behaviour and Turnover Intentions: The Mediating Role of Work Engagement. *Career Development International, 17*(3), 208–230.

Amabile, T., & Khaire, M. (2008). Creativity and the Role of the Leader. *Harvard Business Review, 86*(10), 100–109.

Anderson, N., Potočnik, K., & Zhou, J. (2014). Innovation and Creativity in Organizations: A State-of-the-Science Review, Prospective Commentary, and Guiding Framework. *Journal of Management, 40*(5), 1297–1333.

Aryee, S., Walumbwa, F. O., Zhou, Q., & Hartnell, C. A. (2012). Transformational Leadership, Innovative Behavior, and Task Performance: Test of Mediation and Moderation Processes. *Human Performance, 25*(1), 1–25.

Axtell, C. M., Holman, D. J., Unsworth, K. L., Wall, T. D., Waterson, P. E., & Harrington, E. (2000). Shopfloor Innovation: Facilitating the Suggestion and Implementation of Ideas. *Journal of Occupational and Organizational Psychology, 73*(3), 265–285.

Baer, M. (2012). Putting Creativity to Work: The Implementation of Creative Ideas in Organizations. *Academy of Management Journal, 55*(5), 1102–1119.

Bandura, A. (1986). *Social Foundations of Thought and Action: A Social Cognitive Theory.* Englewood Cliffs, NJ: Prentice Hall.

Beckett, R. C., & O'Loughlin, A. (2016). The Impact of Timing in Innovation Management. *Journal of Innovation Management, 4*(3), 32–64.

Bernerth, J. B., & Aguinis, H. (2016). A Critical Review and Best-Practice Recommendations for Control Variable Usage. *Personnel Psychology, 69*(1), 229–283.

Borman, W. C., & Motowidlo, S. J. (1993). Expanding the Criterion Domain to Include Elements of Contextual Performance. In N. Schmitt & W. C. Borman (Eds.), *Personnel Selection in Organizations* (pp. 71–98). San Francisco, CA: Jossey-Bass.

Brown, T. (2009). *Change by Design: How Design Thinking Transforms Organizations and Inspires Innovation.* New York, NY: HarperBusiness.

Cable, D. M., & DeRue, D. S. (2002). The Convergent and Discriminant Validity of Subjective Fit Perceptions. *Journal of Applied Psychology, 87*(5), 875–884.

Chen, G., Gully, S. M., & Eden, D. (2001). Validation of a New General Self-Efficacy Scale. *Organizational Research Methods, 4*(1), 62–83.

De Jong, J. P. J., & Den Hartog, D. N. (2003). *Leadership as Determinant of Innovative Behaviour: A Conceptual Framework.* Research Report. Retrieved from https://core.ac.uk/download/pdf/7074558.pdf

De Jong, J. P. J., & Den Hartog, D. N. (2007). How Leaders Influence Employees' Innovative Behavior. *European Journal of Innovation Management, 10*(1), 41–64.

De Spiegelaere, S., Van Gyes, G., & Van Hootegem, G. (2012). Job Design and Innovative Work Behavior: One Size Does Not Fit All Types of Employees. *Journal of Entrepreneurship, Management and Innovation, 8*(4), 5–20.

Deng, X., & Guan, Z. (2017). Creative Leaders Create 'Unsung Heroes': Leader Creativity and Subordinate Organizational Citizenship Behavior. *Frontiers of Business Research in China, 11*, 15.

Desouza, K. C. (2011). *Intrapreneurship: Managing Ideas within Your Organization.* Toronto: University of Toronto Press.

Fast Company. (2017, January 24). *Be Inspired By These Creative Leaders Who Are Changing the World.* Retrieved from https://www.fastcompany.com/3067011/be-inspired-by-these-creative-leaders-who-are-changing-the-world

Fischer, T., Dietz, J., & Antonakis, J. (2017). Leadership Process Models: A Review and Synthesis. *Journal of Management, 43*(6), 1726–1753.

Florida, R. (2002). *The Rise of the Creative Class: And How It's Transforming Work, Leisure, Community and Everyday Life.* New York, NY: Basic Books.

Florida, R. (2005). *The Flight of the Creative Class: The New Global Competition for Talent.* New York, NY: HarperBusiness.

Florida, R. (2012). *The Rise of the Creative Class Revisited.* New York, NY: Basic Books.

Forbes. (2018). *America's Most Innovative Leaders.* Retrieved from https://www.forbes.com/lists/innovative-leaders/#59305fd126aa

Fortune. (2019). *World's 50 Greatest Leaders.* Retrieved from https://fortune.com/worlds-greatest-leaders/2020/.

Franičević, V. (1999). Privatization in Croatia: Legacies and Context. *Eastern European Economics, 37*(2), 5–54.

Frese, M., Fay, D., Hilburger, T., Leng, K., & Tag, A. (1997). The Concept of Personal Initiative: Operationalization, Reliability and Validity in Two German Samples. *Journal of Organizational and Occupational Psychology, 70*(2), 139–161.

Griffin, M., Neale, A., & Neale, M. (2001). The Contribution of Task Performance and Contextual Performance to Effectiveness: Investigating the Role of Situational Constraints. *Applied Pscyhology, 49*(3), 517–533.

Halpin, G., Halpin, G., Miller, E., & Landreneau, E. (1979). Observer Characteristics Related to the Imitation of a Creative Model. *Journal of Psychology, 102*(1), 133–142.

Hammond, M. M., Neff, N. L., Farr, J. L., Schwall, A. R., & Zhao, X. (2011). Predictors of Individual-level Innovation at Work: A Meta-analysis. *Psychology of Aesthetics, Creativity, and the Arts, 5*(1), 90–105.

Harari, M. B., Reaves, A. C., & Viswesvaran, C. (2016). Creative and Innovative Performance: A Meta-analysis of Relationships with Task, Citizenship, and Counterproductive Job Performance Dimensions. *European Journal of Work and Organizational Psychology, 25*(4), 495–511.

Hayes, A. F. (2018). *Introduction to Mediation, Moderation, and Conditional Process Analysis: A Regression-Based Approach.* New York, NY: Guilford Press.

Hernaus, T., Černe, M., & Pološki Vokić, N. (2016, June 1–4). Understanding the Nature of Innovative Work Behavior in the Public Sector: Conceptualizing a Static and Dynamic Role of Job Design, *EURAM 2016 Conference: Manageable Cooperation?*, Paris.

Hernaus, T., Marić, M., & Černe, M. (2019). Age-sensitive Job Design Antecedents of Innovative Work Behavior: The Role of Cognitive Job Demands. *Journal of Managerial Psychology, 34*(5), 368–382.

Hoyt, C. L., & Simon, S. (2011). Female Leaders Injurious or Inspiring Role Models for Women? *Psychology of Women Quarterly, 35*(1), 143–157.

Hughes, D. J., Lee, A., Tian, A. W., Newman, A., & Legood, A. (2018). Leadership, Creativity, and Innovation: A Critical Review and Practical Recommendations. *Leadership Quarterly, 29*(5), 549–569.

IBM. (2010). *Global CEO Study: Creativity Selected as Most Crucial Factor for Future Success.* Retrieved from https://www-03.ibm.com/press/us/en/pressrelease/31670.wss

Ilies, R., Scott, B. A., & Judge, T. A. (2006). The Interactive Effects of Personal Traits and Experienced States on Intraindividual Patterns of Citizenship Behavior. *Academy of Management Journal, 49*(3), 561–575.

Janssen, O. (2000). Job Demands, Perceptions of Effort-reward Fairness and Innovative Work Behaviour. *Journal of Occupational and Organizational Psychology, 73*(3), 287–302.

King, N., & Anderson, N. (2002). *Managing Innovation and Change: A Critical Guide for Organizations*. London, UK: Thompson.

Koseoglu, G., Liu, Y., & Shalley, C. E. (2017). Working with Creative Leaders: Exploring the Relationship between Supervisors' and Subordinates' Creativity. *The Leadership Quarterly, 28*(6), 798–811.

Langford, P. H., Dougall, C. B., & Parkes, L. P. (2017). Measuring Leader Behaviour: Evidence for a "Big Five" Model of Leadership. *Leadership & Organization Development Journal, 38*(1), 126–144.

Liden, R. C., Wayne, S. J., & Stilwell, D. (1993). A Longitudinal Study on the Early Development of Leader-Member Exchanges. *Journal of Applied Psychology, 78*(4), 662–674.

Mathisen, G. E., Einarsen, S., & Mykletun, R. (2012). Creative Leaders Promote Creative Organizations. *International Journal of Manpower, 33*(4), 367–382.

Morgenroth, T., Ryan, M. K., & Peters, K. (2015). The Motivational Theory of Role Modeling: How Role Models Influence Role Aspirants' Goals. *Review of General Psychology, 19*(4), 465–483.

Morgeson, F. P., & Humphrey, S. E. (2006). The Work Design Questionnaire (WDQ): Developing and Validating a Comprehensive Measure for Assessing Job Design and the Nature of Work. *Journal of Applied Psychology, 91*(6), 1321–1339.

Motowidlo, S. J., Borman, W. C., & Schmit, M. J. (1997). A Theory of Individual Differences in Task and Contextual Performance. *Human Performance, 10*(2), 71–83.

Mueller, J. S., Goncalo, J. A., & Kamdar, D. (2011). Recognizing Creative Leadership: Can Creative Idea Expression Negatively Relate to Perceptions of Leadership Potential? *Journal of Experimental Social Psychology, 47*(2), 494–498.

Musk, E., & Watson, E. (2016). *Elon Musk: The Greatest Lessons through the Inspiring Life of Elon Musk*. CreateSpace Independent Publishing Platform.

Pološki Vokić, N., Klindžić, M., & Hernaus, T. (2018). Changing HRM Practices in Croatia: Demystifying the Impact of HRM Philosophy, Global Financial Crisis and EU Membership. *Journal of East European Management Studies, 23*(2), 322–343.

Purc, E., & Laguna, M. (2019). Personal Values and Innovative Behavior of Employees. *Frontiers in Psychology*. Retrieved from https://doi.org/10.3389/fpsyg.2019.00865

Ren, F., & Zhang, J. (2015). Job Stressors, Organizational Innovation Climate, and Employees' Innovative Behavior. *Creativity Research Journal, 27*(1), 16–23.

Ricketts, D. (2016). *5 Stories of Innovation and 5 Stories of Dis-integration.* Retrieved from https://www.linkedin.com/pulse/5-stories-innovation-disintegration-david-ricketts/

Scott, S., & Bruce, R. (1994). Determinants of Innovative Behavior: A Path Model of Individual Innovation in the Workplace. *Academy of Management Journal, 37*(3), 580–607.

Serrat, O. D. (2009). *Harnessing Creativity and Innovation in the Workplace.* Manila: Asian Development Bank.

Shalley, C. E., & Lemoine, G. J. (2018). Leader Behaviors and Employee Creativity: Taking Stock of the Current State of Research. In C. Mainemalis, O. Epitropaki, & R. Kark (Eds.), *Creative Leadership: Contexts and Prospects* (pp. 79–94). London, UK: Taylor & Francis Group.

Shalley, C. E., & Perry-Smith, J. E. (2001). Effects of Social-psychological Factors on Creative Performance: The Role of Informational and Controlling Expected Evaluation and Modelling Experience. *Organizational Behavior and Human Decision Processes, 84*(1), 1–22.

Sherf, E. N., Tangirala, S., & Venkataramani, V. (2019, April 8). Research: Why Managers Ignore Employees' Ideas. *Harvard Business Review.* Retrieved from https://hbr.org/2019/04/research-why-managers-ignore-employees-ideas.

Shin, S. J., Yuan, F., & Zhou, J. (2016). When Perceived Innovation Job Requirement Increases Employee Innovative Behavior: A Sensemaking Perspective. *Journal of Organizational Behavior, 38*(1), 68–86.

Škerlavaj, M. (2018). From Creativity to Innovation: Four Leadership Lessons about Capitalizing on High-Potential Ideas. In A. Sasson (Ed.), *At the Forefront, Looking Ahead: Research-Based Answers to Contemporary Uncertainties of Management* (pp. 179–196). Oslo: BI Norwegian Business School.

Škerlavaj, M., Černe, M., & Dysvik, A. (2014). I Get By with a Little Help from My Supervisor: Creative-idea Generation, Idea Implementation, and Perceived Supervisor Support. *The Leadership Quarterly, 25*(5), 987–1000.

Thorndike, E. L. (1920). The Constant Error in Psychological Ratings. *Journal of Applied Psychology, 4*(1), 25–29.

Van de Ven, A. H. (1986). Central Problems in the Management of Innovation. *Management Science, 32*(5), 590–607.

Wen, L., Zhou, M., & Lu, Q. (2017). The Influence of Leader's Creativity on Employees' and Team Creativity. *Nankai Business Review International, 8*(1), 22–38.

West, M. A., & Farr, J. L. (Eds.). (1990). *Innovation and Creativity at Work: Psychological and Organizational Strategies.* London, UK: Wiley.

Wilpers, J. (2015). *Give Your Boss this Story: Innovation Starts with the Leader.* FIPP Connecting Global Media. Retrieved from https://www.fipp.com/news/opinion/innovation-starts-with-the-leader-john-wilpers.

Wright, S. (2012). Is It Lonely at the Top? An Empirical Study of Managers' and Nonmanagers' Loneliness in Organizations. *The Journal of Psychology: Interdisciplinary and Applied, 146*(1–2), 47–60.

Yuan, F., & Woodman, R. W. (2010). Innovative Behavior in the Workplace: The Role of Performance and Image Outcome Expectations. *Academy of Management Journal, 53*(2), 323–342.

Zhou, J. (2003). When the Presence of Creative Coworkers Is Related to Creativity: Role of Supervisor Close Monitoring, Developmental Feedback. *Journal of Applied Psychology, 88*(3), 413–422.

20

Academic Leadership Qualities Towards Innovation Endeavours in an Organisation: A Comparative Study of Malaysia and Singapore Perceptions

Cheng Sim Quah, Sandra Phek Lin Sim, and Wee-Liang Tan

Introduction

The buzz word in the twenty-first century for continual sustainability and success of educational institutions is the ability of leaders to create an innovative climate within the organisation. Thus, the survival of today's educational institutions is different from a decade ago. Amidst the fast pace of technological advancement, in order to sustain a competitive environment, the authors perceived that leaders need to be innovative not only in their own institution but also in the global business world. Innovation has become increasingly popular among staff in organisations to boost organisational performance success and

C. S. Quah (✉)
Institut Aminuddin Baki, Ministry of Education, Nilai, Malaysia
e-mail: csquah@iab.edu.my

S. P. L. Sim
Universiti Teknologi MARA, Cawangan Sarawak, Kota Samarahan, Malaysia
e-mail: sandrasim@uitm.edu.my

W.-L. Tan
Strategic Management at the Lee Kong Chian School of Business, Singapore
Management University, Singapore, Singapore
e-mail: wltan@smu.edu.sg

© The Author(s), under exclusive license to Springer Nature Switzerland AG 2021
A. McMurray et al. (eds.), *The Palgrave Handbook of Workplace Innovation*,
https://doi.org/10.1007/978-3-030-59916-4_20

to survive in this era of technology. Leadership is a catalyst and source of innovation for organisations. Importantly, organisations need effective leadership to encourage innovation. Successful leaders are necessarily innovators (Poonam and Arvind, 2014); thus, a more powerful way to think of leadership and innovation is that innovation and leadership are interdependent. For an organisation to sustain continuous innovation, leaders play a pertinent role to generate creative ideas, provide support and motivate followers.

In this study, the authors postulated universities as organisations, a similar notion held by Brunsson and Sahlin-Andersonn (2000). The term 'endeavours' as used in this study means efforts to do or attain something (Collins English Dictionary, 2015).

Literature Review

Innovation is defined as "the implementation of a new or significantly improved product (good or service), or process, a new marketing method, or a new organisational method in business practices, workplace organisation or external relations" (OECD, 2005, p. 46). According to Zaltman et al. (1973, p. 10), innovation relates to "any idea, practice, or material artifact perceived to be new by the relevant unit of adoption". Similarly, innovation is the creation and implementation of new ideas or improvement in the products, services or processes that could benefit end users (Lousã, 2013; Şena and Erena 2012). According to a general broad definition by Baregheh et al. (2009, p. 1334), "Innovation is the multi-stage process whereby organisations transform ideas into improved products, service or processes, in order to advance, compete and differentiate themselves successfully in their marketplace."

Over the past years, research on factors to enhance organisational innovation has been rampant. According to a few researchers, leaders' characteristics significantly affect organisational innovation (Gumusluoglu & Ilsev, 2009; Makri & Scandura, 2010). Therefore, leadership plays an integral part towards organisational success because without effective leadership in the organisation, innovation will not succeed. Hence, leadership is one of the crucial factors to manage innovation. This stems from the fact that "innovation depends on ideas, and the primary source of ideas is talented individuals" (Leavy, 2006, p. 40). In this respect, effective leadership is vital for an organisation to bring constructive changes to the rapid change in the current environment (Cabeza-Erikson, Edwards, and Van Brabant, 2008; Moo and Yazdanifar 2015).

According to Lousã and Mónico (2018, p. 12), leadership should focus on "an innovation driven culture". That is why good leaders can inspire and cultivate, encouraging an innovative as well as creative climate in an organisation (Denti and Hemlin, 2012; Ionescu, 2014). In line with this, good leadership is vital to support, sustain, encourage and inspire followers to embark on innovation processes in any organisation. It is imperative that an organisation establishes the right leader and leadership structure in place. Hence, leadership is a key factor for facilitating innovation (Chan et al., 2014; Ozorhon et al., 2016; Zheng et al., 2017) as well as significantly affecting organisational innovation (Makri & Scandura, 2010). Therefore, leaders can guide organisations towards becoming more innovative through their actions. Additionally, leadership is a central position to initiate, implement and support innovation by influencing firm strategic decisions, policies and procedures (Mokhber, Wan, & Vakilbashi 2018; Prasad & Junni, 2016).

Moreover, a few prominent leadership qualities associated with innovation also include strategic planning (Bouhali, Mekdad, Lebsir, and Ferkh 2015; Kazmi, Naaranoja, Kytola, and Kantola 2016), executing proper measurement (Human Capital Management, 2011), developing human capital, ensuring adequate allocation of resources, and providing best customer service to garner customer satisfaction, leading to growth of the organisation (Semuel et al., 2017).

Besides that, having the right type of leadership is equally important for organisational innovation (Mokhber et al., 2018, p. 109). Indeed, "not every kind of leadership model is effective in creating this opportunity" (Agbor, 2008, p. 41). Moreover, De Jong and Den Hartog (2007) emphasised that different types of leadership are needed to develop innovation at different organisational levels. Thus, different innovation phases need different leadership behaviours to be effective.

Methodology

This study employed mixed methods to explore the perceptions of university staff pertinent to the contribution of academic leadership qualities towards innovative endeavours. Two types of instruments were used to collect data for this study. The quantitative data pertaining to leadership qualities were based on the instrument adopted and adapted from the questionnaire "Are We Making Progress as Leaders?" by the Baldrige Criteria for Performance Excellence (Baldrige Performance Excellence Program, 2011), whereas the qualitative instrument was designed by the researchers (Quah & Sim, 2016). Simple random sampling was employed to determine the samples representing the population of lecturers in the study, involving 60 lecturers from

Singapore (n = 30) and Malaysia (n = 30). The aim of this study was to examine the comparison between Malaysia and Singapore in terms of the contribution of leadership qualities towards innovation endeavours. In addition, it examined the significance of the relationship between academic leadership qualities and innovation endeavours in both countries. This study also aimed to examine the impacts of innovation endeavour(s) towards organisation, university students and lecturers in both countries. Distribution of frequencies, percentages, means, t-test, ANOVA and multiple regression were used to analyse and describe the results of the research findings.

Research Questions

1. Is there any significant relationship between leadership qualities and innovation endeavours in Singapore and Malaysia?
2. To what extent do leadership qualities contribute to innovation endeavours in Singapore and Malaysia?
3. What are the impacts of innovation endeavour(s) in both countries?

Findings

1. Is there any significant relationship between leadership qualities and innovation endeavours in Singapore and Malaysia?

Findings in Table 20.1 show that there are significant correlations for emphasising the importance of innovation as well as enhancing inspiration on innovative ideas with six of the academic leadership qualities in Singapore. These findings illustrate that Singapore university lecturers emphasising the importance of innovation as well as enhancing inspiration on innovative ideas are positively correlated with a few qualities, namely, leadership, strategic planning, measurement, workforce focus, operational focus and result (p<05). The highest score for Pearson correlation is operational focus with r = .813 and r = .655. The findings showed that there is a strong positive relationship with emphasising the importance of innovation with the operational focus domain (r = .813) and inspiration on innovative ideas with operational focus (r = .655).

Conversely, findings revealed that there is no significant correlation for enhancing inspiration on innovative ideas with any academic leadership

Table 20.1   Correlation between leadership qualities and innovation endeavours in Singapore and Malaysia

Country	Leadership qualities	Innovation endeavours			
		Emphasising the importance of innovation		Inspiration on innovative ideas	
		Sigma (2-tailed)	Pearson correlation	Sigma (2-tailed)	Pearson correlation
Singapore	Leadership	.001	.589	.000	.597
	Strategic planning	.001	.568	.000	.627
	Customer focus	.057	.352	.061	.347
	Measurement	.002	.547	.009	.471
	Workforce focus	.001	.559	.018	.428
	Operational focus	.000	.813	.000	.655
	Result	.000	.643	.000	.655
Malaysia	Leadership	.348	−.177*	.238	−.222**
	Strategic planning	.005	−.501**	.499	.128*
	Customer focus	.029	−.399	.919	−.019
	Measurement	.001	−.564**	.607	.098**
	Workforce focus	.001	−.585**	.254	.215
	Operational focus	.053	−.356**	.576	.106*
	Result	.053	−.356**	.417	.154**

*Correlation is significant at the 0.05 level (2-tailed)
**Correlation is significant at the 0.01 level (2-tailed)

qualities in Malaysia. Nonetheless, there is a significant correlation for emphasising the importance of innovation with six of the academic leadership qualities in Malaysia. This finding illustrates that Malaysia university lecturers' emphasis on the importance of innovation is negatively correlated with strategic planning, measurement, workforce focus, customer focus and result ($p<05$) except leadership. The highest score for Pearson correlation is workforce focus, with $r = -.585$. The finding showed that there is a strong negative relationship, emphasising the importance of innovation with workforce focus.

2. To what extent do leadership qualities contribute to innovation endeavours in Singapore and Malaysia?

Findings demonstrated that there are significant correlations for emphasising the importance of innovation as well as enhancing inspiration on innovative ideas with six of the academic leadership qualities in Singapore. Conversely,

376   C. S. Quah et al.

there is only a significant correlation for emphasising the importance of innovation in Malaysia with academic leadership qualities but not enhancing inspiration on innovative ideas.

In terms of emphasising the importance of innovation, the model in Table 20.2 shows both Singapore, $F(9, 20) = 8.793$; $p < 0.05$, and Malaysia, $F(9, 20) = 3.813$; $p < 0.05$, reached statistical significance, emphasising the importance of innovation (dependent variable) and academic leadership qualities (predictors).

The R^2 value in Table 20.3 shows the amount of variance, emphasising the importance of innovation as explained by the model, which includes the variables of six academic leadership qualities (customer focus, workforce focus, measurement, operational focus, result, strategic planning and leadership). The six academic leadership qualities for Singapore's model contributed 79.8% of the variance in emphasising the importance of innovation. In contrast, Malaysia's independent variables only contributed 63.2% of the variance in emphasising the importance of innovation. The model summary in Table 20.3 on the total R^2 values for both countries illustrates a strong

Table 20.2 ANOVA model on emphasising the importance of innovation for Singapore and Malaysia

Country	Model		Sum of squares	df	Mean square	F	Sigma
ANOVA[a]							
Singapore	1	Regression	25.677	9	2.853	8.793	.000[b]
		Residual	6.489	20	.324		
		Total	32.167	29			
Malaysia	1	Regression	10.614	9	1.179	3.813	.006[c]
		Residual	6.186	20	.309		
		Total	16.800	29			

[a]Dependent variable: emphasising the importance of innovation (Innovative_R41)
[b]Predictors: (Constant), customer focus mean, workforce focus mean, measurement mean, operational focus mean, result mean, strategic planning mean, leadership mean
Significant at the 0.05 level (p < 0.05)

Table 20.3 Model summary

Country	Model	R	R^2	Adjusted R^2	Standard error of the estimate
Model summary[b]					
Singapore	1	.893[a]	.798	.707	.570
Malaysia	1	.795[c]	.632	.466	.556

[a]Dependent variable: emphasising the importance of innovation (Innovative_R41)
[b]Predictors: (Constant), customer focus mean, workforce focus mean, measurement mean, operational focus mean, result mean, strategic planning mean, leadership mean

correlation of academic leadership qualities, emphasising the importance of innovation.

Findings in Table 20.4 illustrate that operational focus (beta = .536) makes the strongest unique contribution to explaining variance in emphasising the importance of innovation in Singapore. Conversely, measurement (beta = –3.82) makes the strongest unique contribution to explaining the variance in emphasising the importance of innovation in Malaysia. Findings also demonstrated that operational focus in Singapore has a part correlation coefficient of .289, indicating that operational focus uniquely explains 8.3% of the variance in explaining the variance in emphasising the importance of innovation. Whereas measurement domain in Malaysia has a part correlation coefficient of –.175, indicating that the measurement domain uniquely explains 3.0% of the variance in explaining the variance in emphasising the importance of innovation.

In terms of enhancing inspiration on innovative ideas, the model in Table 20.5 shows only Singapore, $F(9, 20) = 6.577$; $p < 0.05$, reached statistical significance with enhancing inspiration on innovative ideas (dependent variable) and academic leadership qualities (predictors) and not Malaysia.

The R^2 value in Table 20.6 shows that customer focus, workforce focus, quality measurement, operational focus, result, strategic planning and leadership qualities for Singapore's model contributed 74.7% of the variance in enhancing inspiration on innovative ideas.

Findings in Table 20.7 indicate that the strategic planning domain makes the strongest unique contribution to explaining the variance in enhancing inspiration on innovative ideas. Finding also showed that strategic planning in Singapore has a part correlation coefficient of –.106, indicating that strategic planning uniquely explains only 1.1% of the variance in explaining the variance of enhancing inspiration on innovative ideas.

3. What are the impacts of innovation endeavour(s) in both countries?

Findings in this study revealed that the university lecturers in both countries perceived that innovation works can impact their universities in terms of 'Introduction of new product in the market', 'Customer satisfaction' and 'Up-lifting the image of their university'. Besides that, Singapore university lecturers opined the positive impact of innovation on the university in the aspect of dissemination of knowledge through the creation of journals as a channel to share knowledge with researchers and other interested readers. Some samples of excerpts to illustrate the respondents' responses on the impact of innovation endeavours on the universities are provided in Table 20.8.

Table 20.4 Variance contribution: beta coefficients and part correlation coefficient on emphasising the importance of innovation

Country	Model		Standardised coefficients Beta	t	Sigma	Correlations Zero-order	Partial	Part
Coefficients[a]								
Singapore	1	(Constant)		-2.810	.011			
		Leadership	-.108	-.396	.697	.589	-.088	-.040
		Strategic Planning	-.283	-1.060	.302	.568	-.231	-.106
		Customer focus	.180	1.203	.243	.352	.260	.121
		Measurement	.184	.906	.376	.547	.199	.091
		Workforce Focus	.132	.738	.469	.559	.163	.074
		Operational focus	.536	2.882	.009	.813	.542	.289
		Result	-.116	-.505	.619	.643	-.112	-.051
Malaysia	1	(Constant)		.155	.879			
		Leadership	.134	.784	.442	-.177	.173	.106
		Strategic Planning	.024	.124	.903	-.501	.028	.017
		Customer focus	.063	.358	.724	-.399	.080	.049
		Measurement	-.382	-1.288	.213	-.564	-.277	-.175
		Workforce Focus	-.326	-1.680	.109	-.585	-.352	-.228
		Operational Focus	.146	.595	.559	-.356	.132	.081
		Result	.018	.074	.942	-.356	.016	.010

Significant at the 0.05 level ($p < 0.05$)

Table 20.5 ANOVA model on enhancing inspiration on innovative ideas for Singapore and Malaysia

Country	Model		Sum of squares	df	Mean square	F	Sigma
ANOVA[a]							
Singapore	1	Regression	27.132	9	3.015	6.577	.000[b]
		Residual	9.168	20	.458		
		Total	36.300	29			
Malaysia	1	Regression	6.201	9	.689	2.120	.078[c]
		Residual	6.499	20	.325		
		Total	12.700	29			

[a]Dependent variable: enhancing inspiration on innovative ideas (Innovative_R42)
[b]Predictors: (Constant), customer focus mean, workforce focus mean, measurement mean, operational focus mean, result mean, strategic planning mean, leadership mean
Significant at the 0.05 level (p < 0.05)

Table 20.6 Model summary for enhancing inspiration on innovative ideas

Country	Model	R	R^2	Adjusted R^2	Standard error of the estimate
Model summary[b]					
Singapore	1	.865[a]	.747	.634	.677
Malaysia	1	.699[c]	.488	.258	.570

[a]Dependent variable: enhancing inspiration on innovative ideas (Innovative_R42)
[b]Predictors: (Constant), customer focus mean, workforce focus mean, measurement mean, operational focus mean, result mean, strategic planning mean, leadership mean
Significant at the 0.05 level (p < 0.05)

Based on these findings, the authors concluded that while the university lecturers from Malaysia and Singapore have positive perceptions on the impact of innovative endeavours on their universities, those from Singapore have a more constructive method of reaching out to a wider range of customers globally via the creation of journals to disseminate their innovative works. The findings also revealed that innovation endeavours have promising impacts on the students in Malaysia and Singapore. The respondents from both countries possessed similar views that innovation works in their institutions have enhanced students' learning as well as inspired and motivated students not only to be creative but also to be innovators alongside their lecturers. Some samples of the respondents' responses on the impact of innovation on the students are presented in Table 20.9.

Other than that, innovation endeavours were found to have profound impacts on the respondents from both countries. They viewed that innovation endeavours have provided them a sense of self-improvement, self-motivation, self-satisfaction, self-efficiency and a sense of achievement. Some samples of the respondents' responses on the impact of innovation on the respondents themselves are shown in Table 20.10.

Table 20.7 Variance contribution: beta coefficients and part correlation coefficient on enhancing inspiration on innovative ideas

Country	Model		Standardised coefficients	t	Sigma	Correlations		
			Beta			Zero-order	Partial	Part
Coefficients[a]								
Singapore	1	(Constant)		-.407	.689			
		Leadership	.057	.186	.854	.589	-.088	-.040
		Strategic planning	.400	1.341	.019	.568	-.231	-.106
		Customer focus	-.035	-.207	.838	.352	.260	.121
		Measurement	.104	.460	.650	.547	.199	.091
		Workforce focus	-.387	-1.938	.067	.559	.163	.074
		Operational focus	-.002	-.010	.992	.813	.542	.289
		Result	.050	.197	.846	.643	-.112	-.051
Malaysia	1	(Constant)		-1.146	.265			
		Leadership	-.301	-1.493	.151	-.177	.173	.106
		Strategic Planning	.336	1.462	.159	-.501	.028	.017
		Customer focus	-.059	-.285	.779	-.399	.080	.049
		Measurement	-.048	-.138	.892	-.564	-.277	-.175
		Workforce focus	.296	1.293	.211	-.585	-.352	-.228
		Operational focus	.168	.582	.567	-.356	.132	.081
		Result	-.019	-.067	.947	-.356	.016	.010

Significant at the 0.05 level (p<0.05)

Table 20.8 Impact of innovation endeavours on the organisation

Country	Impact of innovation endeavours on the organisation	Examples of excerpts
Malaysia	Introduction of new product in the market	• Obtain intellectual property of the product for my organisation • Provide more alternative product in the market
Singapore		• Develop the product
Malaysia	Customer satisfaction	• Increase productivity • Reduce costs as the new product is cheaper compared to what is available in the market
Singapore		• Better customer satisfaction • More students' satisfaction and enrolment
Malaysia	Uplift image of university	• Good image for my organisation • Help my organisation to be known outside
Singapore		• Recognition • Increase enrolment in my university • Positive impact. The PISA programmes have been in their nascent stage
Singapore	Dissemination of knowledge	• We created a journal (three of them) to disseminate knowledge about business issues in Asia. We now have over 300,000 readers • Share knowledge of innovative products with others through publications

Table 20.9 Impact of innovation endeavours on the students

Country	Impact of innovation endeavours on the Students	Examples of excerpts
Malaysia	Enhance students' learning	• The products that I have innovated made the work process easier and user friendly • Able to use the product in practical areas
Singapore		• Enhance engagement in students' learning • My experienced students now have a template to do applied research, they understand the needs of applied research are actually harder, often you have to satisfy both academic and corporate worlds
Malaysia	Inspire and motivate students	• Inspire them • Encourage creativity and potentiality • Students also joined force with lecturers to innovate products and bring those innovative products for competitions at national and international levels
Singapore		• More inner reflection and broader view of world • Students also innovate alongside lecturers

Table 20.10   Impact of innovation endeavours on the respondents

Country	Impact of innovation Endeavours on the respondents	Examples of excerpts
Malaysia	Self-improvement	• Teach me to be more innovative • Learning new ideas
Singapore		• I learnt and developed personally • I have learnt a lot on my journey in the PISA programme as well—how to balance the need of quality and pragmatism. Guiding applied research takes both theorised and applied knowledge
Malaysia	Self-motivation	• I become more alert of things around so that I can innovate better products • Makes my mind become more creative
Singapore		• Feels good to be able to teach and innovate products at the same time. That makes me want to be more innovative
Malaysia	Self-satisfaction	• Satisfied with creation • Feel proud and happy, especially when I won the gold medal during the innovation competition
Singapore		• Self-fulfilment • Contented with my creation
Malaysia	Self-efficiency	• Make work procedure or process easier and time efficient • Helps me to be more productive as it improves my task efficiency
Singapore		• My work can be done faster and more efficiently
Malaysia	Sense of achievement	• A bonus to add into year-end assessment • It gives me a sense of achievement
Singapore		• For the honour and glory • Attain success and achievement

Discussion and Implication

Findings showed that there are significant correlations for emphasising the importance of innovation as well as enhancing inspiration on innovative ideas with leadership, strategic planning, measurement, workforce focus, operational focus and result. The findings demonstrated that there is a strong positive relationship with emphasising the importance of innovation with operational focus as well as inspiration on innovative ideas with operational focus. These findings coincide with findings in Gilley et al.'s (2008) study which revealed six sets of leadership skills and abilities that positively influence organisations' success rates in implementing change and driving innovation, namely, ability to coach, reward, involve and support others, promote teamwork and collaboration, communicate and motivate. Their findings concluded that the ability to communicate and the ability to motivate others have the most significant influence to effectively drive innovation and implement change. In addition, according to Horth and Dan Buchner (2009), the essential qualities of leadership for organisational innovation include organisational support, absence of organisational obstacles, leadership support, adequate resources, reasonable workload, courageous work confrontation, cooperation and teamwork. Martins & Terblanche (2003) opined that organisation's support for innovative behaviour is an important factor to mobilise the innovation process. Furthermore, the five fundamental leadership qualities to lead innovation as outlined by Staff (2012) include zeal for innovation, visionary, boldness to encounter and learn from failure, establish linkages with innovators and willingness to endure and support individualist from management. Thus, "knowledge, skills, values, and talents are the key qualities for leaders and followers to make innovative changes" (Şena & Erena, 2012, p. 11).

Findings showed that operational focus and quality measurement make the strongest unique contribution to explaining the variance in emphasising the importance of innovation. These findings are substantiated by Stevenson's (2012) findings that organisational success requires innovation leaders who can inspire a mindset that opens an organisation to discovery and the development of a framework that supports an innovation strategy and empowers people to make the right choices. Moreover, these findings also concur with Pelz and Andrews' (1966) stance that individuals and teams need to be given the autonomy and freedom to generate ideas and be engaged in creative problem solving. This implies that an effective leader plays a pivotal role in navigating the organisation to greater heights by planning and searching for continuous quality improvement to sustain the organisation in the modern market. Furthermore, for effective innovation, tactful balancing between creativity and efficiency needs to be monitored as organisations need to "learn how to walk the fine line between rigidity – which smothers creativity – and chaos – where creativity runs amok and nothing ever gets to market" (Leavy, 2006, p. 42). In other words, leaders need to allow freedom of thinking to innovate and to provide the necessary support to ensure high-quality innovations that are marketable.

In fact, the implementation of operational focus and quality measurement should involve many individuals with various tools and skills to transform the organisation. Barsh et al. (2008) asserted that leaders need to set performance metrics and targets for incremental innovation. According to Bel (2010), innovation requires an IDEA (to generate energy, create commitment and direct individuals towards the vision) and ARMS (to ensure that people really do act accordingly). If we look at the Japanese innovation model, it is based on capability accumulation through mid- and long-term objectives which regard human as the medium of innovation (Yusof and Othman 2016). This implies that the primary role of innovation leaders should be able to create a climate for innovation (Isaksen & Todd, 2006). They need to create an environment for innovation within the organisations as they learn to operate in challenging and unpredictable circumstances because innovation in the workplace represents a return process based on continuous feedback, learning and improvement. Hence, the findings in this study imply that employers need to undergo training to build their skills and knowledge to execute effective strategies in innovation (Freifeld, 2013) and employees also need to attend training programmes to enhance their ability to undertake the required changes in an organisation. In other words, leaders need to create a supportive environment and foster innovative thinking. Moreover, they also need to take a prominent role in making a leap to support innovation by providing avenues to patent new products and avenues for journal publications and commercialisation of the products to stay ahead of others. However, management must bear in mind that some innovations may fail initially, but given time and experimentation, they will succeed.

The findings that both Malaysia and Singapore university lecturers perceived that innovation works can impact their universities in terms of 'Introduction of new product in the market' coincide with the findings in Jafari's (2014) study that organisational innovation has a substantial impact on product innovation, market operation and innovative performance of the organisation. Similarly, Keskin's (2010) and Tajeddini's (2012) studies found that increased innovation produced a positive impact on the organisation's performance. Likewise, Peter et al.'s (2002) study revealed a relationship between innovation and benefits to customers. These findings are substantiated by Amabile et al. (1996) and Chandler, Keller and Lyon's (2000) viewpoint that an organisation that promotes, supports, encourages and explores new approaches has an influence on the innovation in the organisation. This stance is similar to Şena and Erena's (2012) notion that innovation introduces new ideas, creations, services, processes and means as a solution to problems to satisfy human demands. Moreover, the Special Report on Leadership and Innovation by Capozzi (July, 2019) stated that all organisations have pockets of innovation that if tapped can unleash impact. This report showed how leaders can create conditions for greater innovation within and beyond their organisations to increase development impact.

Additionally, the findings that innovation endeavours have promising impacts on the students or stakeholders in Malaysia and Singapore in that innovations helped to enhance their learning, inspire and motivate them concur with Somech's (2006) statement that innovation encourages team reflection processes to stimulate innovative thinking. This is in line with Craig's (2018, p. 3) assertion that "[i]n the digital age, companies challenge themselves to innovate, collaborate and give back". Other than that, the findings that the respondents viewed innovation endeavours to have provided them a sense of self-improvement, self-motivation, self-satisfaction, self-efficiency and a sense of achievement correspond with findings in Simpson et al.'s (2006) study, which found that an innovation-focused environment will possibly lead to more pleasure, self-fulfilment and job satisfaction among the staff in the organisation.

As gathered from the findings, it can be implied that innovation endeavours among the university lecturers of both countries have helped to unleash their self-potential in the world of innovation, encourage their quest for continuous professional improvement and provide them the avenue to feel accomplished upon the recognition of their innovation.

Conclusion

Through the comparison of both countries, the findings provide insights for academic leaders to enhance their innovative endeavours. With the advent of technology in this age of Industrial Revolution 4.0, the ability of leaders to engage their employees in innovation endeavours has become the core business and challenge of many universities to survive. Therefore, the authors concluded that leaders play a pivotal role in creating the right environment to unleash the innovation impact on the universities, staff or lecturers and students. Nevertheless, there are no best-practice solutions to seed and cultivate innovation but holding leaders accountable for encouraging innovation makes a big difference (Barsh et al., 2008). This stems from the fact that different organisations use different types of stimulating factors to promote organisational innovation. Different leadership styles would have different influence on employee motivation and commitment in innovation endeavours. Even though innovation leaders share a common set of qualities and abilities, in complex organisations and environments, leadership roles are diverse and must fit organisation and innovation stage, strategy and organisational level (Bel, 2010). There are no one-size-fits-all types of leadership for positive impact on innovation endeavours; rather, the type of leaders chosen depends on the goals or targets of the organisation. Importantly, innovation and leadership are interdependent as effective leaders will strive and motivate the employees to bring betterment for the university as well as organisation through innovation endeavours.

References

Agbor, E. (2008). Creativity and Innovation: The Leadership Dynamics. *Journal of Strategic Leadership, 1*(1), 39–45.

Amabile, T. M., Conti, R., Coon, H., Lazenby, J., & Herron, M. (1996). Assessing the Work Environment for Creativity. *Academy of Management Journal, 39*(5), 1154–1184.

Baldrige Performance Excellence Program. (2011). *Are we Making Progress as Leaders?* National Institute of Standards and Technology, United States Department of Commerce.

Baregheh, A., Rowley, J., & Sambrook, S. (2009). Towards a Multidisciplinary Definition of Innovation. *Management Decision, 47*, 1323–1339.

Barsh, J., Capozzi, M. M., & Davidson, J. (2008). Leadership and Innovation. *Mckinsey Quarterly*. Retrieved from www.mckinsey.com/insights/innovation/leadership_and_innovation

Bel, R. (2010). Leadership and Innovation: Learning from the Best. Published online in Wiley InterScience (www.interscience.wiley.com). (47–60). https://doi.org/10.1002/joe.20308.

Bouhali, R., Mekdad, Y., Lebsir, H., & Ferkh, L. (2015). Leader Roles for Innovation: Strategic Thinking and Planning. *Procedia - Social and Behavioral Sciences, 181*, 72–78.

Brunsson, N., & Sahlin-Andersonn, K. (2000). Constructing Organisations: The Example of Public Reform Sector. *Organisation Studies, 21*, 721–746.

Cabeza-Erikson, I., Edwards, K., & Van Brabant, T. (2008). *Development of Leadership Capacities as a Strategic Factor for Sustainability*. Karlskrona: Blekinge Tekniska Höogskola.

Capozzi, M. M. (2019, July). *Special Report Leadership and Innovation* (p. 25–28). Development Outreach World Bank Institute.

Chan, I. Y. S., Liu, A. M. M., & Fellows, R. (2014). Role of Leadership in Fostering an Innovation Climate in Construction Firms. *Journal of Management in Engineering, 30*, 6014003.

Chandler, G. N., Keller, C., & Lyon, D. W. (2000). Unravelling the Determinants and Consequences of an Innovation-Supportive Organizational Culture. *Entrepreneurship Theory and Practice, 25*(1), 59–76.

Collins English Dictionary. (2015). (5th ed.). London, UK: HarperCollins.

Craig, W. (2018). 10 Traits of a Client Focused Company. Retrieved from https://www.forbes.com/sites/williamcraig/2018/04/10/10-traits-of-a-clientfocused-company/#65bc024524c6

Denti, L., & Hemlin, S. (2012). Leadership and Innovation in Organizations: A Systematic Review of Factors that Mediate or Moderate the Relationship. *International Journal of Innovation Management, 16*(3), 1–20. https://doi.org/10.1142/S1363919612400075

De Jong, J. P. J., & Den Hartog, D. N. (2007). How Leaders Influence Employees' Innovative Behavior. *European Journal of Innovation Management, 10*, 41–64.

Freifeld, L. (2013). Emerging Training Leaders. *Training, 50*(3), 20–31.

Gilley, A., Dixon, P., & Gilley, J. W. (2008). Characteristics of Leadership Effectiveness: Implementing Change and Driving Innovation in Organizations. *Human Resource Development Quarterly, 19*(2), 153–169.

Gumusluoglu, L., & Ilsev, A. (2009). Transformational Leadership, Creativity, and Organizational Innovation. *Journal of Business Research, 62*(4), 461–473. https://doi.org/10.1016/j.jbusres.2007.07.032

Horth, D. M., & Dan Buchner, C. (2009). Innovation Leadership: How to use Innovation to Lead Effectively, Work Collaboratively and Drive Results. Centre for Creative Leadership. Retrieved from http://www.ccl.org/leadership/pdf/research/InnovationLeadership.pdf

Human Capital Management. (2011). *Organizational Key Performance Indicators—A Management Tool with Bottom Line Effect*. Copenhagen, 1–10.

Ionescu, V. (2014). Leadership, Culture and Organizational Change. *Manager, 20*, 6571.

Isaksen, S., & Todd, J. (2006). *Meeting the Innovation Challenge: Leadership for Transformation and Growth*. Hoboken, NJ: Wiley.

Jafari, N. (2014). *The Survey of the Effect of Organizational Innovation on Product Innovation, Innovative Performance and Market, Financial Management*. Master Thesis, Shahid Chamran University of Ahvaz.

Kazmi, S. A. Z., Naaranoja, M., Kytola, J., & Kantola, J. (2016). Connecting Strategic Thinking with Product Innovativeness to Reinforce NPD Support Process. *Procedia—Social and Behavioral Sciences, 235*, 672–684.

Keskin, H. (2010). Antecedents and Consequences of Team Memory in Software Development Projects. *Information & Management, 46*(7), 388–396.

Leavy, B. (2006). A Leader's Guide to Creating an Innovation Culture. *Strategy and Leadership, 33*(4), 38–45.

Lousã, E. P. (2013). *Liderança empreendedora e cultura de inovação em organizações de base tecnológica e análise comparativa entre setores de atividade*. A Dissertation Submitted in Fulfillment of the Requirements of the Doctor of Philosophy, University of Coimbra, Faculty of Psychology and Education Sciences, Portugal.

Lousã, E. P., & Mónico, L. D. S. M. (2018). How can Leadership and Organizational Culture Predict Innovation in Small, Medium and Large Enterprises? *The Journal of Organizational Management Studies*, 1–15. https://doi.org/10.5171/2018.703891

Makri, M., & Scandura, T. A. (2010). Exploring the Effects of Creative CEO Leadership on Innovation in High-Technology Firms. *The Leadership Quarterly, 21*(1), 75–88. https://doi.org/10.1016/j.leaqua.2009.10.006

Martins, E., & Terblanche, F. (2003). Building Organisational Culture that Stimulates Creativity and Innovation. *European Journal of Innovation Management, 6*(1), 64–74.

Mokhber, M., Wan, K., & Vakilbashi, A. (2018). Leadership and Innovation: The Moderator Role of Organization Support for Innovative Behaviors. *Journal of Management & Organization, 24*(1), 108–128. https://doi.org/10.1017/jmo.2017.26

Moo, J. H., & Yazdanifar, R. (2015). How Effective Leadership can Facilitate Change in Organizations through Improvement and Innovation. *Global Journal of Management and Business Research: Administration and Management, 15*(9), 1–7.

OECD. (2005). *Oslo Manual. Guidelines for Collecting and Interpreting Innovation Data* (3rd ed.). Paris: OECD.

Ozorhon, B., Oral, K., & Demirkesen, S. (2016). Investigating the Components of Innovation in Construction Projects. *Journal of Management in Engineering, 32*, 4015052.

Pelz, D., & Andrews, F. (1966). *Scientists in Organizations: Productive Climates for Research and Development.* New York: Wiley.

Peter, T., Leach, D., Birdi, K., Clegg, C., & Wall, T. (2002). An Investigation of the Contents and Consequences of Major Organizational Innovations. *International Journal of Innovation Management, 6*, 343–368.

Poonam, A., & Arvind, K. S. (2014). Innovative Leadership: A Paradigm in Modern HR Practices. *Global Journal of Finance and Management, 6*(6), 497–502.

Prasad, B., & Junni, P. (2016). CEO Transformational and Transactional Leadership and Organizational Innovation: The Moderating Role of Environmental Dynamism. *Management Decision, 54*(7), 1542–1568.

Quah, C. S., & Sim, S. P. L. (2016). Innovation Initiatives and Its Impact Among Malaysian University Lecturers. In N. Muenjohn & A. McMurray (Eds.), *The Palgrave Handbook of Leadership in Transforming Asia* (pp. 213–232). London: Palgrave Macmillan.

Semuel, H., Siagian, H., & Octavia, S. (2017). The Effect of Leadership and Innovation on Differentiation Strategy and Company Performance. *Procedia - Social and Behavioral Sciences, 237*, 1152–1159.

Şena, A., & Erena, E. (2012). Innovative Leadership for the Twenty-First Century. *Procedia - Social and Behavioral Sciences, 41*, 1–14. A Paper Presented at the International Conference on Leadership, Technology and Innovation Management.

Simpson, P. M., Siguaw, J. A., & Enz, C. A. (2006). Innovation Orientation Outcomes: The Good and the Bad [Electronic Version]. Cornell University, School of Hotel Administration Site. Retrieved from http://scholarship.sha.cornell.edu/articles/604

Somech, A. (2006). The Effects of Leadership Style and Team Process on Performance and Innovation in Functionally Heterogeneous Teams. *Journal of Management, 32*, 132–157.

Staff, B. G. (2012). Developing Innovative Leaders, from World Summer. Retrieved from http://www.billgeorge.org/page/developing-innovativeleaders1

Stevenson, J. E. (2012). Breaking Away—A New Model for Innovation Leadership. *Employment Relations Today, 39*, 17–25. https://doi.org/10.1002/ert.21361

Tajeddini, K. (2012). Effect of Customer Orientation and Entrepreneurial Orientation on Innovativeness: Evidence from the Hotel Industry in Switzerland. *Tourism Management, 31*(2), 21–60.

Yusof, S. M., & Othman, R. (2016). Leadership for Creativity and Innovation: Is Japan Unique? *Journal of Advanced Management Science, 4*(2), 176–180.

Zaltman, G., Duncan, R., & Holbek, J. (1973). *Innovations and Organizations.* New York: Wiley.

Zheng, J., Wu, G., & Xie, H. (2017). Impacts of Leadership on Project-based Organizational Innovation Performance: The Mediator of Knowledge Sharing and Moderator of Social Capital. *Sustainability, 9*, 1893.

21

Frugal Workplace Innovation: A Conceptual Framework

Daniel Etse, Adela McMurray, and Nuttawuth Muenjohn

Introduction

Frugal innovation's value propositions of product or service affordability, substantially low total cost of ownership, robustness, user-friendliness, and others (Basu, Banerjee, & Sweeny, 2013; Tiwari & Herstatt, 2012), as well as its socio-economic and environmental sustainability potentials (Angot & Plé, 2015; Rosca, Arnold, & Bendul, 2017), make it a potentially powerful tool for addressing the global challenges of economic, social, and environmental sustainability. This is particularly salient for the global south, where acute resource constraints remain a major challenge. The surge of interest in frugal innovation among scholars and practitioners (Hyypiä & Khan, 2018; Knorringa, Peša, Leliveld, & van Beers, 2016) may be a reflection of the growing recognition of its relevance as an academic concept and a viable approach to addressing global social challenges. Frugal innovation has been defined as the (re)designing of goods, services, systems, and business models to significantly reduce total cost of ownership and product complexities while fulfilling or exceeding a pre-defined criteria of functionality and quality standards (Leliveld & Knorringa, 2017; Tiwari & Herstatt, 2012).

Though the frugal innovation literature continues to experience substantial growth (Hyypiä & Khan, 2018; Knorringa et al., 2016) issues regarding the

D. Etse (✉) • N. Muenjohn
School of Management, RMIT University, Melbourne, VIC, Australia
e-mail: daniel.etse@rmit.edu.au; nuttawuth.muenjohn@rmit.edu.au

means by which this innovation is embedded into organisational systems and the resultant outcomes remain unaddressed. This state of affairs may leave current and potential adopters of frugal innovation in limbo, as they may lack guidance regarding the approach to employ and to integrate frugal innovation into their organisational systems. To address this lacuna, this chapter proposes a conceptual framework based on the workplace innovation concept to explain the key variables as well as the mechanism involved in embedding frugal and other forms of innovation into organisational DNA.

Taking into consideration key enablers of frugal innovation, including multi-stakeholder approach, co-creation of solutions, flexibility, polycentric process, local knowledge, and social inclusiveness (Knorringa et al., 2016; Meagher, 2018; Prabhu & Jain, 2015; Radjou & Prabhu, 2014), workplace innovation appears suitable as an approach to embedding frugal innovation into organisational systems, as well as facilitating the realisation of intended outcomes. Workplace innovation is a social process which entails the involvement of all organisational members at all levels in decisions regarding the way in which the organisation manages, organises, and deploys people, technology, and other resources (Totterdill & Exton, 2014). It stresses the need for the elimination of any form of barriers to workplace interactions, exchange of ideas, and working together and emphasises flexibility of systems, collaborations within and across levels, as well as the facilitation of employee initiatives, creative thinking, and innovation (Pot, 2011;Totterdill & Exton, 2014). These attributes of workplace innovation appear to align with the enablers of frugal innovation; thus the application of the workplace innovation process may enhance understanding and facilitate the realisation of frugal innovation objectives.

In this chapter we explore the relevance of the concept of workplace innovation to the process and outcome of frugal innovation by developing a frugal workplace innovation conceptual framework. This framework highlights key variables that are likely to create a frugal innovation organisational environment and the relationships between these variables and frugal workplace innovation outcomes. Thus the key objectives of this chapter are to:

1. *Identify the major factors and variables that facilitate frugal workplace innovation.*
2. *Explore organisational outcomes that result from frugal workplace innovation.*
3. *Develop a conceptual framework to illustrate the process and outcomes of frugal workplace innovation.*

A. McMurray
College of Business, Government and Law, Flinders University,
Adelaide, SA, Australia
e-mail: adela.mcmurray@flinders.edu.au

Methodology

Conceptual research, which is the methodology employed in this chapter, is a research approach that focuses on the systematic clarification of concepts as a means of facilitating the description, understanding, and application of complex ideas (Dreher, 2003; Xin, Tribe, & Chambers, 2013). It entails the use of abstract constructs to represent and explain a phenomenon (Xin et al., 2013). Since the purpose of this chapter is to provide a mental representation and understanding of an abstract concept, that is, frugal workplace innovation, the conceptual research approach was considered appropriate for this purpose.

The techniques employed in undertaking this study include exploring the literature in two main domains: frugal innovation and workplace innovation. This was conducted to examine the various definitions and explanations regarding frugal innovation and workplace innovation in order to identify perspectives that provide comprehensive explanations of the concepts. This was followed by a critical examination and logical clarifications of the concepts, as well as evaluation of perspectives that were found relevant for this chapter's purpose. The concepts were then de-composed into appropriate variables in terms of predictor and outcome variables. This was followed by a re-integration of the various variables into a conceptual framework, which shows the interrelationship that exists between the variables. The research process was predicated on a rigorous literature review and critical examination and analysis of relevant concepts. The various literature sources from which information was obtained were carefully referenced, so as to allow cross-checking and verification of information. These processes were followed with the aim of enhancing the scientific quality of the study and ensuring academic openness, good scholarship, and sound judgement (Xin et al., 2013). A schematic presentation of the process is shown in Fig. 21.1.

Figure 21.1 outlines the research process. It highlights the three main activities undertaken, their various outcomes, and the eventual culmination into a conceptual framework. Subsequent sections elaborate on the contents of the framework.

Frugal Innovation

Frugal innovation, an innovation that entails the designing or redesigning of goods or services such that total cost of ownership is significantly reduced and product complexities minimised while fulfilling a pre-defined criteria of functionality and quality standards (Knorringa et al., 2016; Tiwari & Herstatt,

Process & Activities   Focus

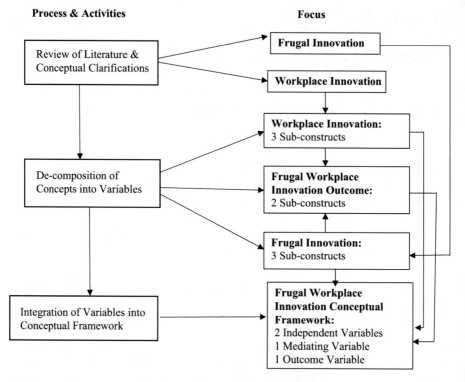

Fig. 21.1 Schematic representation of the research process

2012), has varied and different conceptualisations in the literature. It has often been conceptualised as either a product/outcome, a process, or both. For example, Weyrauch and Herstatt (2016) understand it as a product characterised by substantial cost reduction, concentration on core functionalities, and optimised performance level; Basu et al. (2013) conceptualise it as a design innovation process that develops products and services that are appropriate, affordable, adaptable, and accessible; and Soni and Krishnan (2014) conceptualise it as a mindset, a process, and an outcome. In this chapter, we adopt Soni and Krishnan's (2014) view of frugal innovation, as it appears more holistic and suitable for our comprehensive analysis of the concept.

As a mindset, frugal innovation entails an attitude, behaviour, and lifestyle that combines improvisation and pragmatism to develop solutions for societal needs (Prabhu & Jain, 2015). It has often been referred to using terms such as bricolage, improvisation, jugaad, Gandhian innovation, and inclusive innovation (George, McGahan, & Prabhu, 2012; Radjou, Prabhu, & Ahuja, 2012; Soni & Krishnan, 2014). As a process frugal innovation refers to the concentration on core functionalities and minimisation of non-value adding activities, frills, and wastes, with the aim of maximising customers' value while minimising cost (Sehgal, Dehoff, & Panneer, 2010; Soni & Krishnan, 2014; Weyrauch & Herstatt, 2016). And as outcome it refers to good enough goods, services, and solutions for low-income, cost-sensitive, and sustainability-conscious customers (Prahalad, 2006; Soni & Krishnan, 2014). From the mindset, process, and outcome perspective of frugal innovation, a frugal innovation-embedded organisation or workplace will be one in which employees and other members of the organisation exhibit frugal lifestyle, where organisational processes are underpinned by frugality and where the products and services of the organisation are frugal in nature.

Workplace Innovation

One of the widely used definitions of workplace innovation is that of Frank Pot (Totterdill, 2015), which defines workplace innovation as new and combined interventions in work organisation, human resource management, and supportive technologies (Muenjohn & McMurray, 2017; Pot, 2011). As a concept, workplace innovation describes the embedding of inclusive and participatory workplace practices grounded in a culture of continuing reflection, learning, and improvement relative to employee management, work organisation, and the deployment of technology (Pot, Totterdill, & Dhondt, 2017). It integrates the strategic knowledge of organisational leadership with the professional and tacit knowledge of employees, as well as the organisational design knowledge of experts, with the objective of achieving enhanced organisational performance and improved quality of working life (Pot et al., 2017).

Empirical studies including McMurray, Islam, Sarros, and Pirola-Merlo (2013); Oeij, Dhondt, Kraan, Vergeer, and Pot (2012); Black and Lynch (2004); and Appelbaum, Gittell, and Leana (2011) suggest that workplace innovation enhances the quality of organisational climate; engenders innovative working environment; improves organisational performance and quality of work; and enhances employee commitment. However, the theoretical process by which these outcomes are realised remains unclear. Though studies such as Totterdill (2015) have identified and categorised various determinants of workplace innovation, and developed instruments for its measurement, for example, McMurray and Dorai (2003), it remains unclear the mechanisms by which workplace innovation outcomes are produced. This state of affairs limits the theoretical development of workplace innovation, as the theoretical basis for hypothesising relationships between the antecedents of workplace innovation and related outcomes remains non-existent. To address this theoretical issue, we develop a conceptual framework that provides linkage between independent and dependent variables of frugal workplace innovation by extending the work of Totterdill and Exton (2014) and Totterdill (2015). Though the framework presented in this chapter focuses on frugal workplace innovation, it is relevant to the broader workplace innovation concept.

Frugal Workplace Innovation

Building on Pot, Dhondt, and Oeij's (2012) explanation of workplace innovation, we define frugal workplace innovation as a strategy, process, or situation of inclusive participation in an organisation's practice of managing, organising, and deploying human and non-human resources to achieve organisational mindset, process, and outcomes that align with frugal innovation principles and qualities while simultaneously achieving improved quality of working life. The intent of the definition is to emphasise the relevance of three main factors, that is, the antecedents, the process, and the outcomes, that the phenomenon of frugal workplace innovation entails.

Through the synthesis of empirical studies and relevant literature, Totterdill and Exton (2014) and Totterdill (2015) identified five elements of workplace innovation: these are job design and work organisation; structure and systems; workplace partnership; reflection and innovation; and joint intelligence. According to Totterdill (2015) the first element; job design and work organisation, refers to designing and organising work in such a way as to empower employees to assume responsibility for decisions regarding their work outcomes, as well as provide opportunity for developing work solutions through teamwork. It entails variables such as job autonomy, flexible working, self-managed teams, and integration of technology. The second element, that is, structures and systems, refers to the arrangement of organisational systems such that structures such as ranks, grades, professions, departments, divisions, and units in the organisation do not hinder effective rapport, interactions, collaboration, sharing of ideas, and working together. It entails variables such as fairness and equality, trust, support for employee initiatives, and minimisation of barriers to interaction. The third element, learning, reflection, and innovation, refers to conditions in the work environment that facilitate productive reflection and continuous generation and communication of ideas; its variables include continuous improvement, sharing of knowledge and experience, learning and development, and high involvement of innovation.

The fourth element is workplace partnership and involves collaboration with employees and labour unions to proactively address industrial relations issues. It entails variables such as dialogue, participation of representatives, transparency, effective communication, integrating tacit and strategic knowledge, and involvement of stakeholders in change process. The fifth element is joint intelligence and refers to the collaboration between workplace decision-makers and the research community to co-create organisational vision of high performance and high quality of working life, as well as facilitate their achievement. Totterdill designed a conceptual framework to capture these five elements; this framework is shown in Fig. 21.2.

As comprehensive as Totterdill's five elements workplace innovation framework appears, it does not clarify how the five elements interrelate to create workplace innovation outcomes, as can be seen in Fig. 21.2. In the next section, we modified the above framework to develop a frugal workplace innovation framework that provides linkage between various antecedents of workplace innovation and potential outcomes.

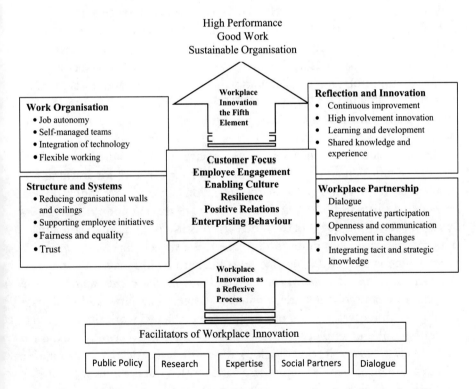

Fig. 21.2 Totterdill's workplace innovation conceptual framework. (Source: Totterdill, 2015)

Frugal Workplace Innovation Conceptual Framework

By critically examining Totterdill's five elements workplace innovation framework, we observed that the five elements relate to three major categories of factors, and we use the terms *organisational arrangements, organisational collaborations*, and *active work situations* to refer to these three categories of factors. Our arguments for the three categories of factors are as follows:

The first element of Totterdill's five elements' concept which is *job design and work organisation* relates to the arrangement of jobs, teams, technology, and other work-related functions, and the second element which is *structures and systems* relates to the arrangement of organisational elements such as ranks, grades, professions, departments, and units to ensure interconnectedness and proper functioning of the organisation. So, the first and second elements of Totterdill's framework relate to arrangement of various organisational aspects, hence our integration of these two elements to form the factor *organisational arrangement*. Furthermore, the fourth and fifth elements of Totterdill's framework relate to collaborations and partnerships; the fourth element which is *workplace partnership* relates to organisational management and leadership's collaboration with trade unions and employees on matters of industrial relations. The fifth element which is *joint intelligence* relates to collaboration or partnership involving workplace decision-makers and the research community; it is a collaboration between practice and research. Since both the fourth and fifth elements relate to collaboration and partnership, we merged them into one major factor, *organisational collaborations*. The third element of Totterdill's framework, that is, *reflection and innovation*, relates to workplace or job situations where workers have sufficient autonomy to control their work demands, as well as discretionary capacity for learning and problem-solving, such that productive reflection and employee innovation are engendered (Totterdill, 2015). Totterdill refers to this situation as *active work situation* (Totterdill, 2015, p. 67), and this constitutes the third major variable of our frugal workplace innovation concept. We suggest that *active work situation*, which is the third major factor, is likely to be influenced by the other two factors: *organisational arrangements* and *organisational collaborations*. This is because organisational systems and job designs that allow and encourage employees' initiatives are more likely to promote active work situations than those that inhibit employee initiatives. Moreover, active work situation is more likely to occur in organisations where there is effective collaboration between management, employees, and other stakeholders than in organisations where management makes decisions unilaterally with no inputs from other stakeholders.

To facilitate the linking of antecedents of workplace innovation to the outcomes, we introduce a fourth major factor, that is, *frugal workplace innovation outcomes*. Drawing on Soni and Krishnan's (2014) concept of frugal innovation, and Pot et al.'s (2012) concept of workplace innovation, we define *frugal workplace innovation outcome* as organisational mindset, process, and outcomes that align with frugal innovation principles and values while simultaneously achieving improved quality of working life. Thus our concept of frugal workplace innovation outcome entails the achievement of organisational mindset, process, and product/services underpinned by frugality, as well as enhanced quality of working life. Consequently, our frugal workplace innovation concept consists of two independent variables: organisational arrangements and organisational collaborations; one mediating variable: active work situation; and one dependent/outcome variable: frugal workplace innovation outcomes. The concept is presented in the frugal workplace innovation conceptual framework in Fig. 21.3

Figure 21.3 is a diagrammatic depiction of theoretical relationships between the antecedents of frugal workplace innovation and related outcomes. It suggests direct relationships between the independent variables, that is, organisational arrangement; organisational collaboration, and the dependent variable; frugal workplace innovation outcomes. It also suggests indirect relationships between the independent variables and frugal workplace innovation outcomes, through the variable active work situation, as the mediator. Related discussions are presented in the next section.

Discussion

The concept of frugal workplace innovation presented in this chapter consists of four key constructs and seven sub-constructs. These constructs are organisational arrangements, organisational collaborations, active work situation, and frugal workplace innovation outcomes. The first two of the above-mentioned constructs are independent variables; the third is a mediating variable; and the fourth is the outcome variable. The seven sub-constructs are job/work organisation, systems and structures, workplace partnership, joint intelligence, organisational performance, workplace quality, and reflection/innovation. The first five of the above-listed sub-constructs are the elements in Totterdill and Exton (2014) and Totterdill's (2015) five elements workplace innovation framework. These were realigned and de-composed into two

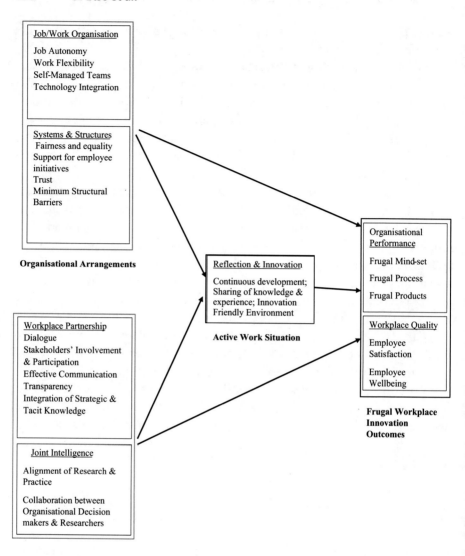

Fig. 21.3 Frugal workplace innovation conceptual framework. (Source: Authors 2019)

independent variables, and one mediating variable, so as to facilitate the theorisation of relationships between the antecedents of workplace innovation and related outcomes. The last two sub-constructs, that is, organisational performance and workplace quality, pertain to the construct frugal workplace innovation outcomes.

Our concept of frugal workplace innovation, as depicted in Fig. 21.3, suggests direct relationships between the constructs: organisational arrangements, organisational collaborations, and frugal workplace innovation outcomes. These proposed relationships are consistent with the extant innovation literature. Regarding the relationships between organisational arrangements and workplace innovation outcomes, studies such as Rothwell (1992) and Jacobsen, Hillestad, Yttri, and Hildrum (2019) suggest direct and positive relationship between organic types of organisations (i.e. organisational systems and structures that are flexible, participative, inclusive, informal, non-hierarchical, and other such attributes) and successful innovation outcomes. Furthermore, studies such as Bos-Nehles and Veenendaal (2019) and Dorenbosch, van Engen, and Verhagen (2005) suggest direct relationships between job design/work organisation and workplace innovation outcomes. Thus our proposition that organisational arrangements will directly influence frugal workplace innovation outcomes has been evidenced in the extant innovation literature. Relative to our proposition of direct relationship between the constructs organisational collaborations and frugal workplace innovation outcomes, studies such as Martínez-Costa, Jiménez-Jiménez, and Dine Rabeh (2019) and Soosay, Hyland, and Ferrer (2008) suggest that collaborations and partnerships within the organisation, as well as externally, have direct and positive influence on organisational innovation outcomes, as they facilitate knowledge sharing, continuous learning, and continuous innovation.

In addition to the proposed direct relationships between the independent variables and frugal workplace innovation outcomes, our frugal workplace innovation conceptual framework suggests an indirect relationship, through the variable; active work situation, as a mediator. The construct "Active Work Situation" refers to a workplace or organisational condition where workers have sufficient autonomy, and discretionary capacity to control their work demands, as well as opportunity for learning, productive reflection, problem-solving, and innovation (Totterdill, 2015). Our proposition is that, organisational arrangements, as well as organisational collaborations, will determine the degree of autonomy and discretional capacity of workers regarding their work and participation in organisational processes and that this will in turn influence frugal workplace innovation outcomes. In other words, the variables: organisational arrangements and organisational collaborations will influence a third variable active work situation, which will in turn influence the outcome variable frugal workplace innovation outcomes. These propositions have support in the extant innovation literature. For example, studies including Bock, Opsahl, George, and Gann (2012) and Laforet (2016) found that systems, structures, and other organisational arrangements influence the innovative culture and climate of organisations. Martínez-Costa et al. (2019) and Sørensen and Torfing (2011) suggest that collaboration fosters innovative organisational environment, which in turn influences organisational innovation outcomes. Furthermore, studies such as Burcharth, Præst Knudsen, and Søndergaard (2017) and Beugelsdijk (2008) found that organisational environments and work situations where employees have sufficient autonomy and discretionary capacity enhance the innovation outcomes of the organisation.

Conclusion

The frugal workplace innovation developed in this chapter has implications for the innovation management field. It highlights various factors that facilitate the creation of workplaces and organisational settings that are innovative and frugal in nature and essence. Furthermore, it postulates relationships between predictor variables of frugal workplace innovation and related outcome variables. The framework is holistic, as it integrates the antecedents and outcomes of frugal workplace innovation. This will deepen theoretical understanding of the frugal innovation and workplace innovation concepts. By linking antecedents to outcomes, this framework provides basis for predicting likely frugal workplace innovation outcomes, with given variables. This testable workplace innovation concept provides foundation for developing a workplace innovation theory.

The insights provided by this theoretical framework may inform management strategy and actions regarding the appropriate means by which organisational structures, resources, and skills can be aligned so as to facilitate the embedding of frugal innovation into organisational systems. Furthermore, by highlighting the mechanism by which organisations can engender workplace innovation outcomes, this theoretical framework may guide management initiatives and actions towards the realisation of improved organisational performance and enhanced workplace quality.

This chapter explored the mechanism by which frugal workplace innovation can be engendered, its resultant outcomes, and relationships between the antecedents and outcomes. Developing instruments to measure the framework's constructs and testing the proposed relationships will be a worthwhile future research project, as this will facilitate verification of the validity and reliability of the conceptual framework, as well as provide inputs for subsequent modification and improvement.

References

Angot, J., & Plé, L. (2015). Serving Poor People in Rich Countries: The Bottom-of-the-Pyramid Business Model Solution. *Journal of Business Strategy, 35*(2), 3–15.

Appelbaum, E., Gittell, J., & Leana, C. (2011). *High Performance Work Practices and Sustainable Economic Growth*. Washington: Centre for Economic Policy Research.

Basu, R., Banerjee, P., & Sweeny, E. (2013). Frugal Innovation: Core Competencies to Address Global Sustainability. *Journal of Management for Global Sustainability, 2*, 63–82.

Beugelsdijk, S. (2008). Strategic Human Resource Practices and Product Innovation. *Organization Studies, 29*(6), 821–847. https://doi.org/10.1177/0170840608090530

Black, S. E., & Lynch, L. M. (2004). What's Driving the New Economy?: The Benefits of Workplace Innovation*. *The Economic Journal, 114*(493), F97–F116. https://doi.org/10.1111/j.0013-0133.2004.00189.x

Bock, A. J., Opsahl, T., George, G., & Gann, D. M. (2012). The Effects of Culture and Structure on Strategic Flexibility during Business Model Innovation. *Journal of Management Studies, 49*(2), 279–305. https://doi.org/10.1111/j.1467-6486.2011.01030.x

Bos-Nehles, A. C., & Veenendaal, A. A. R. (2019). Perceptions of HR Practices and Innovative Work Behavior: The Moderating Effect of an Innovative Climate. *The International Journal of Human Resource Management, 30*(18), 2661–2683. https://doi.org/10.1080/09585192.2017.1380680

Burcharth, A., Præst Knudsen, M., & Søndergaard, H. A. (2017). The Role of Employee Autonomy for Open Innovation Performance. *Business Process Management Journal, 23*(6), 1245–1269. https://doi.org/10.1108/bpmj-10-2016-0209

Dorenbosch, L., van Engen, M., & Verhagen, M. (2005). On-the-job Innovation: The Impact of Job Design and Human Resource Management Through Production Ownership. *Creativity and Innovation Management, 14*(2), 129–141.

Dreher, A. (2003). What Does Conceptual Research have to Offer? In M. Leuzinger-Bohleber, A. Dreher, & J. Canestri (Eds.), *Pluralism and Unity? Methods of Research in Psychoanalysis* (pp. 109–124). London IPA.

George, G., McGahan, A. M., & Prabhu, J. (2012). Innovation for Inclusive Growth: Towards a Theoretical Framework and a Research Agenda. *Journal of Management Studies, 49*(4), 661–683. https://doi.org/10.1111/j.1467-6486.2012.01048.x

Hyypiä, M., & Khan, R. (2018). Overcoming Barriers to Frugal Innovation: Emerging Opportunities for Finnish SMEs in Brazilian Markets. *Technology Innovation Management Review, 8*(4), 38–48.

Jacobsen, D. I., Hillestad, T., Yttri, B., & Hildrum, J. (2019). Alternative Routes to Innovation—the Effects of Cultural and Structural Fit. *International Journal of Innovation Management*, 2050006. https://doi.org/10.1142/s1363919620500061

Knorringa, P., Peša, I., Leliveld, A., & van Beers, C. (2016). Frugal Innovation and Development: Aides or Adversaries? *The European Journal of Development Research, 28*(2), 143–153. https://doi.org/10.1057/ejdr.2016.3

Laforet, S. (2016). Effects of Organisational Culture on Organisational Innovation Performance in Family Firms. *Journal of Small Business and Enterprise Development, 23*(2), 379–407. https://doi.org/10.1108/jsbed-02-2015-0020

Leliveld, A., & Knorringa, P. (2017). Frugal Innovation and Development Research. *The European Journal of Development Research, 30*(1), 1–16. https://doi.org/10.1057/s41287-017-0121-4

Martínez-Costa, M., Jiménez-Jiménez, D., & Dine Rabeh, H. A. (2019). The Effect of Organisational Learning on Interorganisational Collaborations in Innovation: An Empirical Study in SMEs. *Knowledge Management Research & Practice, 17*(2), 137–150. https://doi.org/10.1080/14778238.2018.1538601

McMurray, A., & Dorai, R. (2003). *Workplace Innovation Scale: A New Method for Measuring Innovation in the Workplace.* Paper presented at the Organisational Learning and Knowledge 5th International Conference, Lancaster University, UK.

McMurray, A. J., Islam, M. M., Sarros, J. C., & Pirola-Merlo, A. (2013). Workplace Innovation in a Nonprofit Organization. *Nonprofit Management and Leadership, 23*(3), 367–388. https://doi.org/10.1002/nml.21066

Meagher, K. (2018). Cannibalizing the Informal Economy: Frugal Innovation and Economic Inclusion in Africa. *The European Journal of Development Research, 30*(1), 17–33. https://doi.org/10.1057/s41287-017-0113-4

Muenjohn, N., & McMurray, A. (2017). Design Leadership, Work Values Ethic and Workplace Innovation: An Investigation of SMEs in Thailand and Vietnam. *Asia Pacific Business Review, 23*(2), 192–204. https://doi.org/10.1080/1360238 1.2017.1281642

Oeij, P., Dhondt, S., Kraan, K., Vergeer, R., & Pot, F. (2012). Workplace Innovation and its Relations with Organisational Performance and Employee Commitment. *Lifelong Learning in Europe, Article, 10*(4), 1–15.

Pot, F. (2011). Workplace Innovation for Better Jobs and Performance. *International Journal of Productivity and Performance Management, 60*(4), 404–415.

Pot, F., Dhondt, S., & Oeij, P. (2012). Social Innovation of Work and Employment In. In H. Franz, J. Hochgerner, & J. Howaldt (Eds.), *Challenge Social Innovation.* Berlin: Springer.

Pot, F. D., Totterdill, P., & Dhondt, S. (2017). European Policy on Workplace Innovation. In P. Oeij, D. Rus, & F. Pot (Eds.), *Workplace Innovation: Theory, Research and Practice* (pp. 11–26). Cham: Springer.

Prabhu, J., & Jain, S. (2015). Innovation and Entrepreneurship in India: Understanding Jugaad. *Asia Pacific Journal of Management, 32*, 843–868.

Prahalad, C. K. (2006). The Innovation Sandbox. *Strategy + Business, 44*, 1–10.

Radjou, N., & Prabhu, J. (2014). *Frugal Innovation: How to Do More with Less.* London: Profile Books.

Radjou, N., Prabhu, J. C., & Ahuja, S. (2012). *Jugaad Innovation think Frugal, Be Flexible, Generate Breakthrough Growth* (1st ed.). San Francisco, CA: Jossey-Bass, A Wiley Imprint.

Rosca, E., Arnold, M., & Bendul, J. C. (2017). Business Models for Sustainable Innovation—an Empirical Analysis of Frugal Products and Services. *Journal of Cleaner Production, 162,* S133–S145. https://doi.org/10.1016/j.jclepro.2016.02.050

Rothwell, R. (1992). Successful Industrial Innovation: Critical Factors for the 1990s. *R&D Management, 22*(3), 221–238.

Sehgal, V., Dehoff, K., & Panneer, G. (2010). The Importance of Frugal Engineering. *Strategy + Business, 59,* 1–5.

Soni, P., & Krishnan, R. (2014). Frugal Innovation: Aligning Theory, Practice, and Public Policy. *Journal of Indian Business Research, 6*(1), 29–47. https://doi.org/10.1108/jibr-03-2013-0025

Soosay, C. A., Hyland, P. W., & Ferrer, M. (2008). Supply Chain Collaboration: Capabilities for Continuous Innovation. *Supply Chain Management: An International Journal, 13*(2), 160–169. https://doi.org/10.1108/13598540810860994

Sørensen, E., & Torfing, J. (2011). Enhancing Collaborative Innovation in the Public Sector. *Administration & Society, 43*(8), 842–868. https://doi.org/10.1177/0095399711418768

Tiwari, R., & Herstatt, C. (2012). Frugal Innovation: A Global Networks' Perspective. *Swiss Journal of Business Research and Practice, 66*(3), 245–274.

Totterdill, P. (2015). Closing the Gap: The Fith Element of Workplace Innovation. *European Journal of Workplace Innovation, 1*(1), 55–74.

Totterdill, P., & Exton, R. (2014). Defining Workplace Innovation. *Strategic Direction, 30*(9), 12–16. https://doi.org/10.1108/sd-09-2014-0112

Weyrauch, T., & Herstatt, C. (2016). What is Frugal Innovation? Three Defining Criteria. *Journal of Frugal Innovation, 2*(1). https://doi.org/10.1186/s40669-016-0005-y

Xin, S., Tribe, J., & Chambers, D. (2013). Conceptual Research in Tourism. *Annals of Tourism Research, 41,* 66–88. https://doi.org/10.1016/j.annals.2012.12.003

22

Recognizing the Value of Unsuccessful Innovations: A Case Study from the Dairy Industry in Mexico

Andres Ramirez-Portilla and Erick G. Torres

Introduction

The importance of milk in human nutrition dates back to ancient times and stems from not only milk's nutritional benefits, which affect much of the global population, but also its significant economic and financial impacts. According to the United Nations' Food and Agriculture Organization, more than six billion people worldwide, primarily in developing countries, consume dairy products daily (FAO, 2020). While the per capita consumption of dairy products is expected to be higher in developed countries, the gap between these nations and many developing countries is rapidly narrowing. This phenomenon makes sense since many countries in the developing world have long traditions of milk production, and dairy products play an essential role in the diet now more than ever. Rising incomes, population growth, urbanization, and changes in diets, among other factors, have all fostered a

A. Ramirez-Portilla (✉)
Departamento de Estudios Empresariales, Universidad Iberoamericana,
Mexico City, Mexico
e-mail: andres.ramirez@ibero.mx

E. G. Torres
Departamento de Ingeniería Química Industrial y de Alimentos, Universidad
Iberoamericana, Mexico City, Mexico
e-mail: erick.torres@ibero.mx

© The Author(s), under exclusive license to Springer Nature Switzerland AG 2021
A. McMurray et al. (eds.), *The Palgrave Handbook of Workplace Innovation*,
https://doi.org/10.1007/978-3-030-59916-4_22

407

continuously growing demand for milk and milk products in developing countries in the last decade (Faye & Konuspayeva, 2012).

Different organizations agree that the growing demand for dairy products offers an excellent opportunity for several actors to enhance their livelihoods by increasing production with sustainable practices (FAO, 2020; IDF, 2020; WWF, 2020). These actors include dairy farmers, co-ops, producers, other actors in the dairy chain, and communities in high-potential, peri-urban areas. While all dairy chain actors are vital for industry development, the companies that produce and sell dairy products are the ones setting the industry's pace. However, increasing production and sales in the dairy industry is a matter of not only investing money but having the proper strategy and innovation capabilities to meet market needs. In this regard, though the dairy industry is considered a mature industry that follows a more traditional approach, innovation plays a vital role. Previous research on innovation in the dairy industry has focused on the role of collaborative partnerships in industrial innovation (Hartwich & Negro, 2010), the program team approach to dairy industry innovation (Nettle, Brightling, & Hope, 2013), and the public support of innovations to increase the competitiveness of the dairy industry (Špička, Smutka, & Selby, 2015).

These studies in the dairy industry reflect the majority of innovation literature, which focuses on understanding the positive side of innovation (Fagerberg & Verspagen, 2009; Tidd & Bessant, 2014). However, several authors have studied a variety of specific factors underlying the success and failure of innovation projects (Heidenreich & Spieth, 2013; Van der Panne, Van Beers, & Kleinknecht, 2003). Thus, it is also relevant to explore the less positive side of dairy industry innovation: specifically, the innovations introduced and adopted by dairy companies that are unsuccessful. This chapter presents the case study of Alpura, the second-largest dairy company in Mexico (Alpura, 2020), a country 14th in milk production worldwide, with a complex mix of more than 26 large domestic and international dairy companies. Innovating in this very competitive space is a matter not of choice, but of survival.

The case study in this chapter seeks to describe the dynamics and roles involved in recognizing the value of unsuccessful innovations implemented by the firm Alpura, which, until a few years ago, was the leader in its market for several decades. By focusing on the arrival of a new chief executive officer (CEO) as a change agent and considering the importance of the decision process for innovations, this case study aims to provide an optimistic view of how innovation failures can be capitalized. Therefore, the research question that this investigation attempts to answer is, How can a firm recognize the value of its unsuccessful innovations to avoid similar mistakes in the future? In this context, Alpura's case study is interesting because it shows the importance for any organization of recognizing the value of innovation mistakes for improving future innovation efforts.

The chapter is structured as follows. After this introduction, Section "Theoretical Framework" explains the basis of the theoretical perspectives used to better understand Alpura's dynamics and decisions in recent years. Section "Methodology" describes the methodology used to collect and analyze the data. Section "Results and Findings" presents the main results and insights, which are later discussed in Section "Discussion." Finally, Section "Conclusions" outlines the conclusions, future research directions, and managerial implications of this chapter.

Theoretical Framework

Innovations are an outcome sought by the majority of firms, which devote resources to achieve them. Though firms do not pursue unsuccessful innovations, they are intrinsic to the innovation process (Rhaiem & Amara, 2019); thus, firms must understand how to manage them (Tidd & Bessant, 2014; Tidd, Pavitt, & Bessant, 2001; Van der Panne et al., 2003). However, before exploring the logic of why firms may seek to develop or adopt a potential innovation that later fails, it is relevant to define innovation and unsuccessful innovation. Scholars have agreed that innovation can be both a process and a result. So, on the one hand, innovation can be seen as the process of turning ideas into reality and capturing value through search, selection, implementation, and value capture (Tidd & Bessant, 2014). On the other hand, innovation can be seen as the result of any implementation of a process, product, or management approach that is sufficiently novel to improve current results (Mortensen & Bloch, 2005). Whether innovation is viewed as a process or an outcome, failure can occur at any stage of innovation development (Rhaiem & Amara, 2019).

A recent edition of *The Oslo Manual* (OECD/Eurostat, 2018) defined innovation as "a new or improved product or process (or a combination thereof) that differs significantly from the unit's previous products or processes and that has been made available to potential users (product) or brought into use by the unit (process)" (p. 32). One could argue that an unsuccessful innovation is a proposed new effort that does not fulfill these criteria and which units or users may choose to adopt or not. To better understand why potential users may not decide to use an innovation, it is necessary to also understand the acceptance and rejection of innovations characterized by their adoption processes. In this context, a useful framework for exploring the causes and effects of unsuccessful innovations could be the theory of the diffusion of innovations (Rogers, 1962). For decades, academics from different disciplines have used this theory to understand the process of adoption and rejection of any innovation or new idea (Sriwannawit & Sandström, 2015).

The basis of the diffusion of innovations theory lies in understanding and being flexible about what can be considered an innovation. Rogers (2003) proposed a simple definition: an innovation can be an idea, practice, or object that is perceived as new by an individual or other unit of adoption. Therefore, innovation is a broad term that can refer to a wide variety of outcomes, as long as it is perceived as new by its adopters. The second basis of this theory is the diffusion process. Concerning the disciplines in the social sciences, diffusion is considered the process by which an innovation spreads among potential adopters (Teece, 1980). Within this diffusion process, Rogers (2003) noticed the importance of the selection mechanisms chosen by prospective users and proposed a decision process with five stages key to understanding why and when an individual adopts or rejects an innovation. These five stages of knowledge, persuasion, decision, implementation, and confirmation are always preceded by conditions that trigger the process, such as previous practice, innovativeness, social system norms, and the needs or problems felt by the potential users.

All stages of the process are essential, and, with each one, the user develops a more informed idea about whether to adopt or reject an innovation. However, while this process explains the decision to accept or reject an innovation, the drive to innovate or not is explained by a variety of theories and models focusing on internal and external factors (Van der Panne et al., 2003). A theoretical perspective appropriate for exploring the innovation decision process in firms within the dairy industry is agency theory, due to its notions about the principal–agent problem and the multiple-principal problem. Agency theory not only offers unique insights into incentives and outcome uncertainty when coupled with complementary perspectives, but is ideal for studying the difficulties faced by organizations with a cooperative structure (Eisenhardt, 1989a). Such structures are common in the dairy industry, especially in developing economies, where milk ranchers and dairy producers organize into cooperatives seeking jointly owned enterprises.

Agency theory is also useful in the dairy industry context in developing economies because it assumes that owners and managers follow a classical form of economic behavior within a firm. This behavior considers the organization to be a set of contracts among production factors, with each element motivated and driven first by its self-interest and then by the interests of others (Fama, 1980). This dynamic is often seen as an agency relationship involving a contract between one or more persons (the principal[s]) engaging another person (the agent) to perform some service on their behalf: a relationship that inherently involves delegating some decision-making authority to the designated agent (Eisenhardt, 1989a). However, if both parties are considered to be utility maximizers, there is an apparent rationality to believing that the agent will not always act in the principal's best interests (Jensen & Meckling, 1976). For instance, though the principal may follow a conservative approach to innovation, the agent could be focused on pursuing radical innovations by any means due to the firm's competitive environment.

This conflict of interest between principal and agent is commonly known as the agency problem or the principal–agent problem. Fortunately, the principal–agent problem can be minimized with the appropriate mechanisms. For instance, the principal can limit discrepancies from his or her interest by defining incentives for the agent or by implementing monitoring mechanisms designed to constrain any deviant initiatives (Jensen & Meckling, 1976). These monitoring mechanisms often incur costs, but not having them may cause the agent to make suboptimal decisions from the principal's point of view. Another difficulty of the principal–agent relationship involves the agent reacting more to external influences than the principal's desires. For example, a firm may be disciplined by competition from other firms. Not considering these firms will impact the performance of the agent, regardless of whether the principal is aware of their influence (Fama, 1980). Many managers try to implement innovations that mirror those of their competitors; however, some principals may disagree with this strategy due to the high risks and costs of innovation processes.

Finally, the agent–principal equation becomes more complex when one considers the multiple-principal problem. This problem refers to the scenario in which a firm has multiple collective action problems and must balance the interests of multiple principals or stakeholders (Voorn, van Genugten, & van Thiel, 2019). While some firms (e.g., small- to medium-sized enterprises, or SMEs) have only one principal (the owner) and one agent (the top manager), large firms often have multiple collective problems stemming from multiple shareholders and even multiple agents (Eisenhardt, 1989a). The resulting multiplicity of interactions can complicate the innovation process, increasing the probability of failure. Another explanation for the link between agency problems and unsuccessful innovations concerns the importance of managers' perceived value. In a recent study, O'Connor and Shaikh (2018) found that the firms that continuously struggle with innovation are the ones that also have managers that overinvest free cash flows into innovation efforts with limited commercial value. Despite the high number of probable unsuccessful innovations, the authors agree that this type of opportunistic manager is interested in portraying a high innovation profile for both themselves and the firm they manage, even at the expense of shareholders.

Therefore, in addition to users and their passive and active resistance to innovation (Heidenreich & Spieth, 2013), agents also play a significant role in producing successful or unsuccessful innovations (O'Connor & Shaikh. 2018). However, failing while innovating is not entirely a negative thing, since such experiences can be capitalized. Some authors consider failure to be an essential part of innovation, suggesting that greater exposure to failure might provide more learning opportunities to reduce failures in the future (Rhaiem & Amara, 2019). Figure 22.1 presents a theoretical figure for this chapter that comprises all the above-mentioned ideas relating to the innovation decision process and the role of agents in this process. In Fig. 22.1, the five stages of the decision process proposed by Rogers (1962, 2003) are complemented by more specific communication channels among the different types of actors. The arrows pointing from internal and external communication channels to the various stages indicate the importance of the different actors, including agents, in supporting or undermining the adoption or rejection of innovations within and outside the firm.

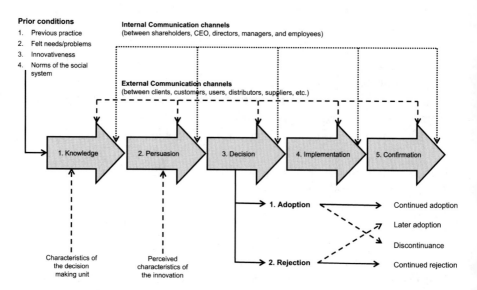

Fig. 22.1 Decision process for internal and external innovation efforts. (Source: Adapted from Rogers, 1962, 2003)

Methodology

To answer the research question of how a firm can recognize the value of its unsuccessful innovations to avoid repeating similar mistakes in the future, an instrumental case study of the firm Alpura was conducted from fall 2017 to fall 2019. An instrumental case study was chosen to support a focus not on Alpura's uniqueness as a firm, but on the processes, dynamics, and rationales of a firm that had lost its long leadership position in the local dairy industry and sought to regain it. The case study was built on qualitative data obtained from a mix of primary and secondary sources. Data from primary sources were collected through semi-structured interviews with decision-makers in top managerial positions within Alpura, and data from secondary sources were obtained to confirm the respondents' assertions. Before the interview sessions, an identical interview script, along with a brief description of the research objectives, was sent by e-mail to each of the target managers. The interview sessions were conducted in the company's facilities (headquarters, production plant, and research center) in Cuautitlan, in the outskirts of Mexico City.

The interviewees included the chief executive officer (CEO), intelligence business officer (IBO), R&D officer (R&DO), commercial officer (COO), quality officer (QO), IT officer (ITO), digital innovation manager (DIM), and production manager (PM). These interviewees were selected because they are the firm's top decision-makers and have the best possible information about the company's operational areas and innovations efforts. Credibility was achieved not only through the nature of the interviewees' positions, but also through their voluntary and open participation. This active and positive participation was evident in the interview sessions, during which interviewees answered freely and extensively, and through their willingness for their words to be quoted both during and after the study. These interactions also allowed a degree of reflexivity, since the researchers were able to revisit some interviewees' responses during other interviews. All the interviews were recorded in a digital format (summing more than 12 hours), which allowed the authors to review them at will.

To facilitate the conduction of the interviews and the subsequent analysis of data, the interview script was divided into two sections with complementary objectives. The first section aimed to identify the information the managers drew from the local and international business environment to shape their competitive strategy and consequent innovation strategy. The second section sought to understand the structure of the managers' innovation frames and

414 A. Ramirez-Portilla and E. G. Torres

procedures for new products and new business process development. The information used to better understand the value of unsuccessful innovation emerged mainly from questions in the second section related to innovation priorities, the roles of internal and external agents in innovation, and the approaches used in the innovation processes. Each department head was asked about their innovation process via a general question: What is the process of innovation for your department? This question was complemented with specific questions inquiring about setting objectives; testing and validating steps; formulating innovation projects; and learning from the outcomes, barriers, and lessons of innovation efforts.

As part of the interview script formulation process, the questions were reviewed by another researcher with vast experience in face-to-face interviews and qualitative data analysis, as well as by two managers of small and medium companies within the dairy value chain. The questionnaire was also thoroughly tested with the plant manager and general director of a medium-sized dairy company in another region in Mexico to assess its external validity. Before its final application, some questions were adjusted following suggestions made during the external validation process. Conceptual saturation was achieved in the case study through two different approaches. First, a set of similar follow-up questions were asked to interviewees during the semi-structured interviews regardless of their first answers. Second, other follow-up questions considered answers from other interviews to crossmatch responses to obtain new data. After the eight interviews, lasting on average more than 1 hour 20 minutes each, it was seen that interviewees did not offer further information.

The secondary data collection was considered to be a complementary step needed to confirm the respondents' assertions and minimize biases within interviewees' responses resulting from the prioritization of recent events. This step was essential to verify whether successful and unsuccessful innovations were considered as such not only by the respondents, but also by the organization as a whole and the market in general. The secondary data collection process followed the logic of using and analyzing multiple sources of evidence to triangulate the initial information obtained (Yin, 1994). The sources were all trusted information sources, including news and articles from recognized online newspapers and magazines, online videos from media, websites from Alpura's competitors, reports from Mexico's dairy industry association, and Alpura's internal annual reports. In addition, the researchers took notes during on-site visits and conducted brief informal interviews and chats with current and former Alpura employees identified and recommended by the human resources department.

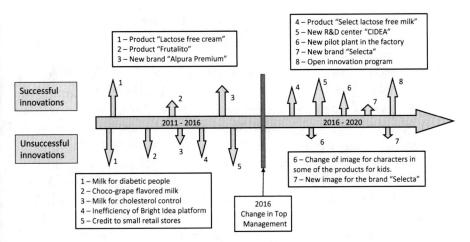

Fig. 22.2 Timeline to analyze and understand Alpura's innovation efforts

The data analysis followed a context-dependency approach to identify singular characteristics of different situations within the case study (Eisenhardt, 1989b). This approach was chosen because, though Alpura lacked clear internal records on its number of successful and unsuccessful innovations, the company experienced a critical event that influenced most subsequent innovation decisions. The importance of this event is depicted in Fig. 22.2, which also presents some of the significant successful and unsuccessful innovations mentioned by the interviewees. The arrows of different sizes represent the interviewees' relative importance to these innovation efforts and indicate a trend from more failures to more successes following the arrival of the new CEO. The data were analyzed using a qualitative content analysis that included open manual coding by each author. The coding process involved structuring the information related to the object of study into themes and later comparing the categories that emerged from the different interviews. To ensure internal validity, the coding and category comparisons were made individually by each researcher and then discussed until a consensus was reached.

Results and Findings

The main findings and insights from the Alpura case can divided into two sections. The first includes vital aspects of the competitive industry environment, Alpura's operative and competitive strategies, Alpura's former innovation strategy, and unsuccessful innovation projects and launchings. The second describes the significant change milestone in Alpura's management, which led to a refocusing of Alpura's innovation strategy, including the identification of barriers to innovation and new ways of measuring innovation within the firm.

To understand the causes of some of its most significant challenges, it is useful to explain the firm's origin. Alpura was created in 1970 through the union of several farmers in different regions in Mexico to more efficiently process and market milk (Alpura, 2020). While Alpura is the company's trade name, its legal name is Ganaderos Productores de Leche Pura (in English, Pure Milk-Producing Ranchers). This legal name reflects how Alpura was born and the nature of the majority of Alpura shareholders. Today, Alpura remains a 100% Mexican cooperative with a family business approach (i.e., many current shareholders are the children and grandchildren of the ranchers who started Alpura). The company employs approximately 5000 direct and 7000 indirect workers and owns 123 ranches in 11 of Mexico's 32 states. The company's dairy herd comprises 140,000 Holstein cows that produce 3,000,000 liters of milk a day. Alpura's product range includes various types and packaging styles of milk, cream, cheese, butter, yogurt, desserts, and local dairy products. Alpura owns transportation for logistics, and its distribution network comprises 30 company-owned warehouses and 63 distributors throughout Mexico.

In Mexico, the current competitive environment in the dairy products market is intense, and rivalry between the participants is expected to increase in the short term. This challenging situation is mainly due to the low organic growth rates expected in coming years, the imminent diversification of products, the critical marketing capabilities of large transnational companies, and the entry of new brands and products. Further, consumers are increasingly demanding immediate perceived benefits and more information about the products and their supply chains. The Mexican dairy industry comprises a complex mix of 3803 firms, of which 61 are big companies and 6 hold more than 50% of the market (CANILEC, 2019). While the big players, such as Lactalis, Nestle, Coca-Cola, Chobani, Danone, and Yoplait, are present in the industry through various brands, two large local companies—Lala and Alpura—lead the market with 21.5% and 10.8% market share, respectively. The interviewees noted that the three strategies all the large dairy companies implement to grow their market share are buying smaller companies, improving existing products, and generating new products according to market trends.

Historically, Alpura's business model was based purely on the industrialization of milk, and the company's competitive advantage depended on the quality of milk and its derivatives. Alpura identifies this approach as operational excellence and clarifies that high quality has been the company's driver and primary strategy since its foundation. Alpura's operational excellence has been possible due to full integration with ranchers, which allows high-quality control (even above regulations) over the entire value chain, from forage and cattle breeding to distribution. As the Mexican market leader for many years, Alpura introduced significant processes and product innovations within both the firm and the Mexican dairy industry as a whole. Some examples mentioned by the interviewees included the first version of Ultra-High Temperature (UHT) or ultra-pasteurized milk in the Mexican market and the production of yogurt through evaporation instead of milk reconstitution. Although these innovations were first in the country, they were not first in the world, emphasizing the foreign import of most new process technologies and product ideas during Alpura's first decades of operation. Alpura is also aware that most product decisions during these decades were product improvements designed as defensive tactics against competition (i.e., flankers), rather than original products created by the firm (i.e., innovations).

In general, consumers consider the dairy industry to be an innovative industry because they see new dairy products and original packaging each season. In an innovative industry, competitors are expected to continually innovate through new products and improvements in the value chain. However, this is not always the case for all dairy industry actors, as was confirmed by the strategy Alpura followed for several years. Until 2015, the group of milk ranchers who serve as the principal shareholders of Alpura were primarily interested in industrializing their product and improving its quality, thinking this was best way to generate value for the company. In other words, Alpura's former innovation strategy was based on acquiring state-of-the-art technology to improve the quality, safety, and sanitation of processes and products. While Alpura did create new products in the past, the company's former approach to innovation and product development was more traditional. For instance, from 1972 to 2014, the firm launched only 17 new or improved products (Alpura, 2020), which translates to one new product every two and a half years. In the last decade, Alpura's main competitor and market leader produced a new product approximately every six months (Lala, 2020).

What was the reason for Alpura's low pace of innovation? While multiple factors influenced the company's traditional approach toward innovations, interviewees consistently mentioned three primary contributors. First, old-fashioned milk ranchers, who form Alpura's principal shareholders, had significant influence over the company's decisions related to growth, expansion, and more secure investments. Second, Alpura's leadership positions, represented by various CEOs and their teams, generally complied with shareholders' desire to focus primarily on quality, without seriously considering other options to increase the firm's value. Third, and likely the most surprising, Alpura viewed unsuccessful innovation experiences as a waste of time and resources and failed to learn from previous mistakes. This is a common issue, since innovation failure does not directly contribute to a company's economic and strategic goals.

While Alpura's approach worked two decades ago, the company is learning the hard way that, in the current dairy market, innovation is not a choice, but a matter of survival. After losing market share for several months, Alpura hired a new CEO at the beginning of 2016. This new CEO differed significantly from the board's previous choices, and within a month, he exhibited a clear transformational leadership style. He made changes in top management and empowered officers and directors that had previously been neglected. He also began to position the customer at the center of decisions and to listen to new ideas from employees. His significant adjustments to top management resulted in immediate changes in how Alpura saw and developed innovation to regain its leadership. A historical diagnosis (requested by the new CEO) allowed Alpura to analyze previous unsuccessful innovations and learn from its failures. The new CEO made it clear to all shareholders and employees that, if properly managed, unsuccessful innovations could serve as learning mechanisms that could add to the firm's capabilities and value.

In the following, we summarize some of the unsuccessful innovations most frequently mentioned by the interviewees and therefore considered to be the most relevant for Alpura. These failed innovations are divided into commercial, product, and process efforts. On the commercial side, there was a proposal to give credits to small retail and mom-and-pop stores to incentivize their operation. Alpura launched a campaign and developed all the financial systems required for this initiative; however, these efforts yielded only meager application. Alpura later understood that the owners of these stores did not need this financial tool and preferred more commercial tools, such as promotions and discounts. On the product side, Alpura suffered three major failed product launches: choco-grape flavored milk, milk for people with diabetes, and dairy that helps to control cholesterol. Although previous market studies and focus groups indicated these products to be viable, subsequent analyses suggested that the failures were rooted in understatements of government regulations, confusing packaging, and improper marketing. Alpura is now aware of the importance of adequately branding new products, understanding official norms, and double-checking every market study. On the process side, the digital innovation department bought the license for a platform called Bright Idea to allow employees to propose new ideas for innovations. In two months, the platform received more than 2000 submissions: an outcome that seemed to indicate success. However, when the ideas were reviewed, only four did not concern correcting broken processes. From this, Alpura learned that it is not necessary to have a state-of-the-art platform for soliciting ideas from employees; instead, the company must first disseminate a culture of innovation throughout the company.

Years after the failed product launches, another study requested by the new CEO and the R&D officer shed new light on the logic behind their failures. The study suggested that consumers often seek immediately noticeable benefits, rather than long-term benefits. For instance, consumers are more interested in lactose-free milk than low-fat milk, milk for controlling cholesterol, or milk for people with diabetes. The reason is that lactose-free milk has immediate benefits during digestion, whereas the other types of milk do not yield valuable results until later. This study illustrates the CEO's new approach toward innovation, which emphasizes that the additional effort and expenditures made to launch these products were still useful in better understanding and learning from the reasons for their failure. Other compelling evidence of the new CEO's refocusing of Alpura's innovation strategy concerns the firm's efforts to begin defining new ways of measuring innovation and identifying barriers to innovation.

For many years, Alpura believed that innovation should be measured primarily by its quality results and the number of new or improved products launched into the market. Innovation by itself did not add direct value to the firm; instead, the benefits were attributed to Alpura's operational excellence and product sales. This has changed since the arrival of the new CEO, and one of Alpura's current goals is for innovation to increase the company's sales by 12%. Until now, there have been no disaggregated indicators of the company's innovation processes, but the company is now working to understanding different ways to measure innovation progress. For instance, in addition to considering the percentage of successful product launches or the percentage contribution to the company's net sales, top management is now also measuring value generation as an increase in profit, a decrease in risk, or cost reductions. Once Alpura has consolidated basic scientific research, it will also measure the number of patents generated. Finally, a significant positive effect of recognizing the value of unsuccessful innovations has been the identification of barriers to innovation. In this regard, Alpura now continuously analyzes its internal structures, people, processes, incentives, external environment, and ecosystems of operation to identify innovation obstacles faced in the past. Using this process, Alpura has already detected several internal and external barriers that slow innovation in the firm (Table 22.1).

Table 22.1   The collected information from Alpura's managers

Barriers	Examples of identified and confirmed barriers
Internal	• Internal strategic decisions that have not foreseen the need for technological updating. • Resistance to change by some employees, managers, suppliers, and even shareholders. • Lack of understanding in the organization of the new collaborative culture for innovation. • Deficiency in the communication of the new approach to the client. • Absence of involvement of operational personnel due to rigid hierarchical structures that inhibit active participation. • Shortage of a specific budget for R&D. • Nonexistence of specific budget for product and process innovation. • Lack of investment in software • Deficiency of training in the use of information technology.
External	• Technological knowledge of transformation processes is not for sale, usually only for rent. • Technological dependence of operation and packaging equipment due to limited suppliers. • The bureaucracy and the politicization in the relationship with universities. • Lack of full knowledge of regulatory restrictions from government institutions • Absence of fiscal support for innovation from government

Source: Own elaboration

Discussion

The dairy industry will continue to grow in the coming years due to unrelenting population growth, inflating income levels, rising health consciousness among consumers, and the burgeoning food and beverage (F&B) sector. According to the IMARC Group's (2019) global dairy market report, the market reached a value of US$718.9 billion in 2019 and is projected to reach US$1032.7 billion by 2024. Being a market leader in the dairy industry can be very valuable; however, as in many other mature industries and sectors, the capacity to innovate is crucial. Mature industries innovate more slowly than emerging and growing industries, implementing more incremental and conservative changes that focus on process innovations rather than product innovations. Alpura's case is an interesting context for analyzing how this traditional view has changed and modern companies in mature industries need to focus equally on both types of innovations. To succeed in these new industry dynamics, Alpura must not only continue using low- and medium-level technologies (i.e., use indirect R&D intensity) to improve its production processes, but also constantly output the types of incremental innovations being pursued by competitors.

However, as Alpura's case shows, following this path is challenging without a change in the firm's mindset as a traditional cooperative dairy company with multiple shareholders. In Alpura, this mindset shift was triggered by the arrival of a new CEO with a vision that differed from that of the shareholders, who are mostly traditional milk ranchers. While an agency problem was identified at the beginning between the agent and the multiple principals (Voorn et al., 2019), this problem has been managed and minimized in recent years. More specifically, the CEO's first action of acknowledging previous unsuccessful innovations was not well received by the shareholders (i.e., risk-averse and heritage-proud milk ranchers). Fortunately, the ranchers were soon open to accepting the new CEO's ideas, since he reminded them that the entire cooperative of ranchers had delegated decision-making authority (Eisenhardt, 1989a) to him to regain market leadership. It also helped that the shareholders and the new CEO defined precise monitoring mechanisms and incentives (Jensen & Meckling, 1976) that helped to establish a clear common ground for the two parties' particular and shared interests.

Together, these actions allowed the new CEO and his team to operate with more flexibility, which enabled them to promptly identify and understand the barriers encountered by employees and customers during the decision innovation process. Now, the company is aware of numerous and complex innovation barriers that were previously not even in the firm's radar. These barriers include resistance to change, the lack of a collaborative culture, rigidities in administrative management, a lack of investment in innovation, technological dependence in the transformation and manufacturing processes, and regulatory constraints, among others. Overcoming these barriers in the coming years will not be an easy task, but Alpura has taken the first steps to better understand how to refocus its innovation strategy by learning from previous mistakes. For instance, the company now accepts new ways of measuring innovation and creating value. Most importantly, it recognizes that a more collaborative and proactive approach toward innovation needs to be the central element of Alpura's competitive strategy, as has been seen in other contexts in the F&B industry (Brunswicker & Vanhaverbeke, 2014; Hartwich & Negro, 2010; Nettle et al., 2013; Špička et al., 2015).

Regarding the causes and effects of unsuccessful innovations in Alpura, it would be unfair to blame previous CEOs' management or the traditional perspectives of the milk rancher shareholders. Instead, the diffusion of innovations theory (Rogers, 1962) suggests that Alpura's previous innovations may have failed because Alpura did not properly manage the adoption process. The organizational and market dynamics into which innovations were launched or implemented can be depicted in Rogers' (1962) five-step decision innovation

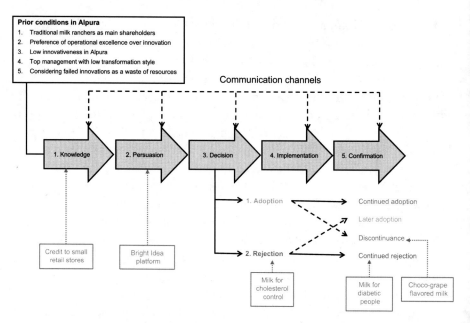

Fig. 22.3 Allocation of Alpura's unsuccessful innovations in the innovation decision process. (Source: Adapted from Rogers, 1962, 2003)

process (Fig. 22.3). For example, the innovation of offering credit to small retail stores was legitimate, but the company failed to educate the store owners on the benefits of such financial tools. In the case of the Bright Idea platform, the high number of submissions that did not offer new ideas or potential innovations suggests that more persuasion was necessary to convince employees to submit valuable rather than numerous ideas. Also, Alpura's decisions to ideate, develop, and launch three innovative products yielded different rejection processes. First, the product idea of milk for cholesterol control was rejected almost instantly during focus groups with consumers stopping its further commercialization. Second, the commercialized product of milk for people with diabetes continued to be rejected even after a campaign to show the product's benefits. Finally, while consumers partially adopted the choco-grape flavored milk sold in stores, this adoption lasted only a few weeks before consumption stopped due to the product's strange flavor and color.

Conclusions

This case study's global insights suggest that Mexico's dairy industry follows a global trend of moderate growth due to an increasing demand for healthy and nutrient-rich food products. The interviewed directors and managers identified similar key aspects and patterns that the whole industry will consider in the future; these are necessary inputs for Alpura's strategic planning in coming years. Some of these critical aspects and trends of which Alpura is aware are the annual demand of milk and derivates; raw yearly milk production and offerings; imminent product diversification of the portfolios of big players; new tendencies toward organic, high-protein, sustainable products; a preference among consumers to buy products of companies that stand for social responsibility; technological manufacturing upgrades; and emerging information technologies along the supply chain. However, knowing these trends is useless if Alpura does not understand how to best explore and exploit them. Thus, it is crucial to recognize the value of previous unsuccessful innovations and innovation failures.

Overall, we were able to answer the research question of how a firm can recognize the value of unsuccessful innovations to avoid similar mistakes in the future. More specifically, by obtaining and corroborating firsthand information from top management, we have shown the crucial role of the CEO and top management in acknowledging the failures of previous innovations and understanding how to refrain from similar mistakes in the future through better information communication during the different stages of the decision process to accelerate the adoption or minimize the rejection of an innovation. Thus, this case adds to the body of literature illustrating the importance of both managing the innovation diffusion process appropriately and having the right mechanisms to allow a good relationship among multiple principals and agents. In addition, the contribution of this case to practitioners is not limited to managers of companies in the dairy industry but may also be useful to managers in other mature and traditional sectors. The Alpura case may also help managers envision their internal and external innovation efforts during the five stages of the innovation decision process. This exercise can help to pinpoint significant issues that may limit organizations' ability to move forward in adopting and diffusing their innovations.

Finally, we acknowledge that this study has some limitations. For instance, the case study could have yielded more insights from not only top management but also employees from all levels. This opens the opportunity for future studies using this collection data approach to understand whether decisions related to innovation by middle managers and operational employees have the same weight in recognizing the value of unsuccessful innovations. It is also necessary to consider the high number of companies realizing the need for a shift in their innovation strategy; thus, it could be interesting to continue studying the causes and effects of unsuccessful innovation in other industries. Other veins for future research include using other theoretical perspectives that complement our understanding of the value of innovation failures, such as learning organization theory (Santos-Vijande, López-Sánchez, & Trespalacio, 2012). This perspective could help investigate whether Alpura, or firms with similar profiles and challenges, can establish proper learning and knowledge management mechanisms after recognizing the value of their unsuccessful innovations.

References

Alpura. (2020). Alpura Group. Retrieved January 15, 2020, from http://alpura.com/corporativo/grupo-alpura.php

Brunswicker, S., & Vanhaverbeke, W. (2014). Open Innovation in Small and Medium-Sized Enterprises (SMEs): External Knowledge Sourcing Strategies and Internal Organizational Facilitators. *Journal of Small Business Management, 53*(4), 1–23.

CANILEC. (2019). Dairy Sector Statistics 2011–2019 (Rep.). Retrieved May 28, 2020, from https://www.canilec.org.mx/estadisticas-2/

Eisenhardt, K. M. (1989a). Agency Theory: An Assessment and Review. *Academy of Management Review, 14*(1), 57–74.

Eisenhardt, K. M. (1989b). Building Theories from Case Study Research. *The Academy of Management Review, 14*(4), 532–550.

Fagerberg, J., & Verspagen, B. (2009). Innovation Studies—The Emerging Structure of a New Scientific Field. *Research Policy, 38*(2), 218–233.

Fama, E. F. (1980). Agency Problems and the Theory of the Firm. *The Journal of Political Economy, 88*(2), 288–307.

FAO. (2020). Milk and Milk Products. Retrieved April 10, 2020, from http://www.fao.org/dairy-production-products/products/en/

Faye, B., & Konuspayeva, G. (2012). The Sustainability Challenge to the Dairy Sector—The Growing Importance of non-cattle Milk Production Worldwide. *International Dairy Journal, 24*(2), 50–56.

Hartwich, F., & Negro, C. (2010). The Role of Collaborative Partnerships in Industry Innovation: Lessons from New Zealand's Dairy Sector. *Agribusiness, 26*(3), 425–449.

Heidenreich, S., & Spieth, P. (2013). Why Innovations Fail—The Case of passive and Active Innovation Resistance. *International Journal of Innovation Management, 17*(05), 1350021.

IDF. (2020). Facts and Figures. Retrieved April 10, 2020, from https://www.fil-idf.org/about-dairy/facts-figures/

IMARC Group. (2019). Global Dairy Market to Reach US$ 1032.7 Billion by 2024, Induced by Adoption of Advanced Management and Production Technologies. Retrieved May 25, 2020, from https://www.imarcgroup.com/global-dairy-market-reach

Jensen, M. C., & Meckling, W. H. (1976). Theory of the Firm: Managerial Behavior, Agency Costs and Ownership Structure. *Journal of Financial Economics, 3*(4), 305–360.

Lala. (2020). Lala Group. Retrieved January 15, 2020, from https://www.lala.com.mx/nosotros/historia/

Mortensen, P. S., & Bloch, C. W. (2005). *Oslo Manual: Guidelines for Collecting and Interpreting Innovation Data* (Organisation for Economic Co-operation and Development, Ed.) (3rd ed.). Paris: OECD Publishing.

Nettle, R., Brightling, P., & Hope, A. (2013). How Programme Teams Progress Agricultural Innovation in the Australian Dairy Industry. *The Journal of Agricultural Education and Extension, 19*(3), 271–290.

O'Connor, G., & Shaikh, I. (2018). Motivating Radical Innovation: An Agency theory exploration. *Academy of Management Proceedings, 2018*(1), 17725.

OECD/Eurostat. (2018). *Oslo Manual 2018: Guidelines for Collecting, Reporting and Using Data on Innovation.* Luxembourg: Paris/Eurostat. https://doi.org/10.1787/9789264304604-en

Rhaiem, K., & Amara, N. (2019). Learning from Innovation Failures: A Systematic Review of the Literature and Research Agenda. *Review of Managerial Science,* 1–46. https://doi.org/10.1007/s11846-019-00339-2

Rogers, E. M. (1962). *Diffusion of Innovations* (1st ed.). New York, NY: The Free Press.

Rogers, E. M. (2003). *Diffusion of Innovations* (5th ed.). New York, NY: The Free Press.

Santos-Vijande, M. L., López-Sánchez, J. Á., & Trespalacios, J. A. (2012). How Organizational Learning Affects a Firm's Flexibility, Competitive Strategy, and Performance. *Journal of Business Research, 65*(8), 1079–1089.

Špička, J., Smutka, L., & Selby, R. (2015). Recent Areas of Innovation Activities in the Czech Dairy Industry. *Agricultural Economics, 61*(6), 249–264.

Sriwannawit, P., & Sandström, U. (2015). Large-scale Bibliometric Review of Diffusion Research. *Scientometrics, 102,* 1615–1645. https://doi.org/10.1007/s11192-014-1448-7

Teece, D. (1980). The Diffusion of an Administrative Innovation. *Management Science, 26*(5), 464–470.

Tidd, J., & Bessant, J. (2014). *Managing Innovation: Integrating Technological, Market and Organizational Change* (5th ed.). Chichester: John Wiley & Sons.

Tidd, J., Pavitt, K., & Bessant, J. (2001). *Managing Innovation*. Chichester: Wiley.

Van der Panne, G., Van Beers, C., & Kleinknecht, A. (2003). Success and Failure of Innovation: A Literature Review. *International Journal of Innovation Management, 7*(03), 309–338.

Voorn, B., van Genugten, M., & van Thiel, S. (2019). Multiple Principals, Multiple Problems: Implications for Effective Governance and a Research Agenda for Joint Service Delivery. *Public Administration, 97*(3), 671–685.

WWF. (2020). Dairy Overview. Retrieved June 1, 2020, from https://www.world-wildlife.org/industries/dairy

Yin, R. K. (1994). *Case Study Research: Design and Methods* (4th ed.). Thousand Oaks, CA: Sage Publications.

23

Innovation and Quality of the Work Life Management: Managers, Purpose of Life and Joy

Ana Cristina Limongi-França, André Baptista Barcauí, Paulo Bergsten Mendes, Rodolfo Ribeiro da Silva, and Wellington Nogueira

Introduction

Innovating means to bring new solutions in the form of products, services and concepts. In this scenario of the third millennium which is impregnated with technology, environmental issues, social and economic diversity, innovation factors have been composed of new technological tools, management values linked to global and local sustainability and—in increasing demand—consumers aware of their needs, rights and duties at the same time we face abysses of economic and political inequality in the "*21st Century Capitalism*", according to by Thomas Piketty (2014).

A. C. Limongi-França (✉)
FEA/USP—Business Department, Universidade de São Paulo, São Paulo, Brazil
e-mail: climongi@usp.br

A. B. Barcauí
Business Management, Universidade Federal do Rio de Janeiro,
Rio de Janeiro, Brazil
e-mail: barcaui@facc.ufrj.br

P. B. Mendes
Aquila Gestão & Arte, São Paulo, Brazil

© The Author(s), under exclusive license to Springer Nature Switzerland AG 2021
A. McMurray et al. (eds.), *The Palgrave Handbook of Workplace Innovation*,
https://doi.org/10.1007/978-3-030-59916-4_23

Frank Pot (2011, pp. 404–405) wrote about innovation: "… the implementation of new and combined interventions in the fields of work organisation, human resource management and supportive technologies. Workplace innovation is considered to be complementary to technological innovation. (…) by introducing workplace innovation, improvement of Quality of the Work Life (QWL) and organisational performance can be achieved simultaneously."

Innovations at the work life management of organizations have occurred in a broad and diversified manner, supported by diverse competences, purposes, organizational values and challenges for enhancing the well-being of the employees' internal and external customers. Innovation, from the perspective of Quality of Work Life (QWL), presupposes recognizing a complex, technologically dense and asymmetric scenario and the skills that take these elements into consideration for the balance and well-being of people and organizations.

This chapter presents three innovative Teaching Cases: the first one a quantitative study on managers coping with stress and their perception of the quality of life (https://rac.anpad.org.br/index.php/rac/article/view/1060/1056), the second from 7waves (https://7waves.me/), a mobile app for planning the purpose and goals of life and the third one based on joy—as an emotion to overcome suffering, sadness and hopelessness, with the activities of the non-governmental organization *Doutores da Alegria* (Doctors of Joy), professional clowns working regularly in hospitals—https://doutoresdaalegria.org.br.

For the methodology, a Teaching Case has been applied, with the analysis of the content of secondary data, as they are innovations already consolidated in the light of the management of quality of work life with the fundamentals and indicators inspired by the biopsychosocial and organizational view of health and well-being in the work environment. We present the following key elements of innovation in the management of quality of life at work: (1) Joy and humanization for behavioural change and company culture *Doutores da Alegria*, (2) Life purposes and definition of personal goals (7waves), (3) Coping with stress in managers for better perception of the quality of work life, as shown in Fig. 23.1, as follows:

R. R. da Silva
7 Waves, São Paulo, Brazil
e-mail: rodolfo@7waves.me

W. Nogueira
Artistic Department, Recursos Humorísticos, São Paulo, Brazil
e-mail: wellington@doutoresdaalegria.org.br; well@wellingtonnogueira.com.br

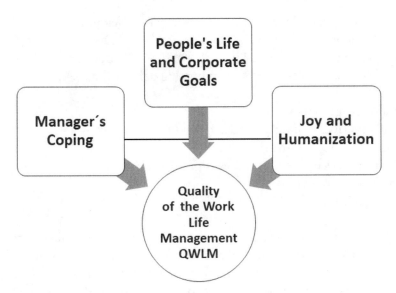

Fig. 23.1 Impacts for innovation in the Quality of the Work Life Management

Theoretical Background

The Evolution of Organizational Behaviour

The new millennium has opened many new doors to personal and organizational changes that address the quality of life at work as something necessary and inseparable to work. However, there are immense dilemmas regarding time, overload, employability, transparency, participation, specialists and use of technology. The large vectors have been insurance, medical costs, multi contractual relationships, strengthening objects and structures specialized in extending life in a multiple and integrated way, both inside and outside work.

The dimensions of the integrated management model of safety and health, added to actions and programs of quality of life can be a response to this new concept of people management at work. The decisions on the workers or their leaders, the involvement of the family and the community must be made consciously and in a highly skilled way. Otherwise, trivialization or even overlapping actions can occur, both of which do not have identity nor consistent goals. And this is a frequent fact. Great efforts often become useless, due to total lack of management or self-management.

This debate about health and quality of life has generated organizational changes. The major milestones are influenced by global movements where behavioural and social support actions stand out to the set of global goals for a better consolidated planet in the Sustainable Development Goals (SDG) and the Organisation for Economic Co-operation and Development (OECD), where good work and satisfaction goals stand out for the workers all over the planet. Historical milestones of quality of life policies (Fig. 23.2):

- Health promotion
- Psychosocial care and stress-related syndromes
- Equity and social justice
- Health knowledge and habits: eating, physical activity
- Affective socio-actions
- Good job for all (Fig. 23.2)

Administrative awareness about people's needs and new challenges at work have stimulated the structuring of quality of life activities in companies, characterizing a new competence. The consolidation of Quality of the Work Life Management—QWLM—in organizations has followed the following logic: perception, choices and management.

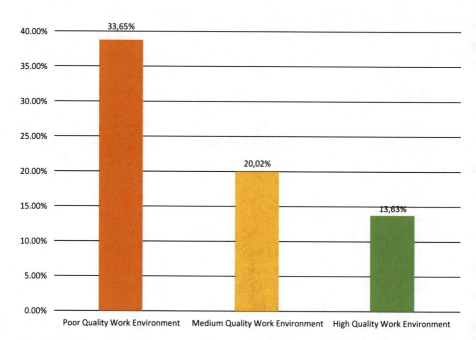

Fig. 23.2 The quality of the work environment affects health and well-being: negative Effect on Health—OCDE 2018 (Source: translate from OECD (2018))

The Concept of Quality of the Work Life Management—QWLM

The Quality of the Work Life Management (QWLM) is a set of well-being choices—unique and personalized—in search of biological, psychological, social and organizational (BPSO) balance, from the legal and psychological contracts with work organizations. This balance, guided by BPSO fundamentals, generates specific markers of each organizational culture and consolidated data in scientific studies and business practices. In general, the following associations between the actions and the BPSO domains are observed:

- Healthy habits are associated with the Biological dimension.
- Self-esteem and recognition with the Psychological dimension.
- Consumption and education with the Social dimension.
- Ergonomics and climate with the Organizational dimension.

The biological, psychological, social and organizational vision is associated with ethics and promotion of the human condition. This integrated attitude meets demands related to quality of life at work issues with an advanced management perspective, which includes:

- The concept of quality of the work life (QWL), considering aspects of the surroundings of the organizations, especially the community and the family.
- The process of developing skills that it finds in the management of quality of work life, aspects of internal and external management to each organization in the design of this competence.
- The development of skills for quality of life at work, based on occupational segments and professional profiles.

The study conducted by Arellano in Fleury (2002) on 27 organizations awarded by the Brazilian Association of Quality of Life (www.abqv.org.br) reveals that most Quality of Work Life programs (88%) were evaluated by specific instruments as indicators of employee's health status and stress, and by generic instruments for the evaluation of Quality of Life and Lifestyle. Regarding productivity, 26% organizations made available information about turnover and 37% on absenteeism. In addition to these data evidences, effective changes in organizational management are observed, more attentive and responsible when it comes to welfare issues.

The BPSO integral vision approach is associated with ethics and improvement of the human condition. Psychosomatic medicine, especially with Lipowisk (1975), proposes an integrated vision of the human being, who acts under the principle that every person is a socio-psychosomatic complex. That is, it has biological, psychological and social potentialities that simultaneously respond to living conditions. From this view, we must work on the specific domains that we conceptualize here. We usually have adopted the term layer, criteria or indicator. However, in order to align the discussions within the scope of quality of life, we now call these skills as domains. For examples of BPSO indicators please refer to Fig. 23.3.

Stress is the process of tension caused when facing a challenging situation (threat or conquest). Stress can characterize a situation of discomfort and illness (distress), or a situation that requires effort, thus requiring necessary responses and performance (eustress). Its result can be positive (when we use this mental or emotional strain to accomplish) or negative (when the response requirements cause burnout). The stress process occurs due to a set of factors, such as: personality, organic constitution, evaluation and perception of the individual, personal expectations, organizational contexts, expectations regarding the environment and strategies for coping with stress.

Methodology Approach: Teaching Case

The methodology approach is Teaching Case. The analysis of real cases from the perspective of added values to the management and practice of quality of life and changes in the organizational culture, for analysis used as a qualitative discourse analysis and quantitative analysis of people.

Slattery (2008) describes: *"teaching case is a rich narrative in which individuals or groups must make a decision or solve a problem. A teaching case is not a "case study" of the type used in academic research. Teaching cases provide information, but*

Organizational	**Biological**	**Psychological**	**Social**
Institutional Image	Occupational Signs and Symptoms Reports	Recruitment and Selection	Business Agreements
Training & Development	Ergonomic Risk Control	Performance Assessment	Free Time and Leisure
Processes and Technology	Labor Gymnastics	Camaraderie	Children Care
Decision Committees	Meals (cafeteria)	Organizational Climate	Basic food Basket
Absence of Bureaucracy	Occupational Health and Safety Commission	Career and remuneration	Private Pension
Personnel Routines		Personal Life	Course Financing
			Free Community Activities

Fig. 23.3 QWLM business indicators with BPSO model for human resources

*neither analysis nor conclusions. The analytical work of explaining the relationships among events in the case, **identifying options, evaluating choices and predicting the effects of actions is the work done by students during the classroom discussion**.*"

The cases studied show new frontiers of perception by the directors, in relation to workshops that promote the expression of emotions, especially joy and happiness. Quantitative data related to life purposes show that there are medium- and long-term plans related to personal care, purchase of consumer goods and investment in professional growth. In conclusion, innovations in quality of life management have new emotional, technological and managerial frontiers.

This chapter presents the account of three situations pertaining to the field of innovation in quality of life management at work: the first, related to facing the health demands of managers in the field of happiness, with quantitative methodology; the second, with behaviour approach activities with emphasis on joy as a regeneration and qualification factor.

Data Analysis and Discussion

Teaching Case 1: Stress, Coping Strategies and Quality of Life—A Survey on Brazilian Managers

In this section we will present the main findings of a study with Brazilian executives on stress, coping and quality of life as part of Barcaui's postdoctoral research and explored in a later study by Barcaui & Limongi-França (2014) postdoctoral research. This study analyses the relationship between perceived stress at work, the coping strategy adopted, and the quality of life of the active managers in Brazilian organizations. Three instruments were applied together: Karasek's Job Stress Scale, Latack's Coping with Job Stress and WHO'S WHO QOL-Brief in a sample with 1290 managers throughout Brazil. An analysis of the correlation between variables—stress, quality of life and coping strategy—was applied.

To evaluate further the relationship between the three dimensions of interest, models of linear and logistic regression were developed. The findings show that most managers find themselves in a high stress level, but share a good social support and a good perception about their quality of life. Most use control strategies to cope with stress. Control strategies and symptoms management significantly influence the perception of quality of life, where avoidance strategies imply a decrease on this perception. Managers with jobs classified as high strain (Karasek &Theorell, 1990) tend to have a poorer quality of life, even moderated by social support.

This proposal basically generated four categories of work: passive (low demand and low control), active (high control and high demand), low voltage level (high control and low demand) and high voltage level (low control and high demand).According to Giga, Cooper, and Faragher (2003), there is no explanatory model about what makes coping strategies effective. Some authors follow a personality trait approach and others emphasize the specific episode of stress to analyse the coping strategy. Therefore, there is some controversy surrounding the concept and mechanisms of coping measurement in literature (Latack&Havlovic, 1992), particularly with regard to its weak predictive power of behaviour (Dewe, Cox, & Ferguson, 1993).

However, if coping is considered as a trait, and therefore relatively stable, research on coping strategies would be poorly practiced in possible interventions and preparation for management of stressful situations (Latack & Havlovic, 1992). The so-called coping is characterized as an action or thought effort to manage or overcome stressful situations (Lazarus & Folkman, 1984). Latack opted for an integrative conception derived from a meta-analysis of models studied by the author. The product of this model review allowed the selection of three new categories of coping strategies:

- Control, including also cognitive reassessments made by the individual in relation to stressful situations (e.g.: talking to colleagues who are also involved in the problem).
- Avoidance actions (e.g.: keeping distance from the situation).
- Symptom management, when referring to behaviours aimed at stress relief (e.g.: physical exercise practice, relaxation or leisure activities).

The coping strategy can be understood in a transactional way between the individual and the environment, at the moment when he evaluates a situation as stressful. Latack (1986) also suggests that the control strategy is positively related to job satisfaction, directly as opposed to the propensity to leave employment and anxiety.

The avoidance and even the strategy of symptom management, according to the author, would induce the appearance of psychosomatic symptoms, which leads us to conclude that the control strategy would be the most appropriate to obtain positive results in stress administration. Haynes and Love (2004) conducted a survey with 100 project managers in the construction area, in which they identified that coping style more focused on the problem tends to fit better compared to that engaged in emotion.

The study can be classified as organizational behavior, to the extent that it reveals new empirical indications about stress in management work and the impacts caused on the lives of these professionals. This evidence can lead to the generation and support of more effective measures to handle stress and consequent increase in perceived quality of life. It can be concluded that most managers have high stress levels, but with high social support and good perception of quality of life. Regarding coping strategies, it was observed that most are characterized by using strategies predominantly of control, followed by avoidance and administration of symptoms.

There is no indication of a relationship between the scores; there is a relationship between the characterizations of managers regarding stress and coping strategy. Coping strategies based on symptom administration and control significantly influence quality of life. At the same time, avoidance strategies suggest a decrease in quality of life perception, corroborating the revised authors (Haynes & Love, 2004).

The administration of symptoms was more positive in relation to the perception of quality of life than to control, which suggests that more studies are necessary so that any predictive action can be recommended more safely. Another characterization of a variable with positive aspect was the definition of the quality of life factor, which brought strength to the relationships between quality of life and coping strategy. In the correlation analysis, many weak correlations appeared and even with two cases of positive signal between the strategy of coping with avoidance and quality of life.

However, in modelling, we observed that the relationship of this strategy with the overall quality of life is, in fact, negative. Hypotheses 3 and 4 of this study were related to moderation between stress and quality of life through symptom control and administration strategies, and how much work framed in the high-voltage category were positively associated with a poor quality of life, respectively. The evaluation was that the strategies—with the exception of avoidance—provide a decrease in the impact on studies considered high voltage and, consequently, improve the perception of quality of life. In addition, it was possible to confirm that the presence of the high-voltage category of the Karasek model (Karazek, Baker, Maxer, Ahlbom, & Theorell, 1981) implies a decrease in the perception of quality of life, regardless of the type of coping strategy. Social support increases the chance of the executive presenting positive strategies (control and administration of symptoms) in stressful situations, which validates the last hypothesis of this work.

The perception of quality of life of managers is associated with coping strategy, and administering the symptoms of stress and adopting control strategies not only mitigates the impact of stress—even in high-tech jobs tension—but also increases positive perception. Avoidance strategies have an exact opposite effect on managers' lives.

Teaching Case 2: Case 7waves: Analytics Applied from People's Life and Corporate Goals

The new economy has demanded from companies the frequent search for innovations to remain competitive (and alive) in the market. Such innovations go through the application of new technologies to internal processes so that they can guide managers in the best decision-making in various aspects, such as for the relationship with customers, for the processes of production and delivery of products and services, but also for the management of their human resources. One of the biggest people management challenges today is the understanding of what motivates a person to work. While in previous decades people valued salary and benefits as main motivators for work, but today people seek purpose, protagonism and quality of work life, so that there is a greater balance between personal and professional life.

In recent years, companies have been increasingly applying, according to Heuvel and Bondarouk (2016), systematic identification and quantification of people's motivators with a focus on solving business problems. This practice, known as people analytics, is gaining increasing notoriety within organizations considering its power to generate valuable insights that generate positive results in company indicators, from the understanding that people are the main assets (and also the main challenges) of companies today.

In this context, a Brazilian startup named 7waves was created in 2017 with the mission of assisting people in managing and monitoring personal and corporate goals through Machine Learning and Data Mining technologies, which recommend actions, content and opportunities that help people to be more effective in their achievements.

Until May 2020 the app had more than 200,000 users in more than 3600 Brazilian cities and 250 cities in 67 other countries. This group of users has more than 450,000 goals registered in the startup database. In a recent study conducted from a sample of 12,633 users in 19 countries, it was observed the goals that will be the focus of people in 2020, as well as the people's procrastination index based in 2019 goals that were not accomplished, as shown in Fig. 23.4.

In an individual analysis of career objectives, we can state that people's goal for 2020 is claiming new positions within the company in which they

Main categories per country

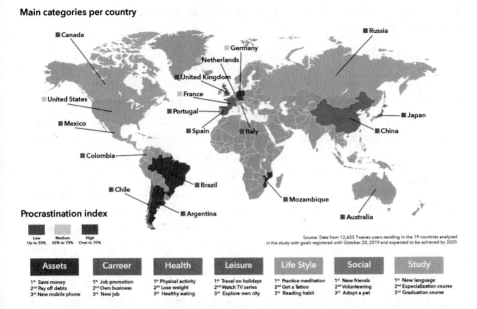

Fig. 23.4 Life categories, main goals and procrastination index for 2020 (Source: 7waves Report 2019)

currently work, which becomes good news for HR managers who are concerned about retention of talents.

On the other hand, it is necessary to analyse the data more robustly to identify insights that lead, in fact, to the retention of talents itself. From this analysis, the data was reviewed and it showed that:

- Four out of ten people who want to "step up" need to "pay off debts";
- about 80% of people procrastinate "eating habits change";
- $28 is the monthly average people can invest to "learn a new language";
- 72% of people living in large cities have as main social objective "making new friends";
- Six kilos is the desired weight for those who want to "lose weight".

Based on this analysis, we have rich insights for HR managers to create actions in their companies to promote the quality of life at work for their employees and, at the same time, create an affective bond with the company for having supported them in their personal achievements. This is the power of people analytics.

Teaching Case 3: Case of the Social Organization Doctors of Joy

Doctors of Joy (www.doutoresdaalegria.org.br) is a non-profit civil society organization that introduced clown art into the healthcare universe, intervening with children, adolescents and other people in situations of vulnerability and social risk in public hospitals. Founded by actor, clown and social entrepreneur Wellington Nogueira in 1991, the association, works in the fields of health, culture and social assistance and is recognized and internationally awarded for the impact of its actions. Since 1991 they have hired professionals trained in performing arts and with specialization in clown theatre language. Doutores da Alegria chooses to work with professional clowns - who go through rigorous selection and training process—in order to organize the knowledge and experience generated by the artistic work developed in public hospitals for future generations of artists.

The clown doctor program is at the heart of the organization and more than 1,700,000 one-on-one artistic interventions have already been carried out with hospitalized children, their parents and healthcare professionals. In weekly visits to children in eight hospitals in São Paulo and four in Recife, duos of clowns intervene in the hospital routine and propose new meanings for the experience of hospitalization. In Rio de Janeiro, the organization works on the concept of Hospital Audiences, where there is the curatorship of a permanent and free artistic program, which includes theatre, music, dance, circus and poetry in seven public hospitals, expanding the relations between art and health.

The Doctors of Joy School offers two training systems—one for the general public and one for artists—with courses, lectures and programs structured from philosophy, values and a practice of more than ten years of acting with diverse audiences. Among its initiatives is the Clown Training Program for Young People, which offers young people in situations of social vulnerability an initiation in the artistic career. The organization also develops public shows and interventions as a way to share its experience with society.

The founder of "Doctors of Joy", Wellington Nogueira, went to study at the American Academy of Dramatic and Musical Theatre in New York, USA. That's when he met the Big Apple Circus Clown Care Unit, founded by actor and clown Michael Christensen in 1984. He joined the cast of the first group of professional clowns who visited hospitalized children around the world, working with the New York company for three years. "Doctors of Joy" has the purpose of intervening in society proposing art as a social minimum for children, adolescents and other audiences in situations of vulnerability and social risk, helping public hospitals and adverse environments, having the language of the clown as a reference. Through this artistic intervention, channels of reflexive dialogues with society are expanded and knowledge produced in the processes of training, research, publications and artistic manifestations contribute to the promotion of Culture and Health, also inspiring universal and democratic public policies for sustainable social development. The values for the management of Doctors of Joy are:

- Art and culture as a right.
- Freedom of expression, cooperation and respect for diversity.
- Ethics, transparency and coherence in action.
- Art, education and research as a way to stimulate a new look and impact realities.
- Search for simplicity and excellence.
- Joy is a state that is built from the encounter with the other—affecting and being affected.
- Search for multidisciplinarity between culture, health, education and social assistance.

The results make it possible to list, consolidate and condense the indicators that guide the organization's studies regarding its artistic action in hospitals and training actions. The evaluation process points to new challenges to further structure the program, so that in fact we can contribute not only to the humanization policy, but also to the promotion of culture in adverse places, such as hospitals. Main results of the project evaluation:

- The Hospital Audiences focuses on the patient, but reaches the hospital. It opens up the possibility of a new concept of hospitals as producers of public health with art.
- Artists created shows for the hospital, which were then performed in theatrical venues outside the hospital, reversing the initial logic, which was to bring theatre shows to hospitals.
- Most professionals, patients and companions actively participate in the proposed artistic activities, from the most debilitated patients, who move their feet, or blink their eyes, to those who sing, dance and play instruments.

In 2016, with a new governance, the Mission of Doctors of Joy was updated to an institutional task that reinforces, among other guidelines, culture as a right of all.

The Innovation: a True Partnership: This case took place at The Children's Institute, the paediatric hospital of the University of São Paulo School of Medicine, a Paediatric Reference Hospital in Brazil, for the treatment of special, challenging medical cases that demand continued study and research, therefore, it counts on the services of top professionals in their fields.

To bring joy to a medical institution of that magnitude required extensive preparation, since joy is also the result of relationships where trust is a key factor and only eye-to-eye conversations, where the details and characteristics of every medical area—oncology, cardiology, specialties, infectology, for instance—could be shared, understood and learned. At these meetings, the "clown doctors" presented the artistic work in detail, so that questions would be answered, do's and don'ts would be learned, such as rules and details of each paediatric unit and doubts about the artistic work be cleared. In this way, with the support of all areas, the itinerary was prepared and submitted to the executive director—Dr Paulo Roberto Pereira—for approval.

A presentation was scheduled for the Wednesday morning General Medical and staff meeting, where Wellington Nogueira could present the planned activities to all medical and administrative teams of the hospital that was considered to be Doutores da Alegria's greatest challenge. Three months after the beginning of the artistic visits, at the first evaluation meeting Dr Paulo Roberto Pereira, the executive director, was present and made a point of letting us know that it was possible to sense a different atmosphere at the hospital. The chief nurse described how she waited for the clowns to finish their visits and then, immediately, talk to the nurses, especially when she had delicate issues to discuss with them; she used that strategy because she observed that after the "clown doctor" visits—which also included the nurses and doctors—the teams turned out to be more open to interact in cooperative ways. Needless to say, the hospitalized children and teenagers responded very well to the "clown procedures", such as red nose transplant and milk-shake transfusions. Sensing the positive atmosphere, Dr Paulo Roberto created the Breakfast with The Director, an activity with the sole purpose to listen to the teams in an informal way and make room for the implementation of ideas and projects created by the staff, that would reinforce the joyful atmosphere.

In his own words: "Doutores da Alegria was my best Management Tool; the regular presence of the clown doctors and the quality of work relationships established with the teams, took the entire hospital to a new level of participation and involvement. One example was the creation of the program known as 'Meetings With The Makers', where children who had medical permission would be taken on a tour of the 'institute's backstage'; the visit to the kitchen was one of the highlights; on several occasions, children took this opportunity to thank the Kitchen Staff for the food, especially, the desserts. 'We make your food with love', said the Chief Cook". Dr Paulo Roberto is not at the Children's Institute anymore, but, to this day—the Clown Doctor program was started in May 1996 and still continues—he says that the regular presence of the clowns—twice a week, from 10am to 4pm—generated an atmosphere of positive changes and cooperation. He saw the opportunity and grabbed it. As a result, everybody could take part in it. Lesson learned: Dr Paulo Roberto had been working on the continuous integration of the work teams. He saw the advent of Doctors of Joy as the "glue" that helped everybody become one team.

Conclusions

People's view, coping with stressors and productivity difficulties and understanding of emotions and life purposes in the work environment are presented here as cases of success in innovation; "joy", "purpose" and "managers" are innovative elements in the perspective of managing quality of work life.

The Teaching Case Methodology used to choose the ones presented here, is close to the teaching case, in which the facts themselves present in their scenario elements of comparison and evidence related to the biological, psychological, social and organizational needs of the organizational actors, and the diversity of management tools, from coping with distress, to ordering life purposes and the performances of joy and expression of emotions in work groups that involve everything from health care to traditional administrative environments. In conclusion, the work routine has experienced changes in people management, far beyond times and movements. Quantitative records that generate big data on life purposes, managers' assessment of coping with stress factors and joy as a new mindset in employee-employer work relationships, open new frontiers of innovation in people management and quality of work life.

References

Arellano, Eliete Bernal in Fleury. M.T.L.org(2002). *As PessoasnaOrganização*. São Paulo: EditoraGente.

Barcaui, A. B., & Limongi-França, A. C. (2014). Estresse, enfrentamento e qualidade de vida: um estudo sobre gerentes brasileiros. Revista de Administração Contemporânea - RAC, Rio de Janeiro, v. 18, n. 5, pp. 670–694. https://doi.org/10.1590/1982

Dewe, P., Cox, T., & Ferguson, E. (1993). Individual Strategies for Coping with Stress at Work: A Review. *Work & Stress: An International Journal of Work, Health &Organisations, 7*(1), 5–15. https://doi.org/10.1080/02678379308257046

Giga, S. I., Cooper, C. L., & Faragher, B. (2003). The Development of a Framework for a Comprehensive Approach to Stress Management Interventions at Work. *International Journal of Stress Management, 10*(4), 280–296. https://doi.org/10.1037/1072-5245.10.4.280

Haynes, N. S., & Love, P. E. D. (2004). Psychological Adjustment and Coping among Construction Project Managers. *Construction Management & Economics, 22*(2), 129–140. https://doi.org/10.1080/0144619042000201330

Heuvel and Bondarouk. The Rise (and Fall) of HR Analytics: A Study into the Future Applications, Value, Structure, and System Support. *Journal of Organizational Effectiveness: People and Performance, 4*(2), 157–178, 2016.

Karasek, R. A., Jr., & Theorell, T. (1990). *Healthy work: stress, productivity and the reconstruction of working life*. New York: Basic Books.

Karazek, R., Baker, D., Maxer, F., Ahlbom, A., & Theorell, T. (1981). Job Decision Latitude, Job Demands, and Cardiovascular Diseases: A Prospective Study of Swedish Men. *American Journal of Public Health, 71*, 694–705.

Latack, J. C. (1986). Coping with job stress: measures and future directions for scale development. Journal of Applied Psychology, 71(3), 377–385. https://doi.org/10.1037/0021-9010.71.3.377.

Latack, J. C., & Havlovic, S. J. (1992). Coping with job stress: a conceptual evaluation framework for coping measures. *Journal of Organizational Behavior, 13*(5), 479–508. https://doi.org/10.1002/job.4030130505.

Lazarus, R., & Folkman, S. (1984). *Stress, Appraisal and Coping*. New York: Springer.

Lipowski Z. J. (1975). Sensory and Information Overload. In: *Psychosomatic Medicine and Liaison Psychiatry* (pp. 47–69). Springer, Boston, MA.

Organisation for Economic Co-operation and Development (OECD). (2018). The Quality of the Work Environment Affects Health and Well-being—Share of Works in Europe Reporting That the Work Environment Affects Their Health, 2015.

Oeij, P. R. A., Rus, D., & Pot, F. (2017). *Workplace Innovation: Theory, Research and Practice*. © Springer International Publishing.

Piketty, T. (2014).*O Capital no Século XXI*, colecção *Temas e Debates*, editor – Círculo de Leitores, ISBN 9789896443047, EAN 978-9896443047, Páginas 912.

Pot, F. D. (2011). Workplace innovation for better jobs and performance. *International Journal of Productivity and Performance Management, 60*(4), 404–415.

Slattery, W. (2008). SERC Pedagogic Service, Starting Point: Introductory Geology, Departments of Geological Sciences and Teacher Education.Wright State University, Dayton, OH. Retrieved from https://serc.carleton.edu/sp/library/cases/why.html

Silva, R. R., & Ferreira, D. J. P. (2019). 7Waves Report 2019. Retrieved from https://7waves.me/. 5 January 2020.

Van Den Heuvel, S., & Bondarouk, T. (2016). The Rise (and Fall?) of HR Analytics. *Journal of Organizational Effectiveness: People and Performance, 4*(2), 157–178. https://doi.org/10.1108/JOEPP-03-2017-0022

24

Impact of Workplace Innovation on Organisational Performance: A Cross Country Comparative Analysis of Entrepreneurial Ventures

Ali Iftikhar Choudhary, Adela McMurray, and Nuttawuth Muenjohn

Introduction

In the last couple of decades, the world has become a global village, and multicultural organisations came into existence. Business practitioners, researchers and leaders are paying attention to the amalgamation of organisational leadership and innovation in the workplace to gain higher organisational performance. Organisations are becoming increasingly aware of the impact of innovation and finding ways to cultivate innovation for performance improvement. Particularly, entrepreneurial ventures are vulnerable to failure in this contemporary competitive business environment and looking for new ways to improve their performance continuously. Innovation is a mean rather than a goal to improve performance (Oeij, Dhondt, Kraan, Vergeer, & Pot, 2012) and many European countries are using workplace innovation as a business growth strategy (Pot, Rus, & Oeij, 2017; Pot,

A. I. Choudhary (✉) • N. Muenjohn
School of Management, RMIT University, Melbourne, VIC, Australia
e-mail: ali.choudhary@rmit.edu.au; nuttawuth.muenjohn@rmit.edu.au

A. McMurray
College of Business, Government and Law, Flinders University,
Adelaide, SA, Australia
e-mail: adela.mcmurray@flinders.edu.au

© The Author(s), under exclusive license to Springer Nature Switzerland AG 2021
A. McMurray et al. (eds.), *The Palgrave Handbook of Workplace Innovation*,
https://doi.org/10.1007/978-3-030-59916-4_24

445

Totterdill, & Dhondt, 2020). This research intends to investigate the above claim, particularly in a developing country.

Workplace innovation is the combined implementation of new and old components from the work organisation, supportive technologies and the human resource management field (Pot, 2011). Innovation within the organisation is conceptualised as a process through which new ideas are generated, products and objects are developed or re-invented or as a tangible organisational outcome (Simmers & McMurray, 2019; Von Treuer & McMurray, 2012). Innovation occurs throughout the organisation as it has roots in organisational culture, structure and systems (Damanpour, Walker, & Avellaneda, 2009). Employees can undertake their roles to connect innovation to all levels of the organisation (Newnham, 2018), yet it is important to establish such an environment where innovation can flourish, and employees can undertake such roles.

This study aims to answer the question, does workplace innovation improves entrepreneurial venture's performance in a developed and a developing country? The purpose of this research is to identify the impact of workplace innovation on organisational performance in Australian and Pakistani entrepreneurial SME ventures, investigating Australia as a developed country and Pakistan as a developing country. Past entrepreneurial studies are based on the Resource-Based View (RBV) theory to explain organisational performance using different organisational elements such as leadership, culture and innovation. RBV theory plays an important role in creating an understanding of the main resources of the organisation and how they are utilised for achieving higher organisational performance. Moreover, external factors like environment and organisational strategies are important. RBV theory is a more robust firm/small and medium enterprises (SME) level theory, mature and ready for interlinkages with other perspectives as a single theory in particular with small businesses or startups (Barney, 2000; Wiklund, 1998).

Literature Review

Context

The recent economic recessions in both developed and developing nations have augmented the role of entrepreneurial ventures in creating better economies and generating more jobs (Molina, Ortega, & Velilla, 2017). Entrepreneurial venture plays a significant role in the economic development of any country (Lim, Ribeiro, & Lee, 2008). Developed countries focused on promoting entrepreneurial culture in their societies, providing big incentive and cultivating youth entrepreneurship worked well for them (Yousaf,

Shamim, Siddiqui, & Raina, 2015). They pay much attention to foster an innovative culture in their organisations that in turn, helps in achieving higher performance for organisations. On the other hand, developing countries are more focused on bringing foreign direct investment through multinational organisations rather than promoting entrepreneurial business culture.

Shaukat, Nawaz, and Naz (2013) argued that impact of process innovation needs to be explored in Pakistani manufacturing sector as the strategic competitiveness can be achieved by continuously upgrading the processes and activities through innovation. Entrepreneurial ventures in developing countries like Pakistan (Akhtar, Ismail, Hussain, & Umair-ur-Rehman, 2015) which have GDP growth rate of approximately 5.7% (2017) should focus on cultivating innovation at the workplace as innovation in entrepreneurial SME ventures is considered more radical and has a strong impact on the overall growth. Innovation is considered as a driving factor for the success of ventures regardless of their size. Pakistani ventures need to focus more on finding innovative ways to cultivate innovation rather than just focusing on product innovation (Anwar, Zaman, & Shah, 2018).

It is believed that new, technology-based, innovative ventures play a pivotal role in overall sustainability, productivity, employability and competitiveness of the firm as they introduced new products, services, markets and business models (Alasrag, 2010; Allocca & Kessler, 2006). Australian entrepreneurial SME ventures are more inclined towards technological innovation. Rapid globalisation and technology advancements helped ventures to capture market quickly by adopting international standards. Particularly in developing economies, improved products, accessible services, and innovation are essential to compete at the global level and to thrive in the international market (Provasnek, Schmid, Geissler, & Steiner, 2017). Without developing robust internal capabilities, ventures can't improve their performance; here the role of workplace innovation becomes essential for keeping the organisation competitive (Pot et al., 2020).

Workplace Innovation

Workplace innovation is an emerging concept among European and American researchers in this decade. It helps in improving organisational performance and creating quality jobs. Workplace innovation is a process of strategic change in organisational behaviour, which helps employees to enrich their work-life and performance (Oeij, Dhondt, & Korver, 2011; Oeij, Vroome, Bolland, Grundemann, & Van Teeffelen, 2014). Workplace innovation is, primarily, the improvement of people's working environments. It enriches people's professional life and improves the quality thereof. There is still a lot of research work required for workplace innovation, and even there is no consensus on the definition. Practical, theoretical and empirical research should be done not only in Europe but in other countries as well (Oeij & Vaas, 2016).

Workplace innovation not only improves the internal dynamics of organisations but also helps in improving the external social and organisational functions as well. Workplace innovation enhances the quality of work, talented human workforce, employability, empowerment, productivity, competitive advantage, and profit and cost improvements (Oeij et al., 2011; Pot, 2011). Workplace innovation is a culturally specific phenomenon and mostly relates to leadership. Workplace innovation has four dimensions namely, organisational, team and individual innovation along with the environment for innovation (McMurray & Scott, 2013; Pot, 2011).

Organisational Performance

Organisational performance is the crucial element for entrepreneurial ventures, researchers shown a keen interest in this field, but mostly the financial aspect of performance has discussed. Efficiency, effectiveness, growth, profitability and market expansion might be an area of interest, but financial performance is the more traditional way, and researchers argued that non-financial aspect should heavily be emphasised (Murphy, Trailer, & Hill, 1996). On the other side, many researchers yet considered the financial aspect of performance as an important strategic performance measurement tool (Ittner & Larcker, 1998).

Organisational performance literature shows that it has been widely used in management research as a dependent variable and is a basic factor in identifying either an organisation is performing well or not. On the other hand, organisational performance is a complex phenomenon because many researchers used it differently. There are no valid criteria to measure performance (March & Sutton, 1997; Richards, Devinney, Yip, & Johnson, 2009). Researchers argue that organisational performance is a tool through which ventures realise that either the objectives are accomplished or not. Organisations continuously try to measure performance through various scales so that they can perform well and remain on the right track (Ho, 2008).

Many researchers identified different dimensions of organisational performance that include effectiveness, efficiency, ongoing relevance, financial viability, profitability measures, operational measures, marketable measures and growth measures (Carton & Hofer, 2006; Lusthaus, 2002). Researchers also argue that financial, profitability and growth measure are the same. Some researchers discussed that business performance could be the operational capability of the organisation to fulfil the cravings of major stakeholders (Smith & Reece, 1999). In this study, the researcher will consider both financial and non-financial aspects of the organisational performance.

Workplace Innovation Relationship with Organisational Performance

Workplace innovation plays a significant role in filling the gap between strategic knowledge of the leadership, professional knowledge of employees and workplace cultures. It helps in achieving higher performance and a win-win situation for all stakeholders (Pot, Totterdill, & Dhondt, 2016). Researchers argued that innovation is vibrant for the survival of entrepreneurial organisations in both developed and developing countries (Batool & Ullah, 2017). They play the central role in achieving economic growth and creating a sustainable environment for small and medium enterprises which in turn helps in attaining higher organisational performance (Olughor, 2015). SME's are considered the economic backbone of any nation; sometimes their full potential remains untapped, but if proper support is provided to them, they could ignite innovation and technological advancements along with creating employment opportunities while reaping impressive profits (Fouad, 2013).

Researchers argue that workplace innovation is a new phenomenon which involves the implementation of mixed concepts of human resource management, work organisations and strategy that improves organisational performance and work quality (Bartram et al., 2020; Oeij et al., 2012; Pot, Dhondt, & Oeij, 2012). Dynamic capabilities, creativity and innovation capabilities have a strong relationship with performance (Ferreira, Coelho, & Moutinho, 2020). Organisations where workplace innovation has more influence on work activities, tend to have higher organisational performance, which states that workplace innovation has a direct positive impact on organisational performance (Pot, 2011) (Fig. 24.1).

Hypothesis: Workplace innovation has a significant positive impact on organisational performance in entrepreneurial SME ventures across Australia and Pakistan.

H1a: Workplace innovation has a significant positive impact on organisational performance in entrepreneurial SME ventures across Australia.
H1b: Workplace innovation has a significant positive impact on organisational performance in entrepreneurial SME ventures across Pakistan.

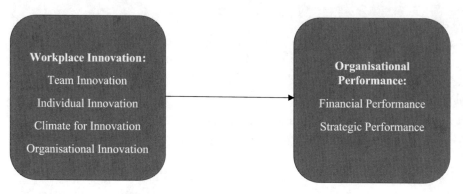

Fig. 24.1 Model

Methodology

Cross-sectional quantitative method was used to collect the data through an online and hardcopy survey. Entrepreneurial ventures are defined as rapidly growing businesses with an innovative idea (Ulhøi, 2005). Entrepreneurial SME ventures are the key driving force enhancing economic growth (Perera & Baker, 2007) of developed and developing countries and the proposed variables have a strong theoretical connection with entrepreneurial ventures as they are the source of creative and innovative design solutions. Hence, entrepreneurial SME ventures working across Australia and Pakistan were used as the population for this study. CEO's, directors and managers working at the executive level in such ventures were served as the respondents. Simple random sampling was employed, and the unit of analysis was SME/Firm level. The formula $SS = (Z^2 * p *(1 - p))/C^2$ provided by Godden (2004) using Z value 1.96 for 95% confidence level, sample size estimated at 384 for each country using 0.05 confidence interval and a 50% average response.

The data was collected using a third-party organisation in Australia, while in Pakistan contact detail was obtained from SMEDA, Federation of Pakistan Chamber of Commerce and different business incubation centres. The data was collected in the first quarter of 2018 from Pakistan and in the second quarter from Australia. The data was collected from 367 respondents in Australia using an online web-based survey, while 396 respondents provided complete responses using a hard copy survey in Pakistan. The data examined through the Statistical Package for Social Sciences (SPSS 25) and Structural Equation Modelling (SEM) using Analysis of Moment Structures (AMOS 25) for reliability, validity, demographics, correlation and regression analysis.

The 24-item scale for workplace innovation (WIS) developed by McMurray and Dorai (2003) has four dimensions—organisational innovation, innovation climate, individual innovation and team innovation—that was measured on five, six, eight and five-item scale, respectively for these dimensions. The Cronbach alpha for workplace innovation in previous studies was $\alpha = 0.913$ (Muenjohn & McMurray, 2015, 2017), which makes it a reliable tool to measure workplace innovation.

Organisational performance (7-item) has two dimensions, financial performance and strategic performance measured on three- and four-item scale, respectively. The alpha score in the previous study was $\alpha = 0.84$ taken from Sulaiman (2016) originally derived from (Porter, 1985; Zou & Cavusgil, 2002). The reliability values more than $\alpha = 0.70$ indicated that the scales were highly reliable (Nunnally, 1994).

There were 13 questions related to respondent demographics, identifying firm characteristics and personal characteristics of the respondents. These personal characteristics questions were mostly related to the respondent's age, gender, marital status, employment status, experience and education. The firm characteristics questions were related to the industry, business ownership, business sector, operation location, number of years in business and number of employees.

Data Analysis and Discussion

The response rate was approximately 18% in both countries. The data was checked for basic Structural Equation Modelling (SEM) assumptions, that is correlation, normality, outliers and common method bias. The data was normal as the skewness and kurtosis were within −1 to +1 range. Harman's single factor was used to test common method bias, and the single-factor variance extracted was well below the threshold of 50% (Pakistan, 9.284%; Australia, 27.591%). Mahalanobis-D test was used to check the outliers, 3 and 7 number of responses were deleted from Pakistan, and Australian data sets respectively. The data was collected using non-identifiable surveys to ensure data integrity and fairness. The scales used in this study were reliable as the Cronbach alpha scores were more than $\alpha = 0.7$ in both countries (Table 24.1).

Basic demographic results were identified after comparing Australian and Pakistani data set with regards to gender, age and education level. More than 50% of Australian respondents were females. More than 65% of Pakistani respondents were in between 18 to 35 years of age. The top three industries were manufacturing, IT and retail in both data set with approximately 80%

Table 24.1   Reliability statistics

Reliability	PK (393)	AU (360)	No of items
WIS	0.733	0.916	24
OP	0.721	0.804	7

of the businesses were in the private sector. A Confirmatory Factor Analysis (CFA) was used to explain the extent to which observed variables represents latent constructs (Hair, Black, Babin, Anderson, & Tatham, 2010). During CFA, based on low standardised estimates, high modification indices and high standardised residual covariances, measurement models were re-specified by deleting items. The re-specified measurement models were then used for structural analysis to test the hypothesis.

Figure 24.2 illustrated the structural model of H1a for Australian data. The GOF statistics were presented in Table 24.2. χ^2/df was below 2, RMSEA and SRMR were 0.048 and 0.038 respectively. Parsimony fit indices were above 0.5 threshold value. GFI and Incremental fit indices, CFI, IFI and TLI were all above the threshold point of 0.9, representing a good fit.

Figure 24.3 represented the structural model of H1b for Pakistani data set, and the goodness of fit indices was tabled in Table 24.2. All the GOF statistics showed a good model fit. χ^2/df 1.142, RMSEA 0.019, SRMR 0.034 and GFI was 0.947. CFI, IFI and TLI in incremental fit indices were 0.973, 0.974 and 0.969 respectively. Parsimony fit indices PCFI and PNFI were 0.858 and 0.724 respectively, which were above the threshold limit of 0.5 and showed a perfect fit.

Table 24.3 illustrated the regression estimates of hypothesis-1 for both data sets. Australian data supported workplace innovation's direct relationship with organisational performance, yet Pakistani data did not support it. The $\beta = 0.757$ in Australia, $\beta = 0.120$ in Pakistan, data results with significant p value = 0.001 for Australia yet p value = 0.233, not significant for Pakistani data.

The findings of H1 showed that workplace innovation has a positive impact on organisational performance in Australia $\beta = 0.757^{***}$ yet Pakistani data did not support this hypothesis as the $\beta = 0.120$ and $p$vlaue = 0.233.

The result of this hypothesis directly links with the research problem. It was discussed that the organisations need to develop an innovative work environment (Totterdill & Exton, 2014), where they can cultivate innovation at individual, team and organisational level, which in turn helps in achieving sustainable organisational performance. It was also identified that the ventures in a developed and developing country perceive this process differently (Alasrag, 2010). This hypothesis revealed two crucial findings that

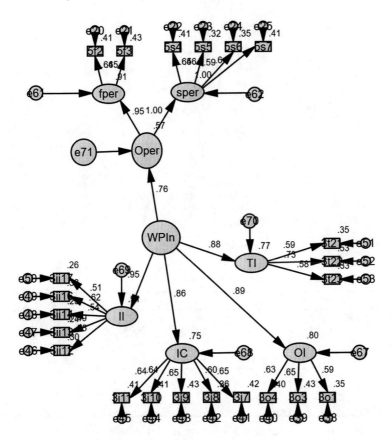

Fig. 24.2 Structural model for hypothesis-1a

Table 24.2 GOF statistics for hypothesis-1

Goodness of fit	GOF statistics	Level of acceptance	Australia (H1a)	Pakistan (H1b)
Chi-Square	χ^2/df	Between 1–5	1.828	1.142
Absolute fit indices	RMSEA	<0.1	0.048	0.019
	SRMR	<0.09 (if CFI >0.92)	0.038	0.034
	GFI	>0.90 or >0.80	0.916	0.947
Incremental fit indices	CFI	>0.90	0.925	0.973
	IFI	>0.90	0.926	0.974
	TLI	>0.90	0.915	0.969
Parsimony fit indices	PCFI	>0.50	0.809	0.858
	PNFI	>0.50	0.744	0.724

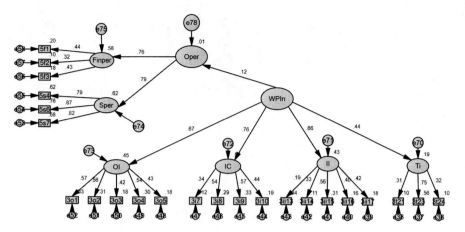

Fig. 24.3 Structural model for hypothesis-1b

Table 24.3 Regression estimates-Hypothesis 1

	Std est.	S.E.	C.R.	p value	Status
H1a—Australia					
WPI → OP	0.757	0.122	7.278	***	Supported
H1b—Pakistan					
WPI → OP	0.120	0.538	1.192	0.233	Not supported

Sig level *** = 0.001

entrepreneurial ventures in a developed country are more focused on designing innovate climate to achieve higher organisational performance, yet on the other side, entrepreneurial ventures in a developing country are not paying attention to reform the organisational structure and environment to cultivate innovation for improved performance. Although, researchers argued that innovation enhances marketing performance in an emerging economy, yet the findings of this research for a developing country does not support this claim (Afriyie, Du, & Musah, 2020). Hence the results demonstrate a significant difference in entrepreneurial ventures working in a developed and a developing country concerning workplace innovation.

Entrepreneurial ventures in a developed country tend to improve organisational performance when they focus on workplace innovation. The finding is aligned with the past studies that argued that developed countries have resources and invest in developing an innovative working environment which leads to higher organisational performance (Alasrag, 2010; Allocca & Kessler, 2006; OECD, 2004; Salavou, Baltas, & Lioukas, 2004). The finding extends the work of Pot (2011) and Oeij, Dhondt, Rus, and Van Hootegem (2019) by linking workplace innovation with organisational performance, particularly in the entrepreneurial venture's context. The finding contradicts to the claim that innovative workplace enhances organisational performance (Pot, 2011) yet that is not the case in a developing country's context.

Task revision, creativity, idea realisation, idea generation and persistence are some key factors which are linked with workplace innovation in the past studies (Simmers & McMurray, 2019), yet there are few studies which identified workplace innovation's linkage with performance (Oeij et al., 2012; Pot, 2011). However, this study focused on workplace innovations' relationship with organisational performance, particularly in entrepreneurial ventures, by comparing a developed and developing country. The results from Pakistani data are significant and proving that the developing nations need to focus on creating a vibrant working environment in their ventures, where they can cultivate innovation by providing quality of working life to their employees.

The finding is significant in a way that it provides a path and direction for policymakers and leaders of entrepreneurial ventures to cultivate innovation at the individual, team and organisational level to enhance their performance. There are two types of entrepreneurial ventures—imitative ventures and innovative ventures—both of the types adds something new yet the innovative ventures offer breakthrough value addition by significantly adding differentiated propositions (Campbell, 2019; Dyer, Gregersen, & Christensen, 2008). These value addition propositions may be at the individual, team or organisational level yet require a climate to capture such innovation to remain competitive. In the United States alone, these high-tech innovative entrepreneurial ventures generate half of the jobs (Campbell, 2019); this is what developing countries require as well. They need to cultivate innovation to remain competitive, enhance organisational performance and to generate more jobs, which are imperative for their economic growth.

The findings of this study extend the knowledge of workplace innovation (Muenjohn & McMurray, 2017) by contributing that the workplace innovation is not linked with cultivating innovation at the workplace through individual innovation, team innovation and organisational innovation only, yet it is also focused on designing a climate for innovation. It should be considered as a core organisational element rather than just a behavioural aspect of workers or organisation (Oeij et al., 2012). It is complementary to technological innovation yet also focuses on quality of working life (Howaldt, Kopp, & Pot, 2012; Pot, 2011). Oeij, Dhondt, Pot, and Totterdill (2018) argued that workplace innovation simultaneously impacts on quality of work, efficiency and effectiveness, which helps organisations in adapting to new environments by creating favourable working conditions to attract talent and to use their capabilities better. It also strives for adopting new technologies, ensuring that organisations and individuals can get benefit out of it (Eurofound, 2015).

Pot (2011) researched Dutch SME's and identified that those SME's focused on developing an innovative work environment, tend to attain higher financial performance as compared to those who do not take such initiatives. The same researcher conducted a couple of other similar research in different organisational set-ups and identified that the different factors of workplace innovation enhance turnover, profit and market share (Oeij et al., 2012). Oeij et al. (2012) argued that empirical evidence is required to support the claim that workplace innovation is linked with strategic performance and productivity. The findings of this hypothesis empirically verified the claim that workplace innovation is linked with strategic and financial performance in a developed country's context yet unable to support this claim from a developing country's perspective.

Conclusion

Entrepreneurial ventures are more focused on maximising their profit, especially in developing countries. They consistently search for identifying ways to improve their performance but usually, they do not have potential resources compared to entrepreneurial ventures in developed countries. This study helps ventures in realising that workplace innovation strategies could play a vital role in their sustainable performance. Allocca and Kessler (2006) concluded from their study that small firms are more innovation orientated. Hence such studies are more insightful and helpful for owners and leaders, which suggests developing a climate for innovation to cultivate innovation for improved performance.

Theoretically, this chapter contributes to the literature on workplace innovation and entrepreneurship. There is a dearth of research addressing workplace innovation with organisational performance, particularly in entrepreneurial ventures context and comparing a developed and developing country. Previous research in these areas focused on developed western countries only (Swierczek & Ha, 2003). This chapter provides ample justification and comparisons of the applicability of these concepts to both developed and developing country entrepreneurial SME ventures and found a significant difference in the results. Cross-sectional data were used in this study, which could be one of the limitations of this research. Further studies can use longitudinal approach. Also, entrepreneurial ventures from the two countries were used as the population for this research. Further studies can use different countries and contexts to replicate this research.

References

Afriyie, S., Du, J., & Musah, A.-A. I. (2020). The Nexus Among Innovation Types, Knowledge Sharing, Transformational Leadership, and Marketing Performance in an Emerging Economy. *Journal of Indian Business Research*, online first. Retrieved from https://www.emerald.com/insight/publication/issn/1755-4195#earlycite

Akhtar, C. S., Ismail, K., Hussain, J., & Umair-ur-Rehman, M. (2015). Investigating the Moderating Effect of Family on the Relationship Between Entrepreneurial Orientation and Success of Enterprise: Case of Pakistani Manufacturing SMEs. *International Journal of Entrepreneurship and Small Business, 26*(2), 233–247.

Alasrag, H. (2010). *Enhance the Competitiveness of the Arab SMEs in the Knowledge Economy*. MPRA (21742).

Allocca, M. A., & Kessler, E. H. (2006). Innovation Speed in Small and Medium-Sized Enterprises. *Creativity and Innovation Management, 15*(3), 279–295.

Anwar, M., Zaman, K. S., & Shah, S. Z. A. (2018). A Study of the Relationship Between Innovation and Performance Among NPOs in Pakistan. *Journal of Social Service Research, 46*(1), 1–15.

Barney, J. B. (2000). Firm Resources and Sustained Competitive Advantage. *Advances in Strategic Management, 17*, 203–227.

Bartram, T., Stanton, P., Bamber, G. J., Leggat, S. G., Ballardie, R., & Gough, R. (2020). Engaging Professionals in Sustainable Workplace Innovation: Medical Doctors and Institutional Work. *British Journal of Management, 31*(1), 42–55.

Batool, H., & Ullah, K. (2017). Successful Antecedents of Women Entrepreneurs: A Case of Underdeveloped Nation. *Entrepreneurship Research Journal, 7*(2). https://doi.org/10.1515/erj-2016-0066

Campbell, B. (2019). *Practice Theory in Action: Empirical Studies of Interaction in Innovation and Entrepreneurship*. New York, NY: Routledge.

Carton, R. B., & Hofer, C. W. (2006). *Measuring Organizational Performance: Metrics for Entrepreneurship and Strategic Management Research*. Cheltenham: Edward Elgar Publishing.

Damanpour, F., Walker, R. M., & Avellaneda, C. N. (2009). Combinative Effects of Innovation Types and Organizational Performance: A Longitudinal Study of Service Organizations. *Journal of Management Studies, 46*(4), 650–675.

Dyer, J. H., Gregersen, H. B., & Christensen, C. (2008). Entrepreneur Behaviors, Opportunity Recognition, and the Origins of Innovative Ventures. *Strategic Entrepreneurship Journal, 2*(4), 317–338.

Eurofound. (2015). *Third European Company Survey-Workplace Innovation in European Companies*. Retrieved from Luxembourg.

Ferreira, J., Coelho, A., & Moutinho, L. (2020). Dynamic Capabilities, Creativity and Innovation Capability and Their Impact on Competitive Advantage and Firm Performance: The Moderating Role of Entrepreneurial Orientation. *Technovation, 92*, 102061.

Fouad, M. A. A. (2013). Factors affecting the Performance of Small And Medium Enterprises (SMEs) in the Manufacturing sector of Cairo, Egypt. *International Journal of Business And Management Studies, 5*(2), 157–166.

Godden, B. (2004). Sample Size Formulas. *Journal of Statistics, 3*, 66.

Hair, J., Black, W., Babin, B., Anderson, R., & Tatham, R. (2010). *Multivariate Data Analysis. A Global Perspective*. Upper Saddle River, NJ: Pearson Prentice Hall.

Ho, L.-A. (2008). What Affects Organizational Performance? The Linking of Learning and Knowledge Management. *Industrial Management & Data Systems, 108*(9), 1234–1254.

Howaldt, J., Kopp, R., & Pot, F. (2012). Workplace Innovation for Better Jobs and Performance. The Most Important Developments in Modern Working Environments. In S. Jeschke, F. Hees, & A. Richert (Eds.), *Prethinking Work: Insights on the Future of Work*. Munster: LIT-Verlag.

Ittner, C. D., & Larcker, D. F. (1998). Innovations in Performance Measurement: Trends and Research Implications. *Journal of Management Accounting Research, 10*, 205.

Lim, S., Ribeiro, D., & Lee, S. M. (2008). Factors Affecting the Performance of Entrepreneurial Service Firms. *The Service Industries Journal, 28*(7), 1003–1013.

Lusthaus, C. (2002). *Organizational assessment: A framework for improving performance*. Ottawa: IDRC.

March, J. G., & Sutton, R. I. (1997). Crossroads—Organizational Performance as a Dependent Variable. *Organization Science, 8*(6), 698–706.

McMurray, A., & Dorai, R. (2003). *Workplace Innovation Scale: A New Method for Measuring Innovation in the Workplace*. Paper presented at the The 5th European Conference on Organizational Knowledge, Learning and Capabilities (OKLC 2003).

McMurray, A., & Scott, D. (2013). Work Values Ethic, GNP Per Capita and Country of Birth Relationships. *Journal of Business Ethics, 116*(3), 655–666.

Molina, J. A., Ortega, R., & Velilla, J. (2017). *Older Entrepreneurs-by-Necessity Using Fuzzy Set Methods: Differences Between Developed and Developing Countries*. MPRA, (76982).

Muenjohn, N., & McMurray, A. (2015). *Leadership, Work Values Ethic and Workplace Innovation: A Comparative Study Between Thai and Vietnamese SME's*. Paper presented at the Asia Pacific Conference on Business and Social Sciences, Kuala Lumpur.

Muenjohn, N., & McMurray, A. (2017). Design Leadership, Work Values Ethic and Workplace Innovation: an Investigation of SMEs in Thailand and Vietnam. *Asia Pacific Business Review, 23*(2), 192–204.

Murphy, G. B., Trailer, J. W., & Hill, R. C. (1996). Measuring Performance in Entrepreneurship Research. *Journal of business research, 36*(1), 15–23.

Newnham, L. (2018). *The Relationship Between Workplace Innovation and Organizational Culture: A Case Study of a Victorian Public Sector Organization*. PhD, RMIT University.

Nunnally, J. C. (1994). *Psychometric Theory*. New York: Tata McGraw-Hill.

OECD. (2004). *Medium-Sized Enterprises in Turkey: Issues and Policies*. Retrieved from Paris.

Oeij, P., Dhondt, S., & Korver, T. (2011). *Workplace Innovation, Social Innovation, and Social Quality* (1757-0344). Retrieved from https://www.berghahnjournals.com/view/journals/ijsq/1/2/ijsq010204.xml.

Oeij, P., Dhondt, S., Kraan, K., Vergeer, R., & Pot, F. (2012). Workplace Innovation and its Relations with Organisational Performance and Employee Commitment. 4.

Oeij, P., Dhondt, S., Pot, F., & Totterdill, P. (2018). *Workplace Innovation as an Important Driver of Social Innovation*. Dortmund: Sozialforschungsstelle TU Dortmund.

Oeij, P., Dhondt, S., Rus, D., & Van Hootegem, G. (2019). The Digital Transformation Requires Workplace Innovation: An Introduction. *International Journal of Technology Transfer & Commercialisation, 16*(3), 199.

Oeij, P., & Vaas, F. (2016). Effect of Workplace Innovation on Organisational Performance and Sickness Absence. *World Review of Entrepreneurship, Management and Sustainable Development, 12*(1), 101–129.

Oeij, P., de Vroome, E., Bolland, A., Grundemann, R., & Van Teeffelen, L. (2014). Investing in Workplace Innovation Pays Off for SMEs: A Regional Innovation Initiative from the Netherlands. *International Journal of Social Quality, 4*(2), 86.

Olughor, R. J. (2015). Effect of Innovation on the Performance of SMEs Organizations in Nigeria. *Management, 5*(3), 90–95.

Perera, S., & Baker, P. (2007). Performance Measurement Practices in Small and Medium Size Manufacturing Enterprises in Australia. *Small Enterprise Research, 15*(2), 10–30.

Porter, M. (1985). *Competitive Advantage: Creating and Sustaining Superior Performance*. New York: FreePress.

Pot, F. (2011). Workplace Innovation for Better Jobs and Performance. *International Journal of Productivity and Performance Management, 60*(4), 404–415.

Pot, F., Dhondt, S., & Oeij, P. (2012). Social Innovation of Work and Employment. In J. Hochgerner, H. W. Franz, & J. Howaldt (Eds.), *Challenge Social Innovation*. Berlin, Heidelberg: Springer.

Pot, F., Rus, D., & Oeij, P. (2017). Introduction: The Need to Uncover the Field of Workplace Innovation. In *Workplace Innovation* (pp. 1–8). Berlin: Springer.

Pot, F., Totterdill, P., & Dhondt, S. (2016). Workplace Innovation: European Policy and Theoretical Foundation. *World Review of Entrepreneurship, Management and Sustainable Development, 12*(1), 13–32.

Pot, F., Totterdill, P., & Dhondt, S. (2020). Workplace Innovation Supports Implementation of European Pillar of Social Rights. *European Journal of Workplace Innovation, 5*(2), 173–185.

Provasnek, A. K., Schmid, E., Geissler, B., & Steiner, G. (2017). Sustainable Corporate Entrepreneurship: Performance and Strategies Toward Innovation. *Business Strategy and the Environment, 26*(4), 521–535.

Richards, P., Devinney, T., Yip, G., & Johnson, G. (2009). Measuring Organizational Performance: Towards Methodological Best Practice. *Journal of Management, 35*(3), 718–804.

Salavou, H., Baltas, G., & Lioukas, S. (2004). Organisational Innovation in SMEs: The Importance of Strategic Orientation and Competitive Structure. *European Journal of Marketing, 38*(9/10), 1091–1112.

Shaukat, S., Nawaz, M. S., & Naz, S. (2013). Effects of Innovation Types on Firm Performance: An Empirical Study on Pakistan's Manufacturing Sector. *Pakistan Journal of Commerce & Social Sciences, 7*(2), 243–262.

Simmers, C., & McMurray, A. (2019). Organisational Justice and Managing Workplace Innovation: How Important Are Formal Procedures? *International Journal of Innovation Management, 23*(03), 1950026.

Smith, T. M., & Reece, J. S. (1999). The Relationship of Strategy, Fit, Productivity, and Business Performance in a Services Setting. *Journal of Operations Management, 17*(2), 145–161.

Sulaiman, N. (2016). *The Impact of Financial Knowledge and Capabilities on SME Firm Performance in Australia.* PhD, RMIT University,

Swierczek, F. W., & Ha, T. T. (2003). Entrepreneurial Orientation, Uncertainty Avoidance and Firm Performance: An Analysis of Thai and Vietnamese SMEs. *The International Journal of Entrepreneurship and Innovation, 4*(1), 46–58.

Totterdill, P., & Exton, R. (2014). Defining Workplace Innovation: The Fifth Element. *Strategic Direction, 30*(9), 12–16.

Ulhøi, J. P. (2005). The Social Dimensions of Entrepreneurship. *Technovation, 25*(8), 939–946.

Von Treuer, K., & McMurray, A. (2012). The Role of Organisational Climate Factors in Facilitating Workplace Innovation. *International Journal of Entrepreneurship and Innovation Management, 15*(4), 292–309.

Wiklund, J. (1998). *Small Firm Growth and Performance: Entrepreneurship and Beyond.* Jönköping: Internationella Handelshögskolan.

Yousaf, U., Shamim, A., Siddiqui, H., & Raina, M. (2015). Studying the Influence of Entrepreneurial Attributes, Subjective Norms and Perceived Desirability on Entrepreneurial Intentions. *Journal of Entrepreneurship in Emerging Economies, 7*(1), 23–34.

Zou, S., & Cavusgil, S. T. (2002). The GMS: A Broad Conceptualization of Global Marketing Strategy and Its Effect on Firm Performance. *Journal of marketing, 66*(4), 40–56.

Theme V

Workplace Innovation and Transformations

25

Innovation Unplugged: The Power of Mindsets, Behaviour and Collaboration in the Quest for Innovation

Mark Boyes and Arthur Shelley

Introduction

According to the World Economic Forum annual report (WEF, 2019), globalisation and technological progress continue to have a profound effect on economic and social systems. Creativity has been highlighted by the WEF as one of the principal critical future skills to drive success in this new ecosystem (WEF, 2018). They call for newer visions of growth, innovation and competitiveness to ensure sustainable growth, productivity and innovation, culminating in this quote about their own practices in their financial statement in the 2019 annual report:

> *The World Economic Forum always acts in the spirit of entrepreneurship in the global public interest, combining the forces of creative thinking, innovative initiatives and intellectual integrity with the will to advance peace and prosperity in the world.* (WEF, 2019)

M. Boyes (✉)
Croydon North, VIC, Australia
e-mail: markboyes@live.com.au

A. Shelley
Melbourne, VIC, Australia
e-mail: arthur@organizationalzoo.com

© The Author(s), under exclusive license to Springer Nature Switzerland AG 2021
A. McMurray et al. (eds.), *The Palgrave Handbook of Workplace Innovation*,
https://doi.org/10.1007/978-3-030-59916-4_25

This chapter explores the importance of a continual quest for innovation. It will not provide a four- or five-step process for innovation, nor will it rehash industry best practice. Instead, it will discuss the roles people play, the necessary mindsets, organisational structures and behaviours to enable collaboration which ultimately shapes our innovation outcomes. Embedded throughout the chapter are case study discussions from three multinational organisations, two of which are highly respected and awarded for their innovations. The third organisation is learning from the other two as they invest in the insights of others' experiences to accelerate what they can achieve.

The Problem with Innovation

How do you keep a wave upon the sand? How to solve a problem like innovation? Proactively exploring complex challenges by questioning what can change and why this is of benefit is a key to an innovative workplace. Most organisations strive for innovation, looking for competitive advantage, efficiency improvements and capitalising on the value novel initiatives can bring. Most, if not all, leaders would like to be more innovative (Barsh, Capozzi, & Davidson, 2008; Horth & Buchner, 2014). However, despite all the good intention, many innovation initiatives fall short of their expectations (Rhaiem & Amara, 2019). In general terms, this occurs due to a lack of understanding of innovation and how it should be managed and successfully executed. Attempts to harness its mystical powers through outdated management methodologies, rigid policies and structural barriers are futile, especially when we try to navigate innovation efforts through tenacious and convergent mindsets that are defending the status quo and are bound by slow-moving decision-making processes. Barsh et al. (2008) highlighted that innovation is a personal and behavioural matter for leaders, stating that, "Members of the top team must agree that promoting it is a core part of the company's strategy, reflect on the way their own behaviour reinforces or inhibits it, and decide how they should role-model the change and engage middle management and front-line workers."

Have you ever heard these words before …? "To be truly innovative, we must encourage innovation" or "we must think outside the box and be more creative". If so, you are not alone. In response we repeatedly hear, "another bloody innovation project" or "here we go again". To kick more goals in football, we might as well say, "we need to encourage more goal kicking" or "kick the ball more accurately". Instead, we may need to recruit players who are great goal kickers, coach them to improve, encourage them to practise, perform together as team and have a strategic game plan. Successfully executing innovation is no different; you need a game plan and the right people who are engaged and have the right capabilities and the right mindsets at the right time. Innovation comes from social interactions; it is organic and it is often triple-coated in the complexities of humanity.

The Problem with Problems

Innovation often starts with a problem, and the people managing the innovation project should have an extensive and comprehensive understanding of the problem that they are attempting to solve. Problems are ubiquitous, but every problem is unique. The problem with problems, is that we attempt to solve our problems with a limited set of often ill-equipped processes, frameworks and methodologies. This limited convergent approach, mostly leaves the original problem partly or completely unsolved and sometimes completely missed.

Formal and modern approaches to innovation management are relatively new—less than 100 years old. The same can be said about project management (PM) methodologies (PMI, 2017). A movement earlier this century to 'rethink' project management (Cicmil, Williams, Thomas, & Hodgson, 2006) set out to challenge the status quo in this domain. However, in PM like innovation management, the firmly established and dominating project management methodologies that we abide by, are extremely tenacious and inwardly focused. They are born from anachronous managerial needs of a different era—an age which laboured to manage efficiency, cost and resources (Atkinson, 1999; Brown, Hyer, & Ettenson, 2013; Kapsali, 2011; Lloyd-Walker & Walker, 2011; Shelley, 2012). The time, cost, scope and quality elements, often referred to as the 'Iron Triangle' in project management, remain as equally important today as they did 50, 100 or even 3000 years ago (albeit not in the formal PM context we experience today). However, in today's ever changing and complex world, this narrow managerial lens is no longer sufficient to be effective (Lloyd-Walker & Walker, 2011).

To solve problems effectively, we benefit from making a paradigm shift away from traditional methodologies. We will benefit greatly from developing mindsets that are able to resist the status quo and engage in divergent thinking before the convergent thinking occurs. A collaboration of diverse and divergent perspectives is key to stimulating creativity and producing valuable innovation outcomes. Equally important is knowing when to converge on a solution, prioritise and execute; the issue is, we habitually do this part first. Iterative cycles of firstly divergent actions (to generate options), followed by convergent (to prioritise and refine the best of these options) is gaining support and has been adopted into practices such as Design Thinking (Brown, 2009; Liedtka, King, & Bennett, 2013; Shelley, 2017).

Methodology

This chapter is positioned from practitioners' (the extensive industry experiences of the authors) points of view and supported by research conducted during the primary author's PhD. This section discusses the research methodology which sat within an interpretivist and inductive inquiry paradigm. The action research program explored how engaging in divergent thinking before convergent thinking can deliver better outcomes. The focus on (intangible) outcomes over (tangible) outputs is an important distinction to make at this juncture.

The authors regularly discover organisations where endeavours are targeted towards producing outputs and they often struggle to deliver desired outcomes. Similarly, outputs are routinely valued over behaviours, leading to ineffective ways of working and poor organisational cultures. The study was designed to investigate the possible impact of a paradigm shift on performance and outcomes, one that is more geared towards leadership, collaboration and behaviour. Research participants from three international settings were engaged during the action research program in which qualitative data was collected and analysed.

One of these organisations was NASA (USA National Aeronautics and Space Administration), where creativity workshops were facilitated by the primary author to assess the impact of creative thinking on options generation and decision making. Insights for the development of the mind-shift model—explained later in this chapter—were taken from this workshop and research interactions at an Australian based service agency. This is significant because even at NASA Goddard Space Flight Centre, which has received multiple innovation awards and regularly voted as the best place to work, additional creative interventions were seen as a positive contribution.

At the time of writing, the findings of the author's research are also being applied to the early stages of a business-wide transformation project for an Australian listed company. The initial assessment of this implementation and real-world application of the mind-shift model and behavioural changes will also be discussed.

Additionally, this chapter shares a case study of a Melbourne-based entrepreneurial small business—Blackmagic Design—which has won many awards in creativity and innovation. Interviews conducted during site visits and discussions with the CEO and cofounder highlight how thinking differently about the way we work can be economically rewarding and game changing for industry.

Creativity Through Collaboration

To address the ever-changing landscape, and to give ourselves the best opportunity to succeed in our quest for innovation, we must embrace a specific set of skills and behaviours, that are not often prevalent in the workplace. The outcome of getting these behaviours in balance is collaboration. Amabile and Khaire (2008) debunked the "Lone Inventor Myth" and stated, "Though past breakthroughs sometimes have come from a single genius, the reality today is that most innovations draw on many contributions." Securing an inclusive collaborative environment moves our activities from managing processes to engaging people in open divergent social interactions (Shelley & Goodwin, 2018). This focus on people interactions can be enhanced with provision of appropriate environment, processes and tools (Gino, 2019; Pisano & Verganti, 2008) and creating these conditions enables elements of workforce engagement.

The good news is that many of these capabilities can develop naturally when we let go of others. The simple act of thinking divergently, before the convergent thinking occurs, is one way to break away from the tenacity of the status quo. This is not a new concept; in the 2000s Sinek (2011) encouraged us to "ask why", in the 1980s Edward de Bono instructed us to put on yellow and green hats before black (de Bono, 1985), meaning creative and optimistic thinking before critical thinking. Earlier still, Guilford (1950) informed us that there are other ways to measure intelligence and that we should embrace the idea of divergence and creativity to survive the challenges of the twentieth century.

It is widely accepted that creative thinking and problem solving are critical capabilities in sustaining a successful business (WEF, 2018). However, the contemporary literature surrounding creativity and the twentieth-century expansion of research in this field has come with a price. Researchers in one discipline such as Neuroscience or Project Management are often unaware of advances in others such as The Arts (Amabile, 1998). Therefore, there is no one agreed academic or practical definition of creativity, which leads to confusion and misinterpretation in the field. For this reason, many organisations are recognising that collaboration—especially across disciplines—stimulates higher performance (ISO, 2017). Connecting people with different perspectives to engage in open conversations around challenges, enables participants to find higher quality options (Shelley, 2017).

Creativity has become an overused buzzword and a catch phrase across several disciplines. Some researchers turn the spotlight onto the creative output and divide it into, disruptive and every day or "Big-C" and "Little-C" (Merrotsy, 2013), while others discussed cognitive abilities and personality traits (Eysenck, 1983). Runco and Jaeger (2012) published an article titled "The Standard Definition of Creativity" to remind researchers that the field of creativity studies predates the digital age and they point future researchers towards early twentieth-century works of Patrick and Stein. Runco and Jaeger propose that these early definitions of creativity are equally valid today and that researchers should pay credit to these early pioneers. To that end, this chapter will use this definition of creativity by Stein (1953):

> The creative work is a novel work that is accepted as tenable or useful or satisfying by a group in some point in time.

By saying 'work' Stein's definition focusses on the output (i.e. a product, artefact, or something tangible), and by novel he explains that the work is original and did not exist before; he clarifies that by saying that not all or any of elements of the 'work' need to be new, but just the combination of or end product. Adding to this definition, modern thoughts on creativity include elements related to the outcomes of engaging in creativity; the intrinsic motivation (Amabile, Barsade, Mueller, & Staw, 2005), mental health benefits and personal growth (Runco, 2007) as examples. Stein maintained that the degree of novelty is how far the work diverges from the status quo. In this statement he provides a nice segue into divergent thinking, which is the generation of multiple possibilities or solutions to a set problem (Guilford, 1950); in other words it is alternative trains of thought away from the status quo.

Divergent Thinking

There is a distinct lack of theoretical and empirical research into divergent thinking within an organisational context; the vast majority (87.9%) of the research (1950–2014) into divergent thinking examines psychological aspects within education, health and social contexts. There are a few pieces of work that provide some insight into how divergent thinking might be used in group settings to improve creative potential and these were drawn upon to provide a theoretical foundation for the mind-shift model. The model was not intended to provide a 'quick fix' to the challenges facing organisations today; it was designed to challenge mind-sets and provide a foundation for constructive, strategic creativity thinking at appropriate times.

Runco and Jaeger (2012) suggested that the notion of divergent thinking is appealing for several reasons. They explain that "it is a good metaphor of the kind of cognition that should lead to original ideas" (p. 68). They also suggest that divergent thinking easily contrasts with convergent thinking, which is an arrangement of predictable and correct solutions as opposed to a degree of original or diverse possibilities. The authors explain that divergent thinking is much more than a metaphor, in that it can be measured and the results are a reliable assessment for creative potential. Runco and Acar (2012) explain that divergent thinking is different from creativity, yet divergent thinking can lead to creative thought. In other words, divergent thinking is not the same as creativity, you can have divergent thinking without creativity, but you cannot have creativity without divergent thinking.

Unplugging Innovation

For the past 50 years it has been widely accepted that divergent thinking was the production of spontaneous ideas which is measured through fluency, flexibility, originality and elaboration. The definition of creativity on the other hand remained as much as a mystery of the universe itself; we know it is there but we cannot agree on how it got there or even why it exists. Early research pioneers such as Guilford (1950) and Christensen, Guilford, and Wilson (1957) defined creativity in terms of the production of ideas or products, while others argued that creativity was an attribute of personality—Barron and Harrington (1981) for example. However, others like Boring (1963) argued that creativity results from social constructs, which steers us towards the human side of creativity and therefore innovation.

One aspect that these scholars conceptually agreed upon is that creativity cannot exist without divergent thinking. Early research focussed on allowing participants to engage in different patterns of thought which may have led to creative output to test whether or not an individual was creative. However, a major shift in attitudes towards creativity occurred during the 1990s, which was steered by creativity activists such as Amabile (1996, 1998), de Bono (1995, 1998, 1999) and Runco (1992, 1995). These scholars challenged the modes of thinking as they proposed that we all have creative talents; you do not need to be famous to be creative (Ripple, 1989). They argued that it is the environment and the culture which is the major influence on whether we engage our creative mind-sets, which in turn highlights the dependence an innovation climate has on, creativity, soft (human) skills and social constructs.

Soft skills such as empathy, collaboration and influence have been on managements' radar since the middle of the twentieth century, when the U.S. Army invested substantial resources into the development of soft skills training procedures. Since the recognition of soft skills in management philosophy, there has been an increasing attention to its value. Characterised by learned behaviours and founded in the individual's predisposition rather than psychological personas, preferences and motivations, soft skills are usually described as non-cognitive abilities (Balcar, 2014). To be innovative, a shift in thinking towards social processes is required, one that is more aligned with the non-linear, soft skills and divergence from the status quo. In other words, to successfully execute innovation, a realignment of authentic soft skills leadership and process management is essential.

The Adobe 'State of Create' study (2012) found that 61% of people surveyed do not consider themselves to be creative, and only 25% feel they are living up to their creative potential. Maintaining the status quo, 75% of respondents felt that they were under pressure to be productive rather than creative at work. If we only applied 'Emotional Intelligence' during specific periods or assigned it to specific people or teams, one could imagine that life at work would be disingenuous and unproductive. Therefore, it is the contention of this chapter that to be truly creative at work we must be freed from traditional patterns of working; creative thinking must be nurtured, encouraged and embedded into the organisational culture and all of the teams, all of the time.

The academic literature and case studies provide overwhelming evidence that creativity and therefore divergent thinking can improve outcomes on many levels: organisational, team, personal and cultural. If we want to be innovative, then creativity must be present at every level of every artistic, technical and operational part of the organisation (Catmull, 2008); creativity is for all of us, all the time.

Increasing innovation opportunities requires an adjustment in the ratios of investment in people, process and tools, as indicated in Fig. 25.1. The overemphasis on tools and process was a common observation in all cases discussed in this chapter, as well in the experiences of the authors across other organisations. The case observations and wider authors' experiences highlight that engaging people in creative divergent activities can assist to break the habits that generate the overemphasis on convergent thinking and overreliance on technology to drive innovation. Rapid advances in technology, focuses on artificial intelligence, the buzz of the fourth industrial revolution and the

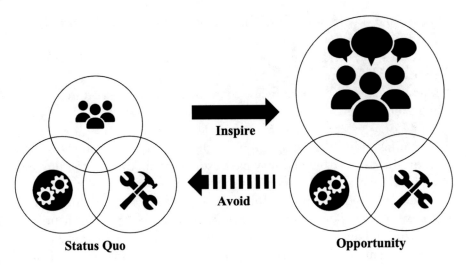

Fig. 25.1 A shift in emphasis to achieve optimal outcomes

promises of machine learning and big data have shifted out focus from people co-creating options to technology-generated solutions. It is not a matter of "this OR that", it is a matter of "this AND that." In our excitement of technology solutions and the reliability of processes, we have stripped the serendipity that happens when people creatively explore possibilities. The effectiveness of iterative cycles has been demonstrated by the success of approaches that maintain a degree of flexibility through the whole cycle, such as Design Thinking and Agile PM. However, to change the momentum of an industry takes considerable effort. We do not want to only inject token creative exercises and then "get on with the real work". To reap ongoing rewards from a more balanced approach, requires a change in mindset of those leading and participating in initiatives.

Changing Mindsets

To engage in divergent thinking before the convergent thinking occurs, we must be able to break away from the over persistent emphases on convergent process and tools. Mostly born from good intent, a myriad of tenacious forces maintain and bolster the status quo. Shifting away from them is a complex challenge for any organisation. To assist in understanding these forces they have been arranged into three categories:

- **Individual**—awareness, fear, focus, motivation, bias, heuristics and personality
- **Culture**—risk aversion, group think, tolerance, recruitment, barriers and embedded behaviours
- **Management**—short term focus, constraints, controls, structure, policies and procedures

Operating within the comfort zone of the status quo, an individual may focus on the task at hand and may have little to no motivation to think of a better way of working. They may not have an awareness of, or want to know, that there is a need to improve. This may be caused by a lack of understanding, a fear of the unknown or their own personal beliefs, biases or heuristics. Supporting and maintaining individual mindsets is the organisational culture which can reinforce risk adversity, group think and an intolerance of failure. Established workplace cultures are created and supported by the behaviours of existing personnel, leadership and recruitment practices. Management which flows from and supports the culture, often includes rigid policies and procedures, hierarchical communication structures, short-term (quarter by quarter) outlooks, increasing tightening of controls and an ever-reducing pool of resources (do more with less approach).

The research findings highlighted how powerful these forces can be; one of the organisations was extremely paralysed, unable to make change without first establishing sub-committees, working groups and producing white papers. 75% of the employees wanted to be more creative at work, yet in contradiction 84% said creativity had no place in everyday work. The overadherence to policy and procedure constructed a 'not safe to fail' mindset across the organisation and shaped an impenetrable barrier to innovation. Participants described how the culture and management had a negative effect on their motivation, most referring to their work as the "daily grind" with limited opportunities for exercising their minds.

In contrast, NASA instilled a 'fail fast, fail safe' policy and encouraged people to challenge the status quo. The result was a highly engaged workforce, 86% of whom thought that the organisation supported creativity. This organisation is highly coveted and awarded for the innovations and often voted as one of the best places to work. The difference between the two organisations is not finance or sector related; in fact both are government agencies. The key difference is the culture and their ability to shift the emphasis towards people, which ultimately determines how innovative they are.

The mind-shift model (Fig. 25.2) was developed from reflecting on the insights in this research and asking how creative interventions can be more

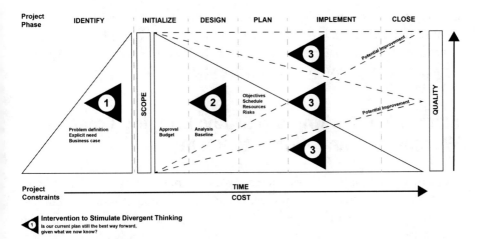

Fig. 25.2 The mind-shift model (Boyes, 2019)

successfully implemented throughout an initiative, such as a project (given that most changes are delivered though projects). Although every project and organisation are different, being mindful of how and when to include divergent thinking and creativity into the process is important. It is easy to get lost in the efficiencies of converging on the problem given the limitations of time and resources. However, many challenges are more effectively managed when a little divergent thinking generates a range of alternatives. The authors have observed in many organisations over the years that creativity and innovation both flourish when time is invested in disrupting the flow with challenging questions and engaging interactions, such as games with a purpose. The Blackmagic Design case, shared later in this chapter, is a good example of this.

Leading Transformational Change

Transformation has been another buzzword for some time with considerable hype in the general literature (Nel, Furr, & Ramsoy, 2018). However, there is no doubt that the pace of change is increasing, and this is generating challenges for traditional organisations. The ubiquitous statement "we are going through a transformation" misses the point. It implies that beyond the transformation there will be a period of stability. In our VUCA world (Glaeser, 2019) we are in constant transformation. The process of change is unrelenting. Whilst this is seen by many as a problem, the more agile and entrepreneurial leaders see this as an opportunity. When nothing is certain and outcomes are unpredictable, the environment favours the flexible and adventurous. Those who can learn and adapt faster than the competitors dominate. A great example is Blackmagic Design, which fits the model of an Applied Social Learning Ecosystem (Shelley & Goodwin, 2018).

Blackmagic Design Case Study: Bringing Creative Workplace Innovation into Reality

Blackmagic Design is an excellent example of implementing the principles of collaboration, creativity and inclusive conversations to stimulate sustained innovation and growth. In the first 16 years of operation, Blackmagic Design moved from a start-up to over USD300 million turnover, with good profitability, no debt and no external ownership. Blackmagic Design is an entrepreneurial broadcast technology enterprise that adapts its products so quickly that competitors can't keep up. By delivering customers' dreams before they become expectations, Blackmagic Design excites the industry and leads the industry big players into reactive tactics. Proof of Blackmagic Design's performance is independently acknowledged with over 400 innovation awards from around the world, including the highly coveted Red Dot 'Best of the Best' award, which represents the top 1.5% of over 5500 entries from 54 countries. Blackmagic Design's broadcast equipment, cameras and editing and colour grading software is acknowledged with preferred supplier status in television stations and at many of the big Hollywood film studios. Blackmagic Design film and colour grading products have been used in many award-nominated and winning films including *Dunkirk, The Florida Project, Three Billboards Outside Ebbing, Hacksaw Ridge, The Martian, Avatar* and many others.

At the largest broadcasting equipment industry trade fair in the world, the Blackmagic Design press conference is completely booked out each year. Everyone in the industry is keen to discover the latest development and how they can access this new technology.

So How Does Blackmagic Design Achieve This Amazing Growth and Innovation Success?

A traditional manager may think such achievements come through strong control and process compliance, not so! In fact, it is the opposite. There is NO management hierarchical structure and no walls of procedural manuals. Blackmagic Design is an inclusive co-creative collaborative ecosystem. Every person in the organisation is directly working on finding creative options to address challenges faced by their customers. Within an hour of any feedback provided to the company, the essence of the challenge is shared in all production facilities on screens. Team members see the comments in real time, and everyone has the opportunity to suggest options for improvement. This means that all employees are directly in touch with what the customers (throughout the supply chain) like about the products and what they desire to improve.

Grant Petty, Blackmagic Design CEO and founder, possesses a very strong vision for the organisation. He has not built the organisation to sell off as quickly as possible, like many start-ups. Petty is passionate about building as an ongoing contributor to the industry and wider society—one that leads innovation and provides career paths for creative people to flourish. Taking a longer-term strategic commitment provides a totally different mindset to what he and his team are trying to achieve. His vision is to create an inclusive professional ecosystem that generates social value for everyone involved— throughout the entire supply chain (and beyond through charitable support). He strongly supports young creative professionals entering the industry as well as creative events that spread the word about the importance of creativity for successful businesses in future.

There are several innovation accelerating elements in how Blackmagic Design operates that can benefit other businesses:

- The CEO has complete knowledge of the detailed technical capabilities of the products and is actively engaged in the development conversations.
- There is an internally built automated management systems technology for the entire development, manufacturing, sales and after-sales support process.
- Real-time customer feedback shared in offices and manufacturing.
- The above means there is no requirement for management hierarchies.
- The products are built around an interchangeable suite to allow flexible installation and upgrades.
- There is a strong sense of identity and belonging within and across teams.
- Integrated self-regulated development teams understand the value of creativity and collaboration and actively participate to optimise outcomes from these.
- Team leaders employ own team members, removing the need for HR.

As a result of these elements there are a lot of synergies generated and a strategic flow of knowledge through the organisation. New knowledge is constantly being co-created in the interactions between teams, which accelerates the innovation process across the entire workplace. Key outcomes of this include:

- Start up to over $300 million (USD) in first 16 years of operation;
- Survived and grew during a complete and ongoing industry disruption;
- Higher quality products for a fraction of competitors' price;
- Consistently perform better than industry growth;
- High demand for products and services and responsive to customer challenges;
- Vibrant consumer support communities in social media.

A strong indication to the open-minded role model that Petty inspires the Blackmagic Design workplace is captured in a few extracts of the 2018 NAB press conference in Los Angeles:

> *"We are creating as much freedom for creativity as we can"*
> *"I don't know what kind of blend of technology and creativity will come together from this ...... I am fascinated to find out ... ""We just do these things and think it sounds right, and it will be interesting to see what happens."*

A key insight for achieving continuous workplace innovation is that within Blackmagic Design there is the inclusion of everyone in an aligned co-creative collaborative purposeful ecosystem. The leadership demonstrates that creativity is not just encouraged, but expected; Blackmagic Design are living role models of what can be achieved through such an approach. The outcomes are internal and external loyalty, fully engaged people and the establishment of a community of passionate supporters around something meaningful, rather than just a "company". Profitable growth is not the focus of the strategy; it is a side effect of getting the ecosystem right.

Conclusions

Without a conscious effort to understand organisational cultural norms and recognise individual cognitive biases, it would be very difficult to break away from status quo decision making within projects. Without proactively injecting creativity into the normal way we work, teams are susceptible to functional fixedness—following the 'known path'. This often results in repeating similar mistakes and operating in a space that is (incorrectly) perceived as being known and controlled, and therefore superficially comfortable. Comfort breeds a mindset of complacency and reduces the desire—but not the need—for creativity.

Shifting the emphasis from processes and tools towards people, then implementing the mind-shift model to embed divergent thinking into team decision making has wide and positive implications, especially for innovation outcomes. Beyond the fiscal improvement, the model offers an opportunity to engage project team members in constructive divergent conversations about the desired outcomes and the way forward. This helps to improve team dynamics, motivation and engagement by involving the team and utilising their intellect and therefore provides an opportunity to improve workplace innovation, overall performance outcomes and opportunities for growth.

References

Amabile, T. M. (1998). How to Kill Creativity. *Harvard Business Review, 1998*, 77–87.

Amabile, T. M., Barsade, S. G., Mueller, J. S., & Staw, B. M. (2005). Affect and Creativity at Work. *Administrative Science Quarterly, 50*, 367–403.

Amabile, T. M., & Khaire, M. (2008). Creativity and the Role of the Leader. *Harvard Business Review, 86*(10), 100–109.

Atkinson, R. (1999). Project Management- Cost, Time and Quality, Two Best Guesses and a Phenomenon, Its Time to Accept Other Success Criteria. *International Journal of Project Management, 17*(6), 337–342.

Balcar, J. (2014). Soft Skills and Their Wage Returns: Overview of Empirical Literature. *Review of Economic Perspectives, 14*(1), 3–15.

Barron, F., & Harrington, D. M. (1981). Creativity, Intelligence, and Personality. *Annual Review Psychology, 32*, 439–476.

Barsh, J., Capozzi, M. M., & Davidson, J. (2008). Leadership and Innovation. *The Mckinsey Quarterly, 1*, 37–47.

Boring, E. G. (1963). The Social Stimulus to Creativity. *Science, 142*, 622–623.

Boyes, M. (2019). *Embedding Divergent Thinking Into Project Team Decision Making.* Doctor of Philosophy, RMIT.

Brown, K., Hyer, N. L., & Ettenson, R. (2013). The Question Every Project Team Should Answer. *Sloan Management Review, 55*, 1.

Brown, T. (2009). *Change by Design: How Design Thinking Transforms Organizations and Inspires Innovation.* New York, NY: HarperCollins Publishers.

Catmull, E. (2008). *How Pixar Fosters Collective Creativity. Harvard Business Review.* Boston, MA: Harvard Business Publishing.

Christensen, P. R., Guilford, J. P., & Wilson, R. C. (1957). Relations of Creative Responses to Working Time and Instructions. *Journal of Experimental Psychology, 53*(2), 82.

Cicmil, S., Williams, T., Thomas, J., & Hodgson, D. (2006). Rethinking Project Management: Researching the actuality of projects. *International Journal of Project Management, 24*(8), 675–686.

de Bono, E. (1985). *Six Thinking Hats*. New York: Penguin Books.

Eysenck, H. (1983). The Roots of Creativity: Cognitive Ability or Personality Trait? *Roeper Review, 5*(4), 10–12.

Gino, F. (2019). Cracking the Code of Sustained Collaboration. *Harvard Business Review, 97*(6), 72–81.

Glaeser, W. (2019). *VUCA World*. Retrieved November 8, 2019, from https://www.vuca-world.org/

Guilford, J. P. (1950). Creativity Research: Past, Present and Future. *American Psychologist, 5*, 444–454.

Horth, D., & Buchner, D. (2014). *Innovation Leadership. How to Use Innovation to Lead Effectively, Work Collaboratively, and Drive Results*. Continuum: Center for Creative Leadership. C. f. C. Leadership.

ISO. (2017). International Standards Organization Standard ISO 44001:2017 Collaborative business relationship management systems — Requirements and framework.

Kapsali, M. (2011). Systems Thinking in Innovation Project Management: A Match That Works. *International Journal of Project Management, 29*(4), 396–407.

Liedtka, J., King, A., & Bennett, K. (2013). *Solving Problems with Design Thinking. Ten Stories of What Works*. New York, NY: Columbia University Press.

Lloyd-Walker, B., & Walker, D. (2011). Authentic Leadership for 21st Century Project Delivery. *International Journal of Project Management, 29*(4), 383–395.

Merrotsy, P. (2013). A Note on Big-C Creativity and Little-c Creativity. *Creativity Research Journal, 25*(4), 474–476.

Nel, K., Furr, N., & Ramsoy, T. Z. (2018). *Leading Transformation: How to Take Charge of Your Company's Future*. Boston, MA: Harvard Business Review Press.

Pisano, G. P., & Verganti, R. (2008). Which Kind of Collaboration Is Right for You? *Harvard Business Review, 87*, 78–86.

PMI. (2017). *A Guide to the Project Management Body of Knowledge (PMBOK® Guide) Newtown Square*. Project Management Institute.

Rhaiem, K., & Amara, N. (2019). Learning from Innovation Failures: A Systematic Review of the Literature and Research Agenda [Electronic Version]. *Review of Managerial Science*, 1–46.

Ripple, R. E. (1989). Ordinary Creativity. *Contemporary Educational Psychology, 14*, 189–202.

Runco, M. A. (2007). *Health and Clinical Perspectives. Creativity: Theories and Themes: Research Development and Practice*. Burlington, MA: Elsevier Academic Press.

Runco, M. A., & Acar, S. (2012). Divergent Thinking as an Indicator of Creative Potential. *Creativity Research Journal, 24*(1), 66–75.

Runco, M. A., & Jaeger, G. J. (2012). The Standard Definition of Creativity. *Creativity Research Journal, 24*(1), 92–96.

Shelley, A. (2012). Metaphor Interactions to Develop Team Relationships and Robustness Enhance Project Outcomes. *Project Management Journal, 43*(6), 88–96.

Shelley, A., & Goodwin, D. (2018). Optimising Learning Outcomes Through Social Co-Creation of New Knowledge in Real-Life Client Challenges. *Journal of Applied Learning and Teaching, 1*(2), 26–37.

Shelley, A. W. (2017). *KNOWledge SUCCESSion. Sustained Performance and Capability Growth Through Strategic Knowledge Projects.* New York, NY: Business Expert Press.

Sinek, S. (2011). *Start with Why: How Great Leaders Inspire Everyone to Take Action.* New York, NY: Portfolio/Penguin.

Stein, M. I. (1953). Creativity and Culture. *The Journal of Psychology, 36*(2), 311–322.

WEF. (2018). *Future of Jobs Report.* World Economic Forum.

WEF. (2019). *Annual Repot 2018–19.* World Economic Forum.

26

The Role of Top Management Team Cognitive Diversity in a Global Sample of Innovative Firms: A Review

Claire A. Simmers

Introduction

The purpose of this chapter is to highlight workplace innovation in a sample of organizations across the globe, particularly describing the generational cohort of the top management team and exploring patterns among a global sample of innovative firms. "Workplace innovation is about creating organizations in which all employees use and develop their knowledge, skills, experience and creativity to the full" (Workplace Innovation Ltd., n.d.). It describes the complex and wide-ranging nature of innovations embodied in workplaces anchored in reflection, learning, and improvements in the way in which organizations manage their employees, organize work, and deploy technologies in the search for innovations in products and services (Van Woensel, Archer, Panades-Estruch, & Vrscaj, 2015). It is a process of organizational actions at the individual, team, and organizational units encompassed within an inventive culture (McMurray, Islam, Pirola-Merlo, & Sarros, 2013) and is "a contextual psychological construct which identifies and measures the behavioral aspects of innovation practices by individuals in their workplace" (Wipulanusat, Panuwatwanich, & Stewart, 2018).

The importance of the top management team to workplace innovation is well established (Bin, Xueqing, & Wen, 2018; Daellenbach, McCarthy, &

C. A. Simmers (✉)
Management Department, Saint Joseph's University, Philadelphia, PA, USA
e-mail: simmers@sju.edu

Schoenecker, 1999; Elenkov & Manev, 2005). However, the role of the generational cohorts of the top management teams in workplace innovation is less understood. According to multi-generational theory, each generation has different approaches to working, idea generation, and values (Mannheim, 1982), and it seems likely that exploring the generational cohorts of the top management teams in innovative companies would contribute to a better understanding of workplace innovation.

According to multi-generational theory, a generation is defined as a group of people, within a range of birth years and events, linked to a specific time period (Arsenault, 2004). These groups not only share a range of birth years but, most notably, share a set of world outlooks attached to social and historical events in their developmental years (Mannheim, 1982). These shared external contexts from the formative years are carried forward as each generational cohort advances in age; these contexts inform expectations, values, attitudes, actions, and beliefs (Cogin, 2012; Parment, 2012). The common generational cohorts are (a) 1935–1945 (Silent or Traditionalist Generation), (b) 1946–1964 (Baby Boom Generation), (c) 1965–1980 (Generation X/Gen Xers), (d) 1980–1999 (Generation Y/Millennials), and (e) 2000 to present (Generation Z). The Baby Boomers, Generation X, and the Millennials constitute the majority of those in the full-time workforce and are the focal generational cohorts in this chapter.

The Baby Boom Generation (the largest generational cohort) is often characterized as competitive, hardworking, often stressed, focused on goal setting, and generally loyal (McGuire, Todnem, & Hutchings, 2007; Zemke, Raines, & Filipczak, 2013). They are entering the typical retirement age, but redefining what retirement means by continuing to work in established or new careers (Kalejta, 2020). Globally, in industrialized regions, this generation has money and time to spend it (Yuan, 2018) and still has major social, economic, and political impacts (Ipsos, 2018).

Generation X is generally portrayed as having lower expectations of success and stronger feelings of alienation, is the first generation widely coming from two income families, is often described as selfish, questioning of authority and is organizational mobile (Corbo, 1997; McGuire et al., 2007; Zemke et al., 2013). Millennials are citizens of the Internet and hence of the globe, they are portrayed as more tolerant of diversity and risk, able to multi-task, and are serious about personal time. In general, their work style and belief systems differ fundamentally from other generations (Hernaus & Pološki Vokic, 2014; Hershatter & Epstein, 2010).

The mix of generations in the workplace presents opportunities and challenges, in attitudes, ambitions, mindsets, and values (Zemke et al., 2013).

While there is no exclusivity among generations, prior research shows it is possible to identify collective memories and define events of these birth ranges representing generational affinities (Zacher, Rosing, Henning, & Frese, 2011). McMullin, Comeau, and Jovic's (2007) qualitative research among information workers found a basis for generational formation and identity focused on computing technology and that generational discourse was invoked to create cultures of difference in the workplace. There is also support for differences among Generation X and Millennials in work values (Twenge, 2010).

Combining workplace innovation strategies with generational cohorts offers an opportunity to further explore innovation through the lens of successful innovative firms. Using more inferential methodologies (a review of publically available documents and the Internet) and a focus on cognitive diversity (represented by generational cohorts) (Reynolds & Lewis, 2017) will further our understanding of workplace innovation. In the following sections, I discuss the theoretical background, methodology, the results and the conclusion, limitations, and areas for future work.

Theoretical Background

Workplace Innovation

The workplace innovation element of the research framework used in this chapter is adapted from Fournier (2019), who proposes sixteen techniques to encourage innovation in the workplace. The sixteen techniques are grouped into seven areas: (1) leadership and management (five techniques), (2) innovation strategy (two techniques), (3) willingness to experiment (three techniques), (4) open communication (one technique), (5) staff well-being (two techniques), (6) workplace design and layout (one technique), and (7) tools and software (two techniques). The first area is leadership and management, and, not surprisingly, this is the most critical factor for innovation. In innovative workplaces, the tone, the culture of innovativeness, and the strategies emanate from the TMT (Kraiczy, Hack, & Kellermanns, 2015). Senior leaders inspire the employees and provide paths and resources to make it possible to take ownership and responsibility for new concepts and solutions (Nieminen, 2018). Fournier (2019) delineates five useful techniques for leadership and management: (1) empower your employees to think about tough problems, (2) adopt a nonhierarchical management approach, (3) give your staff a reason to care, (4) find and motivate intrapreneurs, and (5) encourage your people to think about innovation on a daily basis.

The second area is that senior leaders need to develop and disseminate an innovation strategy. Strategic consensus on the criticality of innovation to the firm strengthens relationships between the TMT and innovation performance (Camelo, Fernández-Alles, & Hernández, 2010). Two techniques in this area are develop an innovation strategy—and use it and accept failure and make it the norm (Fournier, 2019). Failure is an important learning tool in innovation because innovation is the result of an iterative process of learning, iteration, adaptation, and the building of new conceptual and physical models (Hess, 2012).

The third area for successful workplace innovation is a willingness to experiment. "Whether this is through customer co-creation, identifying market adjacencies, or participating in an innovation hub, companies must demonstrate an appetite for new ways of doing things." (Fournier, 2019). A willingness to experiment is essential because experimentation facilitates product and service formations and enhancements (Thomke, 2011).

Open communication is the fourth area Fournier (2019) proposes as necessary for an innovative workplace. Employees need transparency through clear, consistent, and accessible information. Research shows a positive link between open communication and innovation (Kivimäki et al., 2000; Linke & Zerfass, 2011). The fifth area is staff well-being and includes encouraging employees to think multi-dimensionally (Cooper, 1998). More importantly, it is about ensuring that when employees are being creative, they don't feel threatened or at risk. This can be done by recognizing and rewarding innovative behaviors and trying to ensure staff psychological safety with practices that reassure employees that innovation failures and experimentation attempts do not threaten their jobs or career progression (Fournier, 2019; Tong, Liu, Zhang, & Wang, 2018).

The sixth area is workplace design and layout which is increasing in recognition as an important component of workplace innovation. Office upgrades can be either complex as in tearing down walls or as simple as the addition of collaborative spaces, updating furniture and plants (Oziemblo, 2018; Yin et al., 2019). Even rotating work spaces or deciding team work space can positively influence creativity and collaboration (Fournier, 2019). Tools and software is the seventh area to encourage workplace innovation. There are two components to this area: software to automate routine tasks creating more time and space for creativity and innovation software (Fournier, 2019). Automating routine tasks can save time, but it augments the other areas discussed above (Deloitte, 2019). Innovation software collects input from both internal and external sources while also shielding intellectual property and creating a centralized repository for ideas (Bush, n.d.) and thus is helpful in co-creating innovations.

In addition to the seven areas, Fournier (2019) discusses three critical areas where encouraging innovation leads to better outcomes: (1) being more innovative than competitors in finding solutions (competitive advantage); (2) being more innovative in satisfying customer needs, wants, and problems (consumer centric); and (3) being more innovative in satisfying employees (talent satisfaction and retention). Figure 26.1 depicts these dimensions of workplace innovation and how the top management team both directs the dimensions and receives feedback from others in the firm on these areas. In the next section, I discuss the second component of the theoretical background, top management team generational cohorts, and cognitive diversity.

Multi-Generational Theory: Top Management Team Cognitive Diversity

Generational differences influence organizational culture, the work environment and relationships, and thus, the innovation process (Friedrich, Mumford, Vessey, Beeler, & Eubanks, 2010; Stanleigh, 2006). In general, generational

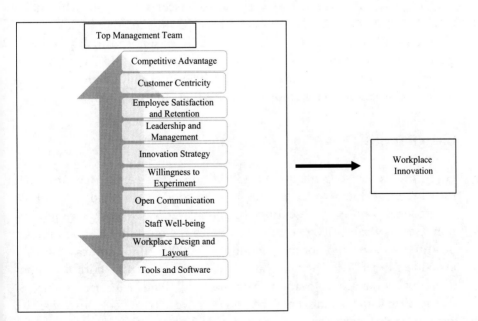

Fig. 26.1 Dimensions of workplace innovation and top management team

differences are important to examine as workplace innovation is a collective process as contributions from many areas and individuals are needed. Multiple generations in a workplace create a form of diversity, with each generation bringing its own worldviews to spur creativity and innovation (Michelson, 2019). Since senior management is particularly relevant to workplace innovation (Oke, Munshi, & Walumbwa, 2009) and there are generational cohorts' differences (Twenge, 2010), linking generational cohorts of top management teams to innovation would provide additional information on workplace innovation.

While there has been some research to question this (Kilduff, Angelmar, & Mehra, 2000), other research supports that generational cohorts, as measured by birth ranges, represent attitudinal and cognitive processes. For example, Eastman and Liu (2012) found significant differences in the level of status consumption by generational cohort with the average level of status consumption highest for Generation Y, followed by Generation X, and then Baby Boomers (p. 1). Twenge (2010) reported no generational differences in altruistic values (e.g., wanting to help others), but did find that Generation X, and especially Millennials, were consistently higher in individualistic traits. Also, Generation X, and especially Millennials, rated work as less central to their lives, valued leisure more, and expressed a weaker work ethic than Baby Boomers and the Silent Generation. In a study of green values and purchasing outcomes, Baby Boomers had higher green value scores than either Millennials or Generations X, which had similar scores (Squire, 2019). McMurray and Simmers (2019) reported that there was a difference in spirituality and religion among generations in the workplace. Generation X and Baby Boomers expressed similar levels of spirituality and religiosity than Millennials; religion was a less important factor among all generations.

Birth Ranges

Given that top management team (TMT) diversity research has produced mixed results (Homberg & Bui, 2013), it is promising to explore the role of generational cohorts, representing cognitive diversity, in workplace innovation. Cognitive diversity, refers to "how much the team shares a common set of attitudes, values and norms" (Kilduff et al., 2000, p. 6). Cognitive diversity introduces expanded viewpoints and intellectual resources—critical components for workplace innovation (Martins, Schilpzand, Kirkman, Ivabaj, & Ivanaj, 2013). The potential positive and negative effects of cognitive diversity were examined by Chen, Liu, Zhang, and Kwan (2019) who found that cognitive diversity encouraged innovative work behaviors via a pathway of reflection, communication, and adaptation (task reflectivity) but impeded innovative work behaviors via disagreements between team members about interpersonal issues including values and preferences (relationship conflict). Olson, Parayitam, and Bao (2007) reported that cognitive diversity encouraged task conflict more than relationship conflict. At the TMT level, the positive effects of task conflict counter, and even outweigh, the potential negative effects of relationship conflict. Their "… findings suggest that although task conflict is positively related to relationship conflict, task conflict still increases decision understanding, decision commitment, and decision quality." (p. 218). Mello and Rentsch (2015) also found that developmental cognitive diversity (individual differences developed over the course of one's life experiences that are relatively enduring over time and across contexts) has been shown to increase conflict. It does not appear to have a clear relationship with subjective or objective performance, but the research on these relationships is scant (p. 639). Such evidence signals the need to further describe situations of cognitive diversity as expressed by generational cohorts and workplace innovation.

Methodology

Sample

A multiple case study methodology was selected as the most relevant to this research for several reasons. It allows for a variety of evidence from both secondary sources (documents, artifacts, web pages, and articles) and organizational viewpoints beyond what might be available from survey data which is often answered by only one organizational member (Zivkovic, 2012). The data can be more holistic, focusing on process and actions. This methodology also can better represent real-life contexts and representations of practitioner experiences and outcomes (Yin, 2014). The use of multiple case studies rather than single case studies helps to develop external validity and assists in limiting researcher bias (Yin, 2014).

Using the illustrative companies from Fournier (2019), combined with Fast Company's (n.d.) the World's 50 Most Innovative Companies in 2019, I compiled a list of thirty-eight firms and matched them with the workplace innovation techniques discussed earlier in the chapter (Fournier, 2019). Of the thirty-eight firms, nineteen are headquartered in the United States, and nineteen are headquartered outside of the United States. I matched the firms to the workplace innovation techniques (Fournier, 2019) based on the information provided by Fast Company (n.d.) and by examining the firm's web pages and other publically available documents like press releases, articles, and others. The assignment to a specific workplace innovation technique does not signify that the firm only excels in that technique, but that it is an outstanding representative of that technique. It can be argued that the reputation for being an innovative company rests on being, at a minimum, excellent in many of the workplace innovation techniques (Cooper, 1998; Tang & Le, 2007). Table 26.1 lists the firms which are particularly stellar examples of the workplace innovation techniques (Fast Company, n.d.; Fournier, 2019). A brief description of each firm is given in Table 26.2.

Data on Firm Characteristics and Top Management Team

Data on firm characteristics and the top management team generational cohorts, which as previously discussed, represents cognitive diversity, were collected from a variety of online sources. These included Internet searches by top management team individual name or the company name, company web pages, LinkedIn, and Wikipedia. The data collected for each company were type of company (private, public, nonprofit), year founded, age of the company calculated from the year founded to 2020, country in which the company listed its headquarters, website for leadership information, number of employees, sales volume, executive name, title, birth year, generation, age as of January 2020, education, company tenure as of January 2020, sex, race, and availability of a photograph, if the executive was an owner/founder and comments, for example, if the executive was described as a serial entrepreneur, if it was noted the executive was leaving the company in 2020, and if an executive was a MBA classmate with another executive in the same company.

If data was either not available or varied from company to company, decision rules were created to estimate the missing or inconsistent information. Number of employees and sales data were used which were closest to January 2020 and were approximations for size. The individuals and the titles for each member of the top management team were based on the information available for each individual company. Thus the size of the top management teams and titles were unique to each company, and these variations were included as data from which I drew conclusions reported in the following section. If an age was not given in any of the sources, age approximations were calculated based on the year entering or graduating from a university; other information

Table 26.1 List of companies by workplace innovation techniques

Workplace innovation techniques	Primary headquarters in the United States	Primary headquarters outside of the United States
Three areas where encouraging innovation has an impact on businesses		
Competitive advantage	Amazon	Meituan Dianping (China)
Customer centricity	Apple	Alibaba (China)
Employee satisfaction and retention	Southwest Airlines	Nubank (Brazil)
Seven areas of techniques		
Leadership and management		
Empower your employees to think about tough problems	Truepic	Lego (Denmark)
Adopt a nonhierarchical management approach	Tesla	Sight Diagnostics (Israel)
Give your staff a reason to care	Duolingo	DHL (Germany)
Find and motivate intrapreneurs		
	Fishbowl Inventory	African Leadership Academy (Mauritius)
Encourage your people to think about innovation on a daily basis	3M	Apli (Mexico)
Innovation strategy		
Develop an innovation strategy—and use it	Microsoft	Oatly (Sweden)
Accept failure and make it the norm	Coca-Cola	Open Bionics (UK)
Willingness to experiment		
Look for market adjacencies	Disney	Grab (Singapore)
Embrace co-creation and open innovation opportunities	Starbucks	Kano (UK)
Participate in an innovation hub	Indigo Ag	Unmade (UK)
Open communication		
Be transparent	Square	Back Market (France)
Staff well-being		
Recognize and reward successful innovations	Westin Hotels	JioSaavn (India)
Ensure staff psychological safety	Beautycounter	Selina (Panama)
Workplace design and layout		
Organize your office for maximum innovation	Google	Snøhetta (Norway)
Tools and software		
Use tools to create time and space to innovate	Studio O + A	Space10 (Denmark)
Consider innovation software	Stitch Fix	AXA (France)

(*continued*)

Table 26.2 Company and description

Company	Description
3M (USA)	The company operates as a diversified technology company. 3M is famous for giving its employees a 15% time allowance every day for constructive daydreaming
African Leadership University (Mauritius)	An institute of higher education designed to teach leadership skills to Africa's best and brightest and to fight the brain drain, which has seen many of Africa's most accomplished young people go abroad to the United States or Europe
Alibaba (China)	China's largest e-commerce company presides over a collection of online platforms. Alibaba has established itself as a global innovator in what it has dubbed "new retail," the blending of digital into real-world shopping experiences
Amazon (USA)	Amazon.com serves consumers through its online and physical stores. It manufactures and sells electronic devices and develops and produces media content. Amazon operates customer service centers and enables sellers to fulfill orders through Amazon
Apli (Mexico)	A Mexico City-based startup and first major job recruiting platform. It was created as a solution to a shortage of restaurant delivery workers digitally connecting workers and employers
Apple (USA)	Apple designs, manufactures, and markets smartphones, personal computers, tablets, wearables, and accessories and sells a variety of related services
AXA (France)	AXA is a worldwide leader in financial protection strategies and wealth management. AXA is a market leader in the traditionally conservative insurance industry
Back Market (France)	Back Market runs an online marketplace based in Paris, connecting refurbished tech to new owners. They give devices a longer life, lessening their impact on the environment and helping customers save money on laptops, smartphones, and tablets
Beautycounter (USA)	Beautycounter, a certified B corporation, selling through its website and through a network of women who can earn up to 35% in commission by selling products. Beautycounter's products don't use chemicals that the brand deems questionable or harmful
Coca-Cola (USA)	Coca-Cola is a nonalcoholic beverage company with products in the following category clusters: sparkling soft drinks; water, enhanced water, and sports drinks; juice, dairy- and plant-based beverages; tea, coffee; carbonated beverages and energy drinks

(continued)

Table 26.2 (continued)

Company	Description
DHL (Deutsche Post—Germany)	Deutsche Post is a mail and logistics services group with four divisions: mail division; express division with services to business and private customers; the global forwarding and freight division which manages the carriage of goods by rail, road, air, and sea; and the supply chain division which provides warehousing, managed transport, and services
Disney (USA)	Walt Disney is an entertainment company. The segments are Media Networks; Parks, Experiences and Products; Studio Entertainment; and Direct-to-Consumer & International, which includes international television networks and channels, direct-to consumer streaming services, and other digital content distribution
Duolingo (USA)	Duolingo is an American platform that includes a language learning website and mobile app, as well as a digital language proficiency assessment exam. The company uses the freemium model
Fishbowl Inventory (USA)	Inventory management software; supplier of manufacturing and warehouse management software to small and midsize businesses
Google (Alphabet) (USA)	Alphabet is a holding company; its primary business is Google. Google's main products and platforms are Android, Chrome, Gmail, Google Drive, Google Maps, Google Play, Search, and YouTube. It also provides advertisers with tools that help them attribute and measure their advertising campaigns
Grab (Singapore)	Grab is a Singapore-based ride-hailing company, who expanded its app to offer food delivery and travel booking but also financial and other services. It added healthcare services as well
Indigo Ag (USA)	Harnessing nature to help farmers sustainably feed the planet Indigo improves grower profitability, environmental sustainability, and consumer health through the use of natural microbiology and digital technologies
JioSaavn (India) Reliance Jio Infocomm Limited, Indian telecomm co. and subsidiary of Reliance Industries	JioSaavn (formerly known as **Saavn** & **JioMusic**) is the Indian online music streaming service and a digital distributor of Bollywood, English, and other regional Indian music across the world. JioSaavn is a freemium service
Kano (UK)	The London-based start-up offers a range of programmable computers that kids as young as 6 can assemble themselves. They then program software, build stuff in Minecraft, and otherwise engage with computing in a way that's active

(*continued*)

Table 26.2 (continued)

Company	Description
Lego (Denmark)	Toy production company best known for the manufacture of Lego-brand toys, consisting mostly of interlocking plastic bricks. There are several amusement parks each known as Legoland and numerous retail stores
Meituan Dianping (China)	Meituan Dianping is an e-commerce platform for services based in the People's Republic of China. It offers over 200 service categories, including catering, on-demand delivery, car-hailing, bike-sharing, hotel and travel booking, movie ticketing, and other entertainment
Microsoft (USA)	Microsoft is a technology company that develops and supports software, services, devices, and solutions. The company provides an array of services, including cloud-based solutions as well as solution support and consulting services. Various software includes operating systems, server applications, business solution applications, and video games. The hardware products include personal computers, tablets, and gaming and entertainment consoles
Nubank (Brazil)	Offers banking solutions for populations that could not or did not access major banks in Brazil. It introduced a credit card to alleviate high interest rates and made the credit process simpler with a virtual, app-based system (and no hidden fees). It expanded into high-interest savings accounts and direct deposit, debit cards, and ATMs
Oatly (Sweden)	Swedish start-up that is a vegan food brand from Sweden which produces alternatives to dairy products from oats. Its Barista Edition Oatmilk delivers the mouthfeel and foamability associated with beverages such as cappuccinos and lattes
Open Bionics (UK)	A bionics company developing affordable, assistive devices that enhance the human body. We've started by introducing the Hero Arm, a stylish multi-grip bionic hand. The mission is to make beautiful, multi-functional bionic limbs more accessible
Selina (Panama)	Selina takes unused spaces and turns them into boutique hotels and co-working spaces catering to travelers at every price point with prices. Selina blends beautifully designed accommodation with co-working, recreation, wellness, and local experiences
Sight Diagnostics (Israel)	At Sight Diagnostics, the aim is to improve health through faster and pain-free diagnostic testing. Sight has developed an artificial intelligence-driven platform for blood analysis and infectious disease diagnostics

(continued)

Table 26.2 (continued)

Company	Description
Snøhetta (Norway)	Snøhetta is an international architecture firm best known for its thoughtful approach to designing public and cultural institutions. They also create landscapes, interiors, product design, and graphic design
Southwest Airlines	A passenger airline that provides scheduled air transportation in the United States and near-international markets. It principally provides point-to-point service, which allows for direct nonstop routing
Space10 (Denmark)	Space10 is IKEA's innovation lab, tasked with dreaming up design solutions for better, more sustainable living. The nonprofit researches and designs innovative solutions to major societal changes expected to affect people and our planet in the future
Square (USA)	Financial services, merchant services aggregator, and mobile payment company. The company markets several software and hardware payments products and has expanded into small business services
Starbucks (USA)	American multi-national chain of coffeehouses and roastery reserves. As the largest coffeehouse in the world, Starbucks is a major representation of the coffee culture
Stitch Fix (USA)	Stitch Fix is an online personal styling service in the United States. It uses recommendation algorithms and data science to personalize clothing items based on size, budget, and style
Studio O+A (USA)	An interior design studio best known for designing stylish offices for tech clients. It also designed a modern workstation which can be configured different ways to function as a freestanding office within an office
Tesla (USA)	Tesla designs, develops, manufactures, and sells fully electric vehicles and energy generation and storage systems and also installs and maintains such energy systems and sells solar electricity
Truepic (USA)	Truepic's software authenticates and verifies images and videos. It aims to accelerate business, foster a healthy civil society, and push back against disinformation by bolstering the value of authentic photos and videos while leading the fight against deceptive ones
Unmade (UK)	Unmade developed technology enabling apparel companies to create personalized, on-demand products. It tracks unique product design and shipping to aggregate orders determining the optimal production schedule to reduce waste and lower costs
Westin Hotels (USA) (Marriott is parent company)	A global leader in wellness, empowers guests to transcend the rigors of travel while on the road through the brand's Six Pillars of Well-being: Sleep Well, Eat Well, Move Well, Feel Well, Work Well, and Play Well

such as dates of the earliest employment were used to provide some degree of confirmation for the age estimations.

Each top management team person was classified into one of the three focal generational cohorts: 1946–1964 ("BB" Baby Boom Generation), 1965–1980 ("X" Generation X), or 1980–1999 ("Y" Millennials). An individual's sex was assigned as binary (male or female) based on visual inspection of digitally available photographs. Race classifications were also made based on visual inspection; the use of visual inspection versus self-reporting race classification research has supported reasonable consistency between visual inspection and self-reporting for racial classifications except for Native North Americans (Kressin, Chang, Hendricks, & Kazis, 2003). The categories used in this study were: Black, Indigenous, and People of Color (BIPOC) and White. This broad level of classification was consistent with the research purposes of identifying general racial diversity in the top management team, rather than specifics within each level.

Data Analysis and Discussion

Companies were grouped by the author according to their business life cycle (Petch, 2016) based on age of the company. Those firms founded pre-1990 were considered in the Maturity business life cycle. Companies formed in the years 1991–2000 were considered in the Expansion phase, and those formed from 2001–2010 were classified as Growth. Start-ups were those firms formed after 2011. Of the thirty-eight firms in the sample, twelve (32%) were in the Maturity phase, five (13%) in the Expansion phase, five (13%) in the Growth phase, and sixteen (42%) of the innovative companies were in the Start-up phase.

The Maturity phase often encompasses building on existing markets with product and service line extensions (Petch, 2016), and leadership challenges focus on continuing to be innovative while building upon previous successes. The Expansion stage involves taking the products and/services to new markets, either geographically or in related product/service lines. The Growth phase involves building on successes in the start-up and working to correct any missteps and improve on efficiencies (Petch, 2016). Often during the Expansion and Growth phases, the top management team increases, and the founders move onto other ventures and are replaced by younger, often outside leaders (Armstrong, 2016). The Start-up phase is when the products and services are launched and is often considered the riskiest stage, with a large number of failures. The owners/founders are concerned with expanding the customer base and generating sufficient cash to meet expenses and balancing hiring and supply to meet demand (Armstrong, 2016).

Of the thirty-eight innovative firms in the sample, nineteen are headquartered in the United States (USA), and nineteen are headquartered in other parts of the world; classifying the firms by business life cycle shows the following geographical distribution. Eight of the twelve (67%) organizations in the Maturity phase are headquartered in the USA, and the remaining four are in Western Europe (France, Denmark, Norway, and Germany). In the Expansion phase, three of the five (60%) are headquartered in the United States, one is in Sweden, and one is in China. In the Growth phase, again three of the five (60%) are in the United States, one in India, and one in China. However, in the Start-up phase, only five of the sixteen (31%) companies are in the United States. Of the eleven other Start-ups, the trend of geographical dispersion continues with the United Kingdom (3) and one each in France, Denmark, Israel, Mauritius, Singapore, Brazil, Panama, and Mexico.

The role of the top management team should complement the life cycle phase. Thus there is a matching of skills and knowledge sets and phases. In the Maturity phase, TMT are described as transformers, who need to take the existing business and continually transform the companies to better meet the changing environment, including evolving technology and customer needs (McSarron-Edwards, 2013; Ward, 2002). The TMT are sustainers in the Expansion phase. They need to sustain what worked, but be willing to be adaptable as the company expands. Knowing what to sustain and what to change as an organization expands is often a challenge (Ward, 2002). Accelerator leadership is best matched with the Growth phase, as the company moves beyond the original business model to new markets. In the Start-up phase, the top leaders are often characterized as creators (McSarron-Edwards, 2013; Ward, 2002). The business life cycle and TMT roles for the 38 innovative organizations are shown in Table 26.3.

Table 26.4 shows the top management team demographics and the classifications of firms based on business life cycle. Those firms in the Maturity phase are highlighted in bold, those in the Expansion and Growth have no highlighting, and those in the Start-up phase are highlighted in italic.

The average number of top management team members in firms in the Maturity phase is 11.5, in the Expansion and Growth it is 6.1, and in the Start-up firms it is 4.7. The average age in Maturity phase organizations is 54.5, in Expansion and Growth organizations it is 46.7, and in Start-ups it is 40.3. The cohorts in the Maturity phase organizations are predominately in the Baby Boomer generation with the remainder in the Generation X. There are no Generation Y cohorts in the top management teams of the Maturity

Table 26.3 Business life cycle assessment

Company	Year founded	Age of company[a]	Business cycle phase[b]	TMT role
AXA (France)	1816	204	Maturity	Transformers
Coca-Cola (USA)	1892	128	Maturity	Transformers
3M (USA)	1902	118	Maturity	Transformers
Westin Hotels (USA)	1930	90	Maturity	Transformers
Lego (Denmark)	1932	88	Maturity	Transformers
Disney (USA)	1938	82	Maturity	Transformers
Southwest Airlines (USA)	1967	53	Maturity	Transformers
Starbucks (USA)	1971	49	Maturity	Transformers
Microsoft (USA)	1975	45	Maturity	Transformers
Apple (USA)	1977	43	Maturity	Transformers
Snøhetta (Norway)	1989	31	Maturity	Transformers
DHL (Deutsche Post Germany)	1990	30	Maturity	Transformers
Studio O+A (USA)	1992	28	Expansion	Sustainers
Amazon (USA)	1994	26	Expansion	Sustainers
Oatly (Sweden)	1994	26	Expansion	Sustainers
Google (Alphabet) (USA)	1998	22	Expansion	Sustainers
Alibaba (China)	1999	21	Expansion	Sustainers
Fishbowl Inventory (USA)	2001	19	Growth	Accelerators
Tesla (USA)	2003	17	Growth	Accelerators
JioSaavn (India)	2007	13	Growth	Accelerators
Square (USA)	2009	11	Growth	Accelerators
Meituan Dianping (China)	2010	10	Growth	Accelerators
Duolingo (USA)	2011	9	Start-up	Creators
Sight Diagnostics (Israel)	2011	9	Start-up	Creators
Stitch Fix (USA)	2011	9	Start-up	Creators
Grab (Singapore)	2012	8	Start-up	Creators
African Leadership University (Mauritius)	2013	7	Start-up	Creators
Beautycounter (USA)	2013	7	Start-up	Creators
Kano (UK)	2013	7	Start-up	Creators
Nubank (Brazil)	2013	7	Start-up	Creators
Back Market (France)	2014	6	Start-up	Creators
Indigo Ag (USA)	2014	6	Start-up	Creators
Open Bionics (UK)	2014	6	Start-up	Creators
Selina (Panama)	2015	5	Start-up	Creators
Space10 (Denmark)	2015	5	Start-up	Creators
Truepic (USA)	2015	5	Start-up	Creators
Unmade (UK)	2015	5	Start-up	Creators
Apli (Mexico)	2016	4	Start-up	Creators

[a]Calculated from January 1, 2020 minus year of founding
[b]Maturity = formed pre-1990; Expansion = 1991–2000; Growth = 2001–2010; Start-up = formed after 2011

Table 26.4 Top management team demographics

Company	Year founded	# in TMT[a]	Average age	Cohorts[b]	Average tenure[c]	Gender[d]	Race[e]
AXA (France)	1816	10	54.1	5 BB; 5 X	12	2 F; 8 M	1 BIPOC; 10 W
Coca-Cola (USA)	1892	12	54.8	5 BB; 7 X	20.9	4 F; 8 M	6 BIPOC; 6 W
3M (USA)	1902	14	52.7	4 BB; 10 X	22	4 F; 10 M	2 BIPOC; 12 W
Westin Hotels (USA)	1930	6	53.5	3 BB; 3 X	8.7	1 F; 5 M	1 BIPOC; 5 W
Lego (Denmark)	1932	8	52.1	1 BB; 7 X	11.1	1 F; 7 M	0 BIPOC; 8 W
Disney (USA)	1938	14	60.5	9 BB; 5 X	18.6	3 F; 11 M	0 BIPOC; 14 W
Southwest Airlines (USA)	1967	16	54.7	9 BB; 7 X	17.4	2 F; 14 M	0 BIPOC; 16 W
Starbucks (USA)	1971	12	55.3	6 BB; 6 X	9.8	6 F; 6 M	4 BIPOC; 8 W
Microsoft (USA)	1975	17	52.5	4 BB; 13 X	20.2	3 F; 14 M	3 BIPOC; 14 W
Apple (USA)	1977	16	54.4	9 BB; 7 X	15.1	3 F; 13 M	2 BIPOC; 14 W
Snøhetta (Norway)	1989	5	55.6	3 BB; 2 X	18.4	1 F; 4 M	0 BIPOC; 5 W
DHL (Deutsche Post Germany)	1990	8	53.4	3 BB; 5 X	21	1 F; 7 M	0 BIPOC; 8 W
Studio O+A (USA)	1992	3	51.3	3 X	20	2 F; 1 M	1 BIPOC; 2 W
Amazon (USA)	1994	6	53.5	6 X	20.2	1 F; 5 M	0 BIPOC; 6 W
Oatly (Sweden)	1994	7	51	3 BB; 2 X; 2 Y	9.9	0 F; 7 M	0 BIPOC; 7 W
Google (Alphabet) (USA)	1998	8	48.8	8 X	15.3	2 F; 5 M	1 BIPOC; 7 W
Alibaba (China)	1999	8	52.1	2 BB; 6 X	11.9	2 F; 6 M	7 BIPOC; 1 W
Fishbowl Inventory (USA)	2001	4	44.8	1 BB; 1 X; 2 Y	14.5	0 F; 4 M	0 BIPOC; 4 W
Tesla	2003	6	43.3	4 X; 2 Y	11.5	0 F; 6 M	1 BIPOC; 5 W
JioSaavn (India)	2007	5	38	2 X; 3 Y	10.2	1 F; 4 M	3 BIPOC; 2 W
Square (USA)	2009	10	45	10 X	8	4 F; 6 M	I BIPOC; 9 W
Meituan Dianping (China)	2010	4	40.8	4 X	7.8	0 F; 4 M	4 BIPOC; 0 W
Duolingo (USA)	*2011*	*4*	*44.8*	*1 BB; 2 X; 1 Y*	*8*	*0 F; 4 M*	*2 BIPOC; 2 W*

(continued)

Table 26.4 (continued)

Company	Year founded	# in TMT[a]	Average age	Cohorts[b]	Average tenure[c]	Gender[d]	Race[e]
Sight Diagnostics (Israel)	2011	5	37.4	1 X; 4 Y	6.6	1 F; 4 M	5 BIPOC; 0 W
Stitch Fix (USA)	2011	9	42.7	6 X; 3 Y	5.9	4 F; 5 M	3 BIPOC; 6 W
Grab (Singapore)	2012	3	37.7	3 Y	7	2 F; 1 M	3 BIPOC; 0 W
African Leadership University (Mauritius)	2013	3	62.7	1 SG; 1 BB; 1 X	7	1 F; 3 M	4 BIPOC; 0 W
Beautycounter (USA)	2013	3	45	3 X	3	2 F; 1 M	1 BIPOC; 2 W
Kano (UK)	2013	4	41.3	2 X; 2 Y	7.3	0 F; 4 M	0 BIPOC; 4 W
Nubank (Brazil)	2013	3	37.3	4 Y	7	1 F; 2 M	2 BIPOC; 1 W
Back Market (France)	2014	3	31	3 Y	6	0 F; 3 M	0 BIPOC; 3 W
Indigo Ag (USA)	2014	9	46.9	1 BB; 7 X; 1 Y	3.2	2 F; 7 M	0 BIPOC; 9 W
Open Bionics (UK)	2014	4	28.3	4 Y	5.5	1 F; 3 M	0 BIPOC; 4 W
Selina (Panama)	2015	3	43	3 X	4.7	0 F; 3 M	3 BIPOC; 0 W
Space10 (Denmark)	2015	10	33.9	10 Y	4.5	4 F; 6 M	0 BIPOC; 10 W
Truepic (USA)	2015	7	40.4	4 X; 3 Y	3.4	0 F; 7 M	2 BIPOC; 5 W
Unmade (UK)	2015	3	33.3	3 Y	5	1 F; 2 M	0 BIPOC; 3 W
Apli (Mexico)	2016	2	40	1 X; 1 Y	4	1 F; 1 M	1 BIPOC; 1 W

[a]Top Management Team = TMT

[b]1935–1945 = Silent Generation (SG); 1946–1964 = Baby Boomers (BB); 1965–1980 Gen X (X); 1981–1999 Gen Y (Y)

[c]Average length of time at the company of the executive team

[d]Female = F; Male = M

[e]Black, Indigenous, and Person of Color = BIPOC; White = W

phase organizations. In the ten organizations in the Expansion and Growth phases, Generation X is the predominate cohort with some Baby Boomers and Generation Y. Thirteen of the sixteen Start-ups have Generation Y in the top management team, and in five of the Start-up firms, the top management teams are all Generation Y. The average tenure is longer in the Maturity organizations than in either the Expansion or Growth or Start-up organizations.

There is more gender diversity in the Maturity firms (average number of females is 2.6) than in Expansion and Growth firms (1.2) and Start-up firms (less than 1). In the Maturity phase companies, there is gender diversity in all of the firms. In Expansion and Growth firms, there are four firms with no women (40%), and in Start-ups there are also four firms with no women (25%). While there are nine firms in the Expansion/Growth and Start-up phases with an all-male top management team, none of the 38 firms have an all-female top management team. Racial diversity in Maturity phase organizations is 58% (seven of twelve organizations) with at least one person who is a Black, Indigenous, or Person of Color (BIPOC). The Expansion/Growth phase has 70% (seven of ten) of the organizations with at least one person who is a BIPOC, and in the Start-up phase, 62% (ten of sixteen) of the organizations have at least one person who is a BIPOC.

Conclusion

The purpose of this chapter is to highlight workplace innovation in a sample of innovative organizations across the globe, particularly describing the generational cohort of the top management team and exploring patterns among a global sample of innovative firms. The sample of thirty-eight organizations shows geographical dispersion in the Start-up phase, with far less geographical variation in the Maturity phase. This may be tied to the increasing dispersion of technology, education, and access to financial resources which facilitates global business creation. The educational experiences of many of the top management team start-ups in this sample are linked through attending graduate schools together, especially Master of Business Administration (MBA) programs.

The average age and average tenure of the top management team is highest in the organizations in the Maturity phase and lowest in the Start-up firms. Cohort dispersion also varies by business life cycle, with a concentration of Baby Boomers in the Maturity Phase and no Generation Y in this phase. It is possible that keeping firms in the Maturity phase from declining and going out of business takes more innovative thought and effort. Thus, contrary to expectations, there is some indication that people are most innovative as they age and have more experience (Bagri, n.d.). This might suggest that having Baby Boomers predominate in the top management team in the Maturity phase with Generation X assistance is helping to keep the older firms innovative and surviving. Generation X is widely dispersed throughout all phases, although there are some organizations in the Start-up phase with only Generation Y in the top management team. Additionally, there is increasingly more variation and Generation Y involvement in the top management teams in the Start-up phase.

Surprisingly, both gender and racial dispersion is highest in companies in the Maturity phase. This could be a function of the larger top management teams, but it also might be a signal of choices to enact the relationship between diversity of the marketplace and workplace and business performance (Hunt, Prince, Dixon-Fyle, & Yee, 2018). Thus while progress is slow in gender and racial participation at the top executive leadership level, there is some indication that innovative firms in the Maturity phase are attempting to increase both gender and racial diversity in the top management teams. This may also be another indication that organizations with a longer history must continue to employ many tools to continue to survive.

This chapter has several implications for the top management team. First, it indicates that firms in the different stages of the business life cycle may have different requirements of the cognitive diversity among the top management team. It appears that the innovative firms in the Maturity phase have less generational and geographic dispersion, but more gender and racial diversity. The concentration on older TMT cohorts and Western headquarters may facilitate innovation to continue marketplace relevancy and thus, potentially, survival of the firm. Baby Boomers bring experience and skill variation that match well with the need for continuous innovation to maintain competitive position. Additionally, the resources (financial, human capital, and customers) are often easier to garner in the more developed Western Europe and the United States. A second contribution in this chapter is that innovative Start-ups are more geographically dispersed but more cohort, gender, and racially concentrated. It could be that this lack of cognitive diversity in the top management team cognitive is necessary to focus on building the product or service in the marketplace, aiding survival in the early years. A third contribution is that TMT cognitive diversity begins to change as the firm moves into the Growth and Expansion phases. In these phrases, the data in this chapter suggest that the firms' TMT cognitive diversity begins a transformation to attract a more diverse talent pool. The owner/founder(s) often exit the firm or move to more advisory roles. A fourth contribution is that TMT cognitive diversity is an important component of workplace innovation and that the trends identified in this chapter should suggest that the selection of the top management team should include different combinations of cognitive diversity as the firm looks to the future.

There were several limitations to this study. First, it was dependent upon secondary data and researcher interpretation and classification of the data. Conducting interviews and having multiple coders would strengthen future work. Second, access to the data was often incomplete; the age of the top management team members was surprisingly difficult to find, and extrapolations from higher education attendance dates was often used with collaboration from other sources where possible. Third, the top management team composition was dynamic with several changes either occurring or announced; thus the date of January 2020 was selected a pivotal date. Following the companies in this work over time would be possible future research to investigate if they survived and how they progress through time in terms of top management team demographics. Fourth, the research is based on a convenience sample of previously identified innovative firms; future research could compare these firms with others not designated as innovative in a comparative study.

References

Armstrong, A. (2016, February 11). *Key Risks of the 4 Stages of a Startup's Life Cycle*. Retrieved June 14, 2020, from https://www.itproportal.com/2016/02/11/key-risks-of-the-4-stages-of-a-startups-life-cycle/

Arsenault, P. M. (2004). Validating Generational Differences: A Legitimate Diversity and Leadership Issue. *Leadership & Organization Development Journal, 25*(2), 124–141.

Bagri, N. T. (n.d.). *Startups Worship the Young. But Research Shows People Are Most Innovative When They're Older*. Quartz. Retrieved October 25, 2019, from https://qz.com/954368/startups-worship-the-young-but-research-shows-people-are-most-innovative-when-theyre-older/

Bin, G., Xueqing, P., & Wen, L. (2018). The Role of Top Management Team Diversity in Shaping the Performance of Business Model Innovation: A Threshold Effect. *Technology Analysis & Strategic Management, 30*(2), 241–253.

Bush, V. (n.d.). *What Is Innovation Software?* Retrieved January 30, 2020, from https://ezassi.com/innovation-software/

Camelo, C., Fernández-Alles, M., & Hernández, A. B. (2010). Strategic Consensus, Top Management Teams, and Innovation Performance. *International Journal of Manpower, 31*(6), 678–695. https://doi.org/10.1108/01437721011073373

Chen, X., Liu, J., Zhang, H., & Kwan, H. K. (2019). Cognitive Diversity and Innovative Work Behaviour: The Mediating Roles of Task Reflexivity and Relationship Conflict and the Moderating Role of Perceived Support. *Journal of Occupational and Organizational Psychology, 92*(3), 671–694. https://doi.org/10.1111/joop.12259

Cogin, J. (2012). Are Generational Differences in Work Values Fact or Fiction? Multi-Country Evidence and Implications. *The International Journal of Human Resource Management, 23*(11), 2268–2294.

Cooper, J. R. (1998). A Multidimensional Approach to the Adoption of Innovation. *Management Decision, 36*(8), 493–502. https://doi.org/10.1108/00251749810232565

Corbo, S. A. (1997). The X-er Files. They're Young, Techno-Hip Job-Hoppers. And Maybe the Perfect Health Care Workers. *Hospitals & Health Networks, 71*(7), 58–60.

Daellenbach, U. S., McCarthy, A. M., & Schoenecker, T. S. (1999). Commitment to Innovation: The Impact of Top Management Team Characteristics. *R&D Management, 29*(3), 199–208. https://doi.org/10.1111/1467-9310.00130

Deloitte. (2019, December 5). *How Companies Are Using Intelligent Automation to be More Innovative*. Retrieved January 30, 2020, from https://hbr.org/sponsored/2019/12/how-companies-are-using-intelligent-automation-to-be-more-innovative

Eastman, J. K., & Liu, J. (2012). The Impact of Generational Cohorts on Status Consumption: An Exploratory Look at Generational Cohort and Demographics on Status Consumption. *Journal of Consumer Marketing, 29*(2), 93–102. https://doi.org/10.1108/07363761211206348

Elenkov, D. S., & Manev, I. M. (2005). Top Management Leadership and Influence on Innovation: The Role of Sociocultural Context. *Journal of Management, 31*(3), 381–402.

Fast Company. (n.d.). *The World's 50 Most Innovative Companies 2019*. Retrieved January 24, 2020, from https://www.fastcompany.com/most-innovative-companies/2019

Fournier, A. (2019, April 26). *16 Techniques to Encourage Innovation in the Workplace*. Retrieved January 30, 2020, from https://www.braineet.com/blog/encouraging-workplace-innovation/

Friedrich, T. L., Mumford, M. D., Vessey, B., Beeler, C. K., & Eubanks, D. L. (2010). Leading for Innovation: Reevaluating Leader Influences on Innovation with Regard to Innovation Type and Complexity. *International Studies of Management & Organization, 40*(2), 6–29. https://doi.org/10.2753/IMO0020-8825400201

Hernaus, T., & Pološki Vokic, N. (2014). Work Design for Different Generational Cohorts: Determining Common and Idiosyncratic Job Characteristics. *Journal of Organizational Change Management, 27*(4), 615–641.

Hershatter, A., & Epstein, M. (2010). Millennials and the World of Work: An Organization and Management Perspective. *Journal of Business and Psychology, 25*(2), 211–223.

Hess, E. D. (2012, June 20). *Creating an Innovation Culture: Accepting Failure Is Necessary*. Retrieved January 30, 2020, from https://www.forbes.com/sites/darden/2012/06/20/creating-an-innovation-culture-accepting-failure-is-necessary/#370a4a86754e

Homberg, F., & Bui, H. T. M. (2013). Top Management Team Diversity: A Systematic Review. *Group & Organization Management, 38*(4), 455–479.

Hunt, V., Prince, S., Dixon-Fyle, S., & Yee, L. (2018, January). *Delivering Through Diversity*. Retrieved June 15, 2020, from https://www.mckinsey.com/~/media/mckinsey/business functions/organization/our insights/delivering through diversity/delivering-through-diversity_full-report.ashx

Ipsos. (2018, August 14). *Baby Boomers*. Retrieved January 30, 2020, from https://www.ipsos.com/en-nl/baby-boomers

Kalejta, T. (2020, January 12). *Reinventing Retirement: The Surprising Increase of Baby Boomers in the Workforce*. Retrieved January 30, 2020, from https://www.potts-merc.com/business/reinventing-retirement-the-surprising-increase-of-baby-boomers-in-the/article_af0b48d0-33f8-11ea-95a4-3f56b419e2f2.html

Kilduff, M., Angelmar, R., & Mehra, A. (2000). Top Management-Team Diversity and Firm Performance: Examining the Role of Cognitions. *Organization Science, 11*(1), 21–34.

Kivimäki, M., Länsisalmi, H., Elovainio, M., Heikkilä, A., Lindström, K., Harisalo, R., et al. (2000). Communication as a Determinant of Organizational Innovation. *R&D Management, 30*(1), 33–42. https://doi.org/10.1111/1467-9310.00155

Kraiczy, N., Hack, A., & Kellermanns, F. (2015). The Relationship Between Top Management Team Innovation Orientation and Firm Growth: The Mediating Role of Firm Innovativeness. *International Journal of Innovation Management, 19*, 1–24. https://doi.org/10.1142/S136391961550005X

Kressin, N. R., Chang, B.-H., Hendricks, A., & Kazis, L. E. (2003). Agreement Between Administrative Data and Patients' Self-Reports of Race/Ethnicity. *American Journal of Public Health, 93*(10), 1734–1739. https://doi.org/10.2105/AJPH.93.10.1734

Linke, A., & Zerfass, A. (2011). Internal Communication and Innovation Culture: Developing a Change Framework. *Journal of Communication Management, 15*(4), 332–348. https://doi.org/10.1108/13632541111183361

Mannheim, K. (1982). *Structures of Thinking*. London: Routledge.

Martins, L. L., Schilpzand, M. C., Kirkman, B. L., Ivabaj, S., & Ivanaj, V. (2013). A Contingency View of the Effects of Cognitive Diversity on Team Performance: The Moderating Roles of Team Psychological Safety and Relationship Conflict. *Small Group Research, 44*(2), 96–126. Retrieved from https://doi-org.ezproxy.sju.edu/10.1177/1046496412466921

McGuire, D., Todnem, B. R., & Hutchings, K. (2007). Towards a Model of Human Resource Solutions for Achieving Intergenerational Interaction in Organisations. *Journal of European Industrial Training, 31*(8), 592–608.

McMullin, J. A., Comeau, T. D., & Jovic, E. (2007). Generational Affinities and Discourses of Difference: A Case Study of Highly Skilled Information Technology Workers1. *The British Journal of Sociology, 58*(2), 297–316. https://doi.org/10.1111/j.1468-4446.2007.00152.x

McMurray, A. J., Islam, M., Pirola-Merlo, A., & Sarros, J. (2013). Workplace Innovation in a Non-Profit Organization. *Journal of Nonprofit Management and Leadership, 23*(3), 367–388.

McMurray, A. J., & Simmers, C. A. (2019). The Impact of Generational Diversity on Spirituality and Religion in the Workplace. *Vision.* https://doi.org/10.1177/0972262919884841

McSarron-Edwards, A. (2013, May 31). *Business Lifecycles and the Need for Different Leaders at Different Times.* Retrieved June 14, 2020, from https://www.hrzone.com/lead/strategy/business-lifecycles-and-the-need-for-different-leaders-at-different-times

Mello, A. L., & Rentsch, J. R. (2015). Cognitive Diversity in Teams: A Multidisciplinary Review. *Small Group Research, 46*(6), 623–658. https://doi.org/10.1177/1046496415602558

Michelson, J. (2019, February 28). *How to Innovate with a Multi-Generational Workforce.* Retrieved from https://www.forbes.com/sites/joanmichelson2/2019/02/28/how-to-innovate-with-a-multi-generational-workforce/#234acaac43f0

Nieminen, J. (2018, November 28). *The Importance of Senior Management Involvement for Innovation.* Retrieved January 30, 2020, from https://innovationmanagement.se/2018/11/28/the-importance-of-senior-management-involvement-for-innovation/

Oke, A., Munshi, N., & Walumbwa, F. O. (2009). The Influence of Leadership on Innovation Processes and Activities. *Organizational Dynamics, 38*(1), 64–72. https://doi.org/10.1016/j.orgdyn.2008.10.005

Olson, B. J., Parayitam, S., & Bao, Y. (2007). Strategic Decision Making: The Effects of Cognitive Diversity, Conflict, and Trust on Decision Outcomes. *Journal of Management, 33*(2), 196–222. https://doi.org/10.1177/0149206306298657

Oziemblo, A. (2018, August 31). *Creating Collaborative Culture Through Office Design.* Retrieved January 30, 2020, from https://www.propmodo.com/creating-collaborative-culture-through-office-design/

Parment, A. (2012). Generation Y vs. Baby Boomers: Shopping Behavior, Buyer Involvement and Implications for Retailing. *Journal of Retailing and Consumer Services, 20*(2), 189–199.

Petch, N. (2016, February 29). *The Five Stages of Your Business Lifecycle: Which Phase Are You In?* Retrieved June 14, 2020, from https://www.entrepreneur.com/article/271290

Reynolds, A., & Lewis, D. (2017, March 30). *Teams Solve Problems Faster When They're More Cognitively Diverse*. Retrieved from https://hbr.org/2017/03/teams-solve-problems-faster-when-theyre-more-cognitively-diverse

Squire, S. (2019). Do Generations Differ When It Comes to Green Values and Products? *Electronic Green Journal, 1*(42), 38–54.

Stanleigh, M. (2006, June 16). *The Impact of Generational Differences on Innovation*. Retrieved January 29, 2020, from https://bia.ca/the-impact-of-generational-differences-on-innovation/

Tang, J., & Le, C. D. (2007). Multidimensional Innovation and Productivity. *Economics of Innovation and New Technology, 16*(7), 501–516. https://doi.org/10.1080/10438590600914585

Thomke, S. (2011, June 6). *How Business Experimentation Fuels Innovation*. Retrieved January 30, 2020, from https://chiefexecutive.net/how-business-experimentation-fuels-innovation/

Tong, L., Liu, N., Zhang, M., & Wang, L. (2018). Employee Protection and Corporate Innovation: Empirical Evidence from China. *Journal of Business Ethics, 153*(2), 569–589. https://doi.org/10.1007/s10551-016-3412-3

Twenge, J. M. (2010). A Review of the Empirical Evidence on Generational Differences in Work Attitudes. *Journal of Business and Psychology, 25*(2), 201–210. https://doi.org/10.1007/s10869-010-9165-6

Van Woensel, L., Archer, G., Panades-Estruch, L., & Vrscaj, D. (2015). Ten Technologies which Could Save Lives: Potential Impacts and Policy Implications. *European Parliamentary Research Service*, 1–22.

Ward, A. (2002). *The Leadership Lifecycle: Matching Leaders to Evolving Organizations: Matching Leaders to Evolving Organisations*. New York, NY: Palgrave McMillian.

Wipulanusat, W., Panuwatwanich, K., & Stewart, R. (2018). Pathways to Workplace Innovation and Career Satisfaction in the Public Service: The Role of Leadership and Culture. *International Journal of Organizational Analysis, 26*, 00–00. https://doi.org/10.1108/IJOA-03-2018-1376

Workplace Innovation Ltd (n.d.). *What Is Workplace Innovation?* Retrieved January 15, 2020, from http://www.goodworkplaces.net/LWIP-What-is-Workplace-Innovation

Yin, J., Arfaei, N., MacNaughton, P., Catalano, P. J., Allen, J. G., & Spengler, J. D. (2019). Effects of Biophilic Interventions in Office on Stress Reaction and Cognitive Function: A Randomized Crossover Study in Virtual Reality. *Indoor Air, 29*(6), 1028–1039. https://doi.org/10.1111/ina.12593

Yin, R. K. (2014). *Case Study Research Design and Methods* (5th ed.). Thousand Oaks, CA: Sage.

Yuan, M. (2018, October 15). *China's Silver Generation Has Money and Time to Spend*. Retrieved January 30, 2020, from https://www.eastwestbank.com/

ReachFurther/en/News/Article/Chinas-Silver-Generation-Has-Money-and-Time-to-Spend

Zacher, H., Rosing, K., Henning, T., & Frese, M. (2011). Establishing the Next Generation at Work: Leader Generativity as a Moderator of the relAtionships Between Leader Age, Leader-Member Exchange, and Leadership Success. *Psychology and Aging, 26*(1), 241–252.

Zemke, R., Raines, C., & Filipczak, B. (2013). *Generations at Work: Managing the Clash of Veterans, Boomers, Xers, and Nexters in Your Workplace* (2nd ed.). New York: Amacom.

Zivkovic, H. (2012). Strengths and Weaknesses of Business Research Methodologies: Two Disparate Case Studies. *Business Studies Journal, 4*(2), 91–99.

27

Design Thinking and Workplace Innovation Interface

Judy Matthews

Introduction

In the fast-changing twenty-first century, workplace innovation continues to be of great importance in commercial and business ventures as well as in private and nonprofit sectors. The many challenges include new technological initiatives that open up new possibilities, the changing demographics and challenging environmental conditions. Workplace innovation in the twenty-first century is relevant in every context, every industry and every constellation of workplace, from manufacturing to services, to health and welfare. Common to each of these contexts is the importance of people, their responses, their ideas and plans for progress and their attempts to create better solutions to make the world a better place.

New approaches from the field of design, design thinking and design-led innovation and the importance of design and its contribution to innovation have come to public attention (Brown, 2008, 2009; Dong, 2015; Gruber, De Leon, George, & Thompson, 2015; Martin, 2009; Verganti, 2009). Design has moved from the aesthetics of products to be intricately involved in the conception of new ideas, as well as the development of new goods and services, with rapid prototyping, testing and implementation. We claim that

J. Matthews (✉)
School of Management, QUT Business School, Queensland University of Technology, Brisbane, QLD, Australia
e-mail: jh.matthews@qut.edu.au

© The Author(s), under exclusive license to Springer Nature Switzerland AG 2021
A. McMurray et al. (eds.), *The Palgrave Handbook of Workplace Innovation*,
https://doi.org/10.1007/978-3-030-59916-4_27

design thinking or human-centred design (HCD) contributes directly and indirectly to both broad and more focused understandings of workplace innovation and provide evidence to support such claims. Given convincing evidence on the contributions of design thinking, as a mindset, a process, as well as a set of methods and tools that begin with a focus on the needs of customers and stakeholders to create more desirable futures, we explore the interface of design thinking and workplace innovation in more detail.

This chapter explores the links between the recent interest in design thinking or human-centred design (HCD), the increasing importance of design and design-led innovation, its contributions to workplace innovation and some potential new directions for research and practice. We begin with a brief discussion of workplace innovation and then present the contributions of design thinking from extant research. Our focus largely describes workplace innovation in developed countries and provides some examples of design thinking for workplace innovation in developing countries.

Theoretical Background

The need for and demonstration of workplace innovation continues to be a strong organisational focus in business (Crossan & Apaydin, 2010; Hobday, 2005) nonprofit (McMurray, Islam, Sarros, & Pirola-Merlo, 2013) and the popular press. Traditionally innovation was closely aligned to ongoing research and development (R&D) (Tidd & Bessant, 2009). Here the focus was to continuously develop and new products to win and retain customers and develop new and better ways of working. While R&D processes retain their importance, they are informed and extended by new processes, purposes and outcomes of innovation (Tidd & Bessant, 2009). Some of the major influences on workplace innovation and how they are changing our understanding of innovation are presented below.

Evolving Understanding of Workplace Innovation

The last two decades have noted increases in the understanding and application of an open innovation paradigm (Bogers, Chesbrough, & Moedas, 2018; Chesbrough, 2003) which recognises and welcomes innovation in the form of multiple inputs to innovation inside and outside the workplace, as well as multiple outputs and applications. Other inclusions have been in new forms of service innovation and open services innovation (Chesbrough, 2011).

The development of new perspectives on innovation is paralleled by the changing definition of innovation. For example, the recent 2018 version of the OECD Oslo Manual has reframed and extended the earlier 2005 definition that included market and management innovation. The 2018 Oslo Manual recognises innovation as both an outcome and as a process, by separating and providing separate definitions for both concepts, regarding innovation activities and business innovation. Eight types of innovation were identified, namely:

(i) R&D activities: (ii) engineering, (iii) design and other creative work activities; (iv) marketing and brand equity activities; (v) intellectual property (IP) related activities; (vi) employee training activities; (vii) software development and database activities; (viii) activities relating to the acquisition or lease of tangible assets and innovation management activities. (OECD, 2018, p. 35)

Workplace Innovation can be found in products, services and systems as well as mobile apps and NetWare. Common themes in workplace innovation include having a strong customer or user focus, exploring incremental and disruptive innovation, building collaborative relationships across teams and joint approaches to problems and challenges. The need and demand for workplace innovation is an ongoing challenge. The multidimensional nature of workplace innovation in diverse contexts can be illustrated with a mind map using Kipling's 'Six Honest Serving Men' of Who, What, Where, When, Why and How as shown in Fig. 27.1.

Our understanding of the multiple dimensions of innovation and the important contributions of design to workplace innovation has been growing and strengthening (Design Council, 2013; Nesta, 2009, 2018). Nesta, an independent United Kingdom innovation charity, was established in 2012, with a mission to help people and organisations bring great ideas to life. Nesta's activities are dedicated to supporting ideas that can help improve our lives, ranging from early stage investment to in-depth research and practical programs: recognising the need to strengthen the foundations for innovation within organisations and that the skills required to bring innovation to life must become part of an organisation's culture to create meaningful impact.

Nesta's overview of workplace innovation methods was structured into four spaces, intelligence, solution, technology and talent and represented in a landscape of innovation approaches (Nesta, 2018). These spaces were built on the premise that in order to create change, you need to make sense and understand reality, as well as develop solutions and interventions to change that reality. For example, the *intelligence space* focuses on approaches that help to

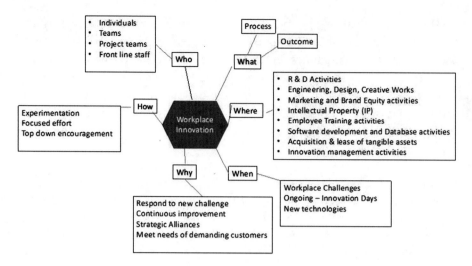

Fig. 27.1 Kipling's 'Six Honest Serving Men' of Who, What, Where, When, Why and How

make sense of and conceptualise reality; the *solution space* focuses on methods that help test and develop solutions; the *technology space* includes approaches and technology that enable action and change, such as digital tools and data-related methods; and the *talent space* focuses on how to mobilise talent, develop skills and increase organisational readiness in order to ultimately make change happen. Processes that contribute to each of these spaces are shown in Fig. 27.2.

Workplace innovation practitioners often use more than one tool or method to initiate, shape, develop and deliver better processes and outcomes. For example, in Fig. 27.2, design thinking is positioned at the intersection of the intelligence and solution spaces and the talent and technology spaces. In practice, design thinking is often used in conjunction with other methods such as open data, ethnographic research, positive deviance, behavioural insights and digital transformation.

The common factor in workplace innovation is the human factor—it is people who create innovations. Innovation in processes and outcomes is created by people: individually, as well as in small groups, teams, project teams as well as research and development teams. The stimulus for innovation may come from multiple influences and challenges. Furthermore, we have learned from studies of workplace innovation that workplaces that continue to innovate often display a number of common characteristics. They have motivated staff who are curious, who engage in creative activities, often in collaboration

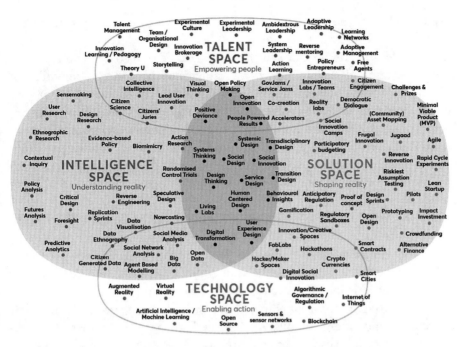

Fig. 27.2   Landscape of innovation approaches. (Version 2. (December 2018))

with other work colleagues; enjoy their work activities; and may work for the benefit of others (Nusem, Wrigley, & Matthews, 2017).

We begin with a brief summary of design thinking and then discuss the design thinking and workplace innovation interface.

Design Thinking

Popularised by IDEO, a well-known design firm as well as other leading design companies and the Stanford d.school, design thinking has become well-known in the management literature. Design thinking or human-centred design can be understood as a mindset, a perspective, a process, a set of methods and tools that begin with a focus on the needs of customers and stakeholders to create more desirable futures. An inclusive approach to design and design thinking is advocated by Herbert Simon, Nobel Laureate in economics, who claimed, 'Everyone who takes an existing situation and attempts to create a more desirable future is a designer' (Simon, 1996). This broad view of designing places each of us in a position with the potential, and perhaps some responsibility, to embrace the design thinking possibilities in shaping the futures that we attempt to create.

Multiple definitions of design thinking have developed from varied discipline backgrounds. A recent review (Johansson-Sköldberg, Woodilla, & Çetinkaya, 2013) identified five interpretations across management and design domains. Within management, the major themes are a set of practices, cognitive approaches and mindsets. In the management literature, a popular definition describes design thinking as 'a human-centered approach to innovation that puts the observation and discovery of often highly nuanced, even tacit, human needs right at the forefront of the innovation process' (Gruber et al., 2015).

Brown (2008) proposed that design thinkers use empathy or a 'people first' approach to imagine solutions that are inherently desirable and meet explicit and latent needs; integrative thinking that combines analytical skills and contradictory factors; optimism and assuming that at least one potential solution is better than existing alternatives; an experimental mindset that poses questions and explores constraints in creative ways that proceed in entirely new directions; and extensive collaboration, perhaps based on a personal background in multiple disciplines and extensive work with other disciplines.

Design thinking gathers deep insights from customers to generate new perspectives and co-create new solutions that are rapidly prototyped, tested and refined and implemented with stakeholders. Research regarding design thinking and its impact has found that clear benefits in workplace innovation arise from its application in business, government and nonprofit sectors.

Characteristics of design thinkers in organisations include an ability to see the whole situation or system, a passion for bringing ideas to life, a willingness to take risks without fully knowing the outcome in advance, being open to visualisation and exploration of all of the senses in seeking solutions and the ability to empathise with the human side of situations (Michlewski, 2008).

Design thinking is often called upon to develop new approach to what seems like intractable or 'wicked' problems (Buchanan, 1992). At times the desired goal or end-state is clear, and what is required is novelty and enthusiasm in looking beyond the existing repertoire of approaches. In other contexts, it is necessary to do a 'deep dive' into the problem space to find core information from stakeholders and to generate energy and insights to create new solutions.

Many of the processes, methods and tools used in design thinking help to overcome the barriers to innovation (Liedtka, 2015) as well as stimulate, progress and enable workplace innovation. For example, using visual tools such as mind maps, rich pictures and visual storytelling stimulates visual thinking (Matthews, 2018; Walter & Gioglio, 2014) and contributes directly to workplace innovation through generating new perspectives, ideas and problem solutions.

Design Thinking and Workplace Innovation

Workplace innovation builds on the notion that innovation is both a process and an outcome (OECD Manual, 2018). If we define innovation as the creation of new sustainable value, then it is clear that innovation not only creates new value for customers and companies, it also needs to capture that value. More recently workplace innovation has been interpreted by European colleagues (Totterdill, 2015) as strongly focused on the direct contributions of employees to the innovation process and innovation outcomes.

Innovation is more likely to be found in contexts where ongoing learning is encouraged (Beckman, 2020; Beckman & Barry, 2007; Cohen & Levinthal, 1989; Høyrup, 2010; Ward, Runcie, & Morris, 2009). Employee engagement, customer engagement, ongoing support, encouragement leadership, monitoring and reflection all play important roles in workplace innovation. We know that ongoing workplace innovation is often related to a broader culture of innovation, which has developed over time, sometimes through particular activities such as FedEx or ShipIt Days, where staff spend an amount of their own time and company time devoted to experimentation on a regular scheduled basis, with the message that such activities are an investment by the company to new ideas, products and services.

Design thinking can also be understood as a *social technology* that addresses the biases and behaviours that limit innovation (Liedtka, 2018, 2020). Common processes of design thinking include customer discovery, idea generation and idea testing with customers. Customer discovery through immersion in the world of users uses ethnographic interviews, observation sensemaking and alignment; idea generation through emergence and articulation; and testing prototypes: pre-experience and learning in action. The desired outcomes of innovation include increased understandings through deep customer insights, better solutions, lower risk and costs and co-created solutions.

Design thinking is a process where hypotheses are developed for potential solutions. Those solutions are made more tangible through rapid prototyping, explored with stakeholders and tested for refinement, gathering the views and perspectives of multiple diverse stakeholders, often many times, before implementation and workplace innovation.

Applications of Design Thinking Through Case Studies

Explorations of design thinking or HCD are found in the *business sector* (Brown, 2008, 2009; Carlgren, Elmquist, & Rauth, 2016; Liedtka, 2011, 2014; Stevenson, Wrigley, & Matthews, 2016; Townson, Wrigley, & Matthews, 2016; Wrigley, Nusem, & Straker, 2020) in the *social sector* (Brown & Wyatt, 2010; Liedtka, Salzman, & Azer, 2017; Nusem, Wrigley, & Matthews, 2017) and *government sectors* (Junginger, 2017). Research into business that successfully applied design thinking for their workplace innovation found common themes of user focus, problem framing, visualisation, experimentation and diversity (Carlgren et al., 2016). These examples are largely located in developed countries. However, examples of applications of design thinking and workplace innovation are also found in developing countries. One interesting example is a not-for-profit organisation using design thinking to address issue of water scarcity in the Thar Desert, the most water distressed and densely populated arid zone, and to build resilient desert communities in this region (Jayakumar, Das, & Srivastava, 2019).

Design thinking contributes to workplace innovation in multiple ways. Its focus on gaining insights regarding needs of stakeholders and specifically customers challenges fixed mindsets and personal biases (Liedtka, 2015). Design thinking as an approach that includes the perspectives and insights of multiple stakeholders may be seen to challenge existing hierarchies, perhaps democratising innovation and contributing to a specific organisational culture (Elsbach & Stigliani, 2018).

Design thinking contributes directly to workplace innovation in creating new value for customers, staff and the organisation (Hobday, Boddington, & Grantham, 2012; Kumar, 2013). An experimental mindset is an important component of design thinking, and such an approach has been well documented in workplace innovation (Brown, 2009; Matthews, 2017; Thomke, 2001, 2003a, b, 2020). Furthermore, design thinking with its focus on experiential learning and experimentation contributes to an organisational culture that values innovation (Elsbach & Stigliani, 2018).

Many of the processes, methods and tools used in design thinking help to overcome the barriers to innovation (Brown & Martin, 2015; Liedtka, 2015; Liedtka & Ogilvie, 2011; Liedtka, Ogilvie, & Brozenska, 2019) as well as stimulate, progress and enable workplace innovation. For example, using visual tools such as mind maps, rich pictures and visual storytelling stimulates visual thinking (Matthews, 2018; Walter & Gioglio, 2014) and also contributes directly to workplace innovation through generating new perspectives, ideas and problem solutions.

Design thinking processes are also used by design teams and more recently, in attempts to embed design thinking, by the acquisition of these teams or even whole design companies. Large companies such as IBM and consulting companies such as Anderson Consulting are not only hiring designers to apply design capability, they are purchasing whole teams and design companies to bring human-centred approaches to the user experiences to enhance their product and service capabilities.

In the era of Industry 4.0, workplace innovation is undergoing multiple changes as the potential of new technologies such as 3D printing, artificial intelligence, machine learning and augmented and virtual reality offers new dimensions and new ways of working. We argue that the workplace innovation that arises from these new technologies is strongly linked to the democratisation of innovation and the importance of human-centred design and the rewards from staff exploring these new potentials. Using design for closer interpretation of the user experiences results in deeper and longer lasting engagement as well as new idiosyncratic structures for stakeholder collaborations and co-creation.

The benefits of design thinking are certainly new and better solutions to intractable issues. However recent research has identified extra benefits. Specifically, *design thinking is a social technology* for exploring new challenges and opportunities (Liedtka, 2020); design thinking as a *process for increased engagement with customers* and deeper knowledge about customer problems and challenges (Wrigley, Nusem, & Straker, 2020); design as a *language for workplace innovation* (Hernández, Cooper, Tether, & Murphy, 2018); design thinking can *increase feelings of creative confidence* (Kelley & Kelley, 2013); design thinking can improve collaboration in teams and organisations (Brown, 2009), and design thinking contributes to organisational culture (Elsbach & Stigliani, 2018).

Addressing Barriers to Using Design Thinking for Workplace Innovation

Many studies have shown the benefits of design thinking and its contribution to workplace innovation in business (Brown, 2009; Carlgren et al., 2016; Martin, 2009) and in nonprofit settings (Liedtka, Salzman, & Azer, 2017; Nusem, Matthews, & Wrigley, 2019). However, introducing new ways of working to established workplaces is not a simple of straightforward process. Barriers can be cognitive (Liedtka, 2015) as well as practice based (Liedtka, 2011). Barriers to implementing design thinking may include traditional workplace specialisation in practices, concern about exploring new not yet proven approaches, a short-term focus on monetary benefits and fear of failure (Kupp, Anderson, & Reckhenrich, 2017).

Nusem, Matthews, and Wrigley (2019) proposed that when organisations are seeking to innovate, design thinking can be used at multiple stages of raising awareness of design, generating interest in design by applying design methods to projects, growing the desire to experiment through applied practice, experiencing first-hand the value of design and increasing confidence in the use of design methods and taking action for innovation. Kupp et al. (2017) found five steps that could be taken to take full advantage of the potential of design thinking: (i) encouraging top managers to champion design thinking initiatives, (ii) including both intuitive and analytical thinkers in teams, (iii) setting clear ground rules, (iv) integrating design thinking into product development processes and (v) redefining desired outcomes to include learning.

This chapter has discussed examples of design thinking and workplace innovation found across many industry sectors and cultural contexts. However, integrating design thinking as a means of driving workplace innovation often requires multiple dimensions of change. Recent research examining the challenges of implementing identified four specific conditions of strategic vision, facilities, cultural capital and directives (Wrigley et al., 2020). Here strategic vision reflects the organisation's long-term strategic goals and intent; facilities refer to the physical spaces and resources that are dedicated to design activities; cultural capital describes the understanding, knowledge and capabilities of the workforce in relation to design; and directives reflect the explicit call for the use of design with accountability for its application.

Conclusion

It is clear from extant research that design thinking contributes directly to workplace innovation and that the nature and evolution of workplace innovation will continue to be of paramount importance to small and large companies and to government and nonprofit organisations. The importance of employee engagement, and human elements of enthusiasm, curiosity, creativity, collaboration, and co-creation in progressing an organisation's agenda for change that are core components of design thinking, is also key to workplace innovation practices.

Where to from Here? Implications for Research and Practice

The potential and benefits of design thinking for organisations has been well demonstrated through multiple and diverse case studies. Summarising research and practice regarding the benefits of design thinking for workplace innovation, we propose that workplace innovation is more likely to be found in organisations with environments that value learning as well as collaboration, creativity and courage. Specifically, such workplaces display the characteristics of design thinking, with a clear user focus, an experimental mindset and an openness to new ways of thinking, encouraging the ability to frame and reframe challenges and issues from a human-centred perspective. However, integrating design thinking into organisations is a long-term but worthwhile program (Björklund, Maula, Soule, & Maula, 2020) that will benefit from further research and experimentation.

References

Beckman, S. L. (2020). To Frame or Reframe: Where Might Design Thinking Research Go Next? *California Management Review, 62*(2), 144–162.

Beckman, S. L., & Barry, M. (2007). Innovation as a Learning Process: Embedding Design Thinking. *California Management Review, 50*(1), 25–56.

Björklund, T., Maula, H., Soule, S. A., & Maula, J. (2020). Integrating Design into Organizations: The Coevolution of Design Capabilities. *California Management Review, 62*(2), 1–25.

Bogers, M., Chesbrough, H., & Moedas, C. (2018). Open Innovation: Research, Practices, and Policies. *California Management Review, 60*(2), 5–16.

Brown, T. (2008). Design Thinking. *Harvard Business Review, 86*(6), 84–92.

Brown, T. ([2009] 2018). *Change by Design: How Design Thinking Transforms Organizations and Inspires Innovation.* New York, NY: Harper Business,

Brown, T., & Martin, R. (2015). Design for Action. *Harvard Business Review, 93*(9), 56–64.

Brown, T., & Wyatt, J. (2010, Winter). Design Thinking for Social Innovation. *Stanford Social Innovation Review,* 30–35, 64.

Buchanan, R. (1992). Wicked Problems in Design Thinking. *Design Issues, 8*, 5–21.

Carlgren, L., Elmquist, M., & Rauth, I. (2016). The Challenges of Using Design Thinking in Industry—Experiences from Five Large Firms. *Creativity and Innovation Management, 25*(3), 344–362.

Chesbrough, H. W. (2003). *Open Innovation: The New Imperative for Creating and Profiting from Technology.* Boston: Harvard Business School Press.

Chesbrough, H. W. (2011). *Open Services Innovation: Rethinking Your Business to Grow and Compete in a New Era.* San Francisco: Jossey-Bass.

Cohen, W. M., & Levinthal, D. A. (1989). Innovation and Learning: The Two Faces of R&D. *Economic Journal, 99*(397), 569–596.

Crossan, M. M., & Apaydin, M. (2010). A Multi-Dimensional Framework of Organizational Innovation: A Systematic Review of the Literature. *Journal of Management Studies, 47*(6), 1154–1191. https://doi.org/10.1111/j.1467-6486.2009.00880.x

Design Council. (2013). *Leading Business by Design: Why and How business Leaders Invest in Design* (pp. 1–90). London: Design Council. Retrieved from https://www.designcouncil.org.uk/resources/report/leading-business-design

Dong, A. (2015). Design × Innovation: Perspective or Evidence-Based Practices. *International Journal of Design Creativity and Innovation, 3*(3–4), 148–163.

Elsbach, K. D., & Stigliani, I. (2018). Design Thinking and Organizational Culture: A Review and Framework for Future Research. *Journal of Management, 44*(6), 2274–2306.

Gruber, M., De Leon, N., George, G., & Thompson, P. (2015). Managing by Design. *Academy of Management Journal, 58*(1), 1–7.

Hernández, R. J., Cooper, R., Tether, B., & Murphy, E. (2018). Design, the Language of Innovation: A Review of the Design Studies Literature. *She Ji: The Journal of Design, Economics, and Innovation, 4*(3, Autumn), 249–274.

Hobday, M. (2005). Firm-Level Innovation Models: Perspectives on Research in Developed and Developing Counties. *Technology Analysis & Strategic Management, 17*(2), 121–146.

Hobday, M., Boddington, A., & Grantham, A. (2012). An Innovation Perspective on Design, Part 2. *Design Issues, 28*(1), 27. https://doi.org/10.1162/DESI_a_00137

Høyrup, S. (2010). Employee-Driven Innovation and Workplace Learning: Basic Concepts, Approaches and Themes. *Transfer, 16*(2), 143–154.

Jayakumar, J., Das, K., & Srivastava, N. (2019). Design Thinking: A Working Strategy for the Third Sector. *Journal of Business Strategy, 40*(5), 28–38.

Johansson-Sköldberg, U., Woodilla, J., & Çetinkaya, M. (2013). Design Thinking: Past, Present and Possible Futures. *Creativity and Innovation Management, 22*(2), 121–146.

Junginger, S. (2017). *Transforming Public Services by Design: Re-Orienting Policies, Organizations and Services around People.* New York, NY: Routledge.

Kelley, D., & Kelley, T. (2013). *Creative Confidence: Unleashing the Creative Potential Within Us All.* Crown Books.

Kumar, V. (2013). *101 Design Methods: A Structured Approach for Driving Innovation in Your Organization*. New York, NY: John Wiley.

Kupp, M., Anderson, J., & Reckhenrich, J. (2017). Why Design Thinking in Business Needs a Rethink. *MIT Sloan Management Review*, 41–44.

Liedtka, J. (2011). Learning to Use Design Thinking Tools for Successful Innovation. *Strategy & Leadership, 39*(5), 13–19.

Liedtka, J. (2014). Innovative Ways Companies are Using Design Thinking. *Strategy & Leadership, 4*(2), 40–45.

Liedtka, J. (2015). Perspective: Linking Design Thinking with Innovation Outcomes through Cognitive Bias Reduction. *Journal of Product Innovation Management, 32*(6), 925–938.

Liedtka, J. (2018, September–October). Why Design Thinking Works. *Harvard Business Review*, 72–79.

Liedtka, J. (2020). Putting Technology in Its Place: Design Thinking's Social Technology at Work. *California Management Review, 62*(2), 53–83.

Liedtka, J., & Ogilvie, T. (2011). *Designing for Growth: A Design Thinking Tool Kit for Managers*. New York: Columbia Business Press.

Liedtka, J., Ogilvie, T., & Brozenske, R. (2019). *The Designing for Growth Field Book: A Step-by-Step Project Guide* (2nd ed.). New York: Columbia University Press.

Liedtka, J., Salzman, R., & Azer, D. (2017). *Design Thinking for the Greater Good: Innovation in the Social Sector*. Columbia University Press.

Martin, R. L. (2009). *The Design of Business: Why Design Thinking is the Next Competitive Advantage*. Boston, MA: Harvard Business Press.

Martin, R. L. (2011). The Innovation Catalysts. *Harvard Business Review, 89*(6), 82–87. Retrieved from https://hbr.org/2011/06/the-innovation-catalysts

Matthews, J. (2017). Experimenting and Innovation: Purposes, Possibilities, and Preferred Solutions. *CERN IdeaSquare Journal of Experimental Innovation, 1*(1), 17–20.

Matthews, J. (2018). Visual Tools for Problem Framing and Problem Solving. In S. Griffith, K. Carruthers, & M. Bliemel (Eds.), *Visual Tools for Cross-Disciplinary Collaboration, Innovation and Entrepreneurship Capacity* (Chap. 4, pp. 45–60). Champaign, IL: Common Ground Research.

McMurray, A. J., Islam, M. M., Sarros, J. C., & Pirola-Merlo, A. (2013). Workplace Innovation in a Nonprofit Organization. *NonProfit Management and Leadership, 23*(3), 367–388.

Micheli, P., Wilner, S. J. S., Hussain Bhatti, S., Mura, M., & Beverland, M. B. (2019). Doing Design Thinking: Conceptual Review, Synthesis, and Research Agenda. *Journal of Product Innovation Management, 36*(2), 124–148.

Michlewski, K. (2008). Uncovering Design Attitude: Inside the Culture of Designers. *Organization Studies, 29*, 373–392.

Nesta. (2009). *The Innovation Index: Measuring the UK's Investment in Innovation and Its Effects*. London: National Endowment for Science, Technology and the Arts.

Nesta. (2018). *Landscape of Innovation Approaches: Introducing Version 2.* Retrieved July 25, 2019, from https://www.nesta.org.uk/blog/landscape-innovation-approaches-introducing-version-2/

Nusem, E., Matthews, J., & Wrigley, C. (2019). Toward Design Orientation and Integration: Driving Design from Awareness to Action. *Design Issues, 35*(3), 35–49.

Nusem, E., Wrigley, C., & Matthews, J. (2017). Developing Design Capability in Nonprofit Organizations, January 2017. *Design Issues, 3*(1), 61–75.

OECD/Eurostat. (2018). *Oslo Manual 2018: Guidelines for Collecting, Reporting and Using Data on Innovation, 4th Edition* (The Measurement of Scientific, Technological and Innovation Activities). Paris and Luxembourg: OECD Publishing and Eurostat. https://doi.org/10.1787/9789264304604-en

Simon, H. (1996). *The Sciences of the Artificial* (3rd ed.). Cambridge, MA: MIT Press.

Stevenson, T., Wrigley, C., & Matthews, J. (2016). A Design Approach to Innovation in the Australian Energy Industry. *Journal of Design, Business & Society, 2*(1), 49–70.

Thomke, S. (2001, February). Enlightened Experimentation: The New Innovation Imperative. *Harvard Business Review*, 67–75.

Thomke, S. (2003a). *Experimentation Matters: Unlocking the Potential of New Technologies for Innovation.* Boston, MA: Harvard Business School Press.

Thomke, S. (2003b). R&D Comes to Services: Bank of America's Pathbreaking Experiments. *Harvard Business Review, 81*(4), 71–79.

Thomke, S. (2020). *Experimentation Works: The Surprising Power of Business Experiments.* Boston, MA: Harvard Business Review Press.

Tidd, J., & Bessant, J. (2009). *Managing Innovation: Integrating Technological, Market and Organizational Change* (4th ed.). Chichester: John Wiley and Sons.

Totterdill, P. (2015). Closing the Gap: The Fifth Element and Workplace Innovation. *European Journal of Workplace Innovation, 1*(1), 55–74.

Townson, P., Matthews, J., & Wrigley, C. (2016). Outcomes from Applying Design-Led Innovation in an Australian Manufacturing Firm. *Technology Innovation Management Review, 6*(6), 49–58.

Verganti, R. (2009). *Design-Driven Innovation: Changing the Rules of Competition by Radically Innovating What Things Mean.* Boston, MA: Harvard Business Press.

Walter, E., & Gioglio, J. (2014). *The Power of Visual Storytelling.* New York: McGraw-Hill.

Ward, A., Runcie, E., & Morris, L. (2009). Embedding Innovation: Design Thinking for Small Enterprises. *Journal of Business Strategy, 30*(2/3), 78–84.

Wrigley, C., Nusem, E., & Straker, K. (2020). Implementing Design Thinking: Understanding Organizational Conditions. *California Management Review*, 1–19. Online. https://doi.org/10.1177/0008125619897606

28

Unleashing Innovation Across Ethical and Moral Boundaries: The Dark Side of Using Innovation for Self-Advantage

Daniel Etse, Adela McMurray, and Nuttawuth Muenjohn

Introduction

Though various unethical practices such as deceptions and factual misrepresentation; unsafe technologies; negligence and lack of duty of care; human rights violations; insider trading; and violations of privacy and confidentiality have been associated with innovation (Fassin, 2000; Henderson & Pearson, 2011; McKinlay, 1981; Sharkey & Sharkey, 2010), there appears to be a low research focus on the ethical dimension of innovation (Fassin, 2000; Mai, Zhang, & Wang, 2019; Schumacher & Wasieleski, 2013). This apparent lack of research focus on this important aspect of innovation is a serious scholarly oversight with grievous theoretical and practical implications, as research on these issues may facilitate the identification of unethical innovation practices

D. Etse (✉)
School of Management, College of Business, RMIT University,
Melbourne, VIC, Australia
e-mail: daniel.etse@rmit.edu.au

A. McMurray
College of Business, Government and Law, Flinders University,
Adelaide, SA, Australia
e-mail: adela.mcmurray@flinders.edu.au

N. Muenjohn
School of Management, RMIT University, Melbourne, VIC, Australia
e-mail: nuttawuth.muenjohn@rmit.edu.au

© The Author(s), under exclusive license to Springer Nature Switzerland AG 2021
A. McMurray et al. (eds.), *The Palgrave Handbook of Workplace Innovation*,
https://doi.org/10.1007/978-3-030-59916-4_28

521

and related antecedents, as well as how these can be prevented, minimised, or managed, and how the resultant knowledge can be employed to inform innovation management theory and practice.

To address this scholarly oversight, this chapter brings into focus the concept of unethical innovation process and explores related attributes and facilitators. Consequently, this chapter responds to the following research questions:

1. *What are the characteristics of an unethical innovation process?*
2. *What are the facilitating factors of an unethical innovation process?*

To explore these two research questions, a thorough examination is made of Theranos, a medical innovation and technological firm which has been investigated and charged for a wide range of corporate irregularities and unethical practices (Carreyrou, 2019; Dunn, Thompson, & Louszko, 2019). The subsequent sections of this chapter are organised as follows: the conceptual review provides a literature overview of the concepts; innovation, unethical behaviours, and practices, as well as a definition for unethical innovation process. This is followed by an organisational profile of Theranos, the case study examined in this chapter. The methodological processes are then presented, followed by the discussion section which explicates the significant findings and their relationships to the extant literature, then the conclusion.

Conceptual Review

Innovation

Innovation is defined in this chapter as the successful implementation of an idea, process, practice, product or service that is perceived as creative or new by the relevant unit of adoption (Amabile, 1988; Kanter, 1983). Over the years, innovation has been one of the major drivers of human development and progress (Mormina, 2019; Wu, Zhao, & Wu, 2019). It remains one of the key areas of significant interests and focus for academia, corporate entities, policymakers, governments, entrepreneurs, as well as individuals, the world over (Damanpour, Sanchez-Henriquez, & Chiu, 2018; Demircioglu & Audretsch, 2017; Drucker, 1985; Uyarra, Zabala-Iturriagagoitia, Flanagan, & Magro, 2020). Innovation has often been conceptualised as a multi-stage process of which the major stages include: recognition of problem/need, research, development, and diffusion (Rogers, 2007; Salerno, Gomes, Silva, Bagno, & Freitas, 2015). Rogers (2007) explains that the development of an innovation often begins with the recognition or identification of a need or a problem, which in turn stimulates research and development aimed at addressing the identified problem. The research stage entails the generation, screening, and selection of relevant knowledge through scientific process to address the perceived need. The development stage is where the generated knowledge is formulated or modelled in a form such that it can be applied for addressing the identified need. The diffusion stage entails the translation of the developed solution into practice, commercialisation, and adoption.

Though innovation entails the development, implementation, or adoption of an ingenious or creative solution for the purpose of addressing a need (Grinbaum & Groves, 2013; Rogers, 2007), the innovation process may not necessarily be devoid of ethical violations and socially unacceptable practices. Various cases of ethical misconducts including deceptions and factual misrepresentation; unsafe technologies; negligence and lack of duty of care; human rights violations; insider trading; and violations of privacy and confidentiality (Fassin, 2000; Henderson & Pearson, 2011; McKinlay, 1981) have been reported in the innovation management literature. Some of the ethical issues of innovation, especially those that relate to healthcare, may seriously jeopardise human life and health (McKinlay, 1981; McLean, Stewart, & Kerridge, 2015). Innovation like any other human invention may be misused, abused, or applied to further selfish and parochial interests at the expense of society. In this chapter, we argue that just as there are unethical scientific experiments (Lefor, 2005), unethical business practices (Ameer & Halinen, 2019), and unethical products (Eisend, 2019), among others, there may as well be unethical innovations. For instance, innovations that are for purposes of committing terrorist acts or trade and business fraud may qualify for the description of unethical innovation.

Unethical Behaviour and Practice

Unethical behaviour is a behaviour that violates generally accepted societal moral norms of behaviour (Jones, 1991; Kaptein, 2011). In other words, something is unethical if it violates generally accepted moral norms of behaviour within a specific culture or context. Following this argument, a process, a product, or a service may be unethical if it violates generally accepted moral norms. Unethical decision or practice usually involves a deliberate choice or action that has the motive of achieving an expected outcome or consequence (Jones, 1991). For example, theft which is an unethical conduct is an act which is deliberately committed with the motive of wrongfully taking possession of something that belongs to others. Unethical behaviours and conducts are numerous and varied and include fraud, cheating, lying, causing harm, stealing, dishonesty, piracy, providing misleading information, falsification of information, greed, and conflict of interest (Belle & Cantarelli, 2017; Kaptein, 2011; Kish-Gephart, Harrison, & Trevino, 2010; Zheng & Mirshekary, 2015).

The extant literature suggests that unethical behaviours and practices are widespread and appear to be on the ascendency with the passage of time (Kaptein, 2011; Kish-Gephart et al., 2010), and the consequences are damaging and disastrous (Belle & Cantarelli, 2017; Kaptein, 2011; Thau, Derfler-Rozin, Pitesa, Mitchell, & Pillutla, 2015). For example, just one type of unethical practice: employee theft is estimated to cost the US economy as much as $40 billion per annum, which is about 10 times the cost of all street crimes combined, including burglaries and robberies (Thau et al., 2015). The devastating effects of unethical practices should be a concern for all, and every possible and legitimate avenue should be sought to address this global canker. Through research, teaching, and community service, the academic community may highlight the relevant issues, develop strategies for addressing them, as well as serve as ethical role models in various communities.

Research suggests that unethical practices and behaviours may be contagious and that people who come into contact with unethical behaviours are themselves likely to become unethical (Francesca Gino, 2015; Gino, Ayal, & Ariely, 2009; Thau et al., 2015). It could be so contagious to the extent that even the most ethically conscious people could succumb to its influence (Zheng & Mirshekary, 2015). This implies organisations that allow or fail to stamp out unethical practices when they occur may cultivate an unethical organisational culture and climate where such negative practices are reinforced and employees as well as other members are corrupted with such behaviours and practices. The major influencing factors of unethical practices include organisational culture and climate; organisational leadership; extent to which people are exposed to unethical practices; extent to which ethical issues are openly discussed; peer influence; moral standards; saliency of ethicality; monitoring; and the use of moral reminders (Belle & Cantarelli, 2017; Gino et al., 2009; Kaptein, 2011). Using the concept of the *fraud triangle*, the facilitators or the influencing factors of unethical practices can be categorised into three main elements: incentives and pressures, opportunities, and attitudes/rationalisations (Cohen, Ding, Lesage, & Stolowy, 2011). These are explained as follows: firstly, managers or employees may be driven to engage in unethical practices when they have an incentive or are under pressure to do so. Secondly, unethical practices and conducts may be engaged in if circumstances that provide opportunity for unethical practices exist. For example, the existence of conditions such as the absence or ineffectiveness of controls, or the ability of management to override such controls, may create opportunity for unethical practices to be perpetuated. Thirdly, the attitude or ability to rationalise unethical conducts may encourage behaviours and practices that are unethical (Cohen et al., 2011).

Unethical Innovation Process

Jones (1991) provides a broad and general definition of unethical decision or behaviour, which he defines as decisions or behaviours that are either illegal or morally unacceptable to the larger community (p. 367). In line with Jones' (1991) definition, we define unethical innovation process as the *process of deliberately developing or diffusing an innovation using illegal or morally unacceptable means usually for the purpose of achieving selfish interests*. The focus of our definition is on the innovation process rather than the outcome or the use to which innovation is put because we reckon that an innovation which is not unethical may be abused or used to produce unethical outcomes; that does not make the innovation unethical, though the way in which it is used may be unethical. For example, an airbus as an innovation may not be unethical; however, a terrorist can use airbus to commit an act of terrorism, which is unethical. The fact that an airbus may be used to commit a terrorist act does not make the airbus an unethical innovation, though the use to which it was put by a terrorist may be unethical. On the other hand, an innovation that was developed or produced using illegal or morally unacceptable means, which we term as *unethical innovation*, may be used to produce useful and morally acceptable outcomes, but that does not make such an innovation ethical. For example, a medical innovation that uses unethical human experimentation to produce a solution to a health condition remains unethical, irrespective of the useful or beneficial medical outcome that it is used to produce.

Thus focusing on the ethicality of how an innovation is developed or produced rather than how it is used will help in distinguishing an unethical innovation from an unethical use of innovation. By our definition we suggest that innovations that are developed using practices or conducts such as fraud, deception, falsification of information, human rights abuses, piracy, dishonesty, and other illegal and morally unacceptable practices are unethical innovations. In the next section, we present the case study of this chapter and highlight the attributes of unethical innovation process.

Theranos as a Case Study

Theranos was a privately held corporation that was in the business of producing blood testing devices as well as providing medical laboratory services (Carreyrou, 2019; O'Donnell, 2018). Theranos' innovation was purported to be a cutting-edge technology that was to revolutionise the medical laboratory industry (Abelson, 2016; O'Donnell, 2018). It was believed to possess the capability of running hundreds of medical tests in real time, with just a pinprick worth of blood from the finger (Dunn et al., 2019; O'Donnell, 2018). The founder and chief executive officer of the corporation is Elizabeth Anne Holmes, a college dropout from Stanford University (Bilton, 2016; Carreyrou, 2019). By means of deceptions, manipulations, provision of false information, falsification of documents, fabrications, fraud, and other unethical approaches, the founder and other members of the management team were able to attract extremely influential personalities, including two former US secretaries of states, high-ranking diplomats, army generals, as well as successful and accomplished entrepreneurs to their governing board (Bilton, 2016; Carreyrou, 2019; Dunn et al., 2019). Through similar means they succeeded in convincing investors to invest huge sums of money into the venture, as well as securing contracts with renowned and powerful entities such as Walgreens, Safeway, Cleveland Clinic, and Capital BlueCross (Dunn et al., 2019; Hartmans, 2018; O'Donnell, 2018).

Theranos' innovation was subsequently found to be ineffective, and its test results were almost always inaccurate (Bilton, 2016; Dunn et al., 2019; Ramsey, 2019). Contrary to claims that Theranos used its innovation to perform the blood tests, it was later found that the technology was unable to perform most of the tests, and instead they relied mainly on laboratory devices procured from third parties (Carreyrou, 2019; Dunn et al., 2019; O'Donnell, 2018). Though the founder knew that the blood analyser she invented did not work, she went about peddling falsehood that the technology worked, and the deception went on for years without being detected (Bilton, 2019; Carreyrou, 2019; Dunn et al., 2019). The technology was eventually commercialised and put to industrial use, even though it was inherently ineffective (Carreyrou, 2019; O'Donnell, 2018).

By 2014, Theranos had successfully raised about $1 billion from venture capitalists and private investors and was valued in excess of $9 billion, with its founder named the youngest female self-made billionaire (Bilton, 2019; Dunn et al., 2019). However, the discovery and exposure of Theranos' fraudulent scheme in October 2015 led to its rapid and sudden collapse, which culminated in its dissolution by September 2018 (Dunn et al., 2019).

Theranos' innovation process appears to have been driven by a chain of unethical behaviours and practices, among which are deceptions and lies; various forms of falsifications, as well as intimidation tactics; and fraud (Bilton, 2016; Carreyrou, 2015; O'Donnell, 2018). It was found that the medical technology company was at the centre of a massive multi-year fraud (O'Donnell, 2018) and that the company often presented false financial reports to prospective investors as a strategy for raising capital (Levine, 2018). The company's staff who were involved in the laboratory activities were encouraged to falsify patients' tests results to make them appear genuine, and staff who raised issues with the unethical practices were harassed and intimidated with legal and other punitive actions (Carreyrou, 2019; Dunn et al., 2019; O'Donnell, 2018). The consequences of Theranos' unethical practices were grave, among other things; they exposed patients to life-threatening hazards by providing inaccurate laboratory test results which doctors may rely on to give prescriptions. Moreover, it resulted in huge financial losses for many investors.

Methodology

Data Collection

Since available information regarding Theranos activities is mainly in textual form, that is, book and media publications, data were collected from relevant publications. They were obtained from 14 key publications which were purposively selected because of their comprehensive coverage of the case study. These publications consist of a 339-page book that provides a detailed account of the various phases of Theranos' development and its eventual demise. This book was authored by the person whose investigation and publications exposed the fraudulent scheme and activities of the company. As such we found this relevant for gaining insights into the innovation's activities. The other publications were 13 media reports from major media organisations including "The Wall Street Journal", "The New York Times," "The Washington Post," the BBC, CBS News, ABC News, *Vanity Fair*, Business Insider, *Wired* magazine, Bloomberg, and *The New Yorker*. Information was obtained from this wide range of sources for the purpose of corroborating the various reports

Table 28.1 The data sources

	Publication	Author, date, and publisher
1	*Bad Blood: Secrets and Lies in a Silicon Valley Startup*	John Carreyrou (2019) (Book) **Picador, London**
2	Hot startup Theranos has struggled with its blood-test technology	John Carreyrou (2015) **The Wall Street Journal** https://www.wsj.com/articles/ theranos-has-struggled-with-blood-tests-1444881901
3	The Theranos deception	Norah O'Donnell (2018) **CBS News** https://www.cbsnews.com/news/ the-theranos-elizabeth-holmes-deception
4	"She never looks back": inside Elizabeth Holmes's chilling final months at Theranos	Nick Bilton (2019) **Vanity Fair** https://www.vanityfair.com/news/2019/02/ inside-elizabeth-holmess-final-months-at-theranos
5	Ex-Theranos CEO Elizabeth Holmes says 'I don't know' 600-plus times in never-before-broadcast deposition tapes	Taylor Dunn, Victoria Thompson, Rebecca Jarvis and Ashley Louzko (2019) **ABC News** https://abcnews.go.com/Business/theranos-ceo-elizabeth-holmes-600-times-broadcast-deposition/ story?id=60576630
6	Bad blood: The rise and fall of Theranos and Elizabeth Holmes	Jamie Robertson (2018) **BBC News** https://www.bbc.com/news/business-43415967
7	Theranos' fate rests with a founder who answers only to herself	Reed Abelson (2016) **The New York Times** https://www.nytimes.com/2016/04/25/business/ theranoss-fate-rests-with-afounder-who-answers-only-to-herself.html?_r=1
8	Elizabeth Holmes, founder of blood-testing company Theranos, indicted on wire fraud charges	Carolyn Johnson (2018) **The Washington Post** https://www.washingtonpost.com/business/ economy/elizabeth-holmes-founder-of-blood-testing-company-theranos-indicted-on-wire-fraud-federal-authorities-announce/2018/06/15/8779f538-70df-11e8-bd50-b80389a4e569_story.html
9	The blood unicorn Theranos was just a fairy tale	Matt Levine (2018) **Bloomberg** https://www.bloomberg.com/opinion/ articles/2018-03-14/ theranos-misled-investors-and-consumers-who-used-its-blood-test

(continued)

Table 28.1   (continued)

Publication	Author, date, and publisher
10 Exclusive: How Elizabeth Holmes's house of cards came tumbling down	Nick Bilton (2016) **Vanity Fair** https://www.vanityfair.com/news/2016/09/elizabeth-holmes-theranos-exclusive
11 Blood, simpler: One woman's drive to upend medical testing	Ken Auletta (2014) **The New Yorker** https://www.newyorker.com/magazine/2014/12/15/blood-simpler
12 Everything you need to know about the Theranos saga so far	Nick Stockton (2016) **WIRED** https://www.wired.com/2016/05/everything-need-know-theranos-saga-far/
13 Theranos founder Elizabeth Holmes faces jail time for fraud charges. Her trial is set to begin in summer 2020.	Lydia Ramsey (2019) **Business Insider** https://www.businessinsider.com.au/theranos-founder-elizabeth-holmes-president-sunny-balwani-trial-date-2019-6?r=US&IR=T
14 The rise and fall of Elizabeth Holmes, who started Theranos when she was 19 and became the world's youngest female billionaire before it all came crashing down	Avery Hartmans (2018) **Business Insider** https://www.businessinsider.com.au/theranos-founder-ceo-elizabeth-holmes-life-story-bio-2018-4?r=US&IR=T

and enhancing the credibility of the information. Table 28.1 presents the list of publications from which the research data were obtained.

Table 28.1 provides a list of the main sources of information from which this study's data were obtained.

Data Analysis

Qualitative content analysis was the approach employed for analysing the documents and publications of interest, as it is an appropriate research technique for analysing written documents and other textual and verbal data (Hsieh & Shannon, 2005; Krippendorff, 1989). The analysis entailed four main processes: (i) initial critical reading through the publications to identify and code the unethical practices that characterised the innovation process and the facilitating factors thereof; (ii) a follow-up reading through the publications to ascertain the completeness and correctness of the data obtained from the initial reading; (iii) clustering of data into well-defined themes on basis of

Table 28.2 Characteristics of Theranos as unethical innovation

	Characteristics	Reference
1	It makes false claims regarding the nature and capability of the innovation	Carreyrou (2019), Bilton (2019), O'Donnell (2018), Dunn et al. (2019), Levine (2018), Ramsey (2019), Stockton (2016)
2	It exaggerates the innovation's capability	Carreyrou (2019), Carreyrou (2015), Stockton (2016), Ramsey (2019), Bilton (2016), O'Donnell (2018), Dunn et al. (2019)
3	It is commercialised whilst not ready functionally	Carreyrou (2019), O'Donnell (2018), Hartmans (2018), Levine (2018), Carreyrou (2015)
4	It is deployed whilst knowing that it poses substantial risk to life or safety	O'Donnell (2018), Bilton (2016), Levine (2018), Dunn et al. (2019), Carreyrou (2019)
5	It uses dishonest and fraudulent means to generate funding for its operations	Carreyrou (2019), Dunn et al. (2019), Bilton (2016), Robertson (2018), Johnson (2018)
6	It encourages unsuspecting customers to use an innovation whilst knowing that the innovation is defective	Levine (2018), O'Donnell (2018), Johnson (2018), Dunn et al. (2019), Bilton (2016)
7	It creates a work environment of fear and intimidation	O'Donnell (2018), Bilton (2016), Bilton (2019), Dunn et al. (2019)
8	It prioritises economic gains over human well-being	Carreyrou (2019), Carreyrou (2015), Bilton (2016), Dunn et al. (2019), O'Donnell (2018)

similarities; and (iv) summarising and presenting the findings in tabular forms for easy identification of key variables. This four-stage process of content analysis is a widely used and recommended approach for content analysis (Bengtsson, 2016; Onwuegbuzie, Leech, & Collins, 2012).

From the analysis, Theranos' process of innovation development was characterised by 8 major unethical practices, and these were facilitated by 11 main factors. Tables 28.2 and 28.3 respectively outline the unethical characteristics and their facilitators.

Table 28.2 above outlines the main unethical practices that characterised Theranos' innovation process. The analysis identified eight major characteristics of unethical innovation process.

Table 28.3 shows 11 factors that were identified as the main facilitators of Theranos unethical practices and conducts. The major findings outlined in the above tables are summarised as follows.

Table 28.3 Factors that facilitated Theranos' unethical innovation

	Facilitators	Reference
1	Organisational culture of extreme secrecy	Auletta (2014), Bilton (2016), Stockton (2016), Johnson (2018), Hartmans (2018), Robertson (2018), O'Donnell (2018), Carreyrou (2019)
2	Autocratic leadership	Abelson (2016), Bilton (2016), O'Donnell (2018), Dunn et al. (2019)
3	Institutional and regulatory grey areas	Auletta (2014), Dunn et al. (2019), Carreyrou (2019)
4	Endorsement and approval of renowned and respected personalities	O'Donnell (2018), Robertson (2018), Dunn et al. (2019), Hartmans (2018), Levine (2018), Abelson (2016), Johnson (2018), Auletta (2014)
5	Favourable and positive media publicity without rigorous investigation	Levine (2018), Bilton (2016), Stockton (2016), Ramsey (2019), Johnson (2018), Dunn et al. (2019)
6	Lack of due diligence on the part of relevant stakeholders	Abelson (2016), Robertson (2018), O'Donnell (2018), Dunn et al. (2019), Levine (2018)
7	Apparent endorsement of powerful and respected institutions	Carreyrou (2019), Ramsey (2019), Stockton (2016), Bilton (2016), Auletta (2014)
8	Deceptions and lies by the organisation	Stockton (2016), Ramsey (2019), Johnson (2018), Levine (2018), Robertson (2018)
9	Manipulation tactics	O'Donnell (2018), Dunn et al. (2019), Carreyrou (2019), Bilton (2019)
10	Intimidation and brutal tactics	Carreyrou (2019), Dunn et al. (2019), Bilton (2016), O'Donnell (2018)
11	Misleading and sophisticated advertisement	Johnson (2018), Dunn et al. (2019), Stockton (2016), Carreyrou (2019), Bilton (2016)

The Findings

From the content analysis, eight characteristics and 11 facilitators were respectively identified from Theranos' example. The eight identified characteristics of unethical innovation process are false claims regarding innovation's capability; exaggeration of innovation's capability; commercialisation of non-functioning innovation; putting innovation to use whilst knowing that its use exposed clients to substantial risks; and the use of dishonest and fraudulent means to generate funding for the innovation's operations. The others are encouraging unsuspecting customers to use an innovation whilst knowing that the innovation was defective; creating work environment of fear and intimidation; and prioritising economic gains over human well-being.

The 11 identified facilitators of unethical innovation process are organisational culture of extreme secrecy; autocratic leadership; institutional grey areas; deceptions and lies; manipulation tactics; failure of due diligence on the part of relevant stakeholders; and favourable media publicity. The other facilitators are the support and endorsement of respected and famous personalities; apparent endorsement of powerful and renowned institutions; misleading and sophisticated advertisements; and intimidation tactics. These findings are discussed in the next section.

Discussions

This chapter sought to ascertain the characteristics of unethical innovation process and explore its facilitating factors. To this end, we introduced the concept of unethical innovation process, which we defined as the *process of deliberately developing or diffusing an innovation using illegal or morally unacceptable means usually for the purpose of achieving selfish interests.* Our discussion focuses on three major issues: it examines the definition of unethical innovation process relative to the nature of Theranos' innovation; it discusses the characteristics of unethical innovation; and it examines the related facilitating factors.

An examination of Theranos' case revealed that the purported groundbreaking innovation that was to revolutionise blood testing and the medical laboratory industry (Abelson, 2016; Dunn et al., 2019; O'Donnell, 2018) was in fact a product of carefully crafted and propagated deceptions, dishonesty, and fraud (Bilton, 2016; Johnson, 2018; O'Donnell, 2018). The purpose for this might be due to the founder's inordinate desire to be rich. Elizabeth Holmes (the founder) is said to have nurtured the ambition to be a billionaire since childhood (Carreyrou, 2019; Hartmans, 2018). Indeed she became one, though it was short-lived. By 2015, with a net worth of close to $5 billion, she was named the world's youngest female self-made billionaire by Forbes magazine (Carreyrou, 2019; Dunn et al., 2019); however, within a time frame of just a year, her net worth had been revised to zero by the same magazine (Herper, 2016). The nature of Theranos' innovation highlights three major attributes: firstly, its design and production process were characterised by piracy of third party technologies, falsification of data, and misrepresentation of information (Carreyrou, 2019; Dunn et al., 2019); secondly, its dissemination or propagation was done by means of peddling of falsehoods, misleading advertisements, manipulations, and false claims (Carreyrou, 2019; Ramsey, 2019; Stockton, 2016); and thirdly, its principal underlying motive was wealth accumulation so as to enable its founder to become the billionaire she always wanted to be (Hartmans, 2018). Our definition of unethical innovation process appears to reflect the nature of Theranos' innovation, as it highlights the unethical nature of the innovation development, the diffusion process, and the egocentric nature of the innovation's underlying motivation.

With regard to the characteristics of unethical innovation process, we observed eight of such characteristics from the Theranos' case, and these are false claims regarding the innovation's capability; exaggeration of the innovation's capability; commercialisation of non-functioning innovation; putting innovation to use whilst knowing that its use exposed clients to substantial risks; the use of dishonest and fraudulent means to generate funding; encouraging unsuspecting customers to use an innovation whilst knowing that the innovation was defective; creating work environment of fear and intimidation; and prioritising economic gains over human well-being (Bilton, 2016; Carreyrou, 2019; Dunn et al., 2019; O'Donnell, 2018). These eight characteristics may be grouped into three major characteristics: dishonesty and falsehood; deliberate decisions and actions with substantially harmful potentials; and inhumane decisions and actions. The following three characteristics: false claims regarding the innovation's capability; exaggeration of the innovation's capability; and the use of dishonest and fraudulent means to generate funding can be placed under the category *dishonesty and falsehood*. This is because all these three characteristics share the attribute of deception, dishonesty, and falsehood. A related specific example is Theranos' use of false financial statements with hugely inflated net revenue for the purpose of attracting investors (Carreyrou, 2019; Levine, 2018).

With regard to the category, *deliberate decisions and actions with substantially harmful potentials*, the following three characteristics may be appropriate: putting innovation to use whilst knowing that its use exposed clients to substantial risks; commercialisation of a non-functioning innovation; and encouraging unsuspecting customers to use an innovation whilst knowing that the innovation was defective. This is because they all entailed wilful action or decision that had potentially harmful consequences. A specific example from the case study is Theranos rolling out the use of its technology in Walgreens and Safeway health clinics whilst its management was fully aware that the technology in question was ineffective and non-functional (Bilton, 2019; Dunn et al., 2019; Ramsey, 2019; Stockton, 2016). The characteristics creating work environment of fear and intimidation and prioritisation of economic gains over human well-being may be grouped under *inhumane decisions and actions* because they entail decisions or actions that are inconsiderate of the interests and well-being of other people. A specific example from the case study is Theranos' use of litigation, humiliation, and swift termination of employment to threaten its employees who raise concern regarding the inappropriate practices of the organisation (Carreyrou, 2019; Dunn et al., 2019; O'Donnell, 2018).

This chapter's second major objective was to explore the facilitating factors of the unethical innovation process. Eleven of such factors were identified, as outlined in Table 28.3. Explanations of these factors are provided as follows: *organisational culture of extreme secrecy*; the reviewed publications suggest that Theranos operated under extreme secrecy (Auletta, 2014; Bilton, 2016; Carreyrou, 2019). Under the guise of protecting its intellectual property and trade secrets, Theranos provided very little information regarding the nature of its innovation, how it functions, or the quality of its results (Auletta, 2014), and even the limited information provided was often fraught with lies and misrepresentations (Bilton, 2019; Johnson, 2018). Lack of transparency and a culture of secrecy may create a conducive environment for criminal and other unethical practices to thrive, as the offenders may not be found and brought to justice. This view is supported by a number of studies, including Nethery and Holman (2016) and Christensen (2012), which respectively found positive relationships between a culture of secrecy and human right abuses, as well as economic and financial crimes. Since there is the possibility of innovators and entrepreneurs to hide behind the guise of intellectual property and trade secrets to perpetuate criminal and unethical practices, there may be the need to find a balance between these two issues, such that inventors do not lose their intellectual property and, at the same time, that the latter is not abused for purposes of unethical and illegal practices. Moreover, it may be important that relevant authorities verify and test the efficacy and safety of innovations before their commercialisation or deployment for public use.

The second factor identified is *autocratic leadership*. It was observed that Theranos' founder had almost total control over decisions and affairs of the organisation (Abelson, 2016; Bilton, 2016; Dunn et al., 2019). Though Theranos' board consisted of eminent and high-profile personalities, the company's decisions, however, were entirely in the hands of Elizabeth Holmes. In December 2013, the founder forced through a resolution that assigned 100 votes to every share she owned, giving her 99.7% voting rights (Carreyrou, 2019, p. 298). This near absolute power permitted her to run the company as she wished and made internal control mechanisms, as well as checks and balances, impossible. This finding agrees with the extant literature which suggests the absence or ineffectiveness of controls or the ability of management to override controls as one of the major factors that facilitate unethical and fraudulent practices (Cohen et al., 2011; Morales, Gendron, & Guénin-Paracini, 2014). The third identified facilitating factor is *institutional and regulatory grey areas* (Auletta, 2014; Dunn et al., 2019). There appeared to be lack of clarity regarding the United States' regulation of laboratory-developed tests (LDTs), where Theranos' operations fell (Auletta, 2014). The Food and Drug Administration (FDA), United States, did not regulate the activities of LDTs, mainly because at the time the relevant Act was amended back in 1976, LDTs were not common; thus they were not specifically captured in the Act (Carreyrou, 2019). As such the LDTs often operate without the direct supervision of the FDA (Auletta, 2014; Carreyrou, 2019). This regulatory grey area might have provided a loophole which Theranos identified and exploited to its advantage.

The fourth identified factor is the *endorsement and approval by renowned and respected personalities*. Theranos' board of governors consisted of high-profile personalities and people of outstanding pedigree, including two former secretaries of states; high-profile diplomats; a distinguished Stanford University academic; a four-star army general; and accomplished entrepreneurs (Abelson, 2016; Auletta, 2014; Carreyrou, 2019; Dunn et al., 2019). The clout provided by the team of distinguished board members might have provided a cloak of credibility and engendered public trust and confidence in the company, and this may have been exploited by the company to perpetuate its unethical practices. The fifth factor is *favourable and positive media publicity*. At a point in time, Theranos became the toast of the media, notably the influential ones such as "The Wall Street Journal", the *Forbes* magazine, CNBC, "The Economists", *Vanity Fair*, Bloomberg, *The New Yorker*, the *Fortune*, the Time Glamour, and a host of others (Bilton, 2016; Dunn et al., 2019; Johnson, 2018; Stockton, 2016). The positive media publicity propelled the company and its founder to stardom (Carreyrou, 2019; Stockton, 2016), and this might have aided the perpetuation of its unethical practices. The sixth factor is the *lack of due diligence on the part of relevant stakeholders* (Abelson, 2016; Dunn et al., 2019; O'Donnell, 2018; Robertson, 2018). It appears the relevant stakeholders, including investors, clients, board members, and the media, took the claims made by Theranos' founder and other spokespersons of the company on its face value without doing due diligence to verify the veracity of the claims. The lack of due diligence might have contributed significantly to the perpetuation of the unethical practices.

The seventh facilitating factor is the *apparent endorsement by powerful and respected institutions* (Auletta, 2014; Bilton, 2016; Stockton, 2016). A number of powerful institutions appeared to have directly or indirectly endorsed Theranos' innovation. For example, Theranos' association with powerful companies such as Walgreens and Safeway might have provided further impetus for the latter's operations. Another example of endorsement by powerful institutions is the nomination of the founder to the Harvard Medical School Board of Fellows (Bilton, 2016; Ramsey, 2019) and the conferment of the Horatio Alger Award on her, making her the youngest recipient in the award's history (Carreyrou, 2019). These endorsements and recognitions might have contributed to the furtherance and continuity of the company's unethical practices. The eighth facilitating factor is *deceptions and lies by the organisation and its founder* (Johnson, 2018; Ramsey, 2019; Stockton, 2016). Deception was not just a characteristic but also a major driver of Theranos' activities. Through deception, dishonesty, and lies, Theranos' founder and other key leaders were able to secure the support of its board of governors, obtain funding from venture capitalists and other investors, secure contracts with powerful clients, as well as gain positive media publicity (Carreyrou, 2019; Johnson, 2018; Levine, 2018; Robertson, 2018). The ninth factor is *manipulation tactics* (Bilton, 2019; Carreyrou, 2019; Dunn et al., 2019; O'Donnell, 2018). Theranos' manipulation tactics are numerous and varied, and examples include the following: whilst it stressed trade secrets and intellectual property as the reason for its extreme secrecy, the real reason was to prevent the detection of its unethical practices (Carreyrou, 2019). Moreover, whilst by its utterances and public statements it pretended to advocate for stricter FDA regulation of laboratory-developed tests (ostensibly to gain the favour of the FDA), in practice, it sternly resisted any suggestion or request for FDA's verification of its activities (Carreyrou, 2019, pp. 121–123).

The tenth factor *is intimidation and brutal tactics* (Bilton, 2016; Dunn et al., 2019; O'Donnell, 2018). By means of tactics such as verbal abuse, humiliation, swift termination of employment, and threat of brutal litigations (Bilton, 2016; Carreyrou, 2019; Dunn et al., 2019; O'Donnell, 2018), Theranos subdued and gagged its employees and others from raising concerns regarding its unethical practices (Carreyrou, 2019; O'Donnell, 2018). The company employed the services of powerful legal firms which are noted and dreaded for aggressive litigation tactics (Carreyrou, 2019). With these intimidation and brutal tactics, Theranos was able to dismantle threats of oppositions and other obstacles that may hinder its unethical practices. The eleventh factor is *misleading and sophisticated advertisements* (Bilton, 2016; Dunn et al., 2019; Stockton, 2016). By means of various forms of advertisements, including a sophisticated website, and appearances on the front pages of reputable magazines such as *Forbes* and *Vanity Fair* (Dunn et al., 2019; Stockton, 2016), Theranos was able to propagate its misleading claims and, through that, succeeded in securing funding, contracts, recognitions, and other benefits (Carreyrou, 2019), so as to continue perpetuating its unethical practices.

Conclusion

This chapter introduced a concept termed *unethical innovation process* and explored related characteristics and facilitators/drivers. Eight major characteristics and eleven facilitators were identified, and the implications of these findings are numerous and varied. Theory-wise, the concept of an unethical innovation process draws attention to the relevance of unethical issues of innovation, a crucial but neglected aspect of the innovation management field. The primary purpose is to engender research interest in unethical issues of innovation, with the hope of providing understanding and insights into important related issues, such as the nature of such innovations, their antecedents, and the consequences, as well as to facilitate the theorisation of valid solutions for addressing such issues.

With regard to practice, the findings have significant implications for corporate governance, innovation policy and regulation, and innovation management. The findings highlighted the monumental failure of the board of governors and the internal control mechanisms in holding office holders of the organisation accountable and responsible, as well as ensuring that the organisation functioned as a credible and responsible corporate entity. Corporate governance might need to put in place mechanisms that will ensure effective internal control systems, and monitoring, as well as effective and functional board of governors for innovation start-ups and other corporate entities. Furthermore, corporate governance may need to ensure that leadership power in innovation/technology companies is not concentrated in the hands of a single or few individuals, since such a situation might be a recipe for clandestine and unethical practices, as exemplified in our case study. Another important implication for practice relates to innovation policy and regulation. There might be the need for relevant policies to be put in place to guard against unethical development, diffusion, and use of innovations. Especially with regard to the issue of trade secrets and intellectual property, relevant authorities in collaboration with inventors and innovators may need to establish guidelines and frameworks that will safeguard intellectual property/trade secrets and at the same time ensure that (potential) innovators do not hide behind the guise of trade secrets to perpetuate illegal and unethical practices. With regard to managers and leaders of organisational innovation, as well as investors in innovation portfolios, the findings highlight the need for due diligence and verification of claims made by innovation companies before making adoption or investment decisions.

Furthermore, the findings draw attention to a sombre question deserving sober reflection, especially for less developed countries where institutions are weak or non-existent and where high level of technological ignorance prevails. And the question is if such serious unethical practices can characterise the innovation process in a country such as the United States, the superpower of effective and time-tested institutions, a global technology giant, and the home of technology experts and technocrats, what might be the situation in the underdeveloped or developing countries?

References

Abelson, R. (Producer). (2016, April 24). Theranos' Fate Rests with a Founder Who Answers Only to Herself. Retrieved from https://www.nytimes.com/2016/04/25/business/theranoss-fate-rests-with-afounder-who-answers-only-to-herself.html?_r=1

Amabile, T. (1988). A Model of Creativity and Innovation in Organisations. In B. Staw & L. Cummings (Eds.), *Research in Organisational Behaviour* (pp. 123–167). Greenwich JAI Press.

Ameer, I., & Halinen, A. (2019). Moving beyond Ethical Decision-Making: A Practice-Based View to Study Unethical Sales Behavior. *Journal of Personal Selling & Sales Management, 39*(2), 103–122. https://doi.org/10.1080/08853134.2018.1544077

Auletta, K. (Producer). (2014, December 8). Blood, Simpler: One Woman's Drive to Upend Medical Testing. Retrieved from https://www.newyorker.com/magazine/2014/12/15/blood-simpler

Belle, N., & Cantarelli, P. (2017). What Causes Unethical Behavior? A Meta-analysis to Set an Agenda for Public Administration Research. *Public Administration Review, 77*(3), 327–339. https://doi.org/10.1111/puar.12714

Bengtsson, M. (2016). How to plan and perform a qualitative study using content analysis. *NursingPlus Open, 2*, 8–14. https://doi.org/10.1016/j.npls.2016.01.001.

Bilton, N. (Producer). (2016, September 4). Exclusive: How Elizabeth Holmes's House of Cards Came Tumbling Down. Retrieved from https://www.vanityfair.com/news/2016/09/elizabeth-holmes-theranos-exclusive

Bilton, N. (Producer). (2019, February 21). "She Never Looks Back": Inside Elizabeth Holmes's Chilling Final Months at Theranos. Retrieved from https://www.vanityfair.com/news/2019/02/inside-elizabeth-holmess-final-months-at-theranos

Carreyrou, J. (Producer). (2015, October 16). Hot Startup Theranos has Struggled with Its Blood-Test Technology. Retrieved from https://www.wsj.com/articles/theranos-has-struggled-with-blood-tests-1444881901

Carreyrou, J. (2019). *Bad Blood: Secrets and Lies in a Silicon Valley Startup.* London: Picador.

Christensen, J. (2012). The Hidden Trillions: Secrecy, Corruption, and the Offshore Interface. *Crime, Law and Social Change, 57*(3), 325–343. https://doi.org/10.1007/s10611-011-9347-9

Cohen, J., Ding, Y., Lesage, C., & Stolowy, H. (2011). Corporate Fraud and Managers' Behavior: Evidence from the Press. *Journal of Business Ethics, 95*(S2), 271–315. https://doi.org/10.1007/s10551-011-0857-2

Damanpour, F., Sanchez-Henriquez, F., & Chiu, H. (2018). Internal and External Sources and the Adoption of Innovations in Organisations. *British Journal of Management, 29*, 712–730.

Demircioglu, M. A., & Audretsch, D. B. (2017). Public Sector Innovation: The Effect of Universities. *The Journal of Technology Transfer, 44*(2), 596–614. https://doi.org/10.1007/s10961-017-9636-2

Drucker, P. (1985). *Innovation and Entrepreneurship: Practice and Principles.* New York: Harper & Row.

Dunn, T., Thompson, V., & Louszko, A. (Producer). (2019, December 14). Ex-Theranos CEO Elizabeth Holmes Says 'I don't know' 600-plus Times in Never-Before-Broadcast Deposition Tapes. Retrieved from https://abcnews.go.com/Business/theranos-ceo-elizabeth-holmes-600-times-broadcast-deposition/story?id=60576630

Eisend, M. (2019). Morality Effects and Consumer Responses to Counterfeit and Pirated Products: A Meta-analysis. *Journal of Business Ethics, 154*(2), 301–323. https://doi.org/10.1007/s10551-016-3406-1

Fassin, Y. (2000). Innovation and Ethics: Ethical Considerations in the Innovation Business. *Journal of Business Ethics, 27*, 193–203.

Gino, F. (2015). Understanding Ordinary Unethical Behavior: Why People Who Value Morality Act Immorally. *Current Opinion in Behavioral Sciences, 3*, 107–111. https://doi.org/10.1016/j.cobeha.2015.03.001

Gino, F., Ayal, S., & Ariely, D. (2009). Contagion and Differentiation in Unethical Behavior: The Effect of One Bad Apple on the Barrel. *Psychological Science, 20*(3), 393–398.

Grinbaum, A., & Groves, C. (2013). What Is "Responsible" about Responsible Innovation? Understanding the Ethical Issues. In R. Owen, J. Bessant, & M. Heintz (Eds.), *Responsible Innovation* (pp. 119–142). Chichester: John Wiley & Sons Ltd.

Hartmans, A. (Producer). (2018, April 21). The Rise and Fall of Elizabeth Holmes, Who Started Theranos When She was 19 and became the World's Youngest Female Billionaire before It All Came Crashing Down. Retrieved from https://www.businessinsider.com.au/theranos-founder-ceo-elizabeth-holmes-life-story-bio-2018-4?r=US&IR=T

Henderson, B. J., & Pearson, N. D. (2011). The Dark Side of Financial Innovation: A Case Study of the Pricing of a Retail Financial Product☆. *Journal of Financial Economics, 100*(2), 227–247. https://doi.org/10.1016/j.jfineco.2010.12.006

Herper, M. (Producer). (2016, June 1). From $4.5 billion to Nothing: Forbes Revises Estimated Worth of Theranos Founder Elizabeth Holmes. Retrieved from https://www.forbes.com/sites/matthewherper/2016/06/01/from-4-5-billion-to-nothing-forbes-revises-estimated-net-worth-of-theranos-founder-elizabeth-holmes/#63a3678e3633

Hsieh, H.-F., & Shannon, S. E. (2005). Three Approaches to Qualitative Content Analysis. *Qualitative Health Research, 15*(9), 1277–1288. https://doi.org/10.1177/1049732305276687

Johnson, C. (Producer). (2018, December 19). Elizabeth Holmes, Founder of Blood-Testing Company Theranos, Indicted on Wire Fraud Charges. Retrieved from https://www.washingtonpost.com/business/economy/elizabeth-holmes-founder-of-blood-testing-company-theranos-indicted-on-wire-fraud-federal-authorities-announce/2018/06/15/8779f538-70df-11e8-bd50-b80389a4e569_story.html

Jones, T. (1991). Ethical Decision Making by Individuals in Organisations: An Issue-Contingent Model. *Academy of Management Review, 16*(2), 366–395.

Kanter, R. (1983). *The Change Masters: Innovation & Entrepreneurship in the American Corporation*. New York: Simon & Schuster, Inc.

Kaptein, M. (2011). Understanding Unethical Behavior by Unraveling Ethical Culture. *Human Relations, 64*(6), 843–869. https://doi.org/10.1177/0018726710390536

Kish-Gephart, J. J., Harrison, D. A., & Trevino, L. K. (2010). Bad Apples, Bad Cases, and Bad Barrels: Meta-analytic Evidence about Sources of Unethical Decisions at Work. *Journal of Applied of Psychology, 95*(1), 1–31. https://doi.org/10.1037/a0017103

Krippendorff, K. (1989). Content Analysis. In E. Barnouw, G. Gerbner, W. Schramm, T. Worth, & L. Gross (Eds.), *International Encyclopedia of Communication*. New York: Oxford University Press.

Lefor, A. T. (2005). Scientific Misconduct and Unethical Human Experimentation: Historic Parallels and Moral Implications. *Nutrition, 21*(7), 878–882. https://doi.org/10.1016/j.nut.2004.10.011

Levine, M. (Producer). (2018, March 15). The Blood Unicorn Theranos was Just a Fairy Tale. Retrieved from https://www.bloomberg.com/opinion/articles/2018-03-14/theranos-misled-investors-and-consumers-who-used-its-blood-test

Mai, Y., Zhang, W., & Wang, L. (2019). The Effects of Entrepreneurs' Moral Awareness and Ethical Behavior on Product Innovation of New Ventures. *Chinese Management Studies, 13*(2), 421–446. https://doi.org/10.1108/CMS-10-2017-0302

McKinlay, J. (1981). From "Promising Report" to "Standard Procedure": Seven Stages in the Career of Medical Innovation. *Health and Society, 59*(3), 374–409.

McLean, A. K., Stewart, C., & Kerridge, I. (2015). Untested, Unproven, and Unethical: The Promotion and Provision of Autologous Stem Cell Therapies in Australia. *Stem Cell Research & Therapy, 6*, 33. https://doi.org/10.1186/s13287-015-0047-8

Morales, J., Gendron, Y., & Guénin-Paracini, H. (2014). The Construction of the Risky Individual and Vigilant Organization: A Genealogy of the Fraud Triangle. *Accounting, Organizations and Society, 39*(3), 170–194. https://doi.org/10.1016/j.aos.2014.01.006

Mormina, M. (2019). Science, Technology and Innovation as Social Goods for Development: Rethinking Research Capacity Building from Sen's Capabilities Approach. *Science and Engineering Ethics, 25*(3), 671–692. https://doi.org/10.1007/s11948-018-0037-1

Nethery, A., & Holman, R. (2016). Secrecy and Human Rights Abuse in Australia's Offshore Immigration Detention Centres. *The International Journal of Human Rights, 20*(7), 1018–1038. https://doi.org/10.1080/13642987.2016.1196903

O'Donnell, N. (Producer). (2018, May 20). The Theranos Deception. Retrieved from https://www.cbsnews.com/news/the-theranos-elizabeth-holmes-deception/

Onwuegbuzie, A., Leech, N., & Collins, K. (2012). Qualitative Analysis Techniques for the Review of the Literature. *The Qualitative Report, 17*(28), 1–28.

Ramsey, L. (Producer). (2019, June 29). Theranos Founder Elizabeth Holmes Faces Jail Time for Fraud Charges. Her Trial is Set to Begin in Summer 2020. Retrieved from https://www.businessinsider.com.au/theranos-founder-elizabeth-holmes-president-sunny-balwani-trial-date-2019-6?r=US&IR=T

Robertson, J. (Producer). (2018, March 15). Bad Blood: The Rise and Fall of Theranos and Elizabeth Holmes. Retrieved from https://www.bbc.com/news/business-43415967

Rogers, M. (2007). Diffusion of Innovations. In V. Hoffmann (Ed.), *Knowledge and Innovation Management* (pp. 37–50). Hohenheim: Hohenheim University.

Salerno, M. S., Gomes, L. A. d. V., Silva, D. O. d., Bagno, R. B., & Freitas, S. L. T. U. (2015). Innovation Processes: Which Process for Which Project? *Technovation, 35*, 59–70. https://doi.org/10.1016/j.technovation.2014.07.012

Schumacher, E., & Wasieleski, D. (2013). Institutionalising Ethical Innovation in Organisations: An Integrated Causal Model of Moral Innovation Decision Processes. *Journal of Business Ethics, 113*, 15–37. https://doi.org/10.1007/s10551-012-1277-7

Sharkey, A., & Sharkey, N. (2010). Granny and the Robots: Ethical Issues in Robot Care for the Elderly. *Ethics and Information Technology, 14*(1), 27–40. https://doi.org/10.1007/s10676-010-9234-6

Stockton, N. (Producer). (2016, May 4). Everyting You Need to Know about the Theranos Saga So Far. Retrieved from https://www.wired.com/2016/05/everything-need-know-theranos-saga-far/

Thau, S., Derfler-Rozin, R., Pitesa, M., Mitchell, M. S., & Pillutla, M. M. (2015). Unethical for the Sake of the Group: Risk of Social Exclusion and Pro-group Unethical Behavior. *Journal of Applied Psychology, 100*(1), 98–113. https://doi.org/10.1037/a0036708

Uyarra, E., Zabala-Iturriagagoitia, J. M., Flanagan, K., & Magro, E. (2020). Public Procurement, Innovation and Industrial Policy: Rationales, Roles, Capabilities and Implementation. *Research Policy, 49*(1), 103844. https://doi.org/10.1016/j. respol.2019.103844

Wu, M., Zhao, M., & Wu, Z. (2019). Evaluation of Development Level and Economic Contribution Ratio of Science and Technology Innovation in Eastern China. *Technology in Society, 59*, 101194. https://doi.org/10.1016/j. techsoc.2019.101194

Zheng, C. S., & Mirshekary, S. (2015). The Power of Australian Small Accounting Firms' Unethical Exposure. *Social Responsibility Journal, 11*(3), 467–481. https:// doi.org/10.1108/srj-02-2014-0018

29

Innovation-Enhancing Leadership in the Australian Tourism Industry

Solmaz (Sally) Moghimi and Nuttawuth Muenjohn

Introduction

According to the literature, the tourism industry has experienced continual transformation under the pressure of global competition driven by social and economic forces, the fast pace of information technology, the growing popularity of new destinations in emerging economies, and customers' rising expectations of service offerings (Mattsson & Orfila-Sintes, 2014; Law, Leung, & Cheung, 2012; Molina-Azorín, Tarí, Pereira-Moliner, López-Gamero, & Pertusa-Ortega, 2015; Orfila-Sintes, Crespí-Cladera, & Martínez-Ros, 2005). Innovation contributes to the hotel industry's financial performance (Chang, Gong, & Shum, 2011), sales growth, and market value (Nicolau & Santa-María, 2013); enhances customer loyalty and satisfaction (Enz, Verma, Walsh, Kimes, & Siguaw, 2010; Ottenbacher & Gnoth, 2005; Victorino, Verma, Plaschka, & Dev, 2005); and sustains a hotel's competitive advantage (Fraj, Matute, & Melero, 2015).

One source of innovation for organisations is their employees' ability, diversity of skills, and knowledge, which can generate new and useful ideas

S. (Sally) Moghimi (✉) • N. Muenjohn
School of Management, RMIT University, Melbourne, VIC, Australia
e-mail: solmaz.moghimi@rmit.edu.au; nuttawuth.muenjohn@rmit.edu.au

(Kremer, Villamor, & Herman, 2019; Jong & Hartog, 2007; Slåtten, Svensson, & Sværi, 2011). There is agreement in the literature that individual innovation contributes significantly to organisational success and effectiveness (Axtell et al., 2000; Kattara & El-Said, 2013; Tajeddini, 2010; Unsworth & Parker, 2003). Ottenbacher, Gnoth, and Jones (2006) have argued that employees are at the heart of change and differentiation in the hotel industry because of their critical role as the organisation's ambassadors. While research frameworks and findings vary to some extent, several researchers have agreed on the imperative role of employees' creativity and innovation for organisational success and effectiveness (Hon, 2011; Nagy, 2014; Ottenbacher, 2007; Zhou & Shalley, 2003).

Given the importance of employee's creativity and innovation, substantial research has been conducted to identify their determinants. Leadership is an important organisational contextual construct, found to be critical in advocating employees' creative accomplishments in the hotel industry as well (Hassi, 2019; Chen, 2011; Slåtten et al., 2011). Despite the agreement that leadership is a significant predictor of employees' creativity and innovation, little research has explored comprehensively the concept of leadership for creativity and innovation (Jovičić Vuković, Damnjanović, Papić-Blagojević, Jošanov-Vrgović, & Gagić, 2018; Gupta & Singh, 2013; Jong & Hartog, 2007).

Therefore, this study seeks to explore the effect of leadership behaviours on employees' creativity and innovation in Australian hotels and resorts industry. More specifically, the study aims to answer the following research questions:

- In what ways, if any, do perceived innovation-enhancing leadership behaviours influence employees' creativity in Australian hotels and resorts?
- In what ways, if any, do perceived innovation-enhancing leadership behaviours influence employees' innovation in Australian hotels and resorts?

Theoretical Background

Creativity and Innovation

Theorists have defined creativity and innovation as two dimensions of the innovation process (Amabile, Conti, Coon, Lazenby, & Herron, 1996; Axtell et al., 2000; King & Anderson, 2002). Creativity occurs during the initial stage of an innovation process and involves the production and generation of new ideas; innovation occurs at a later stage, with the implementation and application of new ideas within an organisation (Amabile et al., 1996; Axtell et al., 2000). Farr and Ford (1990) and West and Farr (1989) have described the full process as innovative work behaviour. The literature suggests innovative work behaviour may be conceptualised as multidimensional, consisting of three to four behavioural tasks associated with different phases of the innovation process (Dorenbosch, van Engen, & Verhagen, 2005; Janssen, 2000; Jong & Hartog, 2010; Krause, 2004; Scott & Bruce, 1994). This study considered all aspects of innovative behaviour and treated creativity and innovation as two distinct dimensions in order to clarify how organisational and individual factors may operate during each phase of the innovation process. For its purposes 'creativity' is the phenomenon that involves generating new ideas and suggestions in order to solve work-related problems, filling gaps in procedures, or developing new products and services for the purpose of achieving organisational goals; 'innovation' is the next stage, which seeks to produce practical outcomes by applying the ideas and suggestions.

Fraj et al. (2015) regarded innovativeness in the hotel industry as the ability to respond faster and more flexibly to environmental changes. Today's challenging and dynamic hotel industry requires organisations to consider innovation and differentiation in their daily practices (Jovičić Vuković et al., 2018; Nagy, 2014) in response to emergent challenges (Chen, 2011; Nagy, 2014; Ottenbacher, 2007; Sandvik, Duhan, & Sandvik, 2014). Innovation is recognised as a means to convert opportunities to new business ideas and increase an organisation's profitability and competitiveness by offering differentiated products and services (Chen, 2011; Ottenbacher, 2007; Slåtten et al., 2011; Sundbo, Orfila-Sintes, & Sorensen, 2007). The literature related to the hotel industry indicates that innovation is a key success factor sustaining a hotel's competitive advantage (Chen, 2011; Ottenbacher, 2007; Tajeddini, 2011; Tsai, Horng, Liu, & Hu, 2015; Wong & Pang, 2003), is a predictor of hotel financial performance (Chang et al., 2011; Kattara & El-Said, 2013; Nicolau & Santa-María, 2013; Sandvik et al., 2014) and of non-financial performance such as customer loyalty (Ottenbacher & Gnoth, 2005), and is an effective response to the ever-increasing demands of customers (Enz et al., 2010; Grissemann, Plank, & Brunner-Sperdin, 2013; Victorino, Verma, Plaschka, & Dev, 2005).

One source of innovation in this sector is in human resources (Chen, 2011; Martínez-Ros & Orfila-Sintes, 2012; Orfila-Sintes et al., 2005; Ottenbacher & Gnoth, 2005; Wong & Ladkin, 2008), using employees' creative ideas to enhance the quality of service offerings and organisational practices (Kattara & El-Said, 2013; Wong & Ladkin, 2008). If the only way for hoteliers to enhance innovation were by improving tangible facilities, that would be relatively simple to achieve (Enz & Siguaw, 2003), but employees in this sector, as in other service industries, are brand ambassadors and service providers, shaping customer's perceptions of service experience (Lopez-Fernandez, Serrano-Bedia, & Gomez-Lopez, 2011; Slåtten, 2011). Within this area of literature, researchers have sought to examine the influence of individual and organisational environmental factors affecting employee' creativity and innovation. Leadership, organisational culture, employees' empowerment, and commitment have been identified as determinants of successful innovation practices within this context (Hughes, Lee, Tian, Newman, & Legood, 2018; Tsai et al., 2015).

Leadership and Innovation

In order to clarify the influence of leadership on innovation, over the years scholars have examined the association between different leadership styles and individual and organisational innovative behaviour in a range of research settings (Hughes et al., 2018). The literature on leadership and innovation follows three main approaches: the collection of quantitative data, the collection of qualitative data, and meta-analyses. Quantitative studies have examined the influence of existing theories and used instruments to measure aspects of leadership (Lee, 2008; Michaelis, Stegmaier, & Sonntag, 2009; Wang & Zhu, 2011). The conceptualisation of transformational leadership has been researched widely as a predictor of employees' creativity and innovation (Cheung & Wong, 2011; Eisenbeiss, van Knippenberg, & Boerner, 2008; Jung, Wu, & Chow, 2008). Other leadership styles such as participative leadership (Krause, Gebert, & Kearney, 2007; Somech, 2006), empowering leadership (Krause, 2004; Slåtten et al., 2011), charismatic leadership (Murphy & Ensher, 2008), and authentic leadership (Valentine, Godkin, Fleischman, & Kidwell, 2011) have also studied predictors of employees' creativity and innovation. The outcomes of this research have not been consistent and convincing; for example, while transformational leadership has been most strongly correlated with innovation (Rosing, Frese, & Bausch, 2011), there are studies that did not find a positive empirical relationship between transformational leadership and individual creativity (Jaffer, 2013) or indicated a negative effect of transformational leadership on group creative performance (Jaussi & Dionne, 2003), and some found that transformational leadership was significantly linked to lower innovation performance (Osborn & Marion, 2009). Similarly, while studies such as those of Volmer, Spurk, and Niessen (2012) and Atwater and Carmeli (2009) demonstrated a positive impact of leader–member exchange theory on creativity, Clegg, Unsworth, Epitropaki, and Parker (2002) found no association between leader–member exchange and idea suggestion. Perhaps employing various approaches and samples in different contexts caused inconsistent outcomes in quantitative studies of the relationship between leadership and innovation.

A second group of literature takes a qualitative approach to the study of leadership for creativity and innovation. Instead of quantitatively testing the impact of different leadership styles, these studies use interviews to understand leadership processes related to creativity and innovation. Following Mumford and Licuanan's (2004) argument, Gupta and Singh (2013) and Jong and Hartog (2007) suggested that existing theories of leadership, originally developed to explore aspects of performance and effectiveness, might not account for innovation in any context. Instead of adopting already developed theories of leadership, these authors conducted in-depth qualitative interviews with managers and supervisors of R&D (research and development) teams and knowledge-intensive firms, respectively, and explored a wide range of leadership behaviours influencing employees' creativity and innovation.

Another set of studies includes those that have reviewed existing literature to identify patterns in the findings related to how leadership influences employees' creativity and innovation (Mumford & Licuanan, 2004; Basadur, 2004; Williams & Foti, 2011). Based on existing literature, Hunter and Cushenbery (2011) proposed a model of leading for innovation, which depicts how leaders directly and indirectly influence innovation at different levels in an organisation including individual and team creativity and organisational innovation. Rosing et al. (2011) meta-analytically integrated the existing literature on leadership and innovation and proposed an ambidextrous model of leadership consisting of opening and losing leadership behaviours that are likely to be related to followers' exploration and exploitation activities.

Methodology

The target population of this study includes three-, four-, and five-star hotels and resorts in Australia. All hotels and resorts graded as three-star, four-star, and five-star, from categories including hotels, hotels and resorts, resorts, and boutique hotels, located in Australia were invited to participate.

This list was developed from the databases of relevant associations and government websites. In Australia 647 qualifying hotels and resorts were identified. An online self-administered survey was used to collect data, given the geographical distribution of the target population. Original contact was made with the identified three-, four-, and five-star hotels and resorts in Australia. To encourage a high response rate, the researchers sent out e-mail reminders or telephoned reminders. A total of 292 usable responses were received, indicating a 45% response rate.

The survey questionnaire was developed, including 89 items in six sections. This study aims to explore leadership behaviours that are likely to influence employees' creativity and innovation. Leadership behaviours were measured using the innovation-enhancing leadership (ILB) instrument. The reliability and validity analysis demonstrated internal consistency (Cronbach's alpha coefficient > 0.70) and divergent and discriminant validity of the instrument.

In terms of employees' creativity and innovation, items were adapted from measures, which have been used widely in the literature with internal reliability and validity established by prior studies. The construct of employees' creativity survey included 11 self-reporting items, which were adopted from Jong and Hartog (2010), McMurray and Dorai (2003), Krause (2004), Janssen (2000), and Dorenbosch et al. (2005). To measure innovation, 11 self-reporting items were adapted from Scott and Bruce (1994), Jong and Hartog (2010), McMurray and Dorai (2003), and Dorenbosch et al. (2005), Janssen (2000), and Scott and Bruce (1994). The employee's creativity and innovation measures were also shown to have acceptable internal reliability (Cronbach's alpha coefficient > 0.70) and evidence of construct validity. All items were measured on a five-point Likert scale that ranged from 1 (strongly disagree) to 5 (strongly agree).

Demographic Distribution of Participants

The numbers of male and female participants were very close (50.3% female = 147, 49.7% male = 145). The sample distribution demonstrates that the vast majority of participants were from the 25–30 age groups. 35.3% of participants were aged 25–30, followed by 34.2% aged 31–40. More than half the respondents had completed a bachelor's degree (54.5%), and 21.6% of the participants had a master qualification, followed by 19.9% of respondents who had certificate/diploma. The respondents were mostly in staff positions (54.4%), while 45.5% held supervisory or managerial positions.

The largest groups of participants were from the hotel category (N: 133; 39.7%), followed by the hotel and resort category (N: 116, 38.7%). The data indicated that just under half of the participants were from international chains (N: 136; 46.6%). The smaller groups were from local chains and non-chain hotels/resorts representing 30.5% and 22.9% of the sample, respectively. Finally, 116 respondents (39.7%) and 98 respondents (33.6%), respectively, represented four- and five-star hotels/resorts. A smaller group of 23.3% were from three-star hotels and resorts sample.

Data Analysis

Regression analysis indicates that perceived innovation-enhancing leadership is positively and significantly related to employees' creativity in Australian hotels and resorts (β, 0.627; P, 0.000), after controlling for demographic variables. Perceived innovation-enhancing leadership explains 39.3% of the variance in employees' self-reported creativity (R-square: 0.393) (Table 29.1).

In order to examine the influence of variables external to the proposed model, the control variables (gender, age, education, organisational level, tenure, hotel category, organisation type, and hotel star rating) were all entered in the first model of regression equation.

The results of the first model explain 3.3% of the variance in the effect of perceived innovation-enhancing leadership on the level of employees' creativity. In the second model, the main effect of perceived innovation-enhancing leadership was entered. The result is significant at (P: 0.000); perceived innovation-enhancing leadership behaviours explain 41.3% of the variance in employees' creativity (R-square, 0.413; adjusted R-square, 0.394) (Table 29.2).

Simple regression analysis reveals that there is a significant relationship between perceived innovation-enhancing leadership and employees' self-reported innovation in Australia hotels and resorts (β, 0.652; P, 0.000), with the construct explaining 42.5% of the variance in employees' innovation (R-square: 0.425) (Table 29.3).

In order to examine the influence of variables external to the proposed model, the control variables (gender, age, education, organisational level, tenure, hotel category, organisation type and star rating) and perceived

Table 29.1 Regression model: innovation-enhancing leadership and employees' creativity, Australian hotels and resorts

Simple regression model	Degree of employee creativity		
	β	t-value	p-value
Innovation-enhancing leadership	0.627	13.713	0.000
R^2	0.393		
Adjusted R^2	0.391		
F-value	188.053		

Table 29.2 Regression model: innovation-enhancing leadership (with control variables), Australian hotels and resorts

	Model 1			Model 2		
	β	t-value	p-value	B	t-value	p-value
Control variables						
Gender	0.047	0.798	0.425	0.055	1.190	0.235
Age	0.038	0.397	0.691	0.145	1.938	0.054
Education	0.029	0.450	0.653	−0.082	−1.595	0.112
Organisational level	−0.113	−1.306	0.192	−0.047	−0.698	0.486
Tenure	−0.024	−0.235	0.815	−0.106	−1.342	0.181
Hotel category	−0.108	−1.687	0.093	−0.045	−0.895	0.372
Organisation type	−0.053	−0.840	0.401	−0.009	−0.181	0.856
Star rating	−0.092	−1.427	0.155	−0.060	−1.203	0.230
Main effect						
Innovation-enhancing leadership				0.640	13.517	0.000
R^2	0.033			0.413		
Adjusted R^2	0.006			0.394		
F-value	1.207			22.062		

Table 29.3 Regression model: innovation-enhancing leadership behaviours and employees' innovation, Australian hotels and resorts

	Degree of employee innovation		
Simple regression model	β	t-value	p-value
Innovation-enhancing leadership	0.652	14.627	0.000
R^2	0.425		
Adjusted R^2	0.423		
F-value	213.953		

innovation-enhancing leadership were all included in the regression equation. The control variables entered in the first model explain 3.2% of the variance in construct on the level of self-reported employees' innovation. In model 2, the main effect of the construct was entered. The result demonstrates a significant influence (P: 0.000): perceived innovation-enhancing leadership behaviours explain 44% of the variance in self-reported employees' innovation (R-square, 0.440; adjusted R-square, 0.423). Analysis of the control variables shows that none is significantly related to the influence of perceived innovation-enhancing leadership behaviours on self-reported employees' innovation ($P > 0.05$). According to the results of the second model, perceived innovation-enhancing leadership is the only independent variable significantly influencing employees' self-reported innovation in Australian hotels and resorts (β: 0.664, P: 0.000) (Table 29.4).

Table 29.4 Regression model: innovation-enhancing leadership and employees' innovation, Australian hotels and resorts

	Model 1			Model 2		
	β	t-value	p-value	B	t-value	p-value
Control variables						
Gender	0.037	0.625	0.533	0.045	0.998	0.319
Age	−0.019	−0.198	0.843	0.092	1.262	0.208
Education	0.017	0.264	0.792	−0.098	−1.956	0.051
Organisational level	−0.149	−1.730	0.085	−0.081	−1.234	0.218
Tenure	−0.009	−0.091	0.928	−0.094	−1.225	0.221
Hotel category	−0.097	−1.523	0.129	−0.032	−0.657	0.512
Organisation type	−0.052	−0.822	0.412	−0.006	−0.128	0.898
Star rating	−0.031	−0.483	0.630	0.001	0.029	0.977
Main effect						
Innovation-enhancing leadership				0.664	14.355	0.000
R^2	0.032			0.440		
Adjusted R^2	0.004			0.423		
F-value	1.155			24.667		

Discussion and Conclusion

The significant positive relationships reported between innovation-enhancing leadership and employees' creativity and innovation in this study are consistent with the literature. Various studies that have dealt with the topic of creativity and innovation have suggested that leadership is one of the important environmental factors determining employees' creativity and innovation (Gupta & Singh, 2013; Qu, Janssen, & Shi, 2015; Wang, Tsai, & Tsai, 2014; Yoshida, Sendjaya, Hirst, & Cooper, 2014). Local leaders who influence employees' attitude to their work environment have a crucial impact on individual creativity (Amabile, Schatzel, Moneta, & Kramer, 2004) as they shape employees' daily experience at work by coaching, defining the scope of their authority and responsibility, influencing interactions with others in the organisation, and providing resources (Jong & Hartog, 2007).

The outcome of this study suggests that the influence of perceived innovation-enhancing leadership on employees' innovation is stronger than its influence on employee's creativity in Australian hotels and resorts. Employees' innovation refers to the implementation stage of new ideas: perhaps this might be due to leaders having more influence at the application stage than at the earlier idea generation stage. Evidence from the qualitative phase also shows that the organisational position of leaders over employees means that they have more access to resources, an essential requirement of successful innovation. The interviewed managers highlighted the vital role of leaders in the implementation process because of their subordinates' limited authority, decision-making power, and access to resources. Given the findings of this research, perceived innovation-enhancing leadership behaviours explain more of the variance in employees' implementation behaviours than idea exploration and generation.

The findings of this study are also consistent with research in the context of the hotel industry (Chen, 2011; Enz & Siguaw, 2003; Nagy, 2014; Slåtten, 2011; Slåtten et al., 2011; Wong & Pang, 2003). For instance, managers' support was found vital in encouraging employees' self-determination and personal initiative and inspiring them to develop creative ideas and solutions in the Hong Kong hotel industry (Wong & Pang, 2003). The quality of relationship between managers and employees was also found to be relevant to employees' innovative behaviour in the Norwegian hotel industry (Slåtten, 2011). In another study in the context of hotels sector in Taiwan, Chen (2011) identified that environmental forces have an important role in shaping innovative behaviours. This study confirmed hotel managers who provide support and recognition, offer encouragement, show tolerance for failure, and encourage employees' novel ideas and suggestions. Similarly Hon (2011), using a sample of 286 employees in 20 hotel companies in China, suggested that social–contextual variables including empowering leadership significantly predict employees' creativity in the industry. Nagy (2014) found that in the context of the Romanian hotel industry, management style that does not encourage employees' involvement and participation in decision-making hinders their innovative behaviour.

The quantitative data analysis provides evidence that supportive leadership behaviours positively and significantly influence employees' creativity and innovation in hotels and resorts in Australia. This finding concurs with Amabile's componential theory (1988) that positive support from supervisors, support from the work group, and recognising individual contributions foster an environment supportive of novel work by employees. Cheung and Wong (2011), drawing on a sample of 182 supervisor–subordinate dyads from the Hong Kong service sector, found that leader support is directly related to employee creativity in such a way that when leaders support subordinates, the latter become intrinsically motivated to think of new solutions to old problems. Further, as creative ventures are associated with risk and difficulties (Hunter & Cushenbery, 2011), support and motivation from above is one of the crucial determinants of employees' creativity and innovation (Jong & Hartog, 2007; Wong & Pang, 2003). The empirical study by Hulsheger, Anderson, and Salgado (2009) demonstrated a positive association between support for innovation and team innovation. The significant relationship between supportive leadership behaviours emphasising a supportive work environment, recognition and reward, and employees' creativity and innovation is similar to that found in the study of Jong and Hartog (2007). Krause (2004) found a leader's support for innovation predicts idea generation and implementation.

The outcome of this research demonstrated the construct of perceived innovation-enhancing leadership positively and significantly influences employees' creativity and innovation in the Australian tourism industry. This result concurs with existing literature that shows leadership positively and significantly influences employees' innovative behaviour (Qu et al., 2015; Wang et al., 2014). In the context of the hotel industry, it is also demonstrated that leadership enhances employees' innovative behaviour (Hon, 2011; Slåtten et al., 2011).

Considering the ongoing development in the hospitality industry, it has long been believed that academic research can assist by providing practitioners with guides that allow them to identify and address managerial and operational deficiencies (Law et al., 2012; Van Scotter & Culligan, 2003). The results of this study may have important implications for practitioners. With a better understanding of potential innovation-enhancing leadership behaviours and the interaction effects of leadership, organisational climate, and personal initiative, hospitality firms will be able to develop strategies to enhance their employees' creativity and innovativeness.

References

Amabile, T. M. (1988). A Model of Creativity and Innovation in Organizations. In B. M. Staw & L. L. Cummings (Eds.), *Research in Organizational Behaviour* (pp. 123–167). Greenwich, CT: JAI Press.

Amabile, T. M., Conti, R., Coon, H., Lazenby, J., & Herron, M. (1996). Assessing the Work Environment for Creativity. *Academy of Management Journal, 39*(5), 1154–1184.

Amabile, T., Schatzel, E., Moneta, G., & Kramer, S. (2004). Leader Behaviours and the Work Environment for Creativity: Perceived Leader Support. *The Leadership Quarterly, 15*(1), 5–32.

Atwater, L., & Carmeli, A. (2009). Leader–Member Exchange, Feelings of Energy, and Involvement in Creative Work. *The Leadership Quarterly, 20*(3), 264–275.

Axtell, C. M., Holman, D. J., Unsworth, K. L., Wall, T. D., Waterson, P. E., & Harrington, E. (2000). Shop-Floor Innovation: Facilitating the Suggestion and Implementation of Ideas. *Journal of Occupational and Organizational Psychology, 73*, 265–285.

Basadur, M. (2004). Leading others to think innovatively together: creative leadership. *The Leadership Quarterly, 15*(1), 103–121.

Chang, S., Gong, Y., & Shum, C. (2011). Promoting Innovation in Hospitality Companies through Human Resource Management Practices. *International Journal of Hospitality Management, 30*(4), 812–818.

Chen, W. J. (2011). Innovation in Hotel Services: Culture and Personality. *International Journal of Hospitality Management, 30*(1), 64–72.

Cheung, M. F. Y., & Wong, C. S. (2011). Transformational Leadership, Leader Support, and Employee Creativity. *Leadership and Organizational Development Journal, 32*(7), 657–672.

Clegg, C., Unsworth, K., Epitropaki, O., & Parker, G. (2002). Implicating Trust in the Innovation Process. *Journal of Occupational and Organizational Psychology, 75*(4), 409–422.

Dorenbosch, L., van Engen, M., & Verhagen, M. (2005). On-the-Job Innovation: The Impact of Job Design and Human Resource Management through Production Ownership. *Creativity and Innovation Management, 14*, 129–141.

Eisenbeiss, S. A., van Knippenberg, D., & Boerner, S. (2008). Transformational Leadership and Team Innovation: Integrating Team Climate Principles. *Journal of Applied Psychology, 93*(6), 1438–1446.

Enz, C., & Siguaw, J. (2003). Innovations in Hotel Practice. *Cornell Hospitality Quarterly, 44*(5–6), 115–123.

Enz, C. A., Verma, R., Walsh, K., Kimes, S. E., & Siguaw, J. (2010). Cases in Innovative Practices in Hospitality and Related Services. *Cornell Hospitality Report, 10*(10), 4–26.

Farr, J., & Ford, C. (1990). Individual Innovation. In M. West & J. Farr (Eds.), *Innovation and Creativity at Work: Psychological and Organizational Strategies* (pp. 63–80). Chichester: Wiley.

Fraj, E., Matute, J., & Melero, I. (2015). Environmental Strategies and Organizational Competitiveness in the Hotel Industry: The Role of Learning and Innovation as Determinants of Environmental Success. *Tourism Management, 46*, 30–42.

Grissemann, U., Plank, A., & Brunner-Sperdin, A. (2013). Enhancing Business Performance of Hotels: The Role of Innovation and Customer Orientation. *International Journal of Hospitality Management, 33*, 347–356.

Gupta, V., & Singh, S. (2013). How Leaders Impact Employee Creativity: A Study of Indian R&D Laboratories. *Management Research Review, 36*(1), 66–88.

Hassi, A. (2019). Empowering Leadership and Management Innovation in the Hospitality Industry Context. *International Journal of Contemporary Hospitality Management, 31*(1), 1785–1800.

Hon, A. (2011). Enhancing Employee Creativity in the Chinese Context: The Mediating Role of Employee Self-concordance. *International Journal of Hospitality Management, 30*(2), 375–384.

Hughes, D. J., Lee, A., Tian, A. W., Newman, A., & Legood, A. (2018). Leadership, Creativity, and Innovation: A Critical Review and Practical Recommendations. *The Leadership Quarterly, 29*(5), 549–569.

Hulsheger, U., Anderson, N., & Salgado, J. (2009). Team-Level Predictors of Innovation at Work: A Comprehensive Meta-analysis Spanning Three Decades of Research. *Journal of Applied Psychology, 94*(5), 1128–1145.

Hunter, S. T., & Cushenbery, H. (2011). Leading for Innovation: Direct and Indirect Influences. *Advances in Developing Human Resources, 13*(3), 248–265.

Jaffer, S. (2013). *Harnessing Innovation in the 21st Century: The Impact of Leadership Styles*. PhD thesis, George Washington University.

Janssen, O. (2000). Job Demands, Perceptions of Effort-Reward Fairness and Innovative Work Behaviour. *Journal of Occupational and Organizational Psychology, 73*, 287–302.

Jaussi, K., & Dionne, S. (2003). Leading for Creativity: The Role of Unconventional Leader Behaviour. *The Leadership Quarterly, 14*(4), 475–498.

Jong, J. D., & Hartog, D. N. (2007). How Leaders Influence Employees' Innovative Behaviour. *European Journal of European Management, 10*(1), 41–64.

Jong, J. D., & Hartog, D. N. (2010). Measuring Innovative Work Behaviour. *Creativity and Innovation Management, 19*(1), 23–36.

Jovičić Vuković, A., Damnjanović, J., Papić-Blagojević, N., Jošanov-Vrgović, I., & Gagić, S. (2018). Impact of Leadership on Innovation: Evidence from the Hotel Industry Management. *Journal of Sustainable Business and Management Solutions in Emerging Economies, 23*(3), 57–67.

Jung, D., Wu, A., & Chow, C. W. (2008). Towards Understanding the Direct and Indirect Effects of CEOs' Transformational Leadership on Firm Innovation. *The Leadership Quarterly, 19*, 582–594.

Kattara, H., & El-Said, O. (2013). Innovation Strategies: The Implementation of Creativity Principles in Egyptian Hotels. *Tourism and Hospitality Research, 13*(3), 140–148.

King, N., & Anderson, N. (2002). *Managing Innovation and Change: A Critical Guide for organizations*. Thomson: London.

Krause, D. E. (2004). Influence-Based Leadership as a Determinant of the Inclination to Innovate and of Innovation-Related Behaviours: An Empirical Investigation. *Leadership Quarterly, 15*, 79–102.

Krause, D., Gebert, D., & Kearney, E. (2007). Implementing Process Innovations the Benefits of Combining Delegative-Participative with Consultative-Advisory Leadership. *Journal of Leadership & Organizational Studies, 14*(1), 16–25.

Kremer, H., Villamor, I., & Herman, A. (2019). Innovation Leadership: Best-Practice Recommendations for Promoting Employee Creativity, Voice, and Knowledge Sharing. *Business Horizons, 62*(1), 65–74.

Law, R., Leung, D., & Cheung, C. (2012). A Systematic Review, Analysis, and Evaluation of Research Articles in the *Cornell Hospitality Quarterly*. *Cornell Hospitality Quarterly, 53*(4), 365–381.

Lee, J. (2008). Effects of Leadership and Leader–Member Exchange on Innovativeness. *Journal of Managerial Psychology, 23*(6), 670–687.

Lopez-Fernandez, M., Serrano-Bedia, A., & Gomez-Lopez, R. (2011). Factors Encouraging Innovation in Spanish Hospitality Firms. *Cornell Hospitality Quarterly, 52*(2), 144–152.

Martínez-Ros, E., & Orfila-Sintes, F. (2012). Training Plans, Manager's Characteristics and Innovation in the Accommodation Industry. *International Journal of Hospitality Management, 31*, 686–694.

Mattsson, J., & Orfila-Sintes, F. (2014). Hotel Innovation and Its Effect on Business Performance. *International Journal of Tourism Research, 16*(4), 388–398.

McMurray, A. J., & Dorai, R. (2003). *Workplace Innovation Scale: A New Method for Measuring Innovation in the Workplace.* Paper presented to 5th Organizational Learning & Knowledge International Conference, Lancaster University, UK, 30 May–2 June.

Michaelis, B., Stegmaier, R., & Sonntag, K. (2009). Shedding Light on Followers' Innovation Implementation Behaviour: The Role of Transformational Leadership, Commitment to Change, and Climate for Initiative. *Journal of Managerial Psychology, 25*(4), 408–429.

Molina-Azorín, J., Tarí, J., Pereira-Moliner, J., López-Gamero, M., & Pertusa-Ortega, E. (2015). The Effects of Quality and Environmental Management on Competitive Advantage: A Mixed Methods Study in the Hotel Industry. *Tourism Management, 50*, 41–54.

Mumford, M. D., & Licuanan, B. (2004). Leading for Innovation: Conclusions, Issues, and Directions. *Leadership Quarterly, 15*(1), 163–171.

Murphy, S. E., & Ensher, E. A. (2008). A Qualitative Analysis of Charismatic Leadership in Creative Teams: The Case of Television Directions. *The Leadership Quarterly, 19*, 335–352.

Nagy, A. (2014). The Orientation towards Innovation of Spa Hotel Management: The Case of Romanian Spa Industry. *Social and Behavioural Sciences, 124*, 425–431.

Nicolau, J., & Santa-María, M. (2013). The Effect of Innovation on Hotel Market Value. *International Journal of Hospitality Management, 32*, 71–79.

Orfila-Sintes, F., Crespí-Cladera, R., & Martínez-Ros, E. (2005). Innovation Activity in the Hotel Industry: Evidence from Balearic Islands. *Tourism Management, 26*(6), 851–865.

Osborn, R., & Marion, R. (2009). Contextual Leadership, Transformational Leadership and the Performance of International Innovation Seeking Alliances. *The Leadership Quarterly, 20*(2), 191–206.

Ottenbacher, M. C. (2007). Innovation Management in Hospitality Industry: Different Strategies for Achieving Success. *Journal of Hospitality and Tourism Research, 31*(4), 431–454.

Ottenbacher, M., & Gnoth, J. (2005). How to Develop Successful Hospitality Innovation. *Cornell Hotel and Restaurant Administration Quarterly, 46*(2), 205–222.

Ottenbacher, M., Gnoth, J., & Jones, P. (2006). Identifying Determinants of Success in Development of New High-Contact Services: Insights from Hospitality Industry. *International Journal of Service Industry Management, 17*(4), 344–363.

Qu, R., Janssen, O., & Shi, K. (2015). Transformational leadership and follower creativity: the mediating role of follower relational identification and the moderating role of leader creativity expectations. *The Leadership Quarterly, 26*(2), 286–299.

Rosing, K., Frese, M., & Bausch, A. (2011). Explaining the Heterogeneity of the Leadership–Innovation Relationship: Ambidextrous Leadership. *The Leadership Quarterly, 22*(5), 956–974.

Sandvik, I. L., Duhan, D. F., & Sandvik, K. (2014). Innovativeness and Profitability: An Empirical Investigation in the Norwegian Hotel Industry. *Cornell Hospitality Quarterly, 55*(2), 165–185.

Scott, S. G., & Bruce, R. A. (1994). Determinants of Innovative Behaviour: A Path Model of Individual Innovation in the Workplace. *Academy of Management Journal, 37*(3), 580–607.

Slåtten, T. (2011). Antecedents and Effects of Employees' Feelings of Joy on Employees' Innovative Behaviour. *International Journal Quality & Service Sciences, 3*(1), 93–109.

Slåtten, T., Svensson, G., & Sværi, S. (2011). Empowering Leadership and the Influence of a Humorous Work Climate on Service Employees' Creativity and Innovative Behaviour in Frontline Service Jobs. *International Journal of Quality and Service Sciences, 3*, 267–284.

Somech, A. (2006). The Effects of Leadership Style and Team Process on Performance and Innovation in Functionally Heterogeneous Teams. *Journal of Management, 32*(1), 132–157.

Sundbo, J., Orfila-Sintes, F., & Sorensen, F. (2007). The Innovative Behavior of Tourism Firms: Comparative Studies of Denmark and Spain. *Research Policy, 36*(1), 88–106.

Tajeddini, K. (2010). Effect of Customer Orientation and Entrepreneurial Orientation on Innovativeness: Evidence from the Hotel Industry in Switzerland. *Tourism Management, 31*(2), 221–231.

Tajeddini, K. (2011). Customer orientation, learning orientation, and new service development: an empirical investigation of the Swiss Hotel Industry. *Journal of Hospitality & Tourism Research, 35*(4), 437–468.

Tsai, C., Horng, J., Liu, C., & Hu, D. (2015). Work Environment and Atmosphere: The Role of Organizational Support in the Creativity Performance of Tourism and Hospitality Organizations. *International Journal of Hospitality Management, 46*, 26–35.

Unsworth, K. L., & Parker, S. (2003). Proactivity and Innovation: Promoting a New Workforce for the New Workplace. In T. D. W. Holman, C. V. Clegg, P. Sparrow, & A. Howard (Eds.), *The New Workplace: A Guide to the Human Impact of Modern Working Practices* (pp. 175–196). Chichester: John Wiley.

Valentine, S., Godkin, L., Fleischman, G., & Kidwell, R. (2011). Corporate Ethical Values, Group Creativity, Job Satisfaction and Turnover Intention: The Impact of Work Context on Work Response. *Journal of Business Ethics, 98*(3), 353–372.

Van Scotter, J., & Culligan, P. (2003). The Value of Theoretical Research and Applied Research for the Hospitality Industry. *Cornell Hotel and Restaurant Administration Quarterly, 44*(2), 14–27.

Victorino, L., Verma, R., Plaschka, G., & Dev, C. (2005). Service Innovation and Customer Choice in the Hospitality Industry. *Managing Service Quality, 15*(6), 555–576.

Volmer, J., Spurk, D., & Niessen, C. (2012). Leader–Member Exchange (LMX), Job Autonomy, and Creative Work Involvement. *The Leadership Quarterly, 23*(3), 456–465.

Wang, C., Tsai, H., & Tsai, M. (2014). Linking Transformational Leadership and Employee Creativity in the Hospitality Industry: The Influences of Creative Role Identity, Creative Self-efficacy, and Job Complexity. *Tourism Management, 40*, 79–89.

Wang, P., & Zhu, W. (2011). Mediating Role of Creative Identity in the Influence of Transformational Leadership on Creativity: Is There a Multilevel Effect? *Journal of Leadership & Organizational Studies, 1*(191), 25–39.

West, M. A., & Farr, J. L. (1989). Innovation at Work: Psychological Perspectives. *Social Behaviour, 4*, 15–30.

Williams, F., & Foti, R. (2011). Formally developing creative leadership as a driver of organizational innovation. *Advances in Developing Human Resources, 13*(3), 279–296.

Wong, S. C., & Ladkin, A. (2008). Exploring the Relationship between Employee Creativity and Job Motivators in the Hong Kong Hotel Industry. *International Journal of Hospitality Management, 27*, 426–437.

Wong, S., & Pang, L. (2003). Motivators to Creativity in the Hotel Industry: Perspectives of Managers and Supervisors. *Tourism Management, 24*(5), 551–559.

Yoshida, D., Sendjaya, S., Hirst, G., & Cooper, B. (2014). Does Servant Leadership Foster Creativity and Innovation? A Multi-level Mediation Study of Identification and Prototypically. *Journal of Business Research, 67*(7), 1395–1404.

Zhou, J., & Shalley, C. E. (2003). Research on Employee Creativity: A Critical Review and Proposal for Future Research Directions. In J. J. Martocchio & G. R. Ferris (Eds.), *Research in Personnel and Human Resource Management*. Oxford, UK: Elsevier.

30

Back to Basics in the Dairy Industry: Building Innovation Capabilities to Allow Future Innovation Success

Erick G. Torres and Andres Ramirez-Portilla

Introduction

The dairy industry is vital for nations not only because of its contribution to population nutrition but also for economic and strategic reasons. Historically, the consumption of milk and milk derivatives has been globally growing. Nowadays, Asia, Europe, and North America are the biggest consumers per capita; however, this industry is relevant in all regions and countries (IDF, 2020). Three main agents of the productive chain are essential to determine the competitive environment of the dairy industry. First, the owners of the stables that produce and supply raw milk. Second, manufacturing companies that transform the milk into diverse products and distribute them. Third, the big retailers and small stores which sell the products available to the consumers. Even though the dairy business is mature, it has not reached its full commercial potential. Since the food and beverage (F&B) companies are exposed to new trends of consumption and changes in the consumers' profile, they are

E. G. Torres (✉)
Departamento de Ingeniería Química Industrial y de Alimentos,
Universidad Iberoamericana, Mexico City, Mexico
e-mail: erick.torres@ibero.mx

A. Ramirez-Portilla
Departamento de Estudios Empresariales, Universidad Iberoamericana,
Mexico City, Mexico
e-mail: andres.ramirez@ibero.mx

© The Author(s), under exclusive license to Springer Nature Switzerland AG 2021
A. McMurray et al. (eds.), *The Palgrave Handbook of Workplace Innovation*,
https://doi.org/10.1007/978-3-030-59916-4_30

559

interested in effectively incorporating the innovation in their competitive strategy (Bigliardi & Galati, 2013; Sam Saguy, 2011).

Firms in the dairy industry are not an exception, and now this mature industry with mostly incremental innovations in processes has changed to become more innovative throughout its value chain. Most dairy industry firms, as the majority of firms, understand that innovation is a process, a coordinated encounter of innovation activities not only from R&D but a complex net of internal and external sources (Tidd & Bessant, 2014). However, few firms truly realize that significant innovation activities come from innovation capabilities, which are the engine of innovation. These capabilities are not inherent to firms, but they need to be acquired, developed, and maintained through time. Moreover, most firms also fail to grasp that innovation capabilities are dynamic and reside in tangible and intangible assets (Teece, 2007). Building innovation capabilities could be a complicated, costly, uncertain, and a long-term journey for a company, but it is essential to deploy an innovation strategy first.

This chapter shows the case of Alpura—the second-largest dairy firm in Mexico—going through a process of creating, building, and reconfiguring innovation capabilities according to a new competitive strategy. The context of the case is interesting since Mexico occupies the 14th place in milk production worldwide (CANILEC, 2019). Only in 2019, the consumption of fluid milk in the country was 4,185,000 tons (SIAP, 2019). The size of the market in 2017 was over 218 million dollars (Euromonitor, 2018). Besides, the Mexican dairy industry is a complex mix of 3803 firms where 61 are big companies with more than 250 employees (INEGI, 2020); and of this, only six hold more than 50% of the market. Two large local companies—Lala and Alpura—lead the market and all the big global players are present with different brands. Thus, the competition is aggressive to be at the top of the consumer's mind, to achieve the best quality and innocuity, and get the optimal location on the shelf of big and small retailers. Only until the last few years, innovation has also become a significant and genuine opportunity for firms to increase profits.

The chapter is structured in the following sections. After the introduction, section "The Relevance of Innovation Capabilities to Allow Firm Success" briefly describes some of the theoretical perspectives used to understand and analyze the relevance of dynamics capabilities such as innovation capabilities to allow firms to compete and have a sustained advantage. Later on, section "Methodology" describes the methodology used to collect and analyze the data in Alpura's case study. Section "Results and Findings" presents the results and main insights from the case study, which are later discussed in section "Discussion". Finally, section "Conclusions" provides some general conclusions, managerial implications, and suggestions for future research.

The Relevance of Innovation Capabilities to Allow Firm Success

Implementing effective innovation strategies is a challenging task in all industries and countries. According to a study performed by the IPADE in 2017, of the 28 interviewed CEOs of some of the most important F&B companies in Mexico—both local and global—all have faced difficulties bringing out innovative products due to internal and external issues. Even though innovation is relevant for the 92% of CEOs, almost one-third acknowledge that they have not expertly embedded the innovation priority into their companies' culture and processes. Also, the consulted CEOs describe that, like in other emerging economies, radical innovation usually comes from the headquarters of international firms. For this reason, their companies generally perform incremental innovation focused on the product (IPADE, 2017). Based on this issue, the establishment and implementation of an effective innovation strategy are necessary for dairy products firms to be successful in the market they perform. According to Porter, five forces determine the competitive dynamics in the industry (Porter, 2004). Hence, an innovation strategy should emerge from a specific context and not a generic one. Even more, in dynamic environments, market structure is the result of innovation and learning (Teece, 2007).

There are multiple perspectives, visions, and frameworks to understand innovation in organizations. Two useful views to analyze innovation in competitive, mature industries and sectors such as the dairy industry are based on market circumstances and the firm's internal resources (Trott, 2012). The first one centered in the market argues that the possibility of innovating depends mostly on the market conditions. The second one, mostly known as the resource-based view, argues that the performance of a firm not only depends on the market opportunities but on the organization's mustered resources (Teece, 1997). Thus, key resources such as capabilities within the company impel or impede innovation. On the organizational capabilities, Dosi, Nelson, and Winter (2002) say: *"Capabilities fill the gap between intention and outcome, and they fill it in such way that the outcome bears a definite resemblance to what was intended."* So, innovation capabilities allow the companies to get new products, production or business processes, new for the world, the market, or, at minimum, new for the firm (OECD/Eurostat, 2018). In the market-based view, innovations efforts from firms are more restrained by the conditions given by the whole industry in general. In the resource-based view, firms can focus on the assets acquired by the organization's sacrifices and investments, for the market rewarding (Teece, 2007).

Capabilities is an essential area because they allow the companies to perform productive activities through the combination and coordination of resources and competences. Lawson and Samson (2001) define an innovation capability as *"the ability to continuously transform knowledge and ideas into new products, processes and systems for the benefit of the firm and its stakeholders."* In other words, innovation capabilities can be seen as a bridge between the innovation stimulus and innovation performance (Projogo, 2006). Building innovation capabilities is both art and science. For this reason, directors have to wisely define the investments in tangible and intangible assets to reinforce the current capabilities and create new ones that allow the formulation, implementation, and maintenance of an innovation strategy. An advantage of having innovation capabilities is that they are dynamic capabilities; thereby, they can be adequate and reconfigured to respond to the environment condition (Teece, 1997).

For the analysis of the case of Alpura, it is used as a pertinent differentiation of capabilities related to innovation. Particularly, Leonard's (1998) approach is considered as it distinguishes the strategic importance of technological capabilities in (a) core capabilities, (b) supplemental capabilities, and (c) enabling capabilities. Core capabilities are essential for the business because they represent the firm's competitive advantage, allows the company to enter a wide variety of markets, contributes to the perceived customer benefits, and cannot be easily imitated (Barney, 1991). Supplemental capabilities add value to the core capabilities by completing or reinforcing them; they are not unique and can be imitated by the competitors (Prahalad & Hamel, 1990). For instance, some particular skills can complement the value offer of the product with striking designs or services. Enabling capabilities are necessary to remain in the market but do not differentiate the company or give superiority over the competitors (Leonard, 1998). For example, in the F&B industry, some certifications in quality management have become indispensable to supply the big retail stores. As we will see in the discussion, these concepts will be useful for understanding and presenting a model of Alpura's transformation to an innovative firm and, more specifically, the capabilities reconfiguration that is going on within the company.

Methodology

The case study was conducted from fall of 2017 to fall of 2019. It included several visits to the firm's headquarters and production facilities in the municipality of Cuatitlan—22 miles away from Mexico City. Eight decision-makers were interviewed to find insights related to the redefinition of Alpura's innovation strategy and the building of innovation capabilities. The interviewees' positions included: Chief Executive Officer (CEO), Intelligence Business Officer (IBO), R&D Officer (R&DO), Commercial Officer (COO), Quality Officer (QO), IT Officer (ITO), Digital Innovation Manager (DIM), and Production Manager (PM). While obtaining different perspectives of innovation within the firm could be insightful, all the positions interviewed were selected because they were directly involved in the formulation of the innovation strategy and responsible for its execution.

The research instrument used for the interviews was a semi-structured questionnaire to obtain more in-depth information. This option for the methodology was chosen since top management in Alpura was open to allow this research approach to collect more integral perspectives than with an online survey. The questionnaire was divided into two sections with complementary objectives to facilitate the conduction of the conversation and the subsequent analysis. The first section aimed to identify the information that managers use from the local and international business environment to shape the competitive strategy and the consequent innovation strategy. Thus, this section contained questions to look into the top management decision process to respond to the customer's necessities and to find out the critical drivers perceived from the competitive environment. The second section's objective was to understand the structure of innovation frames and procedures for new products and new business process development. Therefore, the questions of this section look into the innovation priorities, the role of the internal and external agents for innovation, the innovation processes' approaches, and the building of innovation capabilities required to achieve the innovation goals. After the construction of the questionnaire, it was reviewed by another researcher with vast experience in face to face interviews and qualitative data analysis and by two managers of companies integrated to the dairy value chain. Then, to validate the adequacy of the questionnaire it was applied to the facility manager and general director of a medium-sized dairy company. Finally, before its application to the target company, some questions were adjusted to fit the data collection context.

The questionnaire was sent by mail to each manager before the interview, so they were aware and could prepare the answers. During the session, interviewees answered freely and extensively, and they allowed their words to be quoted; hence much information emerged to enrich the data of the case. All the conversations were recorded in digital format—summing more than 12 hours—allowing the authors to continuously review them to analyze the responses with a qualitative approach. The responses were compared and organized in topics accordingly to the research objective. This goal included evaluating—from a resource-based point of view—the decision-making process to establish the innovation strategy from the company's general competitive strategy and the consequent building of innovation capabilities required to face the future. As shown in Table 30.1, relevant insights related to ten different topics were obtained from most of the interviewed managers. This table shows the number of assertions that every interviewed manager

Table 30.1 The collected information from Alpura's managers

Section	Topic	Relevant insights							
		CEO	IBO	R&DO	COO	QO	ITO	DIM	PM
1. Configuration of the competitive strategy	Relevant factors that affect the competitive strategy	12	3	10	10	7	6	5	2
	Ongoing operative strategy	7	7	–	5	5		3	6
	Implications of new technologies in the operative strategy	2	5	–	–	3	3	3	7
2. Configuration of the Innovation strategy	Basis of the Innovation strategy	9	2	9	1	1	7	7	5
	Frameworks and processes for innovation—Business models	–	–	–	–	–	1	8	–
	Frameworks and processes for innovation—Products and processes	–	–	7	1	3	–	–	10
	Ways to detect innovation opportunities	2	2	4	3	3	4	3	1
	External sources of technological innovation	7	2	14	5	11	2	10	4
	Creation and building of innovation capabilities	13	9	6	6	9	2	4	7
	Successful innovations examples	3	–	–	8	7	2	3	5
Total number of insights provided		55	30	50	39	49	27	46	47

contributed to integrating the listed topics with differentiated relevance insights. Table 30.1 also shows the contrast between the assertions provided by top managers more traditionally involved with innovation (CEO, R&DO, and QO) than other managers. Finally, it should be noticed that some contributions from managers were unique, and some others were crossed confirmations of data.

Results and Findings

Alpura's top management team recognizes an aggressive and dynamic competitive environment on different fronts. They identify the following as the typical strategic issues for the company. First, the well-known but not entirely solved problems of the differentiated seasonality of milk production and consumption. Then, the continuous challenge of increasing productivity and quality as well as the technological ladder dictated by a bunch of specialized international companies. Also, the logistics related to the cold chain and the embedded costs. And last but not least, the correct campaigns of marketing to be on the top of mind of the consumers. Moreover, there are several relevant emerging issues that the managers acknowledge. These obstacles include the recently important acquisitions of local and international firms by transnational corporations moving in on the attractive Mexican dairy market. Also, there is the revolution in product innovation from local and global big players derived from the necessity of product differentiation and fostered by the low-profit margin per unit of legacy products. Finally, top managers consider the continuous threats of substitutes for their products since the battle is for the "share of stomach" of a diverse and demanding consumer. In other words, nowadays consumers want immediate benefits from healthy food and beverages elaborated by companies that practice social responsibility.

Since it was established in 1970, the company's most important strength has been the operative excellence. Alpura's operation is very efficient. It starts with an S&OP process with a horizon of 18 months. The capacity is continuously reviewed, and a project management office (PMO) evaluates decisions to buy new equipment to increase it. The managers take pride in the stable controls of procurement and manufacturing, especially in the excellent milking practices and the innocuity of the fully automated production process. Nevertheless, the quality department is implementing the British Retail Consortium (BCR) quality management system to bolster up the quality assurance along the value chain and comply with the world's strictest regulations. Furthermore, there is an interest in catching up with the information and processes technologies to maintain operative excellence. Thus, techno-logical surveillance focuses on production technologies (PT) and information technologies (IT), triggered by the production staff and the IT staff's initia-tives, respectively. PT priorities are on novelties from the big process equip-ment companies like GEA, SIG, and Tetrapack. IT priorities are on business intelligence applications of SAP and Oracle ERP systems and support soft-ware for maintenance and quality assurance. Alpura exports to the USA and supplies all over México through different channels: distribution centers, retail stores, convenience stores, HORECA, and government.

Nowadays, the company is going through a transformation process to be an innovative firm. Therefore, led by a new CEO with a clear vision of being the best option of dairy products and putting the consumer in the center of the business decisions, a new competitive strategy has been formulated. This new competitive strategy has a horizon of five years and is supported on four pil-lars: innovation, service, leadership, and closeness. Besides, it realigns the cur-rent operations strategy with sales growing as the main driver and four complementary goals: customer satisfaction, operative margin, supply chain conformance, and personnel commitment. With this new set of pillars and operative goals, the expectation is to achieve 30% of sales growth for the next years—18% from organic growth and 12% from innovation. All the inter-viewed managers are aware that the new competitive strategy implies not only a redirection of the business but a profound transformation and a para-digm change.

Alpura's current mission is: *"To satisfy the consumer's needs through the man-ufacturing of high-quality and innovative products, that offers a healthy lifestyle giving the best nutrition and reliance"* (Alpura, 2020). So, the company explic-itly declares its priorities in high quality as well as in innovation. Hence, derived from the competitive strategy, the innovation strategy has been defined with two main objectives: (a) develop digital innovations and create new business models, (b) develop new processes, and launch new products. A specific organization was recently created for each purpose: Digital Innovation (DI) department, depending on the Business Intelligence department, and R&D department reporting to the CEO. The DI department holds the responsibility of achieving both radical and incremental innovations in busi-ness processes and is in charge to manage continuous improvement initiatives for the operation. A consultant guides the implementation of the HiFFi framework (HiFFi Group, 2020) in the DI department, and, for the time being, the efforts are on implementing it to deliver results. The DIM is aware that this can take three to five years since it is required to grow leadership, management structures, and an oriented culture to innovation. Nevertheless, DI is working on the last phase of radical promising projects.

R&D—a former part of the quality department—has recently been restructured and now is an independent department with a new officer who carries out the responsibility of increasing the milk's added value by transforming it into innovative products. The R&D officer is aware of three types of feasible innovations: (a) new products or upgrade current products, (b) new packing, (c) new processes. New dairy products' tendencies aim to be healthy organic food, with high protein and calcium content, added with probiotics, prebiotics, fibers, phytonutrients, and antioxidants. Trends also include products from a unique culture adapted to regular consumer habits, combinations of different products ready to eat, and even new flavors for mature products. New packages aim to be handy according to modern lifestyles, better in functionality and sterility. New processes point to advanced pasteurization methods that enhance the taste of the milk and fractioning processes to obtain specific proteins of high nutritional value. The R&D officer knows that scientific and technical knowledge in food science combined with marketing research is essential to attain innovation in products and processes.

As seen above, DI and R&D departments have different innovations priorities since the objectives are differentiated. Moreover, the nature of the innovation wanted by each one requires distinct methodologies and technical skills. The DI department follows a structured methodology which begins with the detection of the necessity by accompanying individuals in the emotional journey of consumption. Then, it involves the ideation of the solution, conceptualization, and hypothesis of the solution proposed. After an iterative process of prototyping, the prototype's validation and testing takes place, a business model is proposed and evaluated. Finally, the process concludes with the escalation and adjustment of the business model. This process is systemic, and the scope is ambitiously holistic for the whole company. In contrast, the R&D department follows a methodology based on the Stage-Gate® model, adjusted to the company's context, and divided into five phases. These phases are the selection of the ideas and definition of the scope, business case development, prototype development, testing and validation of prototype, and finally launching and commercialization.

The process initiates with a project definition, a fixed budget, and a profitability goal. In addition to these phases, the R&D officer has established a set of guiding questions to advance, along with projects. These questions are: 1. Does the consumer want it? 2. Is it safe and legal? 3. Is it consistent with the innovation strategy? 4. Is it profitable? 5. Can we manufacture it? The fifth question is divided into three more, to inquire more in depth into the availability of the capabilities required to accomplish the innovation projects. The additional questions are: 5.1. Do we own the manufacturing capacity? 5.2. Do we possess the know-how? 5.3. Do we hold the technology necessary? These three last questions allow R&D to find out specific aspects related to the subsequent step of product design. For instance, it helps to recognize the milk volume needed according to the forecasts, the technical knowledge required to manufacture the product, the cost, and the availability of technology. According to the R&D officer, a new product development might take from 12 to 16 months; after that, a launched product is unique for the next three years.

Currently, to detect product innovation opportunities from outside the company, the marketing department conducts market research through focus groups and surveys. The resulting information is analyzed to see if it can become innovation initiatives that could be evaluated by the New Product Committee and the PMO to decide its potential and viability. Similarly, to identify innovations and continuous improvement ideas from within the company, the DI department runs a process supported on a software platform to collect and evaluate employee recommendations. Those employees selected for the more feasible and creative ideas are invited to a family tour to the facilities, and the top management group awards them. Another way to detect innovation and continuous improvement opportunities is by evaluating the complaints received on the 01800-phone number. The managers interviewed agree that these activities are not a part of an articulated system, and there is an opportunity for aligning these efforts to the innovation strategy. However, as part of the new plan of the DI department, a more sophisticated study was recently conducted to detect dairy consuming habits, consumer profiles, and up-coming attitudes and trends of city young people in the center area of Mexico.

There is consensus among the interviewed that external agents are essential to generate new ideas and collaboration to develop new products and processes. Although there is no formal structure to perform networking and cooperation, the interviewed see a lot of potential on the following entities to incorporate them into the innovation initiatives:

- Ingredients suppliers with R&D departments prepared to develop new formulations and perform functional tests.
- Science and technology institutes from universities or supported by the government, willing to share facilities and knowledge to perform applied research.

- Suppliers of process equipment, like GEA, SIG, and Tetrapack, which offer new production and packaging cutting-edge technologies, and training to the operative personnel.

In contrast, other external agents like the raw milk suppliers, industrial associations, competitors, or local SMEs of the dairy industry are not seen as sources for innovation. Significantly, the most thudding action resulting from the new company's strategy is the acquisition of tangible and intangible assets, that shore up the operations and put the base to innovation deployment. The recent investments in operative assets contribute to create and strengthen capabilities to guarantee the continuity of operational excellence, as we can see in Table 30.2.

At the same time, the latest investments that support innovation will contribute to create and strengthen innovation capabilities, as shown in Table 30.3.

Besides the mentioned investments above, the interviewed recognize the importance of soft skills to create and spread the culture of innovation. The CEO has a critical plan to enhance communication inside the company, so a training program is running to increase the officers' and directors' communication abilities. An internal magazine is regularly published to inform the department's social activities and the firm's performance to increase the sense of belonging. Notably, the managers are aware of the great importance of

Table 30.2 Recent investments to shore up the operation

Asset type	Category	Main examples
Tangible assets	Facilities	Macro-distribution center
	Major equipment	Packaging machines for new presentations
	Minor equipment	Laboratory equipment for quality control
		IT devices for salesmen
	Software	ERP modules for logistics, finance, and maintenance
		Software licenses for production planning
		Software licenses for sales control
Intangible assets	Talent recruitment	Financial department head with a risk management orientation
		Personnel specialized in warehouse quality
		Sales managers and supervisors for new channels
	Know-how acquisition	Specialized technical information on sterile packaging
	Consultancy	Warehouse design
		Total productive maintenance (TPM)
		BCR quality management systems
		FDA audits
		New distribution business model
	Training	TPM for operators
		BCR for quality representatives

Table 30.3 Recent investments to shore up the operation

Asset type	Category	Main examples
Tangible assets	Facilities	Facilities of the R&D center
	Major equipment	Pilot plant
	Minor equipment	3D printer for packaging design
		Laboratory equipment for R&D
Intangible assets	Talent recruitment	R&D Officer
		Specialist in sensory analysis
		Specialist in cheese development
	Consultancy	HiFFi innovation framework for DI department
		Teamwork for the R&D department
	Training	Marketing basics for the R&D department
		Ingredient functionality for the R&D department

external and internal workshops, "on the job training," and "learning by doing," to boost the know-how of the company and create the required capabilities to deploy the new strategies.

The new operations strategy has resulted in new forms to perform business processes and has fostered continuous improvement. Some relevant examples are that the quality department is implementing new faster tests to validate the aseptic packaging process. Likewise, the department is leading new cooperative food-safety groups with representatives of the manufacturing departments to assure the BCR compliance. The DI department is leading a new collaborative process to problem-solving using a new software platform to collect and organize different ideas from the manufacturing personnel. The commercial department has established a new business model for the HORECA customers and a new logistic organization by channel using modern information technologies to facilitate the control of the delivering routes. The innovation strategy is on the march, and the results are starting to be noticed. For instance, Alpura has recently achieved significant product innovation hits, such as the 1.5 liter-package, and the infant milk formula—Alpura Kids—for one- to three-years-old kids.

Discussion

The pressure of the business environment has pushed Alpura to redefine its competitive strategy. This shift means recognizing innovation as the main driver for the next years to respond to the aggressive movements of the local leader and closet competitors. The current operations strategy based on operational excellence is still a competitive advantage for the firm, but it is no longer enough to be the industry leader. Thus, the paradigm change is imperative. The brand-new planning developed by the new CEO and his top management team to lay the foundations of a long-term innovation strategy implies a profound transformation of the organization. In Fig. 30.1, we can see the three phases of Alpura's changing into an innovative company, starting with the competitive strategy redefinition followed by the conformation of the innovation strategy, and at last, the expected results.

As seen in the first phase, the actions derived from the competitive strategy shore up the operative strategy and reinforce the operative capabilities. These actions are for two purposes—to keep the operation on-going and to be the launching platform for the innovation efforts. In the second phase, building innovation capabilities and forging an innovative culture represents the major challenge for the organization because of the complexity of the design and the multiple factors implicated. It seems now that Alpura is learning to fly with its new strategical wings. In the third phase, the expectation is to prepare the company for the unexpected with an innovation culture, continually implementing new processes, and launching successful innovative products, flying out to reach the sky and become once again the leader of the Mexican dairy market.

An essential matter of the implantation of the innovation strategy is the building of dynamic capabilities, namely core, supplemental, and enabling capabilities (Leonard, 1998; Prahalad & Hamel, 1990). Innovation capabilities will be the core capabilities that engine the business in the future;

Fig. 30.1 Phases of transformation process into an innovative firm

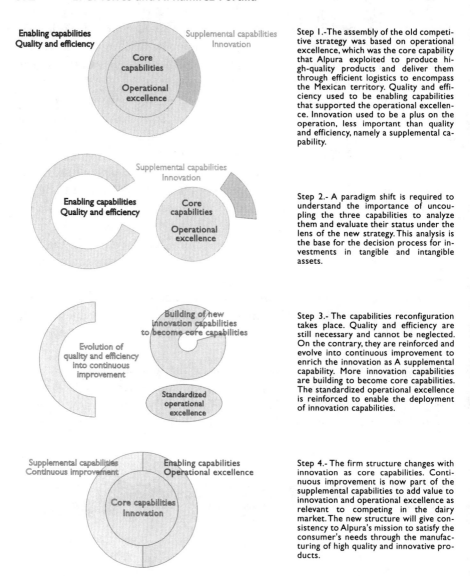

Step 1.-The assembly of the old competitive strategy was based on operational excellence, which was the core capability that Alpura exploited to produce high-quality products and deliver them through efficient logistics to encompass the Mexican territory. Quality and efficiency used to be enabling capabilities that supported the operational excellence. Innovation used to be a plus on the operation, less important than quality and efficiency, namely a supplemental capability.

Step 2.- A paradigm shift is required to understand the importance of uncoupling the three capabilities to analyze them and evaluate their status under the lens of the new strategy. This analysis is the base for the decision process for investments in tangible and intangible assets.

Step 3.- The capabilities reconfiguration takes place. Quality and efficiency are still necessary and cannot be neglected. On the contrary, they are reinforced and evolve into continuous improvement to enrich the innovation as A supplemental capability. More innovation capabilities are building to become core capabilities. The standardized operational excellence is reinforced to enable the deployment of innovation capabilities.

Step 4.- The firm structure changes with innovation as core capabilities. Continuous improvement is now part of the supplemental capabilities to add value to innovation and operational excellence as relevant to competing in the dairy market. The new structure will give consistency to Alpura's mission to satisfy the consumer's needs through the manufacturing of high quality and innovative products.

Fig. 30.2 Building and reconfiguration of innovation capabilities

therefore, Alpura has acquired tangible and intangible assets to integrate robust innovation systems. Likewise, it is necessary to grow appropriate supplemental capabilities to add value to core capabilities. In the past, quality and efficiency have been deeply rooted in Alpura's operation. Nowadays, they have become routines of continuous improvement because of the evolution of production technologies and quality management systems in the food industry.

Thereby, future results from the innovation processes will be systematically enhanced, and the ability to innovate will be enriched with a sense of safety, innocuity, and productivity. As mentioned before, enabling capabilities are required for business continuity. In Alpura, the stable structures of operational excellence are essential to hold a successful supply chain to attain the goals of the operation strategy: customer satisfaction, operative margin, and supply chain conformance. Figure 30.2 shows the planned steps for new capabilities reconfiguration to deploy the innovation strategy in Alpura. Accordingly, to the information of the interviewed managers, Alpura is going through the third step and going forward to the fourth step.

Conclusions

The rivalry in Mexico's dairy industry has increased in recent years due to the entrance of big international players with a history of innovation. Other challenges include the acquisition of local brands by corporations that are expanding the product portfolio and an aggressive repositioning of the national market leader. Even though Alpura is highly reputed in the market, continuous pressure has forced it to redirect its vision while challenging its foundations. For many years, Alpura had a traditional—if not narrow—view toward innovation, so its competitive position has deteriorated. Fortunately, since 2016 due to the arrival of a new CEO, the company has adopted a new vision to embrace innovation and continuous improvement. This vision is supported by current operational strengths built on decades of experience and steady launches of new products.

Innovation in the dairy industry can be of different types and can come from various sources (Bigliardi & Galati, 2013). In any case, consumer satisfaction is the main driver for F&B enterprises to increase the organizational efforts for new products and processes (Sam Saguy, 2011). Innovation is a difficult task to perform, and it can have unforeseen implications, including the need to align the endeavors and make them useful. Therefore, Alpura's top management must structure the innovation strategy corresponding to a clear contextual competitive strategy. In the presented case, we have addressed the steps that the company is taking to arrive at the visualized future (Fig. 30.1), from the restructuration of a new competitive strategy to the shape of the innovation strategy and the expected outcomes. Thus, Alpura is laying the foundations for business processes prepared to respond to changing industry conditions and market upcoming dynamics. The on-going transformation keeps the DNA of quality and efficiency but turned into a more dynamic form of continuous improvement that involves all organizational levels. Likewise, operational excellence is conserved like a competitive advantage that reliably puts the products on the shelf through a stable, robust, and agile supply chain. The center of the organizational transformation is the implementation of the innovation strategy, thus growing a strong base of innovation capabilities is the focus at the time. It is noteworthy to remember that the renewal is happening without interruptions of business as usual, in the context of a mature market, with demanding clients and consumers. Hence, the managers' ability to lead the renewal is a significant innovation capability that allows the others to grow and flourish.

This case shows a close look at the building and reconfiguration of the capabilities required for a rising innovation strategy in the F&B industry in the context of an emerging economy. As we have shown in the literature review, innovation capabilities are, by definition, dynamic, so they can be reconfigured to respond to the environmental conditions. In this case, we use the theoretical differentiation of Core, Supplemental and Enabling capabilities to create a conceptual scheme (Fig. 30.2). This scheme is useful to understand and analyze the managing process of building and reconfiguration of the capabilities to fulfill the implementation of the innovation strategy. Consequently, we can see the challenges of the process exposed. We acknowledge the assembly in the old competitive strategy as a set of managerial decisions and interactions among departments. So the uncoupling process could be seen as a future research activity to indagate where specifically reside the abilities that integrate the capabilities. Hence, building or reinforcing capabilities are investment decisions in tangible or intangible assets with a specific target. At last, the new coupling is a vision to achieve with new interactions. Again, managers have the responsibility to balance the established and new capabilities to allow the transformation flow.

The theoretical contributions of Alpura's case lie in adding to the body of literature about innovation strategy and innovation capabilities. From the resource-based point of view, the building and reconfiguration of the capabilities in a firm is a critical process that determines the possibility to prevail in the market and scale its competitive position. This case clearly shows this building and reconfiguration process, with an ample perspective from eight decision-makers responsible for the leading, designing, and implementing the innovation strategy. The capabilities reconfiguration demonstrates its dynamic nature. Moreover, the case shows useful insights to managers of the F&B industry and other industries of consumer products. These insights highlight the relevance of evaluating and analyzing the implementation path that a company could undergo to catch up with the current environmental conditions of innovation and rapid response. Nowadays, Alpura is advancing in its strategy implementation with concrete actions. For instance, the company has agreed to create the Alpura chair in Tec de Monterrey university—one of the most innovative universities in Mexico. This new alliance with academia will benefit both parties. It will create innovation capabilities like new technologies, patent development, human resources training, boost joint research, and development of dairy products. More than ever, the company is aware of the importance of developing the proper core capabilities to innovate internally and explore and exploit future collaborations in other ecosystems and with different external actors.

From the information obtained from the managers interviewed, we can distinguish some critical gaps in the building of innovation capabilities to become core capabilities. First, the detection of innovation opportunities is not a structured process that gives relevant and specific information to the DI and the R&D department, nor according to critical purposes. In the innovation strategy implementation, it would be a priority to develop a dedicated system to supply with reliable and particular information for innovation and continuous improvement. This system could integrate and align the efforts of technological surveillance performed by the production staff and the IT staff. Second, since innovation is an ample and fuzzy concept, Alpura is evaluating the different innovation possibilities in the product, production processes, organization, and marketing to achieve success on the shelf. For this reason, there are two innovation frameworks—one for DI and another for R&D—that are not connected. This disconnection could compromise the implementation of radical innovations in the company. A new position with the purpose of being a bridge between the two innovation departments is a possible solution for this issue.

Finally, we acknowledge some improvement opportunities in the research methodology for this case. There could be a more profound understanding of the innovation capabilities of Alpura if the study examined some of the critical processes of quality and efficiency in the production and logistic area that support operational excellence capability. Also, it could be interesting to identify the innovation possibilities of Alpura according to the late innovation activity in the Mexican market. Future research opportunities include identifying the challenges of the integration of the innovation strategy considering the organization culture and the soft skills required by the top management team. It would also be interesting to replicate this case with a similar research approach in other F&B companies or from similar industries in other developing countries.

References

Alpura. (2020). *Corporativo Alpura*. Retrieved June 14, 2020, from http://alpura. com/corporativo/filosofia-alpura.php

Barney, J. (1991). Firm Resources and Sustained Competitive Advantage. *Journal of Management, 17*(1), 99/120.

Bigliardi, B., & Galati, F. (2013). Models of Adoption of Open Innovation Within the Food Industry. *Trends in Food Science & Technology, 30*(1), 16–26.

CANILEC. (2019). *CámaraNacional de Industriales de la Leche*. Retrieved June 14, 2020 from https://www.canilec.org.mx/estadisticas%20lacteos%202019.pdf

Dosi, G., Nelson, R., & Winter, S. (2002). Introduction: The Nature and Dynamics of Organizational Capabilities. In G. Dosi, R. Nelson, & S. Winter (Eds.), *The Nature and Dynamics of Organizational Capabilities* (p. 1). Oxford: Oxford University Press.

Euromonitor. (2018). *Euromonitor*. Retrieved February 4, 2018, from www.portal. euromonitor.com

HiFFi Group. (2020). *Hiffi Group*. Retrieved June 15, 2020, from https://www. hiffigroup.org/

IDF. (13 de junio de 2020). *International Dairy Federation. Facts and figures*. Retrieved June 14, 2020, from https://www.fil-idf.org/about-dairy/facts-figures/

INEGI. (2020). *DENUE*. Retrieved June 14, 2020, from http://www.beta.inegi.org. mx/app/mapa/denue/default.aspx

IPADE. (16 de Febrero de 2017). Reflexiones sobre la innovación en el sector de alimentos y bebidas 2016. In *Tercer encuentro sector alimentos y bebidas*. Ciudad de México, Ciudad de México, México: IPADE.

Lawson, B., & Samson, D. (2001). Developing Innovation Capability in Organisations: A Dynamic Capabilities Approach. (I. C. Press, Ed.). *International Journal of Innovation Management, 5*(3), 377–400.

Leonard, D. A. (1998). *Wellsprings of Knowledge: Building and Sustaining the Sources of Innovation*. Cambridge, MA: Harvard Business School Press.

OECD/Eurostat. (2018). *Oslo Manual 2018: Guidelines for Collecting; Reporting and Using Data on Innovation, 4th Edition, The Measurement of Scientific, Technological and Innovation Activities, OECD* (4th ed.). Publishing, Paris/Eurostat, Luxembourg.

Porter, M. (2004). *Competitive Strategy: Techniques for Analyzing Industries and Competitors* (p. 20). New York: Free Press.

Prahalad, C. K., & Hamel, G. (1990, May–June). The Core Competence of the Corporation. *Harvard Business Review*, 79–91.

Projogo, D. (2006). Relationships Between Innovation Stimulus, Innovation Capacity and Innovation Performance. *R&D Management, 36*, 499–515.

Sam Saguy, I. (2011). Paradigm Shifts in Academia and the Food Industry Requiered to Meet Innovation Challenges. *Trends in Food Science and Technology, 22*(9), 467–475.

SIAP. (2019). *Servicio de información agroalimentaria y pequera: Boletín de leche. Enero-Marzo 2019*. Retrieved June 11, 2020, from http://infosiap.siap.gob.mx/opt/boletlech/Bolet%C3%ADn%20de%20Leche%20enero-marzo%202019.pdf

Teece, D. (2007). Explicating Dynamic Capablities: The Nature and Microfundations of (Sustainable) Enterprise Performance. *Strategic management journal, 28*, 1319–1350.

Teece, D. P. (1997). Dynamic Capabilities and Strategic Management. *Strategic Management Journal, 18*(7), 509–533.

Tidd, J., & Bessant, J. (2014). *Managing Innovation: Integrating Technological, Market and Organizational Change* (5th ed.). Chichester: Joohn Wiley & Sons.

Trott, P. (2012). *Innovation Management and New Product Development* (5th ed., pp. 20–21). Gosport: Prentice Hall.

Theme VI

Workplace Innovation Ecosystem

31

Brazil's Innovation Ecosystems: The Role of Cultural Factors

Luiz Marcio Spinosa, Rosana Silveira Reis,
and Marcos Muller Schlemm

Introduction

Brazil is the ninth largest economy in the world (2019), with a nominal GDP of USD 1.89 trillion (WEO, 2019). The economy is large and diversified, based mainly on commodity production, which offers many opportunities to export goods and services. After several years Brazil focused its efforts on a monetary and fiscal policy at the macro level to create a more stable and predictable economic environment for industry. Much progress has been made and today Brazil is a global trader.

Innovation is the basis for economic growth and can be a source of sustainable competitive advantage, being fundamental for organizations that want to remain in focus in the market (Ireland & Webb, 2007). However, in 2018, Brazil ranked only 64th in the Global Innovation Index (GII), published annually by Cornell University, INSEAD, and the World Intellectual Property

L. M. Spinosa (✉)
Federal University of Santa Catarina (UFSC), Florianópolis, Brazil

R. S. Reis
Economics, Market & Society, ISG – Paris, Paris, France
e-mail: rosana.reis@isg.fr

M. M. Schlemm
Business School, Pontifícia Universidade Católica o Paranà, Glendora, CA, USA

© The Author(s), under exclusive license to Springer Nature Switzerland AG 2021   **581**
A. McMurray et al. (eds.), *The Palgrave Handbook of Workplace Innovation*,
https://doi.org/10.1007/978-3-030-59916-4_31

Organization (WIPO). Between 2011 and 2018, Brazil fell 17 places in this ranking, with the worst indicators across the BRIC countries. We suggest that a main challenge to the development of the country's widespread innovation ecosystems is to unlock cultural barriers and foster a culture of entrepreneurship.

Like other countries, Brazil has made consistent efforts to foster innovation ecosystems as a strategic option for socioeconomic development. According to Plonsky (2005), since the 1990s, Brazilian society has tried to build a more effective institutional background for innovation policies. Moreover, Brazil intends to become a coherent part of a globalized knowledge economy, particularly the innovation economy. To this end, Brazil introduced an Innovation Law in 2004 (Law 10.973), establishing a legal framework for cooperation between academia and business. In 2005, the Well Law (Law 11.196) created tax incentives for companies to invest in Research and Development (R&D).

Recently, in 2016, the New Legal Framework for Innovation was endorsed (Law 13.243). It merges the previous legal solutions and creates new and broader instruments for cooperation between government, academia, and businesses. However, the New Legal Framework faces obstacles, mainly from the viewpoint of the control bodies, which have not yet fully understood the nature of the relationship between institutes of science and technology and companies. This creates, among other obstacles, difficulties for innovation diffusion. It is a sign of a lack of innovation culture.

Current initiatives by academia, government, and corporations seek to improve the Brazilian National Innovation System. From a capacity-building perspective, Brazil has in recent years embarked on a large-scale effort to build innovation capabilities. A major strategy has been the creation and strengthening of innovation ecosystems. But once again, the process is held back by the lack of an innovation culture. Culture is key to the fostering of innovation, and the necessary cultural factors must be encouraged and nurtured not only within companies but also across the country as a whole (Kesting & Parm Ulhoi, 2010).

In the context of innovation ecosystems, this chapter presents some results of an ongoing study started in 2015 that aims to answer the question: "What is the status of innovation culture in Brazil, considering a context-based analysis of cultural factors?" Taking into consideration the main constructs from studies of Silicon Valley (USA), we explore the cultural factors observed in some representative entrepreneurial and innovative ecosystems in Brazil, that is, context-based factors impacting these ecosystems.

Background and Significance

A nation's culture affects innovation and may carry important implications for business strategists. Innovation needs a healthy atmosphere to develop. Lee and Peterson (2000) stressed the fact that entrepreneurship and innovation "fit" better with some cultures than with others. One must create an environment that encourages people to think in unusual and creative ways. This is not easy to accomplish when much of business is highly structured and orderly in its processes. A business, whether product- or service-oriented, needs to have standardized routines. Innovation, on the other hand, requires thinking out of the ordinary. These points of view are so antithetical that to foster an effective innovation process, careful attention must be paid to encouraging and allowing unconventional thinking (Baldwin & von Hippel, 2010).

For Taylor and Wilson (2012), there is a linkage between a society's cultural values and its ability to innovate. But, according to them, there is a scarcity of innovation culture research at the national level. Since entrepreneurs often use technological innovation as a basis to build new businesses and industries, the question of whether national culture promotes innovation should be of critical importance. At the same time, Halkos and Tzeremes (2011) suggest that national culture appears to have an impact on countries' innovation efficiency. And, since cultural values are not inborn and must be taught (Hofstede, 1980), they suggest that the biggest challenge for governments and policymakers lies ahead. They must shape countries' national cultural values toward innovation and entrepreneurial norms and ethics.

The existing literature on innovation shows that the production of new technologies is essential for businesses to remain competitive in a constantly changing environment like the current market. However, to produce new technologies, companies need to develop internal competencies to identify, absorb, and produce knowledge (Srivastava & Gnyawali, 2017). Therefore, it is necessary that they invest in domestic knowledge production.

Opportunities to innovate are cultivated when organizations build knowledge and understanding of their cultural values, attitudes, and competencies (Hall & Auernhammer, 2014). A culture of innovation empowers organizations with a vision of the future in which products, processes, and services that are unknown today are envisioned (Skarzynski & Gibson, 2008).

Brief Literature Review

There is general agreement that innovation ecosystems are specific to the context of the region in which they emerge. Their implementation and establishment must necessarily observe local, regional, and national peculiarities. In a country like Brazil, which encompasses many cultural and regional contrasts, there is more than one setting in which such systems might develop. Despite the multiplicity of specificities to consider, we adopt a context-based definition based on a number of ongoing Brazilian initiatives (Spinosa, Schlemm, & Reis, 2015): *Innovation ecosystems are competitive assets in the knowledge-based economy capable of fostering socioeconomic development.*

According to Spinosa et al. (2015, 2018), innovation ecosystems are characterized as follows:

- Specialized organizations that aim to (1) promote the innovation culture and competitiveness of enterprises and research institutions; (2) stimulate and manage the flow of knowledge and technology among universities, R&D centers, businesses, and their markets; (3) facilitate the creation and consolidation of businesses through incubation and spin-off processes; and (4) generate synergy among the various actors, identifying local and regional vocations and seeking economic and technological feasibility.
- Places for knowledge-based businesses to prosper through innovative entrepreneurship and continuous development.
- Spaces for collective learning, the exchange of knowledge and production practices, and synergy among innovation agents.
- Initially based in, but not restricted to, technology parks, science parks, or technopolises.
- Sometimes the cause, sometimes the consequence, of innovation policies issued by government action in order to encourage the production, dissemination, and use of innovation for socioeconomic development.
- An integrated effort by government, academia, corporations, and nongovernmental organizations. The latter are particularly important in Brazil, since they provide several specialized services for both the public and private sectors.

Culture affects innovation (ecosystems) because it shapes attitudes toward novelty, individual initiative, and collective action, as well as understandings and behaviors in regard to both threats and opportunities (Kaasa & Vadi, 2010). Cultural values indicate the degree to which a society considers entrepreneurial behaviors, such as risk-taking and independent thinking, to be desirable. Cultures that value and reward such behaviors promote a tendency toward radical innovation, whereas cultures that reinforce conformity, group interest, and control over the future are not likely to show risk-taking and entrepreneurial behavior (Hayton, George, & Zahra, 2002; Hofstede, 1980).

According to Waarts and van Everdingen (2005), cultures with strong uncertainty avoidance (UA) can be more resistant to innovation. And, to avoid uncertainty, these cultures adopt rules to minimize ambiguity. Reliance on rules may in turn constrain the opportunities to develop new solutions. On the Hofstede scale, Brazil has a high score of 76 on UA (compared with the USA's 46, for example), showing a strong need for rules and elaborate legal systems to structure life. To offset this need, according to Smale (2016), innovation should be analyzed, planned, and managed from a series of perspectives including national culture. For this author, national culture moderates cognition, and behavior becomes salient because creativity, innovation, and initiative are psychological and social processes. National culture is a function of how individuals and groups of people think and behave. Mueller and Thomas (2001) affirm that a supportive national culture will increase the entrepreneurial potential of a country. In addition to support from political, social, and business leaders, a supportive culture must be nurtured to cultivate the mind and character of the potential entrepreneur.

Entrepreneurship is the engine of innovation ecosystems and the effect of encouraging cultural factors. Entrepreneurship is a complex and multifaceted phenomenon. The construct of Hayton et al. (2002) offers an inclusive entrepreneurship definition that helps to capture a broader interpretation of the effects of culture: "entrepreneurship includes new-venture creation that is growth oriented and generates employment, as well as small businesses and micro-enterprises that may provide self-employment but not much employment growth." In a similar way, entrepreneurship also exists within organizations in the form of corporate venturing, strategic renewal, and spin-offs from ideas generated within those organizations (Zahra & Dess, 2001).

Communication without barriers, decentralized authority, and trust are factors that improve innovation culture. Communication enhances invention because much of people's inventive activity requires input from others. An organizational culture that presents clear communication, based on trust, has a positive influence on creativity and innovation development (Barret, 1997). In hierarchical societies, there is less communication between superiors and subordinates than in nonhierarchical societies. Hierarchical societies tend to have centralized authority and control systems based less on trust, and more on rules and procedures, and these controls inhibit creativity and inventiveness. A system of decentralized authority generates more information for the attention of senior managers and gives employees greater incentive to innovate.

According to Abdul Halim, Ahmad, Ramayah, and Hanifah (2014), organizations that make an effort to project their cultures perform better than those that do not. The best strategy for organizations would be to develop cultures clearly based on exploratory learning attitudes and innovation (Ismail & Abdmajid, 2007). In the same vein, Naranjo-Valencia, Jiménez, and Sanz-Valle (2012) affirm that organizational culture can stimulate innovation by influencing employees' behavior. Organizational culture can affect their acceptance of innovation as a fundamental factor in the organization's success, strengthening their commitment to innovation.

Focusing on the Brazilian context, Gomes, Machado, and Alegre (2015) confirm the theory that one of the factors that can stimulate a propensity to innovate is a culture focused on innovation. More specifically, Padilha and Gomes (2016) analyze the influence of a culture of innovation on the performance of products and processes in the textile industry of Santa Catarina in Brazil. They find the presence of determinants of a culture of innovation in companies that encourage flexible work arrangements, commitment, teamwork and multifunctional groups, and support mechanisms (rewards, recognition, and access to information). Another interesting point is that a culture of innovation has a greater influence on performance in process innovation than on performance in product innovation. According to Padilha and Gomes (2016), this influence may be due to the transmission of behaviors and actions that occur within the organization, which disseminates the intention to be innovative, developing an environment and structure in which innovation is supported.

Methodology

With an exploratory qualitative approach, we attempt to achieve a better understanding of the ways in which culture and values influence the building of innovation ecosystems. Following Eisenhardt and Graebner (2007), we build theoretical constructs from case studies and propositions and/or mid-range theory from empirical understandings. The theory is emergent in the sense that it is developed by recognizing patterns of relationships among constructs within and across cases and their underlying logical arguments. We assume that constructs are broad concepts that can be conceptually defined, capturing some meaning in theoretical terms; they are abstract and do not necessarily need to be directly observable.

To this end, we collected data through workshops, semi-structured interviews, and observations, which enabled data triangulation. Triangulation involves the multiple operationalization of the construct. It is a method that allows a phenomenon to be understood by observing it from different points of view and by applying different methods of analysis, always looking for the most suitable explanation.

- **Workshops**: Between September 2014 and February 2016, we organized four workshops—one in San Francisco and three in Brazil. In Brazil, we chose the cities of Curitiba, São Paulo, and Belo Horizonte, considering that they had innovation ecosystems that were typical of the country. The participants comprised five guest groups involved with innovation: entrepreneurs, angel investors, government representatives, academic researchers, and corporate leaders. The discussions were recorded and transcribed verbatim.
- **Interviews**: Between January and February 2015, we interviewed six Brazilian entrepreneurs and CEOs that live in the USA. These interviews were also recorded and transcribed verbatim.
- **Observations**: Between 2013 and 2016, two authors spent time as visiting scholars at Haas Business School at UC Berkeley. They got involved with all kind of activities and events related to innovation in Silicon Valley while registering perceptions, collecting data, and keeping notes from meetings and interviews, as well as other relevant information that served as a basis of comparison with Brazilian culture. Between September 2014 and June 2016, the authors observed Brazilian entrepreneurs. Diverse groups were analyzed, such as academics, industrial innovators, policymakers, and entrepreneurs.

We divided the "coding process" into three phases: (1) content analysis and, with the help of Post-it, NVivo 10, and Excel, fragmenting and categorizing the data (e.g., each paragraph of the transcripts of the workshops and interviews was separately classified); (2) reorganizing the "nodes," putting the data together in new ways, and making connections between categories and subcategories; and (3) integrating the nodes and categories into a coherent storyline.

Findings

The abovementioned process highlighted a set of perceptions about deficiencies, difficulties, and obstacles in the dynamics of the three innovation ecosystems in Brazil. Several innovation ecosystems observed in Silicon Valley are at the base of our analysis, but we do not intend to make a comparison between the three Brazilian innovation ecosystems and the complex and long-standing ecosystems in the USA. The latter merely help us to identify the cultural constructs that foster innovation, which are then analyzed in the Brazilian ecosystems.

In our research on Silicon Valley, we considered the factors that needed to be present and be promoted to create and sustain an innovation culture. As a result, we identified 11 key factors (constructs):

1. *Knowledge dissemination:* Iconic models are prestigious and widespread (people and organizations). Their stories are discussed and disseminated.
2. *Open environment and willingness to experiment:* This involves an acceptance of risk and error and receptivity on the part of teachers, citizens, and leaders to unconventional and unorthodox propositions.
3. *Do things differently:* Understanding that other ways of doing things can be imagined and put to the test.
4. *Collaboration, cooperation, and "pay-forward":* Giving priority to establishing a cooperation based on trust.
5. *Interaction mechanisms:* Meet-ups, contests, project presentations, competitions, start-ups, and others.
6. *Trust:* In relationships, the personal fulfillment of agreements between the parties and the exchange of information and ideas.
7. *Belief in innovation:* Knowing that others have succeeded, there is a built-in belief that you can innovate and there is a chance of success and reward.
8. *Knowledge availability:* Scientific and technological knowledge widely available and cheap.
9. *Plenty of researchers:* A good supply of highly qualified local and foreign researchers living in the region or interacting with it, usually around universities, which also serve as an anchor to maintain critical mass.
10. *Diversity:* Acceptance of a multiplicity of races, colors, creeds, cultural systems, and knowledge from outside sources.
11. *Territorial proximity:* Physical closeness among the different actors in an innovation ecosystem.

As the workshops made clear, the more structured and integrated these constructs are, the greater will be the chance of a successful innovation ecosystem.

Our first main finding is: *Brazil has the basic cultural conditions to foster innovation: diversity, new cultures, presence of immigrants and foreigners*, and *capability to interact*. These conditions emerge when the following basic conditions are met: (1) the region must be open to diversity and new cultures, and (2) the region must have the capability to properly interact with immigrants and foreigners. (See Fig. 31.1.)

Figure 31.1 shows that about 61% of the experts who participated in our study believe that Brazil is open to diversity and integrates new cultures, values, and visions from the external world and that for 50% of them foreigners and immigrants are a common reality in different regions of the country. These perceptions may be explained by the historical sociocultural formation of Brazil, where a medley of cultures was built up over time by various peoples and ethnicities (Bailey, 2002).

No uniform Brazilian culture exists; quite the reverse—the country's socio-cultural profile is the result of a fusion between the cultures of the indigenous people, Europeans (particularly Portuguese), and slaves brought from Sub-Saharan Africa. Migration of people from other countries followed, such as Arabs, Spaniards, Poles, and Japanese (Sanchez-Alonso, 2019). Other ethnicities also contributed to the culture of Brazil in a more limited way. In the cities that are home to innovation ecosystems, particularly in the south of the country, there is a greater influence of Italian and German immigrants.

The second main finding that emerges from these constructs is: *All the factors observed in Silicon Valley are also relevant to Brazil* (see Fig. 31.2). The experts acknowledged the relevance of the whole set of factors, as well as each individual factor. Even *territorial proximity*, which is not relevant for 24% of the experts, is desirable. A possible explanation for its relatively low importance is the existence of a well-developed digital support system (Internet

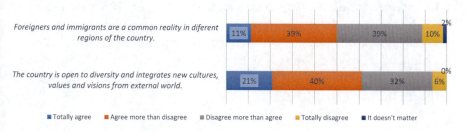

Fig. 31.1 Basic cultural premises fostering an innovation ecosystem. (Source: NPIN Project, based on 59 expert responses)

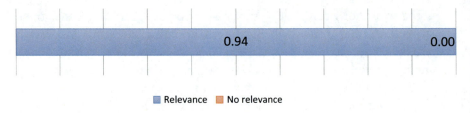

Fig. 31.2 Relevance of cultural factors. (Source: NPIN Project, based on 59 expert responses. Note: range [min=0, max=1]: closer to 0 less relevant, close to 1 more relevant)

access) and a "digital culture" within the analyzed innovation ecosystem. These two factors combine to overcome the barrier of distance between players. For this research, we decided to discard none of the factors, since all of them can help to understand the cultural context in a holistic perspective.

A third finding indicates that *the cultural factors are not fully developed or structured in an integrated way.* There is a consensus among the experts, obtained from the interviews, that all the cultural factors need to exist in a balance and integrated way. When asked about how integrated and balanced the factors were in Brazil, the experts stated that major efforts were needed to attain the required levels.

Nevertheless, there is an order of priority among the cultural factors based on what the experts perceive as essential, desirable, or not important. (See Fig. 31.3.) This paper does not intend to recommend action plans to foster the various cultural factors. However, understanding these priorities helps to identify relevant actions.

A fourth finding is: *Some factors underlie other factors and therefore require immediate attention from innovation managers and policymakers.* The main underlying factors are (1) an open environment and willingness to experiment, (2) belief in innovation, and (3) trust. These are seen as the "most essential" factors for an innovative environment and are prioritized because their deficiency affects many of the other factors. Several studies insist that *trust requires special attention, even considering it as the third most important factor for the experts.* In fact, trust is a key factor for any innovation ecosystems (EDELMAN, 2019; OECD, 2000). It is at the core of the relationship among individuals, enterprises, and their environment. Trust allows a triple helix approach to be implemented (Etzkowitz & Leydesdorff, 1995; Leydesdorff, 2012; THRC, 2011).

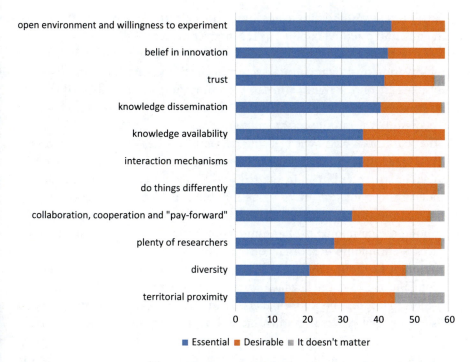

Fig. 31.3   Priority of cultural factors for innovation ecosystems. (Source: NPIN Project, based on 59 expert responses)

Discussion, Conclusion, and Implications

We argue that innovation culture is the basis for the successful performance of innovation ecosystems. How to create, induce, and improve an innovation culture is seen as a challenge in current studies. The right approach to this challenge can have a positive impact on the causes of most of the problems in business, the public sector, and academia and foster mobilization toward innovation.

This research is a first step toward conceiving such an approach and provides some answers to the basic question: "What is the status of innovation culture in Brazil, considering a context-based analysis of cultural factors?" Our main conclusions are as follows:

- A miscellany of peoples and ethnicities is the basis of the sociocultural makeup of Brazil, which makes it a country open to diversity that integrates new cultures, values, and visions from the external world. These attributes are essential to foster innovation. Brazil therefore has the fundamental and essential conditions for innovation ecosystems.

- All the factors observed in Silicon Valley are also relevant to Brazil. The observation of similar cultural factors in Brazil indicates that Brazilian ecosystems are on the right path. The workshops in particular showed that the more structured and integrated these factors are, the greater the chance of successful innovation ecosystems will be.
- The workshops acknowledged the relevance of the whole set of factors in the three innovation ecosystems. However, the factors are not fully developed or structured in an integrated way. We cannot affirm that Brazil considers innovation culture as a glue that binds a myriad of interactions and interconnections, leading to collaborations and interactive dynamics among the components of an innovation ecosystem. These dynamic practices occur mainly in spontaneous, random, and ad hoc ways.
- An open environment and willingness to experiment, a belief in innovation, and trust are the key factors, requiring the priority attention of innovation managers and policymakers. Trust requires special attention, since it is one of the key factors and, at same time, is the basis of several others.

A first essential conclusion emerges. An open environment and curiosity to trial, the believe in innovation, and the trust are key factors. They are at the basis to conduct new experiments requested by innovation dynamics. Without these three factors, the other factors are unlikely to exist. All these factors were observed in Brazilian´s ecosystems. However, innovation while a strategic choice for competitiveness is not completely acknowledged by the actors of the three ecosystems. A documental analysis reveals a significant number of enterprises within the innovation ecosystems that focus on modernizing current actions rather than on developing innovative plans. Strategies and actions aimed at communicating the advantages of innovation could make these enterprises more productive within the innovation ecosystems.

The role of trust is of primary significance in Brazil. The greater the trust, the greater the chances to foster interaction mechanisms, carry out knowledge dissemination, collaborate and cooperate, and create an open environment for experimentation. The more prevalent these factors are, the greater is the chance of generating ideas and balancing interests, which allows the emergence of new businesses. All this is a typical dynamic of start-ups. *How to achieve the relevant trust level* is, however, still a huge challenge in Brazil and several other countries.

These conclusions indicate a clear need to conceive supportive environments to foster the cultural factors that will enable the achievement of success in the innovation process. It is a complex challenge that requires organizations to combine internal and external factors. Internally, cultural factors for innovation require the development and identification of specific resources to organize internal structures and establish clear guidelines. National and/or regional systems of innovation are also required to organize the necessary supportive environment. This emphasizes the importance of the interaction between the players involved in the development of innovation and highlights their respective roles. It explains how institutional arrangements influence the technological progress of a country and so the growth differences between one country and another. These systems are based on the idea that many of the factors that affect innovation activities are internal to countries, such as institutional factors, culture, and values.

This research was made possible by the financial and institutional support of the Coordination for the Improvement of Higher Education Personnel (CAPES), Ministry of Education of Brazil (process N. BEX 6555/14-4 for Senior Internship).

References

Abdul Halim, H., Ahmad, N. H., Ramayah, T., & Hanifah, H. (2014). The Growth of Innovative Performance Among SMEs: Leveraging on Organisational Culture and Innovative Human Capital. *Journal of Small Business and Entrepreneurship Development, 2*(1), 107–125.

Bailey, S. R. (2002). The Race Construct and Public Opinion: Understanding Brazilian Beliefs About Inequality and Their Determinants. *The American Journal of Sociology, 108*(2), 406–439. https://doi.org/10.1086/344812

Baldwin, C. Y., & Von Hippel, E. A. (2010). Modeling a paradgma shift: From producer innovation to user and open collaborative innovation. *Organization Science, 22*(6). https://doi.org/10.2139/ssrn.1502864

Barret, R. (1997). Liberating the Corporate Soul. *HR Focus, 74*(4), 15–16.

Edelman. (2019). Edelman Trust Barometer – Global Report. Edelman Trust Management. Retrieved from https://www.edelman.com/sites/g/files/aatuss191/files/2019-02/2019_Edelman_Trust_Barometer_Global_Report_2.pdf

Eisenhardt, K. M., & Graebner, M. E. (2007). Theory Building from Cases: Opportunities and Challenges. *Academy of Management Journal, 50*(1), 25–32.

Etzkowitz, H., & Leydesdorff, L. (1995). *The Triple Helix – University-Industry-Government Relations: A Laboratory for Knowledge Based Economic Development.* Rochester, NY: SSRN 2480085.

Gomes, G. Machado, D. D. P. N., & Alegre, J. (2015). Determinants of Innovation Culture: A Study of Textile Industry in Santa Catarina. *Brazilian Business Review*, English ed., Vitoria, 12(4): 9-122.

Halkos, G., & Tzeremes, N. (2011). The Effect of National Culture on Countries' Innovation Efficiency. *IDEAS Working papers Series* from RePEc; St. Louis.

Hall, H., & Auernhammer, J. (2014). Organizational culture in knowledge creation, creativity and innovation: Towards the Freiraum model. *Journal of Information Science.* https://doi.org/10.1177/0165551513508356

Hayton, J. C., George, G., & Zahra, S. A. (2002). National Culture and Entrepreneurship: A Review of Behavioral Research. *Entrepreneurship Theory and Practice, 26*(4), 33–52.

Hofstede, G. (1980). *Culture's Consequences, International Differences in Work-Related Values.* Beverly Hills, CA: Sage Publications.

Ireland, R. D., & Webb, J. W. (2007). Strategic Entrepreneurship: Creating Competitive Advantage Through Streams of Innovation. *Business Horizons, 50*(1), 49–59. https://doi.org/10.1016/j.bushor.2006.06.002

Ismail, W. K. W., & Abdmajid, R. (2007). Framework of the Culture of Innovation: A Revisit. *JurnalKemanusiaan, 5*(1), 38–49.

Kaasa, A., & Vadi, M. (2010). How Does Culture Contribute to Innovation? Evidence from European Countries. *Economics of Innovation and New Technology, 19*(7), 583–604.

Kesting, P., & Parm Ulhoi, J. (2010). Employee-driven Innovation: Extending the License to Foster Innovation. *Management Decision, 48*(1), 65–84. https://doi.org/10.1108/00251741011014463

Lee, S. M., & Peterson, S. J. (2000). Culture, Entrepreneurial Orientation and Global Competitiveness. *J World Bus, 35*, 401–416.

Leydesdorff, L. (2012). *The Knowledge-Based Economy and the Triple Helix Model.* University of Amsterdam, Amsterdam School of Communications Research. arXiv:1201.4553. Bibcode:2012arXiv1201.4553L.

Mueller, S. L., & Thomas, A. S. (2001). Culture and Entrepreneurial Potential: A Nine Country Study of Locus of Control and Innovativeness. *Journal of Business Venturing, 16*, 51–75.

Naranjo-Valencia, J. C., Jiménez, D. J., & Sanz-Valle, R. (2012). ¿Es la cultura organizativa un determinante de la innovación en la empresa? *Cuadernos de Economía y Dirección de la Empresa, 15*(3), 63–72.

OECD. (2000). Trust in Government – Ethics Measures in OECD Countries. Public Affairs and Communication Directorate. OECD. Paris. Retrieved from https://www.oecd.org/gov/ethics/48994450.pdf

Padilha, C. K., & Gomes, G. (2016). Innovation Culture and Performance in Innovation of Products and Processes: A Study in Companies of Textile Industry. *RAI Revista de Administraçao e Inovaçao, 13*, 285–294.

Plonsky, G. A. (2005). Bases para um Movimento pela inovaçao tecnológica no Brasil. *São Paulo em Perspectiva, 19*(1), 25–33.

Sanchez-Alonso, B. (2019). The Age of Mass Migration in Latin America. *The Economic History Review, 72*(1), 3–31. https://doi.org/10.1111/ehr.12787

Skarzynski, P., & Gibson, R. (2008). *Innovation to the Core: A Blueprint for Transforming the Way Your Company Innovates*. Boston: Harvard Business Press.

Smale, T. (2016). Why National Culture Should Be at the Heart of Innovation Management. *Technology Innovation Management Review*, Ottawa, 6(4): 18–25.

Spinosa, L. M., Krama, M. R., & Hardt, C. (2018). Desenvolvimento urbano baseado em conhecimento e ecossistemas de inovação urbanos: uma análise em quatro cidades brasileiras. *Eure-Revista Latinoamericana De Estudios Urbano Regionales JCR, 44*, 193–214.

Spinosa, L. M., Schlemm, M. M., & Reis, R. S. (2015). Brazilian Innovation Ecosystems In Perspective: Some Challenges For Stakeholders. *Rebrae. Revista Brasileira De Estratégia (Impresso), 8*, 386–400.

Srivastava, M. K., & Gnyawali, D. R. (2017). When Do Relational Resources Matter? Leveraging Portfolio Technological Resources for Breakthrough Innovation. *Academy of Management, 54*(4), 797–810. https://doi.org/10.5465/amj.2011.64870140

Taylor, M. Z., & Wilson, S. (2012). Does Culture Still Matter?: The Effects of Individualism on National Innovation Rates. *Journal of Business Venturing, 27*, 234–247.

THRC. (2011). *The Triple Helix Concept*. Stanford University Triple Helix Research Group.

Waarts, E., & van Everdingen, Y. (2005). The Influence of National Culture on the Adoption Status of Innovations: An Empirical Study of Firms Across Europe. *European Management Journal, 23*(6), 601–610.

WEO. (2019). International Monetary Fund. 2019. *World Economic Outlook: Global Manufacturing Downturn*, Rising Trade Barriers. Washington, DC. *IMF's World Economic Outlook Database, October 2019.*

Zahra, S. A., & Dess, G. G. (2001). Entrepreneurship as a Field of Research: Encouraging Dialogue and Debate. *Academy of Management Review, 26*, 8–10.

32

A Prototype for Designing Workplace Innovation Within a Care Ecosystem Context

Ezra Dessers and Bernard J. Mohr

Background

Workplace innovation is defined as the implementation of combined interventions in the domains of work organization, human resource management, and supportive technologies, aimed at simultaneous improvement of organizational performance and quality of working life of employees (Pot, 2011). Recognizing the shift in thinking of workplaces as entities that sometimes go beyond a single organization or even formal networks, many countries in Europe and elsewhere are systematically encouraging workplace innovation not only within but between organizations (Alasoini, Ramstad, & Totterdill, 2017).

Much is known already about workplace innovation within single organizations (Oeij, Rus, & Pot, 2017), and gradually the concept is being applied at the level of workplaces that lie within formal organizational networks and value chains (Alasoini et al., 2017; Sels & Van Hootegem, 2019). Since Moore (1996) coined the concept of business ecosystem, it has become clear that economic communities are supported by a foundation of interacting organizations and individuals, including suppliers, lead producers, competitors,

E. Dessers (✉)
HIVA - KU Leuven, Leuven, Belgium
e-mail: ezra.dessers@kuleuven.be

B. J. Mohr
People Powered Innovation Collaborative Portland, Maine, USA
e-mail: bernard@ppicollaborative.org

© The Author(s), under exclusive license to Springer Nature Switzerland AG 2021
A. McMurray et al. (eds.), *The Palgrave Handbook of Workplace Innovation*,
https://doi.org/10.1007/978-3-030-59916-4_32

597

clients, and other stakeholders. Far less is known today about how to engage with this larger and much less formal, often competitive and even difficult to know, constellation of ecosystem workplace actors (Dessers & Mohr, 2019b). This is particularly true when community boundaries are based on the delivery of health and social care, containing, but not limited to, purely economic transactions.

As Dhondt and Van Hootegem (2015) argue, workplace innovation is a broad concept, going far beyond micro-sociological processes at the level of individual jobs and teams. It is rather a concept that asks for a renewal of the understanding of work and workplaces, at different analytical levels. Our research seeks to further the understanding of design activities and steps for co-designing workplace innovation within ecosystems. To develop our STS-based prototype framework of design steps and choices for workplace innovation at the ecosystem level, we used three case studies of ecosystem workplace innovation in the field of health and social care, supplemented by a series of five biweekly, one-hour iterative design dialogues between the authors of this chapter.

Integrated Care Ecosystems and Workplace Innovation

As currently designed, our care delivery systems are increasingly struggling with major new challenges such as rapid aging of the population, the greater longevity of people with multiple chronic conditions, the growing number of medical specialties, the need for changes in the financing mechanisms of hospitals and health and care institutions, technological advancement, and the increased in healthcare costs and expenditures (Goodwin, Stein, & Amelung, 2017). Better integration of care is one of the solutions expected to enable care systems to address this new landscape, by increasing coordination between care providers, reducing the unnecessary costs of duplication of services, and enhancing continuity of care for patients moving from one care setting to another (Dates, Lennox-Chhugani, Pereira, & Tedeschi, 2018). All of this requires that care delivery increasingly becomes a shared outcome of the deployment of multiple actors at the level beyond single organizations or even formal networks, including, but not limited to, patients and multiple health and social care providers.

The ultimate goal of integrated care through workplace innovation at the ecosystem level can be summarized as the Triple Aim (Berwick, Nolan, & Whittington, 2008): (1) to increase care quality, (2) to improve population health and well-being, and (3) to increase the cost-effectiveness of care. Bodenheimer and Sinsky (2014) extended the Triple Aim to a Quadruple Aim, by adopting a fourth objective: to improve the quality of working life of care providers. The addition of this fourth aim is a logical choice, given that workplace innovation manifests itself in empowering job design and the encouragement of entrepreneurial behavior (Ennals, 2019).

We argue that significant improvement movement towards the quadruple aim is unlikely to happen without significant workplace innovation. This requires both a new perspective on what constitutes workplace innovation and practical methods for participative designing beyond the realm of single care delivery organizations (Mohr & Dessers, 2019b). Moreover, we must be able to move beyond what Goodwin (2019) refers to as widely published truisms (about care in the context of single organizations) such as "teamwork is essential," "effective leadership matters," or "success depends on a positive organisational culture."

Fortunately, the ecosystem perspective helps us to better understand complex health system challenges and design better strategies and solutions to address them (Lawer, 2017). In biology, the ecosystem concept is applied to study interactions within and between species and with their environment. As a metaphor, Kelly (2015) defines service or production ecosystems as "dynamic and co-evolving communities of diverse actors who create and capture new value through both collaboration and competition." Actors within an ecosystem perform activities, which contribute to the outcomes at the scale of the ecosystem, leading to observations by Den Hartigh, Tol, and Visscher (2006) that each member of such an ecosystem ultimately shares the fate of the ecosystem as a whole and by Stam (2015) that both ecosystem activities and outcomes will, in turn, affect the entire community of ecosystem actors. When we presume that all kinds of innovation take place at workplaces, we also presume that any workplace is part of a larger totality, making Pålshaugen (2015) conclude that it is impossible to generate knowledge on workplace innovation without taking this larger totality into consideration. In this ecosystem context, the workplace is spread across many boundaries of organization, meaning geography, socioeconomic lines, and so on. This type of workplace creates new challenges that far outstrip what we know about workplace innovation in single organizations, or even in formal organizational networks, which are understood here as groups of three or more legally autonomous partners (organizations or single actors) that deliberately work together to achieve not only their own goals but a collective goal (Provan & Kenis, 2008). Unlike ecosystems, formal organizational networks are the result of an intentional, cross-organizational integration in function of a well-defined, common target, which implies that a formal organizational network has a certain degree of stability in terms of mission, composition (e.g., formal membership), intentional collaboration, and governance (Dessers & Mohr, 2019a). In that sense, for instance, a primary care ecosystem in a certain region is not the result of an intentional effort, knows no clear boundaries or formal membership, may contain as much competition as collaboration, and has no governance structure at the level of the whole ecosystem. And yet, primary care outcomes, in terms of the quadruple aim, are likely to be the result of the functioning of the ecosystem as a whole. Ecosystem-level workplace innovation is the frontier that most calls for new thinking, new frameworks, and new practices.

Design Principles and Process from Socio-Technical Systems Theory

Integrated care, not only at the level of individual organizations but also at the ecosystem level, is an issue of workplace innovation, aimed at organizing the care workplace in a manner that contributes to fulfilling the Quadruple Aim. It has been argued that Socio-Technical System (STS) Design (de Sitter, den Hertog, & Dankbaar, 1997) could offer an approach for developing principle guided workplace innovation (Dhondt & Van Hootegem, 2015; van Amelsvoort & Van Hootegem, 2017). Since the term Socio-Technical Systems was originally coined in the 1950s in the United Kingdom (Trist & Bamforth, 1951), STS theory has been further developed and applied in North America, Australia, Scandinavia, the Netherlands, and Belgium. For a recent overview, see Mohr and Dessers (2019a). The development of the prototype framework described in this chapter represents a potential evolution of Belgian and Dutch STS design theory and practice.

Design Principles

Kuipers, van Amelsvoort, and Kramer (2010) identify five principles for STS designing:

(1) *Parallelization*: Reduce the challenges related to input variation and process complexity by grouping activities around order flows. Create parallel order flows that show homogeneity in terms of business demands, each being maximally interdependent within the flow, but minimally dependent across flow.

(2) *Segmentation*: Cut the parallel flows of orders into segments, in such a way that each segment contains a collection of interdependent activities, which can be entrusted to a work team as a whole task.

(3) *Decentralization*: Increase individual and team control capacity. Create self-managing work teams which are self-regulating at the operational level, with management, preparatory, and supporting activities kept as close to the value-adding process as possible.

(4) *Minimal critical specification*: Specify only minimal critical requirements for production steps and outcomes so as to allow maximal flexibility in adapting to local challenges and opportunities through innovation and creativity by those producing the outcomes.

(5) Build congruent *support systems* (ICT, physical infrastructure, HRM systems, decision support systems, monitoring systems, etc.), focused on providing support instead of controlling and based on diversity of requirements instead of "one size fits all." These principles focus on guiding the content of design choices. Equally important is the process of designing.

Design Process

The overarching principle for guiding the *process* of designing is "co-creation," which can be described operationally as *meaningful participation in the designing of workplace innovations by those who will inhabit the innovated workplace, in partnership with expert resources form the domains of ICT, HR, facilities, and organization design*. In order to put this principle into practice, together with the five principles for guiding the content of design choices, a design process for workplace innovation was developed. This design process consists of a set of design steps, arranged in an intentional successive order (de Sitter et al., 1997; Kuipers et al., 2010; Van Hootegem, 2016). This (Dutch/Belgian) STS design process is based on logical interdependencies between the different design steps, which means that certain design choices need to be made prior to others. An example is that design choices with regard to organizational structures can only be made after strategic goals and core processes have been identified.

The design process contains five design steps:

- *Step 1: Define mission and vision, develop a business strategy, and determine the guiding principles and performance requirements.*
- *Step 2: Map the core process in terms of added value for clients.*

- *Step 3: Design the production/service structure from the macro to the micro level:*

  - *Macro: Create subsets of clients, products, or services, based on common characteristics, in order to define parallel, homogenous flows, for each of which all necessary activities are brought together in the same organizational division.*
  - *Meso: Split the parallel flows into segments of interdependent activities; each segment is entrusted to a work team.*
  - *Micro: Design broad jobs within multifunctional work teams.*

- *Step 4: Design the management, preparation, and support structure from the micro to the macro level: management, preparatory, and supporting activities are kept as close to the value-adding process as possible.*
- *Step 5: Develop support systems which enable the effectiveness and quality of working life for the various individuals and groups that must collaborate together.*

Although originally developed to design single organizations, the Dutch/Belgian STS process has also been used for designing organizational networks (Sels & Van Hootegem, 2019).

Research Question

In this paper, we explore the applicability of the STS design principles and the STS design process for workplace innovation design at the ecosystem level. More specifically, our research question was: "Which modifications are needed to the existing, single organization-focused STS design process, to enable workplace innovation design at the ecosystem level?"

Methodology

In order to answer this research question, we needed to revise the existing STS design process, resulting in a prototype of an ecosystem-level STS design process. We applied two methodological stages in order to build the prototype.

In the first stage, a multiple case study design was developed. A case corresponds to our unit of analysis, which is defined as a Dutch/Belgian STS-based workplace innovation at the level of a care ecosystem, in which multiple actors (holding both formal and informal roles) collaborate across organizational, role, and geographic boundaries to redesign the ecosystem with a focus on improved care integration. Three narrative reports of STS-based ecosystem-level workplace innovation, towards greater care integration, were obtained, two from Belgium and one from the Netherlands. We coded the narrative reports to identify and gather quotes on the different steps in the workplace innovation design process applied, as well as on the level of participation involved. We then thematically grouped the collected quotes, using the five steps of the existing STS design model (as described in section "Design Process") as classification categories, with an additional category for the level of participation. Next, we used the collected quotes to summarize how the ecosystem-level design process dealt with these five steps and with the level of participation. In doing so, we contrasted the design practice found in three ecosystem-level design cases with the existing STS design model for single organization design of workplace innovation and gathered information on the level of participation involved.

In the second stage, starting from the collected case data, combined with the STS design principles as described in section "Design Principles," we developed a prototype of a design process for workplace innovation at the ecosystem level. Prototyping involves moving from the world of abstract ideas to the world of concrete manifestations. A prototype can be usefully thought of as a learning tool which may be used to explore, evolve, and communicate ideas (Coughlan, Suri, & Canales, 2007). Based on findings from our case analyses, using our dual perspectives of an STS practitioner (Mohr), and an academic (Dessers), we developed a prototype of an STS design process for workplace innovation at the ecosystem level in a series of five biweekly, one-hour iterative design dialogues between the authors. We refer to it as a prototype, since we acknowledge that it will need to be further developed and tested.

Findings

In this section, we describe the findings for the two stages in our research design.

Stage 1: Case Analysis

For each of the three cases studied, we present a table, which summarizes how the ecosystem design work was carried out in relation to the existing Dutch/Belgian single organization design model, followed by a short conclusion with regard to the implications for constructing our prototype design process in the next stage.

Table 32.1 Design steps and level of participation in case 1—primary care ecosystem, Belgium (based on: Dessers & Gramberen, 2019)

STS design step 1	An STS-based "canvas tool" for organization design was used as a basis for ecosystem design, in which the design sequence is represented by four steps. In the first step, the added value which the ecosystem aims to deliver was defined. A small change team and a larger change forum representing ecosystem actors consecutively discussed following guiding questions: (1) Why change anything? What is the big why? (2) Why do we exist as a primary care region? What is our added value? What would be missed if we were not there? (3) What are our shared values? (4) Which are the guiding principles for collaboration within our primary care region?
STS design step 2	The first step of the canvas tool (in which the added value which the ecosystem aims to deliver is defined) also covers STS design step 2. Change team and change forum discussed the guiding questions: Which core processes do we need to get organized and for whom? What are the essential characteristics of the core processes? And how can we cluster the activities, in view of their respective target groups?
STS design step 3 STS design step 4	The case description described only the application of the first step of the canvas tool. Future activities are scheduled to involve the redesign of (parts of) selected care processes involving a limited number (i.e., network) of ecosystem actors. Step 2 of the canvas tool covers both STS design steps 3 (*production/service structure*) and 4 (*management, preparation, and support*). The third step in the canvas tool focusses specifically on collaboration and cohesion within teams at the micro level
STS design step 5	Step 4 in the canvas tool matches STS design step 5 (*support systems*)
Level of participation	The design approach was at the same time expert and ecosystem member driven with STS design experts using the canvas tool to involve a broad group of ecosystems actors directly and meaningfully in the iterative steps of ecosystem design

As can be seen from Table 32.1, the ecosystem design process in the first case includes the establishment of mission, vision, and guiding principles at the ecosystem level, as well as an ecosystem analysis and identification of the core processes and target groups. Ecosystem actors were actively involved in a change team and a change forum, supported by STS experts. A next phase is planned to select specific interventions which each involve a limited number of ecosystems actors (i.e., a formal organization network), which will then be designed following the existing STS Design process.

As can be seen from Table 32.2, the ecosystem design process in the second case includes the creation of "collaborative capacity" at the ecosystem level, as well as an ecosystem analysis and identification of the key challenges and

Table 32.2 Design steps and level of participation in case 2—mental healthcare eco-system, Belgium (based on: Sels & Van Hootegem, 2019)

STS design step 1	At the ecosystem level, "collaborative capacity" was built by engaging the ecosystem actors in co-exploring and understanding each other's aspirations, needs, opportunities, and strengths. Conditions for future collaboration between existing actors were explored. The potential of building new collaborative structures, which take into account the challenges and opportunities presented by the ecosystem, were assessed
STS design step 2	The design team was challenged to reflect upon the boundaries of the system to be designed. Topics such as the place of the formal organization network within the ecosystem, the connection between the field of well-being and general healthcare, and the potential need for fusions of organizations were questions in this step of the design. In this step the focus was on the core transformation process of the formal organization network
STS design step 3	The next step was the design of the core process at the macro and meso levels. Not surprisingly, instead of redesigning the entire mental healthcare ecosystem, designing sub-processes around specific client groups was a much more acceptable strategy. Many possible sorting criteria were discussed, which each were tested in respect to their relevance to the network's performance requirements. In the end, the phases in the disease process were used as the basic criterion for sorting. As a result, three key but separate care streams formed the basis of the design work (i.e., first crisis; subsequent crises and associated treatment and guidance; long-term care). Three subsystems within the formal organization network were designed and developed as the outcome of the sorting process
STS design step 4	The case description mentioned the design of the governance and support structures as the next step, but did not describe this step in more detail
STS design step 5	Also the creation of the "internal systems" was mentioned, but not further described
Level of participation	Based upon STS theory and practice, a design team was created as a representative microcosm of the larger ecosystem, for getting "the whole system in the room." Design team members were recruited across organizations and functions, including patient family members and ex-patients. The design team was supported by STS experts

possibilities. After that, and similar to case 1, specific design choices were made, with each involving only a limited number of ecosystem actors (i.e., a formal organization network). These formal networks were then designed following the existing Dutch/Belgian STS design process. A representative design team was created for this and supported by STS experts.

As can be seen from Table 32.3, the design process in case 3 includes the establishment of a common vision for the future, an ecosystem analysis and

Table 32.3 Design steps and level of participation in case 3—caregiver ecosystem, the Netherlands (based on: Verschuur, 2019)

STS design step 1	A. The STS design approach in this case comprised six "stages." First, management level representatives of 25 identified ecosystem organizations co-created a common vision in workshops. In the second stage, core problems, conflicting and common interests, and possible alignment of interests were discussed. A common vision for the future was formulated	
STS design step 2	B. Next, a design team, consisting of a cross-section of all organizations that formulated the vision performed an ecosystem analysis, identifying care fragmentation issues, unconnected control loops, and defective mutual relationships	F. At this point, several multidisciplinary design teams consisting of GPs, district nurses, social workers, and members of volunteer organizations and churches translated the global structure into a detailed design of the network teams. In the first step, they focused on demarcation of the region for each network team, enabling teams to have simple, one-to-one relationships, allowing fast and effective information exchange and communication. The core process of each network is defined in terms of signaling, intake, clarifying the needs, and offering a solution to the caregiver
STS design step 3	C. Then, the design team that did the ecosystem analysis developed a global design for, what is called, a "smart network structure." The first step was to apply parallelization to the primary process, by distinguishing flows for specific types of clients. A separate network for each type of client was defined	G. The design teams then indicated what the internal work organization of the network teams should look like teamwork, tasks, competences, responsibilities, desired internal flexibility within a team, and coordination
STS design step 4	D. The next steps in the global design were allocating and grouping control activities from the micro to the macro level; grouping of supporting and managing activities that cannot be allocated to network teams in the primary process; shaping control junctions and coordination mechanisms; and assessing alternatives. For the overall coordination and managerial link to the home organizations, a governance structure was designed	H. And, the network teams were designed as self-managing teams who are also responsible for controlling their budget, managing volunteers, coordinating and monitoring registered caregivers, developing their network, and so on

STS design
step 5

I. Lastly, consultation structure between network team participants and their colleagues from their own organizations was developed and implemented, as well as a digital information system that can be used by caregivers and network team members, which monitors progress from intake, planning, and execution of actions, thus keeping a digital file for each caregiver

Level of
participation

E. Next was the development of a change plan, in which bottom-up change is combined with direction and support from the top. Workers of all organizations were strongly involved. Each design team received guidance from an STS expert, and multiple large-scale meetings with professionals, nonprofessionals, caregivers, and care recipients were organized during the change process identification of the key issues, and a general design of care service delivery. After that, within the different parts of the ecosystem, "network teams" were designed following the existing STS design process.

In general, evidence from the three cases suggests that designing workplace innovation within ecosystems switches back and forth between the ecosystem level and intervention level (of formal organization networks or single organizations). At the ecosystem level, the following activities can be identified: establish mission, vision, and guiding principles; ecosystem analysis and identification of the core processes and target groups; and identification and selection of required interventions. In the three cases, these interventions are situated at the level of formal organization networks, which are designed following the steps of the existing STS design process (as described in section "Design Process"). But also at the ecosystem level, specific interventions, mainly in terms of support systems (information systems, governance, funding, etc.), can be designed. With regard to the level of participation, we learned from the three cases that the typical STS design approach, being at the same time supported by STS design expert and members of the ecosystem, remains applicable when designing workplace innovation at an ecosystem level.

Stage 2: Prototype Development

Based on the collected insights from the case studies, and inspired by the STS design principles, as described in section "Design Principles," we have developed a prototype design process for workplace innovation at the (care) ecosystem level (Fig. 32.1) in the iterative design dialogues between the authors. We here describe the six steps in this design process.

Frame Purpose

Care ecosystems are complex, potentially never-ending and possibly overwhelming from a workplace innovation view. Framing the ecosystem in terms of common purpose is an essential complexity reducing activity. A basic rule in organizational design theory is that you organize yourself in the function of who your client is and what you want to offer them. The clients of care ecosystems are people with certain care requirements, usually within a certain region. The first step is therefore to frame the ecosystem in terms of its purpose in relation to certain sets of patients or clients. This first step helps us to better understand the way in which the purpose is, or could be, achieved and which interventions could be made to improve the functioning of the ecosystem in the light of the stated purpose.

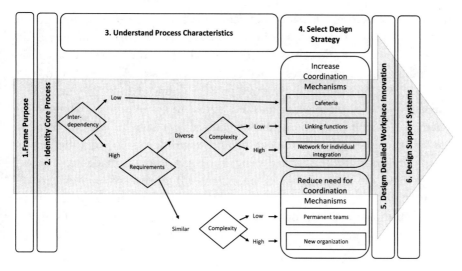

Fig. 32.1   Prototype ecosystem workplace innovation design process

Identify Core Processes

The clients of the care ecosystems are people with certain care requirements. These care requirements can nevertheless vary in complexity. The concrete situation of a specific person with a care requirement influences the breadth of the range of activities and competences needed to provide the care required. By grouping people with comparable combinations of care needs, the enormous variety of individual care needs can be reduced to a manageable range of groups of people with comparable care needs. It is crucially important to identify the different groups of people for whom the care ecosystem wishes to offer specific added value. Target groups are discerned with the help of sorting criteria. *Presence of a chronic condition, illness, place of residence,* and *level of physical impairment* are some examples of possible sorting criteria. For each of the target groups, the care process can then be identified in terms of the various activities that are needed to provide adequate care for the people in that specific target group.

Understand Process Characteristics

To further reduce the complexity, it is necessary for each target group to bring together a collection of care providers who are internally interdependent in view of the care needs of the target group concerned, but who are largely independent from care providers outside their group. In that way, you organize care delivery in parallel streams of activities for each target group. However, full-scale care integration is probably not needed—and not desirable—for each possible care process. Depending on the process characteristics, a different design strategy may need to be chosen. As can be seen from Fig. 32.1, we propose to apply three process characteristics: (1) the level of *interdependency* between activities (and actors) in a care process, determining whether or not the care client can find and self-manage his care provision or not; (2) the uniqueness of the care *requirements*, depending on whether the target group has largely similar care needs or, conversely, is made up of people with diverse combinations of care needs; and (3) the level of *complexity* of the care process (in terms of number of activities, lack of predictability, combination of multiple issues, medical challenges, etc.). Other characteristics may be needed, depending on the specificity and scale of the care ecosystem involved.

Select Design Strategy

As indicated in the previous section, the selection of the design strategy is based on the care process characteristics. Not each of the proposed design tactics results in the same degree of care integration. This approach is similar to the well-known classification of (chronic) care clients applied by care organization Kaiser Permanente: a (small) group of highly complex patients, for which intensive care integration is being organized; a (larger) group of patients with high risk, who receive self-care supported by a general practitioner; and a (very large) group of people with a low risk, for whom mainly primary prevention is put in place (Department of Health, 2007). Figure 32.1 presents five design tactics, grouped into two strategies, building on the process characteristics identified in the previous step.

As Fig. 32.1 shows, in the case of low interdependency between activities and actors in the process (which implies a low need for care integration), the care client is usually able to self-manage his care needs and provision. The *cafeteria* design tactic enables the care client to make his own choice of care providers and professionals in the market. Care integration is hardly required and probably limited to the exchange of information and referrals between different actors. In case of high interdependency between the different activities and actors in the process (which implies a need for care integration), the question remains whether or not the care clients can be bundled in target groups or streams with similar care needs. If not, the care client needs a specific, unique care trajectory. The *linking functions* design tactic enables low-complexity (often long-term) care clients to find the care they need in a coordinated way (e.g., supported by a case manager). The *network for individual integration* design tactic will combine the coordinated efforts of multiple, networked actors, for example, in a temporary, cross-organizational team for an individual care client. If streams of care clients with similar care needs can be identified, the *permanent team* design tactic offers integrated care for (relatively) low-complexity care clients, via fixed, multidisciplinary, cross-organizational teams. The *new organization* design tactic brings all the needed expertise together within a single organization in order to cater for high-complexity care clients via fixed, multidisciplinary teams within this new organization.

Design Detailed Workplace Innovation

It must be clear that, depending on the design strategy and tactic selected in Step 4, a different type of workplace innovation will need to be designed. In the case of the *cafeteria* design tactic, the workplace innovation will likely focus on the challenges related to information sharing, providing the adequate conditions for ensuring accessibility, affordability, and quality. The *linking functions* and *network for individual integration* design tactics mainly require workplace innovations which focus on improving coordination mechanisms, while the *permanent team* and *new organization* design tactics require workplace innovations aimed at redesigning underlying care delivery structures, in terms of changing boundaries that make up the care delivery processes, the associated roles of groups, and the people within them.

Design Support Systems

Only in the final step of the ecosystem redesign process are specific protocols, information systems and machinery, human resource management systems, and planning systems developed. This work enables the workplace innovations which were designed in the previous step. For example, the type of information system you need for a *cafeteria*-based workplace innovation is clearly different from what a *permanent team* would require. Moreover, the way you design these support systems may hamper or stimulate care integration. For example, digital devices can give care clients more autonomy, but they can also make them more dependent on care and technology providers. Ecosystem design may also involve changing support systems at an ecosystem level or beyond (to the extent that ecosystem designers and actors can influence). For instance, the legislative framework may contain impediments or incentives for care integration. In many countries, the area of competence of different professions is rigidly delineated, which leaves little autonomy to care professionals and little room for broadening tasks and sharing responsibilities (Vanermen & Nys, 2017). And of course financial incentives play a large role in the process to achieve more coordination and integration of care, since they have a significant impact on the behavior of care providers (Tsiachristas, Dikkers, Boland, & Rutten-van Mölken, 2013).

Discussion

Using the ecosystem perspective may offer care policymakers, managers, practitioners, patients, and scholars a way to view the bigger picture, in which interdependencies between many different activities and actors come to light and previously hidden possibilities come to the surface. Addressing care fragmentation by identifying target groups of care clients with similar needs and developing specific tactics enables us to tackle the huge, wicked problem of care integration by splitting the problem up in manageable parts.

While the findings clearly show the potential of workplace innovation at the ecosystem level, two limitations are identified and will benefit from additional research. (1) The current study is explorative in nature, and the case selection was based on the response to an open call for book chapters on cases of care ecosystems (Mohr & Dessers, 2019b). Future research may take a more systematic and comparative design, focused on specific aspects (including involvement of people, implementation steps, and outcomes). (2) Readings of our narrative case studies suggest the need for practical and evidence-driven methodologies that enable co-creation among a vast array of ecosystem actors; processes which allow for extensive negotiation of possibilities; processes which build productive relationships among actors; processes which balance emergence and ground-up design with evidence-based principles and theory; and in-stream evaluation processes which from the start manage the tension between pragmatists and innovators and the use of strengths-based, positive approaches. A discussion of initial options is presented by Mohr and Dessers (2019a). Future research may focus on the full integration of this relational process of co-creation with our six design steps at the ecosystem level.

Conclusion

Workplace innovation design at the ecosystem level does not mean "design as a grand plan." Ecosystem workplace innovation is unlikely to be achieved by searching for the one-best-answer resulting from a rational, engineering-type process, but should rather emphasize the iterative and emergent process of designing. A reasonable approach to ecosystem workplace innovation concentrates on design practices leading to viable results, with a focus on users and an attentiveness to the designing process, including an openness for iterations, tests, safe failures, and learning (Bach, 2016). Sovereign entities within the ecosystem may themselves benefit from the adoption of an ecosystem perspective and internal workplace innovation. Raynor, Cardona, Knowlton, Mittenthal, and Simpson (2015) suggest that for individual organizations it is no longer enough to just be organizationally sound—having a vibrant connection to the larger ecosystem is essential. They list three types of capacities needed in that context: the capacity to understand the ecosystem; the capacity to respond to an ever-evolving ecosystem; and the capacity to structure itself in response to its ecosystem. As Iansiti and Levien (2004) say, "the strategy increasingly becomes the art of managing assets that one does not possess." An organization functioning within an ecosystem is part of the ecosystem itself and subject to the same forces of adaptation and evolution as all other actors (Lawer, 2017).

An ecosystem perspective on workplace innovation creates new opportunities for innovation and new design challenges. At the same time, this perspective comes with a multitude of new challenges to the existing practices of workplace innovation at the level of single organizations or formal networks. We are fortunate to be able to explore how existing approaches to workplace innovation such as STS principles and practice might be adapted to the context and challenges of ecosystem workplace innovation. Of course more research into what actually works will further flesh out our understanding of design processes for workplace innovation generally and within care delivery ecosystems particularly.

References

Alasoini, T., Ramstad, E., & Totterdill, P. (2017). *National and Regional Policies to Promote and Sustain Workplace Innovation. In Workplace Innovation* (pp. 27–44). Theory, Research and Practice: Springer International.

Bach, O. (2016). Organizational Design Thinking. Retrieved January 1, 2018, from https://www.managementkits.com/blog/2016/3/1/organizational-design-thinking

Berwick, D. M., Nolan, T. W., & Whittington, J. (2008). The Triple Aim: Care, Health, and Cost. *Health Affairs, 27*(3), 759–769. https://doi.org/10.1377/hlthaff.27.3.759

Bodenheimer, T., & Sinsky, C. (2014). From Triple to Quadruple Aim: Care of the Patient Requires Care of the Provider. *Annals Family Medicine, 12*(6), 573–576. https://doi.org/10.1370/afm.1713.Center

Coughlan, P., Suri, J. F., & Canales, K. (2007). Prototypes as (Design) Tools for Behavioral and Organizational Change: A Design-Based Approach to Help Organizations Change Work Behaviors. *Journal of Applied Behavioral Science, 43*(1), 122–134. https://doi.org/10.1177/0021886306297722

Dates, M., Lennox-Chhugani, N., Pereira, H. S., & Tedeschi, M. (2018). *Health System Performance Assessment-Integrated Care Assessment (20157303 HSPA).* Brussels: European Commission. Retrieved from https://ec.europa.eu/health/sites/health/files/systems_performance_assessment/docs/2018_integratedcareassessment_en.pdf

de Sitter, L. U., den Hertog, J. F., & Dankbaar, B. (1997). From Complex Organizations with Simple Jobs to Simple Organizations with Complex Jobs. *Human Relations, 50*(5), 497–534. https://doi.org/10.1177/001872679705000503

Den Hartigh, E., Tol, M., & Visscher, W. (2006). The Health Measurement of a Business Ecosystem. ECCON 2006 Annual Meeting, 2783565(secretary 2781150), 1–39. Retrieved from http://www.chaosforum.com/docs/nieuws/health.pdf

Department of Health. (2007). *The NHS and Social Care Long Term Conditions Model.* London.

Dessers, E., & Van Gramberen, M. (2019). Designing Primary Care Ecosystems in the Flemish Community (Belgium). In B. Mohr & E. Dessers (Eds.), Designing Integrated Care Ecosystems. A Socio-Technical Perspective. Springer International.

Dessers, E., & Mohr, B. J. (2019a). Integrated Care Ecosystems. In B. J. Mohr & E. Dessers (Eds.), *Designing Integrated Care Ecosystems. A Socio-Technical Perspective.* Springer International.

Dessers, E., & Mohr, B. J. (2019b). Introduction. In *Designing Integrated Care Ecosystems. A Socio-Technical Perspective.* Springer International.

Dhondt, S., & Van Hootegem, G. (2015). Reshaping Workplaces: Workplace Innovation as Designed by Scientists and Practitioners. *European Journal of Workplace Innovation, 1*(1), 17–24.

Ennals, R. (2019). European Journal of Workplace Innovation. Retrieved August 30, 2019, from https://journal.uia.no/index.php/EJWI

Goodwin, N., Stein, V., & Amelung, V. (2017). What Is Integrated Care? In V. E. Amelung, V. Stein, N. Goodwin, R. Balicer, E. Nolte, & E. Suter (Eds.), *Handbook Integrated Care* (pp. 3–24). Springer International.

Goodwin, N. (2019). Improving Integrated Care: Can Implementation Science Unlock the 'Black Box' of Complexities? *International Journal of Integrated Care, 19*(3), 1–3. https://doi.org/10.5334/ijic.4724

Iansiti, M., & Levien, R. (2004). Keystones and Dominators: Framing Operating and Technology Strategy in a Business Ecosystem. *Harvard Business School, Working Paper*, 3–61.

Kelly, E. (2015). Business Ecosystems Come of Age. *Deloitte Business Trends Series, 117*. Retrieved from https://dupress.deloitte.com/content/dam/dup-us-en/articles/platform-strategy-new-level-business-trends/DUP_1048-Business-ecosystems-come-of-age_MASTER_FINAL.pdf

Kuipers, H., van Amelsvoort, P., & Kramer, E.-H. (2010). *Het nieuwe organiseren. Alternatieven voor de bureaucratie.* Leuven: Acco.

Lawer, C. (2017). *Design and Transform Value in Health A Service Ecosystem Framework.* Bloxham: UMIO.

Mohr, B. J., & Dessers, E. (2019a). Designing from a Socio-Technical Systems Perspective. In B. J. Mohr & E. Dessers (Eds.), *Designing Integrated Care Ecosystems. A Socio-Technical Perspective.* Springer International.

Mohr, B. J., & Dessers, E. (Eds.). (2019b). Designing Integrated Care Ecosystems. A Socio-Technical Perspective. Springer International.

Moore, J. F. (1996). *The Death of Competition: Leadership and Strategy in the Age of Business Ecosystems.* New York: Harper Business.

Oeij, P., Rus, D., & Pot, F. (Eds.). (2017). *Workplace Innovation. Theory, Research and Practice.* Springer International.

Pålshaugen, Ø. (2015). Why a European Journal of Workplace Innovation? *European Journal of Workplace Innovation, 1*(1), 5–12.

Pot, F. (2011). Workplace Innovation for Better Jobs and Performance. *International Journal of Productivity and Performance Management, 60*(4), 404–415.

Provan, K. G., & Kenis, P. (2008). Modes of Network Governance: Structure, Management, and Effectiveness. *Journal of Public Administration Research and Theory, 18*(2), 229–252. https://doi.org/10.1093/jopart/mum015

Raynor, J., Cardona, C., Knowlton, T., Mittenthal, R., & Simpson, J. (2015). *Capacity Building 3.0: How to Strengthen the Social Ecosystem.* New York; Philadelphia; San Francisco: TCC Group. Retrieved from http://www.tccgrp.com/pdfs/11-18-14_TCC_Capacity_3.pdf

Sels, C., & Van Hootegem, G. (2019). Designing Networks for Integrated Care Within the Belgian Mental Health Care Ecosystem. In B. J. Mohr & E. Dessers (Eds.), *Designing Integrated Care Ecosystems. A Socio-Technical Perspective.* Springer International.

Stam, E. (2015). Entrepreneurial Ecosystems and Regional Policy: A Sympathetic Critique. *European Planning Studies, 23*(9), 1759–1769.

Trist, E. L., & Bamforth, K. W. (1951). Some Social and Psychological Consequences of the Longwall Method of Coal Getting. *Human Relations, 4*, 3–38.

Tsiachristas, A., Dikkers, C., Boland, M. R. S., & Rutten-van Mölken, M. P. M. H. (2013). Exploring Payment Schemes Used to Promote Integrated

Chronic Care in Europe. *Health Policy, 113*(3), 296–304. https://doi. org/10.1016/j.healthpol.2013.07.007

van Amelsvoort, P., & Van Hootegem, G. (2017). Towards a Total Workplace Innovation Concept Based on Sociotechnical Systems Design. *EWOP in Practice, 1*. Retrieved from http://www.eawop.org/ckeditor_assets/attachments/838/3_vanamelsvoort_vanhootegem.pdf?1494252240

Van Hootegem, G. (2016). Changing the Nature of Work. Toward Total Workplace Innovation. In B. J. Mohr & P. van Amelsvoort (Eds.), *Co-creating Humane and Innovative Organizations*. Portland: Global STS-D Network Press.

Vanermen, E., & Nys, H. (2017). Regelgeving voor samenwerking. In G. Van Hootegem & E. Dessers (Eds.), *Onbezorgd. Naar een geïntegreerd gezondheidsysteem* (pp. 205–229). Leuven: Acco.

Verschuur, F. O. (2019). Designing Smart Network Teams: Supporting Caregivers for People Living at Home. In B. J. Mohr & E. Dessers (Eds.), *Designing Integrated Care Ecosystems. A Socio-Technical Perspective*. Springer International Publishing.

33

Educational Technology at Pivotal Crossroads

Radhika Venkat and Jayanta Banerjee

Introduction

The entrepreneurial drive to explore and innovate has resulted in an exponential rise of startups in both developed and emerging economies across the world. Unable to single-handedly commercialize their business idea (Van de Ven, 1993), entrepreneurs seek the support of the local business environment. This has facilitated the dawn of "entrepreneurial ecosystems" as structured strategies to establish supportive contextual environments that pave the way for sustainable entrepreneurial ventures (Audretsch, Cunningham, Kuratko, Lehmann, & Menter, 2019).

India is host to the third largest and fastest growing entrepreneurial ecosystem in the world (World Economic Forum, 2013). NASSCOM 2019 report on Indian Tech Startup Ecosystem highlights that entrepreneurs in India are leveraging opportunities across high-growth sectors such as EdTech, Fintech, Mobility, Automotive, and Healthtech that are demonstrating a CAGR of over 50% since 2014. The key growth drivers of online education in India is availability of infrastructure due to launch of government initiatives such as SWAYAM, Skill India, and Digital India, internet penetration, proliferation

R. Venkat (✉)
Jain University, Bengaluru, Karnataka, India

J. Banerjee
CHRIST Deemed to be University, Bengaluru, Karnataka, India

© The Author(s), under exclusive license to Springer Nature Switzerland AG 2021
A. McMurray et al. (eds.), *The Palgrave Handbook of Workplace Innovation*,
https://doi.org/10.1007/978-3-030-59916-4_33

of smart phones, increase in disposable personal income, and a large, young, tech-savvy population.

According to Global Skills Index 2019, two-thirds of the world's population is falling behind in critical skills. The report on Education & Training Sector claims that India has over 250 million school-going students and is witnessing a huge demand supply gap, that is, reflecting an additional requirement of 200,000 schools, 35,000 colleges, 700 universities, and 40 million seats in the vocational training centers (IBEF, 2019).

In order to bridge this widening gap, reflected in both primary and secondary school segments in India, and improve the overall student learning outcomes, educational technology startups, commonly referred to as "EdTech," are combining education with innovative technology (Lamine et al., 2018). EdTech startups in India are focusing on technology driven innovations relating to test preparation, tutor discovery, doubt clearance, tech-enabled classroom, digital and vernacular content, gamification, and tracking, with the aim of affecting change and facilitating innovative teaching and learning models in a school environment.

Despite the prevalence of a huge market opportunity for educational technology startups in Bengaluru, India, the industry is encountering growth oriented challenges. The success of an entrepreneurial venture is dependent not just on a startup firm working independently but also based on the ecosystem around which it is discovered, constructed, and operationalized (Elia, Margherita, & Passiante, 2020). Using Isenberg's Entrepreneurial Ecosystem Framework (2011, 2016), the study evaluates the EdTech entrepreneurial ecosystem in Bengaluru, to arrive at key factors affecting the growth of EdTech startups.

The chapter begins with theoretical underpinnings of the entrepreneurial ecosystems (EE) and how it has evolved into a multi-actor, multi-scalar phenomenon using Isenberg's Entrepreneurial Ecosystem Framework (2011), the tenets on which this study rests. Following this, the Research Aim and Scope of this study has been clearly laid out. The section on Research Method takes the reader through the research setting, data collection, and data analysis phases. Findings followed by propositions have been vividly described. Next in the section on "Discussion," the scholars draw reference to "Insights" resulting from the study and build a rational argument to substantiate the findings of the study. This is followed by limitations of the study, practical and theoretical implications, directions for future research, and conclusion.

Theoretical Underpinnings

The theory of entrepreneurial ecosystems (EE) emerged in 1980s and 1990s, when scholars shifted their attention from studying the individual trait and personality-based research on entrepreneurs towards a wider community dimension that included social, cultural, and economic dimensions in the entrepreneurial process (Aldrich, 1990).

Cohen (2006) coined the term "entrepreneurial ecosystem (EE)" and defined it as "a diverse set of interdependent actors within a geographic region that influence the formation and eventual trajectory of the entire group of actors and potentially the economy as a whole." EE comprises of humans, entrepreneurship, society (Prahalad, 2005) and is viewed as a regional economic development strategy (Spigel & Harrison, 2018). Further, they add that it is a conceptualization of a geographical area where social and economic contexts support and influence entrepreneurs. It is also an interactive dynamic community of entrepreneurs and other stakeholders confined within a specific geography where social, cultural, and material attributes influence entrepreneurial growth (Spigel, 2017). Innovation involves the disruption of existing industries and the creation of new ones (Autio, Kenney, Mustar, Siegel, & Wright, 2014).

For an EE to be self-sustaining, various actors in the ecosystem must benefit (Isenberg, 2010). EE involves interaction among many elements of the ecosystem (Acs et al., 2014), and sustainability is perceived to be a key outcome resulting from this process (Sussan & Acs, 2017). Interactions and partnerships between entrepreneurs and their external ecosystem (Adner & Kapoor, 2010) have had a positive influence on new startup firms. EE does not have a formal governance structure around it (Acs et al., 2014). In addition to studying the contextual influences and evolution of EE, scholars are beginning to focus on how various components of EE interact, support, and strengthen the ecosystem (Motoyama & Knowlton, 2017).

Taking this forward, Isenberg (2010), one of the most acclaimed practitioners of EE, claimed that each ecosystem is unique and emerges under very different circumstances. He suggested that in order to build a successful entrepreneurial ecosystem, one must embrace and exploit the local conditions of the specific community (Bouncken et al., 2018).

Isenberg (2010), one of the pioneering practitioners of the Entrepreneurial Ecosystem (EE) Framework, unpacked six key domains of EE Framework, that is, accessible markets, availability of finance, conducive culture, quality human capital, progressive policy framework, and supporting infrastructure, that interact and facilitate and drive entrepreneurial growth. Later in 2011, he claimed that out of the six domains, "accessible markets, availability of finance, and quality human capital" are the most important.

Research further evolved, as scholars proposed that the earlier claims made on important factors were only proximate causes and not fundamental causes for success of the ecosystems (Acemoglu, Johnson, & Robinson, 2005), pointing out that research on ecosystems is underdeveloped and undertheorized. Although entrepreneurial ecosystem (EE) is recognized as a highly variegated, multi-actor, and multi-scalar phenomenon (Brown & Mason, 2017) and remains an important area of research (Borissenko & Boschma, 2016; Isenberg, 2010, 2011), theory remains underdeveloped (Spigel, 2017) and unexplored.

Research Aim and Scope

Isenberg unpacked six key domains of EE Framework, that is, accessible markets, availability of finance, conducive culture, quality human capital, progressive policy framework, and institutional support (Isenberg, 2010), that interact in a complex and idiosyncratic fashion (Mason & Brown, 2014) and facilitate entrepreneurial growth. Isenberg (2011) claimed that out of the six domains, access to markets, availability of finance, and quality human capital are the most important. Later, following extensive research across many countries, Isenberg (2014b) confirmed that the top three challenges facing entrepreneurs are access to talent, excessive bureaucracy, and scarce early stage capital. Modelled on Isenberg's EE Framework, the World Economic Forum (2013) conducted a worldwide survey listing EE-related eight pillars and concluded that market access; resource availability, that is, finance; and human capital are the most important factors that drive growth of entrepreneurial ventures.

This study aims at applying and evaluating Isenberg's EE Framework (2010, 2011) against the context of EdTech entrepreneurial ecosystem in Bengaluru, the Startup Capital of India, to arrive at important factors that undermine the growth of EdTech startups. Instead of arriving at "new theory building," the scholars employ an exploratory, iterative process to unearth the influence of key components of the existing EE theory that has not been applied and evaluated in this context, that is, EdTech entrepreneurial ecosystem in Bengaluru, India. The scope of the study is limited to EdTech startups focused on mainstream education segment, that is, primary and secondary schools in Bengaluru, India.

Research Method

Research setting: According to the NASSOM 2019 report on Indian Tech Startup Ecosystem, Bengaluru, Delhi NCR, and Mumbai are home to over 55% of startups. The company Think & Learn that emerged in Bengaluru owns and operates India's largest EdTech platform, BYJU, which is the world's most valued EdTech startup and one of the five most valued startups in India.

Data collection: To gain a broad and in-depth understanding of the EdTech EE that focusses on primary and secondary schools in Bengaluru, the scholars engaged with a small sample of EdTech entrepreneurs, as well as various members of the education ecosystem. Over a period of 45 days, data was collected vide semi-structured interviews, using purposive and snowball sampling methods. The initial sample interviewed comprised of parents, students, teachers, administration, and institutional mentors of schools in Bengaluru. It was not possible to set up meetings with government bodies, accelerators, incubators, or angel investors. A total of 12 interviews were conducted, of which 6 semi-structured face-to-face interviews were conducted in Bengaluru and 3 interviews via Skype. For triangulation purposes, three more interviews were conducted, that is, higher education institutional mentor and two founders of EdTech startups firms operating in Mumbai and Delhi.

To begin with, the semi-structured interview questions were based on the scholar's prior understanding of Isenberg's (2010, 2011) Entrepreneurial Ecosystem Framework. Since the interviews were totally exploratory in nature, the discussion focused on two important dimensions:

(a) To understand stakeholders' (in the education ecosystem) experience relating to EdTech startup's offerings and transactions
(b) To elicit the current challenges facing the EdTech entrepreneurial ecosystem

Isenberg's framework comprising of accessible markets, availability of finance, conducive culture, quality human capital, progressive policy framework, and institutional support were used as triggers to drive the discussion forward.

The first three interviews helped in acquiring a broad understanding of EdTech offerings and how the education ecosystem works. Six interviews that followed were focused on key themes and sub-themes that emerged from the initial set of interviews. The first author conducted all the 12 interviews in English, and on completion of 9 interviews, a saturation point was reached. The last three interviews contributed towards triangulation as telephonic interviews were conducted with key stakeholders outside Bengaluru. This sample included an "higher education institutional mentor" and two founders of EdTech startups in Mumbai and Delhi. In addition to primary sources, secondary sources were also looked into, that is, government websites, industry updates and reports, news sources, policy documents, school website, and journal articles.

Data analysis: Following transcription of interview data, and in-depth study of interview transcripts, the scholars engaged in drawing meaning out of the lived experiences of various stakeholders. Using quotes, key words and phrases were identified (open coding). The scholars looked into surface level and latent coding to arrive at first-order categories, second-order themes and aggregate theoretical dimensions relevant to the research context. Tables 33.1, 33.2, and 33.3 provide an overview of the data analysis conducted using interview transcripts and coding.

Table 33.1 Data structure: supporting infrastructure and conducive culture

Sl. No.	First-order categories	Second-order themes	Aggregate theoretical dimensions
1	High cost of digital classroom and infrastructure		
	Access to the Internet and bandwidth	Digital infrastructure—access and cost; pricing pressure from schools	Supporting infrastructure: high cost; limited access to infrastructure
	Frequent power shutdowns		
	Minimal access to digital devices		
2	Schools carry a commercial intent, focused on enrolment, examination results	Schools focused on enrolment	
3	Parents not open to digital learning; prefer schools and after-school tuitions	Parents believe in traditional school format	
	Beliefs about traditional school format is strong		
	Parental pressure on students to get a quality job		
	Jobs demand conventional degrees		

(continued)

Table 33.1 (continued)

Sl. No.	First-order categories	Second-order themes	Aggregate theoretical dimensions
4	Schools not open to innovations/new practices, high resistance to change	Schools not open to risk, experimentation, new practices	Conducive culture: stakeholder mindset and beliefs not conducive to adopt EdTech; managing multiple stakeholder mindset and diverse objectives proves to be a challenge
	Schools doubt the sustainability of EdTech firms	Schools uncertain about sustainability of startup firms	
	Schools are exposed to limited use of technology		
5	Teachers not competent with using technology		
	Teaching practices slow to change; acquainted with one-size-fits-all approach		
	Teachers responsible for curriculum-centric teaching, curriculum cramming	Teachers driven by high work load, crammed curriculum, low belief in technology, lack of knowledge	
	Teacher resistance high due to workload		
	Teachers (belonging to an older generation) have a mindset issue with new innovations		
	Low teacher satisfaction with EdTech tools		
	Teachers have low belief in the power of technology		
6	Schools look for attractive board results		
	Schools test knowledge, not skills		
	School promotes rote learning, with no application		
	Peer pressure drives a marks-centric behavior	Students are 'marks centric'	

(*continued*)

Table 33.1 (continued)

Sl. No.	First-order categories	Second-order themes	Aggregate theoretical dimensions
	Indian education system does not promote creative thinking, problem-solving	Parent, schools, and EdTech drive "marks-centric behavior" with no focus on student learning outcomes	Conducive culture: stakeholders' entrenched belief system is not conducive for change; EdTech entrepreneur does not effect change
	Indian education system drives discipline, to the extent of killing creativity		
	Students are driven by fear to perform well in exams	Students driven by fear to perform well in exams; no love for learning	
	Schools focus on marks, not learning outcomes		
	EdTech is not bringing about a change—reinforces marks-driven culture		
	Parental thrust towards marks is high		
7	Price-sensitive market		
	Risk averse society, does not want to experiment		
	Contextual uncertainties such as war and epidemic that disrupt classroom education for a prolonged period may drive acceptance of EdTech due to strong education-centric mindset that prevails		
	Low tolerance for failure; failure is looked down upon	Social and cultural dimensions	Conducive culture: risk averse society, not willing to experiment and not open to new ideas, but with a strong education-centric mindset
	Societal pressure on engg. and medical career choices		
	Indian approach is focused on listening to adults (parents)		
	Multilingual and multicultural society and segments, whose needs vary		

Table 33.2   Data structure: funding

Sl. No.	First-order categories	Second-order themes	Aggregate theoretical dimensions
1	Long sales cycle, slow decision-making and adoption of EdTech in schools and universities		
	Low profitability, high customer acquisition costs, competition from free web sources		
	Market enthusiasm tempered, following Educomp bankruptcy	Huge, attractive market but not sellable and commercially viable	Access to finance: slow adoption of EdTech due to funding-related issues
	Payment issues failing to attract investments, funding issues in the seed stage		
	Business Model is not sustainable—adds value but not sellable		

Table 33.3   Data structure: entrepreneur approach and value addition

Sl. No.	First-order categories	Second-order themes	Aggregate theoretical dimensions
1	Tech. suppliers interaction with academicians is minimal		
	EdTech leading design and development not educationists		
	EdTech entrepreneurs do not understand how the school works	EdTech entrepreneurs score low on interaction and collaboration	Entrepreneur: lack of interaction with stakeholders in the ecosystem (no co-creation)
	Less collaboration, exchange of ideas among entrepreneurs in the ecosystem		
	Mentoring is transactional in nature		
2	EdTech startups have a poor business-related knowledge		
	Poor exit track record; lack ability to scale up		

(continued)

Table 33.3 (continued)

Sl. No.	First-order categories	Second-order themes	Aggregate theoretical dimensions
	Entrepreneurs are not goal/result oriented/fairly emotional		
	Legacy of failed EdTech firm haunting customer—Educomp filed for bankruptcy	Low credibility and lack of standardization on EdTech offerings	Entrepreneur: low credibility (lack of customer belief in entrepreneurial offering)
	Technology only an enabler; EdTech firms setting false expectations		
	Platform-based learning—lack of human touch		
	EdTech does not support in-depth learning		
	Lack of standardization across EdTech product offering		
	Lack of consistent quality across EdTech programs		
	Gradual drop in student engagement rate with e-learning		
3	Lack of performance data on student learning outcomes		
	Focused more on the teaching element, less on student learning	EdTech firms lack performance data on student learning outcomes	Entrepreneur: lack of value addition (does not meet customer's need)
	EdTech firms measure outcome based on teaching inputs and less on student learning and assessment outcomes		

Findings

The findings are based on the Isenberg Entrepreneurship Ecosystem Model (2010, 2011) that consists of over a dozen elements (consolidated into six domains) that dynamically interact in a unique, complex manner and facilitate entrepreneurial growth. This model is being applied to evaluate and explore the key factors affecting the growth of EdTech entrepreneurial

Table 33.4 Challenges facing Indian EdTech startups

Complexity in managing and fulfilling multiple stakeholder objectives (owner, principal, teacher, parent, and student)

↓

EdTech does not collaborate with these stakeholders and understand their need

↓

Similar to traditional system, EdTech drives the "marks-centric behavior" which has no impact on student learning outcomes

↓

EdTech product focus only on "teaching"; no focus on learning and evaluation (TLE) components

↓

Lacks performance data to prove enhanced student learning outcomes (overall not just marks)

↓

Lack of customer belief in the EdTech product offering, which scores low on credibility and standardization

↓

In addition, high cost of digital classrooms and infrastructure hampers EdTech adoption

↓

Schools, teachers, and parents resist change and have low belief in technology

↓

Slow adoption of EdTech in schools and universities

↓

Payment issues and low profitability affecting EdTech ecosystem

↓

Sector does not attract investor funding

↓

EdTech recognizes a huge market opportunity, but unable to realize it

---

ecosystem in Bengaluru. The context involves primary and secondary schools in Bengaluru, which are looking towards embracing educational technology. Using data drawn from interviews and further triangulation, data was analyzed, and causal relationships were drawn up (as indicated by arrows in Table 33.4) to acquire a holistic understanding of the challenges facing EdTech startups. Based on the findings, four propositions have been drawn up.

Following analysis of data, the scholars arrived at four important findings and related propositions, which are discussed in detail in the section that follows.

Finding 1

Managing multiple stakeholder mindset and diverse objectives is complex and challenging for the EdTech entrepreneur.

The education ecosystem comprises owners or founders of schools, principal and teaching staff, administrators, parents, and students. Most EdTech entrepreneurs interviewed and parents with an "education-centric mindset" stated that they are more comfortable with their wards attending the traditional brick and mortar schools and after school tuitions. Their only aim was to ensure that their children secure a job. Similar to parents, employers also look for students who have scored well in school leaving exams (along with their academic scores in degree programs, which is outside the scope of this study). The school administration has most of their efforts focused on impressive results at the board exam (due to its impact on student enrolment). In addition, the directors at schools are risk averse to new innovative solutions and are uncertain if EdTech solutions will eventually enhance student learning outcomes. "High costs" also act as an impediment for adoption of technology in the classroom. The educationists at school also revealed that their biggest fear is the sustained operations of EdTech startups that may encounter a sudden closure. The primary objective of the teacher is to fulfil the unrealistic expectations of the crammed curriculum. Students are pressured by schools, teachers, and parents to score high marks. Hence, the entrepreneurs face a huge complexity in managing the mindsets and objectives of multiple stakeholders in the education ecosystem. These contrasting objectives, mindset in the form of attitudes, and beliefs stand in the way of adoption of educational technology in schools. However, should contextual uncertainties such as war and pandemic (such as COVID-19) cause prolonged disruption of classroom education, such education-centric stakeholders may be quick to embrace educational technology (Livingston & Bucher, 2020).

Proposition 1 Growth of EdTech entrepreneurial firm is dependent upon changing the mindset and attitude of important stakeholders in the ecosystem, that is, students, parents, teachers, and school administration.

Finding 2
2a EdTech entrepreneur does not engage in co-creation, that is, does not collaborate with academia or other actors in the ecosystem.
2b EdTech entrepreneur drives the status quo and does not effect change; the entrepreneur continues to focus on reinforcing "marks-centric behavior."
2c EdTech startups do not offer a holistic solution; EdTech product offerings are not standardized across the industry.

First, according to one of the interviewees, "EdTech entrepreneurs do not know how the school works but they lead the design and development of EdTech products, with little or no engagement with stakeholders." One of the key characteristics of an ecosystem is interaction and mutual interdependence; however, interviewees reported that there was little interaction, knowledge sharing, or bouncing of ideas across actors in the ecosystem. As scholars observe and emphasize, opportunities are not pursued in isolation from their context. The benefits of collaboration are bringing together diverse actors resulting in knowledge expansion and possibility of arriving at innovative solutions (Agranoff, 2004) and solving a complex problem (Lovecek, Ristvej, Sventekova, Siser, & Velas, 2016). A growing body of literature is focusing on entrepreneurial opportunity construction process and various factors that influence this process. According to Dana (1995) context plays an important role in the construction process, with culture of the community influencing the entrepreneur's perception of the opportunity. When these opportunities carry a social dimension, there are important insights drawn on how the context and opportunity construction interact. Actors in the ecosystem co-evolve as they engage in opportunity construction process (Krueger & Brazeal, 1994) resulting in healthy entrepreneurial ecosystems.

Second, through their offerings, EdTech entrepreneurs continue to drive a "marks-centric behavior," a systemic problem that faces the Indian education system. Many interviewees were of the opinion that regulatory and examination boards continue to promote "rote learning and marks-centric behavior," through assessments that test knowledge (i.e., based on rote learning) rather than application of skills. The contextual environment including culture have an influence on entrepreneurs and their product offering. Hence, understanding entrepreneurial phenomena requires taking into account the environment and cultural context of entrepreneurial behavior. Culture can not only influence entrepreneurial activity but can also influence the type of entrepreneurial activities pursued (Dana, 1995). That which is "known" to be desirable and that which is "known" to be feasible can be influenced by local cultural and social norms (Björklund & Krueger, 2016)."

Third, EdTech products fail to address the three pillars on which education rests, that is, teaching, learning, and evaluation (TLE). EdTech offering is centered only on the teaching element and lacks performance data on student learning outcomes (not marks) resulting in an offering that does not address a key issue. According to one of the cofounders of an EdTech startup: "Education technology, or EdTech, is predominately an inputs focused business, with little attention to the output or end result from using all this technology." There is no standardization of courses offered by various EdTech firms. One of the interviewees stated that "startups should not just bring in the best technology to win customers but need to focus on delivering value to the customer i.e. better outcomes for students."

Proposition 2 Growth of EdTech entrepreneurial firm is dependent upon (a) entrepreneurs' interaction, collaboration with actors in the ecosystem, and understanding of customer needs, (b) entrepreneurs developing innovative value-added solutions that challenge the status quo and address current issues that affect the customer, and (c) entrepreneurs developing credible holistic solutions that improve student learning outcomes.

Finding 3
Actors in the education system are reluctant to adopt EdTech products due to (a) high investment costs involved for deploying digital classrooms, (b) limited and uncertain access to the Internet, poor bandwidth issues, and (c) frequent power shutdowns.

Access to infrastructure (telecoms, electricity) remains a relentless challenge for schools operating in many emerging economies, including India. High cost of digital classrooms and poor Internet access serve as an impediment for investment in educational technology solutions (Dutta, 2016).

Proposition 3 Growth of EdTech entrepreneurial firms is dependent upon educationists having access to low-cost digital infrastructure along with government and telecommunication operators addressing infrastructure-related issues and bottlenecks in India.

Finding 4
Payment issues and low profitability in the sector affect growth and sustainability of EdTech startup firms. EdTech recognizes a huge market opportunity in schools but is unable to realize it because sector does not attract investor funding.

Funds are required to grow and sustain such businesses, but cautious investors are seen to be treading very carefully. However, this situation may change and may attract investor funding, should contextual uncertainties such as war, pandemic like SARS, Ebola, COVID-19 and others cause prolonged disruption of classroom education. During the last few years, EdTech entrepreneurs have made an entry sensing the huge market opportunity that exists but have been unable to commercialize it and capture the intended value.

Proposition 4 The growth of EdTech entrepreneurial firms is dependent upon attracting investor funds in the school education segment.

Discussion and Insights

India has the largest population of school-going students, and though enrolment in schools is increasing, there exists a large learning deficit according to a survey conducted by NGO Pratham (n.d.). Structural problems such as inappropriate teacher-student ratio, poor quality of education, teacher absenteeism, teacher incompetence, lack of teaching resource, and poor quality of infrastructure are some of the challenges facing schools in most rural and some urban parts of India. The resolution to these pressing problems is adoption of digital technology-based approach in the classroom.

As indicated in Table 33.5, the study arrives at the following findings as key factors that hinder the growth of EdTech startup firms in Bengaluru, India:

Table 33.5 Important factors affecting growth of EdTech startups

Entrepreneurial ecosystem—domains affecting growth of EdTech entrepreneurial ecosystem	
Lack of conducive culture	Complexity in managing multiple stakeholder attitudes and diverse objectives (principal, administrator, school owners, teachers, students, parent, examination board)
	High resistance to change
	Entrenched belief in current practices: marks-centric behavior, rote learning, curriculum cramming, knowledge-based assessments
	Risk averse society, fear of failure, slow decision-making
	Not open to experimentation, creative solutions, new learning
	Price-sensitive culture
Lack of supporting infrastructure	High cost and limited access to digital infrastructure; minimal access to digital devices; frequent power shutdowns
Unable to access finance	Low profitability, payment issues, failing to attract investment—funding issues in the seed stage
Inadequacies in entrepreneurial approach and value addition	Low interaction with academia; not understanding how a school works
	Lack of collaboration with actors in the ecosystem
	Lack of credibility and standardization of courses
	Not challengers entrenched beliefs—aligning with marks centricity
	Lack of value addition—lack of performance-related data on student learning outcomes

(a) A lack of conducive culture, infrastructure support, and funding
(b) Inadequacies in entrepreneurial approach and lack of value addition in their product offering

Insights from the Study

This study and its findings lends itself to importance because Isenberg (2010, 2011) and later World Economic Forum (2013) through a survey it conducted reiterated that the most important elements in the Entrepreneurial Ecosystem Framework are: Access to Market, Access to Finance and Human Capital. In addition, Isenberg (2014a) also identified that the top three challenges facing entrepreneurs are "access to talent, excessive bureaucracy and scarce early stage capital."

Based on the study of EdTech entrepreneurial ecosystem in Bengaluru, this study identifies "lack of conducive culture, infrastructure support, and finance" as the most important elements that affect the growth of EdTech entrepreneurial startup firms. Isenberg's domains that are recognized as most important, do not include "conducive culture and infrastructure support," though it does include "access to finance" which is part of the study's findings. Though EdTech entrepreneurial firms have "access to market," it is not considered as important as "conducive culture, infrastructure support, and finance."

In addition to the above, the study identifies that other factors that hinder the growth for EdTech startups are inadequacies in entrepreneurial approach and lack of value addition in their product offering.

First, the study points out that under, "a lack of conducive culture," the key challenges facing the EdTech entrepreneur are (a) the complexity involved in managing the prevailing attitudes and diverse objectives of multiple stakeholders in the ecosystem; (b) high resistance to change from key stakeholders in the education ecosystem due to cost, time, sustainability related constraints and low belief in EdTech solutions; (c) stakeholder entrenchment in current practices—marks centricity, curriculum cramming, and knowledge-based assessments which are difficult to change; (d) risk aversion and fear of failing with the new technology-based approach; (e) not being open to creative learning solutions; and (f) price sensitivity and unwillingness to pay for quality solutions.

The study also identified that the second factor that affects the growth of EdTech startups is "inadequacies in entrepreneur's approach and product offering" which is detailed as (a) an entrepreneur's low level of interaction and collaboration with members of the ecosystem and failing to co-create with customers and (b) an entrepreneur's lack of value addition with innovative product offerings that challenge the status quo, that is, marks centricity.

The Organization for Economic Cooperation and Development (OECD) recognized that culture plays a significant role in the success of ecosystems (Boutillier, Carré, & Levratto, 2016). According to scholars, behavior is best predicted by intent (Armitage & Conner, 2001), and intent has its source from attitudes (Ajzen, 2001). Since entrepreneurial ecosystems (EE) are a community of interconnected forces that help in sustaining entrepreneurial activity (Stam, 2015), it is important for EdTech entrepreneurs to understand the intentions of actors in the ecosystem, interact and collaborate with them, and build trust that aids in information exchange, cooperation, and co-creation of offerings that add value to all actors. Such interaction among elements of the ecosystem result in sustainability (Sussan & Acs, 2017). Saxenian (2002) suggests that a culture of greater interdependence and exchange among individuals in the Silicon Valley region has contributed towards a superior innovative performance. He emphasizes that communication between individuals facilitates knowledge transfer among actors in the ecosystem.

Under the finding "lack of conducive culture," the study also identified a huge resistance to change posed by schools, teachers, and parents. The students, unlike parents, teachers, and school authorities, may welcome the change. But the important question to ask at this juncture is "Who drives this transformation or change in approach?" Is it top-down or bottom-up? Will a top-down approach bring in an effective change and eventually improve student learning outcomes? Should parents, teachers, and students not be consulted while bringing in a technology intervention in the classroom? Where in lies the role of the entrepreneur? How does the EdTech entrepreneur align these multiple stakeholders and convince them of a technology-enabled solution that enriches classroom experience and improves student learning outcomes? In order to bring in alignment, the attitudes and mindset of stakeholders must undergo a change, and they be able to see value in bringing technology to the classroom (Krueger & Brazeal, 2018). A growing body of academic literature does confirm that digital technology offers immense opportunity to improve learning processes (Audretsch et al., 2019). Scholarly studies also confirm that entrepreneurial culture is driven by the community's intention towards risk taking, supporting innovation (Audretsch, 2007), creativity, experimentation, and tolerance towards entrepreneurial mistakes and failure.

According to Isenberg (2013) the role of the entrepreneur is to bring to light that the conventional wisdom is wrong, that is, in this case "marks-centric behavior" prevalent among students, teachers, and parents. Entrepreneurial innovation is about affecting change and ensuring value creation for actors in the ecosystem. Similar to "conducive culture," supports such as "access to infrastructure" go a long way in supporting entrepreneurial ventures.

While EdTech focuses on enhancing and strengthening the teaching component with multiple pedagogies, it lacks performance data on student learning and evaluation outcomes. A move towards international partnerships in the development of offerings pertaining to evaluation of student outcomes will be preferred over developing the content from scratch. In addition, the sector faces "funding issues." Low profitability in the segment does not attract investors and funding organizations. However, once the scale improves, funding issues should be resolved.

The 2017 Horizon Report on Higher Education confirms that advancing progressive learning approaches need cultural transformation, that is, promote the exchange of fresh ideas, and collaboration being key for scaling effective solutions. The report also confirms that the focus of higher education should be on achieving lifelong learning outcomes for students, faculty, and staff.

Limitations of the Study

The research context is focused only on Bengaluru, the Startup Capital in India. Due to resource constraints, it was not possible to conduct face-to-face interviews in other parts of India. Nevertheless, as part of the triangulation process, telephone interviews were conducted with stakeholders in Mumbai and Delhi. Though stakeholders in the EdTech entrepreneurial ecosystem also constituted of angel investors, incubators, and accelerators, it was difficult to set up interviews with them. However, in order to ensure validity of the findings of the study, all key stakeholders were interviewed.

Principal Implications for Practice and Theory

From a practice perspective, the study lends insights on the key cultural, social, and behavioral characteristics of ecosystem actors and its resultant impact on the growth and sustainability of EdTech startups. It also throws light on some of the important shortcomings relating to EdTech product offering and lack of value addition thereof. The study is clearly indicative that the offerings from EdTech firms do not address the burning issues impacting the education sector. The study also highlights that EdTech entrepreneurs seem to be working in isolation and are leading the design and development of EdTech products, when in reality, they should be interacting and co-creating solutions with academia in primary and secondary schools. The most important stakeholders in the EdTech landscape are primary and secondary school administration, teachers, parents, and students, who need to be consulted while developing solutions.

One of the most important insights both for practitioners and scholars is that though a huge market opportunity exists, and entrepreneurs recognize that opportunity, there are huge roadblocks in the systematic construction and realization of that opportunity. The impediments are not tangible, but intangible in nature with strong social and cultural connotations, that is, customer attitudes, behavior, and mindset, which make opportunity realization a challenge. However, should contextual uncertainties such as war, natural calamities, or pandemic such as COVID-19 cause prolonged disruption of classroom education, the stakeholders with an "education-centric mindset" will be quick to embrace educational technology solutions (Adnan & Anwar, 2020).

From a theoretical perspective, the findings are important because the study here reveals that though market opportunity exists for the entrepreneur, conducive culture, that is, customer mindset and behavior, and supports, that is, access to infrastructure, serve as key impediments in opportunity realization. The current findings also imply that in different contexts, the relative importance of the various tenets of Isenberg framework (2010) may vary.

Directions for Future Research

Since this is an exploratory study, the findings will have to be empirically tested using a larger sample data, providing avenues for further research in this area. Secondly, there is also wide variation in the attitudes and adoption of EdTech in B2B and B2C sectors. Scholars can take this forward by understanding why such wide variation exists. Third, change must happen for the widespread adoption of EdTech. Who should really drive this change forward? Is this the regulatory authority or the most important actors in the ecosystem, that is, teachers and students? Should the source of change be top-down or bottom-up?

Conclusion

Isenberg (2010), one of the pioneering practitioners of Entrepreneurial Ecosystem (EE) Framework, unpacked six interactive domains of EE Framework, that is, accessible markets, availability of finance, conducive culture, quality human capital, progressive policy framework, and supporting infrastructure, that facilitate and drive entrepreneurial growth. Later in 2011, he claimed that out of the six domains, "accessible markets, availability of finance, and quality human capital" are the most important. The principal aim of the current study was to apply and evaluate the extant theory on EE Framework (Isenberg, 2010, 2011) to the EdTech contextual environment in Bengaluru, India, and bring to light the most important factors affecting the success of startup firms in the EdTech entrepreneurial ecosystem.

Out of the six domains listed under Isenberg's framework, the study revealed that the most important domains affecting the growth of EdTech entrepreneurs are "lack of conducive culture, supporting infrastructure, and availability of finance." The key "culture" related challenges that hinder growth for EdTech Startup firms are: complexity involved in managing the attitudes and diverse objectives of multiple stakeholders, stakeholder resistance to change and entrenchment in current beliefs and practices, fear of failing, and not being open to creative learning solutions. In addition to "culture," "access to quality supporting infrastructure," that is, access to the Internet and frequent power shutdowns, posed a serious challenge. Similar to previous studies conducted by Isenberg (2011), this study also revealed that "access to finance" is an important factor affecting the growth of startups.

The pertinence of this study is reflected via two important dimensions, that is, Isenberg's claim that "access to market, availability of human capital, and finance" are not necessarily the most important domains driving entrepreneurial growth across all sectors. In the EdTech context, the study highlights that though a huge market opportunity exists, it is "lack of conducive culture, supporting infrastructure, and funding" that stand in the way of growth. As a result, we can conclude that the important EE domains driving entrepreneurial success may vary, depending on the context and sectors where it is applied. Secondly, in addition to the above, another key finding that stands in the way of growth, which is outside the scope of Isenberg EE Framework, is "inadequacies relating to EdTech entrepreneurial approach and value addition to the customer." While entrepreneurial innovation is about affecting change and ensuring value creation for actors in the ecosystem, it came to light that most EdTech entrepreneurs failed to interact, collaborate, co-create, challenge the status quo, and offer value-added solutions to customers, that is, the school ecosystem. The "entrepreneur" remains an integral part of the ecosystem, and the quality of action, interaction, and entrepreneur value addition influences the decision-making process of key stakeholders who are responsible for facilitating innovative learning outcomes.

References

Acemoglu, D., Johnson, S., & Robinson, J. A. (2005). Institutions as a Fundamental Cause of Long-Run Growth. *Handbook of Economic Growth, 1*, 385–472.

Acs, Z. J., Estrin, S., Mickiewicz, T., & Szerb, L. (2014). The continued search for the solow residual: the role of national entrepreneurial ecosystem.

Adnan, M., & Anwar, K. (2020). Online Learning amid the COVID-19 Pandemic: Students' Perspectives. *Online Submission, 2*(1), 45–51.

Adner, R., & Kapoor, R. (2010). Value Creation in Innovation Ecosystems: How the Structure of Technological Interdependence Affects Firm Performance in New Technology Generations. *Strategic Management Journal, 31*(3), 306–333.

Agranoff, R. (2004). *Collaborative public management: New strategies for local governments*. Georgetown University Press.

Agranoff, R., & McGuire, M. (2001). Big Questions in Public Network Management Research. *Journal of Public Administration Research and Theory, 11*(3), 295–326.

Aldrich, H. E. (1990). Using an ecological perspective to study organizational founding rates. *Entrepreneurship Theory and practice, 14*(3), 7–24.

Ajzen, I. (2001). Nature and Operation of Attitudes. *Annual Review of Psychology, 52*(1), 27–58. https://doi.org/10.1146/annurev.psych.52.1.27

Armitage, C. J., & Conner, M. (2001). Efficacy of the Theory of Planned Behaviour: A Meta-Analytic Review. *British Journal of Social Psychology, 40*(4), 471–499.

Audretsch, D. B. (2007). *The Entrepreneurial Society*. New York, NY: Oxford University Press.

Audretsch, D. B., Cunningham, J. A., Kuratko, D. F., Lehmann, E. E., & Menter, M. (2019). Entrepreneurial Ecosystems: Economic, Technological, and Societal Impacts. *The Journal of Technology Transfer, 44*(2), 313–325.

Autio, E., Kenney, M., Mustar, P., Siegel, D., & Wright, M. (2014). Entrepreneurial Innovation: The Importance of Context. *Research Policy, 43*(7), 1097–1108.

Björklund, T. A., & Krueger, N. F. (2016). Generating Resources Through Co-evolution of Entrepreneurs and Ecosystems. *Journal of Enterprising Communities: People and Places in the Global Economy, 10*(4), 477–498.

Borissenko, Y., & Boschma, R. (2016). *A critical review of entrepreneurial ecosystems: towards a future research agenda*, No 1630. Section of Economic Geography: Utrecht University.

Bouncken, R. B., Laudien, S. M., Fredrich, V., & Görmar, L. (2018). Coopetition in Coworking-Spaces: Value Creation and Appropriation Tensions in an Entrepreneurial Space. *Review of Managerial Science, 12*(2), 385–410.

Boutillier, S., Carré, D., & Levratto, N. (2016). Reputed Authors in the Field of Territorial Economics. *Entrepreneurial Ecosystems, 2*, 1–41.

Brown, R., & Mason, C. (2017). Looking Inside the Spiky Bits: A Critical Review and Conceptualisation of Entrepreneurial Ecosystems. *Small Business Economics, 49*(1), 11–30.

Cohen, B. (2006). Sustainable Valley Entrepreneurial Ecosystems. *Business Strategy and the Environment, 15*(1), 1–14.

Dana, L. P. (1995). Entrepreneurship in a Remote Sub-Arctic Community. *Entrepreneurship Theory and Practice, 20*(1), 57–72.

Dutta, I. (2016). Open Educational Resources (OER): Opportunities and Challenges for Indian Higher Education. *Turkish Online Journal of Distance Education, 17*(2), 110–121.

Elia, G., Margherita, A., & Passiante, G. (2020). Digital Entrepreneurship Ecosystem: How Digital Technologies and Collective Intelligence Are Reshaping the Entrepreneurial Process. *Technological Forecasting and Social Change, 150*, 119791.

IIndian Brand Equity Foundation. (2019). EDUCATION AND TRAINING. https://www.ibef.org/download/education-and-training-apr-2019.pdf

Isenberg, D. J. (2010). THE BIG IDEA How to Start an Entrepreneurial Revolution. *Harvard Business Review, 88*(6), 40–41.

Isenberg, D. (2011). *The entrepreneurship ecosystem strategy as a new paradigm for economy policy: principles for cultivating entrepreneurship.* Babson entrepreneurship ecosystem project, Babson college, Babson Park: MA.

Isenberg, D. (2013). *Worthless, Impossible and Stupid: How Contrarian Entrepreneurs Create and Capture Extraor-dinary Value.* Watertown, MA: Harvard Business Review Press.

Isenberg, D. (2014a). What an Entrepreneurship Ecosystem Actually Is. *Harvard Business Review, 5*, 1–7.

Isenberg, D. (2014b, October 1). Don't Judge the Economy by the Number of Start-Ups. *Harvard Business Review.*

Isenberg, D. J. (2016). Applying the Ecosystem Metaphor to Entrepreneurship: Uses and Abuses. *The Antitrust Bulletin, 61*(4), 564–573.

Krueger, N. F., & Brazeal, D. V. (1994). Entrepreneurial Potential & Potential Entrepreneurs. *Entrepreneurship Theory & Practice, 18*(3), 91–105.

Krueger, N. F., & Brazeal, D. V. (2018). Entrepreneurial Potential and Potential Entrepreneurs. *REGEPE – Revista de Empreendedorismo e Gestão de Pequenas Empresas, 7*(3), 85–109.

Lamine, W., Mian, S., Fayolle, A., Wright, M., Klofsten, M., & Etzkowitz, H. (2018). Technology Business Incubation Mechanisms and Sustainable Regional Development. *The Journal of Technology Transfer, 43*(5), 1121–1141.

Livingston, E., & Bucher, K. (2020). Coronavirus Disease 2019 (COVID-19) in Italy. *Jama, 323*(14), 1335–1335.

Lovecek, T., Ristvej, J., Sventekova, E., Siser, A., & Velas, A. (2016). Currently Required Competencies of Crisis and Security Managers and New Tool for Their Acquirement. In *3rd International Conference on Management Innovation and Business Innovation (ICMIBI 2016)* (pp. 3–8).

Mason, C., & Brown, R. (2014). Entrepreneurial ecosystems and growth oriented entrepreneurship. *Final report to OECD, Paris, 30*(1), 77–102.

Motoyama, Y., & Knowlton, K. (2017). Examining the Connections Within the Startup Ecosystem: A Case Study of St. Louis. *Entrepreneurship Research Journal, 7*(1).

NGO Pratham. (n.d.). The Annual Status of Education Report (ASER) for 2018.

Prahalad, C. K. (2005). *Learning to lead. Vikalpa, 30*(2), 1–10.

Saxenian, A. (2002). Silicon Valley's New Immigrant High-Growth Entrepreneurs. *Economic Development Quarterly, 16*(1), 20–31.

Spigel, B. (2017). The Relational Organization of Entrepreneurial Ecosystems. *Entrepreneurship Theory and Practice, 41*(1), 49–72.

Spigel, B., & Harrison, R. (2018). Toward a Process Theory of Entrepreneurial Ecosystems. *Strategic Entrepreneurship Journal, 12*(1), 151–168.

Stam, E. (2015). Entrepreneurial Ecosystems and Regional Policy: A Sympathetic Critique. *European Planning Studies, 23*(9), 1759–1769.

Sussan, F., & Acs, Z. J. (2017). The Digital Entrepreneurial Ecosystem. *Small Business Economics, 49*(1), 55–73.

Van de Ven, A. H. (1993). A Community Perspective on the Emergence of Innovations. *Journal of Engineering and Technology Management, 10*(1–2), 23–51.

World Economic Forum. (2013). *Entrepreneurial Ecosystems Around the Globe and Company Growth Dynamics* (Report Summary for the Annual Meeting of the New Champions 2013).

34

Frugal Innovation: A Developmental Implications Perspective

Daniel Etse, Adela McMurray, and Nuttawuth Muenjohn

Introduction

Frugal innovation's value propositions of economic inclusion and substantial affordability (Meagher, 2018; Weyrauch & Herstatt, 2016) are not only relevant in socio-economic sense but also in terms of ethics and social responsibility. Addressing the unmet needs of over 4 billion people around the globe (Angot & Plé, 2015; Prabhu, 2017) does not only create enormous commercial and business opportunities but brings basic needs such as food, water, healthcare, and energy within the reach of poor customers who hitherto could not access these basic needs due to issues of affordability (Prabhu, 2017). Frugal innovation can be defined as the (re)designing of goods, services, business models, or systems to substantially minimise total cost of ownership without sacrificing user value, so as to provide affordable solutions for low-income and cost-sensitive customers (Knorringa, Peša, Leliveld, & van Beers, 2016). It has been hailed as a potentially disruptive innovation which can bring about more inclusive development (Knorringa et al., 2016; Meagher, 2018). A number of frugal innovation solutions are meeting various societal needs in a dramatic way; examples include the MAC 400 handheld ECG machine which has made related services substantially affordable and

D. Etse (✉) • N. Muenjohn
School of Management, RMIT University, Melbourne, VIC, Australia
e-mail: daniel.etse@rmit.edu.au; nuttawuth.muenjohn@rmit.edu.au

accessible to the poor (Rao, 2013); Tata Swach water purifier, which has made safe drinking water accessible to many Indians (Tiwari & Herstatt, 2012a); and the Jaipur Foot, a lower limb prosthetics which has helped in restoring mobility to thousands of physically challenged people the world over (Basu, Banerjee, & Sweeny, 2013).

Frugal innovations' primary markets are the developing countries in Africa, Asia, and Latin America, where the level of socio-economic development is generally low and constraints such as poor infrastructure, ineffective institutions, and weak governance systems are acute and prevalent (Knorringa et al., 2016; Prabhu, 2017). Though frugal innovations have brought goods, services, and other solutions within the reach of poor customers in developing countries, by providing cheap and substantially affordable alternatives (Basu et al., 2013; Kahle, Dubiel, Ernst, & Prabhu, 2013), it remains unclear the extent to which these frugal options address the fundamental developmental needs of these countries. Acute poverty is the main reason why many people in developing countries are unable to access basic needs, as many of these people live on less than $2 a day (The World Bank, 2019), and the pervasive poverty in these countries is mainly due to their poor state of economic and social development (Ayala-carcedo & González-Barros, 2005; Mountjoy, 2017). Thus an effective approach to addressing the affordability challenges in the developing countries might require the provision of solutions that address the economic and social underdevelopment.

While the developmental relevance of frugal innovation remains unclear, related studies remain scarce (Knorringa et al., 2016; Leliveld & Knorringa, 2018), prompting calls from a number of researchers including Leliveld and Knorringa (2018) and Rosca, Reedy, and Bendul (2018) for the need of more research into developmental issues of frugal innovation. Understanding the frugal innovation and development nexus will not only enhance the validity of relevant theories but may as well facilitate improved practical decisions relative to the choice of frugal innovation solutions. The research reported in this paper is an effort towards addressing the aforementioned research scarcity and related clarity issues. It does this by exploring the developmental implications of frugal innovations. Specifically, this research explores the question:

What are the implications of frugal innovation for socio-economic development?

The above research question was investigated drawing on two case studies: the eRanger motorcycle ambulance and the Tata Swach water purifier, which are widely deployed frugal innovations for addressing pressing needs in the health (Hofman, Dzimadzi, Lungu, Ratsma, & Hussein, 2008; Howitt et al.,

A. McMurray
College of Business, Government and Law, Flinders University,
Adelaide, SA, Australia
e-mail: adela.mcmurray@flinders.edu.au

2012) and water (Ramdorai & Herstatt, 2015) sectors, respectively. The health and water sectors are of critical relevance to socio-economic development (Grey & Sadoff, 2006; WHO, 2008), as such insights into frugal innovation's salience in these sectors may provide relevant information for clarifying the research question under investigation.

Frugal Innovation

Frugal innovation appears to be the new kid on the innovation block. This is evident in the surge of researchers' as well as practitioners' interest in this emerging innovation concept (Hyypiä & Khan, 2018; Knorringa et al., 2016; Weyrauch & Herstatt, 2016). It is often defined as the (re)designing of goods, services, business models, and systems with the aim of substantially minimising resource utilisation and total cost of ownership so as to provide good enough and affordable solutions for resource-constrained customers (Leliveld & Knorringa, 2018; Rosca et al., 2018). Its key defining attributes include substantial cost reduction; affordability and accessibility; optimised performance level; and concentration on core functionalities (Basu et al., 2013; Weyrauch & Herstatt, 2016). Frugal innovations are providing solutions to address pressing needs in various sectors. For example, the eRanger, a motorcycle ambulance, facilitates a quick response to prehospital emergency cases, thereby minimising incidence of mortality and morbidity, especially in resource-constrained countries (Hofman et al., 2008; Howitt et al., 2012). The Jaipur Foot, a frugal prosthetics, has helped in restoring mobility to many physically disabled people (Basu et al., 2013), and the Tata Swach water purifier provides access to affordable and safe drinking water, thereby contributing to the reduction of water-borne diseases and related deaths (Ramdorai & Herstatt, 2015; Tiwari & Herstatt, 2012).

Though there is a growing recognition of frugal innovation's potential relevance for developed countries (Agarwal & Brem, 2017; Angot & Plé, 2015), it largely remains a phenomenon of developing countries (Hossain, 2018; Rosca, Arnold, & Bendul, 2017), where socio-economic development is low and affordability remains a major challenge (Leliveld & Knorringa, 2018; Prabhu, 2017). While the extant literature associates frugal innovations with a wide range of beneficial consequences (Albert, 2019), it remains unclear how the innovation directly addresses issues of underdevelopment such as weak infrastructure, low industrialisation, weak technological innovation, low productivity and export, limited access to capital, weak institutions, and poor governance. Understanding the developmental effects of frugal innovations may enhance the quality of relevant decisions and actions.

Frugal Innovation and Socio-Economic Development

In the context of this paper, socio-economic development refers to sustained improvement in the economic and social well-being of a society which manifests in outcomes such as enhanced healthcare, education, income distribution, consumption, welfare, poverty reduction, and environmental well-being (Szirmai, 2015). Weak socio-economic development is a characteristic attribute of developing countries, the primary market of frugal innovation solutions (Prabhu, 2017). Among the major drivers of underdevelopment of these countries are poor infrastructure, low productivity, low industrialisation, weak technological innovation, weak institutions, and poor governance (Myint & Krueger, 2016; Ogun, 2010).

Frugal innovation's relevance appears particularly pronounced in contexts where socio-economic development is low (Meagher, 2018; Prabhu, 2017). This might be because the former makes available affordable solutions to address needs which hitherto remained unmet. While frugal innovations are being deployed to address a wide range of socio-economic needs, it appears the driving motivation has mainly been affordability of the solutions, and little consideration has been given to related developmental implications (Leliveld & Knorringa, 2018; McMurray, Weerakoon, & Etse, 2019). It will be interesting to investigate the extent to which frugal innovations address developmental challenges.

Frugal Innovation and Healthcare

The eRanger, one of the case studies in this research, is a frugal innovation used in the health sector. The health sector was chosen as one of the focus areas of this study because of its critical salience to socio-economic development (Szirmai, 2015; WHO, 2008) and because it is one of the main sectors where frugal innovations are being deployed (Bhatti et al., 2017; Tran & Ravaud, 2016).

Unavailability of health facilities, technologies, and other relevant resources in low-income countries (Howitt et al., 2012)and the escalating healthcare costs in high-income countries (Bhatti et al., 2017) make the need for affordable and accessible alternatives imperative. Frugal innovations have emerged as viable and effective solutions for addressing unmet healthcare needs across the globe (Bhatti et al., 2017; Howitt et al., 2012). These innovations range from simple practices such as the use of mobile phone SMS to identify counterfeit drugs, to high-tech devices such as General Electric's MAC i ECG machine (Tran & Ravaud, 2016). Though frugal innovations facilitate improved healthcare services through the provision of affordable technologies, there might be the need to recognise the multidimensional nature of healthcare delivery, so as to ensure a multidisciplinary approach towards addressing relevant issues effectively and efficiently (Howitt et al., 2012).

Frugal Innovation and Water Supply

Tata Swach, the second case study of this research, is a frugal innovation used in the water sector. The latter's choice was motivated by the critical relevance of water to life's sustenance, and socio-economic development (Grey & Sadoff, 2006; Khan & Malik, 2019), and the fact that it is a sector where some of the well-known frugal innovations have been deployed (Ramdorai & Herstatt, 2015; Tiwari & Herstatt, 2012).

Access to safe drinking water and sanitation is a human right (United Nations, 2016), yet more than 4 billion of the world's population experience scarcity of this basic need in one form or another, and more than half a billion people in developing countries experience all-year round water scarcity (Hyvärinen, Keskinen, & Varis, 2016; Khan & Malik, 2019). With lack of access to safe water comes attendant sanitation and infection challenges which negatively affect the health of around 1.7 billion people and claim the lives of about 525,000 children annually (Pooi & Ng, 2018). Governments and state actors in water-stressed countries appear to be failing in their responsibility to provide this basic amenity, and as a result market participation in the water sector has been on the increase (Annala, Sarin, & Green, 2018). With the increase in private sector participation comes the issue of affordability and the exclusion of many people from accessing this basic need for survival (Annala et al., 2018; Hyvärinen et al., 2016).

Frugal innovation has emerged as a key approach to mitigating the challenge of potable water scarcity and affordability, and many of these frugal solutions come in the form of household water purifiers (Annala et al., 2018; Hyvärinen et al., 2016). While frugal innovations have made safe water accessible to many, governments' failure to improve water infrastructure and the lack of effective regulation of private participation in the sector appear to have negative consequences for the availability, accessibility, affordability, and safety of water (Annala et al., 2018; Hyvärinen et al., 2016). The next subsections provide an overview of the two case studies.

eRanger Motorcycle Ambulance

The eRanger is an innovative motorcycle ambulance designed and produced by the eRanger Production Company Ltd. to meet the need for medical transport in Africa, especially the rural areas. It consists of a motorbike and a stretcher sidecar. Medical transportation is a desperate need in resource-poor countries where medical facilities are often scarce and hard to reach and where access to public or private transport are often unavailable. Due to affordability challenges many health facilities lack access to ambulances. Moreover, because of poor or non-existent transportation infrastructure, standard ambulances are unable to reach many communities, especially the rural areas.

The eRanger is a frugal solution that addresses the issues of affordability and poor transportation infrastructure, as it is substantially affordable to acquire and maintain and at the same time able to navigate the rugged and deplorable roads. It has been deployed in more than 20 countries including Malawi, Kenya, South Sudan, Sierra Leone, Liberia, and Afghanistan, where it has facilitated quick response to health emergency cases and contributed to substantial reduction in mortality and morbidity, especially in maternal healthcare (eRanger, 2019; Hofman et al., 2008; Howitt et al., 2012) (Fig. 34.1).

Tata Swach Water Purifier

The Tata Swach is a point-of-use water purification device introduced in 2009 by Tata Chemicals Ltd. with the aim of addressing India's need for affordable safe drinking water. In India, 76 million people lack access to safe drinking water, and this exposes them to the risk of water-borne diseases and related deaths (The Economic Times, 2016). To address the unmet needs of potable water and reduce associated morbidity and mortality, Tata Chemical Ltd. in collaboration with other companies developed Tata Swach, a low-cost and user-friendly household water purifier.

The filtering component of the product consists of rice husk ash with coating of silver nano particles and is able to eliminate about 90% of contaminants within the water. The use of locally available and inexpensive materials contributes to substantial cost reduction. Tata Swach is believed to be the world's most inexpensive household water purifier, costing about $20 to acquire, and does not require running water or electricity to operate. Thus making it an appropriate product for addressing affordability issues and obviating the challenges of lack of basic utilities such as running water and electricity. The product continues to gain wide acceptance in India and other developing countries (Tata Swach website, 2017; Tiwari & Herstatt, 2014) (Fig. 34.2).

Fig. 34.1 eRanger ambulance. (Source: eRanger website, 2019)

Fig. 34.2 Tata Smart; an example of Tata Swach. (Source: Tata Swach website, 2017)

Methodology

The Design

Qualitative case study was the design employed in this study mainly because little is known about the phenomenon under investigation (Goffin, Åhlström, Bianchi, & Richtnér, 2019; Yin, 2013). This study investigates the socio-economic developmental implications of frugal innovation, a subject about which little is known, hence the appropriateness of qualitative case study approach. Two cases of frugal innovation, that is, eRanger Motorcycle Ambulance and Tata Swach, were purposively selected for in-depth analysis with the purpose of gaining insights into the phenomenon under investigation. Two main considerations informed the selection of the case studies: (1) the cases pertain to sectors (health and water which are of critical relevance to socio-economic development), and (2) the cases are deemed to have contributed significantly to addressing pressing needs in their respective sectors (Hofman et al., 2008; Howitt et al., 2012; Ramdorai & Herstatt, 2015).

Scholarly publications constitute the data of the study. This source of data was chosen with the view of consolidating scientific knowledge on the two case studies, so as to gain relevant insights to facilitate valid deductions. The systematic review approach was employed for data collection with the purpose of ensuring rigour and enhancing validity and reliability (Tranfield, Denyer, & Smart, 2003). The Google Scholar, a widely used web-based academic search engine which catalogues between 2 and 100 million records of both academic and grey literature (Haddaway, Collins, Coughlin, & Kirk, 2015), was the search tool used, as its coverage of scientific and scholarly literature appears more comprehensive than many other major multidisciplinary databases (Martín-Martín, Orduna-Malea, Thelwall, & Delgado López-Cózar, 2018).

Data Selection

The following inclusion and exclusion criteria were followed in the data collection process. For a publication to be included it has to satisfy two conditions: (1) its focus must be on the research objective; and (2) it must be in the English language. Publications were excluded if: (1) they were not in the English language; (2) they did not focus on the issues under investigation; and (3) they were duplicate versions of already selected publications.

The selection process entailed the following activities: the name of the case study was entered into the Google Scholar Advanced search 'with exact phrase' bar and a web search conducted; resultant publications not in the English language were excluded; abstracts and contents of the rest of the publications were examined to determine relevance and focus; publications found to be irrelevant or duplicate/redundant were excluded; and forward and backward linkage of literature was performed to identify other relevant publications. The selection process was replicated by an independent senior academic researcher for purposes of enhancing data integrity, validity, and reliability. The data selection process for the two case studies is summarised in Tables 34.1 and 34.2.

Table 34.1 outlines the process for selecting publications on eRanger motorcycle ambulance. The process yielded 23 relevant publications for the purpose of this study. The data selection process for Tata Swach is outlined in Table 34.2. The process yielded 41 relevant publications.

Table 34.1 Data selection process: eRanger

Activity undertaken	Outcome
1 The word 'eRanger' was entered in the 'exact phrase' bar of Google Scholar Advanced Search and a search conducted	284 initial hit obtained
2 Scanning the publications showed 145 items were not in the English language; these were excluded	139 publications remaining
3 122 of the publications mentioned the case study but did not focus on the issues under investigation; thus they were excluded	17 publications remaining
4 4 of the publications were duplicated; the duplicates were excluded	13 publications remaining
5 5 relevant publications were identified through forward and backward linkage	18 publications remaining

Table 34.2 Data selection process: Tata Swach

Activity undertaken	Outcome
1 The phrase 'Tata Swach' was entered in the 'exact phrase' bar of Google Scholar Advanced Search and a search conducted	243 initial hit obtained
2 Scanning the publications showed 14 items were not in the English language; these were excluded	229 publications remaining
3 180 of the publications mentioned the case study but did not focus on the issues under investigation; thus they were excluded	49 publications remaining
4 8 of the publications were duplicated; the duplicates were excluded	41 publications remaining

Data Analysis

Qualitative content analysis was the data analysis employed because the study's data is textual in nature (Krippendorff, 1989). The analysis followed Bengtsson's (2016) four-stage content analysis process of decontextualisation; recontextualisation; categorisation, and compilations. This process was adopted because of its clarity and systematic nature. The decontextualisation stage entailed reading through the texts to get familiarised with contents and focus. Portions of the texts that contained information of interest were identified and highlighted. The identified relevant information were coded. Texts that did not address the study's aims were excluded from further analysis. At the recontextualisation stage, critical reading of the documents was done a second time to check if any important information was omitted during the first reading. This reading was done alongside the captured information from the initial reading. The categorisation stage entailed merging codes that represented the same ideas into well-defined themes that accurately captured relevant information. This was done to condense the data into manageable units without losing relevant contents. At the compilation stage, the key findings were summarised into frequency tables to facilitate easy identification of key variables. The analysis results are presented in Tables 34.3, 34.4, 34.5, and 34.6 as follows.

Table 34.3 outlines the socio-economic needs that the eRanger motorcycle ambulance was designed to address. The frequency shows the number of publications that mentioned a given socio-economic need. As shown in the table, the need that most of the publications highlighted is poor transportation infrastructure. The solutions provided by the eRanger, as captured by the publications, are outlined in Table 34.4. The frequency indicates the number of publications that mentioned a given solution. As shown in the table, the most mentioned solution is the provision of affordable ambulance.

From the socio-economic needs outlined in Table 34.3, and the frugal innovation solutions provided shown in Table 34.4, we make the following inferences:

Table 34.3 The eRanger ambulance: the socio-economic needs

The needs specified in the publications		Frequency
1	Poor transportation infrastructure	15
2	Financial constraints	8
3	Poor access to health facilities	6
4	Lack of affordable means of transport	6
5	Traffic congestion	2

Table 34.4 Solutions provided by the eRanger ambulance

Solutions provided by frugal innovation	Frequency
1 Provision of affordable ambulance	13
2 Provision of means of transport suitable for poor transportation infrastructure	7
3 Facilitation of fast response to prehospital emergency cases	4
4 Enhancement of emergency healthcare	12
5 Facilitation of community participation in emergency healthcare delivery	5
6 Facilitation of NGOs and international agencies' support for emergency health delivery	5
7 Facilitation of a more efficient use of car ambulances	2

Table 34.5 The Tata Swach: the socio-economic needs

The needs specified in the publications	Frequency
1 Lack of access to potable water	41
2 Lack of water supply infrastructure	20
3 Lack of electricity	16
4 Lack of proper sanitation system	7
5 Financial constraints	4
6 Poor quality of water supplied	3
7 Poor maintenance of existing water supply infrastructure	1

Table 34.6 Solutions provided by the Tata Swach

Solutions provided by frugal innovation	Frequency
1 Facilitates access to affordable potable water	42
2 Reduces the incidence of water-borne diseases and related deaths	25

1. *The frugal innovation provides a solution to the resource constraints/poverty needs by making available an affordable alternative of ambulance.*
2. *The frugal innovation solution facilitates improvement in healthcare delivery.*

However, the frugal innovation is unable to do the following:

1. *Address/rectify the poor condition of the transportation infrastructure.*
2. *Address/rectify the traffic congestion situation.*
3. *Address the situation of inadequacy of health facilities.*

The findings relative to the Tata Swach are presented in Tables 34.5 and 34.6.

Table 34.5 outlines the socio-economic needs that Tata Swach was designed to address. Lack of access to potable water is the most mentioned need by the publications, as indicated by the frequency values. Table 34.6 outlines the solutions provided by Tata Swach to the identified needs highlighted in Table 34.5. Majority of the publications identified Tata Swach's role in facilitating access to affordable potable water.

From the socio-economic needs outlined in Table 34.5, and the frugal innovation solutions shown in Table 34.6, the following inferences are deduced:

1. *The frugal innovation provides a solution to the resource constraints/poverty needs by making available an affordable household water purifying device.*
2. *The frugal innovation facilitates access to potable water.*
3. *The frugal innovation contributes to the reduction in the incidence of water-borne diseases and related deaths.*

However the frugal innovation solution is unable to do the following:

1. *Address the prevalent poor state of water supply infrastructure.*
2. *Rectify the poor sanitation infrastructure.*
3. *Address the unavailability of electricity.*

Summary of Findings

The research findings relate to three broad issues: (1) the socio-economic needs that frugal innovations are deployed to address; (2) the needs that the innovation is able to meet; and (3) the needs that the innovation is unable to meet. Frugal innovations are deployed to address numerous socio-economic needs including lack of access to basic goods and services; poor infrastructure; and acute resource constraints, as shown in Tables 34.3 and 34.5.

In terms of the needs addressed, the findings suggest that frugal innovation makes available affordable alternatives of goods, services, and other solutions to address unmet needs, as shown in Tables 34.4 and 34.6. With respect to the needs that frugal innovations are unable to address, it was found that the main socio-economic development challenges such as poor infrastructure and lack of basic public amenities remained unaddressed. These findings are discussed in the next section.

Discussion

The question this study sought to answer is: *What are the implications of frugal innovation for socio-economic development?* The findings suggest that while frugal innovation is able to provide affordable solutions to address hitherto unmet needs, it appears incapable of addressing the core socio-economic developmental issues, including poor infrastructural development and unavailability of basic public amenities. To be clear, the aim of this chapter was to highlight the developmental implications of using frugal innovations as a solution to systemic developmental challenges. It is by no means suggesting that the case studies examined were purposely designed for addressing the highlighted infrastructural challenges.

The findings regarding frugal innovation's affordable solutions resonates with the extant literature which emphasises substantial affordability as one of the key defining attributes of frugal innovation (Basu et al., 2013; Weyrauch & Herstatt, 2016). Provision of affordable solutions was the most mentioned beneficial effect of frugal innovation in the two case studies, as shown in Tables 34.4 and 34.6. The eRanger motorcycle ambulance, for example, is said to be 19 times cheaper to purchase and 24 times cheaper to operate than a car ambulance (Hofman et al., 2008), and the Tata Swach has been described as the most inexpensive household water purifier in the world (Tiwari & Herstatt, 2014). This underscores the importance which frugal innovation consumers attach to affordability and the centrality of resource constraints/poverty in related decisions. Through their affordable alternatives, frugal innovations make substantial contributions to the enhancement of the socio-economic well-being of poor customers, by helping address basic needs that hitherto remained unmet. The solutions provided, however, appear incapable of addressing the core developmental challenges that give rise to the situations of poverty, acute resource scarcity, and affordability challenges that characterise frugal innovation customers/consumers. As such, these solutions may be more appropriate as temporary/stop gap measures, rather than substantive or long-term solutions to the challenges of socio-economic underdevelopment.

The findings regarding frugal innovations' limitations in terms of socio-economic development indicate that the innovation is incapable or inadequate for addressing the underlying issues of underdevelopment. Frugal innovations provide means for going round or circumventing the underlying socio-economic developmental challenges such as poor infrastructural development, unavailability of basic public amenities, and endemic poverty. For example, the eRanger ambulance provided a means for negotiating poor and deplorable road infrastructure, and the Tata Swach provided a means for circumventing the challenge of unavailability of running water and poor electricity infrastructure. Though the frugal innovations provide ingenious means of going round serious developmental challenges, the challenges remain and may become worse with the passage of time. For example, finding a means of navigating deplorable road networks, as in the case of the eRanger, does not take away the substantive problem of poor transportation infrastructure, and if the situation remains unaddressed, it may worsen over time. In the same way, though Tata Swach provides a means for purifying unwholesome water, the main challenge which is poor water supply and related infrastructural deficiencies does not go away and if left unaddressed may worsen to the point that no water might even be available in the near future for purifiers to treat. Poor infrastructural development is one of the key underlying reasons for socio-economic underdevelopment and low industrialisation (Chester, 2019; Myint & Krueger, 2016), and the failure to effectively tackle this fundamental challenge may continue to pose unsurmountable hindrance to the development efforts of underdeveloped or developing countries. Solutions that circumvent the infrastructural difficulties may be appropriate as short-term and temporary measures; however, the substantive and more effective solution lies in the provision and enhancement of these critical infrastructures.

In summary, frugal innovation's implications for socio-economic development are twofold: (1) it has the potential of enhancing living conditions at the micro-level (i.e. the level of individual consumers and customers, and may be a useful stop gap measure for managing socio-economic development challenges, and (2) it is inadequate as a substantive or permanent measure for addressing the underlying conditions of socio-economic underdevelopment. There might therefore be the need to recognise the capacity and limitations of frugal innovations relative to socio-economic development, so as to facilitate appropriate decision-making and relevant policy formulation.

Conclusion

This study sought to gain insights into the socio-economic developmental implications of frugal innovation, with the aim of providing enhanced understanding regarding the nexus between frugal innovation and development. The findings suggest that while frugal innovation enhances the socio-economic conditions of its customers/consumers, it is inadequate for addressing the underlying and fundamental factors of underdevelopment. This finding has significant implications for theory and practice.

Theory-wise, the findings of this study suggest that frugal innovation's relevance for development is more nuanced: it facilitates the realisation of certain very important development outcomes, and at the same time it is inadequate and limited when it comes to some other developmental needs. Frugal innovation is not as unfavourable to development as some scholars including Dolan (2013) and Meagher (2018) perceive it to be, and at the same time it is not as favourable as others, including Radjou and Prabhu (2014), Kahle et al. (2013), and Prabhu (2017), regard it to be; but rather, it is a mixed bag of positive developmental implications as well as limitations. An example from one of the case studies may clarify this point. The Tata Swach facilitates access to affordable potable water to a large number of households in water-stressed communities, and without it, the alternative might be the drinking of polluted and microbe-infested water, with its attendant risks of fatal consequences. However, the solution provided by Tata Swach does not address the fundamental challenge of poor water supply and related infrastructural needs. So, frugal innovation is capable of addressing certain critical developmental needs, but at the same time, it is incapable of addressing others. This holistic perspective will facilitate a more realistic theorisation and conceptualisation of frugal innovation's developmental relevance.

Relative to practice, this study may influence policies, decisions, and actions at various levels of society. By highlighting the developmental capabilities and limitations of frugal innovations, this study will guide governments and other relevant stakeholders with regard to the appropriateness or otherwise of frugal innovation as solutions to developmental challenges. Moreover, by clarifying the short-term and long-term developmental relevance of frugal innovation, this study may facilitate a more effective deployment of frugal innovations to address developmental needs. Furthermore, the findings may enhance relevant understanding of civil societies and other pressure groups, as well as the general citizenry, so that they can effectively hold governments and political leaders accountable, as well as help prevent the abuse of frugal innovation as a convenient approach to shirking developmental responsibilities.

This research focused on two case studies, the eRanger motorcycle ambulance and the Tata Swach water purifier, and future studies may investigate the developmental implications of other frugal innovations. Furthermore, the use of primary data to verify the insights obtained from the secondary data sources may provide further clarity on the developmental relevance of frugal innovations.

References

Agarwal, N., & Brem, A. (2017). Frugal Innovation – Past, Present, and Future. *IEEE Engineering Management Review, 45*(3), 37–41. https://doi.org/10.1109/EMR.2017.2734320

Albert, M. (2019). Sustainable Frugal Innovation – The Connection Between Frugal Innovation and Sustainability. *Journal of Cleaner Production, 237,* 117747. https://doi.org/10.1016/j.jclepro.2019.117747

Angot, J., & Plé, L. (2015). Serving Poor People in Rich Countries: The Bottom-of-the-Pyramid Business Model Solution. *Journal of Business Strategy, 35*(2), 3–15.

Annala, L., Sarin, A., & Green, J. L. (2018). Co-production of Frugal Innovation: Case of Low Cost Reverse Osmosis Water Filters in India. *Journal of Cleaner Production, 171,* S110–S118. https://doi.org/10.1016/j.jclepro.2016.07.065

Ayala-carcedo, F. J., & González-Barros, M. R. Y. (2005). Economic Underdevelopment and Sustainable Development in the World: Conditioning Factors, Problems and Opportunities. *Environment, Development and Sustainability, 7*(1), 95–115. https://doi.org/10.1007/s10668-003-4012-9

Basu, R., Banerjee, P., & Sweeny, E. (2013). Frugal Innovation: Core Competencies to Address Global Sustainability. *Journal of Management for Global Sustainability, 2,* 63–82.

Bengtsson, M. (2016). How to Plan and Perform a Qualitative Study Using Content Analysis. *Nursing Plus Open, 2,* 8–14. https://doi.org/10.1016/j.npls.2016.01.001

Bhatti, Y. A., Prime, M., Harris, M., Wadge, H., McQueen, J., Patel, H., et al. (2017). The Search for the Holy Grail: Frugal Innovation in Healthcare from Low-Income or Middle-Income Countries for Reverse Innovation to Developed Countries. *BMJ Innovations, 3*(4), 212–220. https://doi.org/10.1136/bmjinnov-2016-000186

Chester, M. V. (2019). Sustainability and Infrastructure Challenges. *Nature Sustainability, 2*(4), 265–266. https://doi.org/10.1038/s41893-019-0272-8

Dolan, C. (2013). Capital's New Frontier: From 'Unusable' Economies to Bottom of the Pyramid Markets in Africa. *African Studies Review, 56*(3), 123–146.

eRanger. (2019). Case Studies. Retrieved February 14, 2020, from https://www.eranger.com/case-studies

Goffin, K., Åhlström, P., Bianchi, M., & Richtnér, A. (2019). State-of-the-Art: The Quality of Case Study Research in Innovation Management. *Journal of Product Innovation Management.* https://doi.org/10.1111/jpim.12492

Grey, D., & Sadoff, C. W. (2006). Water for Growth and Development. In *Thematic Documents of the IV World Water Forum.* Mexico City: The World Bank.

Haddaway, N. R., Collins, A. M., Coughlin, D., & Kirk, S. (2015). The Role of Google Scholar in Evidence Reviews and Its Applicability to Grey Literature Searching. *PLoS One, 10*(9), e0138237. https://doi.org/10.1371/journal.pone.0138237

Hofman, J. J., Dzimadzi, C., Lungu, K., Ratsma, E. Y., & Hussein, J. (2008). Motorcycle Ambulances for Referral of Obstetric Emergencies in Rural Malawi: Do They Reduce Delay and What Do They Cost? *International Journal of Gynecology & Obstetrics, 102*(2), 191–197. https://doi.org/10.1016/j.ijgo.2008.04.001

Hossain, M. (2018). Frugal Innovation: A Review and Research Agenda. *Journal of Cleaner Production, 182*, 926–936. https://doi.org/10.1016/j.jclepro.2018.02.091

Howitt, P., Darzi, A., Yang, G.-Z., Ashrafian, H., Atun, R., Barlow, J., et al. (2012). Technologies for Global Health. *The Lancet, 380*(9840), 507–535. https://doi.org/10.1016/s0140-6736(12)61127-1

Hyvärinen, A., Keskinen, M., & Varis, O. (2016). Potential and Pitfalls of Frugal Innovation in the Water Sector: Insights from Tanzania to Global Value Chains. *Sustainability, 8*(9), 888. https://doi.org/10.3390/su8090888

Hyypiä, M., & Khan, R. (2018). Overcoming Barriers to Frugal Innovation: Emerging Opportunities for Finnish SMEs in Brazilian Markets. *Technology Innovation Management Review, 8*(4), 38–48.

Kahle, H., Dubiel, A., Ernst, H., & Prabhu, J. (2013). The Democratizing Effects of Frugal Innovation. *Journal of Indian Business Research, 5*(4), 220–234. https://doi.org/10.1108/jibr-01-2013-0008

Khan, S. T., & Malik, A. (2019). Engineered Nanomaterials for Water Decontamination and Purification: From Lab to Products. *Journal of Hazardous Materials, 363*, 295–308. https://doi.org/10.1016/j.jhazmat.2018.09.091

Knorringa, P., Peša, I., Leliveld, A., & van Beers, C. (2016). Frugal Innovation and Development: Aides or Adversaries? *The European Journal of Development Research, 28*(2), 143–153. https://doi.org/10.1057/ejdr.2016.3

Krippendorff, K. (1989). Content Analysis. In E. Barnouw, G. Gerbner, W. Schramm, T. Worth, & L. Gross (Eds.), *International Encyclopedia of Communication*. New York: Oxford University Press.

Leliveld, A., & Knorringa, P. (2018). Frugal Innovation and Development Research. *The European Journal of Development Research, 30*(1), 1–16. https://doi.org/10.1057/s41287-017-0121-4

Martín-Martín, A., Orduna-Malea, E., Thelwall, M., & Delgado López-Cózar, E. (2018). Google Scholar, Web of Science, and Scopus: A Systematic Comparison of Citations in 252 Subject Categories. *Journal of Informetrics, 12*(4), 1160–1177. https://doi.org/10.1016/j.joi.2018.09.002

McMurray, A., Weerakoon, C., & Etse, D. (2019). Exploring the Dark Side of Frugal Innovation. In A. McMurray & G. de Waal (Eds.), *Frugal Innovation: A Global Research Companion*. London: Routledge.

Meagher, K. (2018). Cannibalizing the Informal Economy: Frugal Innovation and Economic Inclusion in Africa. *The European Journal of Development Research, 30*(1), 17–33. https://doi.org/10.1057/s41287-017-0113-4

Mountjoy, A. (2017). *Industrialization and Underdeveloped Countries* (2nd ed.). New York: Routledge.

Myint, H., & Krueger, A. (2016). Economic Development. Retrieved January 25, 2020, from https://www.britannica.com/topic/economic-development

Ogun, T. (2010). *Infrastructure and Poverty Reduction*. Helsinki: World Institute for Development Economics Research.

Pooi, C. K., & Ng, H. Y. (2018). Review of Low-Cost Point-of-Use Water Treatment Systems for Developing Communities. *npj Clean Water, 1*(1). https://doi.org/10.1038/s41545-018-0011-0

Prabhu, J. (2017). Frugal Innovation: Doing More with Less for More. *Philosophical Transactions of the Royal Society A: Mathematical, Physical and Engineering, 375*(2095). https://doi.org/10.1098/rsta.2016.0372

Radjou, N., & Prabhu, J. (2014). *Frugal Innovation: How to Do More with Less*. London: Profile Books.

Ramdorai, A., & Herstatt, C. (2015). Study 3: Lessons from Tata: How Leadership Can Drive Disruptive Innovations. In *Frugal Innovation in Healthcare* (pp. 105–130). https://doi.org/10.1007/978-3-319-16336-9_7

Rao, B. C. (2013). How Disruptive Is Frugal? *Technology in Society, 35*(1), 65–73. https://doi.org/10.1016/j.techsoc.2013.03.003

Rosca, E., Arnold, M., & Bendul, J. C. (2017). Business Models for Sustainable Innovation – An Empirical Analysis of Frugal Products and Services. *Journal of Cleaner Production, 162*, S133–S145. https://doi.org/10.1016/j.jclepro.2016.02.050

Rosca, E., Reedy, J., & Bendul, J. C. (2018). Does Frugal Innovation Enable Sustainable Development? A Systematic Literature Review. *The European Journal of Development Research, 30*(1), 136–157. https://doi.org/10.1057/s41287-017-0106-3

Szirmai, A. (2015). *Socio-Economic Development* (2nd ed.). Cambridge: Cambridge University Press.

Tata Swach. (2017). About Tata Swach Retrieved February 13, 2020, from https://tataswach.com/pages/about-tata-swach

The Economic Times. (2016). 76 Million People in India Have No Access to Safe Water: Report. Retrieved February 14, 2014, from https://economictimes.indiatimes.com/news/politics-and-nation/76-million-people-in-india-have-no-access-to-safe-water-report/articleshow/51513761.cms?from=mdr

The World Bank. (2019). Poverty. Retrieved January 23, 2020, from https://www.worldbank.org/en/topic/poverty/overview

Tiwari, R., & Herstatt, C. (2012a). Frugal Innovation: A Global Networks' Perspective. *Swiss Journal of Business Research and Practice, 66*(3), 245–274.

Tiwari, R., & Herstatt, C. (2012b). Assessing India's Lead Market Potential for Cost-Effective Innovations. *Journal of Indian Business Research, 4*(2), 97–115. https://doi.org/10.1108/17554191211228029

Tiwari, R., & Herstatt, C. (Eds.). (2014). *Growing Demand for Affordable Solutions*. Cham: Springer.

Tran, V. T., & Ravaud, P. (2016). Frugal Innovation in Medicine for Low Resource Settings. *BMC Medicine, 14*(1), 102. https://doi.org/10.1186/s12916-016-0651-1

Tranfield, D., Denyer, D., & Smart, P. (2003). Towards a Methodology for Developing Evidence-Based Management Knowledge by Means of Systematic Review. *British Journal of Management, 14,* 207–222.

United Nations. (2016). *The Human Rights to Safe Drinking Water and Sanitation.* United Nations General Assembly.

Weyrauch, T., & Herstatt, C. (2016). What Is Frugal Innovation? Three Defining Criteria. *Journal of Frugal Innovation, 2*(1). https://doi.org/10.1186/s40669-016-0005-y

WHO. (2008). Health and Development. Retrieved February 12, 2020, from https://www.who.int/hdp/en/

Yin, R. K. (2013). Validity and Generalization in Future Case Study Evaluations. *Evaluation, 19*(3), 321–332. https://doi.org/10.1177/1356389013497081

Correction to: Organizational and Individual Reality of Innovation: Similarities and Differences

Shashwat Shukla, Shantam Shukla, and Sonam Chawla

Correction to:

Chapter 14 in: A. McMurray et al. (eds.), *The Palgrave Handbook of Workplace Innovation*, https://doi.org/10.1007/978-3-030-59916-4_14

The chapter 14 was inadvertently published with an incorrect affiliation for the chapter Authors. The affiliations have now been corrected in the revised files as follows,

S. Shukla (✉)
University of Allahabad, Allahabad, Uttar Pradesh, India

S. Shukla
Indian Institute of Management, Ahmedabad, Gujarat, India
e-mail: shantams@iima.ac.in

Also, the affiliation of Adela McMurray has now been corrected on the back cover.

The updated version of the chapter can be found at
https://doi.org/10.1007/978-3-030-59916-4_14

Index[1]

---

[1] Note: Page numbers followed by 'n' refer to notes.

© The Author(s), under exclusive license to Springer Nature Switzerland AG 2021
A. McMurray et al. (eds.), *The Palgrave Handbook of Workplace Innovation*,
https://doi.org/10.1007/978-3-030-59916-4